HUSSERL
Expositions and Appraisals

HUSSERL

Expositions and Appraisals

Edited with introductions by

FREDERICK A. ELLISTON

and

PETER MC CORMICK

UNIVERSITY OF NOTRE DAME PRESS

Notre Dame   London

Copyright © 1977 by
University of Notre Dame Press
Notre Dame, Indiana 46556

Library of Congress Cataloging in Publication Data
Main entry under title:

Husserl : expositions and appraisals.

  Bibliography: p.
  Includes index.
  1. Husserl, Edmund, 1859-1938—Addresses, essays,
lectures. 2. Phenomenology—Addresses, essays, lec-
tures. I. Elliston, Frederick. II. McCormick, Peter.
B3279.H94H88   193   75-19882
ISBN 0-268-01063-3
ISBN 0-268-01064-1 pbk.

Manufactured in the United States of America

To
Dianne and Hélène

Contents

Foreword

In editing this collection of essays devoted to Husserl, Frederick Elliston and Peter McCormick have given a new style to phenomenological studies which should be unreservedly praised—and for more than one reason.

First, by dissociating the study of phenomenology from the study of schools of thought which arose from it but which broke away from it, they make impossible from this time forth those overall evaluations—whether favorable or not—which deal indiscriminately with phenomenology and existential philosophy. By placing at the head of the first section, Philosophical Themes, essays on the philosophy of logic and of language, as well as on epistemology, the editors have placed phenomenology from the beginning within the sphere of those problems which Husserl dealt with from the *Philosophy of Arithmetic* and the *Logical Investigations* to the *Formal and Transcendental Logic* and beyond. The subsequent essays on perception, imagination, time, and history all stand within the limits outlined by Husserl's theory of signification. In the same way, in the second part, Phenomenological Concepts, the two methodological techniques of reduction and eidetic intuition outline the properly phenomenological contours of the "thematic issues" discussed in the following studies, whether it be a question of the noema, the notion of horizon, or the life world. As for part three, Comparisons and Contrasts, it opens with a study that does not hesitate to underscore the incompatibility between phenomenology and existentialism, thereby rejoining the

important distinctions introduced in the second part between the originary role of intuition in Husserl and any return to immediacy (contrary to the vehement reproach against phenomenology articulated by Adorno). In this way the specificity of phenomenology is carefully delineated in the three parts of this collection of essays.

The second merit of this work is that both in title and content, it joins exposition and appraisal. The editors have thereby broken with that purely exegetical tendency which all too often transforms philosophical research into a simple archeology of phenomenology, while at the same time condemning it to remain confined to a circle of the already initiated. This concern not to separate exposition and appraisal is clearly evident in the composition of this volume. Certainly there are more expository articles in the first and second parts, whether it is a question of the theory of signification or the three ways of the Husserlian reduction or the two notions of the life world, while the third part is more directly devoted to "comparisons" and "contrasts." But it is noteworthy that the concern for appraisal which governs the composition of this volume is also found in numerous articles in the first and second parts.

Their authors do not hesitate to reformulate the problems treated by Husserl in a different vocabulary and conceptualization which are not just more familiar to contemporary thought, but which more importantly take account of the considerable changes which have occurred in logic, semantics, epistemology, the phi- losophy of mind, the theory of history, and the many other fields where phenomenology has left its mark. There is no lack of themes which will catch the attention of those readers more interested in the problems themselves than in the history of phenomenology: the refor- mulation of Husserl's antipsychologism in contemporary terms, the comparison between his concept of signification and recent theories of reference, the confron- tation between fulfillment and verifica- tion, between Husserlian intentionality and non-extentionality (or intensionality) as expressed by certain contemporary schools of thought, the interpretation of the Husserlian "noema" in terms of the assertion that $\sim p$, the clarification of the problem of intersubjectivity and the prob- lem of other minds in terms of each other.

Hence this volume as a whole testifies to a remarkable effort to rethink Husserl, which implies that we both think with and against him. Indeed, once such problems are reformulated in different terms, the relation to Husserl ceases to be governed by the rule of orthodoxy, and exposition contains the possibility of appraisal. Some authors, in fact, feel free not only to clarify a Husserlian problem and solution by means of a comparison with problems and solutions arising from other philosophical traditions, but also to add to their reformulation of such problems critical observations which lead to a more or less radical revision of the solution it- self. This freedom in approach means that these authors have addressed themselves "to the things themselves" and not just to Husserl's words.

Another merit, and not the least, of this collection of essays is to bring phenomenology out of its relative isola- tion and to open a discussion with other schools of thought, in particular with the dominant philosophy in the Anglo-Saxon world, analytic philosophy. By clearly distinguishing phenomenology from the philosophy of existence, our authors have already eliminated one misun- derstanding which stands in the way of a discussion of the real problems at issue

between phenomenology and analytic philosophy. Furthermore, in freeing themselves from any purely historical concern and by turning to the problems themselves as they are perceived today, our authors have taken a step in the direc- tion of philosophers in other schools. I cannot praise the editors of this collection enough for their courage in assuming such an undertaking.

For my part, I would like to say how much today it seems to me necessary to undertake an intersecting reading of phenomenology and analytic philosophy. It may look at first as though these two schools of thought take their points of departure in two different regions, that of the speech act for analytic philosophy, and that of lived experience for phenomenology. Upon reflection, how- ever, this opposition is revealed as super- ficial. Indeed, it follows from the program of each of these two schools that the one implies the program of the other. Phenomenology has never pretended to purely and simply reiterate what has been lived. To experience it once is sufficient. To relive it is superfluous. In distancing itself from lived experience through the reduction, phenomenology opens up this experience's field of signification. Moreover, phenomenology has never understood intentionality as a simple di- rectedness to just anything whatever. If it has so insisted upon the primacy of objec- tifying acts, seeming to subordinate af- fects and action to knowing, it is because all intentionality is directed toward a synthetic unity of meaning. There is no intending of chaos.

Finally, if phenomenology undertakes to build up even logic on the basis of the life world, it is not to return to some un- discoverable immediacy, but to use those always anterior syntheses which contain the rough draft and promise of the saya- bility of our world. By these features at least, phenomenology addresses itself to those phenomena which have an affinity for language, which can be brought to discourse, hence which can be articulated in speech acts. At this point phe- nomenology overtakes analytic philosophy. But the latter, in turn, is never just imprisoned in language only to consider its internal functioning in the fashion of structuralism. On the contrary, the analytic philosophers' interest is always turned toward what speech acts are about. Their tenacious and meticulous attachment to the problem of reference testifies to this insistant will to link language to what is not language, whether we call it experience, reality, or the world. For what is the referent of our language if not that lived experience which phenomenology trys to encompass by reducing it to its signification, by analyzing its objective constitution, and by geneti-cally unfolding its synthetic layers? Phenomenology and linguistic analysis, I would say, operate on two different strategic levels: that of the conditions of possibility of meaning and that of the articulation of this meaning in speech acts where it is brought to language.

The honor of the editors of this collection is that after breaking with the archeological style and the spirit of orthodoxy, they have opened the way to such an investigation and no doubt to others very different as well.

Paul Ricoeur
(Translated by David Pellauer)

Preface

In gathering together the following essays, our aim has been to aid, abet, and document the dialogue that is currently under way between Husserlian phenomenology and other contemporary viewpoints.

This new or, more precisely, renewed interest in Husserl within the Anglo-American philosophical community is partly the result of the increasing availability of Husserl's writings, which have been published by Nijhoff with scrupulous editing, as well as the growing list of translations and commentaries. The proliferation of articles, journals, and books on phenomenology is partially due as well to the success of Husserl's successors—notably Martin Heidegger, Jean-Paul Sartre, and Merleau-Ponty. As a result of connecting Husserl's name so intimately with this existential tradition—as the number of books titled simply 'Phenomenology and Existentialism' demonstrates—his original preoccupations with logic, language, and science have ironically been obscured, if not forgotten. Our secondary aim has therefore been to redress this balance by emphasizing these common concerns which align Husserl with the 'analytic' tradition as well.

Of the twenty-three articles included, eleven are published for the first time and six others have been translated especially for this anthology. Our selection was guided by two principles: to represent both the Continental school of phenomenology and its North American counterparts, and to admit essays by both Husserl's defenders and detractors.

We have also sought to maintain a nongeographical or nonideological balance among three types of Husserl scholarship. Like many of the contributions to Marvin Farber's early and valuable *Philosophical Essays in Memory of Edmund Husserl,* some of the following studies are *speculative:* adhering more to the spirit than the letter of Husserlian phenomenology, they seek to resolve shared problems. Like Herbert Spiegelberg's monumental work *The Phenomenological Method,* others have *historical* emphasis: not only do they take account of Husserl's maturing view, they acknowledge the influence of other contemporary figures and movements. Finally, like Robert Sokolowski's *Husserlian Meditations,* the essays are both exegetical and critical: as our title indicates, the task throughout has been to provide both an *exposition* and an *appraisal.*

The essays are grouped into three sections. Part One examines Husserl's treatment of seven general philosophical topics: logic, meaning, evidence, perception, imagination, time, and history. In Part Two the focus shifts to methodological and conceptual issues that are more endemic to Husserl's style of philosophizing: the reduction, eidetic intuition, intentionality, noema, horizon, life-world, and intersubjectivity. Part Three assesses his phenomenological program and its results by contrasting them to other major figures and traditions in contemporary philosophy: Kant, Marx, Heidegger, Frege, and Existentialism, Rationalism, Idealism, linguistic analysis, and formal semantics.

We express our thanks to Union College and the University of Ottawa for their financial support, to the Philosophy Department secretaries for their generous time and effort, to the University of Notre Dame Press for its patience, and to our wives for their tolerance and loyalty during this book's long period of gestation.

The following works offer useful general surveys of Husserl's entire philosophy.

Berger, Gaston. "Les Thèmes Principaux de la Phénoménologie de Husserl." *Revue de Métaphysique et de Morale*, 49 (1944), 23-43.

Biemel, Walter. "The Decisive Phases in the Development of Husserl's Philosophy" in *The Phenomenology of Husserl: Selected Critical Readings*, ed. R. O. Elveton. Chicago: Quadrangle, 1970, pp. 148-73.

Cairns, Dorion. "Phenomenology" in *A History of Philosophical Systems*, ed. Vergilius Fern. New York: Philosophical Library, 1950, pp. 353-64.

Edie, James M. "Revolution in Philosophy: What Is Phenomenology?" *Southwestern Journal of Philosophy*, 2 (1971), 73-91.

Farber, Marvin. "Phenomenology" in *Twentieth Century Philosophy*, ed. D. D. Runes. New York: Philosophical Library, 1943, pp. 343-70.

Findlay, John N. "Phenomenology" in *Encyclopedia Britannica*, 1964 ed., XVII, pp. 699-702.

Fink, Eugen. "Operative Begriffe in Husserls Phänomenologie." *Zeitschrift für Philosophische Forschung*, 11 (1957), 321-37.

Fisher, Alden. "Some Basic Themes in the Phenomenology of Edmund Husserl." *Modern Schoolman*, 43 (1965-66), 347-63.

Gurvitch, G. "Le fondateur de la philosophie phénoménologique Edmund Husserl" in *Les tendances actuelles de la philosophie allemande*, ed. G. Gurvitch. Paris: J. Vrin, 1949, pp. 11-66.

Kockelmans, Joseph J. *A First Introduction to Husserl's Phenomenology*. Pittsburgh: Duquesne University Press, 1967.

Natanson, Maurice. "Phenomenology: A Viewing." *Methods*, 10 (1958), 295-318.

____. *Edmund Husserl: Philosopher of Infinite Tasks*. Evanston: Northwestern University Press, 1973.

Pivcevic, Edo. *Husserl and Phenomenology*. London: Hutchinson and Company, 1970.

Ricoeur, Paul. *Husserl: An Analysis of His Philosophy*, tr. Edward G. Ballard and Lester E. Embree. Evanston: Northwestern University Press, 1967.

____. "Husserl" in *Histoire de la Philosophie Allemande*. Paris: J. Vrin, 1967, pp. 183-96.

____. "Phenomenology," tr. Daniel J. Herman and Donald V. Morano. *Southern Journal of Philosophy*, 5 (1974), 149-68.

Ryle, Gilbert. "Phenomenology." *Aristotelian Society*, Supp. 11 (1932), 68-83.

Schmitt, Richard. "Phenomenology" in *Encyclopedia of Philosophy*, VI. New York: Macmillan, 1967, pp. 135-51.

Schutz, Alfred. "Some Leading Concepts of Phenomenology" in *Essays in Phenomenology*, ed. Maurice Natanson. The Hague: Nijhoff, 1966, pp. 23-39.

Sinha, Debabrata. "The Phenomenology of Edmund Husserl." *The Calcutta Review* (1960), 241-50.

Spiegelberg, Herbert. "The Pure Phenomenology of Edmund Husserl" in *The Phenomenological Movement*, I. The Hague: Nijhoff, 1965, pp. 73-167.

Van Breda, Herman Leo. "Great Themes in Husserl's Thought." *Philosophy Today*, 3 (1959), 192-98.

Wild, John W. "On the Nature and Aims of Phenomenology." *Philosophy and Phenomenological Research*, 3 (1942-43), 85-95.

Zaner, Richard M. *The Way of Phenomenology*. New York: Pegasus, 1970.

Works of Edmund Husserl

Below are listed various works of Edmund Husserl published in German or in English translation that are pertinent to the collection of articles in this volume. At the end of many of these listings are given abbreviated forms employed in some of the articles contained herein, although there will be some variation of reference to these works of Husserl according to the usage of different authors. In some cases reference is made to the *Husserliana* volume number, and in others to the title of the work.

The following Collected Works (the *Husserliana*) of Husserl are based on posthumous writings published, in cooperation with the Husserl archives at the University of Cologne, by the Husserl archives of Louvain under the direction of H. L. Van Breda. English translation editions follow the German original. The dates given for the German works are for the latest editions published by Martinus Nijhoff (The Hague):

1. *Cartesianische Meditationen und Pariser Vorträge.* Edited by S. Strasser. 1973.
   Abbreviated: *Cartesianische Meditationen.*

   [*Cartesian Meditations*, trans. Dorion Cairns. The Hague: Nijhoff, 1960. Abbreviated: *CM.*]

   [*The Paris Lectures*, 2d ed., trans. P. Koestenbaum. The Hague: Nijhoff, 1967.]

2. *Die Idee der Phänomenologie.* Fünf Vorlesungen. Edited by Walter Biemel. 1973.

   [*The Idea of Phenomenology*, trans. W. P. Alston and G. Nakhnikian. The Hague: Nijhoff, 1966.
   Abbreviated: *Idea.*]

3. *Ideen zu einer reinen Phänomenologie und phänomenologischen Philosophie.* Erstes Buch: Allgemeine Einführung in die reine Phänomenologie. Edited by Walter Biemel. 1950.
   Abbreviated: *Ideen I.*

   [*Ideas: General Introduction to Pure Phenomenology*, trans. W. R. Boyce Gibson. New York: Macmillan, 1931.
   Abbreviated: *Ideas.*]

4. *Ideen zu einer reinen Phänomenologie und phänomenologischen Philosophie*. Zweites Buch: Phänomenologische Untersuchungen zur Konstitution. Edited by Marly Biemel. 1952.
Abbreviated: *Ideen II*.

5. *Ideen zu einer reinen Phänomenologie und phänomenologischen Philosophie*. Drittes Buch: Die Phänomenologie und die Fundamente der Wissenschaften. Edited by Marly Biemel. 1971.
Abbreviated: *Ideen III*.

6. *Die Krisis der europäischen Wissenschaften und die transzendentale Phänomenologie*. Eine Einleitung in die phänomenologische Philosophie. Edited by Walter Biemel. 1962.
Abbreviated: *Krisis*.

[*The Crisis of European Sciences and Transcendental Phenomenology*, trans. David Carr. Evanston: Northwestern University Press, 1970. Abbreviated: *Crisis*.]

7. *Erste Philosophie (1923/24)*. Erste Teil: Kritische Ideengeschichte. Edited by Rudolf Boehm. 1956.
Abbreviated: *Erste Philosophie I*.

8. *Erste Philosophie (1923/24)*. Zweiter Teil: Theorie der phänomenologischen Reduktion. Edited by Rudolf Boehm. 1959.
Abbreviated: *Erste Philosophie II*.

9. *Phänomenologische Psychologie*. Vorlesungen Sommersemester 1925. Edited by Walter Biemel. 1968.
Abbreviated: *Phänomenologische Psychologie* or *PP*.

10. *Zur Phänomenologie des inneren Zeitbewusstseins (1893-1917)*. Edited by Rudolf Boehm. 1966.

[*The Phenomenology of Internal Time Consciousness*, edited by Martin Heidegger, trans. by J. S. Churchill. Bloomington: Indiana University Press, 1964.]

11. *Analysen zur passiven Synthesis. Aus Vorlesungs- und Forschungsmanuskripten, 1918-1926*. Edited by Margot Fleischer. 1966.
Abbreviated: *Passive Synthesis*.

12. *Philosophie der Arithmetik*. Mit ergänzenden Texten (1890-1901). Edited by Lothar Eley. 1970.
Abbreviated: *Arithmetik*.

13. *Zur Phänomenologie der Intersubjektivität*. Texte aus dem Nachlass. Erster Teil. 1905-1920. Edited by Iso Kern. 1973.

14. *Zur Phänomenologie der Intersubjektivität*. Texte aus dem Nachlass. Zweiter Teil. 1921-1928. Edited by Iso Kern. 1973.

15. *Zur Phänomenologie der Intersubjectivität*. Texte aus dem Nachlass. Dritter Teil. 1929-1935. Edited by Iso Kern. 1973.

16. *Ding und Raum*. Vorlesungen 1907. Edited by Ulrich Claesges. 1973.

17. *Formale und transzendentale Logik.* Versuch einer Kritik der logischen Vernunft. Edited by Paul Janssen. 1974.
    Abbreviated: *Logik.*

    [*Formal and Transcendental Logic,* trans. Dorion Cairns. The Hague: Nijhoff, 1969.
    Abbreviated: *FTL.*]

18. *Logische Untersuchungen.* Erster Band. Prolegomena zur reinen Logik. Edited by Elmar Holenstein. 1975.
    Abbreviated: *LU.*

* * * * * * * * * * *

Logische Untersuchungen. Erster Band. Prolegomena zur reinen Logik. Halle: 1900; rev. ed. 1913.

Logische Untersuchungen. Zweite Band. Untersuchungen zur Phänomenologie und Theorie der Erkenntnis. Halle: 1901; rev. ed. 1922.

[*Logical Investigations,* trans. J. N. Findlay. New York: Humanities Press, 1970. 2 vols. Based on revised Halle editions.
Abbreviated: *LI.*]

The following are works of Edmund Husserl not contained in the *Husserliana*:

Erfahrung und Urteil, Untersuchungen zur Genealogie der Logik. Edited by Ludwig Landgrebe. Hamburg: Claassen, 1954.

[*Experience and Judgment,* trans. by J. Churchill and K. Ameriks. Evanston: Northwestern University Press, 1973.]

Philosophie als strenge Wissenschaft. Edited by W. Szilasi. Frankfurt: 1965.

["Philosophy as Rigorous Science," in *Phenomenology and the Crisis of Philosophy,* trans. Q. Lauer. New York: Harper Torchbooks, 1965.]

Introduction to the Logical Investigations, trans. with Introductions by Philip J. Bossert and Curtis H. Peters. The Hague: Nijhoff, 1975.

PART ONE

Philosophical Themes

Introduction

The seven articles in Part One, "Philosophical Themes," fall into four groups. The first two articles concern the philosophy of logic and the philosophy of language, while the second two turn to problems in epistemology. The next two articles treat themes from the philosophy of mind, and the last article deals with broader questions about transcendental philosophy. Throughout these papers the dominant stress falls on Husserl's reflections on several recurring sets of problems which are not peculiar to phenomenology but are part of the philosophical tradition.

Dallas Willard's paper, "The Paradox of Logical Psychologism: Husserl's Way Out," looks closely at the question "How can claims about a certain sort of thing fail to draw their evidence from the examination of things of that sort?" The claims in question are logicians' truths—nonnormative statements logicians make about particular conceivings, inferrings, and assertings. The point of the paradox is that statements asserting, for example, that a Barbara syllogism is valid apply to that particular instance, although the evidence for such statements is not drawn from an analysis of that instance of thinking as such. So although the evidence for validity does not consist of empirical generalizations, nevertheless what is judged as valid is a particular empirical occurrence.

Willard points to two examples by showing how both sides of this paradox have occasioned controversy and persistent disagreement. Interestingly, he sets a pattern for the antipsychologistic view by scrutinizing writers such as Bolzano, Frege, Husserl, Russell, Moore, Johnson, Stebbing, and others. The pattern consists of at least nine features, which Willard formulates before he turns to the way Husserl adapted this pattern, especially in *Logical Investigations*.

Husserl's resolution of the paradox of logical psychologism lies in his revision of Bolzano's view of the relation between the mind and the propositions the mind grasps. Bolzano characterized this relation as one of intentionality. Taking his clue from Lotze's criticisms of Plato, by a distinction between reality and validity, Husserl most likely assigned propositions the status of universals in Lotze's sense of entities which exist ideally: they have validity (*Geltung*) but not reality; they do not have existence (*Wirklichkeit*). Hence, for Husserl, propositions become complex referential qualities of acts of thought instead of the acts themselves. So Husserl revises Bolzano's view of the relation between mind and its propositions by substituting instantiation or exemplification for intentionality. The result is that logicians could be held to be saying true things about mental events even if their theories are held to be nonempirical. The point, then, is that logicians' truths are primarily about the character of mental acts and not about the acts themselves. These truths apply to particular mental acts; but their evidence derives from analysis of their character.

Some of the topics behind Husserl's struggles with logical psychologism are treated in J. N. Mohanty's "Husserl's Theory of Meaning." This article discusses the distinction between meaning and reference, the ideality of meanings, and then provides several critical observations.

Mohanty begins by drawing attention to the First Logical Investigation, where Husserl distinguishes between saying something and saying something of something, between meaning and reference. This distinction is proposed as applying not just to nominal expressions but to all linguistic expressions. Husserl's emphasis falls more clearly on the *acts* of speaking, rather than on language as a formal system. And the paradigmatic case of such speaking is not taken as communicative speech but as interior soliloquy. The essence of such speaking is twofold: to express meanings or thoughts *and* to be about objects. But this reduction of language to inner speech, as Derrida and others noted elsewhere, is problematic.

After looking at the traditional view of Husserl's distinction between meaning and reference in the case of names, Mohanty shows that this view is oversimplified. Far from translating into his own terminology distinctions borrowed from Frege's work of 1892 and 1894 (see Frege's 1894 article below), Husserl had used similar distinctions in his work, from 1891 onward, quite independently of Frege. Moreover, Husserl was also concerned with the ideality of meaning, a concern which is not evident in the Frege papers of this time. In fact, despite a shared concern with meaning and reference, Husserl and Frege have a very different orientation, largely because of Husserl's concern with intentionality as well as with acts of expressing. Ultimately, Husserl construes meaning as something other than referent, representation, mental picture, or intuition. Mohanty's strictures (in footnotes 20 and 48) are related to the article by Ernst Tugendhat (see below), when the former discusses the influence of the intentionality theses on Husserl's claims about nominal and predicate expressions. Mohanty holds that Husserl does not treat predicates as names but recognizes the impor-

tant differences between the acts of naming and predicating. Some of these differences become clear when the relevant distinctions are made among "uttering a sentence, saying something about something by that utterance, asserting a proposition, stating a fact, naming the fact so stated, naming the proposition asserted, and naming the sentence uttered." The object of a name is not the objectified meaning of the name, whereas the objective correlate of a sentence is its objectified meaning. Much of the argument for such a distinction, of course, remains controversial. But the detail in Mohanty's discussion of Husserl's view of objective references serves to remind those working in contemporary semantics of the richness of Husserl's work itself (see Küng's article below).

Mohanty turns to Husserl's concept of the meaning-intending act and the ideality of meanings. After noting the extremely controversial status of the second thesis, Mohanty formulates four facts that any satisfactory theory of meaning should recognize: meanings can be shared; they are related to mental life; they serve as media of reference to the world; and they are embodied. Very roughly, this *set* of facts—not just the first—is the needed context for understanding Husserl's claim that meanings are ideal. Husserl, it is true, sometimes talks of meanings in an ontological way, but talks less of meanings as objects of reference and more as media of reference. So the ideality of meanings is neither that of species nor essences, nor even linguistic entities. Husserl blurs his view by introducing misleading terms, such as the contents of meaning-intending or meaning-conferring acts. For Husserl, meaning is always and primarily meaning of an act: meaning is intentional in the sense that an act is directed toward an object in a specific way. Moreover, a meaning is a content in the sense that when I direct an act toward an object, this object consists either of real components of an experience or of intentional correlates which accompany the act. Thus phenomenological theory of meaning, as

Husserl understands it, is concerned with the sense of meanings *as* meaning and with how such sense is constituted.

Mohanty concludes by stressing what he has been at pains to detail throughout: the comprehensiveness of Husserl's theory of meaning; it can accommodate the stress on the identity, objectivity, and communicability of meanings (which is characteristic of Platonic theories) and the stress on the connection between meanings and the mental life of persons, as well as the stresses on the conventional character of language that are features of the non-Platonic theories (whether psychological or nonpsychological). Nonetheless, the following areas of Husserl's theory need modification: the distorting emphasis on the priority of objectifying acts as meaning-conferring, the unclear treatment of nonlinguistic expressions such as "groaning with pain," and the relation between Husserl's structural and genetic phenomenologies of meaning. Some but not all of these topics are touched on below in the papers by Frege, Tugendhat, and Küng.

Shifting the focus from logic and language to epistemology, Henry Pietersma's article, "Husserl's Views on the Evident and the True," sets aside related views in Brentano and Meinong, as well as the development of Husserl's ideas, to concentrate on what Husserl calls *Evidenz*. This term, introduced in *Logical Investigations,* does not refer to evidence but to "a mental state or epistemic situation in which something is evident to the person who is in that state or situation."

Pietersma insists that the context of Husserl's claims about the evident is a theory of justification. We need, however, to distinguish the evident from the nonevident judgment, reserving knowledge—properly speaking—for the first domain. Moreover, in light of Husserl's discussions in the Sixth Investigation, we need to distinguish further between the subject's degree of conviction and the more or less favorable situation with respect to what is being judged. Pietersma calls this second aspect 'epistemic distance', which is not to be under-

stood in a spatial sense but "in terms of whatever cognitive moves are acquired to attain the kind of situation that is optimal for judging." The optimal situation has the character of a fulfillment or achievement, as opposed to an empty possibility. Pietersma construes taking something to be evident in terms of the idea of an optimal situation within his phenomenology of epistemic levels. These levels can be best understood in the context of Husserl's rebuttal of skepticism.

For Husserl, complete skepticism would follow from the view that the evident is "the factual conjunction of judgment and a certain feeling," since two contradictory judgments could be conjoined with an indistinguishable feeling. Without the idea that epistemic levels exist, no resolution for such a conflict would be possible. In *Ideas,* Husserl discusses this optimal epistemic situation in terms of a "primordially presentative seeing." After delineating the optimal epistemic situation and the need to leave no intentions unfulfilled, Husserl denies the skeptic the right to claim to be sure.

How does Husserl view the evaluation of the epistemic subject's claims to certainty in perception? He deals with the justification for our perceptions of material objects when some aspects of that object, say its contexts, are not perceived. This situation is optimal, even though not all sides are perceived, since the epistemic subject can never do everything to perceive all of a material object. Husserl insists on this point, even when, in *Ideas,* he takes account of a perspectival view of material objects. And later, in *Formal and Transcendental Logic,* he talks of the self-givenness of perceived material objects and the fulfillment character of perception (see Welton's article, below). Nonetheless, Husserl continues to call attention to the fallibility of our perceptions and the fact that the existence of the perceptible world is not absolutely evident. Illusion is possible even in these cases, when optimal epistemic situations are achieved. Husserl remains committed to the view that perception justifies knowledge claims, even though perception does not reach the highest epistemic level, namely, perfectly adequate evidence.

In the third section of his paper Pietersma considers some general epistemological features of Husserl's doctrine of essences. Here, as in perception, Husserl holds that the evident is to be understood as an achievement, as a successful traversing of the epistemic distance between intention and fulfillment. However, the optimal epistemic situation is no longer seen in terms of the infinite number of steps the epistemic subject would need for completion but in terms of there being *no other* steps to take. Despite the knowledge claims we make about such essences, Husserl still finds room for epistemic levels, since one can raise questions and doubts even about what is evident.

Is the evident the same as the true? From the standpoint of the searcher after truth, the evident seems to be the true, although Husserl must skirt a correspondence theory. And yet, from the standpoint of what the true is in itself, no such equation seems to be satisfactory. Husserl assumes this second standpoint in both the *Cartesian Meditations* and *Formal and Transcendental Logic*, where he is especially concerned with the total context of consciousness. The true becomes "what in a contextualized situation is held to be true and *continues* to be held to be true." The evident, however, remains part of the passage from intentions to fulfillments in the search for truth. Hence the search for truth, whether empirical or eidetic, terminates in an achievement which is defended against the skeptic with help from the concept of the optimal epistemic situation. This achievement is the evident, an experience of truth. But the true, or as Husserl often calls it, "the true in itself," is what "stands up under *all* the evaluational procedures available to the transcendental subject." What needs further scrutiny is Husserl's highly nuanced understanding of perception.

Donn Welton's paper, "Structure and Genesis in Husserl's Phenomenology," also stresses Husserl's recurring claim that all perception, to be meaningful, requires context—or, to use his somewhat different idea, horizons (see van Peursen, below). Welton's purpose is to consider anew some of the difficulties in Husserl's complex topic of horizons in order to open a related line of inquiry that goes beyond the difficulties in Husserl's theories. Specifically, he proposes to interpret Husserl's reflections about the perceptual horizon, largely as presented in *Husserliana XI*, in terms of Husserl's later development. His aim is to situate meaning, a central concept in Husserl's philosophy (and the subject of Mohanty's paper), within the context of Husserl's deepening analysis of the perceptual *noema* (see Solomon's paper, below, which Welton criticizes).

Beginning with a brief treatment of Husserl's development from a static to a genetic account of sense, Welton shows how Husserl's attempt to apply a logical characterization of the noema to an analysis of perception falters. The difficulties Husserl discovers, especially the movement between intention and fulfillment in the consideration of objective sense, force him to a consideration of passivity. To this must be added, of course, considerations about Husserl's concept of appearance. Husserl argues that "there is a clear difference not merely in function but also in structure between signitive intentions and perceptual fulfillment." To account for the peculiar kinds of syntheses in perceptual fulfillment, Welton turns to Husserl's treatment of association.

Husserl rejects the idea that perceiving entails having sensations and the notion that, when looking "within," one finds either ideas or sense data. What is found, he says, are sensorial moments "integrated from 'below' by passive synthesis and integrated from 'above' by the sense of the object perceived." These syntheses depend on further syntheses—kinaesthetic and associative syntheses. Each is unique, although each consists both of what is synthesized and the synthesis itself. To them must be added the various kinds of temporal syntheses which Husserl dealt with from the period of *Logical Investigations* almost to the end of his life (see Brough's article, below).

So Husserl gives us, at least in his analyses of perceptual sense, a different, multilayer view of the concept of horizon than what his earlier stress on apperception suggested. In the context of an overarching role for the guiding concept of intentionality, Husserl sketches a theory of perceptual horizons which tries to detail both the context and the unity of the three interrelated syntheses.

After providing a tentative schema of this theory, Welton emphasizes three important points about Husserl's view of perception as apperception: his treatment of perception as "a necessary progression and an *optimal* presence," his stress on the future as that which makes perception possible, and the possibility of "an integration of perception and historical praxis"—which others have vigorously questioned (see, for example, Wartofsky's paper, below).

A central topic in Welton's paper is the subject of John Brough's article, "The Emergence of an Absolute Consciousness in Husserl's Early Writings in Time-Consciousness," which discusses the development of Husserl's reflections on the nature and role of the absolute flow of time-constituting consciousness. His discussion takes up the schema "apprehension-context of apprehension" in the early writings (from 1901 to 1907) and then turns to the new interpretation of the constitution of time consciousness in the writings from 1909 to 1911.

The question Husserl is concerned with throughout is "how, in a flow of consciousness, is the awareness of a temporally extended object constituted?" This question applies to any object which is presented to consciousness in a series of phases. Husserl holds that both the object *and* its perception are presented in this way and hence may be roughly called 'temporal objects'. What makes consciousness of such temporal objects pos-

sible is the capacity of consciousness to reach beyond the instant into both the past and the future so as to preserve the actual, elapsed objective phases—that is, the sequences in the past and the future. The subtlety of this analysis can be appreciated by noting that Husserl's theory allows for perception of a melody by distinguishing between the memory of something that is somewhat remote from the instant and the memory of a just-elapsed phase of that instant—between what Husserl calls the just-past phases (primary memory) and the further-past phases (secondary memory). A similar distinction applies to expectation. This perception of the instant (or 'now-perception') and primary memory are constituted "in moments of objectivating apprehension."

Husserl also distinguishes between what is perceived (something external) and what is experienced (something immanent), and holds that while an external object is perceived, "one experiences (*erleben*) immanent sensory contents and apprehensions, or the appearances which the two together constitute." Now-perception, memory, and expectation are constituted in terms of moments of apprehension and context. In short, it is the way a content is apprehended, and not the content itself (as Brentano held), that distinguishes the constitution of the three modes of time consciousness: now-perception, primary memory, and expectation. Brough summarizes: "... the contents and apprehensions belonging to a given slice of consciousness will be as numerous as the objective temporal phases intended through it." This comes to the view that a phase of consciousness contains a continuum of apprehensions and contents.

As his work developed Husserl distinguished two kinds of immanence: that of the identical temporal object and that of its profiles and their apprehension. He claims that the first immanence is constituted within the other. This claim, and the distinction it is based on, results later in rejection of the content-apprehension schema in favor of explicit treatment of the more basic kind of immanence in terms of absolute consciousness, which itself is not constituted and yet constitutes time.

The new theory does not explain time consciousness in terms of the content-apprehension schema. However, it subordinates interest in the constitution of *perceptual* time consciousness to the account of the way that immanent temporal objects are experienced. Part of Husserl's new theory involves terminological changes, such as replacing 'now-perception' with 'primal impression' or 'primal sensations', 'primary memory' with 'retention', and 'primary expectation' with 'protention'. More important, however, is the central distinction between "an absolute constituting flow and a constituted dimension within consciousness itself"—a distinction in part motivated by the gap we experience between our sensory experiences, for example, and our marginal awareness of such experiences. But there is a puzzle here. How can Husserl hold that in the flow of absolute time the temporal object is constituted in its unity, yet the flow constitutes its own unity? How Husserl solves this puzzle remains controversial, despite Brough's excellent exposition. The key to the issue is whether Husserl's concept of the "double intentionality" of the absolute flow is finally coherent. Husserl's talk of the vertical intentionality of the flow's consciousness of the immanent object and the horizontal intentionality of the flow's consciousness of itself is evidently problematic.

Edward Casey's "Imagination and Phenomenological Method" deals with relationships among three paradoxes. The first problem is the continual disparagement of imagination in the history of philosophy and its simultaneous use in the development of that history. The paradox arises by affirming *and* denying the importance of the imagination. This pattern of denigration and acknowledgment is found in many philosophers, such as Aristotle, Descartes, Hume, Kant, and Husserl, who see imagination as critically important yet of doubtful epistemological

value. Imagination, in fact, either is not discussed at all or, when discussed, is viewed as of secondary importance, in contrast with perception. Nevertheless, despite its theoretical denigration, imagination figures importantly in the techniques of Husserl's phenomenology.

The second paradox may be expressed in terms of the need to use imagination to describe imagination. This paradox is peculiar to phenomenology in that imagining is an element of the distinctive methods of phenomenology, in the phenomenological reduction and free variation. In the reduction, imagination is necessary in order to exclude causal and substantial factors from the phenomena and reduce these phenomena to the self-evident and self-given character of the phenomena's transparency to consciousness. In free variation, imagining is even more important because it supplies examples for free variation and systematically alters whatever examples have been chosen, whether fictitious or factual. Sometimes traits are imagined to be lacking; sometimes new traits are imagined for old ones; and sometimes extra traits are imagined to fill out incomplete examples. In each case the aim is to discriminate essential from inessential features. So imagination whether in the reduction or in free variations is a cardinal part of phenomenological method.

The third paradox concerns the variable character of imagination itself. On the one hand, imagination is a liability because it is merely variable; on the other, it is a resource because, as variable, it gives the philosopher another approach to truths. Imagination is either an illegitimate alternative to ratiocination or an essential ingredient in the systematic variation of contexts and contents that helps supplement the work of ratiocination. Casey notes that, unlike other phenomena, imagination would seem not to be invariant. If he is right, a new problem arises: Are any phenomenological accounts of imagination possible if no eidetic features can be found? Casey wants to hold that—the lack of eidetic features notwithstanding—there is still "a case of constant traits" to be found. The practice of free variation is both an example and an illumination of this "ceaselessly variable character of imagining."

The last paper in this section treats this more general and more controversial area: the coherence of phenomenology as a transcendental philosophy. Landgrebe begins his article, "Phenomenology as Transcendental Theory of History," with reflections on problems in interpreting Husserl. He claims that all the recent interpretations which have advanced our understanding of Husserl have used the method of arguing the later against the earlier Husserl. If we propose to understand Husserl's transcendental philosophic design, we must think through Husserl's philosophy to see the limits of the possibility of a transcendental philosophical reflection. This itself is a kind of Husserlian transcendental philosophy, since "transcendental" has for Husserl (as for Kant) the sense of "critique," reason setting its own limits. Because philosophical concepts are more than just theories and because practical principles of behavior come from them, the transcendental critique of these concepts will be, at the same time, a critique of these principles of behavior. For Landgrebe, Husserl wanted his transcendental phenomenology to be understood as a "critique of life." The thesis, then, that Landgrebe argues is that "if phenomenology is to be transcendental philosophy, and this is thought through to its ultimate consequences, then phenomenology is a transcendental theory of history."

For Landgrebe, transcendental phenomenology is primordially concerned with finding the transcendental conditions for the possibility of history; it involves an inquiry into the a priori of history. As a transcendental theory of history, phenomenology will be genetic phenomenology, since it is only as genetic phenomenology that transcendental phenomenology attains its proper development. Also, a transcendental theory

of history presupposes an adequate theory of intersubjectivity—which, Landgrebe tells us, can only be developed as a genetic theory (see Elliston's paper, below).

Landgrebe wants to show that "transcendental genetic phenomenology is, as such, transcendental theory of history" by connecting this thesis to two of Husserl's ideas: the absoluteness of the transcendental ego and the absoluteness of history. The main part of Landgrebe's reflection on these two ideas concerns the second: "history is the grand fact of absolute being," which Husserl wrote in the early 1920s in a manuscript subtitled "Monadology." This leads Landgrebe to look at Leibniz's influence on philosophers of history, and particularly on Herder. Landgrebe sees Husserl's use of the term 'normal' as aiming at the central problem of the grounding of truth—as Herder and Ranke and even today's historians construe this problem.

Looking at the relation between the two ideas, Landgrebe again concentrates on the concept of "monad," which stresses the individuality of each person. For Husserl, the world is historical only through the inner historicity of each person. To understand this, we have to look at the thinking Husserl followed to arrive at these two theses. Transcendental phenomenology as genetic phenomenology is an "investigation of the origin." Rejecting any distinction between epistemological and historical investigation, Husserl views reflection as primarily a turning back toward what we can do. One of the original things we can do as children is move—and without our original familiarity with movement there can be no higher level of reflection. In the experience of motion, both my "there" and the "there" of the other reveal themselves as apodictically certain. For Landgrebe, "only on the basis of this 'there' does the concept of absolute fact achieve its meaning." The "there" is, consequently, the fact beyond which we cannot go: it is the transcendental condition for the possibility of all functions; it must simply be accepted, since one cannot question beyond it. It is here that reflection reaches the limits of its power. Each I-subject finds itself placed in its "there" immediately. It immediately becomes acquainted with itself when it does something. And from the very beginning it experiences its abilities as something to be learned. When it asks "Why?" we get the turn toward history: this inner historicity is the a priori of history.

The question arises as to how others enter this inner historicity—the question of "windows" in the monads. It must be shown that, unlike Leibniz's monads, Husserl's have windows from the very beginning. Though Husserl did not reach a systematic solution to these problems, Landgrebe believes he left some indication of where a solution could be sought. If intentionality is a "primal striving" of the monad, sex, conception, and birth are subjects not just of biology but also of transcendental philosophy—subjects which have impact as conditions of the possibility of history. The winds of the I-monad are to be sought in the proto-impulse which drives one monad to relate to another.

Landgrebe stresses his claim that history is more than just the aggregate of the *res gestae*. He speaks of an abso-luteness—the absoluteness of the "there" and the absoluteness of the earth. In the "there" the ultimate point of transcendental reflection is reached, beyond which it cannot go. The "there" reveals the basis upon which transcendental philosophy criticizes dogmatisms. Since the factualness of history depends on the factualness of the "there" of the individual, "the condition for [our future] is not only acknowledgment of all 'our likes' as equal but also as absolutely individually different." Only recognition of the other and acceptance of one's own factualness are "the ground for the possibility of a human world rather than subjugation under an unpenetrable fate."

Much of the terminology here and some of the claims Landgrebe advances in this speculative paper provoke metaphilosophical questions when we try to evaluate them (see McCormick's paper, below). Before such evaluation can begin however, we need to check our understanding of both Husserl's contacts with major problems of the philosophical tradition and his attempts to formulate his own philosophical problems. These two areas are respectively the subjects of the articles in Part One introduced here and those in Part Two.

The Paradox of Logical Psychologism:
Husserl's Way Out

DALLAS WILLARD

I

Logical Psychologism is the view that the non-normative statements made by logicians engaged in their business both are about, and draw their evidence from the examination of, the particular conceivings, assertings, and inferrings of particular persons—a range of facts commonly thought to belong ultimately to the science of psychology alone. This view enjoyed wide acceptation during the last half of the nineteenth century, being advocated by such men as John Stuart Mill in England, and Sigwart and Erdmann in Germany. More recently, and due as much to misunderstandings and an unfavorable press as to the essential incredibilities it contains, it has suffered an eclipse which is almost total. A part of the purpose of this paper is to show how this eclipse hinders understanding of what Logic is about.

What is here called the "paradox" of Logical Psychologism arises when one sees that, while (1) the class of statements mentioned—we might call them "logicians' truths"—are indeed, in some very important sense, about and applicable to such particular events in personal careers as referred to above, (2) they nonetheless, as Husserl, Frege, and others have

Reprinted with permission of the publisher and author from *American Philosophical Quarterly,* vol. 9, no. 1 (Jan. 1972): 94-100.

shown, do *not* draw their evidence from the examination of such events. Now this seems paradoxical. For *how* can claims about a certain sort of thing fail to draw their evidence from the examination of things of that sort? There seem to be good reasons for believing both (1) and (2). And yet the truth of (1) or (2) seems each to exclude the truth of the other. Thus we have a paradox or antinomy in the classical sense. This paper also proposes to consider a way of resolving the paradox without calling either (1) or (2) into question.

II

Logicians today are likely to feel uneasy about (1). In this respect we seem to be the inverse of most nineteenth-century philosophers, who easily accepted (1), but had difficulty with (2). We today have heard or read many snappy announcements that the laws of logic are not expressions of how we actually *do* think, but of how we *ought* to think. And then—with these ringing in our ears—we fail to notice that logicians in fact fill up large volumes without once saying that anyone ought to do anything at all—just try counting the "oughts" in Quine's *Methods of Logic,* or Mates's *Elementary Logic.* We fail to see that "valid," "invalid," "tautologous," "consistent," "inconsistent," "derivable," and the other terms which form the core of the logician's vocabulary are not used by him at his trade to commend or condemn, to praise or to blame, to exhort or to direct, at all. That an argument, or argument form, is valid or invalid is a point of mere information or misinformation, to which some positive or negative value may or may not be attached. Value considerations have nothing at all essentially to do with whether or not an argument is valid or invalid, or with whether or not an expression is L-determinate.

It is, of course, true that terms from, or closely related to, the core vocabulary of the logician are often given a normative use—are often used to commend or condemn—in the contexts of actual thinking and talking. An example would be the common claim that a certain person at a certain point in an essay or lecture advanced an invalid (or valid) argument, or on a certain occasion made an invalid (or valid) inference. But it is still true here that the normative use is accidental only. A particular instance of the Barbara syllogism, for example, is valid—i.e., no argument of its sort has or can have true premises and false conclusion—regardless of what value may or may not be placed upon it; and, of course, also regardless of how anyone's beliefs may be arranged around the premises and conclusion. *It* is valid, and is known to be valid. That is, the logician's claims (about validity in this case) apply to *it,* the *particular* event of thinking or speaking in the life of a *particular* person. And persons who are logically informed and trained can *know* that *it,* and not merely Barbara syllogisms in general, is valid.[1]

Without this kind of application there would simply be no use at all for what the logician has to teach. If he denies the possibility of such application, he talks himself out of a job. But there is no real danger of that. No logician—even the most hide-bound of anti-Psychologists or Formalists—will assure those whom he would teach that what he has to say is irrelevant to the thinking and speaking which they, or at least *some* persons, may happen to do or meet with. He may have no ready account of *how* it is relevant to actual thinking and speaking, and

may—as many teachers and texts do today—either simply avoid the subject, or content himself with a few remarks about its obscurity (or utter impossibility). But that the remarks he makes at his trade are assumed by him to apply to the actual thought and discourse of himself and others is shown by how he *uses* the logical tools which he has sharpened. He *does* analyze particular arguments and inferences, and he does it *with* the principles and techniques which he has developed. Further, he *expects* others—especially if he has taught them—to do the same. No doubt most students of logic fail to know *why* or *how* what their instructor or text has told them applies to actual thinking and talking; and that is probably why only a minuscule percentage of them do in fact ever make *any* use whatsoever of what they learned from their study of logic.[2] But instructors and texts in logic do yet convey to them the assumption that what they are being taught applies to and informs on actual thinking and talking. To this assumption Logical Psychologism did full and explicit justice; but, with very few exceptions, such as John Dewey, logicians of this century have not even faced up to it.

III

But while a logician working today would, perhaps with some uneasiness, agree with Psychologism so far as to own up to (1), he certainly would also reject Psychologism by asserting, with (2), that the *evidence* which he has for the truths he teaches does not arise from an examination of particular episodes of thinking and speaking. He would assert this simply because he *has* evidence for his truths, but he did not get it in that way prescribed by Psychologism, and because he feels that the *sort* of evidence he has cannot be empirically derived. If Psychologism were correct, then when a logician is speaking, in general and nonnormative terms, about propositions, statements, proofs, arguments or inferences, his claims could have only that degree of probability provided by actual *observation* of instances from the classes of psychical or linguistic facts to which he refers. But he very well knows that his claims are not probability statements at all, and that they are never tested by observation of instances.

For example, Quine says, at the opening of "Part One" of his *Methods of Logic*

The peculiarity of *statements* which sets them apart from other linguistic forms is that they admit of truth and falsity, and may hence be significantly affirmed and denied. To deny a statement is to affirm another statement, known as the *negation* or contradictory of the first.

If, now, we were to approach this (quite non-normative) passage with a consistently psychologistic attitude, the following sorts of questions would have to be asked: How are these claims which Quine makes known to be true? How did he "discover" them? What are the data upon which these claims rest? When were the relevant observations made? What kind of person was making the statements, the denials, the affirmations, etc., observed? And was the observer qualified or trained in the making of such observations? Did he correctly record his observations? Is a margin of error to be allowed for in such observations? If not, why not? If so, what is it? And was it correctly handled in the observations here in question? What were the conditions under which the observations relevant to Quine's statements were made? Were the conditions sufficiently varied to insure that the correlation to be drawn is indeed just between the classes mentioned (e.g., statements, truths, denials, etc.) and not some others?—*If* non-normative logicians' truths belong to psychology—and perhaps, more specifically, to the psychology of linguistic behavior—and *if* psychology is a science in which evidence is ultimately drawn from observations of fact, *then* these questions *must* be asked. Otherwise there simply is no evidence for the logicians' truths in question. And they must, of course, be asked with reference to *all* of the non-normative truths of logic, not

only those stated by Quine above: truths such as "No proposition (or sentence or statement or utterance) is both true and false," "Arguments with inconsistent premises are valid, but never show their conclusion to be true," "The universal quantifier validly distributes through a conjunction, but not through a disjunction," and so on. *All* of the evidence for the truth of these and like claims, as well as for their falsity, must ultimately derive from observation of instances of the appropriate classes of experiences, linguistic and otherwise, if Psychologism is true. But, of course, it simply does not do so. Hence, Psychologism is false. It is wrong about where and how the logician obtains evidence for the truths he teaches.

IV

All of which leaves us with the puzzle of how (1) and (2) can be shown consistent with each other. It is interesting that many philosophers seem not to have been aware of this puzzle, much less worked out any solution for it. Frege, for example, distinguishes very clearly between what he calls an "idea" (a temporalized segment of the experience of some particular person) and what he calls a "thought."[3] As is well known, he takes certain complex "thoughts" to be the bearers of truth, and assigns "to logic the task of discovering the laws of truth, not the laws of asserting or thinking."[4] But as to an elucidation of *how* these "thoughts" and "ideas" are related to one another, especially in such a way that the laws of the former allow us to ascertain (as we constantly do) the logical character of the latter, e.g., valid, inconsistent, etc.—on this Frege has nothing helpful to say. He agrees that something in the individual consciousness must be "aimed at" the thought for us to think it or have it.[5] But he has no analysis of this metaphor of "aiming." He gives the name "apprehension" (*Fassen*) to the relation of mind or "idea" to the thought, but of course has to acknowledge that this too is a metaphor.[6] The puzzle of how logicians' truths apply to and inform us about certain aspects of actual thinking and asserting is left unresolved by Frege, if, indeed, he had any clear perception of it at all. And in this respect he is typical of many of the best logicians and philosophers of recent decades.

Husserl, on the other hand, was driven to work out a solution to this puzzle by his attempts to understand, from what was at first a strongly psychologistic point of view, the anti-Psychologistic view of the *proposition,* as presented by Bolzano.

The pattern for the standard, anti-Psychologistic view of propositions (and concepts as well) was set by Bolzano's *"Satz an sich,"* established by Frege's *"Gedanke,"* and naturalized in Anglo-Saxon countries in the "proposition" of Russell, Moore, W. E. Johnson, L. S. Stebbing, R. M. Eaton, and many other writers. In this pattern (and it is necessary here to think of a *pattern,* which allows some variation in the way it is specified by each writer) a proposition has the following main features:

1. The proposition is not located in space or in time, as, for example, sentences, or events involving sentences, are. This is in part what is meant by saying that they do not have *actual* or *real* existence, but only *ideal being.*

2. The proposition is not identical with a sentence, but the meaning or sense of an (indicative) sentence is a proposition. Propositions may, thus, be "expressed" by sentences, though it is not *essential* to them that they be so expressed.

3. The proposition is not something which can be sensuously perceived—even as a faint "glow" upon meaningful sentences or "living" words—though it *is,* of course, *somehow* known or, to use Frege's term, "apprehended."

4. The *same* proposition can be somehow grasped by the minds of *many* persons. In this capacity the proposition has been invoked as the intersubjective basis of the phenomena of communication and of the objectivity of scientific knowledge.

5. But it *need not* be grasped by the mind of any person at all. Its *esse* is not *percipi.* As Frege says, "In thinking we do not produce thoughts but we apprehend them. . . . The work of science does not consist of creation but of the discovery of true thoughts."[7]

6. When the proposition is related to a mind, its relation is, or principally is, that of an *object* of thought or of the so-called "propositional attitudes," such as belief or doubt. It is "before" the mind. This is sometimes obscurely expressed by saying that it is the "content" of a belief or judgment.

7. Description of a proposition does not *essentially* involve a reference to any particular mind or act of thought with which it may be involved. Its truth value or what it refers to is never affected by such involvement, unless it happens to be a proposition which *refers* to such involvement.

8. But its description does essentially involve mention of its references *to,* or intendings or meanings *of,* certain things, plus description of how these references are related to one another. A proposition essentially consists of a more or less complex set of references, intentions, or meanings, plus the mode of their combination.

9. Finally, the proposition is what is underivatively true or false, while opinions or sentences or statements are true or false only because they have a certain relationship with a proposition.

It would not be worthwhile here to document each point of this pattern in all of the writers mentioned above. The whole pattern appears in subsections 19, 25-26, 34, and 48-50 of volume 1 of Bernard Bolzano's *Wissenschaftslehre.* In Frege's paper "The Thought," already referred to, the pattern once again appears whole. It is almost whole in Moore's *Some Main Problems of Philosophy,* chapter 3; in chapter 1 of W. E. Johnson's *Logic,* part 1; on pages 6-24 of R. M. Eaton's *General Logic;* and on pages 17-20 of Max Black's *Critical Thinking* (2d ed.). Bertrand Russell's "On Propositions: What They Are and How They Mean," in his *Logic and*

Knowledge, as well as chapter 12 of his *Analysis of Mind,* present important phases of the pattern, as well as some modifications of it. So does C. I. Lewis in chapter 3 of *An Analysis of Knowledge and Valuation.* Husserl's *adaptation* of the pattern is nowhere presented more clearly than in chapters 7 and 8 of volume 1, and in subsections 29-35 of the first "Investigation" in volume 2 of his *Logical Investigations.*

V

And it obviously is with an *adaptation* or *modification* of the anti-Psychologistic pattern that we must be concerned, if its concept of the proposition is to be used in a resolution of the paradox at hand. It is clear that if logicians' claims are fundamentally about the "propositions" described, then evidence for those claims could not be derived from a mere inductive survey of particular thinkings and speakings, to which, in the pattern, propositions have only a quite extrinsic and contingent connection. Thus, the pattern supports our (2), and Husserl strongly concurs with it in this respect. But it is equally clear that the pattern, as it stands, gives us no help in reconciling (2) with (1). It gives not the least suggestion of how logicians, having the source and sort of evidence they do have for their claims, do nonetheless succeed in saying something about the actual thinking and speaking of particular human beings. Where in the anti-Psychologistic pattern does the problem lie?

According to Bolzano—and point 6 of the anti-Psychologistic pattern—the relation between the mind and the propositions which it "thinks" or "grasps" is that of *intentionality.* That is, the proposition is the mind's *object*; or, to use one of Frege's terms, it "stands over against" (*gegenübersteht*)[8] the mind thinking it. L. S. Stebbing expresses this view of the proposition's relation to mind in words frequent in logical writings of her time, by saying that "a proposition is anything that is believed, disbelieved, doubted or supposed."[9] Of course the objections to

this position on propositions are quite well known. They are stated, for example, on pages 35-36 of volume 1 of McTaggart's *The Nature of Existence,* and more fully on pages 105-111 of Gilbert Ryle's paper "Are There Propositions?"[10] Perhaps the main points in these objections may be summed up by saying that the alleged "objective" propositions are a queer, or at least superfluous, sort of entity, and that they *are not* always, if they are ever, the objects of our beliefs, doubts, etc.

In fact, these are precisely Husserl's objections to objective propositions. He thought of Bolzano's "propositions in themselves" as "mythical entities, suspended between being and non-being."[11] And he held that when "we make an assertion, we judge about the fact concerned, and ... not about the judgement in the logical sense,"[12] i.e., about the proposition. However, what is principally of interest here is not Husserl's objections to objective propositions, but rather his way of avoiding those objections, while still retaining the essence of anti-Psychologism in *his* view of the proposition and, simultaneously, resolving the paradox of Logical Psychologism.

VI

In the review just quoted from, Husserl indicates that the key for his revision of Bolzano's theory of propositions came from his study of yet another revision: Lotze's revision of Plato's theory of forms.[13] Plato's forms had, like Bolzano's propositions, been persistently called both queer and useless; and the queerness and uselessness alleged seemed mainly to follow upon their being *located in* something at some sort of "distance" from their instances—in some void or Divine Mind or $T\acute{o}\pi o\varsigma$ $o\dot{v}\rho\acute{a}\nu\iota o\varsigma$. Lotze saw that this odd kind of "localization" was not required by the various arguments for universals, and that it indeed made no sense anyway. He held that to say that blueness or triangularity, for example, "exists" or "is" is not to say that a certain color or plane

figure is located somewhere, nor is it to
imply this.[14] It is only to say that certain
discriminable elements of things have
certain (always non-spatial and nontemporal) determinations of their own:
e.g., blueness is a color which is darker
than yellowness (though no blue thing is),
and triangularity is a plane figure involving fewer straight lines than squareness
(though no triangular object is). One—
really not quite correct—way which
Lotze (and later Husserl) had of saying
this was to say that for universals to exist
means only that certain propositions
about them are true.[15] To mark this point
of connection between their existence
and truth, Lotze said that universals do
not have *real* existence, or *Wirklichkeit,*
but only *ideal* being, which he also called
Geltung or *validity.*[16]

Now Husserl does not detail for us precisely *how* this revision of Plato's theory
of forms led to his revision of Bolzano's
theory of the proposition "in itself." One
can see, however, an attractive route
which he may have traveled: If universals
can avoid the charges of queerness and
superfluity by the assignment of ideal
being or *Geltung,* then possibly propositions can escape by being regarded as
universals. Such an identification of propositions with universals (of a certain
sort) must have been rendered more attractive by observing that it conflicted
with the anti-Psychologistic pattern for
the proposition only on point 6, and that
the other points either do not conflict with
it or actually seem to strengthen it, as
does point 4.

In any case, Husserl came to regard the
propositions of which logicians speak,
and for the truth of which, according both
to him and Frege, they discover laws, as
complex, *referential qualities,* which
may or may not be instanced in minds,
but which—following Brentano—are
never instanced by any physical thing. He
said that upon reading Lotze he

saw that under "proposition in itself" is to be
understood . . .what is designated in ordinary
discourse—which always objectifies the
ideal—as the "sense" of a statement. It is that
which is explained as one and the same where,

for example, different persons are said to have
asserted the same thing. . . .And it further became clear to me that this identical sense
could be nothing other than the universal, the
species, which belongs to a certain *moment* or
phase present in all actual assertions (Aussa-
gen) with the same sense, and which makes
possible the identification [of sameness] just
mentioned, even where the descriptive content of the individual experiences (Erlebnisse)
of asserting varies considerably in other respects. The proposition (Satz) thus relates to
those acts of judgment (Urteilsakte) to which
it belongs as their identical intention
(Meinung) in the same way, for example, as
the species *redness* relates to individuals of
"the same" red color. Now with this view of
things as a basis. Bolzano's theory, that propositions are objects which, nonetheless,
have no "existence" (Existenz), comes to
have the following quite intelligible
signification:—They have the "ideal" being
(Sein) or validity (Gelten) of objects which are
universals (allgemeiner Gegenstände); and,
thus, that being which is established, for
example, in the "existence proofs" of Mathematics. But they do not have the real being
(reale Sein) of *things*, or of dependent, thing-
like *moments*—of temporal particulars in general. Bolzano himself did not give the faintest
intimation that these phenomenological relationships between signification, signification
moment, and full act of signifying had been
noticed by him.[17]

And elsewhere Husserl says:

In the actual experience of signification there
corresponds to the unitary signification[18] an
individual aspect, as singular instance of the
signification species: in the same way as in the
red object the red-moment corresponds to the
specific difference, red. If we actualize the act
of signifying and, as it were, live in it, then we
naturally mind the act's object and not its signification. When, for example, we make an
assertion, we judge about the fact concerned,
and not about the signification of the indicative sentence involved, not about the judgment
in the logical sense. This latter becomes an
object for us only in a reflective act of thought,
in which we do not merely look back upon the
real-ized assertion, but rather carry out the
required abstraction (or, better said, ideation). This logical reflection is not. . .an act
which occurs under certain artificially in-
duced conditions. Rather, it is a normal constituent of logical thinking.[19]

We may, therefore, sum up Husserl's revision of Bolzano's view of the proposition as follows: For Bolzano (and most anti-Psychologists) the relation of mind to proposition is *intentionality,* while for Husserl it is *instantiation* or *exemplification.*[20] The obviously increased intimacy of the connection as viewed by Husserl is the essence of his resolution of the paradox of Logical Psychologism.

VII

It seemed paradoxical that logicians could succeed in saying something true of particular events of thinking and speaking, since they do not develop their theories by inductive or empirical analysis of such events. Given Husserl's revision of the concept of the proposition, this fact may be explained as follows: Propositions, on his view, are not particular acts of thought, but complex, referential characters or qualities *of* such acts. These referential qualities also have determinations, among which are truth and falsity and conditions of truth and falsity.[21] But these determinations do not merely have some quite extrinsic and contingent connection with the concrete acts of thinking and speaking which instance their immediate subjects, i.e., propositions. Somewhat as, since red is a color, a red thing—though no color—is necessarily a colored thing, so, we might say, an act of thought or speech which instances a true proposition, though itself no truth, is nonetheless a true judgment or utterance. And the various logical relations which hold between the truth conditions of propositions can similarly be given a natural extension to apply to the

acts of belief or inference which involve instantiation of the propositions in question. The proposition, or set of propositions, introduces its determinations (properties and relations) into the individual acts which instance it.[22]

Because of this connection between universals and their instances, truths about universals, including, of course, truths about concepts and propositions,[23] entail corresponding truths about the corresponding individual things or events.[24] To take examples from logic, the proposition that the proposition that Nixon is a Republican is true, has its transform in the proposition that all judgments or statements to the effect that Nixon is a Republican are true. Or again, the proposition that the premises of a certain syllogism of type Barbara imply its conclusion has its transform in the proposition that all actual inferences from those premises to that conclusion are valid.

What the logician's truths are *primarily* about are, therefore, not mental or linguistic acts, but characters of acts; and it is from the analysis of the truth conditions of these characters (which, as universals, are always the same, no matter what their instances may be) that he obtains evidence for his claims. But his truths also apply informatively to particular acts, and do so precisely because they are about the characters *of* such acts. And *this* is Husserl's way out of the paradox of Logical Psychologism. It is unfortunate that it has been so universally neglected or misunderstood; for it concerns a central issue in the philosophy of logic, and there is perhaps no other philosopher who has worked out a way of reconciling our (1) and (2) that is remotely as plausible as Husserl's way.[25]

NOTES

1. Quine, for one, explicitly says that what admits of truth and falsity—and, by implication, of logical relations—are "individual events of statement utterance" (*Methods of Logic,* rev. ed. [New York, 1959], p. xi). Unfortunately, this statement forms no homogeneous part of his logical theories, but rather is forced upon him by his theory *about* logic, and his

general epistemological views. One who knew only what Quine has said in developing logical theories would not have the least inkling that the theories were theories about utterance events.

2. As a matter of simple fact, few courses more totally—though perhaps many equally—waste the student's time, so far as his own self-betterment is

concerned, than university courses in logic. The irony is that the greater waste is usually made by the very courses which are technically more rigorous. A nice, sloppy course mainly dealing with so-called "informal fallacies" often gives the student a critical handhold (usually involving little *insight*) on some things he subsequently thinks tr hears.

3. "The Thought: A Logical Inquiry," in P. F. Strawson, ed., *Philosophical Logic* (Oxford, 1967), pp. 26-29; and "Der Gedanke," in Gottlob Frege, *Logische Untersuchungen,* Günther Patzig, ed. (Göttingen, 1966), pp. 40-43.

4. Strawson, op. cit., p. 19; Frege, op. cit., p. 31.

5. Strawson, op. cit., p. 35; Frege, op. cit., p. 50.

6. Strawson, op. cit., p. 35n.; Frege, op. cit., p. 49n.

7. Strawson, op. cit., p. 35; Frege, op. cit., p. 50.

8. In "Die Verneinung: Eine Logische Untersuchung," in Frege, op. cit., p. 58.

9. *A Modern Introduction to Logic* (London, 1961), p. 33. Cf. pp. 4-7 of W. E. Johnson, *Logic,* pt. 1 (New York, 1964).

10. *Proceedings of the Aristotelian Society,* 30 (1929-30): 105-11.

11. From p. 290 of Husserl's review of *Der Streit der Psychologisten und Formalisten in der modernen Logik,* by Melchior Palágyi (Leipzig, 1902). This review appeared in vol. 31 (1903) of *Zeitschrift fur Psychologie und Physiologie der Sinnesorgane,* pp. 287-94. An English translation of this review appeared in *The Personalist* for 1972, pp. 5-13.

12. *Logische Untersuchungen,* 5th ed., vol. 2, pt. 1, p. 103.

13. Hermann Lotze, *Logic,* ed. and trans. Bernard Bosanquet (Oxford, 1884), bk. 3, chap. 2, pp. 433-49.

14. *Ibid.*, p. 443.

15. *Ibid.*, pp. 439-46. And for Husserl see *Logische Untersuchungen,* vol. 2, pt. 1, p. 101.

16. Of course, this is no mere *in rebus* or *post rem* doctrine of universals. To deny that universals exist in some place apart from their instances is not at all to hold that they exist only (or at all) in their instances or in minds which have beheld their instances. Nor is it to say that they in any way depend, for their being or their being known, upon their instances.

17. From p. 290 of the review of Palágyi.

18. A "proposition" was one type of "significa-

tion" *(Bedeutung)* for Husserl, as it was one type of "sense" for Frege.

19. *Logische Untersuchungen,* vol. 2, pt. 1, p. 103.

20. The similarity between the views of Husserl and those of Gustav Bergmann on propositions should now be obvious. See Bergmann's *Logic and Reality* (Madison, 1964), p. 34 and elsewhere. The American psychologist R. S. Woodworth also advocated similar views early in this century. On p. 706 of his "Imageless Thought" (in *Journal of Philosophy* for 1906) he says: "There is a specific and unanalyzable conscious quale for every individual and general notion, for every judgment and supposition. These qualities recur in the same sense as red and green recur."

21. Bertrand Russell held a similar view at one point in his career. In "The Limits of Empiricism" he says that there are "facts about universals" which are perceptible, and which extend our knowledge of particulars beyond particulars which have been examined. This is exactly Husserl's view, applied here to what I call "referential qualities." This paper by Russell (*Aristotelian Society Proceedings,* 36 [1935-36]: esp. p. 140), though it makes no mention of Husserl, is an excellent statement of Husserl's view on the limits of Empiricism.

22. *Logische Untersuchungen,* 5th edition, Vol. I. See the sentence spanning pp. 143-143 and the sentence ending the paragraph on p. 151.

23. On p. 342 of *Logische Untersuchungen* (vol. 2) Husserl says: "As to all ideal units [i.e., universals], so there correspond to significations real possibilities and, perhaps, actualities. To significations *in specie* there correspond acts of signifying; and, indeed, the former are nothing but aspects of the latter, taken as ideal *(als Ideal gefasste)*."

24. See subsections 7 and 8 of Husserl's *Ideas* (New York, 1962) for elaboration of this claim. A clear exposition of essentially the same position is found in H. W. B. Joseph, *An Introduction to Logic,* 2d ed. (Oxford, 1916), pp. 282-85.

25. It must be added that the above account is by no means the whole story on Husserl's view of propositions. In *Ideas* (vol. 1; see esp. subsection 93) and in *Formal and Transcendental Logic* (The Hague, 1969), one finds an immensely—and, I think, unfortunately—more complex theory of propositions, which returns to an essentially Bolzanian or "noematic" proposition.

Husserl's Theory of Meaning

JITENDRANATH N. MOHANTY

The concept of meaning is so central to Husserlian phenomenology that it may well provide the best access to its intricacies. The only other concept that is as fundamental is that of intentionality. In fact, in Husserl's thought these two concepts depend upon and enrich each other. This is as it ought to be in any satisfactory philosophy of meaning and mind.

We shall discuss Husserl's reflections on the problem of meaning under two main headings: (a) the distinction between meaning and reference and (b) the doctrine of the ideality of meanings. There will be a concluding section of critical observations.

A. Meaning and Reference

1. The decisive text for this distinction is the following paragraph in the First Logical Investigation:

Each expression not merely says something, but says it *of* something; it not only has a meaning, but refers to certain *objects*.... But the object never coincides with the meaning. Both, of course, only pertain to an expression in virtue of the mental acts which give it sense . . . this distinction means the same as the distinction between what is meant or said, on the one hand, and what is spoken of, by means of the expression, on the other.[1]

1.1. Before proceeding, we may pause to look closely at what Husserl says here. He is talking about *all* expressions, and not merely of names, though he soon tells us that names "offer the plainest examples of the separation of meaning from the relation to objects."[2] Expressions have been a little earlier defined as "meaningful signs,"[3] though this is not very illuminating at this stage, when we do not know what he means by 'meaning' and 'meaningful'. More helpful, provisionally, is the statement that each instance or part of *speech* shall count as an expression, "whether or not such speech is actually uttered, or addressed with communicative intent to any persons or not."[4] He wants to exclude bodily gestures (voluntary or involuntary) and other natural manifestations of mental states (like smiling, groaning, or blushing) and restrict himself to linguistic expressions. But even with regard to language, his primary concern is speech—not written or otherwise documented language. This primacy of speech, of the *act* of speaking, in Husserl's theory of meaning is of utmost importance.[5] Further, Husserl is trying to describe the act of speaking not from the point of view of the third person observer, but from the point of view of the speaker, in whose consciousness—as he tells us—that act of expressing (speaking, uttering) is "phenomenally one with the experiences made manifest in them."[6] It is questionable whether this characterization of an expression (namely, that the act of expressing should be 'phenomenally one' with the experiences expressed in the consciousness of the person performing the act) would serve to exclude all nonlinguistic expressions like gestures, groaning in pain, etc., for it is quite possible that for the person groaning in pain, groaning is not distinguished from his being in pain, or, for the person smiling in happiness, the facial expression is not distinguished from the happiness it expresses. Perhaps anticipating this challenge, Husserl adds that in these nonlinguistic expressions one does not communicate anything to another. But, again, he recognizes that expressions were originally framed to fulfill a communicative function; as is well known, he returns to a solitary monologue where, even in the absence of communicative intent, the expression functions as an expression. Thus the mere absence of the intent to communicate could not disqualify natural or involuntary manifestations of experiences from being 'expressions' in Husserl's sense. Besides, they may serve to communicate even in the absence of the intent to do so. But we have to bear two points in mind. First, when such nonlinguistic manifestations serve to communicate, they do so only insofar as others *interpret* them. We "interpret" groaning to stand for pain, smiling to stand for happiness, and so on. Here groaning is a sign for or an indication of pain. But groaning does not mean pain in the sense in which "pain" does. The second point is that there is "no intent to put certain 'thoughts' on record expressively, whether for the man himself, in his solitary state, or for others."[7] It seems to me that since gestures may be voluntary and may be intentional (i.e., may be accompanied by intention to communicate), the emphasis has to be placed on "thoughts." Nonlinguistic expressions, we may say—slightly modifying Husserl's statement—may be intentional but they cannot *directly* express "thoughts": they may "tell" the interpreter "That man is in pain," and it is what they thus tell, namely, the sentence thus suggested, which alone would express a thought. A gesture, then, may indirectly express a thought by being linguistically interpreted by the interpreter.

Husserl is thus, in the First Logical Investigation, concerned with linguistic utterances, with the acts of speaking. But having come to this point, he takes a step that is almost unique. Although speaking is ordinarily speaking to an audience, one may also speak to oneself in the solitude and interiority of one's inner life—not aloud or subvocally but entirely in phantasy. Now it would be usual to regard audible speaking to an audience as the paradigmatic case where one should look for the essence of speech and then to regard the so-called inner monologues as merely degenerate. But, curiously, Husserl decides that the inner, silent, phantasized speaking is also speaking in the full-fledged sense. If it is, then the essence of expression *qua* expression—now that "expression" has been identified with "speech"—has to be sought here and not in communicative speech situations where more is present than the essence. He is in fact performing a sort of eidetic variation in order to exclude what is not essential to an expression *qua* expression.

The eidetic variation yields the following result. What does not belong to the essence of expression *qua* expression is the function of indicating, intimating, or announcing the speaker's mental states or inner experiences to the hearer. This function surely is of the utmost importance in communicative speech, whose successful performance depends upon the hearer's recognizing the intentions of the speaker.[8] The words of the speaker serve the hearer as signs of those intentions and inner experiences of the speaker. To that extent, words *do* serve as mere signs, indicating or motivating belief in the existence of some other order of reality—much as red spots on one's face may be marks or symptoms of fever or groaning of a state of pain. But expressions are not indicating signs or marks for Husserl. They are, *qua* expressions, meaningful: they express "thoughts." In the inner monologue, the inner experiences of the speaker are being lived by him, so that they need not have been indicated to him. Furthermore, the expressions are not actually existent words but phantasized ones, and so cannot serve as marks in any case—for marks have to be real, existent. Here, then, phantasized speaking is a pure act of expressing:

The word's non-existence neither disturbs nor interests us, since it leaves the word's expressive function unaffected. Where it *does* make a difference is where intimation is linked with meaning.[9]

Their essence, then, consists in (1) expressing meanings or thoughts and (2) being about or referring to some object.

1.2. This turning away from communicative speech to inner and phantasized speech may be regarded either, at best, as the decisive step for all Husserl's subsequent philosophizing[10] or, at worst, as misleading and even untenable.[11] If it is regarded as decisive, it is because the "inner voice" provides the sort of pure self-presence that Husserl needs throughout his philosophical quest, and also because—being unreal—it can be repeated and so can constitute the ideal meanings, whereas actual speech, being real, is evanescent and can never come back again. There is a curious mixture of insight and misunderstanding in this assessment. The reduction to inner speech is in conformity with the general trend of transcendental phenomenology, but what is needed for the ideality thesis is not the repeatability of the speech act—which in the strict sense is never the same (even the acts of phantasizing are individuated)—but that of the meaning.[12] The reduction to inner speech easily leads us to mistake Husserl's intention. First it tends to support looking for the essence of thought in the privacy of one's mental life, while the thesis of the ideality of meanings is meant to rescue us from that privacy and to situate the thinking subject in the communicative world. The objective character and the ideality of meanings are then more apt to be deduced from the communicative speech situation than from the monological. At worst, the turn to inner phantasy is untenable, for phantasy is a parasitical act—a modified act pointing back to perception, actual seeing or hearing. Phantasized speaking then, by

its essence, refers back to actual speaking.

2. An expression, we have been told, "not only has a meaning but refers to certain objects." In what sense—if any—this is true of all parts of speech, and also of all kinds of speech, will be discussed later. For the present, let us restrict ourselves to names. The distinction between sense and reference, at least with regard to names, has become a foundation of modern semantics,[13] and it is commonplace in the secondary literature to trace Husserl's distinction to Frege's. According to the accepted historical judgment, Husserl was made to recognize the objectivity of meanings and the distinction between meaning, object, and subjective mental states by Frege's "Sinn und Bedeutung" (1892) and, more convincingly, by Frege's review (in 1894), of his *Philosophie der Arithmetik*.[14] As a result, Husserl is said to have overcome his early psychologism and to have adopted Frege's distinction with only a changed terminology. This historical judgment, however, does not withstand close scrutiny.[15] In his 1891 review of Schröder's *Vorlesungen zur Algebra der Logik*, Husserl accuses Schröder of failing to distinguish between the meaning of a name, the *Vorstellung* of the object named by the name, and the object itself; and Husserl wants to keep the two questions separate: "whether there belongs to a name a meaning (*Sinn*); and...whether an object corresponding to a name exists or not."[16] The papers on *Inhaltslogik* (1891) make use of the concepts of intension and ideal content.[17] As Husserl himself notes, the concept of 'pure essential lawfulness' is arrived at in his 1891 survey of German logical literature.[18] Only the explicit thesis of the ideality of meanings is lacking. Frege does not have that peculiarly Husserlian thesis.[19] Thus not only did Husserl not get his crucial distinction from Frege, but from the very outset his orientation is quite different. Even when, as in *Logical Investigations*, he has overcome psychologism, his interest nevertheless is in the act—not in the ex-

pressions as physical signs or marks, but in the acts of expressing (*ausdrückende Akte*).[20] The concept of act is inseparable from the concept of intentionality, so that when he extends the results of *Logical Investigations* to all acts in *Ideas,* he is simply applying the Fregean distinction to the entire domain of conscious life. In fact, not having Husserl's concept of intentionality, Frege had a very different notion of the relation between subjective life and objective meanings.

2.1. With regard to names, Frege seems to have been led to his distinction between sense and reference[21] by his attempt to find reasons why the sentences 'a = a' and 'a = b' have different cognitive values: whereas the former is analytic and holds good a priori, the latter—if true—extends our knowledge and cannot always be grounded a priori. Now if the identity were between the things named by the signs 'a' and 'b', then—Frege argues—the two sentences could not have different cognitive values, if 'a = b' is true. Everything is identical with itself, and therefore the sentence 'a = b' would be saying that the signs 'a' and 'b' designate the same thing. The sentence would then be about the two signs. Since, however, our use of signs is arbitrary, in the sense that we could designate the same things with some other signs or some other object or objects by the same signs, the sentence 'a = b' could not express true knowledge. Frege then argues that 'a = b' could have the cognitive value it has only if to the difference of signs there corresponds a difference in the mode of givenness of what is designated by them. Hence besides the designated thing, which may be called the reference of the sign, there is also connected with a sign what may be called its meaning or *Sinn*, which contains the mode of givenness of the referent. The expressions 'evening star' and 'morning star' have the same reference but different meanings.

2.2. To my knowledge, Husserl has not explicitly thematized this Fregean problem. The earliest context in which he introduces this distinction is an examination of Schröder's account of equivocal and univocal names; and it is not surprising, therefore, that the decisive text (quoted in 1. above) occurs in a section in which Husserl returns to the theme of equivocal names. If the meaning of a name were the same as the representation (*Vorstellung*) of the object named by the name, he wrote in that 1891 review,[22] then all common names would be equivocal; in *Logical Investigations* the same identification of meaning with *Vorstellung* is said to yield the consequence that *all* names would be equivocal proper names.[23]

2.3. The Schröder review also takes up the question whether 'round square' is meaningless (*unsinnige*). Schröder thinks it is, and Husserl comments that Schröder is confusing two different questions: whether there belongs to a name a *Sinn* and whether an object corresponding to a name exists or not.[24] Thus to the context of equivocity or univocity of some or all names we may add the problematic—and this becomes increasingly more central in Husserl's thought—of the difference between mere understanding and knowing. The latter distinction is already drawn in the First Logical Investigation and forms the theme of the Sixth; but it has its ancestry in another and, for Husserl, more significant distinction, namely, between "empty," symbolic thinking and thinking that is not so. In chapter 11 of *Philosophie der Arithmetik* Husserl distinguishes between "symbolic" and "authentic" representation, tracing the distinction back to Brentano's lectures:

A symbolic or inauthentic representation is, as the name already suggests, a representation through signs. If a content (*Inhalt*) is not directly given to us as what it is, but only indirectly through signs that *characterize it* uniquely (*eindeutig*), then we have, instead of an authentic, a symbolic representation.[25]

In the *Logical Investigations* we find

Those who locate the meaning-aspect of symbols in intuition must find purely symbolic thinking insolubly enigmatic.[26]

And for those who identify the meaning

with the objective correlate, a name like 'golden mountain' would be meaningless.[27]

In this way Husserl arrives at the distinction between "meaning" (*Bedeutung*) and "reference" (*Gegenstand*). The meaning is neither the object referred o nor a representation of the object, nor a mental picture, nor even an intuition of the object.

2.4. The examples Husserl gives of names are ordinary proper names like 'London' and 'Socrates', names of numbers like '2', definite descriptions like 'the victor at Jena', names of species like 'redness', existence-positing names like 'the statue of Roland in the market place' and 'the postman hurrying by', and non-positing names like 'the supposed S', as well as names of sentences and facts.

For Husserl, the act of naming is a completed act, although it normally functions within the larger context of propositional acts:

If we wish to see clearly what names are and mean we should look at contexts, particularly statements, in which names function in their normal meaning.[28]

A mere noun by itself is not a name, for it does not express a complete act. A name, then, must be a word or group of words that stands or can stand for some complete, simple subject of a statement without undergoing change in its intentional essence. The last clause, 'without undergoing...', is added to exclude such cases as ' "and" is a conjunction'.

This suggests that if we consider a total speech act of assertion, or a propositional act, we shall find that it must contain at least one name. In fact, it consists of an act of naming (nominal act) and an act of predication. The propositional act is not an aggregate of these two-part acts but has a distinctive—and here dominant—act-quality of its own.[29] But since it is necessary that every act have at least one component "objectifying act" (if it itself is not an objectifying one)—according to Husserl's reformulation of Brentano's law about the foundational status of "presentations"[30]—the linguistic ex-

pression of every act whatsoever must contain at least one name, whether the act is one of asserting, questioning, ordering, wishing, or any other act-quality. When the propositional act is what Husserl calls "positing," it is an act of asserting or stating.[31]

Now for Husserl names express referring acts in the paradigmatic sense. But, curiously enough, he also extends the notion of referring to predicate expressions as well as to entire sentences. At this point his semantics appears to run into grave difficulties.

2.5. With regard to "predicate expressions," let us consider the following examples:

1)   Bucephalus is a horse.
2)   The flower is red.

The expression 'a horse', Husserl writes, has the same meaning or sense in different contexts, but the same meaning presents Bucephalus on one occasion and the cart-horse on another (e.g., in 'The cart-horse is a horse'). Now there are uses of 'a horse' which are undoubtedly referential, for example, when it is used in the subject place, as in 'A horse is pulling the cart'. But it is not so obvious that 'a horse' when used as a predicate is also referring to an object. There seems to be two ways of showing that it *is*, the second of which is Husserl's. The first way is to construe 'B is a horse' as an identity statement of the form 'B = a horse', which states that the object designated by 'B' is identical with the thing designated by 'a horse'. Apart from the fact that this would reduce the predicate to a name, there are two difficulties here: first, this construction leaves us with 'identical with a horse' as the predicate, so that if we again wish to reduce predication to identity we have to take a similar step over again, but only at the risk of landing in an infinite regress; and secondly, as Searle has argued,[32] if 'B is not a horse' is construed as 'B is not identical with a horse', we ought to be able to ask "Which horse?" Husserl does not take this way out, but another: the indefiniteness of "a horse" gives it an "extension" which is the "range of possible application,"[33] which is its reference, while the concept "horse" or the property "horseness" is its meaning. The idea of "range" is nothing but "the *logical possibility* of propositions of a certain sort,"[34] so that the predicate 'a horse' determines a range of possible propositions of the form 'X is a horse'. It should be clear, then, that the talk of "being about" in the case of predicate expressions like 'a horse' is somewhat different from the case of names. In *Formale und transzendentale Logik*, Husserl writes that the predicate 'is white' (in the sentence 'This paper is white') goes beyond its own *Sachbezüglichkeit* and comprehends that of the subject, 'this paper'.[35] Possibly he means that while it is true that the reference of the predicate, 'is white', is in itself indefinite, as it functions in 'this paper is white', it is made partially definite insofar as one member of its "range" is specified by the subject term.

The word 'red' functions in

This flower is red. (*predicative use*)
This red flower is beautiful. (*attributive use*)
Being red (*redness*) is a differentiation of colored (*color*). (*nominalized use*)

The original use is predicative; and from this use the other two are derived and always derivable. These are different syntactic formations, underlying which there is a common core with the core forms, which are nonsyntactical. Thus syntactically unformed words like 'paper', 'man', 'horse' have the same nonsyntactical core form, namely the substantival, while syntactically unformed words like 'red', 'green', 'round' have the same nonsyntactical form, the adjectival. It is through their core material that their *Sachbezüglichkeit* is eventually established.

In 'This flower is red' the predicate means a concept and refers to an indefinite range of objects that is partially determined by the reference of the subject term 'this flower'. In 'this red flower',

'red' means the same as before—but refers to a real attribute, a nonindependent moment of this flower. 'Being red' or 'redness' refers to a *species*, a universal object, and again means the concept of redness.

It would not be accurate to say that Husserl treats predicates as if they were names. He recognizes the syntactic differences between names and predicates as well as the fundamental difference between the two kinds of speech acts: naming and predicating. He also sees the difference of both from the speech act of asserting and denying. However, he also holds that each component refers, and not merely the subject expression—even if only the subject expression names. In a certain sense, he also sees that the "object," in the strict sense, is that which is or can be named. By nominalizing the predicate expression we do not continue to have the same reference as before, but constitute a new object in the more appropriate sense of "object." It is because each component has an extralinguistic reference that the entire sentence has one. The extralinguistic reference of the entire sentence is "founded" upon the references of the component expressions. And yet the founded reference alone is independent.

2.6 Other words like 'is', 'or', 'because' are expressions for "moments of meaning" (*Bedeutungsmomente*); they are not unmeaning marks but have only "dependent meanings" which require completion in more or less determinate ways. But they really do lack any *Sachbezüglichkeit*,[36] though again, by virtue of their functions, they participate in the *Sachbezüglichkeit* of the whole sentence. Thus they play distinct semantic roles.[37] Purely formal words like 'something' do not express any "content" or "matter"; rather, they express formal concepts and formal ontological categories.[38] They therefore refer indefinitely to all that is possible, "even if they refer to it quite indeterminately, or as a mere 'something.' "[39] The word 'all' refers to a peculiar semantical form. When made to form the expression 'all A's', it refers to a distributive totality—to all A's but no single A, by itself or directly.[40]

2.7 An indicative or declarative sentence by itself means a proposition (cf. Frege's *Gedanke*) and refers to a fact. The notion of 'object' of such sentences is equivocal. A propositional act is a complex act, in whose case we must distinguish between the objective reference of the act as a whole and the objects to which the part-acts belonging to it refer. In a preeminent sense, a propositional act or an act of judging is *about* an object. The judgment expressed in 'The knife is on the table' is *about* the knife. In this sense, the object is the 'that-about-which' (*Gegenstandworüber*) of the act.[41] It is also called the substrate of the judgment.[42] But the full object of the total act—that which is constituted in the act of predication—is a categorial object, that is, the state of affairs (*Sachverhalt*). Although the state of affairs is the objective *correlate* or the intentional object of the total act of judging, it is not itself presented in the act.[43] The knife is what we judge about; the state of affairs, that the knife is on the table, is what we judge but do not present to ourselves or name. The mode of consciousness of the state of affairs—namely, the act of judging—is a many-ray synthetic positing; it is not as such, however, a single-ray 'presentation' unless and until the original many-ray act is transformed into an act of naming.

We have to distinguish between
uttering a sentence,
saying something about something by that utterance,
asserting a proposition,
stating a fact,
naming the fact so stated,
naming the proposition asserted, and
naming the sentence uttered.

If we pursue the genesis of predicative judgment out of pre-predicative experience, as Husserl does in *Experience and Judgment*, we find that the same passively perceived object is a "source" of relational situations (*Sachlagen*) through acts of internal explication. Such a relational situation is said to "involve" several states of affairs. The example Husserl gives in *Experience and Judgment* is this: the quantitative situation a − b involves two states of affairs, a > b and b < a. Equivalent predicative judgments refer to one and the same situation (*Sachlage*).[44]

When Husserl says that a > b and b < a refer to the same *Sachlage* (as he also says in *Logical Investigations*, 1: 288), what he wants to say is that they state the same fact. If the fact stated by a sentence is nothing but its truth-condition or what makes it true,[45] it would seem that whatever makes one of them true also makes the other true. In this sense of "fact" the *Sachlage* would seem to be the fact that makes them both true. But the same *Sachlage* is explicated by the two judgments in different ways, so that two different syntactical objectivities are constituted by the two acts. These syntactical objectivities are the states of affairs or *Sachverhalten*. These are the objective correlates of the acts, but they are not objectified in them. When a that-clause is formed along with any of the sentences, the resulting expression (e.g., 'That a > b' or 'The fact that a > b') names not the *Sachlage* in the sense of the common truth-condition that 'a > b' may share with some other sentences, but the *Sachverhalt* or the state of affairs in the sense of the syntactical objectivity that is constituted in the act expressed by 'a > b' and not in the act expressed by 'b < a'.

If this interpretation of Husserl is correct, a perceptual statement of the lowest order, like 'This is white', is *about* the thing designated by 'this', *states* the fact (*Sachlage*) which is receptively constituted by pre-predicative explication, and has a syntactical objectivity, a *Sachverhalt* or a state of affairs, as its *correlate*, which is named by 'The fact that this is white'.

The following, then, would seem to be true:

If two sentences have different meanings, they must have different

Sachverhalten as their correlates.

But two sentences with different meanings may refer to the same *Sachlage*.

If difference of meanings entails difference in the *Sachverhalten*, one may well ask how the *Sachverhalt* constituted in a propositional act is related to the meaning of that act. Or, to put it differently, how are "proposition" and "state of affairs" related?

In section 69 of *Experience and Judgment* Husserl distinguishes between the actual state of affairs and the state of affairs supposed as such, and then identifies the actual state of affairs with the true proposition.[46] The proposition, considered apart from the question of its truth or falsity, is the state of affairs supposed as such. It should be remembered that "true" and "false" are, for Husserl, predicates of meanings.[47] The state of affairs (*Sachverhalt*), then, is the objectified propositional meaning. The word 'fact' (*Tatsache*) is used by Husserl sometimes for *Sachlage* and sometimes for *Sachverhalt*, thereby causing difficulties in interpretation.

A difference thus appears to emerge in the sense of "objective reference" with regard to names and sentences.[48] In the case of names the object is never their objectified meaning: a name never names its own meaning, even if the latter has been objectified. (This would seem to be a difference from Frege's semantics: for Frege, a name in oblique contexts—within quotation marks and in act contexts—names its own customary *Sinn*.) But the objective correlate of a sentence is its nominalized and objectified meaning. This difference is due to, and its seemingly ruinous consequences are avoided by, two considerations. First, a name names what it refers to; a sentence does not name its objective correlate. Having an objective correlate, in the case of sentences, is not *eo ipso* naming it. Second, there are two other senses in which a sentence "refers": it is *about* an object and it *states* a fact (*Sachlage*); but in neither case is the object the same as the objectified propositional meaning.

2.8. In the case of names Husserl employs a Fregean type of illustration to *show* that two expressions with different meanings may yet refer to the same object. His examples are 'the victor at Jena' and 'the vanquished at Waterloo'. Does this or any other pair of expressions (e.g., 'morning star', 'evening star') prove that in such cases the reference is the same, while the meanings differ?[49] It may be argued that simply from *understanding* the expressions 'the victor at Jena' and 'the vanquished at Waterloo', one cannot conclude that their reference is the same and therefore that in each case the meaning is different from the reference. It is only by making use of what one may happen to *know* (about European history in this case) that one may be led to conclude that the two expressions refer to the same person, namely, Napoleon. One who simply understands the meaning of 'the victor at Jena' understands it as referring to the victor at Jena; he does not understand it as referring to Napoleon. The same holds for the other expression. Therefore Husserl's use of this example does not prove that meaning is not the reference.

This argument may be met in two stages. First, instead of the pair of expressions used by Husserl let us consider the two expressions 'the victor at Jena' and 'a person who fought at Jena'. It is analytically true that one who understands the meaning of the first understands that it refers to an object which is also referred to by the second. And that they have different meanings may be taken to be obvious. Thus we have, even at the level of *understanding*, a proof of possible identity of reference in spite of difference of meaning.

Next we may consider the sort of examples given by Husserl and Frege. It is significant that Frege was trying to account for the *cognitive* value of 'a = b' when a = b is true. In other words, the identity of reference, to be sure, is established by knowledge and not by mere understanding. That a = b is true in this case has to be ascertained by means other than mere analytical understanding. That the victor at Jena is also the vanquished at Waterloo is a contingent, empirical fact—not a truth of logic derivable from relations among meanings. That, as a result, the two expressions have the same reference is not a necessary truth; yet it is true that they do. If empirical research corroborates that the same person is referred to, then Husserl's thesis is established. I do not quite see why identity of reference, in spite of difference of meaning—in order to be established at all—must be established analytically. One who understands the meaning of 'the victor at Jena' knows that the object referred to is referred to at Jena. He therefore may entertain the possibility that the same person may satisfy *some other* description and so may be referred to by some other synonymous expression. Hence, that *some other* description may be used to refer to the same person is a possibility whose demonstration does not need empirical evidence. However, that in any particular case the same person satisfies a given description can be established only by empirical evidence. It is understandable that in Husserl's thought the idea of "reference" is closely connected to that of "meaning-fulfillment."

2.9. Of course, while separating meaning and reference—and thereby rejecting a referential theory of meaning—Husserl nevertheless wanted to tie the two very closely together. Among the things he says about the relation between the two, the following are worth recalling.

To use an expression significantly, and to refer expressively to an object . . ., are one and the same.[50]

If we perform the act and live in it, as it were, we naturally refer to its object, and not to its meaning.[51]

A meaning "presents" an object.[52]

2.10. We have been examining Husserl's theory of objective reference in some detail and cannot close without a brief reference to sentences other than those in the indicative or declarative mood, or to sentences expressing nonob-

jectifying acts or acts other than the nominal and the propositional. With regard to nonobjectifying acts, Husserl's position may be stated as follows:

A. Since the same "matter" may be taken up into acts with different "qualities," there is a sense in which objective reference does not vary with act-quality. The component naming and predicating acts continue to have their extralinguistic references even when they function as parts of an interrogative act or of an act of wishing. If the "matter" determines objective reference, it may remain unaltered with qualitative variation.[53]

B. It follows from Brentano's principle regarding the foundational character of acts of "presentation" that every nonobjectifying act must be founded upon at least one nominal act, so that the objective reference of a nonobjectifying act would depend upon that of the nominal act which forms its basis.[54]

C. Whereas the above two theses appear to be, generally speaking, unexceptionable, the third thesis is likely to be disputed, and it may even be felt that the very issue to which Husserl is responding is somewhat obscure. He maintains that the "bearer of meaning"—even in the case of nonobjectifying acts—is always an objectifying object. The preceding two theses claim that the objective reference of an act of wishing, for example, is established through the component nominal and predicating acts. The present thesis claims that a sentence expressing a wish or a desire or a question becomes imbued with meaning insofar as the very act that is expressed is also made an object of inner perception. The wish is first objectified in inner perception and only then expressed in a wish-sentence. A consequence of this thesis seems to be that it is not the living desire or the question surging within or the smoldering wish as such that serve to confer meaning. Only some acts of the objectifying sort do so: in the present case, the inner perception of the lived experiences.

As remarked earlier, the very issue that preoccupies Husserl in all this is very obscure. Perhaps we may be able to throw some light on his reasons and purposes for so vehemently defending this position after we have looked into his concept of the meaning-intending act and his thesis of the ideality of meanings.

B. Ideality of Meanings

3. No other thesis in Husserl's philosophy of meaning has been subjected to more unfavorable criticism than the view which, nevertheless, he seems not to have taken back: that meanings are ideal entities. And yet it would seem that by that rather misleading locution he was trying to capture an essential moment of our experience of meanings and our commerce with them. That moment may perhaps be described by the following propositions: first, discourse—and especially, logical discourse—requires that meanings retain an identity in the midst of varying contexts; second, meanings can be communicated by one person to another, and in that sense can be shared; third, in different speech acts and in different contexts, the same speaker or different speakers can always return to the same meaning.

Now any satisfactory theory of meaning should be able to take care of these interrelated phenomena. The theories that reduce meaning to the private experience of the speaker or the hearer cannot explain how it is possible for private experiences (images, for example) of one person to be communicated to and shared by another. Any criterion of identity with regard to such private experiences—by which one could say, for example, "This is the same image as I had last evening"—is difficult to come by. It may be argued that there is in truth no real communication at all, so that each person is enclosed within his own world of private experiences. Such a radical skepticism is different from that moderate skepticism which doubts if we *always* understand each other. The latter position not only does not rule out but, rather, presupposes that sometimes we succeed in communicating or understanding. The radical skepticism, however, is a position

which can hardly be coherently stated, for it would frustrate the possibility of public language and it has to meet all the difficulties connected with the notion of private language, combined with the additional troubles arising out of the denial that there is any public language at all. The so-called Platonic theories of meaning are motivated by the theoretical need for taking into account the identity, communicability, repeatability and—in that sense—objectivity of meanings. But they err by sundering meanings from the concrete meaning experiences (intending, speaking, understanding, etc.), by hypostatizing them into entities that one supposedly inspects when understanding or meaningfully using appropriate expressions. In effect, they reduce expressions to conventional signs for those entities. Thus they cut meanings off from both the subjective life of persons and from the expressions that bear them.

A satisfactory theory of meaning, then, should take cognizance of the following facts: (1) meanings are characterized by a sort of identity and contextual independence, and they can be shared and communicated intersubjectively so that it is legitimate to say of them that they are objective; (2) on the other hand, they stand internally related to the mental life (thought, feeling, and intentions) of the persons participating in them; (3) in spite of their sort of identity, which suggests they do not belong to the real order of temporally individuated events, they nevertheless serve as mediums of reference to things, events, persons, places, and processes in the world; and (4) they are incarnate in physical expressions, words, and sentences, which from one point of view are conventional signs and thus extrinsic to the meanings and yet, from another point of view, are united with the meanings they signify in such a manner that both form a most remarkable sort of wholeness.

Husserl's thesis regarding the ideality of meanings has to be understood in this total context, and not in an isolated manner—namely, only in view of the first above-mentioned fact.

3.1. There is no doubt that on occasions Husserl speaks of meanings in an ontological mode. He divides all beings into the real and the ideal, with temporality as the mark of reality.[55] He then divides ideal objects into those that are meanings and those that are not.[56] In a famous passage he characterizes meanings as species or universal entities:

As a species, and only as a species, can it [a meaning] embrace in unity, $\xi \nu \mu \beta \acute{\alpha} \lambda \lambda \epsilon \iota \nu$ $\epsilon \grave{\iota} s$ $\check{\epsilon} \nu$ and as an ideal unity, the dispersed multiplicity of individual singulars. The manifold singulars for the ideal unity Meaning are naturally the corresponding act-moments of meaning, the *meaning-intentions*. Meaning is related to varied acts of meaning...just as Redness *in specie* is to the slips of paper which lie here, and which all "have" the same redness.[57]

Now this ontological mode of speech is gradually mellowed.[58] To be sure, the meanings are ideal, but their ideality is only "unity in multiplicity";[59] they are media of reference, not objects of reference. In an act of reflection, they are made objects, and when they are made into objects they cease to be meanings and are referred to through some other meanings. Further, all Husserlian essences are not meanings. It is important, for example, to bear in mind the distinction between the meaning of redness and the essence of redness. When Husserl extends the meaning to all acts and derives the concept of *noema*, he tells us that the concern with *noemata* is possible in a phenomenological attitude while the concern with essences is said to belong to an ontological attitude.[60] In *Experience and Judgment*, the characterization of meanings as species is explicitly and unambiguously taken back:

The irreality of objectivities of understanding must not be confused with generic universality...it is a great temptation to think that the proposition belongs to the various acts of which it is the sense by virtue of its generic universality, as, for example, many red things belong to the generic essence "redness"...
But one must say in opposition to this: certainly, the proposition...is not general in the sense of generic universality, i.e. *the general-*

ity of an "extension" ...; it is, therefore, not general in the manner of essences....
....The proposition itself is, for all these acts and act-modalities, *identical as the correlate of an identification and not general as the correlate of a comparative coincidence.* The identical sense does not become particular in individuals; the generic universal in coincidence has particulars under it, but the sense does not have particulars under it.[61]

3.2. If the ideality of the meaning is not that of a species or an essence, it is also to be distinguished from a presumptive ideality of the linguistic entity itself. The same word 'the' recurs. It is *a* word of the English language, though it has infinitely many occurrences. But one may also return from the written to the spoken word, and still be aware that it is the same word. From a purely physical standpoint, of course, each inscription is a distinct physical object, each uttered sound a distinct event, and there seems to be no way to bring them under the same linguistic item, "the same word." The idea of sameness here needs the concept of ideality. Only what is irreal can defy individuation by spatio-temporal location and can maintain identity in multiplicity. It is these considerations that lead Husserl to speak of the ideality of language and of the linguistic.[62] Language has an objective, spiritual being that is handed down by tradition as a persisting, abiding system. The word, the grammatical sentence, considered purely in respect of its "spiritual corporeality" is an ideal unity. The same holds for a symphony in relation to its performances.
This ideality is not the same as that of the meanings those words and sentences bear. One cannot help but ask at this point whether we really need to recognize two orders of ideality in the constitution of an expression: a "corporeal" and an "incorporeal." Is it not possible to take care of the use of "same," with regard to a word or a sentence in its purely "corporeal" aspect, by taking recourse to the distinction between "type" and "token"?
3.3. The ideal meanings are "contents" of the acts, which are called "meaning-

intending" or also "meaning-conferring" acts. Both names are misleading. There is a perfectly ordinary sense in which we may say of a person that he intends to mean such-and-such by the words he is using. His intention is relevant in order to determine what he means when what he says does not quite show what he means. Husserl does not want to use "meaning-intending" in this sense. The second expression, "meaning-conferring," is equally misleading. One may say of an act that it confers a certain right or a certain title on a person—the act, for example, of closing a deed. It is not as if what Husserl calls "meaning-conferring acts" confers meaning on a string of meaningless noises or inscriptions. The metaphors, then, are liable to mislead. The metaphors, however, like all metaphors, are intended to illuminate only within certain limitations. In order to see what Husserl means, let us recall some other characterizations he gives of these acts and their functions.

First, we have to bear in mind that, for Husserl, "meaning" is always and primarily the meaning of an act, namely, of an intentional experience. The senses in which a physical inscription or a thing is or may be said to be meaningful are derivative from this primary sense, inasmuch as we posit some act or other as the source of that meaningfulness. If Husserlian "meanings," like the Fregean *Sinne*, are intensional entities,[63] what I am emphasizing is that for Husserl intensionality derives from intentionality. To say that act is "intentional" is to say that an object is intended by it in a certain manner as being such-and-such: this is to ascribe to it both a sense or a meaning and a reference. It was therefore only appropriate that in *Ideas* the results of the First Investigation were extended over the entire domain of acts.

Second, Husserl says that meanings are *contents* of the acts. If I am perceiving a thing and on the basis of that perception judge 'This is white', the meaning of the sentence I utter is a content of my act of (perceptual) judgment. If I utter the words 'The victor at Jena' and understand what they mean, the act I would be giving expression to is an act of representing to me a certain thing in a certain manner as satisfying a certain description: the meaning of the words is a "content" of that act. The talk of "content" may mean either real *components* of an experience, such that each component itself is a real bit of that experience, or intentional *correlates* which necessarily accompany an act—as the "percept" (the perceived *qua* perceived in the precise manner in which it is perceived) accompanies an act of perceiving, or a "proposition" accompanies an act of judging. The meaning is a "content" in the latter sense; it is not a real part of an act and therefore is not a private particular. For reasons we have already considered, it is also not the object toward which an act may happen to be directed. It is called an *ideal* content. It is not, as it were, that within the corpus of an experience there are elements that are variable and changing and a core of invariant structure which is the meaning.[64] That would have made the ideal meaning a real component of an experience in the same sense in which a sensation, an image, or a feeling may be said to be a real component. But such an assertion is indeed absurd.

Third, subtract from the understanding of a verbal expression (or meaningful use of one) the uncomprehended hearing (or uttering) of it; the surplus is the "meaning-conferring act." Or begin with hearing a string of noises which then grows into comprehension of a structure of meanings: what supervenes is a "meaning-conferring act." Husserl therefore often calls such an act an act of "understanding"[65] which "shines through the expression" and "lends it meaning and thereby relation to objects."[66] A clearer statement is

The soliloquizing thinker "understands" his words, and this understanding is simply his act of meaning them.[67]

At this point the following issue may be raised: a word or sentence is meaningful, no matter whether or not I understand it when it is being uttered. Likewise, if I utter a sentence belonging to a language I do not understand but which I have learned to articulate, the sentence I utter is meaningful even if I do not comprehend its meaning. How, then, can one say that my understanding—whether as the utterer or as the hearer—contributes to making a string of meaningless noises into meaningful expressions? If the expressions are meaningful, it is not because of the acts of understanding by those who may happen to understand them. They may, for example, be meaningful because there *are* rules for their use.

Compare the following with our situation: a physical object is a physical object, irrespective of whether some one perceives it or not. My perceiving it does not make it a physical object, nor does my failure to perceive it make it cease to be one. Or take a specific type of physical object—a tool, for example, a hammer. It is and continues to be a hammer even if no one uses it as one. In what sense, then, is its "being hammer" determined by its use by someone in a prescribed manner?

I think these questions are pertinent for they bring out the real *nature* of a phenomenological theory of meaning. It is often recognized that phenomenology is concerned not with things but with meanings. For example, it is concerned not with physical objects (as the natural sciences are, or even a naive metaphysics would be) but with their sense as physical objects. It seeks to clarify that sense by returning to those intentional experiences in which it is constituted. The same applies to the other concerns of phenomenology. A phenomenological theory of meaning, then, is concerned not with meanings directly but with their sense as meanings: it asks, How is this sense constituted? The sense of the predicate "physical object" is constituted in perceptual experiences of various sorts that are interrelated in certain more or less determinate manners; similarly, the sense of "meaning" is constituted in acts of understanding and certain correlations between "understanding use" of expressions by speakers and "understanding grasp" by auditors. It is in this kind of act-structure that the predicate "meaningful" is constituted. A phenomenological theory of meaning, then, would trace the constitution of meanings as ideal unities to the acts in which these unities come to the sort of givenness appropriate to them by virtue of their sense as "meanings." What about meanings that are not understood or physical objects that are not perceived? Of course, there are unperceived physical objects, and that there are such unperceived physical objects may even be regarded as not an empirical truth but a truth that follows from the sense of "physical objects." Since constitutive phenomenology has to be guided by the sense of the constituted, part of the explication of the sense of "physical object" is to make room for that component of the sense from which the existence of unperceived physical objects appear to follow analytically. Similarly, it belongs to the sense of "meaning" that meanings are not only understood but may be misunderstood, and even be silently ignored.

A phenomenological theory that meanings are constituted in acts of understanding has to be understood and worked out so as to take care of these possibilities.

The comparison with "perception" was very much in Husserl's mind.[68] Meanings are given in acts of understanding, just as physical objects are given in acts of perception. If in the case of perception it is appropriate to say that the sensations which are the primary data are "interpreted" to signify such-and-such perceptual objects, so too in the experience of meanings are such-and-such inscriptions or sounds "interpreted" to signify such-and-such meanings. Thus the meaning-conferring acts are not only acts of understanding but also acts of interpretation.[69] In relation to the tree or the pencil, my perceptual experience is a "presentation." But in relation to the sensory data this experience is an "interpretation." Similarly in the case of meanings: my act of understanding is both an intuitive grasp and an act of interpretation.[70]

3.4. To describe the unity of an expression with its meaning, Husserl often uses the metaphor of the body and its animating soul.[71] The relationship the metaphor is meant to illuminate has two sides. On one hand, the relation is certainly extrinsic in the sense that any other verbal sound or written inscription *could have* done the same job. This "could have" has a very precise force. Certainly—if we take different languages—other verbal sounds, and written inscriptions as well, *in fact* do the job of the English word 'man', for example. But for some other sound or inscription to replace the word 'man' altogether would mean a change in the English language itself. Thus the metaphor of body and soul fails—to the extent that the same soul is not ordinarily supposed to animate many different bodies at the same time; but the same meaning *does* animate many physically different expressions in different languages. On the other hand, if a certain verbal sound bears a certain meaning, the two in fact achieve a remarkable sort of "fusion," so that

We do not find in ourselves a mere sum of acts, but a single act in which, as it were, a bodily and spiritual side are distinct. Just so an expressed wish is no mere *ensemble* of expression and wish...but a whole, an act, which we unhesitatingly call a wish.[72]

Husserl lays great emphasis on this two-sided relationship of a fusion or a wholeness, whose two aspects *could yet have been* separate. This is a phenomenological datum. It is wrong to construe the verbal sound as a physical entity and then to picture the meaning-conferring act as what imparts meaning into it. That picture is indeed misleading. The unity is achieved between the two acts: the act of wishing, for example, and the act of speaking it out. It is this unity of the acts that accounts for the felt nondistinction between words and their meanings.

A further iomplication is that the fusion takes a novel form when the expression names an object that is being perceived. In this case the meaning-conferring act or act of expression and the perceptual act are fused together, so that

the name 'my inkpot' seems to *overlay* the perceived object, to belong *sensibly* to it.[73]

Husserl adds:

Not word *and* inkpot...but the act-experiences...in which they make their appearance, are here brought into relation... the expression seems to be *applied* to the thing and to clothe it like a garment.

All these metaphors are to be taken with their obvious limitations, but only insofar as they serve to illuminate the peculiar experiences they are meant to describe.

4. If all acts—and not merely acts of speaking—have meanings, one has to distinguish between the *Sinn* or *noema* of an act and the conceptualized meaning or *Bedeutung* of the corresponding act of expressing. It is not the case that only by being expressed in words do acts acquire a sense; on the contrary, because acts are intentional and therefore are already imbued with sense, the act of expressing can have its meaning. The meaning of the sentence 'This is white', then, is a conceptualization of the sense or *noema* of the act of (perceptual) judging that is expressed in that sentence. In every intentional experience before it is expressed, its object is intended in a certain manner, which constitutes its sense: the object as it is presented, judged, wished for, etc., or the situation that is desired in its specific way, the state of affairs that is made questionable, etc. Such a sense can by its very nature be "expressed"—namely, transformed into a conceptual meaning of an act of speaking:

Whatever is "meant as such," every meaning in the noematic sense (and indeed as noematic nucleus) of any act whatsoever can be *expressed conceptually* (*durch "Bedeutungen"*).[74]

4.1. According to a well-known theme of the *Logical Investigations*, acts are either signitive or intuitive. (For the present, this division is restricted to objectifying acts.) Now in signitive acts an object is intended symbolically; in an intuitive act it is intuitively experienced precisely as it was, or is capable of being, intended symbolically in a signitive act. The distinction seeks to capture part of the implications of the distinction between "sense" and "reference": one may understand the sense of an expression without being acquainted intuitively with the object referred to. It seems, then, that the concept of meaning thus far elaborated—which is founded on its distinction from "reference"—applies to signitive acts alone, and of course the act of speaking as such is signitive. But Husserl does not wish to limit his theory to signitive acts; he extends the concept of sense thus far expounded to the intuitive acts as well. He thereby derives the concept of "fulfilling sense." Since the acts of perception are fulfilling acts *par excellence,* he also derives the concept of perceptual *noema.* The validity of this notion has recently been seriously questioned.

Thus Hubert Dreyfus writes:

...in the First *Logical Investigation* acts were divided into signifying and fulfilling acts. Then the perceptual act, which one would suppose to be a fulfilling act par excellence, was in turn analyzed into *its* signifying and intuitive components.... Thus a regress develops in which sense coincides with sense indefinitely. At each stage we arrive at a fulfilling meaning for an intending meaning, but at no stage does the fulfilling meaning imply a sensuous filling.[75]

Dreyfus's point is pertinent: if perception is the act in which the object is itself bodily given, it would be strange to introduce within perception a distinction between sense and reference, for then within perception one would have to admit the presence of empty, unfulfilled signifying intentions which need further fulfillments, and hence the infinite regress. Dreyfus ascribes this position to a philosophy of perception that is worked out from the point of view of transcendental phenomenology, and suggests that an existential phenomenological theory of perception, by replacing the transcendental ego by the body subject, may be able to expel conceptual elements from within perceptual experience and restore its

unmediated contact with the object. I will not comment here on the merits of this latter theory but shall only make a few remarks intended to bring out the inner motivations of the Husserlian notion of "fulfilling sense."[76]

A. There is a sense in which one can say that two acts, whether they are perceptions or not, are the same: "the same wish," "the same desire," "the same doubt." These are perfectly legitimate locutions. In *Logical Investigations,* Husserl wants to give a criterion of sameness for acts: two acts will be regarded as identical if and only if they have the same "act-quality" and the same "act-matter," however they may differ in the details of their contents. This concept of matter, we know, becomes the *noema* or *Sinn* of the later works. Without the possibility of distinguishing such a content from the variegated details or *Fülle* (fullness) of an intuitive act, no judgment of identity would ever be possible for such acts.

B. This sense (*Sinn*) does not contain all the fullness of a perceptual experience.[77] It does not include the total descriptive content of that experience.[78] Neither is it the same as the conceptual meaning (*Bedeutung*) of the corresponding expression. To speak of the perceptual sense is not *eo ipso* to inject into the pre-expressive act a conceptual element—unless by implication the Husserlian *Sinn* is identified with the Fregean and so with Husserl's *Bedeutung,* which surely is conceptual. Ideality and conceptuality do not coincide in Husserl's thought.

C. Although in perception the object is bodily given, such bodily givenness never meant, for Husserl, adequate givenness. On the contrary, all perception—at least all outer perception—is perspectival, from which it follows that perceptual adumbrations point beyond themselves to other possible ones and that within the structure of perception the dialectic of sense and presence opens up anew, without destroying the immediacy of perception at any stage.

D. When a perception *does* fulfill a

prior meaning-intention, not every detail of it is relevant for the role of fulfillment. It is not, for example, *qua this* act and *qua mine* that it plays the role of fulfilling the relevant meaning-intention. Rather, any such act (e.g., my perception at some other time or someone else's perception now) could have performed the same function. Hence within a fulfilling experience one should be able to isolate a central core by virtue of which alone this act fulfills that intention and none other. But the same act may fulfill another intention as well. For example, the same perceptual experience may verify not only "This is white" but also "This is not red." In that case, different fulfilling senses are appropriate in each instance.

E. I leave out cases of perceptual judgment—namely seeing *that*—where Dreyfus concedes the need for Husserlian *noema*.

C. Concluding Observations

5. A great merit of Husserl's theory of meaning is its comprehensiveness. Most other theories of meaning err by their sheer one-sidedness and consequent blindness to other sides or aspects. Most theories begin with metaphysical and epistemological preconceptions. For example, many modern theories of meaning begin with a prejudice against the mental and the inner and an epistemological prejudice in favor of public verifiability as a criterion of significance. As a way of verifying reports, introspection is already suspect—and so too all talk about mental acts. Now, not unexpectedly, such theories are "theoretical" in a restricted sense: they are not "descriptive." Husserl's theory of meaning, outlined above, is an attempt to take into account the many facets of our experience of and commerce with meanings, without invoking metaphysical and epistemological preconceptions.

Theories of meaning may be divided into those that consider the intention of the speaker and the auditor's recognition of that intention to be fundamental concepts for explicating the notion of mean-

ing,[79] and those that would appeal to the more objective notion of "rule."[80] One may also, using another principle of classification, classify theories of meaning into those that are Platonic and those that are not—classifying the latter again into the psychological and the nonpsychological. The Platonic theories emphasize the ontological status of meanings conceived as entities which *are*, but not in space or in time; they therefore constitute a Platonic realm of their own, which words contingently signify and which the mind inspects while "thinking" or "understanding." The anti-Platonist theories of the psychological sort, while denying the Platonic myth of subsistent meanings, reduce the meanings to some element of the mental life of the speaker and the hearer (usually imagery). The nonpsychological anti-Platonist theories may take various routes, but the most effective and promising is the attempt to rescue meanings from the privacy of mental life and to account for the meaningfulness of words in terms of the rules of their *use* in a given language.

Husserl's theory is comprehensive enough to accommodate most points of these theories and to put them in their place. The Platonic theory is right to emphasize the identity, objectivity, and communicability of meanings. The psychological theories are right not to want to sever meanings from the mental life of persons; but not having a concept of the mental as intentional, they locate meanings in real parts of the flow of mental life. The theory which tries to explicate the concept of meaning in terms of the intention of the speaker ("S intends to mean *m* by uttering '*u*' ") and the auditor's recognition of that intention remains at the level of communicative speech, and assumes—rather than explains—the locution "The words '*u*' mean *m*." The rule theory knows only what Husserl calls "game meaning" of signs,[81] which presupposes the original conceptual meaning. It does not ask what kind of intentional act "using" or "making a move according to rules" is, what its noematic correlate is, and how, in this "transformation" of the original act of speaking, new noematic senses are constituted which are founded upon—but tend to conceal—the noematic sense of the original act. Both the conventional character of language[82] and its ability to achieve a fusion with meanings that are nonconventional are recognized in Husserl's theory. "Reference" is regarded as an essential function of expressions; but by distinguishing between different senses of "object" and different senses in which words and sentences may be said to "refer," the possible ontological implications are kept within the bounds of sanity.

5.1. There are several points, though, at which Husserl's phenomenology of meaning needs modification. First, there is an overall priority of objectifying acts as meaning-conferring. To a certain extent, this priority is intelligible. Any sentence must contain a name—construing "name" in a wide sense—and this priority of the nominal act is understandable. But when we confront the thesis that all nonobjectifying acts need first to be objectified in inner perception before they can be "expressed," we begin to worry about the phenomenological validity of the thesis. A desire *qua* desire has its noematic sense: namely, the object or state of affairs as desired. It may be that in order to desire an object or a state of affairs, the pertinent object or state of affairs must be "presented." But why should it be that the act of desire, once it occurs, cannot be directly "expressed" in what we may call a desire-sentence, but has to be objectified in "inner perception"? One may have to distinguish between pre-reflective desire which is nonegological—where the object of desire appears "out there" with an appropriate property of "desiredness" and is described not by "I desire it" but by "It is attractive"—and reflective desire whose expression is "I desire it." Only in the latter case do we already have an inner perception or reflection. The former expresses itself directly in the appropriate sentence without any "I."[83]

Part of the reason that may have led Husserl to his thesis may be this: it seems plausible to maintain that whereas the "natural" expression of objectifying acts is a linguistic event (a word, group of words, or sentence), the "natural" expression of a nonobjectifying act (a wish, a desire, a questioning) is not a linguistic event but a bodily movement or gesture (a facial expression, nodding the head, or whatever). If this is the case, then acts like desires and questionings, in order to be linguistically expressible, would need some other supervening factor. But since objectifying acts alone are the sort of acts whose "natural" expression is linguistic, the nonobjectifying acts must be objectified before they can be linguistically expressed; and the most primitive kind of objectification, in their case, is not predicative judgment but an inner glance at them.

This argument would have the force it needs to sustain the Husserlian thesis only if the premise—that the objectifying acts, and they alone, "naturally" express themselves in linguistic acts and not in any bodily manifestations—is tenable. But there seems to be no reason to accept it as true. On the contrary, it appears that there may be "natural" nonlinguistic manifestations of objectifying as well as nonobjectifying acts. In both cases, linguistic expression is a new act-stratum, and there is no reason why a nonobjectifying act by itself cannot provide the material—its own *noema*—for "conceptualization" in linguistic expression.

5.2. It is of course obvious that Husserl's phenomenology of meaning is concerned with linguistic meaning and also with the noematic sense of preexpressive acts. We have seen how he seeks to exclude all nonlinguistic expressions from the scope of his use of the word 'expression'. Although there is a difference in the way groaning means pain and the word 'pain' means pain, the question must be asked: Can the two be kept so strictly apart? Without entering into further discussion of this issue for the present, I wish to mention an additional consideration that Husserl introduces in a different context.

In a manuscript of 1921/22 Husserl writes that language belongs to the group of acts that are cultural but have the form of conventionality. These acts are both conventional and cultural, and these two sides belong together. Then he contrasts language with natural involuntary expressions of the mental in bodily states: these expressions, unlike language, do not succeed in creating such "common possessions"—they do not acquire a "social meaning" that is handed down by tradition.[84]

Now to this I wish to add the following reflection. There seems to be an important sense in which bodily gestures and expressions come to acquire a "social meaning" and become part of an inherited tradition. The same emotions are "naturally" expressed by quite different bodily expressions, gestures, and behavior within different cultural groups. Further, there is a group of bodily movements that acquire symbolic significance and in a certain sense become spiritual objectivities. I have in mind such things as determinate gestures and bodily movements that are institutionalized symbols, for example, those involved in religious rituals or traditional dance forms (e.g., Indian). The point I wish to suggest is that perhaps the distinction between bodily movements of a certain sort and inner mental states breaks down; the former can be intentional, may manifest a nonconceptual significance, may be nonnatural, institutionalized, cultural symbols. How this will affect the overall theory I cannot say at present.

6. Husserl, it must be mentioned, supplements the static, structural phenomenology of meaning (which we have surveyed here) by a genetic account. The genetic point of view comes gradually to the forefront in the later works, without quite requiring a drastic revision of the earlier, solidly grounded theory. The main lines of that new point of view are these:

Every linguistic, as well as prelinguistic, act is performed within a temporal horizon. No intending of a meaning is cut off from that horizon and, in the last analysis, from the horizon of the life-world. This horizon is not a static ground on which we stand but a historical process with which we move. Historicity af-

fects meanings as well, but in a very curious manner. The meanings as ideal objects exhibit timelessness. Language, as the conventionally brought about and traditionally handed-down spiritual objectivity, both determines and is determined by the life-world: language as such, which makes possible intersubjective communication, also makes the sociality of the life-world possible.[85] At the same time, the so-constituted social world determines specific meanings and forms of expression that come into being in the course of history. It is thus that in his essay on the origin of geometry Husserl could say that the questions of origin lead to "the deepest problems of meanings,"[86] and yet, also, that history is nothing but the movement of "the coexistence and the interweaving of original formations and sedimentations of meaning."[87] By following the course of historical genesis we cannot reach an absolute beginning of meaningful discourse, but we can follow the way generated meanings have become "sedimented" into the world and "handed down" by tradition in a manner such that it is always possible for us to "reactivate" their original living constitution. This rather obscure account does not give us a theory of meaning out of meaningless data, but it aims at reviving our ability to recognize that meanings have a genesis from already created meanings, and that those which we "inherit" would be but lifeless shells unless we could relive the acts that constitute them. This sense of historicity is also the abolition of historicity, for past intentions can be relived and thereby be made present for the philosopher. It therefore does not conflict with the thesis of the ideality of meanings. Ideality belongs to the sense of the constituted; historicity to the process of constituting. In *Experience and Judgment* Husserl writes, reflecting on the timelessness of meanings in the context of the all-encompassing phenomenological theme of temporality:

The timelessness of objectivities of the understanding, their being "everywhere and nowhere," *proves . . .to be a privileged form of temporality.*[88]

NOTES

1. E. Husserl, *Logical Investigations*, tr. J. N. Findlay (New York: Humanities Press, 1970), 1: 287 (henceforth cited as *LI*).

2. Ibid.

3. Ibid., p. 275.

4. Ibid.

5. J. Derrida, of all writers, has most clearly seen this. See his *Speech and Phenomena*, tr. David Allison (Evanston: Northwestern University Press, 1973).

6. *LI*, 1: 275.

7. Ibid.

8. E. g., Ibid., pp. 281-82; also H. P. Grice, "Meaning," *Philosophical Review*, vol. 66 (1957):377-88.

9. *LI*, 1: 279.

10. Derrida in *Speech and Phenomena*.

11. See J. N. Mohanty, *Edmund Husserl's Theory of Meaning* (The Hague: Nijhoff, 1969), pp. 15-16.

12. See my "On Husserl's Theory of Meaning," *Southwestern Journal of Philosophy*, V (1974): 229-44.

13. Davidson and Hintikka, among others, recently called this into question. See Hintikka, *Models for Modalities* (Dordrecht: Reidle, 1969).

14. Frege's review was published in *Zeitschrift für Philosophie und philosophische Kritik*, 103 (1894): 313-32, and in this volume.

15. See my "Husserl and Frege: A New Look at Their Relationship," read at the 1974 Husserl Circle meeting, Duquesne University, and now in *Research in Phenomenology*, IV (1974): 51-62.

16. *Göttingische gelehrte Anzeigen*, 1 (1891): 243-78, 250.

17. Husserl, "Der Folgerungscalcul und die Inhaltslogik," *Vierteljahrsschrift für wissenschaftliche Philosophie*, 15 (1891): 168-89, 351-56.

18. *LI*, 2: 446 fn.

19. Here the major influence may be Lotze and not Frege. See D. Willard, "The Paradox of Logical Psychologism: Husserl's Way Out," *American Philosophical Quarterly*, 9 (1972): 94-100, and in this volume, pp. 10-17.

20. E. Tugendhat is right in recognizing that Husserl's theory of meaning begins with the intentional point of view, but wrong when he later charges that the results of the Fifth Investigation affect those of the First. The entire *Logical Investigations*, in fact, was meant to be a phenomenology of "logical experiences" or acts. See Tugendhat, "Phänomenologie und Sprachanalyse," in R. Bubner, ed., *Hermeneutik und Dialektik* (Tübingen: J. C. B. Mohr, 1970) 2: 3-23, and as translated in this volume, "Phenomenology and Linguistic Analysis," pp. 325-337.

21. G. Frege, "Über Sinn und Bedeutung," *Zeitschrift für Philosophie und philosophische Kritik*, 100 (1892): 25-50.

22. *Gött. gel. Anz.*, 1 (1891): 250.

23. *LI*, 1: 368.

24. *Gött. gel. Anz.*, 1 (1891): 250.

25. E. Husserl, *Philosophie der Arithmetik (Husserliana*, vol. 12), p. 193. See also the essay "Zur Logik der Zeichen (Semiotik)" of 1890 in *Husserliana*, 12: 340-73. Incidentally, in this essay, after introducing a distinction between direct and indirect signs, Husserl writes: "In the case of indirect signs, it is necessary to separate: that which the sign means (*bedeutet*) and that which it denotes (*bezeichnet*). The two coincide in the case of direct names" (p. 343). Here proper names, for Husserl, mean what they name—a doctrine he rejects in *Logical Investigations*.

26. *LI*, 1: 303.

27. Ibid., p. 293.

28. Ibid., 2: 625.

29. Ibid., p. 581.

30. Ibid., esp. pp. 648-51.

31. There is a wider use of "proposition" in the context of speech acts according to which the sentences "Sam is smoking," "Is Sam smoking?" "Sam may be smoking," and "Sam should not smoke" express the same propositional content, consisting of the same referring and predicating acts but with different elocutionary forces. See John Searle, *Speech Acts* (Cambridge: Cambridge University Press, 1969), esp. p. 30. Husserl's "act-matter" may correspond to what Searle calls "propositional content," and Husserl's "act-quality" to "elocutionary force."

32. Ibid., p. 27.

33. *LI*, 1: 288, also 371.

34. Ibid., p. 372.

35. E. Husserl, *Formal and Transcendental Logic* (The Hague: Nijhoff, 1969), app. 1.

36. Ibid.

37. *LI*, 2: 502.

38. Ibid., p. 455.

39. Ibid., p. 495.

40. Ibid., 1: 372.

41. E. Husserl, *Experience and Judgment*, tr. James S. Churchill and Karl Amerik (Evanston: Northwestern University Press, 1973), p. 62.

42. Ibid., p. 59.

43. *LI*, 2: 612.

44. *Experience and Judgment*, sec. 59.

45. See G. Patzig, "Satz und Tatsache," in *Argumentationen. Festschrift für J. König* (Göttingen, 1966).

46. *Experience and Judgment*, sec. 69, esp. p. 285.

47. *LI*, 1: 323, 2: 515.

48. Tugendhat draws attention to this in his paper (see fn. 20 above). He thinks this ambiguity destroys Husserl's theory of reference. I do not think it does

49. See John E. Atwell, "Husserl on Signification and Object," *American Philosophical Quarterly*, 6 (1969): 312-17.

50. *LI*, 1: 293.

51. Ibid., p. 332.

52. Ibid., 2: 507.

53. Ibid., pp. 588-89.

54. Ibid., p. 649.

55. Ibid., 1: 353.

56. Ibid., pp. 331, 325.

57. Ibid., p. 330.

58. For the following, see my "On Husserl's Theory of Meaning" (fn. 12 above).

59. *LI*, 1: 331.

60. E. Husserl, *Ideen*, III (*Husserliana*, vol. 5), p. 86.

61. *Experience and Judgment*, sec. 64(d), esp. pp. 261-63. Also *Formal and Transcendental Logic*, sec. 57(b).

62. *Formal and Transcendental Logic*, sec. 2.

63. See D. Føllesdal, "Husserl's Notion of Noema," *Journal of Philosophy*, 66 (1969): 680-87.

64. F. H. Bradley held that the logical idea is part of the content of the psychological idea or image. See his *The Principles of Logic*, 2d rev. ed. (Oxford, 1963), esp. pp. 6-8.

65. *LI*, 1: 302, 327.

66. Ibid., p. 302.

67. Ibid., p. 309 fn.

68. E.g., ibid., 2: 565-66.

69. E.g., ibid., 1: 310, 365.

70. Ibid., p. 568.

71. E.g., ibid., pp. 567, 583.

72. Ibid., p. 583.

73. Ibid., p. 688.

74. Compare what John Searle calls "the principle of expressibility" in *Speech Acts*, pp. 19-21.

75. Hubert Dreyfus, "The Perceptual Noema: Gurwitsch's Crucial Contribution," in Lester E. Embree, ed., *Life-World and Consciousness: Essays for A. Gurwitsch* (Evanston: Northwestern University Press, 1972).

76. See my "On Husserl's Theory of Meaning" (fn. 12 above).

77. *LI*, 2: 738.

78. Ibid., p. 744.

79. This is best found in Grice (fn. 8 above). A more sophisticated development is in Stephen R. Schiffer, *Meaning* (Oxford: Clarendon Press, 1972).

80. P. F. Strawson makes a similar distinction among theories of meaning in his inaugural lecture "Meaning and Truth." See his *Logico-Linguistic Papers* (London: Methuen, 1971), esp. pp. 171-72.

81. *LI*, 1: 305.

82. E. Husserl, *Zur Phänomenologie der Intersubjektivität. Texte aus dem Nachlass. Zweiter Teil: 1921-1928, herausgeben von Iso Kern (Husserliana*, vol. 14) (The Hague: Nijhoff, 1973), app. 24 (of 1921-1922).

83. Compare J. P. Sartre, *Being and Nothingness*, pt. 2, ch. 1, sec. 3; also his *Transcendence of the Ego*.

84. Sartre, *Being and Nothingness*, p. 228.

85. E. Husserl, *Zur Phänomenologie der Intersubjektivität. Dritter Teil: 1929-1935 (Husserliana*, vol. 15) (The Hague: Nijhoff, 1973), app. 12 (1931), esp. pp. 220, 224-25.

86. E. Husserl, *The Crisis of European Sciences and Transcendental Phenomenology*, tr. David Carr (Evanston: Northwestern University Press, 1970), p. 353.

87. Ibid., p. 371.

88. *Experience and Judgment*, sec. 64(c), p. 261.

Husserl's Views on the Evident and the True

HENRY PIETERSMA

My discussion will be limited to what I hold to be the essential features of Husserl's doctrine of the evident and the true. I will not discuss the related views of Brentano and Meinong, though this would be very profitable. Nor will I bring into the discussion the development of Husserl's philosophy, which would inevitably involve dealing with all kinds of issues that are not germane to my topic. I do not think that this limitation amounts to a serious shortcoming because, as far as I can see, the central core of this philosopher's views remains fairly constant throughout his works. When in the course of my discussion I mention Husserl's idealism, I am of course aware that this label does not fit the *Logical Investigations* and earlier works. This context does not emerge until 1913, the year in which the first volume of *Ideas* was published. In this and other respects I have imposed a certain limitation on my treatment of the texts at close range. As any reader knows, the texts present an extremely elaborate and, in some ways, vacillating terminology. To exegete them closely would burden this article with much detail and would leave, in my estimation, insufficient space for an attempt to discern the most fundamental features of Husserl's doctrines. To offer a clear discussion I have tried to conduct my dis-

I am grateful to Professors F. Elliston and J. C. Morrison whose reactions to this paper caused me to rewrite and rethink a number of points. I am also indebted to the former for adding references to English translations to the footnotes.

cussion without inflicting upon the reader the full array of the author's terminology and textual intricacies. For the most part, I present the texts in a fairly consistent interpretative vocabulary.

I should also point out that I have omitted discussion of Husserlian scholarship. There is so much that is confused and confusing that I would need another article to set down what I think is right and wrong in these scholarly discussions.

Finally, I have chosen to use the expression 'the evident' to capture the sense of Husserl's *Evidenz*. What he had in mind is a mental state or epistemic situation, in which something is evident to the person who is in that state or situation. This character, in turn, will be sufficient, I hope, to make clear that the frequently used term 'evidence' is, to say the least, confusing. To avoid excessively complicated circumlocutions I have at times left the term untranslated.

I

In the first volume of his *Logical Investigations* Husserl introduces the term '*Evidenz*' in a passage in which the question is raised: What makes a correct judgment a knowing? We are told that a judgment or assertion, if it is to count as knowing, must involve *Evidenz*, "the luminous certainty that what we have accepted exists or that what we have rejected does not exist." We further learn that the evident is the optimal criterion

(*Kennzeichen*) for the correctness of the judgment and that it has for us the status of an immediate awareness of the truth itself. In other passages of the same work it is stated that when something is evident, what one experiences within oneself, and apprehends as such, is the distinguishing mark that constitutes the justification of the judgment in question. Knowing implies that the judgment is not simply a truth-claim but a claim involving the certainty, on the part of the epistemic subject, that it is justified. This distinguishes the judgment from blind conviction or prejudice. If the evident were in principle beyond our reach, so that a subject never attained that certainty about justification, the distinction between rational assertions and others would vanish. The rational search for truth would cease. Given the concepts of knowledge and knowing subject, we have to insist that the subject can attain an epistemic situation in which what is claimed is also evident to him.[1]

Although these contentions raise many questions, one thing is quite clear and ought to be given emphasis at the outset of our discussion. Husserl's views on the evident are to be understood in the context of a theory of justification. In other words, having certain beliefs or having made certain judgments, we address ourselves to the question whether they are justified, so that we may be in the best position to attain truth. As Husserl says, in our search for truth we assume that such a position can be attained. It seems to me important to highlight this, so that we may be clearly aware of the limits and scope of the discussion about the evident.

Having located the views presented above within the general context of a theory of justification, we should observe that they imply some kind of distinction between evident and nonevident judgments. A nonevident judgment—which is in fact true—does not constitute a knowing and is not a justified judgment. Knowing and justified judgment are not attained until the knower attains a judgment that is evident. To better understand this distinction, we have to turn to another well-

known part of the *Logical Investigations*. What I have primarily in mind is the third chapter of the Sixth Investigation, "On the Phenomenology of Epistemic Levels," which presents us with a phenomenological characterization of the relationships between different epistemic situations. Husserl speaks of a cognitive progression from a so-called 'empty' intention to its 'fulfilment' in what is called, by contrast, a seeing of the object itself. Elaborating a suggestion contained in the term 'level', we might say that Husserl views epistemic situations as occupying different places on a scale. The scale measures what I shall call 'epistemic distance.'

It is crucially important to note the nature of this scale. If we do not keep a firm mental grasp on precisely what is measured, attainment of the highest point on this scale will be confused with other attainments that may be closely related but should, nevertheless, be kept distinct. Let us assume that the different epistemic situations in question exemplify the *same* degree of conviction on the part of the subject. Suppose, also, that the object is posited as a really existing object. Finally, throughout all situations the object is taken to be both numerically and qualitatively the *same* object. In all these respects, then, one would have no ground for distinguishing the situations as different in any important way.

There is, however, one respect in which two otherwise similar situations may differ and thus occupy different places on a scale: epistemic distance. In one situation the subject may be more favorably placed in relation to the object than in the other. For specifically epistemic purposes, one situation affords the subject a better view or grasp of the object. What is believed or said may be the same in both situations; and if we assume that the belief or statement is true, it is true no matter what the epistemic situation. Yet in our epistemic endeavor we accord greater epistemic worth to what is believed or said in a situation in which the subject is nearer the object.

This is the sort of doctrine Husserl puts

forth in the chapter referred to above. The first thing to be observed is that epistemic situations are not merely contrasted from the point of view of an external observer. The contrast between empty intention and fulfilled intention is phenomenological: each situation involves an implicit, if not explicit, awareness on the part of the cognitive subject of the contrasting situation. When the reference to an object or state of affairs is an empty intention, the subject is aware of another situation which, though identical with the present situation in the ways mentioned earlier, nevertheless contrasts significantly with it.

Secondly, that other situation is conceived as attainable by him. In a very simple case, he is aware that he can walk to the place where the object is said to be and see whether it is there and whether it has the qualities ascribed to it.

This leads me to make a third point. When we speak of being far from the object or close to it, we may tend to construe epistemic distance in a purely objective, spatial sense. Husserl's frequent preoccupation with perception of spatial objects may tempt us to do this, but it would be unfair to attribute such naiveté to Husserl. No general theory of knowledge and the search for truth can be constructed with the help of such a notion. To do justice to the author, we have to understand him to mean that epistemic distance, strictly conceived, is assessed in terms of whatever cognitive moves are required to attain the kind of situation that is optimal for judging the real object or the real state of affairs. Traversing an epistemic distance may involve a lengthy process of thinking. In what Husserl calls pure generalities, we are told that we have to go through the process of free, imaginative variation of examples in order to apprehend them.

It is important here to think of a wide range of cases. In respect to whatever truth we seek, we can speak of an epistemic distance one often has to traverse if one is to be in the best position to find the truth. That about which we seek the truth need not always be a perceptible thing.

As Husserl often notes, we also assert possibilities and probabilities: it may or may not be evident that something is possible or that something has such and such a degree of probability. Just as we speak of knowing that S is P or that S is not P, we also speak of knowing that a certain state of affairs has such-and-such a degree of probability. Similarly, Husserl often speaks of evident possibilities.[2] Again, a judgment, as such, may be vaguely apprehended or clearly understood with complete intellectual articulation of the meaning. To know what the judgment really is, we may, accordingly, have to take certain steps in order to become clear about it (which of course is not the same as knowing the objective state of affairs asserted by the judgment).[3]

A final point that tends to be overlooked has to do with the nature of the optimal situation. Husserl characterized it as a fulfillment, as seeing the object itself. In other words, he gives it the character of an achievement. Now if this is to make phenomenological sense, the situation so characterized must involve an implicit, if not explicit, reference to situations other than itself. A subject cannot have a sense of achievement if he has had no sense of failure or if he does not clearly conceive of failure as a possibility. What "seeing the object itself" means can be understood only by grasping very clearly the scale on which it marks an achievement. It is important to make this point because the phrase "seeing the object itself" (and cognate phrases such as "self-givenness of the object") may easily be misunderstood. If I understand Husserl correctly, such a phrase expresses a situation that is experienced as an achievement, in contrast to other situations that are conceived of as mere possibilities.[4]

The above implies, though Husserl does not emphasize it, that a claim to be seeing the object itself can be subjected to critical evaluation. What the subject takes to be the optimal situation for grasping the true nature of something may not in fact be optimal. He may not, in fact, have done all he could, and possibilities for further examination may be pointed out to him. It also seems that this phenomenology of epistemic levels implies a context in which the subject is familiar with a range of types of objects and their corresponding modes of accessibility. In other words, the subject must have a conception of the sorts of cognitive moves on his part that are required to attain a situation that is optimal for various types of objects. He must have a conception of the sorts of moves that are relevant to discovering whether the object is there and whether it has certain qualities or properties. Merely to make some move and merely to fail to see the object clearly have no epistemic relevance.

Though this phenomenology of epistemic levels can only be presented in a highly condensed form, it is essential if we want to advance our understanding of Husserl's epistemological concept of the evident. Taking something to be evident is an optimal situation within the context of empty intentions and their fulfillment. When Husserl employs the term 'Evidenz' he has specifically epistemological questions in mind, but addresses them to the sort of situation earlier characterized by the phenomenology of epistemic levels. But what is the specifically epistemic worth of the kind of situation which is optimal in the sense there indicated? After all, one could treat the distinction between empty and fulfilled intention as a merely phenomenological distinction. It seems to me that the specifically epistemological aspects of Husserl's thought appear in his discussion of skepticism,[5] and it takes the form of a defense of the epistemic worth of these optimal situations.

One form of skepticism he considers treats Evidenz as nothing more than the factual conjunction of a judgment and a certain feeling.[6] Such a view, according to Husserl, amounts to complete skepticism. To appreciate the full force of this skepticism, we have to remember that what is at stake is the epistemic worth of a situation which is genuinely optimal in terms of the scale that measures epistemic distance. We have to suppose that the subject has done all he could to obtain a good grasp of what he intends. This implies that he not merely thinks he has but that no critical evaluation has been able to show that he has powers he did not fully exercise, or that the nature of the case requires exploration he has not undertaken. In short, the subject cannot conceive of anything he could still do. In more Husserlian language, there are no 'intentions' still calling for 'fulfillment'. This disposes of the argument that a feeling of certainty is a sign of truth, since this situation clearly presupposes a situation in which such a correlation first became known to us.

Supposing, then, that the epistemic situation is truly optimal, let us adopt for a moment the suggested feeling-theory. Now the subject who judges may well ask himself whether, in some other mind, a judgment contradicting his own might not be conjoined with a feeling indistinguishable from the one he now has in connection with his own judgment. This would lead to a conflict of belief which (in principle) could not be resolved, since we have supposed that neither could be shown how to improve his epistemic situation. Hence skepticism would be the last word, if the feeling-theory were adopted.

In opposition to this theory, Husserl formulates his view by stating that, for one who makes an evident judgment, it is evident that the belief or insight of somebody else cannot conflict with his judgment insofar as both are genuinely evident.[7] The point he wants to make is that the evident—strictly as such—is trustworthy. It is, as he says in the same context, an experience of truth. If a particular claim is to be called into question, this must be done by showing that the epistemic situation was not genuinely optimal. And in order to show this shortcoming, the one whose judgment is called into question must be shown steps he did not take but could have taken which would cast doubt on his judgment or show it to be false. The feeling-theory, on the contrary, legitimates doubt when, ex hypothesi, there is no way in which the search for truth can be carried further. In the terminology of epistemic levels, a situation in which one sees the object itself excludes all meaningful doubt. Doubt makes sense if what is before the mind is not self-given. In such a case, however, there is an intentional reference to what is not self-given, and for that reason it is within the range of the subject's powers to seek fulfillment of the empty intention, id est, to continue the search for truth. The matter can be settled by steps he is either already aware of as possible or which can be shown to him to be possible. And in this way the trustworthiness of seeing and self-givenness as such remain beyond dispute. To reject this trustworthiness, however, is to reject "every ultimate norm, every basic criterion that gives knowledge its meaning." Any argument against the skeptic makes use of the trustworthiness of self-givenness or the epistemic worth of the evident. And the skeptic, for his part, cannot argue without claiming to see grounds or reasons, and in this way he also trusts what is evident.[8]

What all this comes to is formulated as the so-called Principle of all Principles in the first volume of *Ideas*. Every primordially presentative seeing (*originaer gebende Anschauung*), we read here, is a source from which we may derive the justification for a knowledge-claim.[9] The expression "primordially presentative seeing" is another designation of the highest epistemic level. Further on Husserl formulates a slightly stronger version when he states that this mode of givenness, on the one hand, and the acceptance of the object as real (*Setzung*), on the other, belong together as a unity which is not a case of a mere general matter of fact but of "rational motivation." It is an "act of reason in the highest sense."[10] It would be unreasonable not to accept what is evident.

I have already shown that the subject whose claim implies that he takes what he asserts to be evident can be called to account. He is not considered infallible. In fact, a subject who is utterly committed to rationality should reflect on his epistemic

situation and submit it to critical scrutiny. He should ask himself whether the situation really has that character of perfection which his cognitive claim implied. Has his cognitive intention been completely fulfilled or does the object intended have components which are in some way referred to but not self-given? If nothing whatever is ascribed to the object beyond what is actually seen, Husserl calls it a case of *adaequate Evidenz*. Or, as one might prefer to say, in this case what is referred to is completely evident. If no further exploration in any direction is indicated and if no criticism can show him otherwise, this subject may "defend" his position as follows.

When I see as I do now and when I keep this fact before my mind, I simply cannot conceive the possibility that what I see might not be or that it might be different from what I see it to be. If I try to deny it or to consider it doubtful, it immediately becomes completely evident to me that non-being or being doubtful is impossible. I cannot imagine that doubt might be warranted here. I cannot imagine that its being and so-being might be merely possible in the sense of there being something that could be said in favor of a contrary possibility. I cannot conceive the possibility that it might turn out later that what I see did not exist. To be sure, such things are in one sense conceivable. But I can only apprehend the nonexistence of the object or state of affairs as a possibility that is evident, provided I ignore the fact that I am now seeing the way I do.[11]

How must these emphatic statements be taken? The preceding discussion has prepared us for the answer. To safeguard the meaningful search for truth, Husserl has characterized an epistemic situation and defended it against skeptical doubts. A situation in which one believes something or makes a statement about something usually involves indications for further exploration and verification. If we want to justify our belief or our statement, we have to follow up some of those indications (in Husserl's language "empty intentions") in order to verify whether they agree with the facts. Let us now envisage, I take Husserl to be saying, an optimal epistemic situation. The subject is not aware of anything further he might do in his search for truth. And no criticism can show that in his search for truth he has left unexplored a relevant dimension whose exploration might adversely affect the belief or the statement. To be sure, he has not told us what object or facts, if any, can be apprehended in this way. The discussion has been very generally concerned with the search for truth, epistemic situations, rationality, and the like. If the search for truth is to be meaningful, we were told, we have to insist on the attainability of that kind of optimal situation.

The situation was also defended against skepticism. In that sort of situation it would be unreasonable to entertain doubt. To the skeptic Husserl seems to be saying: Either you must be able to suggest further meaningful explorations or I have the right to be sure.

Now the strong language in the above statements must be appreciated as a way of characterizing the optimal situation envisaged. Given the stipulations about the situation of the epistemic subject, that confident language would seem to be appropriate. When doubt can no longer be considered a reason for further exploration, it can only be rejected as evidently without ground.

This point is very important and gives us a significant insight into Husserl's philosophy as a whole. Let us note, first of all, the clear attempt to formulate a position that does not expose itself to a skepticism that would attack the trustworthiness of our cognitive powers. Men like Descartes and Pascal, for example, struggled with that kind of skepticism—and they were convinced that even our highest cognitive achievements could not be accepted as revealing to us what reality is like unless knowledge of the author of our being is somehow available to us. To get rid of the evil genius, we must know that God has given us trustworthy instruments for knowledge. Husserl, however, does not share that conviction; he does not allow an evil genius to suggest

some reason for doubt. Descartes' proof for the existence of a veracious God is set aside as "a theological theory of *Evidenz*."[12] Doubt which springs from the realization that reality is mind-independent and that it is not obvious that our being is a fit instrument for attaining truth about a nonmental reality is not tolerated. Husserl's position emphatically excludes the recognition of reality that would be transcendent in the sense that it would elude the grasp of our cognitive powers and thus in principle be beyond the reach of all experience possible to us. And he therefore cannot, in terms of his view, lend an ear to a skepticism that somehow is nourished by the wonder about such transcendence. For him it is the essence of doubt that there be something within our experience that speaks against that which is in doubt.[13] But for one thing to be taken as a reason for doubting something else, the trustworthiness of our cognitive powers is presupposed, not called into question.

These considerations of course involve the idealism of the Husserlian position: the scope of the mind defines reality. To be sure, Husserl recognizes a kind of transcendence. But what he has in mind is simply the fact that something may lie beyond the scope of a particular epistemic situation or even a finite series of such situations. It is a transcendence that calls for further exploration. In fact, in recognizing it the mind ascribes to itself the powers necessary for that exploration. From his point of view, there is no need for proof of a veracious author of our being because there is no transcendence of the kind that might suggest an evil genius. The being of the knower need not be safeguarded by a reference to its author since it is transparent to itself, with respect both to its status and the sufficiency of its powers. What Husserl affirms as a very remote analogy to Descartes' proof of the existence of God is the Principle of Principles, mentioned earlier.

II

The completely rational subject, we

noted in the preceding section, has to submit his epistemic situation to critical scrutiny (guided by the general principles outlined in that section). Such scrutiny will either reveal dimensions that ought to and can be further explored or give warrant for perfect confidence and a certainty that can be seen to be unshakable. In this section we shall consider what Husserl says about the outcome when specifically different directions of human inquiry or search for truth are evaluated in this manner. Let us begin with the perception of material objects.

Husserl emphasizes the achievement character of a perceptual situation. If the inquiry concerns really existing material things—in contrast to possibly existing material objects—perceiving one of these things is in some sense an optimal situation. Yet he puts equal emphasis on the fact that perceiving, as an achievement, must be intrinsically limited in scope. Perceiving a material object involves references to a context that is not actually perceived but nonetheless is held to be real. The percipient commits himself to taking, as really existing, not just the thing as actually perceived but the whole thing, including its unperceived aspects.[14]

Can these two emphases be reconciled? How can one maintain that the object itself is perceived when it is obvious that the object has aspects that are not perceived? Here, of course, it is important to recall a point made earlier. On what scale do we place perceiving when we call it a seeing of the object itself?[15] We compare it, as noted before, with inferior epistemic situations. The examples Husserl usually gives are merely linguistic references and pictures of the perceptible object. In contrast to such situations, *perceiving* takes on its achievement character, and on *this* scale of epistemic distance it is optimal. If we ask, however, whether the subject has done all he could, the answer seems to be negative. That he can do more is indicated by the references to the unperceived. But this does not count against achievement character because there is a sense in which a subject can never achieve more than perceptions. He can certainly seek further perceptions, following the indications implicit in his situation, but, given the fact that his inquiry is directed to material reality, he can never transcend being in a position in which there is more to reality than what he perceives.

In paragraph 43 of *Ideas* Husserl deals with what he calls an error of principle. In view of the perspectival character of our perceptions of material objects, it might be suggested that perception is not a mode of access to the material thing itself but that it is accessible to an apprehension of a different sort. God, who possesses absolutely perfect knowledge, may be supposed to perceive a material thing all at once and in all its aspects. Unlike ourselves, he would not perceive the thing through "appearances." Husserl's reaction to this view is revealing.

The suggestion, and the disqualification of our perceptions which it entails, is declared absurd (*widersinnig*). It is absurd because it is contrary to what is meant by a material object. To say that a spatial thing might be apprehended in a nonperspectival way is tantamount to saying that a spatial thing is not what it is. Instead of being a spatial thing it would be an experience, a mental occurrence, in the divine mind. "Not merely for men but also for God," Husserl holds, a material thing is an entity that can be apprehended only through appearances.[16] It is inconceivable that a spatial object might be given in the kind of perception appropriate to mental events, whether the intellect involved is human or superhuman. It is a poor service to God, he says; to allow him to make five an even number and, similarly, every absurdity a truth.[17]

Although the perceptual mode of a spatial reality's givenness is inadequate, a different mode of givenness is absurd. The former is inadequate in the sense that the search for truth must go on; but the mode cannot be disqualified for all that. ('Inadequate' should not be construed as meaning we are dealing with a "contingent defect" a superior mind could overcome.)[18] To be sure, the mode entails the fallibility of such perceptions, and the existence of a material thing is never entailed (*notwendig gefordert*) by a perceptual mode of givenness—not even by a series of perceptions that confirm one another. In spite of its being evident to the perceiver, it is an open possibility that it might not exist. Husserl uses 'open possibility' to mean that this is not an alternative for which there is specific evidence; it means merely that the perceptual situation does not exclude the possibility that the evident might later become doubtful.[19] But this is not to be construed as a reason for doubt *while* we have perceptions of material objects. In *Formal and Transcendental Logic* Husserl maintains that Descartes lost sight of the fundamental sense of perception as self-givenness because of his heavy emphasis on the possibility of error. He lost sight of the achievement character of perceptual experience, Husserl says, because he never asked what it means to be a material object.[20] To be a material object, in Husserl's view, means to be accessible through sense perception, even though this implies fallibility and an unending search for truth.

As noted a moment ago, the open possibility of the nonexistence of an object of perception does not mean that we always have reasons to doubt. There is, in fact, no reason to doubt the veridicality of a particular perception until other perceptions (those counted on to fulfill the empty intentions) reveal details that are incompatible with those intentions. If a given perception is to be called into question, this can only be on the strength of other perceptions.

Through our perceptual experience we have before us a familiar spatio-temporal world that endures through change. What has come to be believed, and has not been repudiated, survives as the familiar spatio-temporal world in which things exist and change and in which we ourselves live and move. A particular perception is limited and fallible, because what is believed on the basis of it is believed to be an item having status within this broad context. At times we recognize some of our beliefs about its details as erroneous, but the world as a whole remains consistent in spite of such corrections. And in Husserl's view there is a certainty about the world that goes beyond its being thus-and-so. Even if extensive doubts arise, we somehow are sure there is a world that can be further explored in order to resolve our doubts and settle our disputes—in the long run. There is, on one hand, what is called an 'empirical indubitability' of the world, while experience of it retains its essential unity in spite of corrections because it is apodictically impossible to believe in, the nonexistence of things and the world while experience continues. As we noted, belief that there is something that speaks against another belief is essential to doubting.[21] There is, on the other hand, an "unshakable belief regarding the world" (*unzerbrechlicher Weltglauben*), no matter how extensive our doubts become.[22] It envisages the world as the reality whose exploration would resolve our doubts. This belief is unshakable in the sense that it is a determinant of this style or pattern of experience as a whole; *within* this experience it is not, and indeed cannot be, subjected to verificatory procedures that might confute it. Another way of saying the same thing: Experience as a whole is pervaded by the conviction that illusion will not have the last word but that truth will be attained beyond the illusion.

Yet, according to Husserl, if we are utterly rational and consider perceptual experience of the world in light of the principles defining the absolutely optimal epistemic situation, we have to hold that neither the existence nor nonexistence of the world is absolutely evident. On the contrary, what is absolutely evident is that existence as well as nonexistence is possible.[23] Even while we continue to experience a unified world, we can arrive at the insight that it is possible that this world might not exist. As he states, this is not to be understood in the way the contingency of facts is usually understood. He does not mean to say that although the world in fact exists, it might not have existed. What he means he formulates as follows: *Although* I perceive the world (in whatever degree of perfection), *although* my certainty of its existence is never shaken, and *although* I cannot entertain doubt about its existence, it is nevertheless true that its givenness does not in principle exclude its nonexistence.[24] It is possible that this world-experience might be a mere illusion.

He stresses that this is not like saying that perhaps the world does not exist— using 'perhaps' to suggest that this is quite possible, if not altogether likely. Talk about possible nonexistence should not be taken to suggest that we be prepared for the end of the world. The possibility in question is not like the possibility we have in mind when we say that a clear sky may cloud over. According to the straightforward sense of our perceptual experience, there is no doubt whatever about the existence of the world. Skeptical argumentation should not lead us to lose sight of this; nothing speaks in favor of the nonexistence of the world.[25] Nevertheless, despite the percipient's firm belief that possible error will not be the last word and that further experience will correct our errors, it is not apodictically necessary that experience continue in a pattern whereby, through corrections, a unified world remains before us. It is conceivable that experience should dissolve into ultimate discontinuity and a chaos of ultimately incoherent appearances. It is conceivable that experience should be such that there could be no question of correcting errors and illusions and arriving at a truth beyond them. If one supposed the subject retains memory of experience as it is now, he would remember the earlier coherent experience and its corresponding world but he would no longer be able to assert its existence. For him it would be a transcendental illusion or a coherent dream. The author deliberately uses 'transcendental' to indicate that this recognition of illusion, quite unlike others, would not presuppose the subject's recognition of what is really the nature of the world. All this, we are told, can be appreciated as an open possibility;

it is free from absurdity (*widersinnsfrei*) and is not incompatible with the undoubted empirical belief in the existence of the world which characterizes our ordinary perceptual experience.[26]

How are we to take what I have so far expounded? What is Husserl doing in this epistemological evaluation of our experience of the external world? It is clear that, on one hand, he takes pains to defend it against views that would totally discredit it as a reliable mode of access to truth about material reality. He has contended that it would be contrary to the recognized character of this form of reality to demand a radically different approach; a transcendence that would give grounds for such a suggestion has been firmly rejected. A perception of the world, therefore, is a form of *Evidenz*: it justifies a knowledge-claim. On the other hand, he is concerned to point out that in this direction of inquiry the subject can never attain the epistemic situation in which it would be appropriate to use the strong language which was said to be appropriate in the absolutely optimal situation discussed in part I of this paper. Such knowledge-claims always go beyond what is actually perceived. Therefore, what is asserted *can always become* doubtful and *can be* in error, although it would be unreasonable, in light of the above, to assert that it *is* doubtful or false while we have, and continue to have, perceptions of it. In fact, belief is so firmly entrenched that even when conflicting claims arise and doubt and uncertainty prevail, the belief remains unshaken that a world exists whose nature can be established. That is to say, it is constitutive of the percipient to believe that there is a world whose exploration will settle conflicts of view and that it is within his power to find truth beyond all possible error. From the percipient's viewpoint, this is a belief he will never give up, and in this way it is quite different from beliefs about particular items within the world.

Husserl, however, affirms the nonexistence of the world as an open possibility. It seems to me important to recognize that in affirming this he goes *beyond* the framework of the percipient. Since the nonexistence of the world would entail the nonexistence of the percipient as such—that is, as a being endowed with powers of exploring the world—he is affirming the open possibility of the nonexistence of the entire framework constituted by the percipient and his world. It is not a possibility which, strictly speaking, is part of the framework; it does not function as a possibility within that framework. The percipient *cannot* give up belief in the existence of the world. It is nevertheless a belief which, from an external viewpoint, can be seen to be defeasible.

III

In the preceding section I discussed Husserl's evaluation of a very important range of epistemic situations, namely, those directed upon the empirical world which we experience through perception. To establish his conclusions with respect to that world and our experience of it, Husserl made various claims. He claimed, for example, that a spatial object can never be perceived all at once. He likewise claimed that it is impossible to believe that something does not exist in a situation in which the object in question is perceptually given. What sorts of claims are these? Since they were used in an inquiry about all empirical knowledge of the external world, it is obvious that they cannot be general empirical claims about the world. If the conclusions are to be cogent, they must have a different status. Since Husserl was one of the most methodologically self-conscious philosophers, the point did not escape him. Such statements, he said, are eidetic. They are about essences.

In this section I want to discuss some epistemological features of Husserl's doctrine of essences. Philosophy is not the only discipline that talks about essences. When we affirm that 2 is less than 3 or that 5 is a prime number, we make an eidetic statement. Similarly, when in logic we talk about relations between propositions, we make eidetic state-

ments. Now in all inquiry directed to essences the epistemically optimal situation is most often designated by the author as apodictic *Evidenz* or insight (*Einsicht*). It is, again, an epistemic achievement, defined by reference to an epistemic distance that may have to be traversed from mere meaning or intention, as Husserl would have it, to its fulfillment. The required steps will of course depend on the subject matter, the "object of the intention." In each case, however, the inquiry is directed to the nonempirical. In no case does the subject presuppose or assert an empirical fact about the world. No observation can invalidate this kind of claim to knowledge. The optimal epistemic situation is typically "defended" by reference to one's inability to think otherwise about the matter in hand. How are we to take this description?

In *Logical Investigations* Husserl emphatically rejects views that would interpret this description in a purely psychological manner. It is essentially the feeling-theory discussed earlier in this article. An epistemically optimal situation would thus be characterized in terms of a subjective necessity which is only a fact about our thinking, in all likelihood obtaining whenever we make a claim about anything at all. According to our author, the awareness of not being able to think otherwise is to be taken as a presentation to the subject of "objective-ideal necessity." It shows that this or that cannot *be* otherwise; hence if a subject thinks about it otherwise, he will be wrong.[27] In other words, Husserl insists on describing the situation as one of seeing an objective necessity, as an insight into the pure essence of things.

Since empirical facts (i.e., empirical instantiations) do not fall within the scope of this inquiry, the limitations inherent in the earlier situation are not present. It would therefore seem that the sort of situation envisaged in part I of this article is attained. What is asserted cannot be falsified by the facts of empirical existence. It would appear that the epistemic worth of the situation might be defended in the language used earlier to characterize the absolutely optimal situation. The search for truth has, in this direction, really reached its goal; beyond it there is nothing further to look for.

There is a sense in which Husserl affirms this. Yet as long as we think of essences in terms of disciplines such as logic, mathematics, and regional ontologies, there remains, in his view, something unsatisfactory in eidetic knowledge-claims, as indeed in everything he calls "positive knowledge" (*positive Erkenntnis*). Mathematical *Evidenz*, however perfect, has a side that can raise questions and doubts. However evident things may be in the various directions of inquiry carried out by the "positive" sciences, the entire enterprise is "surrounded by transcendental and metaphysical mists in which skepticism and mysticism have their day."[28] A naiveté is inherent in "positive" searching for truth (*Wahrheitsbegründung*). He also speaks of abstractness, one-sidedness, and transcendental naiveté—terms that have approximately the same force. Again, he urges that a distinction be made between what is evident from the "positive" point of view (*Evidenz der Positivität*) and what is evident from the point of view that affords clarity about transcendental origins (*Evidenz der transzendentalen Ursprungsklarheit*).[29]

To make sense of all this we should perhaps begin by noting Husserl's term *Blickrichtung*, which I translate somewhat freely by 'direction of inquiry'.[30] When we pursue a certain direction of inquiry, there comes a point at which, in terms of the methodology or framework within which the inquiry is conducted, we can confidently maintain the truth of our beliefs or judgments. In the case of eidetic claims, the object can become completely evident. Thus there is no point in going further in that particular direction of inquiry; the search for truth in *that* direction has ended. Even if we grant this, however, there are determinants that do not lie within the scope of the inquiry now considered to have been finished but are, nevertheless, essentially involved. They are involved in the sense that they consti-

tute what is taken for granted and are relied upon by the epistemic subject in the situation in which he makes his confident claims. They do not fall within the scope of the inquiry, inasmuch as no explicit claims are made about them and verificational procedures do not test what is taken for granted. What the authorn in the final analysis, has in mind is the nature and status of the epistemic subject itself. As he puts it in one passage, the subject who sees and claims "I see this and that" does not, *ipso facto*, have knowledge, perhaps not even an idea, of everything subjective that makes this "I see" concrete.[31]

However, unless clarity is also attained in this direction, even evident eidetic knowledge-claims are vulnerable to the skeptic. Psychologism, for example, is precisely such a skeptical attack on logic and mathematics. It is not an attack on knowledge-claims that are made within the framework of these inquiries; it does not dispute specific claims which, within the framework, are held to be justified and true. Psychologism would discredit the entire framework from a point of view external to it.[32] From this point of view, the subject who makes claims in logic and mathematics is interpreted as an object whose nature can be finally determined by empirical psychological inquiry. The epistemic situation in which something is evident is treated as merely a psychological fact about that object. That it is a mode of access to truth about objects other than itself (e.g., essences and essential states of affairs) must now appear as an unreasonable assumption. Yet this is exactly what is taken for granted in inquiries such as logic and mathematics. To employ terminology introduced earlier, psychologism is a skepticism because it attacks epistemic situations which are trusted in those inquiries as establishing that something is or is not true.

Now as long as an epistemic achievement, though optimal within its own framework, is exposed to this sort of attack, it is epistemically deficient. As noted, the author speaks here of one-sidedness, positivity, and transcendental naiveté. That it is vulnerable to attack from a direction other than that of its own inquiry is due to the fact that the nature and status of the inquiring subject remain unclarified. To overcome this deficiency and this vulnerability to the skeptic, we have to explore that dimension of subjectivity which is left unexplored in "positive" inquiries and on which the psychologistic skeptic draws for his contentions. Such exploration, according to Husserl, leads to the conclusion that the subject, who ultimately is responsible for all knowledge-claims, is transcendental. He is "outside" the world to which his cognitive claims are directed. Every framework in which the subject appears otherwise (e.g., as a psycho-physical entity in the world) can be shown to be constituted in transcendental subjectivity. Only by virtue of being outside can the inquiring subject's claims be justified in such a way as to be secure from skeptical attacks. When the mists hanging over the status and nature of that subject have been driven away by transcendental clarification, the absolutely optimal situation envisaged by the discussion of part I has been attained.

What was said here about the need for further (i.e., transcendental) exploration, even when in one direction of inquiry an optimal situation has been reached, applies equally to the type of situation discussed in section II. Erroneous views about the nature and status of the subject (e.g., psychologism) can equally endanger perceptual experience as a mode of access to truth about things and other empirical objects. Here, too, naturalism with regard to the subject must be countered by transcendental clarification.

IV

Is the evident the same as the true? From the viewpoint of one who searches for truth, the evident is in fact the true, because it is evident he holds it to be true. If he is aware that in holding something to be true he commits himself to more than the evident, he will be prepared for the possibility of error. But this implies the conviction that the evident is the true.

Because he has defined the evident as an experienced relation of agreement between what is meant and what is self-given, Husserl is able to assign a sense to the old formulation according to which truth is the adequation of the thing and the intellect.[33] That this is not a final endorsement of the correspondence theory of truth should be clear. Both *relata* lie within experience. In the context of a theory about the search for truth, however, this relation is fundamental in the way we experience that search. If there is a sense in which we search for truth, there must be a phenomenological sense in which, having started somewhere else, we arrive at a point which is a finding of truth.

Yet there is also a sense in which Husserl distinguishes between the evident and the true. I am thinking of those passages in which he insists that there is a truth in itself. In spite of the unquestionably idealistic tone of *Cartesian Meditations*, we read this statement:

Every entity is, in a very broad sense, 'in itself,' in contrast to its accidental being 'for me' in a particular act. Similarly, every truth is, in this very broad sense, 'truth in itself.'[34]

A single experience, characterized as *Evidenz*—something's being evident to someone on some particular occasion—cannot be taken as an indefeasible grasp of a truth in itself.[35] As it is stated, it does not yet create for us an entity that endures. Every situation in which something is evident to me, to be sure, founds (*stiftet*) a lasting possession for me, but this is only because I anticipate being able to come back and reaffirm what I now affirm.[36]

In *Formal and Transcendental Logic* the same point comes up in slightly different language.[37] Here Husserl wants to emphasize that every single intentional experience, including *Evidenz*, is a function within the total context of consciousness. Its peculiar contribution or achievement (*Leistung*) requires context. It cannot be appreciated as such when the experience is considered in its sheer particularity. A situation of something's being evident to someone, as I stressed earlier, is what it phenomenologically is, because of its implicit references to other, epistemically inferior situations. The author emphasizes in the passages just mentioned that being conscious of something as evident is contextual in still another sense. It includes reference to what he calls a synthesis of recognition: the subject who takes something to be evident to him presumes he can return and be in a position to find it still evident once more. As an apprehension of the true on a particular occasion, in a particular epistemic situation, *Evidenz* has to be completed (*vervollständigt*) through repetition.

The specifically epistemological import of this becomes clear when, in these same paragraphs, Husserl touches on the problem of error. In a general way, he mentions views that consider *Evidenz* an experience without context in the totality of subjective experience, and that attribute to it the property of giving us "an absolute criterion of truth," an "absolute security from error." This seems to him to be an utterly disastrous view of *Evidenz*, and he devotes many pages to showing how wrongheaded such a construction is. Much of what he writes, however, is very difficult to understand. He emphasizes that it is a construction and that it will not stand up under phenomenological analysis. It is a construction that takes its point of departure from the presupposition of truth-in-itself, contending that if we are to have truth and knowledge at all, we must have an absolute *Evidenz*. Husserl of course approaches this matter from a different angle altogether. Truth for him, one might say, is revealed in the fulfillment of intentions; it emerges from the search for truth as a belief that can be defended and justified. The epistemological, rather than ontological, features of truth are primary. Truth is what, in a contextualized situation, is held to be true and *continues* to be held to be true. *Evidenz*, as a particular apprehension of truth, is to remain embedded in the total process involved in

the search for truth: intentions, fulfillments, anticipations, recognitions, etc.

A particular experience called *Evidenz*, then, is not an "absolute criterion of truth." Error, in other words, is possible. Husserl states quite plainly that "even an *Evidenz* that professes to be apodictic may be revealed as error."[38] The point seems to be this: When a particular claim is made, it is judged by an independent standard; even though the subject who makes the claim thinks he has satisfied the requirements laid down by the standard, what he asserts can be tested and therefore can be shown to be in error. This applies to *all* particular epistemic situations, even those in which something is claimed to be apodictically evident. This does not mean that the concept of the apodictically evident is abandoned by Husserl. He clearly says that if a particular claim is to be refuted, it can be refuted only on the strength of accepting something else as more apodictically evident. In the event of such a refutation, only a particular claim to be apodictically evident is rejected.

The skepticism here envisaged as confronting *every* claim to truth is of course not a treat but rather a stimulus to the search for truth. It urges the seeker to do all he can, that is, to test his claim and to allow it to be tested. The trustworthiness of the standards is not in question but only the claims which imply that they have satisfied those standards. We recall that the attempts of Husserl to refute the skeptic were concerned with epistemic situations that were characterized as situations in which the epistemic subject had done all he could do. Only in such cases is skepticism a serious threat to the search for truth. It is not necessary to hold that every claim, based on what is taken to be evident, is infallible. There is no more ground for skepticism in this case than in the case of the fallibility of sense experience. In either case, an expression of skepticism, when it meets a claim, can only lead the person who makes the claim to a further effort to make sure. The essential point in all this was included in the discussions of part I.

The trustworthiness of the evident, it was stated, cannot be rejected without rejecting "every ultimate norm, every basic criterion that gives knowledge its meaning." But it was also apparent that the situation in which something is implied to be evident is to be subjected to critical scrutiny.

Although there is, then, a sense in which every truth is *an sich*—not essentially related to any actual experience in which it might be taken to be evident—there is an important qualification. In *Cartesian Meditations* the statement about truth-in-itself is immediately qualified as follows. The sense of "in itself" may not include reference to any particular experience, but it does include reference to potentialities of repetition grounded in the life of the transcendental ego.[39] Truth is defined by the scope of this ego, as is reality itself. Truth is verifiability in the sense of performability of the act of verification (*Ausweisung*) on the part of transcendental subjectivity.

V

This discussion of what I take to be the fundamental principles of Husserl's theory of knowledge might be summed up as follows. Part I culminated in the characterization of an epistemic situation which is envisaged in every search for truth. If the search continues, in a certain direction of inquiry, it continues precisely because that kind of epistemic situation has not been attained. If the search for truth is deemed to have come to an end, the attainment of truth must be defended by reference to the general principles that define the absolutely optimal situation.

I have placed emphasis on Husserl's attempts to safeguard the search for truth against skepticism. A skepticism that would undermine it by disqualifying it as meaningless is rejected as unreasonable since it must share in the search for truth to find its own arguments. Skepticism that stimulates this search, however, is taken very seriously. In sections II and III we noticed that the search for truth, both as empirical and as eidetic inquiry, cannot be safeguarded against a disastrous skepticism without transcendental inquiry into the nature and status of the epistemic subject. If we do not direct inquiry to this dimension of subjectivity, where the issue essentially concerns the subject's powers of access to truth, all other inquiry will remain exposed to skeptical attack. We touch here, it seems to me, on a very fundamental sense of Husserl's Cartesianism, his search for the indubitable or for what cannot be wrong. Unless we seek this, Husserl believes, the search in which we can be wrong cannot be defended as meaningful.

In section IV the relation between the evident and the true was discussed. On one hand, truth appears to the subject as what is evident to him; as Husserl put it in his *Logical Investigations* and elsewhere, *Evidenz* is experience of truth. On the other hand, what is asserted as true on the basis of its being evident to the subject on a particular occasion can be tested again and is fallible. Even a claim that implies that something is apodictically or "adequately" evident can, in this sense, be shown to be mistaken, if it can be shown that it was not really evident.[40] Can what is really evident be false? Since what is really evident is that which stands up under *all* the evaluational procedures available to the transcendental subject, and since truth is defined in a way that makes it relative to the cognitive powers of that subject, the answer is negative.

NOTES

1. *LU* (2d ed.; Halle, 1928), 1: 12-14, 110-11, 143, 152, 186 [*LI*, 1: 60-64, 135-36, 159, 166, 191]. For a much later formulation of these ideas, see *Husserliana*, 8: 363-68.

2. The matter is never treated at great length, but in a number of places he makes fairly clear statements regarding it, e.g., *LU*, 1: 13 [*LI*, 1: 61], and *Husserliana* 1: 93 [*Cartesian Meditations*, 57-58] and 3: 259-60, 275-76, 278-79, 289, 341-43 [*Ideas*, 300-1, 317-18, 320-22, 331, 387-89].

3. *Formale und transzendentale Logik*, sec. 16a

[*Formal and Transcendental Logic*, sec. 16a].

4. For a more elaborate presentation of this point and most of what I said on this business of epistemic levels, see my article "Intuition and Horizon" in *Philosophy and Phenomenological Research*, 34 (Sept. 1973): 95-101.

5. Skepticism, Husserl maintained, is essentially subjectivism. In principle it involves the following train of thought. Everything objective is only there for the knower, because he experiences it. To experience it, however, means that it somehow appears to him in some subjective mode of appearing. That which is in itself is not experienced apart from subjective modes of appearing. Skepticism constitutes a motif of universal significance because, with the entrance of skepticism, the naive, antecedent givenness of the world becomes problematic, and this in turn gives rise to questions concerning our ability to know it and concerning the sense of the being in itself of that world. The novelty of Cartesianism and all subsequent modern philosophy consists in the fact that it took up the battle against skepticism in a completely new way. The development of modern philosophy aims at overcoming the paradoxical, playful, frivolous subjectivism of the traditional skepticism by way of a novel, serious subjectivism that can be absolutely justified, namely transcendental subjectivism. In other words, Husserl seems to be saying that skepticism is important in that it forces us to come to terms with subjectivity, a dimension that can easily be overlooked, but from which skepticism draws its arguments. For the above, see *Husserliana*, 7: 58-63.

6. The matter is discussed in the following places: *LU*, 1: 180, 189ff. [*LI*, 1: 187, 194ff.]; 2: ii, 127 [2: 772]; *Husserliana*, 2: 59f. [*The Idea of Phenomenology*, 44ff.]; *Husserliana*, vol. 3, sec. 21, 145 [*Ideas*, sec. 21, 145]; *Husserliana*, 7: 65, 131; *Formale und transzendentale Logik*, pp. 140, 245 [*Formal and Transcendental Logic*, pp. 156, 277].

7. *LU*, 1: 191 [*LI*, 1: 196]. The text uses the term *Einsicht* (insight), but the context explicitly designates this as a synonym of *Evidenz*. We should be prepared for this variation in terminology in view of the already indicated connection between the evident and the notion of seeing that emerges from the phenomenology of epistemic levels. Cf. *LU*, 1: 91 [*LI*, 1: 120].

8. See *Husserliana*, 2: 35, 49-50, 61 [*The Idea of Phenomenology*, 28, 39-40, 49]. Cf. *Husserliana*, 7: 335f., 341f.

9. *Husserliana*, 3: 52 [*Ideas*, 92]. See also *Husserliana*, 3:44 [*Ideas*, 84]. In a later text we find this mentioned as the most general principle of justification (*Husserliana*, 8: 32).

10. *Husserliana*, 3: 334-36 [*Ideas*, 380-82].

11. I constructed this lengthy "defense" from various passages. "Gibt es *absolute* Anschauungen, so muessen sie so geartet sein, dass ich, waehrend ich sie urspruenglich im Vollzug habe oder noch habe, mir schlechthin nicht vorstellen kann, dass das Erfahrene nicht sei oder zweifelhaft sei oder nur moeglich sei in dem Sinne, der eine Gegenmoeglichkeit, fuer die auch etwas spricht, neben sich hat" (*Husserliana*, 8: 368).

In another passage this is called apodictic indubitability and characterized as follows: "Wo ich sehe, wie ich sehe, und dies festhaltend, dass ich so sehe, da kann ich mir nicht einmal die Moeglichkeit, dass das Gesehene nicht sei oder anders sei, denken; somit etwa auch die Moeglichkeit, dass sich hinterher herausstelle, dass das Gesehene nicht sei. Dergleichen kann ich mir denken; ich kann es nur einsehend als Moeglichkeit erschauen, wenn ich mir dazu denke, dass ich nicht sehe und in dieser apodiktischen Art sehe" (ibid., p. 50).

"Versuche ich, eine adaequate Evidenz zu negieren oder als zweifelhaft anzusetzen, so springt, und wieder in adaequater Evidenz, die Unmoeglichkeit des Nichtseins oder des Zweifelhaftseins... hervor" (ibid., p. 35).

In *Cartesianische Meditationen* we read: "Eine apodiktische Evidenz aber hat die ausgezeichnete Eigenheit, dass sie nicht bloss ueberhaupt Seinsgewissheit der in ihr evidenten Sachen oder Sachverhalte ist, sondern sich durch eine kritische Reflexion zugleich als schlechthinnige Unausdenkbarktei des Nichtseins derselben enthuellt; dass sie also im voraus jeden vorstellbaren Zweifel als gegenstandslos ausschliesst." ["An *apodictic* evidence, however, is not merely certainty of the affairs or affair-complexes (states-of-affairs) evident in it; rather it discloses itself, to a critical reflection, as having the signed peculiarity of being at the same time the absolute unimaginableness (inconceivability) of their non-being, and thus excluding in advance every doubt as "objectless," empty."] (*Husserliana*, 1: 56 [*Cartesian Meditations*, 15-16]).

It should be noted that in the above quotations Husserl admits that there is a sense in which it is conceivable that what is seen might not exist. Though he does not elaborate on this point, I take it that he means that a proposition to this effect is not self-contradictory. It is a possibility, he says, which becomes evident only by abstracting from the specific nature of the epistemic situation in question. What he clearly wants to deny is that to *the subject in that situation* it is evident that he can be in error. One might make the point this way. For this subject it would be wrong to *assert* "It is possible that this is not so," implying by that assertion that he did not know that it is so. For him to use this locution would be wrong in the sense that it would imply a wrong assessment of his situation. For the general possibility of error, see sect. 4 below.

12. *Husserliana*, 7: 341.

13. *Husserliana*, vol. 3, sec. 47-48 [*Ideas*, sec. 47-48]; *Husserliana*, 8:50.

14. *LU*, 2: 2: 56 [*LI*, 2: 712]. *Husserliana*, 3: 88, 338 [*Ideas*, 127]. Cf. *Husserliana*, 8: 44 and 11: 3.

15. "Seeing the object itself" is here strictly a technical phrase, defined in terms of the phenomenology of epistemic levels. The fact that in its ordinary sense it is at home in the area now under discussion should not lead us to forget that.

16. *Husserliana*, 3: 98, 101, 371; cf. pp. 341, 191 [*Ideas*, 136, 138, 418; cf. pp. 387, 229].

17. *Husserliana*, 11: 18f. Cf. *Formale und transzendentale Logik*, p. 250.

18. *Husserliana*, 11: 19.

19. *Husserliana*, 3: 108 [*Ideas*, 144]. Cf. *Husserliana*, 1: 56 [*Cartesian Meditations*, 15-16]. For the distinction between open possibility and so-called problematic possibility, see *Erfahrung und Urteil*, para. 21c [*Experience and Judgment*, para. 21c]].

20. *Formale und transzendentale Logik*, p. 249f.; cf. pp. 144f. [*Formal and Transcendental Logic*, p. 282; cf. p. 161f.].

21. *Husserliana*, 3: 109 [*Ideas*, 144]. Cf. *Husserliana*, 8: 50, 53, 368.

22. The expression "unzerbrechlicher Weltglauben" occurs in *Husserliana*, 8: 54.

23. Ibid., 7: 336.

24. Ibid., 8: 50.

25. Ibid., p. 54.

26. Ibid., 3: 114f. [*Ideas*, 151]; *Husserliana*, 8: 48-58, 64-68; 1: sec. 7.

27. *LU*, 2: 1: 239 [*LI*, 2: 446]. Cf. *LU*, 1: 107, 134, 142, 183, 185 [*LI*, 1: 133].

28. *Husserliana*, 8: 38.

29. Ibid., pp. 27-38.

30. I am here putting weight on a passage that in German reads as as follows: "Meine Erkenntnis soll aber auch eine in jeder Hinsicht evidente sein: auch in jeder moeglichen Hinsicht, die jetzt oder normalerweise nicht fuer mich aktuelle Hinsicht ist; das Erkannte soll nicht ihm wesentlich zugehoerige Bestimmungen haben, die ausserhalb der Blickrichtung meiner sonst vollkommenen Evidenz liegen und vermoege ihrer Unbekanntheit verfaengliche Unklarheiten, Raetsel, Zweifel mit sich fuehren" (Ibid., p. 31).

31. Ibid., p. 289.

32. Its having external status may be only apparent. If it directs claims against a framework while being unable to sustain them without that framework, it is of course self-stultifying (*widersinnig*, as Husserl would say). See various arguments to this effect in the first volume of *Logical Investigations*.

33. *LU*, 2: 2: 118; cf. p. 122 [*LI*, 2: 762; cf. p. 765].

34. *Husserliana*, 1: 96 [*Cartesian Meditations*, 60].

35. Cf. *Formale und transzendentale Logik*, p. 245 [*Formal and Transcendental Logic*, p. 277].

36 *Husserliana*, 1: 95f. [*Cartesian Meditations*, 59].

37. *Formale und transzendentale Logik*, sec. 59, 60; cf. also, in this connection, sec. 105-7 [*Formal and Transcendental Logic*, sec. 59, 60; cf. also sec. 105-7].

38. *Formale und transzendentale Logik*, p. 140 [*Formal and Transcendental Logic*, pp. 156-157]. Cf. *Husserliana*, 8: 364, where apparently the same point is made about insights (again, as it were, in passing).

39. *Husserliana*, 1: 96 [*Cartesian Meditations*, 60]. In *Logical Investigations* we also read that "A is true" is evidently equivalent to "It is possible that someone or other should make the evident judgment that A is the case" (1: 184). But he adds that this is an ideal possibility which holds, even if in the order of nature it should be impossible for such an intelligence to exist (cf. ibid., p. 129). In his later idealistic works this point will obviously require qualification. In the *Ideas*, for example, he will also state that a possible ego belongs to the possibility of truth, but the explanations that follow indicate the change of view (*Husserliana* 3: 123f. [*Ideas*, 159]).

40. The only exception to this which Husserl admits is the assertion of the existence of the transcendental ego itself. It is a claim emphatically said to be confined to existence, excluding the nature or character of this existent subject. Although the distinction remains somewhat obscure, the point of the exception just noted makes sense. This existence claim cannot be wrong since it involves the existence of that which is presupposed as subject in all epistemic appraisals whatsoever (*Husserliana*, 1: 59 *Cartesian Meditations*, 19]). It is presupposed as existing subject even in those inquiries in which it tries to become clear about its own nature and its cognitive powers.

Structure and Genesis in Husserl's Phenomenology

DONN WELTON

Perception does not consist of staring at something located in consciousness nor at something which, through some kind of senseless miracle, is stuck into consciousness as if there were first something there and then consciousness somehow surrounded it. Rather each objective existent [Dasein] with its specific sense-content is, for each conceivable subject, an accomplishment which must be new for each new kind of object.[1]

In Adam Smith's world of pre-established economic harmony commodities are governed by irrevocable laws that regulate their flow and their relation to the entire system of self-expanding values. Smith's laws are primarily laws of production and growth, not laws of distribution, yet they are only able to incorporate labor as a variable within the larger movement of capital. Much like the laws of gravity, one tampers with Smith's laws only at the risk of having the entire factory cave in.

The genius of Marx's criticism, instituted in the 1844 manuscripts and fully developed in the first volume of *Capital,* consists not so much in showing that Smith is mistaken but in showing that the reality which Smith describes *conceals* its structure beneath a web of appearances. When Marx "breaks open" the essence of the commodity, he does not find things with additive properties and

relations but rather coagulations of human labor. The fetishism of commodities consists not primarily in endowing things with the qualities of commodities but of endowing commodities with the qualities of things. For Marx, the essence of the commodity *is* human labor and the laws governing commodities are the laws of *human* production and its exploitation.

Husserl's turn to a transcendental analysis of the perceptual world takes root in his conception of phenomenology as interrogation, as interrogation not of facts and things but of meaning. Just as Marx overturns the fetishism of commodities and sees them as congealments of human labor, Husserl is able to explode the fetishism of things and to see their meanings as accomplishments (*Leistungen*) of human consciousness in view of human interests.

Husserl is convinced that the autonomy of things cannot be broken without the transcendental turn. "Intentional analysis is something totally different than analysis in the usual sense.... Intentional analysis uncovers the activities and potentialities in which objects are constituted as unities of sense."[2] In this analysis we do not withdraw from the world into the ego as its creative source; rather we merely disengage our living out toward the world in order to apprehend the manner in which the world is present to us and to thematize those affective and active accomplishments which cohabit this presence. The purpose of the turn to subjectivity is not to dissolve the world but to break its fetishism. And when Husserl speaks of bracketing the existence of the world, he does so in order to gain its *presence* and to open its meaning. The objects remain; even things (*Dinge*) remain. But now they function as transcendental clues to the analysis of the many-layer syntheses in which "new types of objects and new individual objects are constituted."[3]

Husserl's phenomenology attempts to show that all perception, in fact all human praxis, takes place within horizons, within horizons without which the world would cease to be significant. Husserl, more than any of his predecessors, was likewise able to show that the presence of a field of objects and facts already presupposes the unseen co-functioning of this horizon. But problems of untold complexity arise for this phenomenology when one turns to the questions of the constitution of the horizon itself. How is it formed and how, exactly, does it "make possible" our perception of objects?

It is this issue that I would like to take up in this paper. And while I believe that it will be possible to give this problem a new and fresh consideration and, perhaps, to resituate it in the larger context of Husserl's progressive radicalization of his own method and results, still I find abiding ambiguities and difficulties in his position. What I propose, then, is to sketch a line of thought which I hope others will complement and correct.

The notion of meaning, as is well known, is the heart and soul of Husserl's *Logical Investigations*. The concept of the perceptual horizon, however, does not find its proper place in his phenomenology until after the first book of *Ideas*, until Husserl, at one of those critical junctions in writing and thought, takes up "the colossal problem of individuation," as one of the letters to Ingarden put it in 1918. During this period he begins reworking the lectures on time-consciousness and the first draft of *Ideen*

II and writing what we now have as his "Lectures on Transcendental Logic" (also called the "Lectures on Genetic Logic").[4] In these lectures we find Husserl carefully moving into a consideration of pre-predicative perceptual experience and attempting, unlike *Logical Investigations* and *Ideas*, to study in detail the structures and dynamics of this dimension. Rather than characterizing perceptual sense along the lines of linguistic meaning, Husserl now concentrates on the unique structures of perceptual fulfillment.[5] In Husserl's language this requires an analysis of passivity, an analysis he spoke of as distinctively noematic: "The first of all phenomenological investigations—that investigation which specifies itself as distinctively noematic—is that of the passively given object."[6] This is, at the same time, an analysis of individuals qua individuals: "In the sphere of those objects passively pregiven and receptively experienced we have to do exclusively with individual objects."[7] With his new interest in a "transcendental aesthetic" we also find an extensive discussion of sensation and its relationship to perception—what Husserl now speaks of as affectivity and action, of the body, and of motivation. From these new investigations—and this is why they are important for us—emerges a notion of perceptual meaning or—to use his term—sense, a notion Husserl was unable to disclose in the static analysis of the earlier works. Husserl's breakthrough, it must be emphasized, is incomplete and truncated. While following the movements and structures of the field he is surveying, he discovers new and interesting terrain. But integrating this into his earlier system, when giving the contours of this terrain a philosophical articulation, Husserl robs his insights of their proper development, of their weight and values.[8] In this paper I will attempt to follow Husserl's new discoveries, and rather than simply cast them in terms of his older distinctions I will try to link them to the later movement of his phenomenology.

In doing this I hope to place the future

discussion of Husserl's concept of *Sinn* on solid ground. The present debate concerning the status of the noema, as exemplified by Professor Solomon's paper in this volume, has taken place *outside* any serious consideration of Husserl's deepening of his analysis of the perceptual noema and *within* the confines of his static methodology. The question whether *Sinn* is a concept (an intensional, mental entity which could be fully expressed by the appropriate syntactically well-formed expression in a critical language) or a percept (a pre-linguistic perceptual structure or schema underlying and perhaps giving rise to concepts) has become hopelessly entangled precisely because (a) perception is treated as a member of the class of signifying intentions (judgments) and not as a class of acts having a structure and an intending component different from signification; (b) the form-content schema is equivocally applied to all kinds of acts; (c) sensations are still treated as devoid of immanent structure and organization (*Sinn*) and consequently are taken as that which is organized by the signifying intention; (d) no distinction is made between passive perception and what Husserl calls attentive or explicative perception; and (e) correspondingly, the lived-body (*Leib*) is treated merely as a vehicle of cognition. In view of Husserl's later work I suggest that all of these assumptions underlying the concept-percept debate are false. In this paper I hope to open a new approach to these issues.

To situate our considerations, let me begin with a brief sketch of Husserl's initial definition of sense.

From a Static to a Genetic Account of Sense

Is not my original discussion of the immanent sphere with immanent data that finally "come to apprehension" through the passive accomplishment of association but a vestige of the old psychology and its sensationalist empiricism? But how can one express it otherwise? There are no sense-data without apprehension. Being apprehended, being "a representation" is innate [to them]. But what can one make out of this? What does the associative constitution really accomplish?[9]

When Husserl speaks of intentionality as the fundamental structure of consciousness he treats the act as that which is always directed toward an object (*Gegenständlichkeit*). Within this terminus, however, it is possible to distinguish between the "sheer object" and the "object in the manner of its determinations." And since in the case of speechacts it is possible to make this distinction without such an object even existing, Husserl spoke of this object as an *intentional* object:

Expression	X(a)	X(b)	X(c)
Meaning	"X(a)"	"X(b)"	"X(c)"
Intentional object		/ X (a, b, c, . . .) /	

This scheme gives Husserl a logical and formal characterization of the intentional object: it is that which is referred to through the meaning of an expressive act. As such it is a *possible* object,[10] or, in the case of counter-sense, no object at all. This also gives Husserl a logical characterization of the noema: it is that meaning which is bestowed or taken up by the expressive act (noesis).

When Husserl attempts to apply this scheme to an analysis of perception, however, he runs into serious difficulties. On the one hand, we can contrast the "self-same" object I perceive to the varying and different profiles of the object I see. This contrast, however, is not a contrast within a possible object but rather one made with an individual real object in view. And this starting point moves precisely from what the logical characterization of the intentional object excluded, namely, a concrete object of perception. On the other hand, Husserl wants to speak of this perceptual contrast between the same object and its profiles not merely as a difference "in" the fulfilling object but as a difference in the perceptual act, as a difference which, in fact, makes the perceptual contrast possible.

Out of this arise two problems. First, when Husserl begins with a perceptual characterization of the object, he tends to revert to a logical characterization of it when discussing the interplay of intention and fulfillment, when attempting to account for it by the correlation of noesis and noema. As a result, the perceptual object is seen as a "filled in" intentional object. As long as the coincidence between *Darstellungsinhalt* and the given was *adequate*[11] and as long as meaning, logically characterized, was considered symmetrical with the unmodalized perceptual object fulfilling or ratifying it, Husserl had no reason to be concerned with the unique structure of the perceptual object. But once it is seen as inadequate, even for the immanent sphere, we are left with a nasty split between intentional and perceptual object, between "mental" object and concrete object. And second, rather than giving full range to the unique and different way in which a perceptual noema functions, the sense is still characterized as that which the act must animate and bestow. And as a result we are left with the puzzling problem of how that which we do not directly intend is nevertheless seen and how it can itself initiate a perceptual act.[12]

These difficulties also have a disturbing effect on Husserl's discussion of sensation and sense-data. In *Ideas* the hyletic data are considered to be a formless, timeless, immanent, noetic content of consciousness which the act then animates with a representative function. They accounted for the fact that we can see the same color, for example, with different intensities and textures—for what Husserl spoke of as adumbrations or profiles. What is amazing, however, is that Husserl considered them not something excluded by the transcendental reduction but rather a noetic "residue" to which we have immediate access from within the reduction. This creates not merely an insurmountable methodological problem[13] but it also seems to transpose— once the split between intentional object and real object is forced—all the problems of Hume's empiricism into a transcendental phenomenalism.

These tensions and persisting dilemmas carried Husserl into an extensive study and reevaluation of his treatment of perceptual sense. It is in this context that the turn to genetic analysis and to a direct consideration of passivity finds it source. What I want to emphasize in this section is the new methodological approach Husserl takes to the analysis of sense, an approach which, to be sure, he did not clearly formulate but which is immanent in the many manuscripts from the early 1920s and in the "Lectures." This approach begins by establishing contrasts and then progressively follows them into a definition of the central concepts of his genetic analysis. This is a genetic phenomenology which implicitly substitutes relational definitions of his concepts for substantival definitions of them. And it is an approach which lets these concepts arise from the pulsations of experience: rather than stylizing the logical limits of experience, it traces the synthetic *Leistungen* that are actually engaged in the perceptual process.

The starting point of Husserl's genetic analysis of perceptual sense is located in the *opposition* between intentional and fulfilling perceptual acts, traversed by the coordinating concepts of absence and presence, identity and change, solicitation and encroachment. In that this opposition does not merely define an exchange of "information" but rather an interlocking expansion of both the sense and the presence of the world, I want to speak of their interplay as *dialectical*.

I return home—to use a simple example—and discover something new in the aquarium. It is a goldfish. The fish has caught my eye and I walk over to take a closer look. I notice the shape of its head, its colors, the contours of its back, the position of its dorsal fin, the length of the caudrals. Throughout these changing perspectives I see the same object but always differently. Or perhaps I look for nothing but merely let the object lead my perception, merely let the side I notice lead me to the side I do not see, let the configuration of the tail lead me to the shape of the head.

If, instead of following the object, I attempt to study it as an object of perception; if, instead of living in the object, I ask how this object is perceived according to a familiar style, I do so by means of a reflection which (a) disengages my normal living *in* the object, (b) takes the object as the terminus of a set of perceptions, and then (c) studies the relationship between object and perceptual act in its effort to account for the perceptual significance the object seems to possess.

The thing is a goldfish. What I see, and everything I *will* see, is organized by this overarching perceptual significance, this sense of the whole, or what Husserl calls an "objective sense" (*gegenständlicher Sinn*). Whether I pursue the object or whether I give in to the object, the objective sense provides the framework within which my perceptions take place. Once this framework is established, the objective sense both guides the sequence of further perceptual acts and—since we are now dealing with individual concrete objects—is itself specified in the course of these acts. The objective sense, Husserl says, "is an essence (sense-essence) which is specified in its own way according to two fundamental modes: in the mode of that which is intuited (*Anschaulichkeit*) . . .and of that which is not intuited (*Unanschaulichkeit*), the empty."[14] The objective sense, however, is not merely a collection of what is intuited and what is not intuited. For what is given is itself permeated by absence, by what is not given. Thus, as Husserl puts it, "in the case of inadequate perception, which necessarily includes all outer perception, we have a standing tension between sense and fulfilled sense."[15] Whatever is intuited (fulfilled sense), whatever is directly given to perception, points to or *implicates* other determinations or a range of other determinations which, at that moment, are not given but are "empty." These, then, are fulfilled (or disappointed), but again only in the context of yet other implicated senses. In this movement between fulfilled sense and implicated sense the objective sense is not a summation of what is past and

what is present, nor is it merely the addition of what is given and what is not given. Rather, it is that which remains *identical* throughout a family of past and present intuitions. As what is identical throughout a family of perceptual phases, the objective sense is also the *difference* between what is given and what is absent.

Objective sense as that which is identical can be characterized as that which arises through a continual *congruence* of past and present phases or acts of perception. Similar blends with similar to form not only the material unity of a given phase but also to form the identity of sense throughout phases.

Besides this progressive congruence of past and present, the objective sense also bears the *difference* between what is present and what is absent, between fulfilled sense and what always remains implicated in fulfillment. The impossibility of adequate perception bears this out. Were "outer" perception adequate, the tension would collapse and the objective sense would become the completely fulfilled sense. In this event the interplay between implicated and fulfilled sense would be exhausted and there would be nothing more which *could* be perceived. The fish that I see would itself be the essence. In view of this impossibility, however, Husserl speaks of the perceived object as an "approximation." "We always have the external object 'in person' (we see, grasp and grip it) and yet it always remains infinitely far from us." This line of thought is continued in the following words: "What we grasp of the object pretends to be its essence; it is it also; but only as an incomplete approximation which, in grasping something about the object, also reaches into an emptiness, an emptiness which itself moves toward fulfillment."[16] The objective sense, then, is never exhausted in *a* fulfillment but rather it is present only in the reiterative and expansive movement between fulfillments and intentions, between fulfilled senses and implicated senses.

Once the consideration of objective sense is taken in the context of the movement between fulfilled and implicated sense, we have the key to Husserl's treatment of objective sense. The relationship between implicated sense and fulfilled sense is completely different from the relationship between signifying meaning and perception. For in the dialectic of fulfillment and implication and of *perception* and *apperception* the objective sense is discovered as a sense found *in* perception, and yet as a structure organizing the ongoing process of perception:

1. The objective sense is, first of all, found *in* perception, not as that which is given but as that which is *announced*:

The course of actual experience...exposes a sense actually determining itself, a sense thought of as final, a sense harmoniously clarifying and radifying itself in this course of experience. It would be thought of as final not inasmuch as it directly exhibits itself as an appearing picture but as inasmuch as it is a sense above and beyond the appearances, a sense announcing itself in the appearances of the fulfilling process with increasing distinctness and clarity, a sense which exhibits and validates itself with increasing completeness in a kind of originality peculiar to it.[17]

(This "originality" that is peculiar to objective sense will be taken up in the next section.)

2. The objective sense, on the other hand, is that which *directs* the course of perception. As the difference between fulfilled and implicated sense, the objective sense is *future*; that is, it is present only as future. Perception, in turn, can be fulfillment only by being *anticipation*. Fulfillment as incomplete is at the same time intention. Husserl expresses this— in a way which has led to much misunderstanding—by saying that if we ask what is thereby *present* in the intention ("Now") we discover only an X, a pole which prescribes the ongoing course of perception. In one of the E manuscripts this is brought out in the following way:

All physical being is given in anticipation and, seen exactly, is shot through with anticipations so that the intentional unity with its content of determination is not actually constituted[18] but rather "anticipated" through and

through. Obviously in a special sense. The thing which has already appeared is pre-given as a momentary appearance of a thing being always newly determined in possible, new appearances. Here the existing thing, even when it is apprehended, is given only in a *Vorgriff,* and it is not actually constituted in the soul but [constituted] only as the idea of something perduring and being more exactly determined as identical in the mode of consequent harmony throughout ever new possible *Vorgriffen.* What is thereby in the soul is the apperception itself and the harmonious style of its changes, and the object-pole known therein as [the] X of the actual determinations, determinations arrested in openness, determinations of the further horizon.[19]

Thus far we have characterized the *gegenständlicher Sinn* or *Seinssinn* as the identity between past and present fulfillments, and as the difference between presence and absence. We have seen that this *Seinssinn*, or "total-structure," perpetuates a continual movement from fulfilled sense to intended sense, to an intended sense not carried to the object from without but an intended sense implicated from within the fulfilled sense.

Our clarification of sense thus far is *genetic* but *structural*. It needs to be expanded by a consideration which is *genetic* and *material*. This is provided by taking up the concept of appearance.

Husserl's initial treatment of appearances, as we have mentioned, played with the idea of an immanent hyletic content which was given a representative function by the act. After its animation, after it was given an exhibitive role, the sense-data functioned to fill out a sense with its material qualities and the result was a profile or an appearance of an object. This led to two not entirely compatible ideas: (a) the data themselves were internally unaffected by the sense; at most, they were externally organized in a certain way in view of a particular function, and (b) the appearances could be linked to any number of acts, even different kinds of acts.

With the genetic turn, however, we find a certain movement in Husserl's phenomenology pushing it toward a closer integration of act and appearance on the one hand, and toward a *noematic* treatment of sense-data on the other.

The earlier characterization of sense-data had the advantage of showing a continuity between perception and phantasy.[20] In both worlds we could speak of the appearance as a gestalt filled out with animated sense-qualities. But with this advantage came the distasteful disadvantage of being unable to contrast these two worlds. Husserl realized this, and in a provocative passage from D19 he states that if we abstract from our position (*Stellungsnahmen*)—what we will see shortly as our kinaesthetic, bodily relation to the world—we are not able to distinguish phantasy from reality. "Appearances are not something in addition to our position." If we want to speak of them as such, we are talking about "mere abstracta."[21] Whereas perception, modeled along the lines of the speech-act could easily contrast position and context,[22] Husserl realizes that such an opposition greatly distorts his treatment of appearances. These arise precisely because perceptual senses are schematizations of our *bodily* relationship to the object.

According to our discussion so far, an implicated sense has both a precise direction and a determinate range of possible fulfillments. When Husserl speaks of it as "empty" he does so because it is not filled out by an intuitive content, because it is not yet, in his terms, an appearance or a profile of the object we are looking at. But while Husserl still speaks of the appearance as "the presentational content in its intuitive plentitude,"[23] he does not think of it as a composite of sense and raw materials. Resorting to a contrast, he says: "Only by contrasting empty and full sense do we gain the differences [between sense and *Fülle*]."[24]

It is with this strategy at hand that Husserl takes up the analysis of appearances and sense-data in the early parts of the "Lectures." This discussion is situated within a distinction between that which I, an experiencing subject, *have* and that which I *perceive*. I do not perceive sense-data. Rather I "live" them. Nor do I directly perceive appearances (profiles). What I perceive are objects and their properties. On the other hand, I experience or have sense-data; and I have the interplay between them and kinaesthetic data as well as my own mental acts. All of these, Husserl claims initially, are directly or immediately experienced; and there is no difference between my experience and that which I experience, between *percipi* and *esse*. It is at this point, however, that the difficulties arrive: I do not directly perceive "exhibiting appearances" or profiles, nor do I have them immediately.

	Haben		*Wahrnehmen*
The act	Appearances		Thing Properties
Sense-data			
Kinaesthetic data			

Two alternatives are open to Husserl, neither of which proved satisfactory. I could say that in perception I perceive the thing, but what is actually seen is the profile. However, according to Husserl's own admission this only obscures the way in which perception is "an original consciousness of an individual, temporal object."[25] Or I could claim that the appearance is not *directly had* but *indirectly had* as "a partially fulfilled intention which contains unfulfilled indications."[26] The profile would then "exhibit" the transcendent object. "We live through (*durchleben*) the appearances. Our attentive perception, however, runs through them and is directed to the pole; to the object itself and then to the pole of its properties, to the thing's color, gestalt and so on."[27] This second alternative is what Husserl chooses. At the same time, he is no longer satisfied with the talk of an animating apprehension. Even though the data functions as moments of the *object,* as profiles, only by virtue of an apperception, Husserl is now looking for a new way to understand this:

It is dangerous to speak of that which is represented and that which represents, of an interpretation of sense-data, of a projecting function taking place through this "interpreting." *Being adumbrated or exhibited in sense-data is totally different from significative interpretation.*[28]

Whereas *Investigations* and *Ideas* stress the similarity in structure between perceptual acts and linguistic acts by taking both as signitive acts, Husserl is now arguing that there is a clear difference not merely in function but also in structure between signitive intentions and perceptual fulfillment. At the same time, this opens a way to contrast properly the signitive intention and the intentional side of perceptual acts.[29] As a result, we find Husserl maintaining the identity of *Empfinden* and *Empfundene*, or sensation and sense-data, and—at the same time—he pushes toward an integration of sense-data and the noematic appearances of the object. This movement in Husserl's thought is made possible by the introduction of the concept of "associative intentionality"[30] and by a reinterpretation of the horizon of sense. Through the first he comes to see the hyletic complexes *not* as formless data, as "dead stuff"[31] devoid of all sense. Through the second he moves beyond the static characterization of the horizon as a formal structure and now sees it as a complicated system of motivations, of noematic motivations. What appears in each fulfillment and is present is shot through with empty horizons which take the form of a perceptual demand:

A new empty horizon, a new system of determinate indeterminacies, a new system of progressive tendencies with corresponding possibilities...belongs to each appearing [sic] of the thing in each perceptual phase. The aspects are... nothing for themselves, they are appearances-of only through the intentional horizon which is inseparable from them.[32]

It is in view of the noematic organization of the horizon that noetic acts are engaged. Once this is admitted, the data are no longer treated as formless and timeless materials making profiles possible. Rather they are themselves the result of a constitution arising from aesthetic syntheses in view of *perceptual* functions.

In *Phänomenologische Psychologie*, which consists of lectures and manuscripts Husserl worked on between the time of his "Lectures" and *Formal and Transcendental Logic,* we find the same strategy at work. Husserl begins his characterization of perceptual *Erlebnisse* by using his older form-content scheme—only to turn his attention then to the more accurate analysis of the hyletic constituents of perception. It seems that when Husserl is speaking of constitution as that which makes possible the *referential* function of consciousness, and when he has the functional contrast between appearances and the various way of apprehending them in view, he disregards the hyletic constitution of the appearance and takes it as a given upon which the *Auffassung* operates. The hyletic data are given in sensation and the subjective function which makes them an appearance-of "does not affect their own being."[33] But, on the other hand, it seems that when Husserl speaks of constitution as many-layer temporal *synthesis*, as *"synthetische Leistung,"*[34] then each datum or complex of data has both a *unity* and a *field,*[35] has a "proto-apprehension" which "precedes" its apprehension and, in fact, *founds* the apprehension.

What is thereby founded? Precisely what we speak of as "apprehending as", i.e., the inner time-consciousness constituting the datum of sensation is founding for the specifically different (*neuartig*), thus higher-level act of apprehending; or, correlatively, the datum of sensation functions as a profile of a color, etc. In the reflection upon the sense-datum it does not [so] function but the apprehension is there in a modified form.[36]

The apprehension, then, accounts not for the composition of a given phase or hyletic moment but for the fact that such a phase functions as appearances of a single object:

In the concrete unity of an *Erlebnis* the phases and pieces cannot be just any appearances but rather the appearances must fit together in order to form a unified intentional *Erlebnis* in which an object can appear. One cannot simply amass appearances from outer perception arbitrarily. To put it exactly, the visual data belonging to each perceptual thing have an immanent hyletic unity, the unity of a closed "sensuous" field-gestalt. This is also the case with the tactual and other hyletic fields which may run parallel to the visual field. But the data of different *fields* do not form a sensuous or hyletic unity with one another. This changes, however, if we also consider the apprehensional characters, i.e., if we take the concrete appearances into consideration. The synthesis is grounded in the intentional characters of the hyletic data and it is through this that these data become adumbrations.[37]

What accounts, one immediately wants to know, for the hyletic synthesis itself? How does it function? The only hint we are given here is that there is a synthesis corresponding to each *homogeneous* group of hyletic data. To discover what this means, however, it is necessary to turn to a systematic treatment of association.

Action and Affection

The ego is the ego of affections and actions, the ego which only has its living in the stream of the *Erlebnisse* because, on the one hand, it exercises intentions in these intentional *Erlebnisse*—thus it is directed to its intentional objectivities and is occupied with them—and because, on the other hand, it is allured by these objectivities, is affected by them as objects of feeling, is drawn to them, is motivated by them to action.[38]

Husserl's discussion of sensation is situated within an explicit rejection of classical empiricist accounts: (a) perceiving does not entail having sensations which would, in some way, depict the object or whose combination would be the object, and (b) if one does reflect and look "within" one discovers neither ideas nor hard data but rather a "complex" or sensorial moments that are integrated from "below" by passive syntheses and integrated from "above" by the sense of the object perceived. The first thesis had been argued from the time of the *Investigations*. The second thesis, however, developed gradually, beginning with "Lectures on Internal Time-Consciousness" and their reworking between 1905 and 1910.[39] Sensations have a temporal constitution, one which breaks up their hard presence into a duration depending upon deeper-lying temporal syntheses (retention-impressional now-protention). What we discover in "Lectures on Transcendental Logic," however, is that their formation and function as appearances depends upon yet other syntheses; and these fall into two groups: (a) kinaesthetic syntheses and (b) associative syntheses of homogeneity and heterogeneity. The first integrates the body into phenomenological analysis. The second opens the way to seeing perception as the interplay of receptivity and activity.

1. After setting aside a consideration of "reproductive" associations which would account for our recollection of past objects, Husserl turns his attention to those "primal" associations which explain the sense-data as hyletic complexes organized according to certain structural syntheses. Sense-data are formed—disregarding kinaesthetic constitution for the moment—for two reasons: (a) there is a temporal continuity of the complex, a duration arising from originary time-consciousness, and (b) there is synthetic coincidence or congruence of the complex, and this according to the limits of complete congruence (identity) and incongruence (degrees of contrast). In the event of congruence, the complex is a "blended" complex and is said to be "similar"; in the case of incongruence, the complex becomes "emphatic" or "lifted out" and is said to be "contrasting" with other elements or with the entire blended field.[40]

Three sounds are detected. Each of these sounds has a duration and, regardless of whether we are attentive to them or not and regardless of the changes of their intensity and quality, they are organized as successive. Each sound, however, did not drop into this succession but was formed by elementary material syntheses which organize the note's intensive and qualitative features according to homogeneity and heterogeneity. In the case of homogeneity (blending), these features do not form *independent* parts of the datum. If they did, we would have several data, or we would have only pushed the problem back another step. Rather, they are *dependent moments founding each other*. At this level of analysis the whole they form is treated as founded upon them and not founding them. Were there a break, were there a change in either intensity or quality, we would no longer have a sound but sounds. In Husserl's discussion there is a distinction between syntheses and what is formed in these syntheses; yet each synthesis is of a unique type. It is structurally different from that synthesis taking place between speech-act and fulfillment, and it is also different from the synthesis of profile and object. It is a synthesis that takes place within the profile, and rather than the apprehension determining the perceptual function of the content, the content leads the associative synthesis. The synthesis, however, is not an identifying coincidence ["*identifizierende Deckung*"[41]], nor does it have relata in the same sense in which the others do. While there is a distinction between synthesis and what is formed in the synthesis, the relative independence of "content" and apprehension does not exist at this level. Undergoing associative syntheses is equivalent to having sensorial complexes, and there cannot be a single identical complex which could remain the same throughout various associative syntheses. To put it in a way which clashes with Husserl's static analysis, the syntheses are productive. Each change in synthesis is a change in "content." Thus the primary unit of this analysis is the complex or the unified datum, and we can speak of its mutually founding "constituents" only from a highly focused or (what Merleau-Ponty calls) analytic attitude.

Once the complex character of sensation is admitted and once its "content" is seen as affective, the first step on the way to establishing the continuity between affection and perception is taken. Rather than affection providing the raw material upon which perception must work, it is a complement to perception and takes its bearings and task from it. And rather than syntheses of similarity and contrast providing elements which must be fashioned into profiles, we see that the profile is formed only by the interlocking of both affective and kinaesthetic syntheses. Husserl's later treatment of sensation, then, seems to prescribe an option that is open to perception. *Absolute Sinnlichkeit*, in turn, becomes a limiting concept [*Grenzbegriff*].[42] What is emphatic, what is lifted out, "exerts an affective power or tendency upon the ego."[43] It is by virtue of these autosyntheses that something comes to have an ambiguous and distant attraction to us.

In Husserl's account in "lectures," sensation does not create a perceived object, nor does it create a proxy standing for one. Rather, sensation accounts for the fact that once certain thresholds are reached, we *follow* the pulsations and organization of the perceptual field. Rather than our actions leading us to the object, rather than our perceptions being "explicative," these noematic constituents bring the object to us and introduce its presence for us. The three sounds draw us and become a song, a song which, although only initiated, is still perceived as a whole. And at the same time that one "content" becomes prominent, the rest of the perceptual field falls away and, while unified, becomes a vague horizon:

The unity of the field of consciousness is always produced through sensuous interconnections, sensuous connections of similarity and sensuous contrast. Without that we would not have a "world" which is there. We could put it as follows: the sensuous similarity and the sensuous contrast. . .is the resonance which grounds all which has already been constituted.[44]

2. So far, however, our consideration of associative syntheses and of affectivity still lacks that which gives them their roots in existence. This is what Husserl's treatment of the body provides. The body, in this account, is both in the world and yet not merely another object of the

world. Contrasting the body to the things perceived, Husserl speaks of it as the invisible limit of the world, the *Nullpunkt* that gives the world its position. Right-left, over-under, back-front are the coordinates which determine the "entire three-dimensional continuum of orientations."[45] In fact, it is in terms of these coordinates that the difference between interiority and "exteriority" is situated. And it is in terms of these coordinates that the perceptual field as a field of action is organized. With this new emphasis, perception is seen as a mode of praxis, and passivity, in turn, as a style of possible actions.

We suggested above that associative syntheses produce a sensorial complex with a unified field. This field is sometimes characterized as a two-dimensional field without movement and without perspectives.[46] Once we relinquish the abstractions that make such an analysis possible and once we reintroduce the kinaesthetic dimensions into the account, the continuity between this characterization and our normal perceptions is regained: what Husserl speaks of as a two-dimensional hyletic field is seen as a *dependent* system, one which is founded upon our normal perceptual orientation, which, in turn, is founded upon purpose. The associative organization of the hyletic complexes, therefore, is complemented and, in fact, restructured by a kinaesthetic organization, one which affects both the unity and the function of the complexes. The unity is affected in that the abstract configuration and limits organizing the hyletic field depend upon a stationary bodily position, depend upon a modality of bodily action (rest). The function is affected in that the complexes are integrated into the total spacial presence of the object.

This brings us back to our initial treatment of appearances. The kinaesthesen—the movements of the arm, the turns of the head—do not merely parallel the appearances. They are possibilities [*Vermöglichkeiten*] of appearances.[47] They and the appearances are constituted in and through each other,

and this in a double way: (a) once I institute a perceptual series, once I first move toward the goldfish, or once I perceive the sounds as notes, the appearances lead my perceptions and I am not "free" in relation to the coming appearances; and yet (b) the appearances are in themselves nothing apart from the lived-body. In an especially lucid passage Husserl says:

The appearances form *dependent* systems. Only as that which is dependent upon the kinaesthesen can they continually move over into one another and constitute a unity of sense. Only by running-off in such a way do they unfold their intentional indications. Only through this interplay of *dependent* and *independent* variables do they constitute the appearing [something] as a transcendent object of perception, an object which is more than what we directly perceive, an object which both vanishes from and perdures in my perception.[48]

The three sounds are perceived as a melody by virtue of the organization or, to put it more accurately, the reorganization of their significance. As notes of a melody they indicate and point to each other. The unsuccessive fulfillments, in turn, follow a horizon which they determine and sustain. Abstractly considered, the sound is an associative whole of dependent contents mutually founding each other. Concretely considered, however, the sounds are themselves organized by the orientation of our body and by the demands of the objective sense. This, within limits, extends to the affective syntheses and gives them their organizational possibilities. As Husserl put it in *Formal and Transcendental Logic*: "The perceptually awakened does not affect in and of itself nor does it become a thematic object by itself. Rather that which is awakened now has the character of a component."[49] The sounds are notes only as notes-of, notes of a song, notes of a song which is here and soft and not there and biting.

In Husserl's later analysis the associative and the kinaesthetic syntheses are co-founding and the former are not autonomous contributors to the perceptual process but rather contribute in view of their organization in an appearance which, in turn, is dependent upon the kinaesthesen for its form and function. Generally Husserl speaks of the objective sense as a "rule" which in a full act of perception "prescribes" the transition from one appearance into another and from one implicated sense to another. But what we now find is an aesthetic motivation immanent to the appearance and based on the homogeneity and heterogeneity of its complex: the "apprehension" is there in a "modified" form[50] as associations which create tendency, allurement, and distant attraction according to an *implicit sense,* a *style* which is both given and indeterminate. A hyletic field, so to speak, organizes *itself* in this way, and there is a residual aesthetic sense which no perceptual consciousness can destroy without destroying itself. This, I believe, is the origin of perceptual types and of the perceptual horizon in Husserl's phenomenology.

Thus in Husserl's extensive reworking of perception during the 1920s the earlier mentalistic image of *Auffassung* is dislodged by the aesthetic images of temporal, associative, and kinaesthetic syntheses. As a result, he came to see that even the most elementary sensuous syntheses are not pre-horizonal, are not syntheses creating elements which find a "meaning" subsequent to their formation. In the event that the content is "blended" and in the event that we have a uniform profile, we have an implicit noematic identity, an implicit aesthetic "What."[51] The various homogeneous elements within a profile or a field are such that they "resonate" with each other and they tend to call each other forth.

While our analysis has dissected perceptual consciousness into three kinds of interlocking syntheses, we must be careful to point out that Husserl does not view perception as the sum of these three, as would be the case in a typical empiricist account. What is found in the whole which is not isolatable in any of its parts is precisely that which is phenomenologically primary, id est, intentionality. It is this underlying structure of consciousness which both integrates and directs the various dependent passive syntheses we have discussed in this paper.

By way of summarizing these various levels, let me, with some misgivings, suggest this depiction:

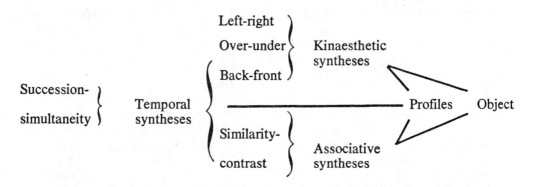

To make the ties with the movement of Husserl's later phenomenology, I would like to suggest three points by way of concluding this paper.

1. The horizon-determining perception is seen by Husserl as a system of interlocking objective senses. In normal perception this system of senses—what Husserl also calls types—establishes the lines of possible fulfillments in view of possible actions. As such, it is said to *motivate* the progressive movement from implicated to fulfilled to implicated sense. In order to bring this immanent movement out to perception and to emphasize the dialectic of appearance and object,

Husserl speaks of perception as *apperception*.

2. The horizon, however, is composed not only of possibilities but of *Gegenmöglichkeiten*. Because perception always remains open to this horizon, it is never possible to speak of a "final, enduring Self of the object." In place of finality and adequate presence, Husserl treats perception in terms of a necessary progression and an *optimal* presence. That which determines the optimal in this case is *praxis*:

The thing itself in its saturated plentitude is an idea found in (a) the sense which it has for consciousness, and (b) the style of its intentional structures. It is, to a certain extent, a system of all optimals which would be discovered by sketching in its optimal framework. The thematic interest which lives itself out in perception is, in our scientific life, led by a practical interest.... That which suffices practically counts as the Self [of the object].[52]

Husserl's thesis that perception is always presumptive and perspectival is not equivalent to the phenomenalist's suggestion that we never perceive the object but only a proxy that stands for the object. When Husserl speaks of profiles and appearances, he does so with the clear understanding that we do not *perceive* appearances and that in optimal perception the appearance is *effaced* into the side of the object directly present. The usual depiction of consciousness as that which bridges a void between the object and itself is highly inaccurate. Husserl's later analysis suggests that the perceptual field is not one which has to be traversed by consciousness but, rather, is a field inhabited by consciousness. The object serves as a pole of consciousness not in the sense that it can never be approached but in the sense that every successful appropriation of it always can be complemented. The choice to terminate the explication is determined by human interests and goals.

3. In "Lectures on Transcendental Logic" Husserl's analysis of passivity leads him into a characterization of perception in terms of the unique structure and function of protention. With the suggestion that passive experience engages a complicated group of interlocking associative syntheses came the simultaneous recognition that they are intentional and that, as such, they are grounded in protention, not retention:

It is only in the protentional line of primitive time-constitution that association does its work....Retentions, as they originally occur, do not have intentional characters.[53]

Becoming aware of something follows the protentional continuity. The process of becoming aware of something (*Das Gewahren*) engages our being-directed-forward already lying in passive perception. As opposed to this, however, there is no being-directed running through the retentional continuity.[54]

Syntheses of homogeneity and heterogeneity, of blending and contrast, take place in view of *protentional* functions. They are engaged and motivated by the objective sense specifying itself in the perception and by a "striving" toward that which is missing in every fulfillment.

The ongoing opposition between retention and protention and the ongoing resolution of protentions into retentions within a phase ("Now") define the temporal structure of the *appearance*. Considered in abstraction from the future and in relation only to affectivity, the objective sense would be a mere echo, a mere reverberation of the style of the past. It would be no more than the identity of past and present, and as such it would be a gestalt of associative components giving rise to each other. At most, the third sound could only anticipate another like itself or another like those retained. At most, the future could only be a repetition of retentions. But taken in relation to the future and to action, the objective sense is that which *founds* the associative syntheses and engages them in terms of a perceptual task. The objective sense is the difference between "Now" and protention, between the fulfillment of a protention and that protention's escaping every fulfillment. In this way Husserl came to see the future as productive: the objective sense announced in every fulfillment is not only a reverberation of the past but is that which motivates and solicits the past. As such, Husserl speaks of it as an "in-itself." The in-itself drawing perception is the presence of the object as future. "The thing has its true being in an infinite, systematic multiplicity of real and possible appearances striving toward it. Accordingly the order of the system is tele-ological."[55] Once the in-itself is seen as the goal of perception and once the future becomes that which makes perception possible, perception is always a form of action. And once perception is seen as a form of action, Husserlian phenomenology is on the way to an integration of perception and historical praxis.

NOTES

1. Edmund Husserl, *Analysen zur passiven Synthesis: Aus Vorlesungs und Forschungsmanuskripten 1918-1926*, ed. Margot Fleischer, *Husserliana* (The Hague: Nijhoff, 1966), XI: 19.

2. *Cartesianische Meditationen und Pariser Vorträge*, ed. S. Strasser, *Husserliana* (2d rev. ed.; The Hague: Nijhoff, 1963), I: 19 [*The Paris Lectures*, 19].

3. Ibid., p. 22. Rather than eliminating the world, it is only by holding fast to the world of synthetic object-types [*den synthetischen Gegenstandstypus Welt*] that we can uncover the "endless structure of our intentional experience of the world" (p. 21).

4. These lectures were given three times between 1920 and 1926. They, along with other supporting texts from this same period, have been published as *Passive Synthesis*. It is only the second draft of *Ideen II*, completed in 1918, that contains the important sections on passivity and the body. Cf. the editor's introduction to Edmund Husserl, *Ideen zu einer reinen Phänomenologie und phänomenologischen Philosophie*, bk. II: *Phänomenologische Untersuchungen zu Konstitution*, ed. Marly Biemel, *Husserliana* (The Hague: Nijhoff, 1952), IV: xviii. Because "Lectures" presents a much more unified theory, I will use it as the basis for my discussion.

5. As I am concerned with a phenomenology of meaning which is "pre-linguistic" I will consistently use the terms 'sense' or 'perceptual meaning' when speaking of this level. The term 'meaning' is usually restricted to expressive acts (speech-acts) or acts of judgment. In another paper I attempt to define the relationship between language and perception, between "meaning" and "sense," for a Husserlian phenomenology (cf. "Intentionality and Language in Husserl's Phenomenology," *Review of Metaphysics*, 27 [December 1973], 260-97). My treatment of this relationship there, however, underplayed the protentional side of perceptual (vs. expressive) reiteration. In this paper I will consider perception apart from its relationship to language.

6. *Passive Synthesis*, p. 291.

7. Ibid.

8. This is due, in part, to an ongoing struggle Husserl has with his own terminology. In "Lectures" Husserl overturns both the empiricist and the rationalist statements of perception and yet we often find him falling back into Kantian imagery.

The terminology is pushed beyond itself; it, so to speak, explodes from within. Such terms as 'empty content', "empty appearances", 'empty horizons of an empty content', etc., rupture the limits of the language of his tradition. Yet the weight of this language continually pulls at Husserl's most revolutionary insights.

9. Edmund Husserl, B I 13 (1932), p. 8, as quoted in Elmar Holenstein, *Phänomenologie der Assoziation: Zu Struktur und Funktion eines Grundprinzips der Passiven Genesis bei E. Husserl, Phanenomenologica* (The Hague: Nijhoff, 1972), 44: 95f.

10. Husserl's initial characterization of this in para. 131 of *Ideas I* (*Ideen zu einer reinen Phänomenologie und phänomenologischen Philosophie*, bk. I: *Allgemeine Einführung in die reine Phänomenologie*, ed. and expanded by Walter Biemel, *Husserliana*, vol. III [The Hague: Nijhoff, 1950] [*Ideas: General Introduction to Pure Phenomenology*, trans. Boyce Gibson (New York: Collier Books, 1962)]) tends to confuse meaning and reference—a contrast he clearly holds—and to mistake use with mention. There Husserl says that the intentional object *is* the subject of its possible predicates. To avoid a use-mention fallacy, however, it is necessary to speak of the intentional object as either that which would be denoted by the expression or as the meaning of the expression. In the latter case we would run afoul of Husserl's persistent theme that we refer to the intentional object by means of or through the meaning. The intentional object, then, must be that which would be referred to by the expression, and this must be what Husserl has in mind when he speaks of it as "the subject" of its possible predications. As such it is a possible object.

11. See Guido Antonio de Almeida, *Sinn und Inhalt in der Genetischen Phänomenologie E. Husserls, Phaenomenologica* (The Hague: Nijhoff, 1972), 47: 85-92, for a much more detailed discussion of the problem of "adequate" fulfillment.

12. This synopsis considerably oversimplified the treatment of signitive and perceptual acts in *Logical Investigations* (*Logische Untersuchungen* [2d rev. ed.; 2 vols.; Halle: Max Niemeyer, 1913 and 1921]: *Logical Investigations*, trans. J. N. Findlay [2 vols.; New York: Humanities Press, 1970]) and *Ideas*. I have attempted to do justice to its complexity in another paper: "Toward a Phenomenology of Per-

ceptual Sense" (forthcoming). Whereas that paper attempts to show the historical development of Husserl's analysis of perceptual sense, this paper delivers a promise made in that paper. Here we suggest, against the interpretations of Follesdal, Dreyfus, Smith, McIntyre, and Solomon, that Husserl makes a clear distinction between signitive or expressive meaning (concept) and perceptual sense, and we will give a detailed characterization of the latter based on the difference in *structure* between signitive and perceptual acts.

13. Asemissen has described this problem with clarity and force: "Without the corporality of the body (*Leiblichkeit*) the sensations are absolutely nothing. The body (*Leib*) is the medium of their being. In that Husserl bracketed the body in the reduction in order to gain the pure ego and pure consciousness as the proper domain of phenomenology, he, at the same time, without knowing it, also bracketed the sensations. . . . Just as the pure ego does not have a body, so it also does not have and cannot have sensations. And just as the body is not an immanent (*reel*) content of consciousness, so neither can the sensation be such. Husserl's talk of sensations after the bracketing of the body as content of pure consciousness is not a phenomenological discovery." Herman Asemissen, *Strukturanalytische Probleme der Wahrnehmung in der Phänomenologie Husserls*, Kantstudien Erg. H. (Cologne, 1957), 73: 34.

14. *Passive Synthesis*, p. 363. Husserl speaks in "Lectures" of an "absolutely individual essence," thereby resurrecting a concept much discussed in medieval philosophy. Cf. p. 21.

15. Ibid., p. 363.

16. Ibid., p. 21.

17. ". . .der Gang der wirklichen weiteren Erfahrung. . .einen sich wirklich bestimmenden Sinn herausstellt, einen als endgültig gedachten und einstimmig in diesem Gand sich klärenden und bestätigenden. Als endgultiger wäre er gedacht, sofern er sich zwar nicht als Erscheinungsbild direkt darstellt, aber im Erfüllungsgang der Erscheinungen sich immer deutlicher und klarer bekundender übererscheinungsmässiger Sinn, sich in Evidenz, in einer ihn eigenen Art der Originalität immer vollkommener herausstellt und bewährt." A VIII 22 (1926), p. 35a (transcription p. 70).

18. Reading *konstitutiert* instead of *konstruiert*.

19. ". . .alles dingliche Sein ist gegeben in Antizipation und, genau besehen, ist alles daran mit Antizipation durchsetzt, sodass die intentionale Einheit mit ihren Bestimmungsgehalt nicht wirklich seelisch konstruiert ist sondern durchaus 'antizipiert'. Freilich in einem ganz besonderem Sinn. Vorgegeben ist das schon erscheinende Ding als momentane Erscheinung eines in möglichen neuen Erscheinungen sich immerfort neu bestimmenden. Das Seinde ist hier in gewisser Weise, auch wo es erfasst ist, nur in einem Vorgriff gegeben, und es ist nicht in der Seele wirklich konstituiert sondern nur als Idee eines in immer neuen möglichen Vorgriffen sich identisch in der Weise der konsequenten Einstimmigkeit Durchhaltenden und Näherbestimmenden. Was in der Seele dabei vorliegt, ist die

Apperzeption selbst und der Stil ihrer Wandlungen in Einstimmigkeit und der darin bewusste Gegenstandspol als X der jeweiligen mit Offenheiten behafteten Bestimmungen und der weitere Horizont dazu." E III 2 (1920 or 1921), p. 18b (transcription pp. 37f.). Cf. Edmund Husserl, *Phänomenologische Psychologie: Vorlesungen Sommersemester 1925*, ed. Walter Biemel, *Husserliana* (The Hague: Nijhoff, 1968), IX: 153.

20. In *Logical Investigations* Husserl stressed the parallel between perceptive and imaginative adumbrations in contrast to signs in expressive acts and he spoke of both as presenting or representing contents. *Logische Untersuchungen*, II/s: 56-58, 78-79 (Eng. trans., II: 712-15, 730-31).

21. *Passive Synthesis*, p. 350. See the discussion on pp. 349-50.

22. Cf. the current contrast between illocutionary and propositional acts.

23. Ibid., p. 36.

24. Ibid., p. 363.

25. See the fn. on p. 18 of ibid.

26. Ibid., p. 19.

27. *Phänomenologische Psychologie*, p. 153.

28. *Passive Synthesis*, p. 17. Italics mine.

29. See the next section for the latter.

30. *Passive Synthesis*, p. 429. See also Edmund Husserl, *Formale und transzendentale Logik: Versuch einer Kritik der logischen Vernunft. Mit Ergänzenden Texten*, ed. Paul Janssen, *Husserliana* (The Hague: Nijhoff, 1974), XVII: 321 [*Formal and Transcendental Logic*, trans. Dorian Cains (The Hague: Nijhoff, 1969), p. 322].

31. Edmund Husserl, *Ding und Raum: Vorlesungen 1907*, ed. Ulrich Claesges, *Husserliana* (The Hague: Nijhoff, 1972), XVI: 46.

32. *Passive Synthesis*, p. 6.

33. *Phänomenologische Psychologie*, p. 163. Cf. pp. 150-63.

34. Mohanty has noted this contrast between intentionality qua self-transcendence and intentionality qua synthetic production by speaking of constitution₁ and constitution₂ and by viewing the genetic turn as the movement from one to the other. Cf. his "Husserl's Concept of Intentionality," *Analecta Husserliana*, 1 (1970): 111.

35. *Phänomenologische Psychologie*, pp. 165, 172-73.

36. Ibid., p. 424.

37. Ibid., p. 173.

38. Ibid., pp. 208-9. Cf. *Ideen*, II: 216, 225.

39. On this development cf. the excellent article by John Brough, "The Emergence of an Absolute Consciousness in Husserl's Early Writings on Time-Consciousness," *Man and World*, 3 (August 1972): 298-326 [see this volume, pp. 000-000].

40. *Passive Synthesis*, pp. 140-41. See pp. 117ff. for an extensive treatment of these topics. Also cf. *Phänomenologische Psychologie*, pp. 78-81. The recent book by Holenstein, *Phänomenologie der Assoziation*, is helpful in situating these concepts in the larger development of Husserl's phenomenology. As he points out, between *Investigations* and "Lectures" there is a shift in emphasis from syntheses of contiguity to similarity (blending)

and contrast (bringing into emphasis). I suggest that this arises because Husserl emphasized the animating role of *Auffassung* in the early work. The data were givens and the apprehension bestowed a sense uniting them into presentations *of* the object. Since the sense-data were devoid of an immanent sense—were, in Husserl's language, formless—the only kind of association which could be operative would be contiguity. Once Husserl understands sensations to be a synthesis, however, there is a corresponding shift in emphasis to associations of similarity and contrast precisely because these syntheses have a field and an implicit aesthetic What.

41. *Phänomenologische Psychologie*, p. 424.

42. B III [?], pp. 11f quoted in Iso Kern, *Husserl und Kant, Phaenomenologica* (The Hague: Nijhoff, 1964), XVI: 63.

43. *Passive Synthesis*, p. 131.

44. Ibid., p. 406.

45. Ibid., p. 298. Cf. *Ideen*, II: 127f.

46. *Phänomenologische Psychologie*, p. 164.

47. Husserl, C 13 III (1934), transcription p. 4.

48. *Passive Synthesis*, pp. 14-15.

49. *Formale und transzendentale Logik*, pp. 321 (Eng. trans. pp. 322-23).

50. *Phänomenologische Psychologie*, p. 424.

51. *Passive Synthesis*, p. 130.

52. Ibid., p. 23.

53. Ibid., p. 77.

54. Ibid., p. 74.

55. "Das Ding hat sein wahren Sein in einer unendlichen systematischen Mannigfaltigkeit wirklicher und möglicher gegen es hinstrebender Erscheinungen. Das muss danach sagen, die Ordnung des Systems ist eine teleologische." A VII 22 (1926), p. 35b (transcription p. 72).

Imagination and Phenomenological Method

EDWARD S. CASEY

Fiction constitutes the vital element of phenomenology as of all eidetic sciences.

Husserl

There has been a close link between imagination and method in Western philosophy and science, both of which not infrequently appeal to imagination in an effort to explain the genesis of ingenious hypotheses, bold thought-experiments, brilliant inferences, and the like . But the appeal typically occurs as a move of last resort: "imagination" more often names a mystery than a truly explanatory mental process. Phenomenology has been no exception in this regard, since it too appeals to imagination in its methodology. Yet the exact role of imagining within phenomenological method has been for the most part neglected by phenomenologists.[1]

Accordingly, my task will be to investigate in some detail the relationship between phenomenological method and imagination. This will be done by discussing a group of three closely related paradoxes. The first paradox is rooted in the way Western philosophy has traditionally conceived the relationship between imagination and the philosophical enterprise. As we shall see in section I, phenomenology is in this regard illustrative of a pervasive trend which at once devaluates and draws upon imagination. But, as will be shown in section II, a second and even more crucial paradox is

the fact that phenomenological method must make use of imagination in order to describe the nature of imagination itself. In section III a final paradox will be analyzed—a paradox which stems from the way in which imagining combines the freely variable with the strictly invariant.

Exploring all three paradoxes will enable us to take a close look at phenomenological method as such and, at the same time, glimpse the outlines of an adequate phenomenology of imagination.[2]

I

To study imagination in a philosophical context is to land immediately in the first of the paradoxes mentioned above, which can be expressed in the following way. On one hand, philosophers have adopted an official attitude toward imagination which ranges from Platonic contempt to contemporary indifference. There is a remarkably widespread tendency to denigrate imagination, to condemn it as cognitively dangerous: "the mistress of falsehood and error," said Pascal, or to belittle it as wholly inconsequential: philosophical thinking, proclaims Heidegger, is "charmless and image-poor."[3]

In a climate of continual and continuing disparagement, any latent sympathy for imagination expresses itself in an effort to give imagining an exaggerated role in some enterprise *other than* philosophy, as an example, in artistic creation or in scientific discovery. Only rarely has it been suggested that imagination might have a central role to play within philosophy itself. With few exceptions, the Western tradition in philosophy has been so overwhelmingly logocentric in orientation that imagination has not been considered of critical significance in gaining philosophical insight.[4] Indeed, it has often been considered as obscuring or preventing such insight.

On the other hand, in its actual practice, namely, its working method, the very same tradition has been inextricably bound to the *use* of imagination. This use is more extensive than is generally admitted. It occurs, above all, in the preliminary procedures which philosophers have employed in the pursuit of their cherished logocentric aims. The result is a paradoxical pattern of denial-*cum*-acknowledgment in which an express denigration is accompanied by a covert recognition of the considerable value of imagination in the very process of philosophizing. This pattern may be observed in the ambivalence with which a number of Western philosophers, including Aristotle, Hume, and Kant, view imagination. All of these thinkers were acutely aware of the importance of method in philosophy, and all accorded imagination a privileged position in methodology—a position which has no sanction or support in other parts of their philosophy.[5]

We shall center our attention upon the particularly pertinent case of Husserl, who follows in the footsteps of the philosophers just cited. But before we come to Husserl let us look briefly at the position of Descartes, who is the first modern philosopher to exemplify the paradox of denial-*cum*-acknowledgment. In his *Meditations* Descartes describes his method as one in which he has "put aside every belief in which I could *imagine* the least doubt."[6] Further, he sets out to "pretend" or "suppose"—two mental acts which are closely allied, though not identical, with imagining—that all of his former beliefs are "entirely

imaginary and false" and that he is being deceived by an omnipotent evil genius.[7]

Now to perform such sweeping acts of doubt requires not only a suspension of ordinary beliefs but a forceful use of imagination. The fact that such doubt is solely methodological in character only underlines the essentiality of imagination's role. For it is not through having discovered new evidence or logical reasons for doubt but by an act of imagination that Descartes effects the methodological suspension of belief: he tries to imagine that the world is the kind of place in which the normally unquestioned validity of everyday beliefs does not obtain. Yet there is scarcely any basis for such a crucial recourse to imagination in Descartes' theory of mind, in which imagination is regarded as adventitious and eliminable. Thus, later in the *Meditations*, he condemns imagining as "in no way necessary to my nature or essence, that is to say, to the essence of my mind."[8] Hence imagination, which earlier in the same work had been invoked as fundamental to certain initial methodological moves, is declared inessential to the mind, even though Descartes meanwhile has been driven to draw upon specific imaginative capacities. In this rapid turnabout we observe a striking instance of at once acknowledging and denying human powers of imagining: what is granted with one hand is taken back by the other.

Husserl presents an even more paradigmatic form of the denial-*cum*-acknowledgment paradox. Himself a professed admirer of Descartes, his work exhibits to an acute degree a similarly deep-seated ambivalence toward imagination—an ambivalence which involves both recognition of its critical importance in philosophical method and disparagement of its epistemological value. This disparagement is expressed, first of all, by a conspicuous neglect: only rarely do we find a detailed description of imagining in Husserl's published writings. Even the often-cited Dresden gallery example in *Ideas* involves a mixture of imagining, remembering, and signifying.[9] When imagination *is* singled out, as in *The Phenomenology of Internal Time-Consciousness*, it is given a decidedly secondary role. Its basic operation is conceived as that of "presentification" (*Vergegenwärtigung*), which is only a modification of a directly giving, presentative consciousness such as is found in perception.[10] In fact, insofar as perception is considered the "basic" or "simple" act (to use the terms of the *Logical Investigations*), Husserl endorses the primacy of perception: a primacy in terms of which imagination is necessarily secondary in status.[11]

Furthermore, Husserl's professed aims in philosophy are such that imagination appears to be excluded *ab initio* from the pursuit of objective knowledge. To the extent that phenomenology is a "rigorous science," it aims at describing

a universal conformity to laws of structure on the part of conscious life, a regularity by virtue of which alone truth and actuality have, and are able to have, sense for us.[12]

Such conformity and regularity leave little room for imagination's arbitrary adventures. If objective, conceptualizable truth is found in the nonvarying content of experience, imagination cannot, by its own action, embody such truth. For imagination signifies the variable *per se* (a theme to which we shall return in section III). Its divagations, when unchecked, distract and divert us from what is "absolutely invariable."[13] To use Husserl's metaphor, the imprint or seal of conceptual truth must be placed *upon* all lower cognitive strata, including the strata of expression and imagination.[14] In this manner, the logically apodictic is ranked above the actual or the possible, the conceptually necessary above the empirically contingent. Logos, god of reason, triumphs—at least in theory—over Eros, god of imaginative desire.

I say "at least in theory" for a closer look at Husserl's writings reveals a very different aspect of his attitude toward imagination. Despite his doctrinal commitment to a resolute rationalism, Husserl takes a surprisingly open stance toward the act of imagining. For in his actual practice of philosophy—namely, in the use of phenomenological method—imagination, although still distrusted in the realm of reason, comes into its own. Since phenomenological method, especially as formulated and constantly reformulated by Husserl, is exceedingly complex, we shall limit ourselves to the claim that a case can be made (and will be made more fully in section II) that this method is significantly parallel to the spontaneous operation of imagination while also involving the exercise of imagining in its own operation. In both respects, the role of imagination is considerably enhanced and enlarged, compared with its strictly secondary status in Husserl's theory of mental activity. For its primary product, fiction, taken in the broadest sense, is shown to be essential to the successful prosecution of phenomenological method, and imagination is thereby elevated to a position of the first rank. Perhaps more than any other post-Romantic philosopher, Husserl accords imagination a place of prominence in philosophical methodology. In this methodology, imagination is responsible for securing "all essential necessities and essential laws—all genuine intuitive *a priori*."[15]

It is therefore perplexing that Husserl, while granting imagination full play within phenomenological method, is not willing to recognize it as an independent act in its own right. What is essential to the gaining of eidetic insight becomes a mere mode of presentification in the context of epistemology. There could be no starker contrast than that between the role of imagination in phenomenological method and its subordinate role in Husserl's model of the mind. In the latter it is restricted to modifying memory, from which it is thereby held to be derivative. It makes little difference that this is "memory in the largest sense" or that imagination is said to be indefinitely reiterable.[16] These concessions to the scope of imagination are minor when compared to the compass the same mental operation is given for the sake of pursuing eidetic insight. The contrast remains, reminding us that, for all his obstinate originality, Husserl does not overcome the schizophrenic attitude with which other Western philosophers have also viewed imagination.

Nonetheless, unlike these other philosophers, Husserl at least intimates a way of breaking out of the paradoxical pattern of denial-*cum*-acknowledgment, and for this reason he merits further consideration. For closer scrutiny will suggest a possible exit from the stalemate in which Husserl's predecessors—typified by Aristotle and Descartes, Hume and Kant—were caught. All of these latter figures are trapped in the initial paradox of asserting and denying, at one and the same time, the importance of imagining. By contrast, though Husserl does not entirely escape this paradox, he indicates a means by which it might be avoided: *phenomenological method itself*. For it is precisely by making use of imagination that phenomenological method allows us to view imagining unambivalently and in its full significance.

Yet this very realization brings us abruptly to a second paradox: it is advisable to *use* imagination in order to give an adequate descriptive account *of* imagination. But in contradistinction to the previous paradox, this second paradox is positive and promising. Where the first paradox is dominated by a desire to suppress the significance of imagination, the second displays an interest in imagination for its own sake. And where interest in imagining is at best indirect and surreptitious in the classical philosophers in the Western tradition, in Husserl's instance imagination is explicitly taken as a theme of philosophical interest. Yet it receives this attention not because of its importance in mental activity in general but because of its special role in phenomenological method. Hence Husserl grants imagination a status of its own—but only within the specific philosophical method he advocated.

II

As a consequence of the second paradox, any attempt at a phenomenology of imagination finds itself in a peculiar position. Since imagining is a basic phenomenological technique, the phenomenologist will utilize the very capacity he aims to elucidate. Does this paradoxical circularity subvert the possibility of carrying out a phenomenology of imagination? Not insofar as imagination is a mental act like any other and thus a perfectly legitimate object of phenomenological description. To the extent that it is merely one mental act among others, it is as amenable as the others to the basic investigative procedures of phenomenological method. In this respect, imagination has no special position of advantage—or disadvantage. For, in principle at least, there are no privileged entities in phenomenology; every object, act, or event counts equally as what Husserl calls a "pure phenomenon."[17]

Nevertheless, imagination is not a mental act *just* like any other. In particular, it possesses an extraordinary elusiveness which is not found in other acts. This elusiveness (which accounts for our tendency to describe most imaginative experience as "fleeting") makes imagining not only difficult to pin down but unlikely as a source of philosophical insight: on both counts, imagination poses special problems. Yet, however difficult these problems may prove to be, they do not justify dispensing altogether with imagination as an aid in phenomenological description. In spite of its evanescent and often obfuscated character, it may still be a valuable tool for analysis—and precisely for its *own* analysis. Indeed, explicit awareness of its role in phenomenological method will help to make its own description more accurate. Accordingly, we turn now to a consideration of two principal procedures of phenomenological method, with both of which imagination is closely allied.

A. Phenomenological Reduction.
What is the nature of this fundamental, and yet highly controversial, phenomenological technique? At the

very least, it involves (in Husserl's well-known terms) the "bracketing" of the "natural attitude"—that is, suspending the naively held belief that mundane objects exist in themselves in such a way as to be strictly transcendent to our consciousness of them. By a simple but radical change of outlook, we disengage the natural attitude's stranglehold upon almost all aspects of lived experience. This attitudinal change, which is not meant to be permanent, is effected by an abstention from—an *epochē* of—our untutored tendency to posit objects, events, or mental acts as transcendent presences or (more generally) as real (where "real" means to be grounded in transphenomenal factors). To escape the hold of the transphenomenal—that is, of factors which are conceivable exclusively in causal or substantial terms—we must cease, at least temporarily, to posit things as transcending consciousness. We put out of play our natural and naive belief in the independent existence of objects of consciousness, and this allows us to realize that the *meaning* (*Sinn*) of these objects can be made evident without reference to their *being* (*Sein*).

There are, in fact, two aspects or phases of the phenomenological reduction: the reduction proper ("reduction *of*" the natural attitude), which is excluding in character, and the attainment of the sphere of immanence ("reduction *to*" this sphere). The sphere of immanence is the region of reduced phenomena, that is, of phenomena in a state of transparency to consciousness: a state characterized by "self-evidence" (*Evidenz*) and "self-givenness" (*Selbstgegebenheit*).[18] Consequently, the function of phenomenological reduction as a whole is, in Herbert Spiegelberg's words, "to free the phenomena from all transphenomenal elements, notably from all beliefs in transphenomenal existence, thus leaving us with what is indubitably or 'absolutely' given."[19] In short, phenomenological reduction leaves us with pure phenomena which make no claim to a transcendent status.

It is phenomenlogical reduction prop-

er, and not the subsequent disclosure of the sphere of immanence, that is of greatest moment for our present purposes. For this initial and basic stage of reduction displays several features which are remarkably parallel to certain traits of imagining. In both reduction proper and in imagining, belief in transphenomenal entities is suspended: we abstain from believing in them as abidingly real. This decommissioning of doxic commitment is so extensive as also to exclude any supposition as to the *non*-existence of presented phenomena. Husserl distinguishes a Cartesian positing of *non*-existence—namely, active denial of ontic status as in Descartes' first *Meditation*—from his own attitude of sheer suspension. For any act of positing, even one which posits non-existence, is effected on the basis of a world in which belief continues to be placed, however implicitly.[20] Similarly, we do not posit the strict non-existence of phenomena in imagining, and this is so even when what we imagine (e.g., a unicorn) does not in fact exist. Rather, we simply contemplate imagined objects or events as possible: existent or not, an imagined unicorn is a purely possible beast.[21] Finally, as a result of suspending doxic commitment there is a fundamental similarity of stance in reduction proper and in imagining. In both, we forgo active involvement in what immediately surrounds us. Thus what Husserl says of reduction proper could just as well be said of imagining: "all [our] natural interests are put out of play."[22]

Husserl pointed to what he called the "close kinship" between imagination and phenomenological reduction.[23] But he was also keenly aware of differences between the two activities: he denies, for instance, that reduction is an operation of "merely imagining something in thought" (*sich bloss denken*) or of sheer supposing (*annahmen*).[24] Moreover, imagining is regarded as significantly similar to "neutrality-modification," since the ontic status of imagined content (unlike perceived or remembered content) is neutral in character and since imagination is conceived as a modification of memory.[25] Now even if phenomenological reduction is ontically neutral, it does not, strictly speaking, *modify* anything previous or pregiven. Rather, in reduction the phenomenologist seeks to let what is given appear as pure phenomenon. And this means that the world, far from being modified and transcended as in complete acts of imagination, remains before the phenomenologist, only now as reduced:

... the world, exactly as it was for me earlier [i.e., before the reduction] and still is, as my world, our world, humanity's world, having validity in its various subjective ways, has not disappeared.[26]

In imagining, contrariwise, the world as perceived or remembered *does* disappear; it forms no part of imagined content, which is confined to strictly imaginal presences.[27] It is at this point, then, that the parallelism between imagination and reduction reaches its limit.

We may conclude this brief comparison between phenomenological reduction and imagination by suggesting that an adequate account of imagining as such would eliminate at least one of the above-mentioned differences between the two activities. On the basis of such an account, which Husserl fails to provide, imagination would no longer be viewed as akin to neutrality-modification—or to *any* sort of modification of other mental acts. Thus imagining would be seen to possess an essential independence of its immediate context—an independence which is reminiscent of reduction proper. For context-independence is involved both in abstaining from committed belief in transcendent objects and in positing imagined objects as purely possible. Further, such independence makes possible the evidential certitude of both experiences.[28]

But the parallel stops here, and any further analysis would have to acknowledge the differences that remain between the two activities, including the fact that imagining is subject to reduction in a way that differs inherently from the manner in which reduction can become the subject of an imaginative experience: I can im-

agine how it is to reduce without actually performing a reduction, but to reduce imagination I must apply the reduction to an actual act of imagining.

B. Free Variation in Imagination. If the relation between imagination and phenomenological reduction is one of limited parallelism at best, this is no longer the case with what Husserl calls "free variation in imagination."[29] In this latter procedure, imagination becomes an intrinsic part of the methodology. This occurs in two ways. First, as the source of what Husserl terms "fiction" (i.e., any product of imagining which exceeds the factual), imagination supplies the phenomenologist with a considerable portion of the examples which are the starting points of free variation proper. For the phenomenologist may begin his investigation with an example which is either factual or fictitious. If he is unable to find an example of a given phenomenon within present or past experience, he is perfectly free to invent an example as a point of departure in an eidetic analysis. Second, and more important, the factual or fictive example is then subjected to a systematic variation in imagination. It is this critical move which may be considered free variation proper, and in it imagination is, in Paul Ricoeur's words, "the main weapon in the tactic of the example."[30] For it is by employment of imagination that an example is freely and yet methodically varied until the essential structure of the phenomenon which is displayed in the example is made apparent. The full procedure of free variation proper (hereafter referred to simply as "free variation") consists in one or more of three complementary methodological moves:

(1) The attempted *removal* of all significant traits from the phenomenon in the example—that is, the effort to imagine such traits as absent from the phenomenon. This is the most direct and decisive mode of free variation. For those traits that *cannot* be removed in this way are, by virtue of their undissociability, shown to be essential to the phenomenon.

Together they form its *eidos,* the resistant core which is its invariant structural nucleus.

(2) The *substitution* of new traits for the original ones. Here one imagines different traits in place of those that are initially given as characterizing the phenomenon; instead of simply removing the original traits, the phenomenologist attempts to see if they can be replaced by *other* traits. If he fails in this effort, he is given assurance that the original traits are indeed essential to the structure and identity of the phenomenon in question. If he succeeds, this is taken as an indication that the traits are only contingent.

(3) The *productive imagination* of additional traits which are not given in the initial grasping of the example and which do not merely replace those that are. These extra traits act to fill out an example that is incomplete or ambiguous as first presented. But their imaginability is not, as such, a definitive indication of their essentiality; it is only an aid in determining the essential character of the phenomenon illustrated in the example.[31]

Now it cannot be denied that it is perception and not imagination which plays a privileged role in phenomenological method by serving as a model for direct givenness: "the intuition of essences is an originary giving act and is in this respect the analogue of sensible perception and not of fiction."[32] But perception is analogous only to the final grasping of an essence, that is, to what Husserl calls "eidetic insight" (*Wesensschau*). It is neither analogous to, nor is it necessarily utilized in, the preparation for this ultimate insight. As we have just seen, it is imagination which is most crucial in the preparatory stages. More than either perception or memory, imagination allows for the unrestricted invention and exfoliation of examples—and for the detailed development of aspects of examples—which form the basis for eidetic insight. What Husserl says of the geometer is equally true of the phenomenologist:

On the plane of imagination he has the incomparable freedom of being able to change arbitrarily the form of his fictive figures, to run through all of their possible configurations.[33]

Of course, he does not have to run through every one of them *ad infinitum.* This would be an impracticable requirement, and all that counts in any event are the significant variations, id est, those that represent genuinely different versions of a given phenomenon.[34] To bring forth these variations by means of imagination becomes essential to the phenomenological enterprise: "freedom in the investigation of essences necessarily requires that one operate on the plane of imagination."[35]

Imagination is also called for because of its ability to project manifold possibilities—possibilities which are "pure" by virtue of their independence of the realm of fact. Here we need only note that common to both the act of imagining as such and to free variation is precisely an ability to entertain such pure possibilities, whether by treating already existing objects or events as sheerly possible or by projecting altogether new possibilities. In the pursuance of phenomenological method, each variation is regarded strictly *as* a possibility, not to be compared with pre-existent realities but only with other possibilities: as merely one possibility among others. In this way the work of the phenomenological reduction is reinforced by severing all connection with the posited realities of the natural attitude. The phenomenologist comes, in short, to inhabit what Husserl terms a pure "world of imagination."[36] And it is precisely in such an unlikely locale that he is in the best position to grasp essences:

[it is] a world of absolutely pure possibilities, each of which can then serve as a central structure for possible pure variations in the mode of the arbitrary; and from each [such possibility] results an absolutely pure *eidos.*[37]

Therefore, essences or essential structures are obtained not by foraging or surveying the real but by disengaging oneself from mundane realities (i.e., from the fixations of the natural attitude) and by concentrating upon pure possibilities. What Husserl calls "eidetic reduction" or (less frequently) "ideating abstraction" refers to this general movement from fact to essence via free variation.[38] Along with phenomenological reduction, free variation allows the phenomenologist to obtain access to essences. But it is above all in free variation that imagination comes into prominence as a central feature of phenomenological method itself. For it is only here that the phenomenologist can "let imagination have free rein"[39] in the confident expectation that it will aid him in achieving eidetic insight—and yet without drawing him into a debilitating dalliance in the imaginary, a dalliance against which the mainstream of Western philosophy has so incessantly inveighed.

III

As a result of our discussion of phenomenological method, we are now in a position to observe the curious way in which Husserl leads us, through a strictly methodological concern with imagining, toward an insight into its essential structure—which he himself fails to achieve when he approaches imagination outside the context of method. This insight concerns imagination's essentially *variable* character. Now it is precisely in its variability that imagination has occasioned a deeply ambivalent attitude on the part of philosophers. On the one hand, as the merely variable—as the shifting and inconstant—it has been subjected to a continual critique in Western philosophy ever since Plato announced that "a theoretical inquiry no more employs images than does a factual investigation."[40] For what varies in form or substance is held to be incommensurate with strict standards of objective knowledge. Such standards admit of no exceptions and thus of no significant variations from the norms they embody. These standards themselves are regarded as necessarily invariant—indeed, as the invariant *par excellence*. Such invariancy is held to be constitutive of the highest objects of reason, whether these be forms, categories, or other a priori structures. Western logocentrism, to which Husserl firmly and sometimes fiercely adheres, dictates that anything that strays from the invariant is *ipso facto* suspect. Locked within this logocentrism, philosophers of a rationalist persuasion have regarded imagination in its inherent variability as a primary source of distraction from objective truth. Thus Descartes describes imagination as "a vagabond who likes to wander and is not yet able to stay within the strict bounds of truth"; and Kant laments that the image is "determined by no assignable rule."[41] These two indictments of imagining are not unrelated to each other: to be intellectually vagrant is to be ruleless, unruly. Imagination is seen as tending always to overextend itself and to lose its bearings when it ventures beyond the secure confines of reason; its intrinsic errancy marks it as a basically aberrant mental act.

Yet, on the other hand, imagining's variability has also been viewed as offering a legitimate avenue to truth. Precisely as variable, imagination provides a prelude to insight into a priori structures. In this spirit, it is even admitted that what seems to be a diversion from truth may end by being the most revealing approach to it. In any case, it is just this distinctly different attitude toward the variability of imagining which Husserl adopts in promulgating the method of free variation in imagination. For the value of variability is presupposed in this method, and an appreciation of this value allows us to realize that there may be more than a single inroad into truth—namely, that truth can be attained not only by sheer ratiocination but also by a systematic variation of content and context. Thus by varying the forms of facts or fictions in his imagination, the phenomenologist may discover what is truly unvarying in a given series of variations, and thereby knowing the invariant structure, he knows the objective truth about the phenomenon he is investigating.

It is both curious and crucial to observe that where most phenomena yield an invariant—a rule, a law, a certain type of objectivity—at the end of a series of free variations in imagination, *imagination itself*, taken as an object of phenomenological investigation, shows itself to be radically variable in character—so variable, in fact, that it seems to possess on invariant structure of its own. Or we might say that imagining is invariant precisely in its own radical variability of content and aspect. Such variability is constitutive of imagining itself and not merely of our mode of access to it. In this important respect, imagination as a phenomenon is to be distinguished from both essences and perceptual objects which may involve the variable as an avenue of approach but which are not themselves constituted by continually varying factors. In these latter two cases, the invariant is sought amid the variations. In the case of imagination, we have to do with variations within the invariant itself—that is, with the variable *as such*, with that which cannot fail to be varied at our merest whim and which presents itself in ever-varying appearances.

Thus a final paradox suggests itself: a distinctive invariant feature of imagination is its very variability. Free variation, then, is not only a special phenomenological technique but is, in itself, of the essence of imagining as a total phenomenon. Yet insight into the inherent variability of imagining—an insight upon which Husserlian methodology capitalizes—does not prevent the ascertainment of stable features alongside shifting ones. Even if imagination's variability is in fact a constant characteristic, this does not preclude other, non-varying factors. Indeed, any prolonged phenomenological description of imagination must be devoted to discerning precisely such stable features. But it should be kept in mind throughout any such description that these features, however unchanging in ultimate form and function, do not exclude the essential variability of imagination's modes of appearance and expression. In their noematic nucleus, such features are rigidly invariant; but, as appearing to the mind, they are always varying and variant.[42]

In sum, we may say that in its freedom of enactment, in its projection of pure possibilities, and in the unanticipatable wealth of its products, imagining manifests itself as a mental act which is incurably variable.

Any full picture of imagination, then, must do justice to *both* of its dimensions: to its essentially variable appearance, content, and aspect as well as to a core of constant traits (which themselves appear in varied ways). And it is by recognizing this duality of dimensions that the force of the final paradox is diminished: variability is not the *only* invariant feature of imagination, even if it is the most conspicuous and general such feature. Moreover, the sense in which the variability of imagination is itself invariant is not only as an *eidos* which is present as such to eidetic insight but also as an uneliminable aspect of the *experience* of imagining. In imagining, we experience the variable directly in terms of the unexpectedness of the onset of the act and in its ever-changing course and direction. Therefore, the very *way* we experience imagination is itself radically variable, and imagination's variability cannot be confined to such objective features as pure possibility or independence of perceptual parameters. Both the imaginer and the imagined are caught up in a dialectic of incessant transformation. But if this is so—if variability is built into imagining as act and as object—it cannot be claimed that the third paradox possesses the same significance as the two primary paradoxes explored in the previous sections. [43]

IV

The foregoing reflections on phenomenological method and imagination may be brought to a close by stressing that an insight into the ceaselessly varying character of imagining is facilitated by the actual use of one of the principal procedures of this method. Free variation in imagination both exemplifies and illuminates this character. Husserl seized on the intrinsic variability of imagining as possessing supreme methodological value, despite the fact that imagination as a mental act occupies only a secondary position in his philosophy of mind. Such is the paradox of denial-*cum*-acknowledgment. But if we wish, as phenomenologists, to do justice to imagination—namely, to recognize its independent status as a mental act—we are led ineluctably to the second paradox: to describe imagination adequately, we must employ imagining as part of our procedure. As we have seen, this employment of imagination (as method) to describe imagination (as phenomenon) draws on imagination's intrinsic powers of variation; and we land in a third (and tamer) paradox when we realize that such variability is a constant characteristic of imagining, even in its everyday enactments. Thus we arrive, by a series of paradoxes arising from considerations of method, at a basic grasp of the nature of imagining itself *qua* variable. At the same time, we come to appreciate the fact that questions concerning phenomenological method on the one hand and the character of imagination on the other are not so distinct as they might at first appear to be. Indeed, we begin to suspect that they are closely intertwined. And the important implication is that, just as phenomenological method makes prominent use of imagination, a philosophical study of imagination cannot afford to ignore the question of a proper philosophical method.

I say "*a* proper" and not "*the* proper" method because it cannot rightly be claimed that phenomenology provides the only satisfactory method for achieving an adequate philosophical account of imagination. Wittgenstein is justified in asserting that "there is not *a* philosophical method, though there are indeed methods, like different therapies."[44] But we can at least claim, as this essay has attempted to show in part, that phenomenological method is unusually well situated to investigate imagination insofar as one of its basic techniques involves the direct and active use of imagining itself. In this respect, what is at

first sight paradoxically circular—id est, has to utilize imagining in the description of imagining—may end by being a specific strength. For phenomenological method is in an especially favorable position for giving a general account of imagination. Through its use of free variation and (to a lesser extent) its practice of phenomenological reduction, it is already intimately acquainted with the process of imagining and, above all, with its capacity for endless variety. A method that rigorously excluded a technique such as free variation would find itself at a disadvantage in treating imagination, which would appear as merely one mental act among others. Indeed, a militant stance of scientific objectivity which disdained recourse to imagination as an exploratory technique—as in many contemporary conceptions of methodology—would find itself approaching imagination as an alien and often highly suspicious mental activity.[45]

However controversial the place of imagination may be in an enterprise which, like much modern science, highly values objectivity, its crucial role in art, in philosophy and in everyday human activities is more difficult to deny. This does not mean, however, that we are entitled to assume that the special role of imagination in art (e.g., as stressed by Romantic poets) or in philosophy (as emphasized by Husserl) provides a definitive model for imagining in all its avatars. Moreover, even if the use of imagination is more extensive in art or in philosophy than in other comparable human activities, this should not be allowed to prejudice the outcome of a general project of describing imagining in its eidetic structure. Such a project aims only at offering an accurate account of imagining in its minimal and yet seminal form—a form which, despite its many guises and possible extensions, can be viewed as a unified structure or series of structures.

Phenomenological method presents itself as an especially appropriate and promising basis for discovering and delineating this phenomenon's primary traits, among which variability figures prominently. And this is so not because phenomenological method is of supreme value in the description of all phenomena but because, self-consciously employing imagination in its own methodology, it finds itself more familiar with and more sensitive to this particular phenomenon than alternative methods which abjure its role in philosophical method. Whatever the paradoxes arising from the central place of imagining in phenomenological method, this method presents itself as a privileged means of elucidating imagination's *eidos*. Consequently, if phenomenological method calls for the use of imagination, eidetic insight into imagination calls for the use of phenomenological method.

NOTES

1. For some recent efforts in this direction, however, see David Levin, "Induction and Husserl's Theory of Eidetic Variation," *Philosophy and Phenomenological Research* (1968), 29: 1-15; Donald Kuspit, "Fiction and Phenomenology," *Philosophy and Phenomenological Research* (1968), 29: 16-33; Richard M. Zaner, "The Art of Free Phantasy in Rigorous Phenomenological Science," in F. Kersten and R. Zaner, eds., *Phenomenology: Continuation and Criticism* (The Hague: Nijhoff, 1972), pp. 192-219; and Richard M. Zaner, "Examples and Possibles: A Criticism of Husserl's Theory of Free-Phantasy Variation," *Research in Phenomenology* (1973), 3: 29-43. In varying degrees, all of these essays are critical of Husserl's notion of the role of imagination in phenomenological method, and in this regard they complement the present essay.

2. This essay forms part of my book, *Imagining: A Phenomenological Study* (forthcoming, Indiana University Press).

3. Pascal, *Pensées*, ed. L. Lafuma (Paris: Seuil, 1962), p. 54; Heidegger, *Vorträge und Aufsätze* (Pfullingen: Neske, 1954), p. 229.

4. The term "logocentric" is borrowed from Jacques Derrida, *De la grammatologie* (Paris: Minuit, 1967), pp. 21ff.

5. To glance at these three classical cases: (a) In Aristotle's model of the mind, sensing and thinking are elevated to positions of supreme epistemological value. Imagination, caught in the middle, is said to be "for the most part false" (*De Anima*, 428a 11). Yet in practically the same breath Aristotle adds that imagining is necessary to the soul, which "never thinks without an image" (ibid., 431a 16). This rapid promotion of imagination to a position where it is necessary to thinking in general (and hence to philosophical thinking as well) occurs unexpectedly and yet with firm insistence.

(b) Similarly, Hume begins by asserting that nothing is more dangerous to reason than the flights of the imagination," and calls for "a resolution to reject all the trivial suggestions of the fancy, and adhere to the understanding" (*A Treatise of Human Nature*, ed. Selby Bigge [Oxford: Oxford University Press, 1955], p. 26). Yet it turns out that the understanding itself is conceived by Hume as "the general and more establish'd properties of the imagination" (ibid. Cf. also p. 165: "the memory, senses, and understanding are therefore, all of them founded on the imagination"). Thus Hume comes to acknowledge the essential ingrediency of imagining in the very activity of understanding, which is in turn crucial to philosophical thought.

(c) Following the same pattern, Kant denounces the merely "visionary" imagination, which is said to produce "empty figments of the brain," yet contrasts it with an "inventive" imagination, which has the merit of operating "under the strict surveillance of reason" (*Critique of Pure Reason*, trans. N. K. Smith [New York: Humanities Press, 1950], p. 613). In the end, imagination is elevated to a position of central prominence within Kant's epistemology: "a blind but indispensable function of the soul, without which we should have no knowledge whatsoever" (ibid., A 78 B 103). It is indispensable because it is the source of all intellectual synthesis in the understanding, and such synthesis is what "first gives rise to knowledge" (ibid., A 77, B 103). Consequently, imagination is again made basic to understanding, id est, to the faculty of knowledge, and thus to philosophical activity itself.

6. Descartes, *Meditations on First Philosophy*, trans. L. J. Lafleur (New York and Indianapolis: Bobbs-Merrill, 1961), p. 23. My italics.

7. Ibid., p. 21.

8. Ibid., p. 69.

9. Husserl, *Ideas*, trans. B. Gibson (London: Allen and Unwin, 1931), sec. 100.

10. Cf. Husserl, *The Phenomenology of Internal Time-Consciousness*, trans. James Churchill (Bloomington: Indiana University Press, 1964), appendices 1 and 2.

11. Cf. Husserl, *Logical Investigations*, trans. J. N. Findlay (New York: Humanities Press, 1970), pp. 606-610, 642-47, 682-88, 760-63, and esp.773-95.

12. Husserl, *Cartesian Meditations*, trans. Dorion Cairns (The Hague: Nijhoff, 1960), p. 59.

13. Husserl, *Phänomenologische Psychologie* (The Hague: Nijhoff, 1962), p. 73.

14. Cf. Husserl, *Ideas*, sec. 124.

15. Husserl, *Phänomenologische Psychologie*, p.72.

16. Cf. Husserl *Ideas*, sec. 111-12. To be more exact: imagination is a strictly *nonpositing* mode of presentification, in contrast with memory, which is conceived as positing (i.e., existence-establishing) presentification. Whereas imagination is a modifica-

tion of memory, memory in turn is a modification of perception or direct sensory presentation. In the end, then, all presentification, whether imaginal or mnemonic in character, is a form of re-presentation (Re-präsentation) of content originally given in sensory experience. (Re-präsentation is interchangeable with Vergegenwärtigung for Husserl. Cf. Phenomenology of Internal Time-Consciousness, sec. 17.)

17. The term "pure phenomenon" occurs with emphasis in The Idea of Phenomenology, where Husserl writes: " The truly absolute datum is the pure phenomenon" (The Idea of Phenomenology, trans. W. P. Alston and G. Nakhnikian [The Hague: Nijhoff, 1950], p. 5).

18. These terms first occur in Logical Investigations V and VI; they are also employed in The Idea of Phenomenology and in almost all of Husserl's later works.

19. Herbert Spiegelberg, The Phenomenological Movement (The Hague: Nijhoff, 1965), 1: 134.

20. Cf. Ideas, sec. 31, but also The Crisis, where Husserl takes himself to task for having, in Ideas and in Cartesian Meditations, adopted "the Cartesian way" to the reduction. (Cf. The Crisis of European Philosophy and Transcendental Philosophy, trans. David Carr [Evanston: Northwestern University Press, 1970], p. 155; hereafter cited as The Crisis.)

21. For a development of this point, see my articles "Imagination: Imagining and the Image," Philosophy and Phenomenological Research (1971), 31: 476-80, and "Toward a Phenomenology of Imagination," Journal of the British Society for Phenomenology (1974), 5: 16-18.

22. Husserl, The Crisis, p. 152.

23. The full statement is "The close kinship of the two forms of consciousness is evident" (Ideas, sec. 31 [I have modified Gibson's translation, here as in other instances]).

24. Ibid. On the subject of annahmen, see Alexius Meinong, Über Annahmen (Leipzig: Barth, 1902).

25. On neutrality-modification, see Ideas, sec. 109-14. The crucial difference between imagination and the neutrality-modification is that only imagination can reiterate itself (cf. ibid., sec. 112).

26. The Crisis, p. 152.

27. As Wittgenstein says, "While I am looking at an object I cannot imagine it" (Zettel, trans. G. E. M. Anscombe [Oxford: Blackwell, 1967], sec. 621).

28. On the last feature, see Paul Ricoeur's discussion of "the certitude of intuition" which is found in phenomenological reduction. in his translation of Ideas: Idées (Paris: Gallimard, 1950), p. 100, n. 3.

29. The original discussion of free variation is to be found in Ideas (sec. 70), but a more complete account is offered in Experience and Judgment, trans. J. Churchill and K. Ameriks (Evanston: Northwestern University Press, 1973), sec. 39-42. Cf. also Aron Gurwitsch, The Field of Consciousness (Pittsburgh: Duquesne University Press, 1964), pp. 191ff., 390f.

30. Ricoeur, in translation cit. supra, p. 223n.

31. It should also be noted that Husserl sometimes adds another step: the apprehension of a basic "similarity" or "congruence" between the variant versions of the example. The essence is here conceived as the invariant factor which remains the same through all the variations. It is that common factor which resides in the overlapping (Deckung) of variants, hence in their similarity. But it seems clear that the determination of such similarity must involve a cognitive operation that goes beyond imagining proper. Thus it may be said to build on the activity of imagining without itself being an act of imagination. Cf. Experience and Judgment, sec. 87e, and Phänomenologische Psychologie, p. 71f.

32. Husserl, Ideas, sec. 23.

33. Ibid., sec. 70.

34. The variations should nevertheless be viewed as "endless" in the sense of open ended and freely produced. Cf. Phänomenologische Psychologie, sec. 9, and Experience and Judgment, p. 173.

35. Ideas, sec. 70.

36. Phänomenologische Psychologie, p. 74.

37. Ibid. Cf. also Experience and Judgment, p. 351.

38. Strictly speaking, ideating abstraction and free variation differ in detail as procedures, but the two are closely associated in eidetic inquiry since free variation is frequently a necessary adjunct to ideating abstraction. Cf. Gurwitsch, Field of Consciousness, pp. 191-193, 390.

39. Phänomenologische Psychologie, p. 71.

40. Phaedo, 100a.

41. Descartes, Meditations, p. 29; Kant, Critique of Pure Reason, p. 613.

42. On the notion of noematic nucleus, see Husserl, Ideas, sec. 90-91.

43. In fact, this third paradox may even be considered an extension of the second primary paradox. If it is paradoxical to use imagination to describe imagination, and if this use is precisely that of free variation in imagination, then we would expect to discover variability as an intrinsic feature of imagining—since we have already made use of this ability to vary in previous applications of the method. A separate paradox arises only insofar as this variability is held to be an invariant feature of imagining. But is it deeply paradoxical to hold that a constant feature of something consists precisely in its constantly changing state? At least it is no more paradoxical than the nature of the universe itself as described by Heraclitus: "Everything flows and nothing abides. . . .It is in changing that things find repose" (fragments 20 and 24 in the translation of Philip Wheelwright [Princeton, N. J.: Princeton University Press, 1959], p. 29).

44. Ludwig Wittgenstein, Philosophical Investigations, trans. G. E. M. Anscombe (Oxford: Blackwell, 1967), p. 51.

45. It is worth noticing that a compromise is sometimes effected in the philosophy of science: the process and the effects of imagination are tacitly recognized, but they are assimilated to a procedure which is held to have nothing in common with the supposedly haphazard character of everyday imagining. For example, in their discussions of Gedankenexperimente both Karl Popper and Norwood Russell Hanson admit the importance of imagina-

tive hypothesis-formation; but this creative act is not brought into connection with everyday acts of imagining. It is as if there were a special faculty of strictly scientific hypothesizing which, though undeniably imaginative, has little or no relation to the use of imagination in other human activities. See Karl Popper, *The Logic of Scientific Discovery* (New York: Basic Books, 1961), appendix 9, and N. R. Hanson, *Patterns of Discovery* (New York: Cambridge University Press, 1965), pp. 126, 137, 140.

C. S. Peirce, by contrast, allows for a continuity between the everyday and the scientific utilization of the basic inferential procedure which he calls "abduction" or "hypothesis"; and since abduction relies on a special conjectural ability, it involves the projective powers of imagining. As Peirce himself writes, "the [abductive] hypothesis should be distinctly put as a question, *before* making the observations which are to test its truth. In other words, we must try to see what the result of predictions from the hypothesis will be" (*Collected Papers*, eds. C. Hartshorne and P. Weiss [Cambridge, Mass.: Harvard University Press, 1931-35], I-II, p. 380 [sec. 2.634]). To envisage results by way of prediction in Peirce's sense requires the use of imagination. (On this topic see also K. T. Fann, *Peirce's Theory of Abduction* [The Hague: Nijhoff, 1970], and Rulon Wells, "Distinctively Human Semiotic" in *Social Science Information* (1967), vol. 6, no. 2.)

The Emergence of an Absolute Consciousness in Husserl's Early Writings on Time-Consciousness

JOHN B. BROUGH

The collection of Edmund Husserl's sketches on time-consciousness from the years 1893-1917, edited by Rudolf Boehm and published as Volume X in the Husserliana series,[1] affords significant new material for the study of the evolution of Husserl's thought. Specifically, the sketches suggest that in the course of analyzing the consciousness of temporal objects Husserl became convinced that a distinction must be drawn between an ultimate or absolute flow of consciousness and the immanent temporal objects or contents—sense-data, appearances of external things, acts of wishing, judging, etc.—constituted or known within that flow. Further, the texts indicate that the emergence of the absolute dimension was connected with the development during this period of two distinct interpretations of the constitution of time-consciousness. Husserl apparently worked out the first of these during the years 1901-1907, and only towards the end of this period did the notion of an absolute consciousness, absent in earlier texts, make its appearance. And no

sooner did it emerge than Husserl undertook a critique of his first interpretation which ultimately culminated in its rejection. In the new position which then appeared, around 1909, the absolute flow of time-constituting consciousness, and its distinction from temporal objects both immanent and transcendent, was unequivocally affirmed. We propose now to discuss this evolution and the emergence and nature of the absolute flow of consciousness.

1. Husserl's Interpretation of Time-Consciousness in Terms of the Schema: Apprehension—Contents of Apprehension (1901-1907)

A. Succession and Time-Consciousness. Husserl's interpretations of time-consciousness may be understood as attempts to answer the question: How, in a flow of consciousness, is the awareness of a temporally extended object constituted? An alternative formulation, characteristic of Husserl's analyses dating from the first five years of the century, would be: How, in a succession of consciousness, is the consciousness of succession constituted? For a "temporal" object, no matter what its material character may be, is precisely an object presented to consciousness in a series of phases. Thus in listening to a violin concerto, I hear the first measure as Now,

Reprinted with permission of the publisher and author from *Man and World*, vol. 5, no. 3 (Aug. 1972): 298-326.

*The author acknowledges a debt of gratitude to Professor Robert Sokolowski of Catholic University and to Professor Louis Dupré of Georgetown, both of whom helped him in clarifying his thoughts about Husserl's early writings on time.

and then successively perceive another section as Now while the earlier one is experienced as just past, and so on as the music develops. A house too is presented successively insofar as I now see the front and in the next moment see the side or continue to see the front. The temporal object, then, is presented to consciousness in a continuum of phases with the "fundamental temporal distinctions: Now, past (future)" (211).

But the perception (*Wahrnehmung*)[2] of the temporal object, Husserl insists, "is itself a temporal object" (232). It too develops in a continuum of phases which run off successively, one of which will be Now or actual, while others will have elapsed, or will have not yet appeared. Nor is this an accidental characteristic: "the consciousness of time itself [requires] time, the consciousness of duration, duration, the consciousness of succession, succession" (192). Clearly, if an object is to be *perceived* in its temporal extension, then as each phase of the object appears successively as Now, there must be present a corresponding phase of the perception through which it is perceived as Now. The perception must endure or develop successively as long as the object is perceived.

B.   Conditions of the Possibility of the Consciousness of Temporal Objects. The above observations merely serve to clarify our question. We must now discuss Husserl's attempts at explaining how in the succession or flow of perceptual phases the consciousness of an object in the modes, Now, past, and to come, is possible.

1. The Overlapping Intentionality of Time-Consciousness. The primary requirement is that "consciousness must reach out beyond (*hinausgreifen*) the Now" (226). And this overlapping intentionality must be accomplished in each moment of the developing perception. "Each perceptual phase has intentional reference to an extended section of the temporal object, and not merely to a Now-point necessarily given in it and

simultaneous with it" (232).[3] The momentary perceptual phase or "Querschnitt" (231), a term used by Husserl in 1904,* is therefore not simply consciousness of the Now-phase of the object. If it were, one would never perceive an extended temporal object such as a melody, for such perception must include consciousness of the *past* phases of the object as well as of the Now-phase. Accordingly, the Querschnitt or perceptual slice, while conscious of the objective Now-phase, at the same time "encompasses the hitherto elapsed part of the temporal object in a *definite way*" and also bears "an intention towards what is yet to come (*Kunftiges*), even if not towards continuations of the same temporal object" (232).

That the single perceptual phase is consciousness of the elapsed objective phases in a "definite way" is a further important condition of the possibility of the perception of temporal objects. For example, if in the hearing of three successive tones, *a* is perceived as coming before *b*, and *b* as coming before *c*, then this order will be preserved in the consciousness of the elapsed phases. If this were not the case, then tones which, objectively speaking, had succeeded one another, would appear as simultaneous in the past. One would thus hear one tone as Now, and experience at the same time an elapsed tonal chaos. Further, the preservation of the order of succession will occur in connection with constant modification. That is, the preserved moments will be intended in continuously changing modes of the past. Thus when tone *b* is heard as Now, tone *a* will be perceived as just past with respect to *b*; in the next moment, when tone *c* is heard as Now, tone *b* will be perceived as just past with respect to *c*, and tone *a* as "just" just past with respect to *c*. Obviously, the actual Now-phase has a certain privileged position (168) in the process of continual

---

*"Querschnitt" may be translated as "cross section" or "slice" (of the extended perception). We will frequently use the terms "cross section" or "slice" as concise expressions for the momentary phase of perception or consciousness.

modification, for elapsed phases are perceived in definite modes of the past *relative* to the Now. The elapsed Now-phase, Husserl writes, remains the same, "except that it stands forth as past in relation to the momentarily actual and temporally new Now" (179).

2. Time-Consciousness as Originary Consciousness in a Threefold Sense. According to Husserl, then, perception of succession would be impossible if each slice of the extended perception were exclusively consciousness of the *Now*-phase of the object. The perceptual slice must also be conscious of past and future phases of the object. And that consciousness must be authentically *perceptual* in character if *perception* of succession is to arise through it. Indeed, Husserl argues that Franz Brentano denied authentic perception of temporal objects precisely because he restricted the sense of perception to perception of the Now-phase alone (13). The consciousness of elapsed or future phases of the object, according to Brentano, would be memorial or imaginative in character, not perceptual. Thus one would perceive tone *c* as Now and at the same time remember tones *a* and *b* in the way in which one might remember a melody heard a week ago. The consciousness of a temporal object would be in the main memory and expectation, and only in smallest part perception (23). One could not claim to perceive more than a single note of a melody, if that.

Husserl, on the other hand, argues that one may rightfully be said to perceive a melody, or at the least an extended portion of one (151-52). [4] He secures his position by pointing to an evident phenomenal distinction between the memory of an event or act that occurred at a moment relatively remote from the actual Now, and the consciousness of the just elapsed phases of a temporal object which one is presently perceiving. The latter intentionality is "originary consciousness of the past" (417), and can legitimately be called perception insofar as perception is "the act in which all origin lies, which constitutes originarily"

(41). The former consciousness, however, which is memory in the ordinary sense or "representation" (Repräsentation), "does not place an object itself before the eyes, rather just represents (*vergegenwartigt*) it" (41). Through the "originary" or perceptual consciousness, the past itself is *perceived* (39) or presented; through the representational consciousness it is simply remembered or represented. Indeed, memory presupposes prior perception—including perception of the past—insofar as what is remembered is intended as having been perceived.

It is of course true that the perceptual consciousness of elapsed phases as past differs from the Now-perception. In the latter, a phase of the temporal object is presented as Now, as "there itself" (232).[5] In the perception of the past, however, the phase of the object is no longer given as Now or even as there itself. It is, after all, a past phase. But it *is* "still present as just past" (212) relative to the actual Now; its being past is "something perceived" (213).

In the period 1901-1909, Husserl fixes the distinction between the two types of consciousness of the past by referring to the perceptual consciousness of just past phases as "primary memory" (41).[6] Memory of the further past is often termed "secondary memory" (418)[7] or, as we have seen, "representation." The immediate or perceptual consciousness of what is not yet Now is called "primary expectation" (39), in distinction from "expectation" of events or acts anticipated in the distant future.

Primary memory and primary expectation belong, together with the Now-perception, to the actual "slice" or momentary phase of consciousness. Indeed, it is precisely through primary memory and expectation that perception in *each* of its phases "reaches out beyond the Now. While the Now-perception "constitutes the pure Now," primary memory constitutes " 'a just having been', something preceding the Now intuitively" (41). Each slice of time-consciousness, then, *is* perception of the

Now-phase of the object, primary memory of elapsed phases, primary expectation of phases yet to come.

The threefold intentional structure of the individual phase of consciousness carries certain implications. First, a clear distinction must be drawn between the phases of the *object* intended in the various temporal modes and the intending slice of *consciousness* composed of Now-perception, primary memory, and primary expectation. Second, the primary memory and expectation belonging to a given phase of consciousness are not themselves past or future relative to the Now-perception belonging to that phase. Rather, they are all, one may say, "co-actual" or equally "Now."[8] On the other hand, the past or future phases of the object intended through primary memory and primary expectation *will* be past or future relative to the object's Now- phase intended through the Now-perception. These implications, we note in passing, have not always been appreciated by the commentators concerned with Husserl's early sketches on time—a fact which we will have occasion to discuss in a later section.

Finally, Now-perception, primary memory and expectation, forming the intentionality of a dependent momentary phase of consciousness, are not and cannot be independent acts in the sense in which an extended perception is.

Thus the perception of succession through a flow of consciousness is possible because each phase of the perception intends an extended part of the temporal object, preserves elapsed objective phases in the order in which they ran off for consciousness, and does so in an authentically perceptual manner.

C. *The "Schema 'Content of Apprehension–Apprehension' " as a Model for Constitution.* The structure of Husserl's theory described to this point will also hold, with some changes, in the case of his later interpretation. What distinguishes his first position is the explanation advanced for the *constitution* of Now-perception and primary memory.

That is, the explanation of the intentionalities of Now-perception and primary memory in terms of those elements and factors which make them possible. The model of constitution which Husserl applies to time-consciousness until about 1908 will be familiar to readers of the *Logical Investigations*: it is the "schema 'content of apprehension—apprehension'."[9] "*Time*," Husserl writes, "is a form of objectivity, it constitutes itself in moments of objectivating apprehension" (417).

1. The Schema Applied to Perceptual Experience. In order to facilitate the understanding of its application to time-consciousness, we will first illustrate the schema's role in the explanation of perceptual experience. According to Husserl, when we perceive an external object, a red barn, e.g., the transcendent reference is established through the animation of sensory "contents" *immanent* to consciousness by an appropriate "apprehension." The animation of such contents constitutes an immanent perceptual appearance (*Erscheinung*), or simply the perception of the object.[10]

The key to this conception of constitution rests in two connected theses. The first is that the immanent sensory contents, considered in themselves, are *neutral* with respect to external reference as such, or reference to any particular object. This neutrality thesis implies that the *same* content can furnish the basis for the perception of qualities of *different* external things—e.g., of the pink skin of a person or the pink painted surface of a department store mannequin.[11] The second thesis is that external intentional reference and the role the content will in fact play in a given instance depend upon the supervening apprehension.[12] As neutral materials for animation, the contents alone constitute neither transcendent reference nor, beyond a certain material quality (e.g., "pink"), the specific character of such reference. Those functions are the privilege of the animating apprehension.

It bears repeating that neither the contents nor the apprehensions are external objects; they are rather "immanent" to consciousness. They are therefore not perceived, except in specific reflective acts; they are instead "experienced" (*erlebt*), which is a nonthematizing or *marginal* form of consciousness. Thus while one *perceives* (*wahrnehmen*) the red barn one experiences (*erleben*) immanent sensory contents and apprehensions, or the appearances which the two together constitute.[13] Husserl is claiming, in effect, that consciousness is always self-consciousness, that when I perceive a red barn, I am aware not only of the barn but, in a marginal way, of my seeing it.

2. The Schema Applied to Time-Consciousness.

How, then, does Husserl apply this schema in explaining the constitution of time-consciousness, specifically of Now-perception, primary memory and expectation?

According to the schematic pattern, each of these modes of consciousness will be constituted through appropriate moments of content and apprehension. The locus of these constitutive elements will be the "Querschnitt" or slice of consciousness, insofar as the latter's threefold intentionality is Now-perception, primary memory, and primary expectation. The two connected theses discussed above—that the immanent contents are neutral materials and the specific intentional reference derives from the character of the apprehension which animates the contents—will be operative in the schematic interpretation of time-consciousness. Thus the apprehensions will play the decisive role in determining whether the consciousness constituted is Now-consciousness, consciousness of elapsed phases of the object, or consciousness of phases yet to come. Indeed, as early as 1901, in the course of discussing Brentano's theory that the origin of time-consciousness and the distinction between what is known as Now and what is known as past should be sought on the side of the content, Husserl writes that "I am inclined to place the distinction in the mode of apperception"

(174). And Husserl is so inclined because he believes that the contents are devoid of all temporal determinations—they are neither Now, nor past, nor future. Considered in themselves, they are simply "nontemporal material" (*Unzeitliche Materie*, 417) for time-constituting apprehensions. Just as the "pink" sensory data mentioned above were neutral in the sense that they could be animated by different thing-apprehensions, so the contents in the case of time-constitution are neutral with respect to the time-apprehensions.

But what is the nature of these apprehensions and how do they account for the constitution of Now-perception, primary memory, and primary expectation? To the extent that the three modes of time-consciousness are differentiated, they must be constituted through distinct moments of apprehension, and to the extent that they are all "perceptual" or "originary," their constituting apprehensions must possess that character as well. "An act which claims to give a temporal object itself," Husserl writes, "must contain in itself 'Now-apprehensions,' 'past apprehensions,' etc. specifically in the mode of originally constituting apprehensions" (39).[14] Thus if a melody is presented to consciousness and if through the present slice of the perception tone c is perceived as Now, the Now-perception will be constituted through the animation of a "c" content, often termed a "sensation" (*Empfindung*, 231) by a "Now-apprehension" (*Jetztauffassung*, 230). Further, the perception of c as Now will be accompanied by the primary memory of b as just past with respect to c. The apprehension responsible for the consitution of the primary memory will be a "past-apprehension" (*Vergangenheitsauffassaung*, 232) or "primary memorial apprehension" (319). This apprehension will animate a "gradually shaded content of apprehension" (234)—"shaded" because tone b, unlike the Now-tone c, has elapsed and therefore can no longer have an original sensory correlate in consciousness.[15]

It should be clear from the exposition

to this point that the contents and apprehensions belonging to a given slice of consciousness will be as numerous as the objective temporal phases intended through it. Since only one objective phase is intended as Now through any single perceptual phase, there will be only one Now-apprehension and only one "sensation" in a given perceptual slice. But since several objective phases will be perceived as elapsed in varying degrees, the perceptual phase will contain several past-apprehensions and corresponding contents. For example, in addition to the apprehension and content through which the primary memory of tone b as just past is constituted, the perceptual phase will contain another apprehension and content constituting the primary memory of a as still further past, and so on for whatever other objective phases are primarily remembered through that "Querschnitt".[16] There will be, in addition, a "future apprehension" (*Zukunftsauffasung*, 232) which will account for the constitution of primary expectation. Husserl, however, says little about this apprehension, never explaining whether there would be a plurality of such apprehensions in a given perceptual phase or what kind of contents they would animate, if any.

The sense of the schematic interpretation, then, is that each momentary phase of consciousness contains within itself a Now-apprehension, several past-apprehensions, future-apprehension, which in animating the proper contents together constitute the immediate consciousness of what is Now, of what is just past, and of what is not yet.

Each momentary slice of consciousness, in other words, really embraces, simultaneously, a double continuum—a continuum of apprehensions and a continuum of contents (231). In the intentional unity of these continua, "the originary past is constituted in continuous connection with the perceived Now" (234). Further, since the perceptual act is a continuum of phases or slices, and since each of these phases contains a continuum of contents and a continuum of

apprehensions, the total perception may be described as "a continuum of these continua" (231). Finally, returning to our original question, according to the schematic interpretation it is time-apprehension which accounts for the consciousness of temporal objects in the perceptual continuum, in the perceptual flow of phases springing into life and immediately dying away: "Only through the *temporal apprehension* is this becoming, for us, becoming in the mode of arising, passing, *enduring* and changing in the duration" (296).

D.   The Schematic Interpretation and the Absolute Consciousness. In the foregoing outline of Husserl's interpretation of time-consciousness in terms of the schema, a matter of fundamental importance has been left hanging fire. We observed, following Husserl, that the perception of a temporal object is itself a temporal object. Presumably, then, one is or could be conscious of its temporal character. For on what other grounds could the phenomenologist claim that it possesses such a character? According to principles already laid down in the *Logical Investigations* and noted earlier by us, the immanent act, and the contents and apprehensions constituting it, would be *experienced* (rather than perceived) temporal objects. We must ask, then, if Husserl's schematic interpretation is an explanation both of the perceptual consciousness of external temporal things or events *and* of the experiential consciousness of immanent temporal objects. The question, as we will see, is connected with the role of an absolute dimension of consciousness in Husserl's first interpretation. The conclusions we advance in regard to these matters, because of the difficulty and obscurity of Husserl's analyses, will involve a considerable degree of speculation and should be taken as tentative

1. The Focus of Husserl's Analysis prior to 1907. In texts written prior to 1907, texts in which the schematic interpretation predominates, Husserl cer-

tainly recognizes the distinction between *experienced* immanent contents and *perceived* external objects. Further, he affirms implicitly that there is an immanent time or time of consciousness by his claim that perception is itself a temporal object and by his insistence that the time of the perception and the time of the perceived object coincide (226) and further, that the temporal determinations of the external object are presented through those of the perception (179-80). Yet throughout this period, Husserl's attention seems to be focused, not on the constitution of the experiencing of immanent temporal objects, such as the perception or the sensory contents involved in it, but on the consciousness of the transcendent objects appearing through the perception or through its reproductive modifications, such as secondary memory or imagination. His vocabulary, his examples, the very model of the schema itself tend to support this conclusion. Of course, it might be argued that since each succeeding phase of the perception recapitulates within itself (in modified form) moments of content and moments of apprehension which had belonged to its predecessors, a consciousness of the extended perception is implicitly constituted within each of its phases. Husserl, however, does not appear to make this claim. He may, of course, have taken the matter for granted, but that would only buttress the suggestion that his main concerns at the time lay elsewhere. Finally, prior to 1907, Husserl is silent about the question of an absolute time-constituting consciousness immanent even to the experienced appearances, contents and apprehensions. The analyses rather seem restricted to two dimensions: that of the appearing transcendent temporal object and that of the perceptual act or appearance.

2. The Emergence of the Theme of the Absolute Consciousness. However, in a sketch written early in 1907 (or perhaps late in 1906),[17] in which a modified version of the schematic interpretation is developed, Husserl's attention does turn towards the consciousness of immanent temporal unities and, of signal importance, the theme of an absolute dimension of consciousness emerges for the first time. In the sketch in question, Husserl focuses on the "really immanent perception" (272) of an *immanent* tonal content. "Immanent tonal content" here signifies the sensory content which together with an appropriate "thing"-apprehension would constitute, for example, the perception or appearance of a violin-tone. In this case, probably in order to avoid discussion of transcendent reference, Husserl abstracts from the violin-tone apprehension and simply reflects on the perception of the pure tonal content.[18] The sense of that "perception," however, is obscure; it may be a synonym for "experiencing" (*Erleben*), although it is unlikely that it is quite that, or it may signify reflection, a thematizing act of consciousness. In the light of later analyses, it appears that Husserl has probably not clarified his position on the question. Despite the obscurity, however, the sketch leaves little doubt that Husserl now seeks to cope directly with the consciousness of the immanent temporal object, and it is obviously a key transition analysis in the direction of Husserl's more mature position.

An immanent temporal unity, of which the tone is an example, is, Husserl affirms, an authentic temporal object. "On both sides, that is both in the immanent as in the transcendent spheres of reality, *time is the irreducible form of individual realities* in their described modes" (274).

Husserl then proceeds to explain the consciousness of the immanent tone, as he earlier explained the consciousness of the transcendent object, in terms of the schema. Each moment of the immanent perception will "really"[19] contain a continuum of time-apprehensions and a sensation and series of shadings or profiles (*Abschattungen*) of former sensations which will serve as "representants" respectively, for the Now-phase and elapsed phases of the tone (282-83). Now the further conclusions drawn by Husserl about these contents and apprehensions can be understood only if it is appreciated that the temporal object "perceived" through them is immanent and not transcendent. Husserl insists, it will be recalled, that there is a fundamental distinction between the perceptual flow and its contents and apprehensions on the one hand, and the appearing transcendent object on the other. *He now proposes to draw a parallel distinction on the side of immanence itself*: "Immanence of the identical temporal object, the tone, must surely be distinguished from the immanence of the tone-profiles and the apprehensions of these profiles, which make up the consciousness of the givenness of the tone" (283). Husserl therefore differentiates two dimensions of immanence, *two dimensions within consciousness itself*, and claims that within one the consciousness of the other is constituted. Against the background of this distinction, Husserl introduces, for the first time in straightforward fashion, the notion of an absolute consciousness: "*Immanent can indicate the opposition to transcendent* [and] then the temporal thing, the tone, is immanent; but it can also indicate what exists in the sense of the absolute consciousness, [and] then the tone is not immanent (284). The immanent tone is not "given as *constituent of the absolute consciousness*" (284), it is rather intended by virtue of the contents and apprehensions which *are* constituents of that consciousness. And lest there be any doubt about the constitutive function of the "absolute consciousness," Husserl remarks with respect to any individual (immanent) object that "it pertains to the nature of this unity as temporal unity to be constituted in the absolute consciousness" (284). Finally, Husserl characterizes this ultimate constitutive dimension as a "flow of consciousness" (*Bewusstseinsfluss,* 284).

Thus only a short time before rejecting his schematic interpretation, Husserl points to a dimension of immanent conscious life which is ultimate in the strictest sense, which is not itself constituted, and which is the absolute foundation for the constitution of the consciousness of immanent temporal objects and presum-

ably through the latter (when a thing-apprehension comes into play), of transcendent objects. Nonetheless, the conception of the absolute time-constituting consciousness which here emerges probably does not coincide exactly with the sense of the ultimate dimension discussed in later texts. The sketch, we noted, is concerned with "immanent" or "adequate *perception*," a mode of consciousness which seems closer to objectivating reflection (if not identical to it) than to the experiencing (*Erleben*) of immanent objects, which is a marginal and not objectivating mode of consciousness. Indeed, the final sentence of the sketch—All non-objectivated objectivation belongs in the sphere of the absolute consciousness"—is not as it stands an adequate account of the relationship of the absolute consciousness and the experiencing of immanent objects as Husserl will express it later. For experiencing, as we will see, is the original consciousness of the immanent object and is identical with the absolute flow, but does not "objectivate" its correlate, if that term signifies a thematizing mode of awareness.

3. Early Elaborations of the Theme of the Absolute Consciousness. The distinction developed by Husserl in the 1907 sketch is confirmed in other texts of the period, apparently written before the rejection of the schematic view. Thus in a short sketch, dating from about 1907, Husserl distinguishes:
1. The flow of "consciousness"
2. The pre-empirical "time" with past, "Now," and after, and the pre-empirically "existent" (*Seiende*), the enduring and changing (tone as "content of consciousness")
3. The levels of empirical being (286-87)[20]

And in a sketch perhaps of somewhat later date Husserl clearly draws the line between two different kinds of content, a distinction quite in keeping with the segregation of two levels of immanence. We must not confuse, Husserl writes, "the contents in the sense of immanent temporal things, of individual objects in time—and the contents of the ultimate temporal flow, which do not endure and are not temporal objects, rather precisely the ultimate flow of consciousness" (293). No doubt his interest in the consciousness of the immanent content and his continued allegiance to the schema compel Husserl to affirm the difference. For as the immanent tonal content runs off for consciousness certain of its phases will have elapsed and will be known as past. And as Husserl said as early as 1901, "where we bestow the predicate *past*, or apprehend as past, there what is past is also really past"(152). The elapsed tonal phases therefore cannot be present as contents of apprehension in the actual momentary phase of consciousness. Yet according to the schema some content must be present if the elapsed phases of the immanent object are to be presented as past. Hence the necessity of affirming the "contents of the ultimate flow" which are distinct from, while serving as representants for, elapsed immanent objective phases. Further, while the enduring immanent tone is a temporal object, the representing contents of the flow do not endure and are not temporal objects in the authentic sense. Husserl very likely draws the latter conclusion because he thinks the contents disappear when the phase of the ultimate consciousness to which they belong flows away.[21] We will have occasion to note the prominence in later texts of the thesis that the absolute consciousness is not temporal in the sense of what is intended through it.

Before turning to the examination of Husserl's criticism of his interpretation of time-consciousness in terms of the schema, we venture the following conclusions about the role in that interpretation of an absolute consciousness and the awareness of immanent temporal objects. First, the schematic interpretation seems to have been concerned originally with the constitution of perceptual time-consciousness, i.e., the consciousness of transcendent temporal objects. Second, late in the development of the interpretation Husserl's attention turns towards the immanent domain, towards the consciousness of immanent temporal unities although he refers to the "perception" rather than the "experiencing" of such unities. Third, coinciding with the emergence of the new focus of attention is the appearance of the notion of an absolute consciousness. We also offer the following anticipation: the introduction of the absolute consciousness is followed rapidly by Husserl's criticism of the schematic interpretation, and the unambiguous focusing on the *experiencing* of immanent unities. We will now discuss Husserl's critique of his first position.

E. Criticism and Rejection of the Schematic Interpretation. Texts in which Husserl directly criticizes his first interpretation of the constitution of time-consciousness date from approximately 1908. Husserl's argument focuses on the schematic interpretation's thesis that each slice or momentary phase of consciousness actually contains, in the form of "real components" (*reelle Bestandstucke*, 232), series of contents and series of apprehensions. Through these moments, as we know, the extended temporal object supposedly is brought to givenness in the appropriate temporal modes. *In truth, however, the implication of such real containing is that consciousness of elapsed objective phases–in effect, consciousness of succession–would be impossible.* For the contents and apprehensions inhabiting the actual *Querschnitt* are themselves actual, are experienced as Now, as simultaneous (322). Husserl accordingly asks: "Can a series of *coexistent* primary contents ever bring a *succession* to intuition? A series of simultaneous red-contents a duration of red, of tone *c* and the like? Is that possible *in principle*?" (323). Husserl replies unequivocally that it is not (322-23). The point of the criticism is that the contents, contrary to the schema's requirements, are not *temporally* neutral. Since they are actually contained in the momentary phase of consciousness, since they are actually on hand, they are experienced as Now, and no time-apprehension can alter their temporal character. As *Now*-moments of the actual phase of consciousness, they cannot serve as representants for elapsed or future phases.

This argument would apply both to the experiencing of immanent temporal objects and the perceiving of transcendent objects, although in the sketches critical of the schema Husserl again does not clearly differentiate the two forms of consciousness. As far as the consciousness of the elapsed phases of the immanent perception is concerned, the moments of content experienced as "Now" cannot serve as representants for the past phases *as* past. Even if replications of the contents and apprehensions which had belonged to elapsed moments of consciousness were present in the actual conscious slice, they would be experienced as Now and not as past. No experiential consciousness of the extended act or appearance would be constituted. And since transcendent temporal phases are brought to appearance through the immanent moments or contents, and with the same temporal determinations as the latter, the consciousness of the extended external object would also never be constituted.

There are two further criticisms of the schematic interpretation latent in Husserl's discussions but never explicitly developed. The first concerns the arbitrary character of temporal apprehension. *If* the contents were genuinely neutral with respect to time-determination, then tone *a*, for example, which objectively is Now, could in principle be apprehended as past (317). That it is in fact apprehended as Now is a piece of good fortune for which the theory does not account. The second argument raises the spectre of an infinite regress. If the contents occupying a given *Querschnitt* are experienced as Now, then this consciousness must be constituted by yet another level of constituting consciousness with its own momentary phases embracing experienced contents and apprehensions, and so on without end. It should be added that if this were the case, there could be no talk of an

absolute foundation of time-consciousness.

The schematic interpretation which was intended to account for the constitution of "outer" time-consciousness and perhaps of "inner" time-consciousness as well thus fails of its purpose. Its fundamental defect, as well as the new direction of analysis opening up, is probably best indicated by Husserl's exhortation: "One should not materialize (*verdinglichen*) the structure of consciousness, one should not falsify the modifications of consciousness" (324). Husserl came to view his schematic interpretation as just such a falsification. The generating and real containing in each momentary phase of consciousness of bits of temporally neutral content, and the "stamping"[22] on them of temporal determinations by apprehension, were materializations of consciousness which Husserl could no longer accept after 1908.

II. Husserl's New Interpretation of the Constitution of Time-Consciousness (1908-1911)

Husserl's new interpretation of the constitution of time-consciousness appeared for the first time in its main outlines in approximately 1909,[23] and seems to have reached maturity in 1911.[24] Two characteristics especially set it apart from the schematic view. First, it does not explain time-consciousness in terms of apprehensions and contents, of whatever sort. Second, it is primarily and unambiguously a theory of the *experiencing* of immanent temporal objects, and includes the identification of experiencing or inner time-consciousness with the absolute time-constituting flow.[25] Let us reflect first on the latter theme.

A.   Identification of Experiencing with the Absolute Time-Constituting Flow. Distinction between the Flow and the Immanent Object. In a sketch written sometime after the abandonment of the schema as a useful explanatory model for time-consciousness, Husserl mentions that in the *Logical Investigations* he had dealt with experiences (*Erlebnisse*) in the sense of *already constituted* immanent objects, and that they formed a "closed domain" (127). His attention thus directed, he did not distinguish between the experiencing or "sensing" (*Empfinden*) of immanent contents and the contents themselves, e.g., between the sensed "red" content and the sensing of it. This also seems largely true of those sketches in which Husserl advances his first interpretation of time-consciousness.[26] Exceptions might be those relatively late texts cited above in which the notion of an absolute consciousness is introduced while the schema is still maintained. No doubt Husserl's thought is evolving in those sketches, but they remain, as we noted, fundamentally ambiguous.

With the rejection of the schematic interpretation, however, Husserl breaks out of the "closed domain" decisively, and the ambiguity is dispelled. Indeed as early as 1908, Husserl distinguishes between the constituting "primal consciousness" (*Urbewusstsein*, 292), which is identified with experiencing or sensing, and the experienced or sensed contents, which are constituted " 'immanent' temporal unities" (292).[27] Husserl thus draws a sharp distinction *within consciousness itself* between two dimensions, one constituting in the ultimate sense, the other constituted but still immanent. And if the immanent object has a transcendent reference, then a third level would have to be distinguished: that of the transcendent temporal object.[28]

This distinction of intentional levels or dimensions and the shift of Husserl's attention towards the ultimate time-constituting flow is continually affirmed in the later sketches in which the new interpretation emerges: "We regard sensing as the original time-consciousness; in it is constituted the immanent unity, color or tone, the immanent unity wish, …etc." (107). And the texts leave no doubt that this "original time-consciousness" is the absolute consciousness, "the absolute time-constituting flow of consciousness" (73).

1. A New Terminology. If Husserl's new interpretation is above all an account of the experiencing of immanent objects, it follows that "Now-perception," "primary memory," and "primary expectation" will stand for the fundamental modes of *inner* time-consciousness. In fact, in 1909 when the new position emerges, Husserl's terminology undergoes a significant change, evidently reflecting the theoretical evolution. "*Now-perception*"—a misleading term when marginal inner consciousness is at stake—is much less frequently used after 1909. It is regularly replaced by "*primal impression*" (*Urimpression*) or "*primal sensation*" (*Urempfindung*). The primal sensation, Husserl writes, is "the *absolutely originary consciousness*" in which the actual phase of the immanent object "stands forth as present itself, as bodily now" (326). "*Primary memory*" and other synonyms for the immediate consciousness of the past, while still appearing in later texts, will frequently be replaced by "*retention*"[29] after 1909. And "*primary expectation*" will ordinarily give way to "*protention*." Thus each momentary phase of the ultimate consciousness will be at once primal sensation, retention, and protention. The intentional *correlates* of these three fundamental forms of inner time-consciousness will be the phases of the immanent *object* experienced in the modes *Now, past,* and *to come.*

2. Confusions in Interpretation. The distinction between primal impression, retention, and protention, and the temporal determinations Now, past, and future correlated with them, deserves special emphasis insofar as commentators on Husserl's early writings on time have often overlooked it. Thomas Seebohm, for example, situates the *Now* on the *same level* with retention and protention.[30] Seebohm in addition arranges the Now, retention, and protention in the form of a succession on a horizontal line: "Formula I: R— J— P," where "R = Retention; J = Jetzt; P = Protention."[31] But according to Husserl, retention and protention are *not* past or future with re-

spect to the Now; they are on a level dimensionally different from the Now and are co-actual with the primal impression which *intends* or experiences the Now moment. Alvin Diemer seems guilty of the same confusion when he writes of the "Now with all its horizons, with its retention as with its protention."[32] The Now, to be sure, does have a horizon, but that horizon is formed by past and future phases of the immanent object, not by retention and protention which, again, are on a different level. Finally Robert Sokolowski writes of the "now—retention—protention structure" which he calls "the unchanging form of inner consciousness."[33] Husserl's sketches, however, make it quite clear that the "unchanging form of inner-consciousness" is the threefold intentionality expressed by the terms *primal impression* (or sensation), *retention*, and *protention*. The Now should not be placed on the same level with retention and protention. The Now is rather the intentional *correlate* of primal impression and belongs properly with the past and future on the constituted immanent plane. The proper formulation would thus be: primal impression, retention, and protention, through which phases of the immanent object are experienced in the modes Now, past, and to come.

The terminological confusions discovered in the commentators are probably rooted in a deeper oversight: the failure to appreciate fully the distinction Husserl draws between the level of constituted immanent objects and that of the absolute time-constituting flow of consciousness. Robert Sokolowski writes, for example, that: "Intentional consciousness *is* a Now-point on the time continuum, and retentional consciousness is a retention point on this continuum. Each of them is a temporal phase."[34] This conception would indeed lead one to align the Now with retention and protention. But the view becomes plausible only if the distinction between absolute subjectivity and immanent temporal objectivity is suppressed. Husserl's point, however, is that primal sensation, retention, etc., are

not temporal phases themselves but *do* intend such phases. "The *primal sensation*," Husserl wrote in 1911, "with which the Now of the tone is constituted, cannot be the Now-red [sic] itself" (382). Subsequent sections of this paper will hopefully clarify further the distinction between the absolute flow and what it constitutes.

3. Descriptive Grounds for the Distinction between Two Dimensions within Consciousness. Husserl's insistence on the distinction between an absolute constituting flow and a constituted dimension within consciousness itself may initially strike the reader as peculiar. Husserl himself, in the writings on time we are considering, never directly justifies the difference on descriptive grounds. Yet one may offer a plausible account of what Husserl has in view. He is evidently arguing from the premise that consciousness is self-consciousness. That is, there is a kind of fissure between my acts, my sensory experiences, and so on, and the marginal awareness of them that I continually possess. Perhaps this gap is best represented by the implicitly recognized *abiding* character of the life of consciousness itself over against the implicitly recognized *transitory* character of any one act of consciousness or state of mind. This does not mean, of course, that one could be conscious without experiencing some act or state of mind. Husserl often affirms the inseparability in principle of the moments of the absolute flow and the moments of immanent content intended by them. Specifically, while it may be true that there is some difference between my present perception of a house and the ultimate stream of my consciousness, it is inconceivable that my perceiving should cease and only "pure consciousness" remain. Should my present perceiving not be followed by some act of feeling, etc., I would no longer be concious at all. Thus with his doctrine of the absolute consciousness, Husserl apparently attempts to live with two dimensions of consciousness which are indeed inseparable, but in some sense still distinct.

If the above account offers some justification for Husserl's distinction, it does not explain how the absolute consciousness is conscious of immanent objects. Nor does it explain how the awareness of the absolute flow itself is constituted—and some explanation must be forthcoming if the talk of an absolute flow is to be justified. Let us turn, then, to the question of the constitution of inner time-consciousness in Husserl's second interpretation.

B. The New Conception of Constitution. The new interpretation, developed against the background of the inadequacy of the schematic view, will of course not explain the constitution of inner time-consciousness through the animation of contents by special temporal apprehension. There will be no more talk of contents of the ultimate flow of consciousness, for the slice or momentary phase of the flow is purged of all contents: it "really" contains nothing but experiential consciousness. It simply *is* experiencing. Accordingly Husserl writes that retention of an immanent tone "is not to be dissected into 'sensed tone' and 'apprehension as memory' " (312). No moment of tonal content is "really on hand" (314) in primary memory, rather it "really contains consciousness of the past of the tone" (312). And that is all it contains.

1. The Double Intentionality of the Absolute Flow. The above consideration, however, does not reveal the distinctive character of the constitution of inner time-consciousness. That character is expressed in Husserl's new interpretation by the notion of the "double intentionality"[35] of inner consciousness, and particularly of retention. It is by virtue of the absolute flow's twofold intentional reference that, on the one hand, the temporal object, in some sense distinct from the flow itself, is constituted in its unity and, on the other hand, the unity of the absolute flow itself is constituted. "In the one, single flow of consciousness the immanent temporal unity of the tone is constituted and at the same time the unity of the flow of consciousness itself" (80).

The idea that the flow constitutes its own unity, in effect making itself known, may at first sight appear "scandalous," Husserl claims (378). The scandal evidently would derive from the apparent violation in this case of a principle which for Husserl is otherwise binding: what is intended, and what intends, belong to different dimensions. Thus the transcendent object, the red barn, is dimensionally different from the perceptual act through which it is known. So too the immanent act or content is in some sense distinct from the ultimate flow through which it is experienced. The ultimate flow itself, however, while indeed known in a marginal way, is not known through any dimension of consciousness different from or more ultimate than itself. "The self-appearance of the flow does not require a second flow, rather it constitutes itself as phenomenon in itself. The constituting and what is constituted coincide" (381). If this were not the case, Husserl would be forced to admit an endless series of successively more "ultimate" levels or dimensions of consciousness. It is the double intentionality, explaining how the flow can constitute within itself its own self-appearance while also accounting for the constitution of the marginal awareness of immanent objects, which will banish at once the scandal of self-constitution and the specter of infinite regress.

What is the specific organization of the flow, then, which makes possible the double constitution? We know that the absolute flow may be viewed in terms of a passage of phases or slices, one of which will be actual while the others will be post-actual. Each of these "absolute" phases possesses intentional reference to some *phase of an immanent object*, or phases of several immanent objects insofar as one may simultaneously experience a plurality of acts, feelings, etc. But each phase of the flow in addition is intentionally related to *other phases of the flow*. In approximately 1911, Husserl points to this difference in intentionality by distinguishing between two sorts of retention, and between what he calls the "vertical" and "horizontal" intentionalities of consciousness.

a. The vertical intentionality of the flow. Primal sensation, we noted, is that intentional moment of the absolute flow by virtue of which a phase of the immanent object is experienced as Now. When the immanent Now-phase has elapsed it is still retained in consciousness, but now in the mode of the just past. The immediate consciousness of this elapsed phase of the immanent object Husserl terms "consciousness of the past" (*Vergangenheitsbewusstsein,* 377). Distinct from secondary memory, this mode of intentionality might be described as a "species" of what Husserl ordinarily simply terms retention or primary memory. Together with the primal sensation and protention of the immanent object, it forms the "vertical intentionality" (*Querintentionalität,* 380) of the flow—that is, the flow's consciousness of the immanent object in the modes Now, past, and to come. That the intentionality is termed "vertical" signifies that the intending absolute consciousness is of a different and more ultimate dimension than the immanent object which it intends.

b. The horizontal intentionality of the flow. Turning now to the absolute dimension itself: when a constituted phase of the immanent object has elapsed, the constituting phase of the ultimate flow which originally experienced the objective phase as Now (in primal sensation) will have also elapsed, and will have been replaced by a new actual slice of the ultimate consciousness which experiences a new objective moment as Now. The just elapsed phase of the absolute flow, however, is no more lost to consciousness than the just elapsed phase of the immanent object. *It too is retained by the new actual phase of the absolute consciousness.* Thus Husserl distinguishes a second immediate consciousness of the past the consciousness "*of the earlier primal sensation* (Now-consciousness)" (377), which he terms "retention," apparently applying the name of the genus to the second of its species. *Thus the actual phase of the absolute flow has intentional reference to the just elapsed phase of the flow.* And not simply to the moment of primal sensation of the elapsed phase, as the citation above might suggest. For the elapsed phase, just as the actual one, possesses its own retentional moment, and that too is retained. Thus Husserl speaks of "retention of retention" (81), which makes possible within the flow an awareness of an extended series of its phases in the order in which they emerged into actuality and subsequently elapsed. Put concretely, if the third of three successive phases of the absolute flow is actual, then that "third phase [is] once more new primal sensation with retention of the second primal sensation and retention of the retention of the first, etc." (81).

The retention of retention is, in effect, the flow's *self-retention* and thus is at the core of the constitution of the flow's self-appearance. As early as 1909, Husserl writes that as the flow develops, "*a steady continuum of retention* is engendered *such that every later point is retention for every earlier one*" (29). Husserl does not mean thereby that each retention is actually a continuum of phases, or that it really contains such a continuum. Rather, each is "*consciousness* of a continuum," more precisely "consciousness which continually bears within itself intentionally all earlier memorial consciousness in modification of the past" (327). Insofar as this intentionality extends throughout or along the flow itself, Husserl describes it as "horizontal intentionality" (*Längsintentionalität,* 379), in distinction from the flow's vertical intentionality directed towards the immanent temporal object. Through the horizontal intentionality, the flow itself becomes "apprehensible in the flowing" (381) and both the apparent scandal of self-constitution and the specter of infinite regress are banished. And we may add, reverting to terms familiar from the investigation of the schematic interpretation, that thanks to the horizontal intentionality the succession of consciousness *is*, in this case, the consciousness of succession (332).

2. Inseparability of the Two Inten-

tionalities. The preceding discussion of the two intentionalities of the absolute consciousness may suggest that they are separable. The vertical intentionality has been described as the flow's consciousness of the immanent object; the horizontal intentionality as the flow's consciousness of itself. Husserl's texts indicate, however, that while the two may be distinguished, they are not separable in principle. Thus, following a description of the two intentionalities, Husserl writes that they are "inseparably united, requiring one another like two sides of one and the same thing, and are interwoven into the one, solitary flow of consciousness" (381). No doubt the inseparability of the intentionalities derives from the inseparability of their intentional correlates, the absolute flow itself and the dimension of immanent objectivity. We earlier discussed Husserl's thesis that within consciousness itself there can be distinguished two dimensions, and we alluded to certain descriptive grounds which might justify the thesis. But in drawing the distinction, Husserl does not lose sight of the fact that in the end *one* consciousness is in question, which constitutes itself as an immanent temporal flow on the one hand, embracing its own contents, while abiding on the other hand in itself as sheer experiencing of what it constitutes, a kind of endless reservoir of conscious life. It is in the *one* flow of consciousness, we recall, that "the immanent temporal unity of the tone is constituted and at the same time the unity of the flow of consciousness itself" (378). Thus the two constituting intentionalities are no more separable than the immanent content and the experiencing of that content. But they will be two—for that follows logically from Husserl's thesis that the one consciousness does possess two dimensions: "Two kinds of retentional series must be given, therefore in addition to the constitution of the flow as a unity through the 'inner' retentions, a series of 'outer' [retentions must be given]. The latter constitutes the objective time (a constituted immanence, external to the first but nonetheless immanent)" (118).

3. Horizontal Intentionality as a Condition for Vertical Intentionality. In his discussion of the flow's intentionalities, however, Husserl seems to go further than the mere citing of their inseparability. He appears—the provisional language is intended—to claim in addition that the horizontal intentionality is a *condition* for the vertical intentionality. Thus he writes in 1911 that retention intends "what was previously known in the mode of the Now, in a primal sensation. ... *In a certain way*, however, it represents the earlier time-point known in the mode of the Now by presenting the primal sensation" (376; italics mine).

This implies, as we understand it, that elapsed immanent *objective* phases are retained insofar as the elapsed phases of the ultimate flow, which originally intended the objective phases, are also retained. Thus the (vertical) intending of tone *a* as just past is conditioned by or dependent upon the (horizontal) intending of the elapsed phase *of the flow* originally correlated with tone *a*. As for elapsed objective phases preceding tone *a* in some definite order, they would be experienced in the appropriate temporal modes of the past by virtue of the retention of retention which is proper to each phase of the flow. "Retention of a retention has intentionality not only in relation to what is immediately retained [that is, the just elapsed phase of the flow], rather also in relation to what is retained of the second level in the retaining [that is, the "next" phase of the flow] and ultimately in relation to the primal datum [the objective phase correlated with the retained flow-phase]" (81; remarks in brackets are mine). Thus the horizontal intentionality, preserving in proper sequence the elapsed phases of the absolute flow, at the same time preserves the intentional correlates of those phases on the immanent objective level, thereby making possible the flow's vertical intentionality. In the last analysis, then, to be aware of the absolute flow *is* to be aware of the extended temporal objects correlated with it. The horizontal and vertical intentionalities are indeed two sides of one and the same thing. This need not appear paradoxical if it is kept in mind that, according to Husserl, the flow simply is the experiential awareness of the immanent object, and thus that there could be no awareness of the elapsed immanent object *as elapsed* apart from our present (implicit) awareness that we had been aware of it earlier. But such present awareness of our having been aware of the object just *is* awareness of the flow. If one were not thus aware of the flow, one could not be aware of the elapsed object or *any* temporal object at all. There is reason, then, for the claim that the two intentionalities are two sides of the same thing.

C. *The Absolute Flow of Consciousness and Temporality.* In order to complete the discussion of the absolute flow of consciousness something must be said about its relation to temporality. It will be recalled that when Husserl introduced the concept of an absolute consciousness into his schematic interpretation he hesitated to say that the absolute "contents" were themselves in time. With the emphasis on the absolute flow in the new view, its status with respect to time becomes of central concern.

The temporal predicates "Now, before, after" apply to individual objects or processes, to an immanent tone, for example. All such individuals, as temporal objects, begin, endure, cease, change in various ways. The phases of the absolute flow, however, are not individuals in that sense, and so "the predicates of such cannot be meaningfully attributed to them" (370). Apparently for this reason, Husserl states typically that "the consciousness of the immanent tone as originary inner consciousness can have no immanent temporality" (96).

But inevitably, in light of the description of the ultimate consciousness as a flow or succession of phases, Husserl has more to say on the matter. For if the flow is a succession of slices or phases, each in its turn replacing its predecessor as the privileged moment of actuality, each preserving those phases which have gone before and anticipating those which are not yet, then certain of the phases will be known as *elapsed* or as *to come*, while one will be experienced as *actual*. So there is a kind of temporality constituted in and proper to the flow itself, but "for all this we have no names" (371), presumably because the "names," the temporal predicates, are applied already and with full legitimacy to the constituted immanent objects. But Husserl does not for that reason feel condemned to silence about the ultimate flow's "temporal" character: "This flow is something which we speak of *in conformity with what is constituted*, but it is nothing temporally 'objective' " (371). The point Husserl seeks to establish is that we are forced to apply to the flow itself a vocabulary which appropriately belongs to the vertical intentional *correlates* of the flow, the immanent objects, but that this may be done if it is recognized that the terms do not apply to the two dimensions "in the same sense" (370). Put differently, it must be kept in view that the absolute consciousness, despite the application of "objective" predicates to it, is constituting in the ultimate sense and thus distinct from the constituted objective dimension, even though that dimension is itself immanent. Indeed, Husserl on occasion does try to convey linguistically the distinction between the two temporalities by the use of certain prefixes and qualifiers. Through the flow's vertical intentionality, he writes, "the immanent time, an objective time, an authentic time" (381) is constituted, while through the horizontal intentionality, the flow itself is constituted "as a one-dimensional quasi-temporal order" (380). Or he claims that the flow is possessed of a "pre-phenomenal or pre-immanent temporality" which "constitutes itself intentionally as the form of the time-constituting consciousness and in it itself" (381). The "temporal order" is "quasi" because the flow does not possess the properties of constituted temporal objects. But there is a kind of temporal order to the extent that the absolute flow does break down into phases, into actual and pre-actual and

post-actual phases, running off in perpetual succession. Further, the flow's
temporality is "pre-immanent" insofar as
the flow is the *consciousness of* the immanent object in immanent time. Husserl's description of the flow's temporality as "pre-phenomenal" is more
troublesome at first glance, however. Indeed, Husserl observes in the same
sketch in which "pre-phenomenal"
temporality is mentioned that the absolute flow "constitutes itself as a phenomenon in itself" (381). But Husserl probably means by "pre- phenomenal" simply
that absolute subjectivity brings *itself* to
givenness, and thus too *its* temporality,
while the phenomenal time of the immanent object is brought to givenness by a
flow of consciousness other than itself.
Again, the terminology aims at distinguishing the constituting and constituted
dimensions. Admitting that distinction,
Husserl's point is that just as immanent

objects are invariably experienced
through absolute subjectivity in the
threefold temporal form of Now, before,
and after, so analogously the absolute
flow of time-consciousness and its phases
are self-given in the form of the actual,
pre -actual, and post-actual—that is, in a
pre-immanent, quasi-temporal order.

The purpose of this discussion has been
the exposition of the development and
main features of the notion of an absolute
consciousness in Husserl's writings on
time during the first decade of the century. What relation this notion might bear
to the later concept of transcendental subjectivity, or whether it might illuminate
the nature of Husserl's egology, are questions not answered here—but they certainly become intriguing questions in the
light of what Husserl had to say about
time-consciousness, "that most difficult
of all phenomenological problems" (276).

NOTES

1. Edmund Husserl, *Zur Phänomenologie des Inneren Zeitbewusstseins* (1893-1917), ed. Rudolf
Boehm, *Husserliana X* (The Hague: Nijhoff, 1966).
Page numbers of texts cited or directly quoted from
Husserliana X in this article will be given in parentheses immediately following the reference or
quotation.
2. From 1901 through at least 1907 Husserl ordinarily employs "Wahrnehmung" to express the
"original" time-consciousness in opposition to
memory, expectation, or imagination. We will say
more about Husserl's terminology as we continue.
3. Meinong, Husserl claims, held that each phase
short of the final one intends *only* the Now-point of
the object. Thus one would not hear an extended
melody until the *end* of the perception.
4. "The *entire melody* is perceived" (38).
5. Es das Wesen der Jetztwahrnehmung ist, das
Jetzt direkt zur Anschauung zu bringen" (41).
"Jetztwahrnehmung" is a common term in Husserl's texts through at least 1906. A synonym for
"Wahrnehmung" or "Jetztwahrnehmung" infrequently used at this time is "Impression" or
"Urimpression" (67). Later, the vocabulary of
"Wahrnehmung" will be largely replaced by a terminology built on "Impression" and "Empfindung."
6. "*Primary memory (primäre Erinnerung) is
perception.* For only in primary memory do we *see*
what is past, only in it does the past constitute itself,
namely not representatively but presentatively
(*präsentativ*)" (41). Among the synonyms for "pri-

mary memory" employed during this period is
"frische Erinnerung." See, e.g., p. 165.
7. "Die sekundäre Erinnerung." Synonyms include "Reproduktion," "Wiedererinnerung." Occasionally Husserl will use "Erinnerung" without
qualifying it, or some other terminology which may
suggest *secondary* memory, when he is in fact discussing *primary* memory. The context ordinarily
makes clear the sense in which the term is being
used.
8. Husserl will occasionally say that primary
memory is "Now" (cf. 175), meaning that it is co-
actual with the Now-perception in forming a single
phase or "Now" *of consciousness.*
9. Husserl also refers to the schema as "meine
Repräsentationstheorie" (p. 319).
10. "Es ist der Aktcharakter der die Empfindung
gleichsam beseelt und es seinem Wesen nach
macht, dass wir dieses oder jenes *Gegenstandliche*
wahrnehmen, diesen Baum sehen, jenes Klingeln
hören..., *Logische Untersuchungen* (5th ed.;
Tubingen, 1968), II, 1, p. 385. "Aktcharacter" is a
synonym for "Auffassung." Another common
synonym is "Apperzeption."
11. Edmund Husserl, *Erfahrung und Urteil*
(Hamburg, 1964), pp. 99-100.
12. Thus Husserl writes in a sketch dated approximately 1908 (*Husserliana X*, no. 48): "Alles bloss
Unterschiede der Auffassung, die sich an den übri-
gens erlebten und im Bewusstsein seienden Inhalt
nur anschliesse, ihn 'beseelend' " (319).
13. *Logical Investigations*, p. 385. Around 1907

Husserl wrote: "Jedes Erlebnis ist 'Bewusstsein,' und Bewusstsein ist Bewusstsein von... Jedes Erlebnis ist aber *selbst erlebt,* und *insofern* auch 'bewusst'. *Dieses* Bewusst-sein is Bewusstsein vom Erlebnis" (*Husserliana X* [291]). "Erlebnis" here refers to anything immanent to consciousness: sensory content, apprehension, appearances or acts. In the same sketch (No. 41), Husserl distinguishes between "erleben" and thematizing acts of consciousness such as perception in terms of "being directed towards." We are directed towards the house in a perceptual act, but not towards the experienced immanent house-appearance (289). We anticipate later discussion by noting that the experiencing of immanent contents and objects will be of central significance in Husserl's final interpretation, and will in fact be identical with the "absolute flow" of consciousness.

14. Husserl indicates that the time apprehension is an apprehension "in a fundamentally different sense" (320-21) from the "thing-apprehension" which in animating a sensory content constitutes an appearance of a transcendent object. Indeed, the appearance phase—and therefore the "thing-apprehension"—would be temporally neutral material for the time-apprehension. For example, the fact that a violin-tone appears depends upon a violin-tone apprehension. But that the tone appears as Now, or as elapsed, depends upon the Now-apprehension or the past-apprehension. Thing-apprehensions could not exist apart from time-apprehensions insofar as perceived external objects always appear as temporal.

15. At one point Husserl suggests that the content of apprehension in the case of primary memory would be a "phantasm" (233-34), but later rejects that suggestion (296), probably because he understands phantasms to be contents which serve in the constitution of *secondary* memory. Elsewhere Husserl does not distinguish at all between the contents for Now- and past-apprehensions (e.g., no. 46, 310-11). Husserl probably never quite made up his mind about the contents which enter into the constitution of primary memory.

16. In one text (66-67), Husserl appears to distinguish two different types of time-apprehension, one accounting for the preservation of elapsed objective phases in a definite order, the other for the appearance of the phases in continuously changing modes of the past relative to the Now. Whether or not Husserl actually intended to distinguish two apprehensions here, it remains true that time-apprehension, whatever its form, will exercise these two functions.

17. No. 39, 269-86.

18. The sensory content, apart from apprehension, lacks transcendent reference. The appearance (*Erscheinung*) constituted through the animation of the content by the apprehension does have such

reference, and is itself an immanent object.

19. "Reell" (276). The term signifies that the elements in question actually exist in or compose the *Querschnitt* or momentary phase of consciousness, and are not merely intended by it. The term will be important in Husserl's criticism of the schematic interpretation.

20. In the edition of 1928 a version of this text, probably revised by Edith Stein, appears in *Husserliana X,* no. 34, 73. There the flow is called "den absoluten zeitkonstituierenden Bewusstseinsfluss."

21. There is a hint of this position in an earlier text (1904) written before Husserl clearly distinguishes two levels of immanence. The text concerns the *apprehensions* belonging to a given phase of consciousness: "To the act-form corresponds the categorical moment of time; is is the act-form of the 'object,' of the temporal content. But is this moment itself time? That is surely impossible" (229).

22. Husserl wrote in 1905 that primary memory "simply holds what has been generated in consciousness and stamps (*prägen*) on it the character of the 'just past' " (37).

23. In no. 50, *Husserliana X,* pp. 324ff.

24. In no. 54, *Husserliana X,* pp. 368ff.

25. "Flow" is of course a metaphor, and Husserl is aware of that: inner time-consciousness "is *absolute subjectivity,* and has the absolute properties of something to be designated *metaphorically (im Bilde)* as 'flow' (*fluss*)" (371).

26. "Empfindung" in earlier sketches indicated a *content* and not the sensing *of* an immanent content as it usually does in later texts.

27. In about 1909 Husserl wrote that "sensation...designates the whole time-constituting consciousness, in which an immanent sensuous content is constituted" (326, n. 1).

28. Key later references to the three levels are found on p. 358 and p. 371.

29. As Boehm points out, the term "retention" was first used unambiguously in the sense of "primary memory" in about 1909, in no. 50, the first sketch in which the new interpretation appears (333).

30. Thomas Seebohm, *Die Bedingungen der Möglichkeit der Transzendental-Philosophie* (Bonn, 1962), p. 115.

31. Ibid., p. 120.

32. Alwin Diemer, *Edmund Husserl: Versuch einer Systematischen Darstellung seiner Phänomenologie* (rev. ed.; Meisenheim am Glan, 1965), 2: 125.

33. Robert Sokolowski, *The Formation of Husserl's Concept of Constitution* (The Hague, 1964), p. 85.

34. Ibid., p. 88.

35. The "double intentionality," Husserl writes, is the "essential constitution" of the flow (378).

Phenomenology as Transcendental Theory of History*

LUDWIG LANDGREBE

I

This title indicates the thesis to be established in the following remark: *If phenomenology is to be transcendental philosophy and is thought through to its ultimate consequences, then phenomenology is a transcendental theory of history.* This thesis leaves in the background—one might even say "brackets"—the question whether phenomenology should or must be *transcendental*. As is well known, this question was debated by Husserl's students from the time he made the so-called "transcendental turn" in his *Ideas*. But resolution of this controversy presupposes that the meaning of the word 'transcendental' for Husserl has been made clear, and that this meaning is to be fathomed solely in the context of his work. One cannot simply grant this expression the meaning it had *before* Husserl. Thus the following remarks will refer to Husserl, but they can be understood as a contribution to Husserl-interpretation only with reservations.

There is already an unmanageable number of conflicting interpretations. It is almost as if their differences depend on the passages and quotations that are cho-

*Translated by José Huertas-Jourda and Richard Feige, with many thanks to Mr. Harry P. Reeder for his invaluable help in tidying up the English and typing the manuscript.

sen from the multilayer texts of Husserl to support these interpretations. This controversy touches almost all the fundamental operative concepts of Husserl which have been shown not to be unequivocal. But most of the recent investigations of Husserl's phenomenology have a common basis in his later works and the manuscripts of the last period, which interpret the early works as steps on the way to his final insights. In doing so they follow a fashion according to which only the late work of a thinker produces the final and decisive thoughts, on the basis of which all his previous results are merely preparation. Furthermore, this methodological principle has shown its fruitfulness especially here, inasmuch as it can demonstrate that no break can be found in the development of Husserl's thoughts. Rather, from the beginning they follow a guiding intention, which, of course, in its development only slowly achieves clarity about what it aimed at from the beginning.

That this should be so accords with Husserl's notion of intentionality and the relation of intention to fulfillment as a path from darkness to clarity. The procedure according to which one argues against the earlier Husserl on the basis of the later one has been used by all the recent investigations, which has advanced matters in some way and has been proved justified through its success. Consequently, a critical examination of Husserl's transcendental philosophical design must miss its goal if it rashly uses a standard which arises from a different philosophical starting point. With all the possibilities it contains, Husserl's position must first be completely thought through. Only then can one see where, roughly, the limits of the possibility of a transcendental philosophical reflection lie and where one has to go beyond them with other procedures.

Should the demarcation of these limits be gathered from Husserl's later reflections, his philosophy could justifiably lay claim to the title "transcendental philosophy"—"transcendental" in the sense that under this heading a manner and method of knowledge is to be understood which makes it possible for knowledge initially to lay down its own limits. This concept of "transcendental" would also agree with what Husserl stated in a manuscript that apparently was written after the conclusion of—and looking back on—the *Crisis* and that is related, above all, to the "Galileo Appendix" (appendix IX of the *Crisis,* pp. 389-400). He spoke there of the acute difficulties of this text: that "in such a historical method of questioning things there will gradually arise a style of philosophic questioning which is new in principle, and a new method of philosophical work." To its complete meaning belongs

the interweaving of historical investigations and the systematic investigations they motivate, arranged from the start according to that peculiar sort of reflexivity through which alone the self-reflection of the philosopher can function—the philosopher, who is in the position of not being able to presuppose any pregiven philosophy, his own or another.[1]

Husserl's use of the word 'transcendental' is formally equivalent to the Kantian use, namely, "critical": a critique of the use of traditional philosophic concepts, the question concerning the *quid juris?* (legitimary) of their use for explaining our experience. In this sense 'transcendental' means nothing but absolute opposition to any type of dogmatism whatsoever—not only the

dogmatism of metaphysics, which was what Kant attacked, but also the critique of the hidden metaphysical implications of the modern anti-metaphysical positions.

Generally speaking, therefore, a transcendental philosophy entails the *critique of any unexamined usage of all traditional philosophic concepts* by means of which the understanding of our world, and ultimately a comprehensive cosmology, might be achieved. In this sense it is at the same time both a critique of linguistic usage and a theory which critically examines metaphysical and anti-metaphysical cosmological theories. Since all attempts at a cosmology, in their original sense, were not mere theories but—far more—attempts at reaching an understanding of the world in order to find the right way to live in it, such theories always entailed practical principles of behavior. Accordingly, the transcendental critique of these theories is at the same time a critique of the principles of behavior which follow from them. This intimate connection could obviously be demonstrated in the coining of the concept of *theoria* by Aristotle. Husserl too wanted his transcendental phenomenology understood as a "critique of life."

So much for the provisional understanding of the concept "transcendental" and the sense in which phenomenology should be understood as transcendental theory. Nothing has as yet been said about "history" (*Geschichte*) as the theme of this transcendental theory. As is well known, the word 'history' has at least two senses: it can mean *res gestae* (historical event) as well as *historia rerum gestarum* (the science of history). The proposed thesis does not claim that transcendental phenomenology will be discussed only insofar as it is a theory about the scientific knowledge of history, nor, even, that it will be limited to such a theory, which belongs to the formerly so-called humanities and social sciences (*Geisteswissenschaften*). For if such a theory is understood as a philosophical problem, a level of reflection is thereby indicated which is subordinate to transcendental philosophical reflection and which can only be founded upon it. Transcendental phenomenology is above all concerned with the question "What is history?"—or "*What are the transcendental conditions for the possibility that such a thing as history exists for us,* which can then be the object of scientific research?" In this sense, Husserl has inquired into the "*a priori of history*." This a priori will now be shown to have its very own character.

A transcendental philosophical reflection cannot simply accept the boundaries between the particular sciences as given since, for the most part, these boundaries stem from the requirements of their modes of inquiry and have become, for the most part, questionable. Because of this, neither can we resort to Husserl's outline of regional ontologies in the second volume of *Ideas,* which pioneered Heidegger's orientation in *Being and Time,* since this outline accepted the then valid division of the scientific fields simply as given. This outline stems from a static observation. Transcendental phenomenology, however, reached its full meaning only as *genetic* phenomenology—which requires no further justification here.[2] Accordingly, phenomenology as transcendental theory of history can only be *genetic* phenomenology. Certainly its results will be shown to be important *also* for the theory of scientific knowledge, and history will be shown to include more than the aggregate of the *res gestae.* Therefore the sense in which history is spoken of in this thesis must be held in suspense for the moment.

A transcendental theory of history presupposes an adequate theory of intersubjectivity. This too can only be developed as a genetic theory. It has now been proved that Husserl's theory of intersubjectivity in the Fifth Cartesian Meditation failed because Husserl attempted to develop it through static phenomenology.[3] Nor have his later attempts, available now in volume XV of *Husserliana,* reached this goal, although some of his

later reflections indicate how this gap can be closed. We shall return to this later.

II

After these introductory remarks, let us proceed to establish this thesis, which must now be somewhat expanded: *Transcendental genetic phenomenology is, as such, transcendental theory of history.* This thesis is connected to two of Husserl's thoughts, which at first glance appear incompatible with each other. The first concerns the character of the transcendental "Ego," whose world-constituting achievements (*Leistungen*) are the subject of phenomenology. The phenomenological reduction leads back to the apodictic self-certainty of this Ego (*Ich*), which is present immediately to itself in this reflection. In this self-presence of its constituting functions it is apodictically certain of itself and can know, in eidetic variations, these functions as necessarily belonging to any thinkable Ego at all. Of course, Husserl stressed repeatedly from the outset that such a reflection is always carried out by a self which in fact exists. But according to the doctrine of essences developed earlier in *Ideas*, a particular fact is accidental by contrast to its essence. Only after 1931 is this thesis reversed in manuscripts (in part unpublished):

"The eidos transcendental Ego is unthinkable without a transcendental Ego as factual" (*Husserliana*, XV: 385), "for I myself, who reflects, varying himself in free phantasy and thereby releasing himself through variations on his own factual reality, am apodictically the Ego of factual reality, and am the Ego of abilities which in particular I have acquired for myself in fact as an I eidetically thinking and seeing. The possibilities of phantasy as variants of the eidos are not free floating but constitutively relate to me in my factuality, with my living present which I 'live' factually."[4]

Therefore "the apodictic structure of transcendental reality [is] not one that is contingent in virtue of that ability to vary himself in phantasy—[it is not] an accidental factuality with an essential framework of other possibilities which might equally well have existed. Hence this Ego, which I myself am, must be called an *absolute fact* (*absolutes Faktum*)" (ibid., p. 148).

"I am the proto-fact (*Ur-Faktum*) in this course of questioning back ... the absolute, which has its foundation in its self and in its groundless being it has its absolute necessity as the one 'absolute substance.' Its necessity is not the necessity of essences, which would leave the accidental open. All essential necessities are much more aspects of its factuality (*seines Faktums*) ...[they] are ways of understanding or being able to understand one's self" (*Husserliana*, XV: 386). "The absolute that we reveal is an absolute matter of fact (*absolute Tatsache*)" (ibid., p. 403).

At first sight these theses seem strange. With them, do we not go beyond the limits of a transcendental philosophy and pass into a metaphysics of the Absolute which might recall Schelling's "positive philosophy"? Eugen Fink previously rejected such an interpretation.[5] He was familiar with these thoughts from the time of their origin (1931) when Husserl was working on the attempt (which he later abandoned) to revise the German text of *Cartesian Meditations*. It is in no way a question of a transition to speculative metaphysics; rather it is a question of a "perplexed conception of philosophic borderline cases," which stem from the tireless attempt to catch red-handed, so to speak, the living process of transcendental consciousness through reflective analysis. If it succeeded, this would be a special strengthening of the justification of phenomenology's claim to the title "transcendental." It would thereby have demonstrated that it is in a position critically to make evident to itself its own limits.

To gain clarity in this, let us juxtapose the thesis about the absoluteness of the transcendental Ego with the thesis about history which is found in the concluding paragraph of a research manuscript on "the transcendental reduction and abso-

lute justification." This thesis is "History is the grand fact (*das grosse Faktum*) of absolute being,"[6] and this concluding paragraph has received the subtitle "Monadology" in Husserl's manuscript. First of all, two pertinent points are to be noted:

1. This manuscript was written in the early twenties; it is therefore not true that Husserl discovered the bearing history has on phenomenology only in the last phase of his thought. This discovery must be understood not as a break in his thought but as a consequence of his earlier transcendental philosophical point of departure.

2. The manuscript also indicates the context from which Husserl's thesis about history arises: the *Monadology*. Interpretations up to now have paid too little attention to this title and therefore have ignored the problem that is hidden under the adoption of the Leibnizian term. In the adoption, the meaning of this term is changed. Leibniz's monads have no "windows"; however, in the context of transcendental phenomenology they designate the transcendental Ego. In this sense, Husserl speaks of transcendental intersubjectivity as the totality of monads.

Two questions follow from this:

1. What is the justification for using "monad" for the "transcendental Ego" which is an "absolute fact" in its apodictically certain presence of itself to itself?

2. How are the two theses about the "absolute" compatible with each other, or how do they go together to complement each other, and what follows from this for understanding Husserl's talk of "absolute" and for the transcendental-phenomenological concept of history?

It becomes apparent that the two questions cannot be dealt with separately. The very fact that they "go together" is *the transcendental-phenomenological problem of history*, which will subsequently be sketched in rough outline. In preparation for this, let us stress the *sense which the introduction of the concept of monad has for the scientific theory of history*.

One must remember that the fundamental thought of Herder's philosophy of history was demonstrably inspired by Leibniz's *Monadology*: the thought of individuality *per se* and of the temporal uniqueness of what is historical. It has its absolute sense in itself, and cannot be criticized only in consideration of its aftermath in history. Herder has thereby criticized the Enlightenment's theory of progress, and especially *Voltaire*'s, and thereby prepared the ground for the modern science of history. This critique is guided by interest in individual being. Leopold von Ranke repeated Herder's thesis in almost the same terms in lectures he delivered before King Maximilian of Bavaria on the periods of recent history. The credo of the science of history alone can provide understanding of the sense of objectivity required by it. This requirement of Ranke's was fought by the proponents of "political history," in particular by Gervinus: History must serve the interests of the day, the nation's interest in survival. Ranke emphatically opposed this thesis because he saw its relativistic consequences and the end of history as a science. In this confrontation it becomes apparent that *it is not the thought of individuality but, rather, ignoring it which leads to relativism* and which blocks the way to the truth of history.

This may suffice to show that mention of the controversy between Ranke and Gervinus is not a mere historical reminiscence but a fundamental problem about historical knowledge, which remains unsolved even today. In the early fifties, when the *Historische Zeitschrift* reported a discussion among American historians about the methodological principles according to which the Japanese attack on Pearl Harbor should be depicted, the very same positions were opposed to each other that had been taken up by Ranke and Gervinus. One might also recall the Bolsheviks' dealings with history, which, as is well known, has to be rewritten again and again according to the interests of the party. The issue is whether the truth of what is to be historically transmitted is limited to what is meaningful for the interests prevalent at a particular time or

whether—above all other issues—it must be appreciated in its individuality "as it actually happened." The theory of history of the southwest German school of neo-Kantianism exhibited strong awareness of this problem since it attempted to differentiate "ideographic" historical knowledge from the "nomothetic" knowledge of the natural sciences. Discussion of the way in which the neo-Kantian theory attempted to solve the problem of individuality by the concept of value-relation must be omitted here, even though it might be of real import today because this theory of value-relation still has repercussions in the controversy over value-free social theory.

It is not claimed here that Husserl was influenced in his "discovery" of history by the development of the theory of history since Herder: nothing allows the conclusion that he was in any way concerned with this development or, in particular, with Herder. *His own investigations led to the "primordial fact" of individuality in history,* and he can be shown to have discovered a better foundation for historical truth by following this path than if he had followed the path offered by the neo-Kantian theory of history. From this it should be apparent, first of all, that the appropriation of Leibniz's term 'monad' to designate the absolute fact of the transcendental Ego in its living self-presence is not the introduction of a mere "expression born of perplexity"; rather, with this term's introduction *the central problem of the grounding of truth is envisaged, just as it is present to historians even today.* But it is not just a problem about the scientific theory of history: beyond that, it concerns the relationship between men of each epoch or group and their history even *before* their history is known scientifically. The problem has special urgency at a time that is threatened by the loss of history and by tendencies to turn away from it.

III

This said, let us turn to the second question, which deals with the relation between the two theses—the first about the absoluteness of the "Ego" and the second about the absoluteness of history—as well as to the ensuing transcendental-phenomenological concept of history.

It has been pointed out that both Herder's philosophy of history and Husserl's "Monadology" harken back to Leibniz's thoughts about the monad. The historical background of Leibniz's monadology is the reformist thought of the immediacy of each man before God. This immediacy demands that each human monad be dependent on nothing other than God, who has created it. Therefore it must be "without windows"—enclosed upon itself. Only a preestablished harmony can ensure that the monads enter into commerce (*commercium*) with one another. However, transcendental phenomenology is not permitted such a metaphysical foundation for the theory of the monad and its commerce (*commercium*). By means of the reflection upon subjectivity that is characteristic of it, phenomenology must ground the introduction of the monad concept in such a way that the thesis about absoluteness retains its legitimacy. But in spite of this, the monad's commerce can occur. To do so, monads must not be thought of as without "windows." The task of phenomenological analysis is therefore to find the place where one is to look for "windows." For this, as we said, a theory of intersubjectivity is required which can answer the question about "windows."

To bring the problem into focus more sharply, we must first deal with the objection that unavoidably arises from the reference to the historical origin of the theory of the monad: Is such reflection not just a result of the modern history of thought, with its particular presuppositions which go back to Descartes— presuppositions which, in turn, are rooted in the still more remote history of Western thought? Other cultures, as is well known, have not developed this manner of reflection. The concepts of singularity and uniqueness, and in this sense the absoluteness of each human being, as a being equipped with the ability to think and reflect, are foreign to them. Thus we have to ask whether this concept of singularity is simply the result of a very specific Western cultural development and history—a thought which could only be formulated under very definite historical conditions. Therefore, can what is merely a historically conditioned matter of fact lead to apodictic insight into the unconditionally universal and necessary—a question already posed and answered negatively by Lessing?: "Historical facts can never become the proof of eternal truths." Therefore, can the reflective recourse to the "I am," as historically conditioned, lay any claim at all to being the path to insight into what we all are as members of the human race? This, at bottom, is the question Husserl posed for himself in the *Crisis*—the question about the universal meaning of the European manner of reflection according to its origin.

This question can now be formulated as follows. This way of inflecting leads Husserl to the thought of the absoluteness of the "transcendental Ego" as monad and, concerning its relation to history, to a remark which must be understood as the ultimate answer to his question about the "a priori" of history: The world is *historical* only "through the inner historicity of each particular person who, as an individual, is in his inner historicity, communalized with the other people."[7]

"Inner historicity" denotes, in Husserl's sense, a character of the monadic quality of singularity of each individual personal subject. Inner historicity is, accordingly, the "a priori," that is, the structure on the sole basis of which there is for us "*the one* history." Up to what point is a relationship thereby designated which holds for any personal subject whatever with apodictic generality, and which allows us at last to talk about a "history of mankind"? Why can the converse not be asserted if, on the other hand, it is held to be true that "history is the grand fact of absolute being?" The converse would have to read: History is the a priori presupposition of the inner historicity of each individual ego-subject. This would be possible only if the "monad" were already found in the context of history. Expressed in modern jargon, the inner historicity is nothing other than the internalization of history. Only under very definite historical conditions would such an internalization become possible and a concept of "historicity" be formed. It would, accordingly, have no binding force whatever beyond the realm of Western culture.

Only if it can be shown how transcendental phenomenological reflection is in a position to make a binding decision on these alternatives can the way Husserl's two theses belong together be understood and the claim that transcendental genetic phenomenology is a transcendental theory of history be established. To do this, we must now trace the meaning of the path of reflections by which Husserl was led to his two theses. One has to look more closely at the peculiar form of reflexivity which, according to the previously cited quotation, is characterized by intervening historical investigations and the systematic questioning back they motivate.

Husserl, who calls transcendental phenomenology in its full development into genetic phenomenology an "investigation of the origin," also calls it, ultimately, an "archaeology" of consciousness, since genetically it has for its subject the "deep layer" of passive preconstitution. The origin of all our presentations of what we experience and recognize is the constitutive functions of subjectivity that are accessible to reflection. For Kant, transcendental philosophy was guided by the question of the origin of our presentations. Trying to answer this question he distinguished this origin in reason and in time.[8] This distinction, however, is rejected by Husserl: "The current dogma of the separation in principle of epistemological explication from historical explanation and from genetic origin is . . .fundamentally mistaken."[9]

What, then, is the peculiar form of reflexivity in terms of which this claim can

be substantiated? It is not to be found in the list of current concepts of reflection which H. Wagner has assembled in his article "Reflexion."[10] To be sure, the Husserlian form of reflection is given there as "constitutive reflexion" ("Konstitutions reflexion"); it is the reflective tracing back from the noema as product to the producing and constituting acts. This characterization holds for Husserl's own understanding of his procedure: it is always directed by the schema of the constitution of objects in which the object forms itself as the synthetic unity of its manners of appearance. According to this model, he attempts to grasp the self-constitution of the Ego as identical throughout the performances of its constitutive acts. In this sense, reflection is always a "retrospective perception," a subsequent turning oneself back upon the already enacted functions.[11] However, the concept of reflexivity which was developed in this manner is a static one. Husserl, in fact, early went beyond the limits of static procedures in his genetic analyses, but never thematized this step beyond in its systematic import. Let us now sketch this in a simplified manner.

Static reflection cannot lead to the origin of the acquaintance between ourselves and our constitutive function, which precedes all reflection upon already performed acts. This peculiar sort of reflexivity, as a prior acquaintance with ourselves, can be understood if we look at the way whereby we are moved in everyday life to interrupt the performances of our acts to reflect on their success or failure. This occurs primarily when we encounter difficulties in the performance of an act. Then the naive performance is stopped with the consideration which might be formulated in such words as "Why were you unable to do this?" Thus *reflection* is primarily, and always, *a turning back toward what we can do.* But we find out what we can do by exercising our capacity to do what we can do. Husserl was on the verge of discovering this fact when, in the analysis of kinaesthetic ability [*Vermögen*] in the second volume of *Ideas* (p. 163), he said·

"The 'I move' precedes the 'I can'." This is true even at an early level of prelinguistic development in the child, while the goal-oriented movement of the parts of its body are practiced and copied. In such activity—with its success or failure—the child experiences itself, even at this early stage, as a center and source of spontaneous motion whereby he can bring about, grasp, push away, etc., something in his environment. All presentations of acting forces have their origin in this experience, in which a "because . . . there" is experienced in an original way. The polarization of "I" and "thou" in this center of spontaneous motion and effect is, genetically, a later development. The child is already this individual existence, and knows itself as such in terms of experiencing the ability to control his body in the gradually learned ability to govern its motor system. This ability provides the child with its first access to its environment.

To be sure, one might ask whether this kind of prelinguistic acquaintance with oneself as the center of a spontaneous ability to move is something specifically human, or should it be ascribed to animals as well? Does it not apply to any biological organism as a unity that is capable of self-direction? One can only say that they evidently function as centers of motion, but are not aware of themselves as such. Husserl speaks in this sense, following Leibniz, of "sleeping" monads. However, it would lead us too far afield to deal with this problem further.

What is meant by this reference to the origin of all our knowledge of an ability [Können] is merely that, without this original familiarity with kinaesthetic abilities, there cannot exist a higher level of reflexivity which maintains the sense of reflection on an ability, its range, and limits. This *ability to move itself is the most elementary form of spontaneity,* and a theory of action which does not stem from it can only arrive at an abstract and global concept of action. Even speaking, which alone allows the ability to think to be articulated, has the structure of the kinaesthetic performance of motion. Thus the kinaesthetic motions, without which there can be no constitution of time, are the most fundamental dimension of transcendental subjectivity, the genuinely original sphere, so that even the body (*Leib*), as functioning body, is not just something constituted but is itself constituting as the transcendental condition of the possibility of each higher level of consciousness and of its reflexive character.[12]

Husserl did not explicitly draw this conclusion. But when he speaks about the "natural side" of subjectivity and about the fact that transcendental subjectivity can only be called an "I" by equivocation, he indicates that he did not want "nature" to be understood as something opposed to subjectivity but as subjectivity itself at its most basic level. So understood, it is not nature objectified as the totality of real existence "outside us" but nature as we immediately experience it with our bodily functions. Although it is this control of our kinaesthetic functions which provides our first access into our world, it would be incorrect to say that it is the body which individualizes. It does so only insofar as one knows it as *one's own* body, over which one has control within certain limits. Husserl recognized this, too, when (p. 258) he says: "The discovery of *mine* precedes the discovery of 'I'." But he did not draw the conclusion which follows from this for understanding the meaning of the absoluteness of the "transcendental Ego" and for seeing into the primary practical sense of reflection as reflection upon abilities.

The ability to move oneself is the deepest-lying transcendental function whereby time constitutes itself as one. Consequently, there is a reason why the first extended analysis of time—Aristotle's—takes place in the context of the question about motion. In experiencing this ability in operation, *my* undeniable *there* ("Da") or the undeniable *there* of the other reveals itself as apodictically certain of the operative living present. *From this "there" the concept of absolute fact first achieves its meaning:*

On the one hand, the ultimate functioning Ego is already there before any performance of free variation and ideation upon "ego-ness as such" and before the positing of an all-temporal *nunc stans*; the Ego encounters, so to speak, this "there," which it is itself. On the other hand, one must say that this "there" is not pregiven the way sense stimuli precede higher-level experiences in constitution.[13]

This means that in order to receive sense stimuli, this "there" is required.

This point must be understood correctly: whenever we talk about our "there," this demonstrative always means, at the same time, a "there" in its temporal place, which is preceded and followed by other "theres." But this talk stems from a retrospective reflection in which this "there" is already objectified as one among others to which the "staying and remaining Ego," which persists through all the "theres," corresponds. It is the very reflection which gives the impetus to Hegel's dialectic of sense-certainty which is to demonstrate that this supposed immediacy is itself mediated. Here, by contrast, it is a matter of proving that this operative, living present is an apodictic certainty that cannot be crossed out, a *fact beyond which one cannot question further,* and in this sense *immediate and absolute,* as an absolute fact which is *the deepest-lying transcendental condition for the possibility of all functions and their performances.*

The constitutive functions are always "abilities to..." But abilities are only "there" for us insofar as they are enacted. If this functioning becomes an object of reflection which, as such, is always retrospective perception, it is no longer grasped as what it is in its living enactment. Only in its living enactment is it "itself there." To be sure, this apodictically certain "itself there" does not meet the requirements Husserl set on the regress to ultimate apodictic certainty. For him self-presence meant to be present in intuition through phenomenological reflection. But a *function as ability cannot be intuited*; it can be an object of consciousness in its self-presence only as it is enacted. Here, to be sure, *a limit is reached to the retrospective reflection, the reflection which has for object the perceived,* beyond which

there is, so to speak, something immediately apodictically certain—something certainly prelinguistic. Were this reflection to be articulated, the articulation would already be subject to the compulsion to reify, which is inevitably tied to speech, since the meaning of words is always related to previously constituted entities and not to the ultimately constitutive functions. To be sure, this absolute "there" is not to be something merely inferred but something that is known and certain even in its functioning, as certain as the unavoidability of the "there" before which we always stand at bay and which we are forced to face. In this sense it is an absolute fact which must simply be accepted and beyond which one cannot question. "The ultimate functioning Ego cannot catch up with itself as something which endures. The ultimate functioning Ego is always ahead of its own reflexive present" (Held, op. cit.).

With this brief and rough outline we have sketched the path of the genetic reflection of the transcendentally meditating Ego the monad. This path leads to *the "there" that cannot be annihilated as the ultimate ground for the apodictic certainty of itself* as living present of function. This ground cannot itself be made subject to further reflection. Rather it is *experienced as the limit* which transcendental reflection encounters and upon which it founders. If reflection has primarily the sense of a reflection upon ability, here it reaches the *limits of its ability* against which all ability (*Können*) is powerless (*machtlos*) and which it simply must accept. Thus each "I subject," in the performance of its constitutive functions, finds itself placed in its "there" immediately—or in the language of Heidegger's *Being and Time*, "thrown." Thus it becomes acquainted with itself immediately through its performances as the center of its functions and abilities. Accordingly, it experiences what it is able to do, and from the very beginning it experiences its abilities as something to be learned and exercised. The *turn toward its life-history* is already contained in this experience: the ability whereby it experiences itself is experienced as *something acquired* through the history of experience in which it has found this very ability. This history can become known to it in reflection primarily as its life history, which has always already happened and been operative anonymously, before reflection upon it begins. Such a reflection can be expressed thus: "Why did it happen this way, why did I do this?" Consequently, Husserl can say: "The question 'why' is the original question about 'history' " (*Husserliana*, XV: 420). It is the question about the "inner historicity" which precedes and is the transcendental ground for the possibility of all explicit recollection and all autobiography.

This "inner historicity" can be found through an "egological" reflection and a genetic retrospective question. It is found as the historicity of each individual life, which cannot be substituted for any other life and is unavoidably separate from that of any other by means of its "there." But, according to Husserl, the "inner historicity" is supposed to be the "a priori" of *the* history, whether it be understood as the history of the family, of one's own people, of one's own epoch, or in quite general terms as the history of "mankind," but always *the* history which everybody shares with others. How do others enter into the "inner historicity" of each individual, or how can they be shown always to be included in it already? This question is none other than the one about the "window" of the monad. Only if some such thing can be proved—not just as something inferred or postulated but as something experienced from the first—can each individual "inner historicity" be claimed as the a priori of *the* history and the compatibility of the two theses about the absoluteness of the monad, as well as the absoluteness of history, become understandable.

IV

It is the task of the transcendental genetic theory of intersubjectivity to clear the way for answering these questions. As

was mentioned in the introduction, Husserl failed in the first comprehensive exposition of his theory of intersubjectivity, in the Fifth Cartesian Meditation, because he tried to develop it statically. We must now return to this point with at least a few remarks (a full examination would go beyond the limits of the present discussion).

The three volumes of Husserl's analyses of intersubjectivity (*Husserliana*, vols. XIII-XV), which are now available, show that in 1927 Husserl had already gone beyond the limits of a purely static analysis in that he attempted to trace the constitution of intersubjectivity through the appresenting analogizing apperception (*appräsentierende analogisierende Apperzeption*) back to its passive preconstitution in its associatively founded appresentation. But even this attempt leaves open the question whether, in the case of such an associative analogizing, the monad's differentiating itself from the "thou," from the "us," and from the "other" in general is already presupposed. Can its own "there" correspond with the "there" of the other, so that its own individual temporality and inner historicity remain a priori in relationship with that of the other, and so that a common time becomes possible? Can one justifiably talk about a proto-intersubjectivity which originates simultaneously with each separate "proto-Ego" ("Ur-ich") in such a way that one cannot be without the other? Husserl must also answer the question "How do the others enter into my own proto-temporality" (*Husserliana*, XV: 356), so that each "soul" "is certainly in and for itself, but has sense only within a plurality grounded in and unfolding from itself?" (op. cit., p. 341).

Husserl did not develop and answer these questions systematically, but some of his late manuscripts give some indication of the direction in which these solutions can be sought. In these manuscripts Husserl's earlier characterization of intentionality as a "primal striving of the monad" is somewhat more concrete: "May or must we not presuppose a universal intentionality of impulse (*Trieb-Intentio-nalität*), which constitutes unitarily each original present as an enduring temporalization which advances from present to present in such a way that all contents are contents of the fulfillment of impulse, and are intended in approaching the intentional aim?" (op. cit., p. 595).

"The structural analysis of the original present (the constant living stream) leads us to the Ego-structure and to the continually operative level of the ego-less stream which grounds it. [This ego-less flow of consciousness] brings us back to the *radically pre-egoic level* through a subsequent retrospective question about what presupposes and makes possible the sedimented activity" (op. cit., p. 598).

In this sense, Husserl attempts to understand the sexual impulse "as an intuitive primal intentionality of communalisation."[14] As a primal impulse it is from the outset related to the other (self) and finds in it its response. "A relation to the other as other is found in the impulse *per se* and to its correlative impulse." In its "primal fulfillment we do not have two fulfillments that must be separated into the one and the other primordialities, but a unity of both primordialities which produces itself through the inter-penetration of fulfillments" (op. cit., pp. 593ff.).

Let us try to complete these thoughts by pursuing them a little further.

The result of the fulfillment of each "primal impulse" can be the birth of a new man with his own, unique history, whose possibilities, however, are largely determined by the inheritance of his ancestors.[15] Thus *conception* and *birth* are not merely subjects of biology *but are also of transcendental philosophical import as conditions for the possibility of history*. This grounds the differences among generations, through which what they have in common appears in different perspectives on the basis of the different times of their lives. The common history of a family, a people, an epoch, etc., thereby arises: each member, through his birth and development, has *his* time, which is granted to him. Only through such a return to the deepest-lying genetic structures, which could only be hinted at

by summary indications, can Husserl's statement be given a concrete content: "History, from now on, is nothing other than the living movement of the collectivity and the permeation of original constitution and the sedimentation of sense."

The "windows" of the Ego-monad are therefore not to be sought just *above* in apperception, or *lower* in associative analogizing, but in the "proto-impulse" which, as such, has always been related to the "other" and finds its fulfillment and response in him. The possibility of the analogy of the collective present and the self-presence is founded in its primal-unification in duality, which Held discussed in his critical examination of Husserl's theory of intersubjectivity (which was mentioned earlier). The certainty of the "there" of the other precedes, therefore, all apperceiving and all associations. Its ultimate foundation is not the "a priori" of the I-thou relationship which Waldenfels examined—who was well aware of that, since he inquired, ultimately, into the "fundamental basis (*Untergrund*)" of the dialogue. This *prior unity and simultaneously absolute separation is originally experienced passively in the performance of the striving toward the other, which finds its response in him. This experience is an absolute experience,*"[16] and *upon its ground history is absolute.*

But this is more than history in the sense of *res gestae* (historical events); it includes what precedes all *res gestae*: the transcendental oneness in duality which, in turn, leads to a new oneness, to a new absolute monad which carries within itself the generative common traits. They are common because the fulfillment of the original intentionality of impulse produces a "unity of both primordialities," that of the one and of the other. Each has its "there" in the stream of performances—a "there" which becomes common in fulfillment. This "there" is the "there" of the corporeal self-moving subject. In their corporeal self-moving, "nature" is open to them from the first, since they themselves, as corporeal things, belong to it. It is a "there" in its "place" in nature, and consequently is related to the "earth," which "blends into a universal 'history of nature' into which man reaches as a life form."[17]

However, history is in no way merely a history of nature. True indeed: "natural occurrences" form its ground; but not at all in the sense of "matters" that could not be further defined. Rather, they are known to us as the *"earth,"* that is, as the *totality of the conditions which set the boundaries for all the activities of man and consequently for his history in the sense of "res gestae."* This is the situation in which we find history today: as this limitation on all human possibilities has become more explicitly conscious, the process of mastery over the earth has progressed. To the absoluteness of our "there" belongs the absoluteness of the earth as the limit on any possible "there." Let us not talk about space travel here; it will probably never occur in any way other than "connected to the earth." "Earth," in this sense, is a *transcendental limiting concept.* It is a fundamental structure of the human lifeworld and denotes, at the same time, the limit with reference to which all our talk of "nature" can gain only for us an intuitively fulfillable sense. It is a limiting concept which, at the same time, precludes the possibility of speculation about a nature ruling in and for itself. The history of earth and the history of nature exist only inasmuch as we, through our individuation, are historical beings to whose individual "there" all temporal determinations of natural events are ultimately related.

In this *universal sense,* which includes even natural events, the statement about history as the grand fact of absolute being has to be understood. The static-flowing happening, the "transcendental life," experiences itself *as* happening only through the separation and, at the same time, unification of the initially anonymously moving center of motion (the "monads").[18] In this sense "the Ego is to be understood as always already prior,

but at the same time the stream is always prior."[19] The sense in which the statement that "nature" is itself a form of transcendental history (*Husserliana* XV: 391) must be understood in terms of this. Hence only the transcendental subjects, or monads, are "historical," and only subsequently does something like a history and then a science of nature exist for us. These could constitute themselves, in the modern sense, only by methodical abstraction from this transcendental relation. In this sense, therefore, one must understand *the compatibility of the absoluteness of the monad and the absoluteness of history.*

To what extent, then, is the definition of the "absolute" or "there" transcendental and, accordingly, an a priori definition? And, as a result, to what extent is phenomenology, which leads to this peak, a transcendental philosophy? It is transcendental philosophy because it leads to what has always preceded anything else of which we can say, in any sense at all, "It is." The factualness of this "there" is a structural principle (Aguirre, op. cit.). Its precedence is in its anonymous "priorness"; consequently, "anonymous" and "there" are *transcendental definitions* whereby the ultimate point of transcendental reflection is reached. It is the point at which transcendental reflection *finds* its self-imposed limits, beyond which it cannot go. It cannot go behind what comes first.

This discovery reveals the basis *upon which* transcendental reflection and transcendental philosophy are to be understood as critiques of *any* dogmatism. This critique is not merely a critique of the old, pre-Kantian metaphysics but, at the same time, a critique of the hidden metaphysical implications of the modern positions which consider themselves anti-metaphysical. It also forbids the transgression of the limits it has found by means of a science of postulates in the Kantian sense. But it in no way leads, therefore, to an absolute skepticism. Precisely with the conditions for the possibility that there "be" for us something like history, it leads to an insight into what is required for us as the highest principle for the direction of life in the face of this *condition humaine,* which can be determined through its limits in unconditional generality and binding force.

We have attempted to show that the factualness of history depends upon the factualness of the "there" of the individual existence, singularized in each case.[20] If there is to be a future for this "humanity," bound in its "there" upon the "earth," and if its history is not to be at its end, the condition for this is *not only* *the acknowledgment of all "our likes" as equal but also, at the same time, as absolutely individually different.* The unconditionally general, binding requirement is thus *acknowledgment and respect of each individual existence,* of each of "our likes," and those of historically evolved groups, peoples, tribes, and nations in their "collective" individuality. Only this acknowledgment, namely, the acceptance of one's own facticity, is the ground for the possibility of a human world rather than subjugation under an impenetrable fate.

NOTES

1. *Husserliana,* VI, supp. II, p. 364—in the English translation by D. Carr (Evanston, 1970), p. 351.

2. See also A. Aguirre, "Genetische Phanomenologie und Reduktion," *Phaenomenologica,* 38: esp. pp. 153ff.

3. Cf. K. Held, "Das Problem der Intersubjektivität in 'Perspectiven phänom. Forschung,' " *Phaenomenologica,* 49: 1ff.

4. Manuscript K III-12, p. 34—quoted in Held, "Lebendige Gegenwart," *Phaenomenologica,* 23: 147.

5. "Husserl-Gedenkband," *Phaenomenologica,* 4: 133.

6. For an explicit interpretation of this thesis, see the author's "Meditation über Husserls Wort 'Die Geschichte ist das grosse Faktum des absoluten Seins,' " *Tijdschrift voor Filosofie,* XVI/I: x90ff. (Louvain, 1974), and its English translation in *Southwestern Journal of Philosophy,* 5(1974): 111-126. The following remarks may be seen as a variation on this theme, in part expanding it, in part improving it.

7. Quoted from "Vom Ursprung der Geometrie" of 1936, supp. III in *Crisis,* p. 381—n. 1 in Carr's translation (p. 372).

8. "Religion innerhalb der Grenzen der Vernunft," *W. W.,* VI: 39.

9. "Vom Ursprung der Geometrie," *Husserliana,* VI: 379; in Carr translation, p. 370.

10. *Handbuch philos. Grundbegriffe,* IV (Munich, 1973), pp. 1203ff.

11. Cf. the author's *Der Weg der Phanomenologie,* pp. 192ff.

12. Cf. the author's "Reflexionen zur Konstitutionslehre," *Tijdschrift voor Filosofie,* XXXVI/3: 466ff.

13. Held, "Lebendige Gegenwart," p. 149. For the "there" as fundamental determination of the existing ego see also Alfred Schütz, "Collected Papers, Vol. I," *Phaenomenologica,* 11: xxxi (editor's introduction).

14. Manuscript E III-10, p. 1, quoted according to Waldenfels, "Das Zwischenreich des Dialogs," *Phaenomenologica,* 41: 298.

15. Concerning the problem of "heredity" as empty horizon see *Husserliana,* XV: 640ff.

16. Cf. the author's "The Phenomenological Concept of Experience" in *Philosophy and Phenomenological Research,* 34 (1973): 13ff.

17. Manuscript CI and B III, I, quoted according to Waldenfels, op. cit., p. 336. Cf. also *Krisis (Husserliana,* VI: 304).

18. Cf. *Husserliana,* XV: 373ff.

19. Manuscript, C VII-1, p. 18.

20. Cf. also the author's "Faktizität und Individuation" in *Sein und Geschichtlichkeit: Festschrift f. Volkmann-Schluck* (Frankfurt, 1974), pp. 275ff.

Further References

Psychologism

Bachelard, Suzanne. *A Study of Husserl's Formal and Transcendental Logic*, tr. L. E. Embree. Evanston: Northwestern University Press, 1968, pp. 92-113.

Eley, Lothar. "Life-World Constitution of Propositional Logic and Elementary Predicate Logic." *Analecta Husserliana*, 2 (1972), 333-53.

Mortan, Günter. "Einige Bemerkungen zur Überwindung des Psychologismus durch Gottlob Frege und Edmund Husserl" in *Atti XII Congr. intern. Filos. XII*. Florence: Sansoni, 1961, pp. 327-34.

Natorp, P. "Zur Frage der logischen Methode. Mit Beziehung auf Edmund Husserls Prolegomena zur reinen Logic" in *Husserl*, ed. H. Noack. Darmstadt: Wissenschaftliche Buchgesellschaft, 1973, pp. 1-15.

Puhakka, Kaisa, and R. Puligandla. "Methods and Problems in Husserl's Transcendental Logic." *International Logic Review*, 2 (1971), 202-18.

Schupe, W. "Zum Psychologismus und zum Normcharakter der Logic. Eine Ergänzung zu Husserls Logische Untersuchungen" in *Husserl*, ed. H. Noack. Darmstadt: Wissenschaftliche Buchgesellschaft, 1973, pp. 16-34.

Wild, J. W. "Husserl's Critique of Psychologism: Its Historical Roots and Contemporary Relevance" in *Philosophical Essays in Memory of Edmund Husserl*, ed. Marvin Farber. Cambridge: Harvard University Press, 1940, pp. 19-43.

Willard, Dallas. "Concerning Husserl's View of Number." *Southwestern Journal of Philosophy*, 5 (1974), 97-109.

Meaning

Atwell, John E. "Husserl on Signification and Object." *American Philosophical Quarterly*, 6 (1969), 312-17.

Cairns, Dorion. "The Ideality of Verbal Expressions." *Philosophy and Phenomenological Research*, 1 (1941-42), 453-62.

Derrida, Jacques. "La forme et le vouloir-dire: note sur la phénoménologie du langage." *Révue de Théologie et de Philosophie*, 21 (1967), 277-99.

Dreyfus, Hubert. "*Sinn* and Intentional Object" in *Phenomenology and Existentialism*, ed. R. C. Solomon. New York: Harper-Row, 1972, pp. 196-210.

Gendlin, Eugene T. *Experiencing and the Creation of Meaning*. New York: Free Press, 1962.

Küng, G. "World as Noema and as Referent." *The Journal of the British Society for Phenomenology*, 3 (1972), 15-26.

Mohanty, Jitendranath. *Edmund Husserl's Theory of Meaning*. The Hague: Nijhoff, 1964.

Orth, Von Ernst Wolfgang. *Bedeutung Sinn Gegenstand*. Bonn: H. Bouvier and Co., 1967.

Sokolowski, Robert. *Husserlian Meditations*. Evanston: Northwestern University Press, 1974.

Thyssen, J. "Husserls Lehre von den Bedeutungen und das Begriffsproblem." *Zeitschrift für Philosophische Forschung*, 13 (1959), 163- 86; 438-58.

Volkmann-Schluck, K. H. "Husserls Lehre von der Idealität der Bedeutung als metaphysisches Problem" in *Husserl et la pensé moderne*. Actes du deuxième Colloque international de Phénoménologie, Krefeld, 1-3 novembre 1956, édités par les soins de H. L. Van Breda et J. Taminaux. The Hague: Nijhoff, 1959, pp. 230-41.

Evidence and Truth

Adorno, Theodor W. *Zur Metakritik der Erkenntnistheorie. Studien über Husserl u. d. Phänomenologie.* Stuttgart: Kohlhammer, 1956.

Bjelke, J. "Der Ausgangspunkt der Erkenntnistheorie, eine Auseinandersetzung mit Husserl. "*Kantstudien 55* (1964), 3-19.

Chisholm, R. M. "Introduction" *Realism and Background of Phenomenology.* New York: The Free Press, 1960, pp. 3-36.

Dupré, Louis. "The Concept of Truth in Husserl's *Logical Investigations." Philosophy and Phenomenological Research,* 24 (1963-64), 345-54.

Hein, K. F. "Husserl's Criterion of Truth." *Journal of Critical Analysis,* 3 (1971), 125-36.

Levin, David M. *Reason and Evidence in Husserl's Phenomenology.* Evanston: Northwestern University Press, 1970.

———. "Husserl's Notion of Self-Evidence" in *Phenomenology and Philosophical Understanding,* ed. Edo Pivcevic. London: Cambridge University Press, 1975, pp. 53-77.

Mall, Rom Adhar. *Experience and Reason.* The Hague: Nijhoff, 1973.

McGill, V. J. "Evidence in Husserl's Phenomenology" in *Phenomenology: Continuation and Criticism Essays for Dorion Cairns,* ed. Frederick Kersten and Richard Zaner. The Hague: Nijhoff, 1973, pp. 145-66.

Patzig, Günther. "Kritische Bemerkungen zu Husserls Thesen über das Verhältnis von Wahrheit und Evidenz." *Neue H. Philos,* 1 (1971), 12-32.

Spiegelberg, Herbert. "Phenomenology of Direct Evidence." *Philosophy and Phenomenological Research,* 2 (1941-42), 427-56.

Zaner, Richard M. "Reflections on Evidence and Criticism in the Theory of Consciousness" in *Life-World and Consciousness: Essays for Aron Gurwitsch,* ed. Lester E. Embree. Evanston: Northwestern University Press, 1972, pp. 209-30.

Perception

Asemissen, Hermann Ulrich. *Structuranalytische Probleme der Wahrnehmung in der Phänomenologie Husserls.* Cologne: Köln Universität Vertag, 1957.

Chapman, H. M. *Sensations and Phenomenology.* Bloomington: Indiana University Press, 1966.

De Almeida, Guido Antonio. *Sinn und Inhalt in der Genetische Phänomenologie E Husserls.* The Hague: Nijhoff, 1972.

Dreyfus, Hubert. "The Perceptual Noema" in *Life-World and Consciousness: Essays for Aron Gurwitsch,* ed. Lester E. Embree. Evanston: Northwestern University Press, 1972, pp. 135-70.

Føllesdal, Dagfinn. "The Phenomenological Theory of Perception" in *Handbook of Perception* I, ed. E. C. Carterette and M. P. Friedman. New York: Academic Press. 1974, pp. 381-85.

Gurwitsch, Aron. *The Field of Consciousness.* Pittsburgh: Duquesne University Press, 1964.

———. "Contribution to the Phenomenological Theory of Perception" in *Studies in Phenomenology and Psychology,* ed. Aron Gurwitsch. Evanston: Northwestern University Press, 1966, pp. 332-49.

Holenstein, Elmar. *Phänomenologie der Assoziation. Zu Struktur und Funktion eines Grundprinzips der passiven Genesis bei E. Husserl: Phenomenologica 44.* The Hague: Nijhoff, 1972.

Landgrebe, Ludwig. "The Phenomenological Concept of Experience." *Philosophy and Phenomenological Research,* 34 (1973-74), 1-13.

Larrabee, M. J. "Husserl on Sensation." *The New Scholasticism,* 47 (1973), 179-203.

Lingis, Alphonso. "Hyletic Data." *Analecta Husserliana,* 2 (1972), 96-101.

Imagination

Casey, Edward. *"Imagining: A Phenomenological Study.* Bloomington: Indiana University Press, 1976.

Dufrenne, Michel. *The Phenomenology of Aesthetic Experience.* Evanston: Northwestern University Press, 1974.

Graumann, Carl Friedrich. *Grundlagen einer Phänomenologie und Psychologie der Perspektivität.* Berlin: de Gruyter, 1960.

Kuspit,   Donald.   "Fiction   and
    Phenomenology." *Philosophy and
    Phenomenological Research,* 29 (1968-
    69), 16-33.
Meinong, Alexius. *On Emotional Presenta-
    tion,* tr. M.L.S. Kalsi. Evanston: North-
    western University Press, 1972.
Oosthuizen, D.C.S. "The Role of Imagination
    and Judgment of Fact." *Philosophy and
    Phenomenological Research,* 29 (1968-
    69), 34-58.
Saraiva, Maria Manuela. *L'imagination selon
    Husserl.* The Hague: Nijhoff, 1970.
Sartre, Jean-Paul. *The Psychology of Imagi-
    nation,* tr. Bernard Frechtman. New
    York: Philosophical Library, 1948.
————. *Imagination: A Psychological
    Critique,* tr. Forrest Williams. Ann Ar-
    bor: University of Michigan Press, 1962,
    pp. 127-43.
Zaner, Richard M. "The Art of Free Phantasy
    in Rigorous Phenomenological Science"
    in *Phenomenology Continuation and
    Criticism: Essays in Memory of Dorion
    Cairns,* ed. J. J. Kockelmans and Theo-
    dore Kisiel. Evanston: Northwestern
    University Press, 1970.

Time

Berger, Gaston. "A Phenomenological Ap-
    proach to the Problem of Time," tr. D.
    O'Connor in *Readings in Existential
    Phenomenology,* ed. Nathaniel Law-
    rence and Daniel O'Connor. Englewood
    Cliffs, N. J.: Prentice Hall, 1967, pp.
    187-204.
Brand, Gerd. *Welt, Ich und Zeit.* The Hague:
    Nijhoff, 1955.
Bröcker, Walter. "Husserls Lehre von der
    Zeit." *Philosophia Naturalis,* 4 (1957),
    374-79.
Canon, J. H. "The Phenomenology of Tem-
    poral Awareness." *The Journal of the
    British Society for Phenomenology,* 1
    (1970), 38-45.
Eigler, Günther. *Metaphysische Vorausset-
    zungen in Husserls Zeitanalysen.*
    Meisenheim a. Glan: Hain, 1961.
Findlay, John. "Husserl's Analysis of the
    Inner Time-Consciousness." *Monist,* 59
    (1975), 3-21.
Granel, Gérard. *Le sens du temps et de la
    perception chez E. Husserl.* Paris: Gal-
    limard, 1968.
Held, Klaus. *Lebendige Gegenwart.* The
    Hague: Nijhoff, 1966.
Huertas-Jourda, José. "The Genetic Con-
    stitution of Reality from the Innermost
    Layer of the Consciousness of Time."
    Cultural Hermeneutics, 1 (1973), 225-50.
Kates, Carol A. "Perception and Temporality
    in Husserl's Phenomenology." *Philos-
    ophy Today,* 14 (1970), 89-100.
Minkowski, Eugene. *Lived Time,* tr. K.
    McLaughlin. Evanston: Northwestern
    University Press, 1970.
Spicker, Stuart F. "Inner Time and Lived
    Through Time: Husserl and Merleau
    Ponty." *Journal of the British Society for
    Phenomenology,* 4 (1973), 235-47.

History and Transcendental Philosophy

Boehm, Rudolf. "La phénoménologie de
    l'histoire." *Revue internationale de
    philosophie,* 71-72 (1965), 55-73.
Carr, David. *Phenomenology and the Prob-
    lem of History: A Study of Husserl's
    Transcendental Philosophy.* Studies in
    Phenomenology and Existential Philoso-
    phy. Evanston: Northwestern University
    Press, 1974.
Fink, Eugen. "Welt und Geschichte" in *Hus-
    serl et la pensée moderne.* The Hague:
    Nijhoff, 1959, pp. 143-59.
Funke, Gerhard. "Phenomenology and His-
    tory" in *Phenomenology and the Social
    Sciences,* ed. Maurice Natanson.
    Evanston: Northwestern University
    Press, 1973, pp. 3-101.
Hohl, H. *Lebenswelt und Geschichte.*
    Munich: Alber, 1972.
Janssen, Paul. *Geschichte und Lebenswelt.
    Ein Beitrag zur Diskussion von Husserls
    Spätwerk.* The Hague: Nijhoff, 1970.
Kaufmann, Felix. "The Phenomenological
    Approach to History." *Philosophy and
    Phenomenological Research,* 2 (1941-
    42), 159-72.
Kersten, Frederick. "Phenomenology, His-
    tory and Myth" in *Phenomenology and
    Social Reality: Essays in Memory of
    Alfred Schutz,* ed. Maurice Natanson.
    The Hague: Nijhoff, 1970, pp. 234-69.
Klein, Jacob. "Phenomenology and the His-
    tory of Science" in *Philosophical Essays
    in Memory of Edmund Husserl,* ed. Mar-
    vin Farber. Cambridge: Harvard Univer-
    sity Press, 1940, pp. 143-63.
Landgrebe, Ludwig. *Phänomenologie und
    Geschichte.* Darmstadt: Mohr, 1967.
————. A Meditation on Husserl's Statement:
    'History is the Grand Fact of Absolute
    Being.' " *Southwestern Journal of Phi-
    losophy,* 5 (1974), 111-25.

Lowe, Donald M. "Intentionality and the Method of History" in *Phenomenology and the Social Sciences,* ed. Maurice Natanson. Evanston: Northwestern University Press, 1973, pp. 103-30.

Morrison, James. "Husserl's 'Crisis': Reflections on the Relationship of Philosophy and History" in *Philosophy and Phenomenological Research,* forthcoming.

Pazanin, Ante. "Das Problem der Geschichte bei Husserl, Hegel, und Marx" in *Phänomenologie Heute. Festschrift für Ludwig Landgrebe.* The Hague: Nijhoff, 1972, pp. 173-203.

Ricoeur, Paul. "Husserl and the Sense of History" in Paul Ricoeur, *Husserl: An Analysis of His Phenomenology.* Evanston: Northwestern University Press, 1967, pp. 143-74.

Shiner, L. E. "Husserl and Historical Science." *Social Research,* 37 (1970), 511-32.

PART TWO

Phenomenological Concepts

Introduction

As Part One has shown, Husserl's treatment of traditional philosophical problems is couched in a terminology which marks phenomenology off from other movements in contemporary philosophy. This new vocabulary arises not only from Husserl's attempt to develop a rigorous yet comprehensive method but from the application of this method. The following section's exploration of the concepts and issues that are central to phenomenology can be divided into two groups. The first deals with two methodological techniques: the reduction (Van Breda, Kern) and eidetic intuition (Patocka). The second group deals with thematic issues: intentionality (Olafson), noema (Solomon), horizon (Van Peursen), the life-world (Carr), and intersubjectivity (Elliston) .

I

Though many commentators have discussed the technical intricacies of the phenomenological reduction, Father Van Breda's "Notes on the Reduction and Authenticity" is a rare and profound commentary on its spirit. By this device, central to the phenomenological style of philosophy, Husserl seeks to overcome the fetishism of the everyday world, viewed from the natural attitude, in order to live an authentic life which recognizes the source of beliefs and values in transcendental subjectivity. Its negative moment, which calls the commonplace into question, is complemented by the discovery of the sources of meanings that are sedimented within daily life. This re-trieval of the constants within consciousness is the philosopher's infinite task.

Iso Kern focuses on the details of the three paths Husserl concurrently pursued to the goal Van Breda has articulated. The first is Cartesian: as a response to the skeptic's challenge, the reduction is a search for an absolute foundation for knowledge. The second path proceeds through psychology: by abstracting from everything physical, the reduction uncovers subjectivity, which becomes the domain of phenomenological inquiry after further purification of everything positive. Ontology provides the third route: as a critique of formal logic, positive science, and the life-world, the reduction yields transcendental subjectivity as the intentional correlate of whatever actually exists.

According to Kern, the first two paths fail to reach their objective. The first does not yield subjectivity in its full breadth, which includes both others and a temporal horizon of past and future. The second is obstructed by the paradox that a process of abstracting should provide what is most concrete. Only the third way, through ontology, avoids these pitfalls and the dead end of psychologism in its various forms.

After the reduction, eidetic intuition is perhaps Husserl's second most celebrated methodological technique—and Jan Patocka defends it against two recent attacks from dialecticians.

Adorno has argued that Husserl's appeal to eidetic intuition erroneously assumes that things and their essences can be isolated and immediately ap-

120

prehended. Husserl's subsequent attempt to bridge the gap thereby created between the realm of facts and the realm of essences succumbs to a circular logic: particulars presuppose the universals of which they are instances. Husserl's mistake is said to stem from a classificatory logic he unwittingly assumes, despite his disclaimers.

Patocka rejects Adorno's characterization of Husserl's intuition in terms of 'immediacy' and appeals to 'originality' instead. The latter contrasts not so much with mediated consciousness as with empty intentions which present things only obliquely and partially. Through imaginative variation and the harmonious fulfillment of expectations, eidetic intuition achieves insight into the general features that are shared by particular things, and thereby makes it possible to compare and classify them.

Lothar Eley interprets Husserl's transcendentalism as an unsuccessful effort to relate facts and essences that founders on the ossification of the dialectical tension between these two domains. Patocka, conceding this dialectic, credits Eley with an explanation for the unity of Husserl's thought: the transcendental motive animates both the intuition, which discloses essences, and the reduction, which discloses the consciousness that constitutes the factual world. By countering the tendency to absolutize essences and their apprehension, Eley has helped to restore the vital balance to Husserl's philosophy.

II

If we shift from procedural to thematic issues, most critics and interpreters of phenomenology agree that intentionality is the central concept in Husserl's philosophy. Yet his views shifted as the concept developed, though not all phenomenologists have appreciated the changes. In its mature form it provides a fruitful context for the recent debates on thought and language, though few non-phenomenologists have appreciated its virtues.

Frederick Olafson rectifies these two deficiencies by analyzing Husserl's theory of intentionality in its contemporary perspectives. Recent attempts to interpret intentionality as a logical feature of certain kinds of sentences (i.e., as intensionality) have equated it with nonextensionality. This failure to reduce the intentional to the extensional has led other philosophers to try to eliminate all intentional idioms from language. To resolve this impasse, Chisholm tried to derive the intensionality of language from the intentionality of thought. But the ensuing referential opacity and nontruth functional character of the constituents of statements of belief have appeared to his detractors as a roadblock to the scientific world view.

Olafson offers Husserl's more constructive and positive theory of intentionality as an alternative resolution of this dilemma. By discounting the mentalistic features of the concept in Brentano, along with his preoccupation with the ontological status of non-real objects and the common features of all mental phenomena, Husserl developed a theory which made intentionality the vehicle of all objective reference. Because of his greater interest in epistemology rather than psychology, Husserl subordinated the contingent features of mental acts and their correlates—for example, their date, duration, location, or intensity— to their logical and referential function (see D. Willard's discussion of psychologism in Part One). Also, he modified Bretano's concept of intentional object by distinguishing between the object that is intended and the object as it is intended.

The initial mentalistic overtones in the latter concept diminished as the doctrine developed: talk of sensations and sense data, which Husserl (like Bretano) had taken as intrapsychic, yielded to the concept of the noema, which is the correlate rather than the content of consciousness. (See Solomon's article, below, on the concept of noema.) Also, the ambiguous and obscure relation between signitive and intuitive intentions in *Logical Investigations* was clarified in *Ideas* through the notion of fulfillment. (See Pietersma's discussion of evidence in Part One.) Husserl was forced to concede that the categorical syntheses characterized not only the higher-order objectivities, such as sets, but sensible objects themselves. (See Welton's discussion of perception.)

The theory of intentionality eventually merges with the full theory of constitution whereby objects with a persisting identity and nature are conceptually formed. (For the role of time consciousness in the process, see Brough's article, above.) Husserl's mature theory emphasizes, in Kantian fashion, that a conceptual system is the mediating condition for the apprehension of the world. (Other Kantian motifs are examined in Kockelmans' article in Part Three.) His final position is more radical than Chisholm's, inasmuch as Husserl holds that all language is intentional. Yet it stands in opposition to linguistic analysts who would confine intentionality to language. (See Tugendhat's comparisons in Part Three, as well as Mohanty's article in Part One.)

As Olafson notes, the concept of intentionality is inextricably tied to that of the noema. Robert Solomon carefully delineates two competing interpretations: taking perception as his paradigm, Gurwitsch contends that the noema is the perceived as such; appealing to judgments instead of sensory experiences, Føllesdal interprets the noema as an abstract intensional entity. In each view the noema is part of the solution to a problem. For Gurwitsch, the problem is the reidentification of particulars experienced at different times; for Føllesdal, the problem is the opacity of reference in judgments, which precludes substitution *salva veritate* and allows false statements (which denote no actual state of affairs) to be meaningful. Gurwitsch's interpretation leaves the Individuation Problem unresolved: How can particular noeses and noemata be identified? Taking the noema as an 'abstract' entity (by which he means 'not perceived'), Føllesdal is forced into the absurdity that the perceived, as such, is not perceived.

Solomon attempts to preserve the particular insights of each interpretation (while acknowledging their differences) by taking Husserl's radical thesis as Kantian. He emphasizes the similarity between asserting 'that-p' and seeing 'that-p': the noema is 'that-p'; the thetic component is assimilated in the first case to the different sentences which could be used to assert 'that-p' and, in the second case, to the perspectival structure of perception. In a similar spirit, Solomon argues against the extreme polarization of meaning (*Sinn*) and its expression in language (*Bedeutung*), thereby mediating as well the divergence between phenomenology and the analytic tradition.

Each noema is situated within an inner horizon (the other aspects of the perceived as such), an outer horizon (other possible objects of consciousness), and a temporal horizon (other experiences within the stream of consciousness). Conceding the ambiguity of the term 'horizon', C. Van Peursen details the way it cuts across various dichotomies. It bridges the polarization of man and world inasmuch as it belongs to neither, taken by itself, but only to their dynamic interrelation. It recalls the boundaries of man's finitude while connoting his constant efforts to transcend them. It marks the current context which gives shape to man's intellectual quests, as well as the future possibilities still to be uncovered. Because of the horizon, man is bound to a perspective which restricts what he can apprehend to an aspect of things; and yet it makes all these things perspicuous in human terms. As the source of a meaningful coherence, the horizon makes it possible both to distinguish and to unite the elements of the whole.

The possibilities foretold in the horizon have their basis in man's anticipations and recollections, which in turn are based on time. Paradoxically, then, the spatial contours of the horizon point back to lived time as their source. A world without this temporal horizon would be meaningless. (See Brough's article, above, for a fuller discussion of time consciousness.)

Not only does man exist solely as a

projection into the world, reality exists only as the correlate of this activity in its various human forms. Any absolute or hidden world, behind what manifests itself to man, is a betrayal of this insight.

The horizon invites us to explore what is beyond, if not behind it. Reality is not exhausted by the instantaneous, and always reaches out toward the possibilities yet to be realized.

Van Peursen summarizes these themes with the Heideggerian expression 'to dwell'. The horizon supplies a protective context within which man makes himself at home in the world. The occasional loss of orientation in moments of anguish emphasizes the human need for a framework which, in the form of culture, marks the boundary between the familiar and the unknown.

According to Van Peursen, the horizon is both spatial and spiritual: the literal and the figurative meanings are continuous. Carr examines this continuity in his critique of Husserl's concept of the life-world.

Carr grapples with the paradox that science, as a spiritual accomplishment, should be based on the life-world and yet be an element within it. He resolves the paradox by distinguishing two notions of the life-world: as the realm of immediate experience, the life-world supplies the *sine qua non* for higher cultural formations; yet, as the pretheoretical realm of daily practice, it includes the sciences among its mundane facts. Failure to note this ambiguity easily generates mistakes in Husserl scholarship, and confused phenomenological programs.

Husserl's philosophy has been charged not only with ambiguity but with incoherence, because of the way he tries to resolve the transcendental problem of intersubjectivity. Elliston's examination of empathy provides a defense against this charge. After cataloguing the four constituents of the sense 'alter ego', he analyzes the process of analogizing apprehension whereby this sense is constituted. The objection that the reduction cannot be carried out because it lacks the linguistic means confuses the philosopher with the object of his philosophizing. The claim that the analogy fails, because the similarities between self and others are lacking, overlooks its indirect and counterfactual character. Furthermore, Husserl's account avoids the rationalistic biases in current discussions of the "problem of other minds" and provides a fruitful model for explanations in the social sciences.

A Note on Reduction and Authenticity According to Husserl

H. L. VAN BREDA

1. In what is called the *natural* attitude (*natürliche Einstellung*), man leads an inauthentic existence because he unconsciously lives in the absolute belief (*Glaube, Hingabe*) in "what is constituted" or "what is founded" (*we* prefer the term *canonized*, which Husserl rarely uses) without justifying this belief or clarifying its foundation.

2. The phenomenological reduction in general, *the transcendental epoche* in particular—*and these alone*—disclose to us the *constituted* character of the world in which we naturally live. They allow us to catch sight of the *intentional genesis* of the content and the values of the given world. The reduction is thus presented as the only possible way to escape the inauthentic existence of the natural attitude, to retrieve the original meaning of the given, and to rediscover the intentional constitution of the world.

3. The phenomenological reduction is *by rights* the *first* and the most fundamental of the steps to be carried out by the philosopher, because it alone allows us—at least in principle—to rediscover the origins of conscious life and to understand its intentional history.

4. The essential elements which

This article originally appeared in *Revue de Métaphysique et de Morale*, 56 (1951): 4-5. Translated by permission of the Société Française de Philosophie and the author. Translated by F. Elliston and P. McCormick. © 1976 Elliston and McCormick.

characterize the phenomenological reduction in all its forms (which allow us to consider it as a philosophic method, as *one* method, notwithstanding the undeniable variety of forms it presents) are as follows:

a. The suspension (epoche) of definitive value judgments concerning all conscious meaning (or conscious meanings taken as a whole) whose intentional constitution (intentional history) has not been reconstructed in terms of the first and original data of consciousness and whose intentional explication by and for the transcendental ego has not been understood.

b. The sustained attempt first to *discover* (*ent-decken*) the given, prior to the intentional point of view, which is overlaid *in* and then concealed (*verdeckt*) *by* the subsequent given intentionality (*in* and *by* the "constituted" or "canonized"*) and, secondly, then to *reduce* what is intentionally subsequent to the source of its meaning. As a result of the *natural* character of the *natural attitude* and of the irresistible and innate tendency of the human mind to objectify the content of consciousness in an absolute way and to settle there, the reduction must always be repeated and it can never be considered definitively achieved.

5. The phenomenological reduction is a *multi-formed* philosophic method whose concrete structure will be determined:

a. By the meaning or group of meanings

whose intentional genesis is studied and which are to be reduced to their intentional origin;

b. By the structure of the acts in which the considered meanings become conscious.

6. The transcendental reduction shows us that every meaning is necessarily meaning *for* the transcendental Ego and that it is always and necessarily grasped by an *active* Ego (*Konstituirendes Ego*).

7. The transcendental reduction shows that all meaning is either the content of an intuitive act or the explication of such a content. The intuitive acts are *multi-formed* but imply, as does each intuitive act, a *cognitive* grasping *of an intellectual character*. This cognitive grasping is fundamental (*fundierend*) in relation to other aspects of these intuitive acts.

8. The philosopher—by definition the man who tries to know the origins of everything given and who is at pains to live the authentic life—ought to exercise the phenomenological reduction, if he does not want to betray his calling. The transcendental epoche is thrust on his freedom in a catagorical and imperative way.[1]

NOTES

1. The author intends to complete these theses in another article.

The Three Ways to the Transcendental Phenomenological Reduction in the Philosophy of Edmund Husserl

ISO KERN

The question raised here concerns the constitution of philosophical knowledge: Through which steps in thinking does philosophic cognition (*Wissen*) arise? How does knowing emerge from the aphilosophical life and become genuinely philosophical?

Philosophy has been perceived historically as a break with the natural life, and, to be sure, just as much by non-philosophers as by philosophers themselves. For the former, this break is taken as a kind of "becoming abnormal" or "going crazy" (as a breaking away from the norms of sound conduct established by the natural life)—as "being turned on one's head." Philosophers, on the other hand, experience this break as taking leave (*Verlassen*) of the superficial realm of empty appearances and shadows in the cave and as emergence into full and true actuality—as a revolution in the naive way of thinking. How is this leaving of the cave of shadows accomplished? What is the meaning of these allegories and images?

No philosopher in history has occupied himself with these particular questions so

This article originally appeared in *Tijdschrift voor Filosofie*, 24 (1962): 303-49. Translated by permission of the publisher and author. Translated by F. Elliston and P. McCormick.© 1976 Elliston and McCormick.

earnestly and so adamantly as Edmund Husserl. He discusses them under the heading "The Transcendental Phenomenological Reduction." The following explications seek to study the "geographical maps" for the ways of access into the land of true actuality which that indefatigable philosophical traveler has left behind for us under this heading. In addition, these explications try to set foot on these same paths and to test whether they lead to the promised goal.

Eminent interpreters have distinguished in Husserl four different paths to the transcendental phenomenological reduction: (1) the Cartesian way, (2) intentional psychology, (3) the critique of the positive sciences, and (4) ontology.[1] As we will show, the third and fourth ways are ultimately the same type of path, so that we can speak in principle of only three different ways. Let us remark at the outset that in Husserl they are not always sharply and clearly separated but often appear entwined with one another.

A. The Cartesian Way

The Cartesian way, like the other two types, appears in Husserl in various modifications, yet it has a more or less stable underlying structure which we will try to delineate in advance. This structure of the Cartesian way is determined by the following steps in thinking.

1. At the outset is the idea of philosophy as an absolutely grounded science that is built into an absolutely grounded procedure from an absolute beginning (from an "Archimedean point," as Husserl says). Also settled at the outset is that this beginning must consist of absolute evidence (*Evidenz*), of evidence which is absolutely indubitable, clear, and unenigmatic (*rätsellos*).

2. Now it is necessary to look for absolute cognition or evidence. The result of a universal critique of transcendent knowledge of the world is that in principle no such knowledge corresponds to the demand: that belief in the existence of the world, which underlies all knowledge of it, does not possess that absolute evidence. The philosopher who begins absolutely must exercise an epoche on the belief in the world and thereby also on all knowledge of the world, be it of scientific or prescientific nature; that is, he must refuse to accept such belief or knowledge as valid (*ausser Geltung setzen*).

3. The question arises whether any valid cognition remains if all knowledge of a transcendent world is no longer accepted as valid. The question can be answered in the affirmative: there remains the "cogito" of the one who philosophizes, the object of immanent cognition, and this is absolutely evident. The absolute beginning is secure.

4. The "cogito" bears intentionally, and in this sense immanently, the whole world as a "cogitatum" in itself. Although the world and its entire content have been suspended as valid by the beginning philosopher, this world nevertheless continues to exist for him (*Bestehen*), though no longer in its original (*ursprünglichen*) validity but merely as "*cogitatum qua cogitatum*"—that is, as mere "phenomenon." Pure subjectivity is thereby grasped in its full range. The latter should not be confused with man, who is a mere transcendent "cogitatum" of this subjectivity.

Let us pursue this Cartesian way in a survey of Husserl's philosophic work.

Its beginnings are already found in the second volume of *Logical Investigations* (1901), namely, in the seventh section of the introduction, which bears the heading " 'Freedom from Presuppositions' as a Principle in Epistemological Investigations." In it Husserl demands that the theory of knowledge must exclude "all statements not permitting of a comprehensive *phenomenological* realization,"[2] that it return to the "adequate fulfillment in intuition":[3] that is, it must "be performed on an actual *given* basis of experiences of thinking and knowing."[4] Thus we encounter the demands which characterize the Cartesian way for a beginning in absolute evidence and for excluding all that is not absolutely evident. In the *Logical Investigations*, only the lived experience (*Erlebnis*) with its *real* content is claimed as the "sphere of what can be phenomenologically realized fully and completely." But its *intentional* content, namely the "cogitatum," is not taken in this way. Subjectivity in its full sense has not yet been attained. In addition, subjectivity is still spoken of as psychological, for phenomenology is taken as "descriptive psychology."

The thought of including the "cogitatum" in the absolute realm of phenomenology or theory of knowledge emerges in a text from 1904 which calls upon Descartes.[5] The Cartesian way of the phenomenological reduction is thereby clearly staked out in principle. But it is systematically worked out first in the "Five Lectures," *The Idea of Phenomenology*, of the summer semester of 1907. The Cartesian way begins in the second lecture, where the demand is made at the outset that the theory of knowledge must have an absolute beginning which "must contain nothing of the unclarity and the doubt which otherwise give to cognition the character of the enigmatic and problematic."[6] After setting forth this demand, Husserl begins with the Cartesian doubt[7] (*Zweifelsbetrachtung*) and affirms that the "cogitationes" are the first things that are given absolutely. The "cogitatio" is "unenigmatic,"[8] "absolutely clear and indubitable cognition,"[9] an "absolute,"[10] the "ultimate standard of what being and being given can mean."[11] It is thus able to form the absolute starting point for a theory of knowledge. The "cogitatio" or lived experience as what is really (reell) immanent in consciousness seems to present for the first time—as Husserl notes—the sole absolute givenness, or what is the same, the sole pure immanence. As a result, the phenomenological reduction (as the exclusion of all that is not given absolutely) appears as the exclusion of everything that is really transcendent. This is again the standpoint of the Logical Investigations.[12] But after stressing that the absolute "cogitatio" should not be understood as a psychological "cogitatio" (which as a component of transcendent man is not given absolutely),[13] the subsequent lectures show that things that are really transcendent as well belong in the realm of absolute givenness, or of pure immanence, namely, the general essences of the "cogitationes,"[14] which are seen in ideation, and the intentional object as such (the "cogitatum qua cogitatum").[15]

Consequently, the idea of phenomenological reduction acquires a more narrow and more profound determination and a clearer meaning. It means not the exclusion of the really (reell) transcendent (perhaps even in some psychologico-empirical sense), but the exclusion of the transcendent as such as something to be accepted as existent, i.e. everything that is not evident givenness in its true sense, that is not absolutely given to pure seeing.[16]

In conclusion, let us emphasize that the "Five Lectures" do not proceed beyond one's own subjectivity and thus they persist in a certain "solipsism."

We have hereby indicated in broad outline the Cartesian way of the "Five Lectures." Let us note in advance that it does not exclusively determine the sense of the phenomenological reduction in those lectures, but that even quite different lines of thinking, determining its sense, are still at work. But of this I shall speak later.

The lectures "Basic Problems of Phenomenology," which Husserl delivered in the winter semester 1910/11, form an important stage in the development of his idea of the phenomenological reduction.[17] In them Husserl extends the phenomenological reduction to intersubjectivity for the first time. But the Cartesian way plays no role in these lectures!

In contrast, "The Fundamental Phenomenological Outlook" of Ideas, which develops the transcendental phenomenological reduction, is strongly imprinted once again with motifs of the Cartesian way. To be sure, this fundamental outlook is not initiated with the demand for an absolute beginning. But its structure is nevertheless typically Cartesian in that it begins "by placing out of action," "disconnecting," or "bracketing"[18] belief in the world. As a result, the question arises: What still remains[19] as validly existing? This question about the "phenomenological residuum" remains the leading point of view of the following investigations, which do not themselves bracket the belief in the world but, in merely psychological reflection on consciousness, try to show the following.

First, that consciousness "is to be grasped as an open endless sphere of being which is yet closed up for itself."[20] Second, that "just this sphere of being remains unaffected by the phenomenological disconnection described above."[21]

The first of these two aims, namely the proof that consciousness is closed or different from transcendent things (Dinglichkeit, or transcendent world), is attained in the second chapter of the section. It is determined "that a unity determined purely by the proper essence of the experiences themselves can be only the unity of the stream of experience."[22] This stream of lived experiences constructs the object of immanent cognition, while the transcendent thing is "without any essential unity"[23] with the (transcending) act of cognition. Consciousness (the stream of lived experience) is thereby found to be a closed unity. The difference is then determined through the following closely connected comparisons.

First, lived experiences can be apprehended immanently, whereas it is impossible to apprehend real things immanently (where "immanence" means, as here, being really contained in).[24] Second, real things (what is transcendent) are given in a merely phenomenal way (i.e., they are given through one-sided "ways of appearing" or "aspects"), whereas the lived experiences (what is immanent) are given absolutely. And, Husserl immediately adds, what is transcendent exists merely phenomenally, whereas what is immanent exists absolutely.[25] Third, from this it follows that transcendent things are doubtful, whereas the immanent lived experiences are indubitable.[26]

After the differentiation between consciousness and reality has been worked out in the second chapter, the third chapter states that consciousness is *absolute*, as opposed to the transcendent world; namely, consciousness is "modified, to be sure, by a nullifying of the thing-world, but would not be affected thereby in its own proper existence,"[27] while the transcendent thing as something which exists merely intentionally is related throughout to actual consciousness.[28] The course of thinking has thereby achieved its goal, and Husserl can conclude: After the exclusion of the transcendent world, we still have "the whole field of absolute consciousness."[29] "It is this which remains as the *phenomenological residuum* we were in quest of."[30] With this, he stresses that this "residuum" includes worldly transcendence in itself as an intentional correlate.[31]

The Cartesian way is begun in its purest form in the lecture "Erste Philosophie" [First philosophy] from the winter semester 1923/24. Under the guiding principle of apodictic or adequate[32] evidence, Husserl is seeking the absolute beginning ("Archimedean point")[33] for philosophy.[34] The critique of experience of the world brings to light[35] its inadequacy in principle, so that the demand ensues to include the world in the "universal overthrow" of the phenomenological reduction.[36] The specifically Cartesian question is now to be posed: What would be

left unaffected and would perhaps exist as apodictic if the whole world did not exist?[37] Husserl responds that in reflections about the possible non-being of the world the ego, as that which experiences the world, along with its experiencing life, was presupposed.[38] It thereby proved for Husserl that the ego, with its life, "is a sphere of being which can be posited by and for itself—, even if the whole world does not exist or even if every position taken on its existence is inhibited."[39] It is significant that here—in contrast to the "Five Lectures" and to *Ideas*—Husserl does not yet claim absolute, namely, adequate and apodictic, evidence for this transcendental ego.[40] But he demands that this ego submit to the apodictic critique.[41] With the transcendental ego, the Archimedean beginning point of philosophy has not yet "eo ipso" been attained. In what follows, Husserl tries to achieve a beginning for such an apodictic critique which should lead to an apodictic reduction.[42] But, as a matter of fact, this critique is never carried out but is put aside "ad calendas Graecase."[43] The subsequent explications are devoted to an analysis of the phenomenological reduction whereby, at the same time, a new way to the phenomenological reduction is opened which is completely independent of the Cartesian one:[44] through psychology.

In *Cartesian Meditations* we find a situation similar to the one in the lectures "Erste Philosophie." Here too at the outset is the demand that philosophy begin with apodictic evidence.[45] The evidence for the world is proved not to be apodictic and is included in the "Cartesian overthrow."[46] An apodictic critique is demanded for the transcendental ego which remains and which includes in itself the world as "phenomenon." But then this critique is put aside as a "problem for higher stages" and is carried out no further.[47] Even in *Cartesian Meditations* the Cartesian way does not achieve its goal: the absolute starting point of philosophy.[48]

In his final work, the *Crisis*, Husserl explicitly dissociates himself from the

Cartesian way and points to this lack.[49] As a matter of fact, this way had appeared questionable to him (at the latest) even in the 1920s. In what follows let us examine the aspects of this way which must have made it questionable in Husserl's eyes.

A first and extremely grave failing of the Cartesian way consists of the fact that in it the transcendental reduction has exclusively the character of a *loss* and that consciousness is made to appear as *something left over* (*Übrigbleibendes*, or "residuum"). Even though at the end of the Cartesian way Husserl at times stresses that the world has not at all been lost, since it lies in the phenomenologist's field of research as the intentional correlate of the "cogito,"[50] nevertheless this claim is unjustified *from the viewpoint of the Cartesian way itself*. For even if the world is retained as a "phenomenon," nevertheless it is retained merely as a "phenomenon"—namely, only as "subjective representation"—for no other sense can justifiably be given to the term "phenomenon" on the Cartesian way. After the belief in the existence of the world has been checked along the Cartesian way, Husserl's follower constantly expects that he may return *again* to this belief after an appropriate justification. In the course of his philosophic investigations Husserl makes no such attempt to secure this belief in the world anew and renounces such attempts as misunderstandings.[51] And in *Cartesian Meditations*, after securing the ego as the "residuum," he explains that the world is nothing at all but a "phenomenon" for this ego.[52] When Husserl does this, his follower feels duped, and with full justification. For on the basis of the motifs of the Cartesian way, the suspension of belief in the world could be only a matter of a methodological stepping back or surrendering, which must necessarily have a provisional character. It is guided of necessity by the thought that the being of the world must be disregarded in order to try anew to secure it alter on the basis of apodictic reflections. In the Cartesian suspension of experiences of the world and the sciences which investigate the world, Husserl speaks of "making valid once again" (*Wieder-in-Geltung-Setzung*).[53] In the further explication, though, he does not think about it. Therefore the objection has been justifiably raised against him that, after the *epoche*, he never returns to the being of the world. But this objection ultimately rests on a misunderstanding: it considers the sense of Husserl's phenomenological reduction to be determined in principle by the motif of the Cartesian way. But as we will see, this is not at all the case. The proper meaning of Husserl's transcendental phenomenological reduction contains nothing of a stepping *back behind* the belief in the world so that making it valid once again must appear as the goal of philosophizing which is proposed and still to be sought. The proper meaning of the phenomenological reduction is not to be attained by the Cartesian way.

Even the correlate of this loss of the actual existence of the world, namely "consciousness" characteristic of being "something left over" or a "residuum," is extremely misleading. For what can be left over besides a part, or a component, or layer? And what can consciousness as a part, component, or layer be—other than the psychic consciousness, the psychic "morsel of the world"? We need not enlarge on how often Husserl's transcendental consciousness has been interpreted in the psychological sense, and also been most severely criticized in this interpretation.

Husserl realized that talk of "excluding the world" and of "consciousness as a residuum" which results from the Cartesian way was questionable. In a text from 1924 he indicates that this kind of talk easily gives the impression that the world itself *in its true being* does not belong to the realm of transcendental phenomenology and that the "ego cogito" is only the layer of the psyche which has been abstracted from the world.[54] The same thing is said in section 43 of the *Crisis*, which is explicitly kept at a distance from the Cartesian way: this path leads to the transcendental ego by way of a leap, but in the beginning leaves the one who travels this path at a loss as to *what* is achieved with this transcendental ego. "As the reception of my *Ideas* has shown, one succumbs all too easily and too quickly right at the outset to the very great temptation to fall back into the naive natural attitude."[55]

A second basic lack of the Cartesian way consists of the fact that on it the *full* subjectivity—be it the psychological or transcendental—cannot legitimately be attained.

First, the Cartesian way does not reach intersubjectivity (which, according to Husserl, alone constitutes full subjectivity). Other subjects or co-subjects are only given, according to Husserl, through "indications" or "appresentations"—by means of the real things which I experience as animate organisms (*Leiber*).[56] If the world —and along with it, of course, the things which I experience as animate organisms—is no longer accepted as valid on the Cartesian way, or if, as Husserl argues on the Cartesian way, the world were to be "nihilated" (*vernichtet*), then of course nothing of another's subjectivity remains in the *residuum*. For the animate organism of another (*fremd*) can indicate or appresent to me a subjectivity which is *valid* (*geltende*) only if it itself is valid for me. If I consider animate organisms completely nihilated, so too is the subjectivity of the other. On the Cartesian way, the subjectivity of another is reached only as a "mere phenomenon." Husserl has been justifiably reproached in many critiques for not being able in his phenomenological philosophy to take account of the being that is proper (*Eigensein*) to the subjectivity of another. By way of anticipation, we must say again that this critique is justified *only* from the point of view of the Cartesian way which has not attained the genuine sense of Husserl's transcendental phenomenological reduction.

In his lecture "Erste Philosophie" (1923-24) Husserl himself points to this failing. As an advantage of the new non-Cartesian way to the transcendental subjectivity which Husserl expounds in this lecture, it is explicitly stressed that it sec-

ures transcendental intersubjectivity, which was not the case in the previous Cartesian way.[57] In the same lecture Husserl notes that for years he saw no possibility to conceive the phenomenological reduction as leading to an intersubjective one[58]—events in his development which Husserl indicates are shown by a text from the lecture mentioned. Here Husserl speaks of an "error which is not easily made transparent" (in his introduction to the phenomenological reduction in 1907) and remarks that "it [this error] was annulled through the 'extension' of the phenomenological reduction to the monadic intersubjectivity in the Fall lectures of 1910."[59] This error of which Husserl speaks (besides another about which we shall speak later) has to do with the limitation of subjectivity to what is purely my own subjectivity (at first taken psychologically) as it was carried out on the Cartesian way of the "Five Lectures" of 1907. The lecture of fall 1910 (which is mentioned above as "Basic Problems of Phenomenology"), which overcomes this limitation, diverges markedly from the Cartesian way.

If the Cartesian way does not lead to intersubjectivity, does it at least lead to my own full subjectivity, which is not just a subjectivity of the present but also possesses a past and future? This question must be answered in the negative.

In this context, Kant's acute "Refutation of Idealism" may be recalled.[60] Kant here discusses Descartes' problematic idealism which regards only the object of *inner* experience as immediately and completely certain: the object of *outer* experience is taken to be disclosed only indirectly and to be problematic. Kant shows that inner experience as a determination of my existence (*Dasein*) is possible only in time on the basis of something that endures (in time). This is bound up with my existence only from *outside* me and thus can be only an object of outer experience. Outer experience, then, is at least as immediately proved as inner experience. In other words, Kant shows that the subjective time determination is possible only on the basis of the objective. Only the consciousness of my own existence (of the "I am"), which accompanies all thinking, does not presuppose any outer experience, according to Kant. But, according to him, this consciousness is not an intuition, and consequently it is not a cognition and is therefore completely empty. On the basis of these reflections of Kant we can say: If the Cartesian way depends on "not accepting as valid" the world and, along with it, objective time, or even on thinking about it as "nihilated", then this way cannot achieve subjectivity as the stream of consciousness which possesses a temporally determined past and future.

But does Husserl not achieve, on the Cartesian way of the "Five Lectures" and of *Ideas*, just that stream of consciousness in its full temporality? Without doubt, Husserl claims to have done so in these texts. But in critical remarks from the 1920s Husserl says that he does not show in those writings how he comes to the stream of experience[61] but, rather naively, presupposes it.[62]

In what follows, let us look at a text in which Husserl shows exactly how it is possible to reach the transcendental life stream in its full temporal extent. By doing this we will corroborate our thesis that the Cartesian way is unfit for this end. Husserl speaks in detail about the way in which this goal can be attained in his lecture course "Erste Philosophie" (1923/24). It contains extraordinarily deep analyses of the phenomenological reduction. Here he shows that the past and future life of subjectivity is to be grasped only through a double reduction. Through a first radical reflection and transcendental reduction I secure—and secure *only*—my actual, conscious life of the present. As its horizon, this actual conscious life possesses the world in its past, present, and future. The transcendental ego thus possesses in its present, as horizon, the universe of all objectivities which are valid for it. To a certain extent, it even possesses those which are going to be valid for it in the future. It has the possibility of bringing this world closer to it in recollection and expecta-

tion. According to Husserl, then, this world horizon is the condition for the possibility that I can attain something transcendentally pure of the past and the future. This horizon, then, as Husserl explains, is not something I am allowed "no longer to accept as valid".[63] For what is transcendentally pure (e.g., the past) I secure only by first grasping myself *in* my past horizon as a *human* ego which has lived in its surrounding world (*Umwelt*), which is now past, and has lived in intentional relation to it. I recall, for example, how in yesterday's walk I traversed a certain region and saw these and those things. By means of the first reduction I take my actual recollection as *transcendental*. But I do not yet have the content of this recollection, namely my perception yesterday of that region I walked through, as something transcendental but only as the perceiving of the *human* ego which steps about in the world of yesterday. If I want to grasp this perception as transcendental, I must exercise a second reduction which reaches *into* the reproductive content of my recollection.

Doing this, if I go along the chain of my recollections and let myself be at the same time guided continuously by an emerging recollection to the actual present and I practice the transcendental reduction on the series of recollections which are continuously awakened, then I thereby see my continuous transcendental past right up to the now.[64]

Something analogous holds as well for securing the future of the transcendental life stream. What is decisive for us is that in securing my transcendental life of the past and future it is the past and future world in its objective temporality which presents the *necessary* "clue."[65] If there were for me no past and future world in which I lived or were going to live, there would be for me as well no past and future transcendental life. In order to secure my past and future transcendental life as something valid, the past and future world as well must have validity for me. The objective time determination is thus the condition for the possibility of the subjective time determination. Or "outer'' experience is the condition for the possibility of "inner" experience, which can exist merely as a reflection of the outer. This expresses nothing other than the radical intentionality of consciousness.[66]

By means of these reflections the inadequacy of the Cartesian way, which takes from the world the validity of its existence, becomes clearly evident. What is especially questionable is the argument for the "nihilation of the world" which is brought forward along this path. Husserl writes in *Ideas*: Through a nihilation of the world of things, the being of consciousness, indeed of any stream of experience whatever, would

be inevitably modified by a nullifying of the thing-world, but would not be affected thereby in its own proper existence. Modified, certainly! For the nullifying of the world means, correlatively, just this, that in every stream of experience (the full stream, both ways endless, of the experiences of an Ego) certain ordered empirical connexions, and accordingly also systems of theorizing reason which take their bearings from these, would be excluded. But this does not involve the exclusion of other experiences and experiential systems.[67]

On the basis of the reflections of 1923/24, this thought from *Ideas* is correct only in a very limited way. The existence of consciousness does not become obliterated by the nihilation of the world. But after the nihilation of the world, this existence which remains does not have any duration; namely, it no longer has a past and future, but is diminished to the present. Indeed, since this present is such always bears past and future in itself by means of retention and protention, even this present would be reduced to a point and thereby to something untemporal.

Whether Husserl ever became fully conscious of this inadequacy of the Cartesian way is not clearly evident, although there are some indications for it. Above all it must be kept in mind that Husserl never thought that the phenomenological reduction was determined purely by means of the Cartesian way. Rather, other non-Cartesian elements are always tied to its meaning, so that the questionableness of that way could perhaps never merge into complete clarity for him.

The Cartesian way has still a third failing, which is related to its demand for an absolute beginning to philosophy. We have already indicated that in the "Five Lectures" (1907) and in *Ideas* Husserl claimed absolute evidence for the subjectivity attained on the Cartesian way. Thus he believed he was able to fulfill the demand for an absolute beginning. But in the lectures "Erste Philosophie" (1923/24) and in *Cartesian Meditations* he deviates from this claim and puts aside the proof for an absolute givenness "until later." By means of this postponement, which is recognized as necessary, the Cartesian idea is shown to be illusory. Philosophy cannot begin at an absolute point. Neither will the apodicticity of this beginning be shown afterward in the further development of the inquiry. Rather, it is shown that the "cogito," as something temporal, does not possess any absolute *content* whatsoever which can be grasped scientifically.

The absoluteness of the evidence, which is supposed to stand at the beginning of philosophy, according to the Cartesian way, signifies absolute indubitability or apodicity.[68] It further signifies absolute adequation as well, insofar as adequate and apodictic evidence are treated as equivalents.[69] The *Cartesian Meditations*, of course, dissociates itself from this equivalence.[70]

At least since the 1920s, Husserl is clear that there can be no talk of apodictic evidence for the content of the past and future of my stream of lived experiences. For recollections and expectations can be fundamentally deceptive.[71] Only the *form* of past and future, and thus the temporal form of the stream of lived experience, possesses apodicticity according to the explications of the later Husserl.[72] For an apodictic content, only the living-flowing present enters into consideration.[73]

Now what is this living-flowing present? With it, I do not have the infinitude (*Unendlichkeit*) of my life, "much less my ego itself—as the I 'which I am'. I am not just the life which I have lived but the subject of capacities and of the life which is thereby possible for me."[74] I do not have my concrete subjectivity as the content of this living present, not even the concrete subjectivity of the present. For my concrete subjectivity of the present exists only as the identical one which has already lived in the past.[75] Concrete subjectivity exists, even in its present, only as something *presented* (something mediated) through the living-flowing present.[76]

Is there in this living-flowing present an actual (*seiendes*) lived experience which can be grasped apodictically? The later Husserl denies even this. If a lived experience may have something apodictic which cannot be annulled so long as it continues to be lived, this lived experience, nevertheless, is not thereby an existing one, since the particular perception can never be conclusive evidence for an existing entity. For to the *being* of the lived experience belongs the idea that it can be identified in recollections,[77] which—as was said—are in principle subject to error. Thus a content from the flowing present as such cannot provide apodictic evidence to serve as the point of departure for a science which ascertains what is (*Seiendes*).[78]

Following Husserl, we can go still further. Since the living-flowing present is grasped only in retention and protention as flowing, it exhibits, as such, a mediated structure, so that here too the apodicticity becomes problematic.[79]

Finally, only two apodictic moments of my "cogito" remain: the temporal *form* and the *existence* of my self.[80] These two moments are not contents, for Husserl can write:

Cognition, and in particular scientific cognition, would be absolutely satisfied if and insofar as it attains absolutely final validity in apodicticity in a simultaneous *adequation to an apodictic content*. But no factual knowledge—no *mundane* and no *phenomenological*-subjective knowledge—*is of this*

sort. No temporal being can be known with apodicticity: not only is it impossible for us to do so; it can itself be known apodictically that it is impossible.[81]

It is ultimately *temporality* which makes the apodictic knowledge of my subjectivity impossible.

We do not need to discuss the extent to which the impossibility of an apodictic factual knowledge of my transcendental subjectivity can still leave open (according to Husserl) the possibility of an apodictic knowledge of the essence of this subjectivity. For, in any case, the meaning of Husserl's phenomenological reduction cannot consist simply of going back to an apodictic knowledge of essences. For example, apodictic knowledge of essences exists, according to Husserl, in mathematical knowledge.[82] But this falls under the reduction, something which, moreover, cannot be motivated by means of the Cartesian way. In his Cartesian way, Husserl never begins with a knowledge of essences.

B. The Way through Intentional Psychology

In this discussion of the second way let us try at the outset to indicate its basic structure.

1. This way begins with a reference to the physical sciences, which are interested *purely* in the physical and *abstracts* from everything psychic. In opposition to these sciences, Husserl conceives the idea of a *complementary* science which is interested *purely* in the psychic and *abstracts* from everything physical.

2. This complementary abstraction of psychology cannot be of the same structure as the abstraction of the natural (physical) sciences. For while in natural experience I have mere bodies, I do not have anything *purely* psychic, since the natural attitude grasps the intentional relation of lived experiences to objects as *real* relations—namely, on the paradigm of relations between bodies. I can secure a pure lived experience only by withholding my interest in the actuality of the in-

tentional object of the lived experience. That is, I must establish myself opposite it as a disinterested onlooker and refrain from taking the object of the lived experience as valid.

3. But in practicing the *particular* epoche on validity or in the particular inhibition of interests on the particular objects of particular lived experiences and connections of lived experiences (be it of myself or of the other), I still do not get to the purely psychic. For an analysis of the horizon of consciousness in lived experiences shows that every lived experience takes the *world*, by way of an intentional implication, as valid. To secure the purely psychic, I must inhibit my interest in the world in a *universal* epoche—"at one stroke" as it were. By means of this universal epoche I reach the all-embracing context of the pure psyches, which as a community intentionally includes the generalized "phenomenon" world. This intersubjectivity proves to be transcendental. Thus working out the idea of a pure psychology leads to transcendental philosophy.

Husserl first set out systematically on the way through intentional psychology in the lecture "Erste Philosophie" (1923/24). In this lecture course he annexes it to the exposition of the Cartesian way, but declares it to be deeper and richer than the latter,[83] and completely independent of it as well.[84] The *pure interest* in the subjective is taken as the guiding thought of this new way.[85] To achieve the purely subjective in the sense of *psychology*, in this lecture Husserl regards the particular reductions as sufficient—namely, the step-by-step exercise of inhibiting interest in the being of particular intentional objects of the particular lived experience or series of experiences.[86] But, amplifying on this, he points to the insufficiency of the particular reductions in which hidden validities always remain as intentional implications.[87] To overcome this inadequacy, Husserl demands a universal inhibiting of interest "with respect to the whole world that one is conscious of in the distant

horizon, with respect to the totality of all realities and idealities."[88] This universal inhibiting of interest—which is to be carried out at one stroke—Husserl calls the "transcendental reduction."[89] In critical remarks and discussions on this lecture, which could hardly have been written more than a year later, Husserl corrects himself by rejecting the particular reductions as inadequate for *psychology* as well, especially with reference to the validity implications hidden in the particular lived experiences. According to Husserl's remarks, even psychology requires the *universal* reduction from the start.[90]

Husserl, furthermore, has systematically trod the way through intentional psychology in the *Crisis* as well, whose presentation begins with the idea of an *abstraction* which would "complete" the universal abstraction upon which the natural (physical) sciences rest, in that it seeks to grasp the purely psychic.[91] He speaks of the epoche which makes possible that complementary abstraction for which the particular reductions (on the particular intentional objects of particular lived experiences) are taken, indeed, as a necessary beginning.[92] Yet, on the other side, it is immediately pointed out that these particular reductions are inadequate. To attain the closed universe of the purely psychic the psychologist requires an epoche of the whole world, through which he sets out in the "abstract" attitude of the disinterested onlooker.[93] "Psychology, the universal science of the purely psychic in general—therein consists its abstraction—requires the epoché, and for all psyches it must reduce their consciousness of the world in advance."[94] After Husserl has pointed to the meshing of intentionalities of pure psyches in the consciousness of *one* world for *all*, which has become the generalized "phenomenon" in the epoche, he writes:

Thus we see with surprise, I think, that in the pure development of the idea of a descriptive psychology, which seeks to bring to expression what is essentially proper to souls, there necessarily occurs a transformation of the phenomenological-psychological epoché and reduction into the *transcendental*.[95]

Now that we have completed a survey of this way to transcendental subjectivity, we want to pose the question: Does it indeed lead to what it is supposed to lead to, or, like the Cartesian way, is it not affected by a fundamental inadequacy?

The way through psychology is free of the second and third failings of the Cartesian way. Of course, this claim will have to be shown in more detail—but, as we must assert, it includes a lack which is the precise analogue to the first failing of the Cartesian way. By the second path, the meaning of the transcendental reduction is defined as an *inhibiting of interest* and as an *abstraction*. The main difficulty is now the following: How can a procedure of abstracting lead to the most concrete of all sciences?—for Husserl takes transcendental phenomenology to be just that. Through abstraction and one-sided interest, do we not incur the loss of a part of total reality, namely, of full concretion? In other words, can the way through psychology lead further than to psychology, namely, to the *partial* science of the purely psychic? Does not Husserl's thesis—that the world is nothing other than the "phenomenon" for this subjectivity, achieved through abstraction—occur as an unfounded claim similar to the unfounded claim of the natural scientist who suddenly declares his abstraction to be the whole reality, and thereby slides into materialism? We are convinced that *if* the meaning of the phenomenological reduction is ultimately determined by the way through psychology, these questions must be answered in the affirmative. But we must be on the lookout to see whether Husserl himself was conscious of the failing of this way.

After Husserl introduced the universal reduction in the text of the lecture course "Erste Philosophie" and characterized it as a transcendental reduction, in a critical marginal notation (which could hardly have been written more than a year after the delivery of that lecture) he writes: "Now the true character of the transcendental-philosophic reduction as opposed to the universal psychological reduction is missing."[96] Thus Husserl

seems to see quite clearly that the psychological epoche, as well as a universal one, does not lead into the transcendental realm—that it is *not* exactly true that "in the pure development of the idea of a descriptive psychology...there necessarily occurs a transformation of the phenomenological-psychological epoché and reduction into the *transcendental*."[97] As this quotation from the *Crisis* shows, Husserl seems in this final work—whose fragmentary character should of course always be kept in mind—to be no longer conscious of this difference between the psychological and the transcendental reductions. In this work he even notes that *pure* psychology is identical with transcendental phenomenology[98]—so that, in terms of this identification, the above quotation is of course quite correct.

The questionableness of this identification of a scientific outlook, which is achieved by means of abstraction and thus is necessarily partial, with the philosophic outlook, which is characterized as directed toward the totality, is immediately striking. But let us stress that this extremely doubtful identification by Husserl was not always defended, and can be explained simply by the incomplete character of that work, which issued from the mind of someone who was almost eighty years old. In a text from the middle of the 1920s—as in the *Encyclopaedia Britannica* article (1927/28)—Husserl places strong emphasis on the distinction between *pure* psychology, which rests on a universal *epoche*, and transcendental psychology. He explains that although the psychologist has reduced the world as a totality, the world in its naive validity continues to exist for him in the background as that which determines meaning, and in this validity it confers the horizon-index of "pure psychical" to the subjective.[99] According to this text, the *transcendental* character of subjectivity can only be grasped through the knowledge of its absoluteness, of its priority, and of its character as an origin (*Ursprungscharakters*), as opposed to the world.[100] These properties of subjectivity, however, are not grasped through a psychology which abstracts from the being of the world.

C. The Way through Ontology

For this way also we shall give the basic structure at the outset.

1. This way begins with positive ontology or logic. Various things can be meant by this: (a) formal logic and ontology ("mathesis universalis"), which contain the formal principles of the sciences (thus functioning as a general theory of knowledge); (b) material or regional ontologies, which, taken together, present a closed unity and form the particular principles or a priori norms of the particular positive sciences (thus playing the role of particular doctrines of science); (c) the ontology of the life-world, which forms the basis of all scientific ontologies and logic.

According to which of these different and basic kinds of ontologies the way through ontology is instituted, it appears as a way through formal logic, as a way through the critique of the positive sciences, or as the way through the ontology of the life-world. According to Husserl, the ontology of the life-world is the most fundamental—the one to which all other ontologies ultimately refer back in some way or other. Hence it forms the most basic point of departure for the way through ontology. But it is an idea of the late Husserl.

In all positive or objective ontological a priori, an ultimate unclarity can be felt which becomes the occasion for imputing mistaken meanings and for misinterpretations. This unclarity has its source in the "abstract" character of the positive ontological knowledge, which disregards the relationship to subjectivity of all objective a priori. The relationship to the subject is repeatedly announced—without, however, being clearly grasped—in the consciousness of the thinker, if only in the form of a subjectivistic skepticism which dissolves ontological principles into "something merely subjective" and robs them of their objective validity.

2. From the task which arises in clarifying the ontological a priori (and thereby subjecting the conception of this a priori to a critique) results the demand for a *radical reflection* which overcomes the one-sidedness (abstractness) of positive ontological knowledge and views the ontological a priori in its correlation to subjectivity. This radical reflection has the character of a truly revolutionary *change of attitude* (*Einstellungsänderung*): the glance is no longer directed in a naive, one-sided, or "straightforward" fashion to the positively ontological (as the principle of positivity or objectivity) or to the world (as the embodiment of the positivity or objectivity). Rather, the glance is directed to subjectivity, in whose manifold life the positive is "presented" ("constituted"). This change of attitude is *not a loss* of any kind of positivity; on the contrary, it is a *gain*, a "widening," since now positivity is seen in its correlation to subjectivity—namely, as something which is presented objectively or is constituted objectively in the subjective life. In other words, the "theme" of the objective attitude is contained in the "theme" of the new universal attitude. This new theme is not joined together from two "themes" (from an objective and a subjective one). Rather, the objective "theme" is implied intentionally in the subjective "theme" (in the intentional life of subjectivity). The change of attitude is to be compared with the transition from the second to the third dimension of space, which contains in itself the second dimension. This subjectivity, in which everything objective is constituted, is the *transcendental* one. It is exhibited as an intersubjectivity, made communal through the common objectivity. It is exhibited as temporal (historical) since the objectivity which is constituted in it has a history.

3. The exploration of the universal transcendental life, in which worldly objectivity, with its ontological a priori, is constituted, is by no means an easy matter. It is extremely difficult to accept and to adhere in complete purity to the revolutionary new attitude, which has the

character of a "conversion" of the direction of thought. For the transcendental investigator is always tempted to grasp the subjective life in a positive ontological way: he is tempted, to a certain extent, "to realize it." Because he is accustomed to the flat dimension of his natural life, he is constantly inclined to level out the dimension of depth. He always has the tendency to "explain" the transcendental life through objective science. Of course, this procedure is absurd or nonsensical (*Widersinn*), since he is always confronted with the task of explicating these objective laws by going back to subjective life. In other words, the transcendental philosopher is constantly threatened with a "metabasis eis allo genos"—that is, a metabasis from the transcendental character in the positive, from the transcendental attitude to the objective mundane one, from three-dimensionality to two-dimensionality. There is only one means by which the transcendental investigator can escape this danger: the transcendental epoche of everything with positive validity.

This epoche signifies precisely the following: the transcendental investigator must constantly be conscious of the meaning (*Sinn*) of his own investigations. Thus he ought not to succumb to the absurdity of seeking to explain the transcendental life by means of any positive "statements" (validities). For him, no positive statement in this sense can have validity. No positive statement, no positive validity can play the role of a premise in transcendental investigation. Only as the intentional correlate of the subjective life is any objective validity situated in the transcendental realm. The epoche of what is positively valid does not ensue because what is valid lacks apodicticity (cf. the Cartesian way), nor because I am interested *only* in the subjective and disengage my interest in the being of the world (cf. the way through psychology). Rather, it comes about because I see that it is nonsense to explain the transcendental life by positing something positive. On this basis alone is the meaning of the transcendental epoche determined here.

Let us now follow the history of this way through ontology in Husserl's philosophic development.

Certain starts on this way are found in the *Logical Investigations*, and in the introduction to the second volume Husserl writes as follows about the theory of knowledge:

According to the presentation of the Prolegomena [volume one of *Logical Investigations*], it is nothing other than the philosophical completion of *pure Mathesis*, understood in the widest conceivable sense, which includes all apriori categorical cognition in the form of systematic theories.[101]

Theory of knowledge, which represented the immediate goal of Husserl's earlier phenomenology, is here seen in strict interconnection with "mathesis universalis" (formal logic and ontology). This interconnection acquires a certain determination through the idea, already alive in *Logical Investigations*, of a strict correlation between the objective and the subjective a priori.

What now is the position in the "Five Lectures" of 1907 (*The Idea of Phenomenology* which are so decisive for Husserl's philosophic development? In our discussion of the Cartesian way we have shown that it occupies a dominating position in those lectures. Yet this way is taken up for the *first* time in the *second* lecture. The first lecture, however, begins with the statement "In earlier lectures I distinguished between *science of the natural sort* and *philosophic science*. The former originates from the natural, the latter from the philosophic attitude of mind."[102] All of the first lecture revolves around the thought that a theory of knowledge (or philosophy) must lie in a "wholly new dimension," as opposed to natural science (objective science), and must form "in principle a new unity."[103] "In contradistinction to all natural cognition, philosophy lies, I repeat, within a *new dimension*."[104] As Husserl explains in the first lecture, it lies in the thought that

pure philosophy, within the whole of the critique of cognition, and the "critical" disciplines generally, must disregard, and must refrain from using, the intellectual achievements of the sciences of a natural sort and of scientifically undisciplined natural wisdom and knowledge.[105]

This "exclusion" (*Ausschaltung*) of objective knowledge has thus the sense of a protection from a metabasis of the (philosophic) cognitive dimension into the natural-objective one.

In a surprising way, Husserl determines the phenomenological reduction by means of this sense immediately *after* the construction of the Cartesian way in the second lecture—even though the sense is not at all that which results from this way but even stands in a certain opposition to it. Husserl declares that the "sufficient and full deduction" of the epistemological (or phenomenological) reduction, which loads down all objective transcendences—even if they are completely certain—with the "index of exclusion," of "indifference," of "epistemological nullity," results from two moments: first, from the *meaning* of the epistemological investigations which discuss the possibility of objective cognition and, second, from the "extraordinarily strong inclination to make a judgment oriented to transcendence and thus to fall into a 'metabasis eis allo genos' (a change into some other kind) in every case where a thought process involves transcendence and a judgment has to be based on it."[106] Husserl adds that "all the basic errors of the theory of knowledge go hand in hand with the above mentioned 'metabasis'—on the one hand the basic error of psychologism, on the other that of anthropologism and biologism."[107]

Even more clearly, the proper sense of the phenomenological reduction, as protection against a *metabasis* of the philosophical dimension (or attitude) to the natural-objective one, is expressed in Husserl's synopsis in these "Five Lectures." Referring to the end of the second lecture, he writes:

Meanwhile the proper *meaning of one principle* (the phenomenological reduction) is in the constant challenge to stay with the objects as they are in question *here* in the critique of cognition and not to confuse the problems here with quite different ones. The elucidation of the ways in which cognition is possible does not depend upon the ways of objective science.[108]

Thus we are able to establish that in the "Five Lectures" Husserl ultimately intended a meaning for the phenomenological reduction which did not correspond to the Cartesian way, which was the only one up to here explicated, but to the way through ontology, which can also be termed the "way though objectivity."[109]

That the proper meaning of the phenomenological reduction consists in a protection against the metabasis was also portrayed by Husserl in other texts from the important year 1907:

The main thing is to be clear about this, that the current (epistemological) investigations lie outside the domain of all objective science and in a certain sense of any science whatsoever. The phenomenological reduction means: constantly to be conscious of this state of affairs and not to rush on with a naturalistic chain of thoughts where epistemology is being investigated. I may not make any thetic use of the existence of nature not because I am not certain of it or because it is not clear to me in what sense it exists, but rather because the finest and best clarity is of no avail to me here.[110]

The 'phenomenological reduction' signifies nothing other than the demand constantly to remain aware of the meaning of the investigation proper and not to confuse theory of knowledge with the (objectivistic) investigation of the natural scientist.[111]

The way through ontology plays a very important role in Husserl's lectures of the winter semester 1910/11. Here, *for the first time*, this path is trod systematically and is completely dissociated from Cartesian thoughts. In a text from the year 1923 Husserl records the basic structure of this way and then explains that he had developed this way during that winter semester:

The world which is given, given in intuition, the universal ontology of the world with all particular ontologies leads to a universal world-intuition as eidetic world observation. The axioms of the universal ontology must be the descriptions of the essence of any possible world whatsoever. Therefore nature leads to corporeality (*Leiblichkeit*), to the psychic, and to the subjectivity which guides the spiritual. It leads to the insight that subjectivity is world-constituting, transcendentally absolute, and that all being 'is' the correlate of transcendental subjectivity, which embraces everything objective as the correlate of subjective constitutions. And it leads to the insight that all being stands in a universal subjective genesis, etc.[112]

Strictly speaking that is the way of my introductory lecture in the winter semester 1919/20. It was already the way of my Göttinger lectures on the theory of science, logic of 1910/11.[113]

In the above-mentioned lecture of 1910/11 ("Logic as a Theory of Cognition") Husserl sketches this way with the following words:

The path goes from sciences of a natural kind to ontologies right up to the most universal ontology (to the analytic) and then further to the noetic which comes after all these ontologies and explains their principles and methods. All particular scientific cognition is then explained by means of the noetic. Then all cognition is transformed into absolute cognition. It is metaphysical cognition. Thus the noetic is the epistemological in the highest sense and at the same time it is the very discipline which makes possible a final and highest fulfillment of our cognitive needs.[114]

In correlation with ontology, this noetic is for Husserl nothing other than transcendental phenomenology.

The following is of great importance. During the same period as the lecture "Logic as a Theory of Knowledge," Husserl delivered a two-hour lecture, "Basic Problems of Phenomenology," in which he succeeded for the first time in extending the transcendental phenomenological reduction to intersubjectivity.[115] Now this very important step is taken in the way through ontology.[116] The continuously existing world, with its a priori structure, is taken as an *index*, not just for an actual stream of consciousness but for a whole system of actual and possible lived experiences which succeed one another in time[117] and which, as representations, are rooted in actual lived

experiences. But additional systems of experience which are not just my own are indicated by means of the world—namely, the lived experiences of *others* (*fremde Erlebnisse*).[118] In its basic structure (or ontological structure), the world in these elucidations of Husserl is thus necessarily the clue for the mediation of intersubjective systems of experience in which the world is constituted.[119] On the basis of these considerations, Husserl comes to a definition of the meaning of the phenomenological reduction which is possible only in the way through ontology:

The phenomenological reduction is nothing but a change of attitude in which consequentially and universally the world of experience is seen as the world of possible experiences—and that is this experiencing life; the experienced itself is at any given time—and universally—the sense of experience in a determinate intentional horizon.[120]

Let us now turn to *Ideas*, where we find the same situation, in principle, as in the "Five Lectures." The Cartesian lines of thinking are in the foreground in the second section of this work ("The Fundamental Phenomenological Outlook"), which is devoted to the idea of the phenomenological reduction. But before Husserl develops these lines of thinking, he opposed—in the last paragraphs of the first section (sec. 26)—"sciences of the dogmatic and sciences of the philosophic attitude."[121] He explains that "theory of knowledge is needed as a science having a *direction of inquiry peculiar to itself.*"[122] On the other hand, in section 61 of this work, which bears the title "The Methodological Importance of the Systematic Theory of Phenomenological Reductions" and which concludes the exposition on the "fundamental phenomenological outlook" (which has encompassed more than thirty paragraphs), Husserl states that the phenomenological reduction is univocally and exclusively determined as protection against a *metabasis* (i.e., against the contamination of the transcendental-phenomenological dimension of subjectivity by means of objective cognition of the natural sort). Here we find the statements that the explicit "bracketings" of the phenomenological reduction

have the methodical function continually to remind us that the relevant spheres of being and knowledge lie *in principle* outside those which should be studied transcendentally and phenomenologically, and that every intrusion of premises belonging to those bracketed domains is a sign pointing to a non-sensical confusion, to a genuine *'metabasis'*.[123]

Thus even in the "fundamental phenomenological outlook" of *Ideas* there is an authoritative meaning for the phenomenological reduction which cannot be derived from the Cartesian way (which was undertaken). Rather, it belongs to the way through ontology.

Furthermore, as we know, Husserl undertook the way through ontology in the winter semester 1919/20—namely, in his lecture "Introduction to Philosophy."[124]

This way is used anew in the article "Kant and the Idea of Transcendental Philosophy," which Husserl wrote immediately after the lectures "Erste Philosophie" in the winter semester 1923/24 (in which the Cartesian way and the way through psychology were expounded). Here he proceeds from a description of the presupposition inherent in the natural worldly life: that the world exists in itself and forms the standard for our knowledge. He poses the question: How is this belief in a world existing in itself constituted in the life of consciousness? He explains that if consciousness were studied purely in itself under the guidance of this question, one would already be operating in the transcendental attitude.[125] Moreover, he demands still further—and hereby aligns himself against Kant—that this naive transcendental attitude must be secured by means of a methodic reflection (through the transcendental reduction). According to him, one thereby consciously comprehends the purity of transcendental subjectivity, and all psychological and naturalistic interpretations are kept at a distance.

Husserl's *Formal and Transcendental Logic* is determined exclusively by means of the way through ontology. Let us try to determine the broad outlines of the second section of this work, which executes the about-turn from objective logic and ontology to transcendental phenomenology. After Husserl has outlined (in the first section) the idea of a formal logic in the comprehensive sense of a *"mathesis universalis,"* he begins to show (in the second section) that a purely *objective* logic "remains stuck fast in a naiveté which shuts it off from the philosophic merit of radical self-understanding and fundamental self-justification,"[126] and is subject to deception and displacement which make impossible the clarity which alone is able ultimately to determine its scope and the range of justifiable application.[127] In these terms, Husserl demands a grounding of logic through investigations directed toward the subjective, which, moreover, he characterizes as a "Critique of Reason."[128] In addition, he proceeds to exhibit the concealed (implicit) presuppositions of logic, always with the intention of demonstrating the necessity of the subjective investigations and of freeing the subjective problematic. This proof finally leads Husserl to the *world* as the unity of possible experience which is always tacitly presupposed by traditional logic.[129] Consequently, the elucidation of the meaning of the world is shown to belong to the elucidation of the fundamental logical concepts.[130]

Let us stress that, up to now, Husserl quite deliberately said nothing about the proper character of the subjective investigations—even when he spoke extensively of the genetic constitution.[131] At the outset of this proof, he had explained that the disclosure of that character would itself take place through reflection on the *logical requirements* of subjective investigations.[132] This reflection then takes place in sections 93 and 94. If the meaning of the fundamental logical concept "world" must be clarified in the subjective investigation, then the world in its naturally objective sense of being ought not simply to be tacitly presupposed as its own horizon. The subjectivity, in which this sense of being is constituted and achieved, ought not to be naively burdened with this sense of being; rather, the world is "to be called into question." The subjectivity which is investigated cannot, then, have the sense of "world"; that is, it cannot be a psychological subjectivity. Rather, it can only be apprehended as a world-constituting one; that is, as a transcendental one.

In conclusion let us stress again that, in this movement toward transcendental subjectivity in *Formal and Transcendental Logic*, no motif enters which stems from the Cartesian or from the psychological way. Nowhere is there recourse to the apodicticity of the subject or to the demand for an absolute beginning to philosophy. The "exclusive interest in the purely psychic" plays just as little role. There is no talk even of the ambiguous opposition "immanence-transcendence", which is typical of the Cartesian way. It is replaced with the opposition between "mundane" (or "objective") and "transcendental." The whole line of thinking is determined by the task of clarifying or criticizing objective logic and ontology, and by the solution of this task through the investigation of the operative (*leistenden*) intentionality, whereby the correlation between the ontological and the phenomenological a priori is repeatedly indicated.

Finally, the way through ontology occupies a very important place in Husserl's last work, the *Crisis*. For "The Way into Transcendental Phenomenological Philosophy by Questioning Back from the Pre-given Life-World," which forms section A of the third part of the work, is nothing other than a particular form of that way, of course the most fundamental. In three successive thrusts, Husserl pushes forward to transcendental subjectivity. In a certain sense, each of these thrusts poses a new beginning but, at the same time, rests on the prescriptions and indications of what has preceded in order to penetrate to greater concreteness.

The first of these thrusts comprises sections 28 to 32 and stands under Kant's auspices. In "Philosophizing with Kant,"[133] Husserl points to the subjective courses of world-constitution which are disclosed by the inquiry into the sense of being and validity of the world, which is constantly presupposed and taken for granted in the natural-objective life. He speaks of the "superficial" and "shallow" character (*Äusserlichkeit*[134] and *Flächenhaftigkeit*[135]) of the natural-objective outlook on the world. He takes the anonymously functioning subjectivity in it, which constantly raises a world to valid existence through an unceasing change in itself, as a region of being of a "new dimension,"[136] which, in contrast to the "two-dimensional character" of the natural-objective world-life, he characterizes as "dimension of depth" (*Tiefen-dimension*)[137] or as a "third dimension."[138] Kant's theory of the "formation" of the world through the transcendental operations pushes in this direction of depth, according to Husserl, but without actually (i.e., methodologically) disclosing it.[139] Husserl now takes this disclosure as a task—a task which is antagonistic to the interests of the natural-objective world-life. For this reason "it had to remain concealed to humanity and even to the scientists for millennia."[140]

The second advance toward transcendental subjectivity, which is already more concrete, comprises sections 33 to 42. It concerns, above all, the "problem of the way in which the life-world is"[141]—as part of the more general problem of a complete grounding of the objective sciences. The former problem is drawn from this latter problematic, in order to treat it as an independent one.[142] But then what is at issue with it is finally realized to be not a partial problem but a universal philosophical problem which includes the objective sciences as phenomena *in* the life-world.[143] Husserl then begins to look for the *kind* of scientific method in which the problem of the life-world can be discussed and to show in this respect that *objective* science, to which psychology belongs as well, is in principle unable to grasp it.[144] To safeguard the problem of the being of the life-world from foreign intrusion[145]—namely, in order "not to allow entities in the sense objective science understands them to be substituted where entities of the life-world are in question"[146]—Husserl demands an epoche in regard to the cognition which is carried out in the objective sciences.[147] Here this epoche has the exclusive sense of making a *metabasis* secure. To indicate the formal object of this new type of scientificity, Husserl points to the ontological and phenomenological a priori structures of the life-world and of experiences of the life-world. He then speaks of two ways to make the life-world a theme: by the naive natural attitude directed straight to what is ontologically objective (but not to what is scientifically objective) and by the resultant reflective attitude directed toward the way the life-world is given in various modes.[148] The theme of the second attitude, which touches on a "complete reversal of interest,"[149] includes the life-world in its ontological structure as well. But here it is correlated to the universal operative (*leistenden*) life in which the world is situated, namely, in terms of which the world attains its sense of being and being valid as the correlate of universal synthetically bound achievements which can be researched. After Husserl has pointed to this new, ensuing reflective attitude, which is none other than the transcendental phenomenological one, he places it in relation to Kant:

One path which is historically motivated has led us from the interpretation of the problematic operative between Kant and Hume[150] to the postulate to investigate the universal prior given world as the basis for all objective *praxis* whatsoever. It has thus led us to postulate that new kind of universal science of the subjectivity which grants the world antecedently.[151]

After Husserl had outlined the transcendental attitude, or what is to be investigated in it, he penetrates its inner demands and determines that these investigations cannot be carried out on the basis of the natural attitude. The consciousness which constitutes the sense and validity of the world cannot be studied in the natural attitude because the natural attitude always presupposes the sense and validity of the world as something not yet questioned. Consequently there is need of a universal epoche on our naive belief in the validity of the world.[152] The new attitude stands *beyond* the pregivenness of the world as valid and *beyond* the universal life of consciousness (the individual subjective and intersubjective life) in which the world is "there" for those who naively live in it.[153] The second projected way to transcendental subjectivity concludes with the demand for a *concrete* indication of the way to carry through the transcendental reduction.

The third plan, which is formed in sections 43 to 55, begins with a critique of the Cartesian way[154] in order to describe more concretely in what follows that very way which was sketched in the previous plans. To investigate the ways in which the world is given, an "*epoché* which is offered in the first place quite obviously as immediately necessary"[155] is demanded with respect to the actuality of *things* belonging to the life-world.[156] Analyses follow of the various basic phenomena of consciousness in which the thought of the correlation between the ontological and phenomenological a priori—or the thought of function of the ontological a priori (of the ontology of the life-world) functioning as an index or a clue—forms the leading idea.[157] The final four paragraphs *consciously* take the subjectivity investigated as transcendental. They begin with the explanation that the survey of the correlation problematic yields insights (*Erkenntnisse*), which with the complete *methodic assurance*, signify a radical new formation of our whole conception (idea) of the world.[158] In view of this assurance, Husserl undertakes a reflection on the basis of the ultimate presuppositions in which the whole correlation problematic is rooted. Grasping on the strength of the obviousness of natural-objective life the constituting subjectivity as human, he encounters the paradox that a portion of the world constitutes the whole world, that the subject portion of the world absorbs, so to speak, the whole world and thereby itself.[159] The resolution of this paradox ensues by distinguishing between the *objective* subjectivity as a portion of the constituted world and the *transcendental* subjectivity which constitutes the world.[160] The objective-psychological apprehension of the constituting subjectivity as a human subjectivity is explicitly rejected as a nonsensual intrusion of the natural-objective attitude and is thus rejected as a *metabasis*.[161]

It is especially to be emphasized that in this context Husserl achieves a definition of the meaning of the transcendental attitude and epoche which completely frees the latter from any impression of a loss or limitation. With respect to the question whether the world is lost in the transcendental epoche, Husserl realizes that in the epoche even the philosopher must in a certain way "naturally live through" the natural life in which the world is posited. Husserl realizes that, as distinct from the man of the natural attitude, the philosopher does *not* allow his cognitive purposes to be *terminated* in the world. Rather, he goes back to the subjectivity which constitutes the world, which he can no longer grasp as worldly. Consequently, for investigating it, he may use nothing worldly as *premises*.[162]

At the end of our presentation of Husserl's way through ontology, we can state the following. This way is not in itself marred by the failure which made the other two ways appear questionable; not only is full subjectivity achieved along it, but the transcendental reduction no longer appears, above all, as a loss or limitation to a special region of being. *On the contrary*, the transcendental reduction appears here as *breaking through limitations*, namely, the limitations of natural objective cognition, which is shown to be "one-sided," "abstract," "superficial," and "shallow." To use words which hark back to Hegel, it is the transition (*Übergang*) from the limited character of natural consciousness, which sees objects only positively as stat-

ic, fixed, foreign things standing over against, to philosophical thinking, which recognizes the world as the proper achievement of consciousness, changing and developing throughout various forms. This phenomenological reduction thus attains validity as a step into the "comprehension," the "concrete," the inner, the depths (which includes the "superficial" in it). Its basic character consists of the *reversal* (*Umstellung*) of a radical reflection which breaks through the natural-objective life of the world. The epoche then emerges as a *dependent* moment: it follows as a logical demand of the reversal which wants to remain faithful to itself and does not want to intrude into the newly opened dimension with views ("categories") which belong to the life of the natural-objective world. Only this relationship between the transcendental reversal and epoche allows the transcendental reduction to appear not as a loss or return to a special sphere of objective actuality. The opposite is necessarily the case when the epoche independently precedes the transcendental reversal, as it does on the Cartesian and psychological ways. Thus only the ontological way actually grasps even subjectivity as transcendental.

The meaning of the phenomenological reduction, as it issues from the way over ontology, is the one Husserl ultimately had in mind whenever he speaks of the phenomenological reduction itself—even when he crosses other ways (as in *The Idea of Phenomenology* and *Ideas*). Whenever he tries to grasp the final meaning of the phenomenological reduction, he uses the concept of reversal.[163] Indeed, he explains that the phenomenological reduction is nothing but a change of attitude.[164] Thus the epoche signifies the following: ". . . to exclude the world means not to want to pass judgment on it straightway."[165] In this way it signifies further protection against the corrupting realization of transcendental consciousness:

Consciousness is not a psychic lived-experience, not a mesh of psychic lived-experiences, not a thing, not an appendage (condition, activity) in an object of nature. To think so is the basic mistake which makes up the final basic mistake of psychologism (to which not only all empiricists but also rationalists succumb). Whoever saves us from the realization of consciousness is the saviour of philosophy, indeed the creator of philosophy.[166]

In our opinion, nothing has so harmed the understanding of Husserl's phenomenological reduction as conjoining it (as Husserl himself does) with the Cartesian reflections on doubt. On the basis of the occurrence of dreams and the hyperbolic assumption of the "evil genius" Descartes *doubts* the existence of the world (or at least tries to do so). For him, the "cogito" is the first secure member or basic axiom by means of which he tries to win back that which is lost. But Husserl does not doubt for a moment the being of the world and the sciences of the world. He explicitly explains that no doubt at all is possible concerning the existence of the world.[167] Even on the Cartesian path, Husserl denies that the epoche signifies a doubt and that through it we surrender our convictions.[168] When he speaks of the dubitability of transcendent being, he does not thereby want to say that the latter *is* doubtful but only the possibility in principle that this being could at one time *become* doubtful.[169]

In the epoche it is also not a question about the "being posited there" of neutral consciousness. Especially in *Ideas*, Husserl sees an interconnection,[170] but later he denied this view.[171] The mistake in these interpretations of the epoche consists of deriving it from the *natural* attitude. Doubt and neutral consciousness toward worldly being belong to the natural attitude. But along the Cartesian way, where the epoche independently precedes the transcendental reversal, the epoche can only be grasped in a "natural" sense—namely, as doubt or neutralized consciousness—since even by carrying through the epoche on this route something other than the natural-objective attitude is not reached. If Hus-

serl denies that it is a matter of a doubt or of a neutralized consciousness, he can do so only because he does not think of the epoche as determined by the Cartesian way. In its essence, Husserl's philosophy is scarcely Cartesian at all. At most, its basic tendency toward an apodictic and absolute evidence provides a general and vague parallel with Descartes. In Husserl's philosophy it is not a matter of guarding entities against a skeptical spirit; rather, the issue is to understand entities. The phenomenological reduction therefore does not have the meaning of calling the world into question "to show its actuality, but to bring out its possible and genuine sense."[172] In *The Paris Lectures* and *Cartesian Meditations*, Husserl explains that his philosophy could be taken as a new Cartesianism; but in so doing he lets himself be pulled too strongly by a single idea, as well as by the purely external context in which the lectures were delivered. In the *Crisis* he sees more clearly

It is naturally a ludicrous, though unfortunately common misunderstanding, to seek to attack transcendental phenomenology as "Cartesianism", as if its *ego cogito* were a premise or set of premises from which the rest of knowledge (whereby one naively speaks only of objective knowledge) was to be deduced, absolutely "secured". The point is not to secure objectivity but to understand it.[173]

It must nevertheless be noted that Husserl's divergence from the Cartesian way or his setting out on the way over ontology by no means signifies abandonment of the ideal of philosophy as a rigorous science. Of course, this ideal thereby becomes modified in principle: philosophy does not have absolute evidence as its starting point; rather, its course consists of seeking absolute evidence through increasingly more radical reflection and self-critique. Absolute evidence is not something given but something to achieve—an idea, as Husserl clearly recognized in *Formal and Transcendental Logic*.[174] In the radical subsequent pursuit of this idea, philosophy is shown to be rigorously scientific. It knows that the absolute evidence *in itself* (*kath auto*) is the first, or the ground (*arche*), of the cognition for which philosophy strives. On the other hand, it knows as well that this absolute evidence *for us* (*pros egas*) can only be the last (the "result"). In *Formal and Transcendental Logic*, Husserl explains the transcendental self-critique of transcendental phenomenology, through which absolute (because totally reflected) evidence is achieved, as the *in itself* first critique of knowledge.[175] But at the same time he expresses the insight that this critique of knowledge, which is first in itself, cannot be the first for us; rather, transcendental philosophy must of necessity begin in a certain naiveté and tentativeness.[176]

Now that we have become familiar with the three ways of Husserl's phenomenological reduction, we return to the question which was our point of departure: By what means is the constitution of philosophical knowledge carried out?

On the basis of experiences which we have undergone along the routes traversed by Husserl, we can say the following.

Philosophy obviously does not arise in the subsequent extension of a positive science, such as psychology—to cite Husserl's example. Positive science rests on an *abstraction* which makes it possible and grounds it. All knowledge, which subsequently remains within the framework of a positive science and strictly accords with what is demanded by the character of a definite positive science, is always infected with the basic character of the abstractedness which makes it possible. For this reason such abstract knowledge is never able to become philosophical knowledge, which, according to its very nature, proceeds to *concrete* and *total* truth. According to their essences, positive sciences have the character of being founded upon abstraction. This foundedness proves that the scientific concept of philosophy is nonsense.

But it is obvious, as well, that philosophy does not arise in a way prescribed by Descartes. On the Cartesian line of thinking, the contradiction ultimately consists of the fact that *absolute* philosophical truth—that is, concrete total (adequate) truth—is claimed for a *single* cognition (the "cogito") which is *separate* from all remaining cognitions. A single cognition, separated from the rest, cannot be concrete and total; that is, it cannot be absolute philosophic truth. For absolute philosophic truth is the *whole*. What an individual is ultimately is determined first by its relationship to the whole; thus an individual can only be recognized absolutely in the whole. For this reason philosophy does not have an absolute beginning but only an absolute end, which lies at infinity. The Cartesian concept of philosophy, which is mathematical (since it wants to begin with an absolute axiom), is just as contradictory as the scientistic.

Clearly, philosophy arises through radical critical reflection which is constantly making itself radical (as transcendental self-knowledge and thereby, at once, as transcendental knowledge of the world). This reflection emerges from the natural, historical mundane life. It does not turn away from the latter, but, by means of a new viewpoint; this reflection seeks the true meaning (*telos*) of this mundane life and makes the latter for the first time visible in its naive and historical nature and in its entire concretion.

On the one hand, philosophy finds itself historically in a necessary antagonism with natural mundane life, since philosophical reflection radically calls into question and thereby disrupts the straightforward absorption throughout life and work into the world. Out of anxiety about the loss of absolutizing and idols, mundane *praxis* resists in the face of radical critical reflection. The *praxis* seeks to bring the philosopher to betray his truth (*metabasis*) or to release itself from him by making him ridiculous or by condemning him. Seen from the point of view of the natural mundane life, philosophical reflection has the character of a loss. But this loss is in itself a loss of limitations—that is, a win.[177] Philosophical truth has a superiority over the merely one-sided and situation-dependent mundane interests and mundane truths of men. Therefore it cannot have its criterion of truth in the mundane *praxis* of the positive sciences or the community. "Philosophy" which arises purely in a natural mundane interest is not philosophy. It is either bad scientific hypothesis or ideology which does not arise above its particular historical situation and thereby passes away with it.

But, on the other hand, philosophy does not lack inner cohesion with an individual historical epoch—and not just because philosophy is a constant going beyond (transcending) the historically conditioned situation and never an actual, complete being beyond (absolute transcendence). Rather it lacks this cohesion because, as self-reflection, philosophy reflects on the definite historical situation of the spirit out of which it has arisen and which always remains its present, its fertile soil, and the partner it seeks. Philosophy is therefore actual, but it is not absorbed in this actuality—as ideology is. Rather, it has the eternal for its horizon and therefore has the unending task of bringing the present to its *telos*, of bringing limited reason to complete reason and thereby sublating the antagonism between the naive mundane life and philosophy.[178]

NOTES

1. Cf. the introduction by R. Boehm to *Edmund Husserl: Gesammelte Werke*, edited under the direction of H. L. Van Breda (8: xxxiii ff.), and the appendix by E. Fink in *Edmund Husserl 1859-1959* (The Hague: Nijhoff, 1959). Hereafter *Gesammelte Werke* is referred to as *Husserliana*.

2. *LU* (Halle edition referred to throughout), 2:19; *LI*, 1: 263.

3. *LU*, 2:21; *LI*, 1:265.

4. *LU*, 2:19; *LI*, 1:263.

5. Cf. the original manuscript, preserved in the Husserl archive (Louvain) (MS orig.), B II 1, p. 47a (16 June 1904).

6. *Husserliana*, 2:29; *The Idea of Phenomenology* (The Hague: Nijhoff, 1964), p. 22. Hereafter this English translation, by W. P. Alston and G. Nakhnikian, will be cited as *Idea*.

7. *Husserliana*, 2:30; *Idea*, p. 23.

8. *Husserliana*, 2:34; *Idea*, p. 27.

9. *Husserliana*, 2:33; *Idea*, p. 26.

10. *Husserliana*, 2:31; *Idea*, p. 24.

11. Ibid.

12. *Husserliana* 2:35ff; cf. p. 5; *Idea*, pp. 27ff.; cf. p. 2.

13. *Husserliana*, 2: 43ff.; *Idea*, pp. 33ff.

14. *Husserliana*, 2:49; *Idea*, p. 39.

15. *Husserliana*, 2:67, 72; cf. p. 11; *Idea*. 52, 57; cf. p. 8.

16. *Husserliana*, 2: 9; *Idea*, p. 7.

17. The manuscript for these lectures is preserved in the Husserl Archive under the heading F 1 43.

18. *Husserliana*, 3:65; *Ideas*, p. 108.

19. *Husserliana*, 3:70; *Ideas*, p. 112.

20. *Husserliana*, 3:72.

21. Ibid.

22. *Husserliana*, 3:86; *Ideas*, p. 125.

23. Ibid.

24. *Husserliana*, 3: 95ff.; *Ideas*, pp. 133ff.

25. Cf. sec. 44.

26. Cf. sec. 46.

27. *Husserliana*, 3:115; *Ideas*, p. 151.

28. *Husserliana*, 3:116; *Ideas*, p. 152.

29. *Husserliana*, 3:118; *Ideas*, p. 154.

30. Ibid.

31. *Husserliana*, 3:119; *Ideas*, p. 155.

32. In the lecture course "Erste Philosophie" (1923/24) apodictic and adequate evidence are treated as equivalents; cf. *Husserliana*, 8: 35.

33. *Husserliana*, 8:69.

34. Cf. Ibid., sec. 32.

35. Cf. ibid., sec. 33, 34.

36. Ibid., p. 68.

37. Ibid., p. 69.

38. Ibid., pp. 70-73.

39. Ibid., p. 76.

40. Ibid., pp. 71ff.

41. Ibid., p. 80.

42. Ibid.

43. Cf. ibid., pp. 126, 171ff.

44. Ibid., p. 127; cf. Husserl's critical remarks on this point, app. [app. for appendix (Beilage)] 2, p. 312 (and pp. 81ff).

45. Cf. *Husserliana*, vol. 1, sec. 6; apodictic and inadequate evidence are here no longer taken as equivalent (cf. loc. cit., p. 55). References to the English translation by Dorian Cairns, *Cartesian Meditations* (The Hague: Nijhoff, 1960), will be abbreviated *CM*.

46. *Husserliana*, vol. 1, sec. 7.

47. Ibid., sec. 8.

48. Ibid., sec. 9.

49. Ibid., 6:157-58.

50. Cf. ibid., 3:119; *Ideas*, p. 155.

51. Cf. *Erste Philosophie (1923/24)*, pt. 2; *Husserliana*, 8: 174; app. 30, pp. 479ff. (about 1924).

52. *Husserliana*, 1:60; *CM*, p. 21.

53. *Husserliana*, 8:pt. 2, p. 68.

54. Cf. loc. cit., app. 20, pp. 432-33 (1924).

55. *Husserliana*, 6:158.
56. Cf. *Husserliana*, 8, *Erste Philosophie*, pt. 2, sec. 53, 54; *Husserliana*, 1, *Cartesian Meditations*, Fifth Meditation.
57. *Husserliana*, 8:129; cf. app. 2, pp. 312-13.
58. *Husserliana*, 8:174n.
59. Ibid., app. 20, p. 433 (1924).
60. *Critique of Pure Reason*, B XXXIX ff. Remarks on pp. 274-79.
61. Cf. *Husserliana*, 3: critical app., p. 468. Remarks to p. 79, 2.
62. Cf. ibid., app. 13, pp. 399ff. (1929), and critical app. to the text, p. 467. Remarks to p. 75, 33. Cf. also *Husserliana*, 8: app. 20, p. 433 (1924).
63. *Husserliana*, 8, *Erste Philosophie*, pt. 2, p. 159.
64. Ibid., pp. 85-86.
65. Ibid., p. 158.
66. For carrying out the above, cf. ibid., pp. 84ff., 132ff., 157ff.
67. Ibid., 3: 115; *Ideas*, p. 151.
68. *Husserliana*, 2, *Five Lectures*, pp. 29ff.; *Husserliana*, 8, *Erste Philosophie*, pt. 2, pp. 33ff.; *Husserliana* 1, *Cartesian Meditations*, 17, 18.
69. *Husserliana*, 8, *Erste Philosophie*, pt. 2, p. 35.
70. *Husserliana*, 1: 55.
71. Cf. ibid., 3: app. 13, p. 409 (1929); *Formal and Transcendental Logic*.
72. Cf. *Husserliana*, 8: app. 28, pp. 469ff. (2 Nov. 1925); *Cartesian Meditations*, pp. 28-29.
73. Cf. *Husserliana*, 3. In this text it is a matter of a remark from the 1920s, which was taken up in the Louvain edition of *Ideen I*.
74. *Husserliana*, 8: app. 28, pp. 469ff. (2 Nov. 1925).
75. Ibid., p. 468.
76. Ibid., p. 466.
77. Cf. ibid., 3: 107. It has to do with a completion from the twenties which was taken up in the text of the Louvain edition of *Formale und transzendentale Logik*, p. 254.
78. *Husserliana*, 8, *Erste Philosophie*, pt. 2, p. 175.
79. Cf. *Husserliana*, 1, *Cartesian Meditations*, p. 67; *Husserliana*, vol. 2, critical remarks on the text, p. 91 (on 35, 30).
80. Cf. *Husserliana*, 8: app. 13, pp. 397ff. (1925); *Cartesian Meditations*, pp. 28-29.
81. *Husserliana*, 8: app. 13, p. 398 (1925).
82. Cf. *Husserliana*, 8, *Erste Philosophie*, pt. 2, pp. 35, 109.
83. *Husserliana*, 8: 165.
84. Ibid., p. 127.
85. Ibid., pp. 108, 127.
86. Ibid., pp. 128, 141-42.
87. Ibid., pp. 144, 153.
88. Ibid., p. 162.
89. Ibid.
90. Cf. ibid., app. 2, p. 317, to pp. 127, 9-17; to pp. 127, 26-29; to pp. 128, 6-13; to pp. 129, 143; and to app. 23 (probably 1925).
91. *Husserliana*, 6, *Krisis*, 66.
92. Ibid., p. 252.
93. Ibid., pp. 242-43.
94. Ibid., p. 256.
95. Ibid., p. 259.
96. Ibid., 8: app. 2, p. 319.
97. Ibid., 6, *Krisis*, p. 259; *Crisis*, p. 256.
98. *Husserliana*, 6, *Krisis*, pp. 261, 263, 268; *Crisis*, pp. 257, 260, 264.
99. Cf. *Husserliana*, 8: app. 23, pp. 446-47 (1925), and *Encyclopaedia Britannica*, vol. IX; art. 4 (final) draft, sec. 13ff.
100. *Husserliana*, 8: app. 23, pp. 448-49 (1925).
101. *LU* (1st ed.), 2: 20-21.
102. *Husserliana*, 2: 17; *Idea*, p. 13.
103. *Husserliana*, 2: 24; *Idea*, p. 19.
104. *Husserliana*, 2: 25; *Idea*, p. 21.
105. *Husserliana*, 2: 24; *Idea*, p. 19.
106. *Husserliana*, 2: 39; *Idea*, p. 31.
107. *Husserliana*, 2: 39; *Idea*, p. 31.
108. *Husserliana*, 2: 6; *Idea*, pp. 4-5.
109. Ontological principles are indeed nothing other than the principles of objectivity.
110. Original manuscript B 2 1, p. 5b (1907).
111. Loc. cit., p. 14b (Sept. 1907).
112. *Husserliana*, vol. 8, treatise: "Way into Transcendental Phenomenology as Absolute and Universal Ontology through Positive Ontologies and the Positive First Philosophy." p. 225 (1923).
113. Ibid.
114. Original manuscript F 1 12, p. 69a (1910/11).
115. Cf. manuscript F 1 43.
116. In our presentation we are following a summary of this lecture, which Husserl wrote about 1924 and which is published in *Husserliana*, 8, as app. 20.
117. Ibid., p. 434.
118. Ibid., p. 435.
119. Cf. (above) our explication of Husserl's method for securing transcendental intersubjectivity.
120. *Husserliana*, 8: 436 (1924).
121. Ibid., vol. 3, heading of sec. 26; *Ideas*, sec. 26.
122. *Husserliana*, 3: 56; *Ideas*, p. 96 (Kern's underlining).
123. *Husserliana*, 3: 144-45 (cf. *Ideas*, p. 179).
124. Cf. original manuscript F 1 40.
125. *Husserliana*, 7: "Kant und die Idee der Transzendentalphilosophie," pp. 254-55 (1924); cf. "Kant and the Idea of Transcendental Philosophy," *The Southwestern Journal of Philosophy*, 5 (1974), 9-56.
126. *Formal and Transcendental Logic*, p. 153 (hereafter abbreviated *FTL*).
127. Ibid., p. 267.
128. Ibid., pp. 162-71.
129. Ibid., p. 218.
130. Ibid., p. 229.
131. Cf. ibid., sec. 85.
132. Ibid., pp. 155-56.
133. *Krisis*, p. 114; *Crisis*, p. 111.
134. *Krisis*, p. 116; *Crisis*, p. 113.
135. *Krisis*, pp. 121, 122; *Crisis*, pp. 118, 119.
136. *Krisis*, pp. 115, 120, 123; *Crisis*, pp. 112, 119, 120.
137. *Krisis*, p. 121; *Crisis*, p. 118.

138. *Krisis*, p. 126; *Crisis*, p. 123.

139. *Krisis*, pp. 120-21; *Crisis*, pp. 117-18.

140. *Krisis*, p. 121; *Crisis*, p. 118.

141. *Krisis*, p. 125; *Crisis*, p. 123.

142. *Crisis*, sec. 33.

143. Ibid., sec. 34e, f.

144. Ibid., sec. 34.

145. *Krisis*, p. 137; *Crisis*, p. 135.

146. *Krisis*, p. 129; *Crisis*, p. 127.

147. *Crisis*, sec. 35.

148. *Krisis*, sec. 38.

149. Ibid., p. 147.

150. By the expression "problematic operative between Kant and Hume" Husserl has in mind Kant's "reacting against Hume's positivism of data"—i.e., Kant's doctrine that not only sense data are found in sensory experience (as Hume had in mind) but unities rationally formed by means of the hidden functioning understanding. Loc. cit., pp. 96-97, 100.

151. *Krisis*, p. 150; *Crisis*, p. 148.

152. *Crisis*, sec. 39, 40.

153. Ibid., pp. 153, 155.

154. Ibid., sec. 43.

155. *Krisis*, p. 157; *Crisis*, 154.

156. Ibid., sec. 44.

157. Ibid., sec. 46, 48, 51.

158. *Crisis*, p. 175.

159. Ibid., p. 179.

160. See ibid., sec. 54.

161. *Krisis*, pp. 157, 183, 187; *Crisis*, pp. 154, 179, 184.

162. *Krisis*, p. 180; *Crisis*, p. 177.

163. Cf. *Krisis*, pp. 202, 247; *Crisis*, pp. 199, 246.

164. Cf. *Husserliana*, 8: app. 20, p. 436 (probably 1924).

165. Cf. ibid., app. 23, p. 448 (probably 1925).

166. Original manuscript A 1 36, p. 193a (1920).

167. *FTL*, p. 251.

168. *Husserliana*, 3: 65, *Ideas*, p. 108.

169. *Ideas*, sec. 46.

170. *Ideen I*: 266; *Ideas*, p. 308.

171. See the remarks about the text in *Husserliana*, 3: 479, ad. 266, 11.

172. *FTL*, p. 229.

173. *Krisis*, p. 193; *Crisis*, p. 189.

174. *FTL*, p. 287.

175. *FTL*, p. 289.

176. *FTL*, pp. 270-71; cf. *Krisis*, p. 185; *Crisis*, p. 182.

177. The failure of the Cartesian way consists of its showing only a loss, and not dealing with a negation of a "negativity" (loss of boundaries).

178. In *Husserl und Kant: Studie über Husserl Verhaltnis zu Kant and zum Neukantianismus* I have dedicated more detailed investigations to the connections and ties to Kant which frequently emerged in our analysis of the ontological way of Husserl's phenomenological reduction. This work was published by Nijhoff in 1964. The present article presents the essentials of some paragraphs from this study.

The Husserlian Doctrine of Eidetic Intuition
and Its Recent Critics

JEAN PATOČKA

For many years analysts and commentators on Husserlian thought concentrated on the transcendental basis of knowledge and on the constitution of being (*l'être*) in transcendental consciousness. During the existential vogue, one rapidly passed over the doctrine, expressed in the *Logical Investigations* and developed systematically in the first chapter of *Ideas*, in the *Formal and Transcendental Logic* and, in the *Experience and Judgment*, of an eidetic intuition as a major process yielding general theses which are independent of empiricism in the current sense (that is to say, appealing to particular facts as arguments in their support). The Husserlian theory of access to the essential and of intuition of essences was nonetheless regarded by Husserl himself as an integral part of the theories of transcendental phenomenology.

All phenomenological analyses claim eidetic generality. If Husserl developed in *Ideen* III certain very novel considerations in comparison to *Ideas* he certainly was not under the impression that they were incompatible with his primary thesis. If he did not believe the exposition of *Ideas* to be complete and irreproachable, he probably never believed that he

This article appeared originally as "La Doctrine husserlienne de l'intuition eidetique et ses critiques recents *"Revue Internationale de Philosophie*, 71-72 (1965): 17-33. Translated by permission of the publisher and author. Translated by F. Elliston and P. McCormick. © 1976 Elliston and McCormick.

was obliged to sacrifice the very crux of what he had conceived from the beginning as his doctrine of the *eidos* and of an eidetic knowledge.

All the same, the general impression was that if Husserl's transcendental doctrine presupposed the eidetic reduction and if all the constitutive analyses take place at the level of eidetic universality, the doctrine of the *eidos*, on the contrary, was logically independent of transcendental considerations.

Nowadays, when some believe that the time has come for a review of the whole philosophical effort of the earlier, prewar generation,[1] the Husserlian doctrine of the *eidos* arouses a new interest—that of minute and severe criticism. In this sketch we react to two recent criticisms of this kind which have a common denominator: dialectic thought. The critics of the Husserlian eidetic whom we are going to discuss are dialecticians. These two recent critics Adorno and Eley,[2] bring to the surface a similar fundamental objection: a fixation of a universal which would like to be concrete but does not overcome its isolated abstraction.

Let us start by setting forth Adorno's point of view. The Husserlian doctrine of the *eidos* seeks to escape the need to traverse the field of extension in order to arrive at conceptual generality.[3] In contrast to the traditional doctrine of abstraction, Husserl's doctrine seeks to place itself in the immediate act of seizing a universal. This makes Husserl accept without criticism two nonexistent immediates: something given to the senses as isolated—the moment "red" in a visual presentation, for example; and the universal which would be no less immediately given as one and the same in a specific intellectual act.

Husserl is mistaken about the sense of the experience, which he poorly analyzes. He does not see that the moment "red," insofar as it is isolated from its spatio-temporal context, possesses no generality[4]—whereas the conceptual moments which comprise it, for example, the property of an object which belongs to the class of red things, possesses no immediacy.[5] Thus he forges his concept of eidetic intuition by contaminating the two moments of real (réelle) experience, which are in fact inseparable but which, fundamentally, are conceptually distinct. According to Adorno, this genesis of the Husserlian eidetic is valid for the Second Logical Investigation.

Later, during the period of *Ideas*, Husserl realizes the inconsistency of his first doctrine, which makes the *eidos* a useless reduplication of the individual. The individual fact is envisaged from the beginning as an "example" of the *eidos*. But to go from fact to essence, a specific process of variation must be carried out in the free field of imagination. The *eidos* or univeral essence, insofar as it is invariable, is supposed to result from this process of variation.

But the example of fact, taken as a point of departure for the research into the *eidos* in the imagination, annuls the point of departure of the whole doctrine—the fundamental difference between fact and essence. The idea of example is borrowed from this abstract and classificatory logic, against which the original doctrine had revolted.[6] According to that logic, the concept was only form without essential content. And the variation tries in vain to substitute an a priori terrain for a factual development of fact. The concrete content is borrowed from experience and the substance of the variation is drawn from this fountainhead.[7]

By contrast, the objects fictitiously constructed would count for nothing as regards the essence of the acts, which take them formally as intentional poles.[8]

The critic of Husserlian thought realizes, at a given moment, that the Husserlian effort basically seeks to assert that the concept is in no way external to the thing, that it is not arbitrarily built up by abstraction. Rather, the concept constitutes the life of the thing itself. But, according to Adorno, Husserl overlooks the moment of mediation and, instead of reflecting on the scientific concept at its very basis, dogmatically opposes to this concept a different procedure.[9]

It is quite possible that the Husserl of the *Logical Investigations* and of the article "Philosophy as a Rigorous Science" had been strongly impressed by the emphasis positivism placed on the immediately given. But his idea of an *intuition that gives originally* (*originairement*) is very different from that of positivism. The intuition which gives originally is that which offers the thing itself, by contrast to a simple "representation," whether the latter be actual or nonactual, directed toward the thing as present or as absent.[10] It is not the idea of an atomic given which directs the Husserlian conception but that of a harmony or agreement between what is aimed at and what is actually present. The presence itself is not dogmatically affirmed, but constitutes a phenomenon to be analyzed and to be defined (in the course of researches into time-consciousness).

The Husserlian doctrine does not presuppose a dogmatic thesis about the nature of the given. What is presupposed is the idea of *a meaningful act with universal intention* (*acte significatif à visée universelle*). The meaningful act is not an act of cognition, but it opens the possibility for all cognition; it puts someone on the track of possible knowledge. The connection, which is in no way a purely factual one, between what is intended and the fulfillment of an intention puts us on the track of an important distinction in the case of the meaningful act which intends something universal. This intention can be fulfilled *in certain cases* by an intuition—that is, by the original (*originaire*) presence, like that of a shade of red no longer considered, as in the case of a simple perception as an individual property, but taken in its generality as something which can be realized at any place and at any moment.

Thus it is completely false to say that Husserl *contaminates* the conceptual moment with the raw given of perception in his theory of the *eidos*. The conceptual moment is the general goal. Now this intention can evidently be fulfilled in the case of seeing or hearing. What then appears to us is neither the class of realizations of this type of consciousness nor some member of this class as such. Consequently, there remains only one possibility: to affirm that one grasps in the given presentation precisely that which makes possible the grouping of realizations of the type in question into the same class.

At the same time, it can be seen why Husserl speaks of red as one and the same without falling into contradiction. Red is primarily identical neither with the different parts of an extended thing nor with different objects where it forms a heading for a particular property. And at the same time it can fulfill the two functions. It fulfills the intention of a *shared* aspect on the basis of which a class of objects can be constituted. A class is not constituted without such an aspect. It is of primary importance in relation to the class intended.

Adorno's point of view consists of saying that Husserl claims to separate the understanding of the concept from its extension. This viewpoint is without foundation since the *act of universal intention* itself, which is presupposed by apprehending the essence, contains the moment of extension. It is expressed by a term which by no means applies to particulars. On the contrary, the *Second Logical Investigation*, which Adorno attacks for failing to take extension into account, speaks of equality and comparison;[11] it speaks of the possibility of having presented to the mind a multiplicity of objects which have the same trait. With Husserl it is not a question of revolt

against the traditional theory of concepts but of an attempt to deepen it.

This deepening consists of stating that the common aspect which can constitute a class is itself amenable to special reflection, which in turn can decide if it is a matter of a factual or fictitious intention (as in the case of the class of inhabitants of the moon), of a set of characteristics with no necessary connection (whatever the empirical class may be), or of a set of characteristics internally connected. The last is a case of eidetic intuition. It should be noted that, despite appearance, eidetic intuition is by no means simple—even if it is a question of an eidetic singularity.

One would not know how to apprehend a shade of *red* without regard to something more general than the shade itself. One would not know how to grasp the shade of red without a certain extension which in turn grounds it. A particular tone *necessarily* has duration, intensity, coloration, and a certain affective character: the eidetic apprehension is not an atomic given, even in the cases which are most amenable to such criticism. Jean Hering has drawn attention to the phenomenon of a mixture in the domain of the *eidos*, represented, for example, by the *eidos* "bitter-sweet" or "brownish-red," whose color—with its precise shade and the mixed quality of the form—could serve as examples.[12]

What must be remembered also is the fact, often emphasized by phenomenologists, that to grasp the essence, it by no means suffices to fix on it. Rather it is necessary to immerse oneself in it, follow its suggestive connections and indications—in short, to comprehend its intelligible content.[13]

It is also useful to remember that Husserl's Sixth Logical Investigation contains a description of a simple act of apprehension, applicable either to sensible perception or to the apprehension of essence, which expressly mentions all that is implicated in these acts. Their simplicity constitutes a phenomenal quality which is by no means metaphysical. It is precisely this phenomenal quality which allows envisaging even the 'immediate' givens as something mediated. Adorno emphasizes this fact a good deal and with good reason.[14]

Husserl is criticized for needlessly duplicating the sensory given, purely and simply. The rebuttal of this criticism, which is traditionally addressed to the defenders of the general concept of being, is contained in the preceding elucidation. By no means does sensory perception thematize; namely, it does not yield intelligible, necessary relations.

But if this is so and if it is not a question of a revolt against traditional logic and of a radical separation of the intension of the concept from its extension, then Adorno's reproach, which should be balanced with the first, charges that Husserl used examples as points of departure for the procedure of eidetic variation. But since the example is nothing other than a particular realization of the *eidos* in question, it is natural to begin with the analyses of an example and to free it from the contingent characteristics which affect it in its real (*réelle*) facticity. Husserl does not seek solely to determine the qualitative content of certain objects or experiences. He wants to reach intelligible and necessary structures and connections which are necessary. But to try to extract these relationships from the worthless stone of the contingent is precisely to force oneself to imagine things in ways other than they are usually given. An attempt must be made to change different moments of the thing and to combine all the changes the object can undergo without ceasing to be itself. This is the whole of the principle of variation.

Of course, this is not a revolution against logic and the traditional methodology of scientific research. On the contrary, it is an attempt to deepen it. Maurice Merleau-Ponty has illuminated what Husserlian research into essences has in common with inductive procedures—if induction is understood as it really is, divorced from what positivism makes of it.[15] Induction, he asserts, does nothing more than pursue in the domain of facts the search for the essential undertaken by Husserl beyond

the factual. Despite the distinction (fundamental, according to Husserl) between *eidos* and fact, there is also a continuity between essence and reality. The reason for this is that the contingent itself could be known as such only on the basis of the necessary and of the rational, and that the realities of facts themselves are by no means *given* but are constructed by means of *ideas* in order to satisfy the demands of the rational on the one hand and of the data of experience on the other. The ideas which are formed in order to understand reality are structural complexes which definite essential relations make possible. Thus Newton constructed the idea of a universal gravity in terms of material masses as substrata endowed with the universal property of mutual attraction in space according to a specific mathematical law. The material substrata of properties, space, and mathematical laws are components of this idea. These components are pure essences, malleable wherever any kinds of contingent factors can enter. Their mutual connection is ultimately possible only by virtue of a structural eidetic law.

Some of Husserl's disciples from the Göttingen period, for example Jean Hering and Roman Ingarden, in commenting on the distinction in *Ideas* between *what* is present in the particular entity and its ideation,[16] distinguished between the individual nature of a thing (its qualitative import—its *Sosein*, expressed by τί and ποῖον) and the pure *eidos* freed from its reality. They ask themselves the question: How could the nature of things be derived from pure essences?

This problem about the a priori character of the pure *eidos* and its relation to factual reality very much preoccupied Husserl. He made an effort not only to make this relation comprehensible in its generality but also to make intelligible the way in which this relation secures a place for itself in the historical evolution of science. Here again it is necessary to rebut the criticism that Husserl substituted metaphysical constructions for reflections on real science. Nevertheless, it is quite possible that the expressions "regional ontology" and "formal ontology" lend to the confusion. If it is true that Husserl does not try to reform knowledge by purely philosophical speculations but to reflect on the real processes of science, then the "ontologies" in question are by no means a priori constructions, arising from concepts in the sense of the old rationalistic metaphysics, but disciplines which make explicit the a priori conditions of experience in the Kantian sense.

This relationship between the *eidos* as a priori and reality is precisely the major problem which the second critic of Husserlian thought takes as his object. We now turn to Lothar Eley, whose criticism operates at a more profound and exacting level. It is not a question of proving errors in logic, or of accusing Husserl of having a false theory of concepts, but of discovering the hidden dialectic of all Husserl's work in order to rectify it, if possible, and to make phenomenology avoid the false paths which confuse its way.[17]

Criticism of the Husserlian *eidos* forms the core of Eley's analysis. According to Eley, who raises a rather new thesis with this point, the internal tensions of the *eidos* determine the entire construction of Husserl's transcendentalism. The prior and distinct unity of *Wesen* (essence) and *Dies-da* (this-here) is affirmed by the Husserlian doctrine of transcendentalism. Transcendentalism is called upon to make this unity evident, and it is precisely this unity which it is prevented from attaining at the very moment it affirms it, because it makes this unity an object and reifies its moments.[18]

The Husserlian *eidos* is quite different from the Aristotelian or scholastic *eidos*, which is simply the objectivity of the universal. Above all, the *eidos* is what makes the given rational, namely, what facticity is earlier connected to and what provides it with the necessary casing against which its contingent side can be contrasted. But it is also a special object, an object which has its particular way of being given, as we have seen. The *eidos* is therefore the framework within which the experience of an object unfolds—what gives it its quality as such-and-such an object—and

at the same time it is the object itself. But this very feature constitutes the apex of a subtle contradiction which prevents the *eidos* from being a simple objectivity and which forces Husserl to envisage therein, step by step, its irreconcilable aspects.

One of these aspects is a concrete logic, a conduit conducting the research into the real. If a fact must exist as fact, that is, as something determined (however contingent it may be), it could not be reduced here and now to a pure given. It is necessary that it have its essence, the universal of which it is an example; it must therefore be related a priori to this universal. But experience presents us with individual facts. If they relate to the essence, there must be a reason why they are so related. This reason can be contained neither in the essence and the intuition of the essence nor in the knowledge of the individual as such. There must therefore be a sphere between the *universal knowledge of the particular fact* and the particular fact itself. Thus the fact is the result; that is, fact involves mediation.

There is in the fact at first the understanding of a *detached* universal which tells us what the fact is. Then there is the understanding of the connection between the universal and the *concrete and individual eidos in general*. Finally, in the fact the concrete given is again attached to this double universality. In this way one can understand why the given in experience, the "this-here" (*Dies-da*), is an individual. To do so, it by no means suffices to see in the fact the realization of a highest universal, an "eidetic singularity." By doing so, one sees no further than the universal itself. The relation between the *eidos* (the universal essence) and the pure "this-here" (*Dies-da*) does not imply a *duality* but a *triplicity*.[19]

But it is certainly true that Husserl sees clearly that facts are related to essences and that they are therefore a result. (Here Eley parts company with Adorno.) *At the same time, he denies this position by envisaging the eidos as an objectivity sui generis*, totally separated from the fact. It is true that Husserl would like this separation to be unilateral: the facts depend on the essences; but the *eidos* does not depend on facts. But in reality he allows the *eidos* no other necessary connections than with other eidetic unities. He thereby makes two separate complexes: factually real things and the realm of essences. The reality of fact is divided—cut into eidetic singularities on the one hand and into a pure "this-here" on the other. If the essence does not have the power to connect itself to the factually real, then at the same time it loses its internal rationality.

This is the very fate to which the Husserlian *eidos* finds itself delivered: it is given to a pure view of the universal; but on the other hand it proceeds as if factual experience were connected to it—without being able to provide the reason for this connection. The variation itself, which is the principle for grasping the *eidos*, is conceived at one time as dependent on eidetic particularization and at another time as a function of the real which is individualized in its spatio-temporal connections as a possible framework of the variation. The regional *eidos* is the rule and norm of experience, giving it the form which by no means is drawn from empirical givens. But on the other hand its relation to empirical generalities is conceived on the model of a classification and the classification proceeds from the comparisons among the factually given.

Finally, the *eidos* and the actual reality figure as so many independent objects. If one forgets the contradiction of the *eidos*—conceived from one side as an a priori penetrating the fact in its pure factuality and from another side as a general object closed on itself—then one is ready to construe the *eidos* and the *reality* as *Sosein* and *Dasein*; the fact that reality exists and the "how" of its existence. The two belong to what is factually given. They are only distinctions of reason, as Nicolai Hartmann would say one day.[20]

But what conditions the thesis of the immediate grasp of the *eidos*—that which is at the root of the tension described above? Why does Husserl burden his doctrine of the a priori with such a heavy

mortgage? It is because he is trying to avoid a contradiction which is at the heart of his understanding of the way in which the a priori or regional eidos (*Wesen*) determines the experience of the "this-here." This determination or precedence of the a priori in relation to experience is the universality of the a priori, of the regional *eidos*. What results from it is a determinate universal—for example, a stone, this stone here. The experience of the "this-here" is the milieu, the synthesis of the *eidos,* and the fact as such.

The "this-here," seen from the point of view of the universal, must therefore be at once universal and nonuniversal. But how can it be both at the same time? According to Husserl—as Eley interprets him—it is necessary to envisage the two contradictory components of the "this-here" as *fixations* of one side by means of an "as." As long as the "this-here" is apprehended, one does not see what is prior—the universal a priori. And vice versa: apprehending the universal prevents apprehension of the fact. Aiming at the "this-here" is thus aiming at the universal as a nonuniversal. But grasping the universal is conditioned by this grasping of the *"this-here."* So conceived, the universal is itself conditioned by the sensory.

Thus apprehension of the *eidos* is itself apprehension of a fixed object and by no means the apprehension of the true universal, which would never be given as "peaceful and simple essence." Thus apprehension of the true universal requires opposite and contradictory points of view. But this true universal, which cannot present itself as a pure object, is transcendentality in its character as subjectivity-objectivity—as a subjectivity which makes itself objective and which transcends itself toward the world. The interpretation of the Husserlian *eidos* must be approached from there and by no means from its first partial result: the universal apprehended as an immediate object.

There is also the true meaning of the critique which Husserl directs to his own theory of the *eidos* in the sixth supplement to the first chapter of *Ideas* I. There he envisages the regions—the *summa genera* of eidetic universality—as universal structures of the world. The world is the totality of real things, such that each "this-here" which one encounters in it necessarily possesses the character of an objectively determinable entity. In its character as a rational fact, the world is the veritable field of the *eidos*.

We must be thankful to Eley for having illuminated in Husserl this unavowed dialectic which is found at the basis of his doctrine of the *eidos*. His study, which at first glance seems to be a review of contradictions and misunderstandings which permeate the Husserlian doctrine in a tight network, makes one see that all the apparent weaknesses of the doctrine start from a philosophical plan which is fully justifiable although not complete. The doctrine, which seemed to be set in an abstract formalism takes on new life. One begins to understand that the fixation of *Wesenschau*, the intuition of essences, does not constitute the central point inasmuch as one has gone past the fixation and attained the unconditional universal—what the Husserlian doctrine truly has in sight. The intuition of essences is in reality a moment of spiritual reflection which accomplishes its own objectivity—a moment necessary to assure its progress, but which would be dangerous to institute as a closed and completed objectivity.

Eley's theses bear directly on problems which Husserlian thought poses—above all on the question so often debated about the relation between Husserlian transcendentalism and the "ontological" phase of the doctrine. A break between the two has often been attempted, and Husserl (whose first intention would have been to deliver philosophy from formalist isolation, where modern subjectivism confined it, by opening an avenue to the things themselves) has been accused of falling back into the subjectivism he originally intended to repudiate. But what Eley shows is the contrast to this rather extensive view. It is precisely the doctrine of the absolutized *Wesenschau*

which threatens the doctrine with a radical separation from reality. And if the doctrine of the *eidos* fails there, it fails precisely by virtue of the transcendental motive it implies as a doctrine of the a priori. It is of little importance for this philosophical insight if the doctrine of the *Wesenschau* chronologically precedes the doctrine of the *Wesen* as a priori. What is decisive is that one would not know how to justify the tensions and contradictions which the intuition of essences implies except by invoking the transcendental motive. The unity of Husserlian thought is thus philosophically established.

Moreover, Eley's critique calls for reflection on the role that description plays in Husserl. Does description simply reproduce the given through abstract terminology? Is it the transposition of a set of facts into the sphere of the universally communicable *logos*? It *would* be if subjectivity were conceived as a field of processes ready to be grasped, which only need to be looked at for one to follow their articulations. But phenomenological description demands, above all, the discovery of a point of view, from which these processes can become something to be described and grasped objectively. Thus intentionality, which is the main object of Husserlian description, is not a *property* of object—a consciousness which would characterize the latter as the color red characterizes a posy. Consciousness is not intentional; it is not intentionality. Consciousness is *intentionality in the forgetfulness of itself*, intentionality masked by itself and become something other than it is.

Insofar as it is worldly, subjectivity is alienated subjectivity, and this alienation is itself the result of a subjective function which, having already *understood* us, prevents us from *understanding* ourselves. To discover intentionality and to subject it to description is, at the same time, to understand the meaning of the relationship between the subjective life and objectivity. It is to be beyond description, since the piercing of illusion and the destruction of masks do not describe themselves but are *carried out* (by phenomenological reduction).

But Eley believes he must note in Husserl the exclusion of the thematization and operation (execution): the operative (*exécutante*) consciousness does not thematize; the thematizing consciousness (the transcendental observer) is not operative. But if what we have just said is true, what is carried out by the thematizing consciousness is precisely the apprehension of the point of view from which operative consciousness becomes thematizable through the discovery of its forgotten and alienated operations in an understanding reified by itself.

What certainly must be subjected to a new examination, under the impulse of Eley's criticisms, is the relationship between essence and the "this-here" factually given. Eley shows us in the fact itself the result of a mediation which reconciles the universal and the abstract individual. They negate and exclude one another at the heart of the absolute universal transcendental consciousness. But it should be noted that the opposition, so deep in Husserl, between *Tatsache* (fact) and *Wesen* (essence) has long since been proved hardly convincing. That does not mean that the problem noted by Eley of a horizon within which the relation between essence and "this-here" must be located has already been solved. But in confronting the opposition between *Tatsache* and *Wesen*, essential necessity versus factual contingency, a dissatisfaction has long been felt which may be clarified by dialectical interpretation. Here "dialectical" signifies that the opposition in question is not static; the essential and the necessary on the one hand and the contingent and the factual on the other could not be distinguished once and for all. It is a matter of *process*, in the course of which the experience of facts is penetrated by the essential and the necessary.

The distinction made by such philosophers as Hering and Ingarden between *Wesen* and *Wesenheit* (essence and *eidos*) seems to accord with the sense of a less rigid relation. The definition in *Ideas* speaks of the *Wesen* as the peculiarity (*Eigenart*) of a thing, as the "set of essential properties which belong to it so that the other secondary accidental properties can be attributed to it." This definition obviously applies only to individual essences and in no way to the *eidos* as such. It should be noted, however, that if one speaks of essences individualized to such an extent, as in "the essence of the politics of Richelieu," it becomes increasingly more difficult to determine them or to separate them from the remaining properties and to "transpose them into ideas." The problem is definitely there, but it tends indefinitely to approach the inexhaustible task of grasping the individual as such.

But if the *eidos does not have an essence*, but *is* the essence or the "primary substance" of things, it becomes even more urgent to delimit the eidetic necessity and contingency in relation to others, for the *eidos* is purely essential. Thus it can seem at first glance that it is pure necessity. But that is to take up the metaphysical notions of necessity as defined by the tradition. Metaphysical necessity is either τὸ ἐξ ἀνάγκης ὄν what cannot not exist, or what cannot be otherwise, τὸ οὐκ ἐνδεχόμενον ἄλλως ἔχειν. These two types of necessity exclude all contingency.

Eidetic necessity is quite different. It deals with traits of one or several objects of our experience which are connected in a way that is accessible to intuition. The connection is not accidental (i.e., a conjunction allowed but not required). The exclusion is not a separation of fact but one which can be seen to be impossible in trying to understand the contrast. For example, it is impossible to imagine a visible tone—the two determinations exclude each other. But, on the other hand, the tone is one specification which is only possible—and is by no means required—by the "audible" type. It is an original specification, to be sure, and is not contained in the type itself. It contains an element of contingency in relation to this type on which it depends. In relation to it, it is in no way a ο’κ ἐνδεχόμενον ἄλλως ἔχειν but a possibility which excludes others and is coordinated with them. Thus the contingency itself is relative to a necessity and is based on it. The contingency is therefore itself an essential relation. It is what is permitted (not excluded) and at the same time required, but solely as a member of many coordinated possibilities.

It thus becomes impossible to conceive the order of εἴδη itself without contingency. This is one of the reasons why Husserl has admitted, in *Ideen* III, that the material essences themselves contain some contingency and that all material essences and their determinations are contingent—with the exception of a core of meaning that is absolutely indispensable if an experience of the world is to be possible. It is what forces Husserl to admit a distinction between the substantial regional *eidos* and the accidental regional *eide*, where the latter are characterized by their lack of this primary necessity.

It must be said that in *Ideas* Husserl analyzes eidetic necessity only in relation to the generality ("Charakter der Wesensnotwendigkeit und damit Beziehung auf Wesens-Allgemeinheit," sec. 2). He is occupied solely with the relation *Wesen-Tatsache* (*eidos*-fact). He fails to define what gives the essence its character as essence. This character certainly does not come from the fact that the *eidos* is unreal and atemporal—and thus from a certain point of view eternal. It comes from the fact that the rule of essences involves the relations between their members, relations which can be intuited and which tie these members together. This does not mean that an essence forms a single totality, one and inseparable. These are precisely the relations of contingency which make the breaks no less natural than the ties. But an essence as such is always formed by distinct traits which nonetheless control themselves and react on one another.

The definition Husserl gives in *Ideas* of *Wesen* neglects altogether this internal connection between the moments of the essence and does not speak of "a set of

predicates." But a set of predicates that are not related in a regulated way is not an essence, not even the essence of an empirical nature such as humanity or horseness. It is surprising that there are phenomenologists who believe there can be essences which lack this necessary internal connection.[21] Precisely the essences which Hering cites to support this thesis, for example horseness, have long been the objects of analyses which show the reciprocal play of the functions and forms which are mutually presupposed. (Since Cuvier, for example, the reconstruction of animal fossils from partial remains would have been impossible without such relations.)

In the *Logical Investigations*, by contrast, Husserl analyzes certain relations of essential necessity, but neither completely nor systematically. Here it is a matter of fundamental relations, which according to him are the origin of every relation of the whole to the parts and of the parts to the whole—be it a matter of real parts or of moments. But the foundation he examines is prior to all relations of coexistence. But there must also be analogous relations of succession. It is also doubtful that all relations of the type Hering calls "mixtures" (*Wesensverschmelzungen*) lead to fundamental relations (unilateral).

Thus, for example, "bitter-sweet" is not a whole composed of bitter and sweet but a reciprocal penetration of a special sort. The same applies to "brownish-red." The color of a tint is not an isolatable thing, even abstractly; rather, it is present in a whole like a substance in a solution. The more or less close kinship of certain traits in an *eidos* which results in their being based on an "original form" (*Urmorphe*, in Hering's sense) also rests on similar relations. Likewise, the kinship between certain qualities and certain forms which are based on them (the rough, the glossy, the pithy, the pungent in taste) are relations that are difficult to define with the help of the foundation.

In any case, Husserl never systematically treated the other universal relation of necessity, that is, *exclusion*. Above all, despite certain rudiments and fragmentary efforts, his *Logical Investigations* did not treat the main, necessary relations which cannot all be reduced to cases of objective necessity—correspondence between experience and the experienced. The latter will become the major theme of phenomenology (under the title "constitution"), without which its nature and its structure are never completely elucidated.

Husserl has thus treated the essential productive relations of contingency in *Ideas* and certain productive relations of necessity in *Logical Investigations*. But he never thought of establishing them in a systematic totality. For this reason the theory of essential necessities and their relations to the contingent fact fails; he never gave systematic grounding to the "ontology" whose idea he proclaimed. This has allowed his treatment of essences to be given this atomic and almost substantialist aspect, of which it should be relieved. The rule of essences is not that of substrata but of relations.

NOTES

1. H.-G. Gadamer, *Philosophische Rundschau* (1959), p. 6.

2. Theodore W. Adorno, *Zur Metakritik der Erkenntnistheorie. Studien über Husserl und die phänomenologischen Antinomien* (Stuttgart, 1956), esp. chap. 2, "Species und Intention," pp. 100-134; L. Eley, *Die Krisis des Apriori bei Edmund Husserl* (The Hague, 1962).

3. Adorno, *Metakritik*: "Bemühung, das Wesen dem Umfang zu entreissen..." (p. 126).

4. Ibid., pp. 109, 117.

5. Ibid.: "Momente...die nicht 'da', nicht anschaulich, kein absolut Singulares sind, sondern von Anderem abgezogen" (p. 111).

6. Ibid., p. 131.

7. Ibid., p. 134.

8. Ibid., p. 133.

9. Ibid., p. 126.

10. *Ideen*, 1: 10-11 [*Ideas*, 51-52].

11. *Logische Untersuchungen*, 2: 114.

12. Jean Hering, "Bemerkungen über das Wesen, die Wesenheit und die Idee: *Jahrbuch für Philosophie und Phänomenologische Forschung* (1921), 512ff., 519ff.

13. In the case of Hering, consider the way in which he introduces the idea of a *"noyau eidetique"* (eidetic level) and a *"morphe originelle"* (original form).

14. *Logical Investigations*: "No doubt ideas of such supplementary properties, not given in perception, are 'dispositionally excited'....But just as the thing does not appear before us as the mere sum of its countless individual features..., so the act of perception also is always a homogeneous unity.....The unity of perception comes into being as a *straightforward* unity, *as an immediate fusion of part-intentions, without the addition of new act-intentions"* (2:789).

15. "Le probleme des sciences de l'homme selon Husserl," title of a 1953 course of the Sorbonne.

16. *Ideen*, 1: 13 [*Ideas*, 54].

17. Eley, *Krisis*, pp. 135, 138.

18. Ibid., p. 36.

19. Ibid., pp. 32-33, 36-37.

20. Ibid., p. 43.

21. Hering, "Bemerkungen": "Dass überhaupt eine zusammenhängende, nach inneren Notwendigkeiten begreifbare Struktur *jedem* Wesen innewohne, kann keineswegs behauptet werden" (p. 503).

Husserl's Theory of Intentionality in Contemporary Perspective

FREDERICK A. OLAFSON

In this paper I want to give an account of Edmund Husserl's theory of intentionality and to do so in a way that clarifies its relationship to current discussions of that topic. The latter differ from most earlier treatments of intentionality, Husserl's included, by virtue of a widely shared disposition to conceive intentionality primarily in linguistic terms and, more specifically, as a logical feature of certain sentences with verbs like "believe" and "hope" whose truth-value is independent of the truth-value of the propositional objects such verbs take. While there has been broad agreement on this characterization of intentionality, there has been much controversy as to the wider philosophical implications.[1] One body of opinion holds that intentionality, even in this sober linguistic version, remains irreconcilable with the principle of extensionality and thus with a fundamental logical requirement of the scientific world view; and basing itself quite explicitly on these wider philosophical considerations, it calls for a sweeping conceptual reform which would eliminate all vestiges of intentionality. On the other side the difficulties of such an undertaking have been very clearly demonstrated; but for the most part the defenders of intentionality have seemed to lack a wider philosophical perspective compar-

Reprinted by permission of the author and of the Editor of NOUS, 9 (1975): 73-83.

able to that of their opponents. As a result, the narrow, though powerful, conception of intentionality they defend, focussed as it is on cases in which we intend what may not exist, lends itself all too readily to its opponent's view of it as an ingeniously contrived roadblock in the way of the scientific worldview. I suggest that a more substantially motivated defense of intentionality requires that the current way of conceiving it be broadened in such a way as to embrace the positive, object-referring functions of intentionality as well as its admittedly important capacity for failure in such reference, and to do so in such a way as to exhibit the interdependence of these two facets of one underlying function. If this suggestion has merit, then there cannot be much doubt about the relevance to such an undertaking of Husserl's theory of intentionality which in the context of a general theory of mind and mental acts presents just such an integrated account of the two aspects which are now artificially separated.

There are, of course, serious philosophical inhibitions against widening the concept of the intentional; and these presumably account for the almost total neglect of Husserl's work on the subject by philosophers working in the logico-linguistic mode.[2] These come to a head in the charge of "mentalism" which is held to be the common fate of philosophies that associate intentionality with a general theory of mind. If charges of this kind were brought against Brentano rather than against Husserl, they might well be justified; but they miss altogether the distinctive shift in the interpretation of intentionality that Husserl effected, a shift which begins with his fundamental reconstrual of the concept of the intentional object he inherited from Brentano. That concept has to be understood in the context of Brentano's wider philosophical concern with a range of entities—relations and aggregates among them—about which true statements can be made, but which do not have the kind of reality that things do. At the same time he was interested in finding the distinguishing feature of psychic or mental phenomena as such, and the two concerns came together in the conception of the intentional or mental inexistence of the object—the contemplated horse as distinct from the actual horse—as this distinguishing feature. For Brentano the term 'intentional' applies primarily to this inexistent object which is also described as 'immanent' or intramental; and, secondarily, it applies to what Brentano calls the 'relation' to such intramental objects. The important point here is not so much that the intentional object can exist even if the external, nonmental object does not; it is rather that the latter has no place in Brentano's theory of the intentional act at all. (Current interpretations of intentionality follow Brentano in this respect, but they differ importantly from him since they drop the notion of the inexistent object yet preserve the notion of the intentional as applying to the act of perception or thought, while Brentano abandoned the term 'intentional' altogether when he gave up the notion of intentional object as well as of other nonreal entities). The external nonmental object plays no part in Brentano's account of the intentional object because he understands the former in basically dualistic, representationalist terms as that which causally produces sensations in the mind and is itself posited as existing by a reciprocating causal inference. In other words, the adjective 'intentional' applies exclusively to an intramental object and to an equally intramental act in its relationship to that object, while the broader question of the mind-world relationship is handled by Brentano in perfectly conventional realist and dualist terms. In this version which sequesters *both* the intentional act and the intentional object in a mind which is known only through first-personal acts of reflection, the doctrine of intentionality is indeafeasibly and objectionably "mentalistic"; and it was precisely this aspect of the doctrine that Husserl was to attack.

Unlike Brentano, Husserl was not particularly interested in working out a criterion of the mental as such, and he was in any case convinced that there were elements in consciousness—sensations, for example, and some states of feeling—that are not intentional in either Brentano's sense or his own. More significantly, Husserl does not appear to have been influenced by concerns relating to the ontological status of nonreal objects as Brentano and Meinong were. He was not at all disposed to argue that since we are able to think of unicorns although none exist in actual fact, there must be a special kind of subsistent unicorn to which our thought is directed. Husserl *does* on occasion speak of ideal objects and essences, but he subsumed all such matters under the question that most deeply engaged his thought—the question about the nature of the intentional act—and they raised ontological issues for him only in the context of the latter. From the beginning Husserl understood intentionality in terms of the object-referring or "objectifying" function of mental acts, and he made the crucially important distinction between two senses of "intentional object," namely, between the object that *is* intended and the object *as* it is intended. The latter is explicated by Husserl's conception of the "matter" of the intentional act to which I will turn in a moment. The former is the "real," external object which, as Husserl repeatedly emphasizes, may or may not exist; and as early as the *Logical Investigations* it is clear not only that the relationship in which we stand to it is intentional in character but also that competing theories of a causal or dualist type are unacceptable to Husserl. Intentionality is thus no longer the relationship of a mental act to its intramental object, but rather the basic vehicle of objective reference generally and thus of our knowledge of the world that Husserl speaks of as a comprehensive intentional object.

Although Husserl's conception of the intentional object is in conflict with the mentalism of Brentano's theory, the account Husserl gives of the intentional act itself retains a heavily mentalistic cast. He bases himself on what he takes to be an intuitively obvious distinction between "perceptual contents in the sense of presentative sensations"[3] and the "perceptual taking" or interpretative act which supervenes upon such data. Sensations are not intentional in nature nor are they intentional objects themselves, but they are "experienced" and have the status of "immanent contents"—a locution which inevitably invokes the dualistic framework in which it originates. Once this framework is imposed on the discussion, the function of the interpretative act has to be construed as the transformation of the "experienced" sense-datum into a property of the "perceived" object. The questionable aspect of this account is not just Husserl's continuing use of the concept of sense data while rejecting other elements in the general theory of experience from which it derives, notably the causal theory of perception and the inferential status of objects. The more serious problem is that Husserl commits himself to the very dubious view that intentionality understood as objective reference always involves a reinterpretation of an immanent datum, its transformation into something that is not immanent at all. He thereby makes the concept of intentionality dependent upon the concept of sense datum which, as he was to recognize late in his career, is vulnerable to many objections. Nevertheless, the main tendency of Husserl's theory is belied by these survivals from earlier theories of mind, and although I cannot make a detailed case here for the line of interpretation I will follow, I will concentrate my exposition on the elements in Husserl's theory that rise above the psychological assumptions with which he rather uncritically associated it.

An "act" properly understood, Husserl tells us, is an intentional experience, an experience that refers to an object. As an experience it is datable: it occurs at a time within a certain sequence of other experiences. As an experience, moreover, it is not a publicly observable or behavioral event, and any social or behavioral dimension it may assume is incidental and must not be incorporated into the phenomenological account we give of it. But if, as experiences, intentional acts are anchored in time and in the life history of a self, their central function is semantic and referential in nature; and Husserl insists again and again that no account of that semantic function can be given in psychological terms, namely, in terms of sensuous or imaginal content. An especially vital question that arises here is whether these restrictions preclude any effort to understand the intentional act by analogy with the speech act, but I will postpone consideration of this question until later. What is definitely being excluded is any effort to interpret the semantic or representational properties of the intentional act on the model of what Husserl calls its "real" (reel) or psychological properties: its sensuous content, its date of occurrence, or its being the act of a particular ego which as Husserl says "lives in it." These are properties of the act that can be described in abstraction from the object of the act, namely, without any implication as to the nature and locus of the object arising from the description of the act. The representational functions of the act cannot be described in this self-contained way. Even if we confine our description to what Husserl calls the act-quality as distinct from the act-matter—that is, to the act simply as a perception or a recollection rather than as a perception, say, of a particular object—it is apparent that these different act-qualities can be described only by a kind of borrowing from the temporal or logical modality in which the object is being posited. In other words, the distinguishing mark of the intentional for Husserl is not, as some have proposed, the fact that the truth values of "I believe that p" and "p" are independent (although he would agree that they are), but rather the fact that no one can say "I believe that p" and "not p."[4] It is, of course, not the case that every intentional act "attains" the world if that is understood to mean that the statement about the world and the statement of the intentional act cannot be disjoined. But it does not follow from the fact that an act of reference may be unsuccessful that it can be described otherwise than as an act of reference and thus in terms that imply, for the person whose act it is, something about the world.

The semantic characteristics of the intentional act center, of course, in its matter as distinct from its quality, in its character as a perception or recollection of just such and such an object as contrasted with its character as a perception or a recollection. In the *Logical Investigations* Husserl spoke of the matter of the act as an "act-character," a locution which has the disadvantage of suggesting that the act carries its conceptual freight in much the same way as it does its differentiations into acts of perception, of imagination, etc.; and while the act-quality and the act-matter are both intentional, they are also quite different from one another. Later, Husserl made a much sharper distinction between, on the one hand, the act as such for which the term 'noesis' was devised and, on the other, the representation of the object of which it is the vehicle. The latter Husserl called the 'noema'. What is plain throughout these differing formulations is the categoreal character of the act-matter, or nuclear noema, the essentially conceptual character of the operations it involves. It may be that certain overly concrete connotations of the term 'object', as well as Husserl's persistent emphasis on intuition as a kind of "seeing," stand in the

way of a full appreciation of this categoreal element. But we miss Husserl's point entirely if we understand the matter of the intentional act—the object as it is intended—as the counter-part of a direct, nonconceptual intuition rather than of a conceptual operation.[5] When Husserl speaks of the categoreal character of the act-matter, he means that the latter represents its object as an identical something—a something that is one and the same for all the many references, in the several different modalities, that can be made to it, and a something that is in principle susceptible of further logical determination. Objects as intended are elements in an order of signification rather than in the order of reality, and in the former as contrasted with the latter the otherwise distinct concepts of an "object" and a "state of affairs" become correlatives, as Husserl's tendency to use the term 'objectivity' (*Gegenständlichkeit*) to cover both indicates. Although it is true that Husserl holds all objectifying acts to be nominal in nature, it does not follow from this that all his intentional objects must be logical subjects and thus incapable of coming together in even the simplest of syntactical relationships. Instead, he strongly emphasizes the "perfect analogy" which must "obtain between nominal and propositional acts" and which is of such a nature that it must always be possible to pass directly from an initial nominalization to a corresponding proposition.[6] In other words, the "object" that is set up by the intentional act is, not some compact chunk of matter impervious to anything but physical modification, but rather a conceptually determinable identity that lends itself to categoreal operations in which its internal structure and its place in higher order objects like sets are set forth. Comprehensively, the world as it is represented in the matter of an intentional act is, not a congeries of syntactically formless objects that stand in isolation from one another, but a logical space in which objects that are in principle susceptible to logical articulation serve as nodal points in a system of propositions.

In the *Logical Investigations* Husserl associated this conception of the semantic function of the intentional act with a distinction between two basic types of intentions which he calls as the signitive and the intuitive. The former are those that refer to the object in its absence while the latter themselves directly apprehend that object, although not necessarily in a complete or exhaustive way. The reference of the signitive intention to the object is thus also a reference to the intuitive intention which will fulfill and confirm it in the event that the semantic essence of the two acts is one and the same; and Husserl often speaks of the relationship of the one to the other in teleological terms. A problem arises here because Husserl describes our sensuous apprehension of the object in terms implying that this apprehension is "straightforward" (*schlicht*) in some sense that excludes anything in the nature of categoreal organization. On this view such organization would supervene only after sensuous objects have been apprehended without it, and it then proceeds to form more complex objects for which, however, the independent noncategoreal unity of the sensuous object cannot be claimed. All of this is quite consistent with Husserl's assumption at the time that phenomenology was to concern itself exclusively with the *Gegebenheitsweise* of the object, our modes of reference and intuitive access to it, and not with the object itself. Nevertheless, the sense in which an intuition without categoreal organization could correspond with one defined precisely in categoreal terms remained obscure as did the sense in which such an intuition deserved to be called an intention at all. It may be that Husserl merely wanted to make the point that there is no complexity on the side of acts in the apprehension of a sense-object, no sub-acts or subdescriptions corresponding to the "individual percepts" which we run through and which add up to the single selfsame object. If so, his point would be perfectly consistent with the view that the identity of the object, though not constructed out of the matter of its sub-acts, is, nevertheless, itself conceptual in nature. Even on this interpretation, however, the status of intentionality would be in effect reduced to that of a structure of our reference to objects in their absence and the sense in which we can apprehend only what we (categoreally) intend would not have been made out.

These ambiguities were resolved in Husserl's later writings. As already noted, a distinction was made in the *Ideas* between the noetic and the noematic components of the intentional act, the former comprising the act as such, whether of perception, imagination, or whatever, and the latter in effect uniting within itself what had previously been distinguished as the object-that-is-intended and the object-as-it-is-intended. The notion of a "straightforward" apprehension of the sensible object-that is of the object that is intended-was dropped, and the categoreal synthesis that was previously restricted to the constitution of "higher-order objectivities" became a necessary element in the apprehension of sensible objects.[7] This shift made it necessary for Husserl to conceive this categoreal function no longer exclusively in terms of explicit logical operations which I can be aware of myself as carrying out and to admit the notion of a passive synthesis, namely, a mapping of our experiences that yields an object but is not an act of the self. The noema itself, comprising as it does not only what would ordinarily be called the concept of an object but also the temporal and logical modality in which it is posited, is a complex of conditions in terms of which the existence and nonexistence of objects is determined. Since there can be no experience of an object in which such conceptual conditions are not involved as that which determines *what* object the experience is an experience of, the noema can no longer be said to have a referent that is ontologically independent of it. The same noema can, of course, apply to many different objects, but in each case the identical something to which we refer is one for which the logical conditions defining its identity are the ones laid down in the noema itself.[8] In this sense a reference to the object as an identical something is, as Husserl says, an internal feature of the noema.[9]

With this shift the sense in which we may speak of intentionality as a constitution of objects begins to emerge, and it differs fundamentally from both the sense Brentano gave the term and also from Husserl's earlier interpretation. Intentionality is neither a relation to an intramental object nor is it the reference that a signitive act makes to its intuitive fulfillment and thus, at least ideally, to a nonintentional apprehension of its object. It would also be a mistake to suppose that in its constitutive function intentionality is a literal production or creation of the object, since it may very well turn out that the constituted object does not exist and this it could hardly do if it owed its existence to the intentional act. To constitute an object is rather to construct it conceptually, to go through the passive and active syntheses for which the object serves as the identical logical substrate and in which it takes on its proper judgmental or categoreal forms. The object is thus not a preconceptual somewhat to which our conceptual and logical apparatus is somehow to be made to apply; it is in every respect the creature of its concept, and its existence can be established only to the extent that that concept can be deployed through the full range of judgmental syntheses proper to the object in question. There is thus a strict correlation between the elements in the object domain—the world—and the intentional activity that constructs them conceptually, a parallelism expressed in the formula "ego cogito cogitatum," in which the *cogitatum* denotes the object understood as comprehending not merely the qualitative differentiation that is not attributable to judgmental and conceptual operations but also the formal or categoreal elements that are in Husserl's view inseparable from such judgmental operations and thus from the *cogito*. The *cogito* in the form of these operations is thus the necessary noetic condition for the apprehension of objects whose formal noematic structure is defined precisely in terms of conceptual syntheses, and mental activity is intentional just to the extent that it provides the necessary conceptual condition for the identification of objects.

It may now be possible to characterize in both positive and negative terms the relationship between Husserl's conception of intentionality and the much more restricted "linguistic" interpretation noted at the beginning of this paper. On the positive side, one may note that Husserl's noematic construal of the object presents a kind of rough analogue to the linguistic criterion of intentionality which relates to the lack of existential implication in intentional sentences. Both have the effect of tieing the object of the intentional verb to that verb—Husserl would say to the intentional act expressed by the verb—in such a way that the question of the independent truth of the object clause or the independent existence of the object does not arise. What the precise sense of that "tieing" is in the two cases and whether for example it needs to be interpreted in any way that could provide support for Husserl's much discussed "idealism" are matters I cannot take up here.[10] Even more indicative of a possible affinity between the two interpretations is another "linguistic" criterion, not previously noted, which turns on the referential opacity of certain expressions that may occur in intentional sentences. The point is that if I do not know of the equivalence of two expressions A and B and use A in a statement of belief, like "I believe that A is C," it cannot be inferred from the latter that "I believe that B is C" is also true. Here it is not the object that is tied to the verb as with the first criterion, but the verb or intentional act that is tied to its object, or rather to the object under the description used in conceptualizing it. What this comes to is that in interpreting their objects intentional acts are also interpreting themselves and in such a way that statements about these acts may change their truth-value when the description of their object is changed. A parallelism of this kind in which the description of the act and the description of its object are conceptually yoked together is profoundly consonant with the deepest tendency of Husserl's thought, for which human consciousness is an intentional system in precisely this sense, a system whose elements are acts, and acts described in a way that can change only if the description of the part of the world they are addressed to changes.

These are significant affinities between the Husserlian and the contemporary linguistic interpretations of intentionality, but they are subject to serious qualifications. For those who develop the above points entirely as theses about the logic of certain sentence types, the conclusions reached must remain dependent upon the explicit employment of such intentional verbs as "believe" and "think" or their cognates; and if a way could be found to bypass these locutions, or to reinterpret them in an extensionalist sense by some such strategy as inscriptionalism, the case for intentionality would fall to the ground. For Husserl, by contrast, the employment of these verbs is of secondary importance because the intentional act is not identified with the linguistic act and because his conception of the intentional act treats all language use in all its forms, from the most complete and explicit speech acts to the most private soliloquy, as itself intentional in nature. The answer to the question raised earlier about the relationship of intentional acts to speech acts is therefore as follows: the two are not identical since not all intentional acts are speech acts, although all speech acts are intentional acts. The point of making the distinction between them is not to claim that they designate parallel and distinct series of events, physical and mental, that intersect only incidentally, but rather to bring out the full range of events or acts that carry a semantic function and thus to draw attention to the way that function can persist through the most drastic variations of its physical and imaginal accompaniments. In this connection Husserl uses our ability to perceive words and not just physical marks, and to perceive words as to-

kens of a type as evidence for the conclusion that language use pervasively involves a perceptual taking of the same kind that is involved in all perceptual experience. He also insists upon the looseness and variability of the bond that ties semantic functioning to the physical aspects of linguistic activity and upon the fact that it is possible to substitute word images for words and more generally to abbreviate the sensuous side of language very drastically as is typically done "in uncommunicated mental life" in which "the word floats before us in imagination although in reality it has no existence."[11] In other words, the wider intentional act that subtends language-use as such is not the localized intentionality that is peculiar to certain verbs (and in this sense, as I have said, internal to language) nor is it a function of the organism or of the nervous system in any sense that would imply that it can be described exhaustively by means of concepts drawn from the sciences that deal with one or another of both of these.

Here Husserl's theory of intentionality begins to point toward ontological conclusions relating to mental acts just as unmistakably as it was shown to do earlier in respect of objects. I cannot pursue either issue here, but I feel I must notice at least briefly the most sophisticated contemporary alternative to the line taken by Husserl.[12] This is the view which combines a recognition of intentionality as a logical feature of the conceptual system laid down in our language with a radically physicalistic ontology. What a thought is *of* in its representational function is held to pose no restriction on what a thought itself may *be* as an entity or event, and it follows that there can be no reason not to identify a thought or any intentional act with a brain-state and to describe it by means of physical and logically extensional concepts. Husserl could certainly accept the premise of this agreement, namely, that thoughts need not resemble their objects. But he would surely have pointed out that the fact that thoughts and other intentions have representational functions at all may impose such restrictions even though what they are representations of does not. He would also have reminded us that brain physiology knows nothing of representational properties or intentionality and that our knowledge of the latter derives instead from reflection upon our own conscious activities. It is one thing to say that these activities would not be possible if we did not have brains; it is something else (and a serious mistake) to suppose that we can vault over the conceptual divide that separates physical from representational properties and forcibly unify them in the concept of a single physical entity, the brain. The independent provenience of the intentional and nonintentional components in that hybrid concept will inevitably assert itself, and the concept itself will not do much more than symbolize, in the manner of Kant's ideas, a unity of ontological understanding which we may desiderate but have certainly not achieved.

NOTES

1. The literature to which I am referring here is both vast and relatively well-known, so I will cite only a recent anthology in which many of the most important contributions to this discussion have been collected: A. Marras, ed., *Intentionality, Mind and Language* (Urbana: University of Illinois Press, 1972). The exchange of letters between Professors Roderick Chisholm and Wilfred Sellars which originally appeared in H. Feigl, M. Scriven, and G. Maxwell, eds., *Concepts, Theories and the Mind-Body Problem* (Minnesota Studies in the Philosophy of Science, vol. 2) (Minneapolis: University of Minnesota Press, 1958), pp. 529-39, is reprinted in the Marras collection and can be taken as an exemplary statement of the two positions I sketch below.

2. An indication of this neglect is the fact that only one reference is made to Husserl in the Marras anthology and that reference is a purely bibliographical one.

3. *Logical Investigations*, translated by J. N. Findlay (London: Routledge & Kegan Paul, 1970), 2: 566.

4. Strictly speaking, this formulation is appropriate only to the so-called "doxic" modalities of belief, assertion, etc. and not to the modalities of, say, hope or imagination in which the intention is of such a nature that its object may very well not exist.

5. This seems to be the view taken by Ernst Tugendhat in his essay, "Phänomenologie und Sprachanalyse" in R. Bübner et al., ed., *Hermeneutik und Dialektik: Hans-Georg Gadamer zum 70. Geburtstag*, vol. 2 (Tübingen: J.C.B. Mohr, 1970, pp. 3-23. See this volume, pp. 325-337, for a translation of this essay, "Phenomenology and Linguistic Analysis." For an interesting and, I think, sound reply to his criticisms of Husserl see Donn Welton, "Intentionality and Language in Husserl's Phenomenology," *The Review of Metaphysics*, 27 (1973-74): 269-97.

6. *Logical Investigations*, 2: 627.

7. This evolution of Husserl's thought is most clearly displayed in *Formal and Transcendental Logic*, translated by Dorion Cairns (The Hague: Martinus Nijhoff, 1969).

8. In speaking of the "same" noema as applying to many different objects here I am of course referring to what Husserl calls the nuclear noema or noematic *Sinn* and not to the full noema.

9. See, for example, *Ideen zu einer reinen Phänomenologie und phänomenologischen Philosophie* (The Hague: Martinus Nijhoff, 1950), 1: 318.

10. Whatever confusions Husserl may have been guilty of in this connection, the distinctions he should have made are surely the ones made by Roman Ingarden in "Die vier Begriffe der Transcendenz und das Problem des Idealismus in Husserl" in Anna Teresa Tymieniecka, ed., *Analecta Husserliana*, vol. 1 (Dordrecht: D. Reidel, 1971), pp. 37-74.

11. *Logical Investigations*, 1: 279.

12. See, for example, the discussion of these matters in Arthur Danto, *Analytical Philosophy of Action* (Cambridge: Cambridge University Press, 1973), pp. 66-72.

Husserl's Concept of the Noema

ROBERT C. SOLOMON

The eye of the intellect sees in all objects what it brought with it the means of seeing.

Thomas Carlyle

1. Two Interpretations

It is generally agreed that the concept of the *noema* is one of the themes, if not the central theme, of Edmund Husserl's phenomenological philosophy. Yet like many of Husserl's key concepts, "noema" changed its meaning many times throughout his repeated attempts to reformulate and strengthen his philosophical position. From its introduction in the first volume of *Ideen*[1] in 1913 until his later writings, this concept receives no definitive and unequivocal characterization. It is variously described and employed in such ways that several very different interpretations have become defensible on the basis of published as well as unpublished Husserlian texts.

On the one hand, following Husserl's examples and his characterization of the noema as "the perceived as such" (*Ideas*, sec. 88), several of Husserl's leading students, notably Aron Gurwitsch[2] and Dorion Cairns,[3] have characterized the noema with special reference to certain problems of perception, for example, the identification and reidentification of particulars. On the other hand, following an equally documented Husserlian insistence that the noema is a "generalization of the notion of *Sinn* to the field of all acts" (*Ideen III*, p. 89), a heretical group of more "analytically" minded philosophers, notably Dagfin Føllesdal,[4] has paid special attention to the close relationship between Husserl and his (more or less) philosophical colleague, Gottlob Frege. In this interpretation the noema becomes an abstract intensional entity which is not perceived at all.

At first glance, no two interpretations could seem more opposed, and considerable antipathy between the two has consequently emerged. One might wonder whether the "perceived as such" and this Fregean abstract *Sinn* are in fact interpretations of one and the same conception. Our problem here is to understand the source of these differences and to develop a conception of the noema that does justice to both. Of the greatest importance, of course, is our need to understand the role of the noema in Husserl's own thinking—or at least in that phase of his thinking that produced the conception of the noema in *Ideas*.

This is not the place to trace the vicissitudes of Husserl's difficult conception; this has been accomplished elsewhere[5] and will not help us here. We may grant from the outset that the concept is to be found in several different contexts and that different emphases may reinforce different interpretations. One pair of contexts, however, stands out from all the others—a basic ambivalence that underlies all of Husserl's thought. Husserl entered philosophy from the foundations of mathematics with an interest in the nature of certain "ideal" entities (e.g. numbers) and the nature of certain necessary truths (e.g. arithmetical propositions). But, like Frege, with whom he had considerable correspondence,[6] Husserl was drawn into the broader philosophical arena, particularly to the problems of epistemology. Though his interests were always tied to the former, his examples and his concerns often emerged from the latter.[7] His work in logic and the foundations of necessity is often brilliant, comparable to the work of Frege; his suggestions in the field of perception are typically sketchy and incomplete and are never pursued with the intensity of his more formal concerns.[8] The problems of logic and the problems of perception have their mutual dependencies, of course, but the paradigms they provide for philosophical analysis are worlds apart. (The historical "schools" of rationalism and empiricism, which Husserl, like Kant, attempted to synthesize, provide an apt illustration of the divergence which this choice of paradigms entails.) Attempting to solve problems indigenous to one sphere by using paradigms more appropriate to the other gives rise to spectacular confusions (as the history of modern philosophy is again quick to prove). Husserl's concept of the noema is an attempt to establish a common ground for both the problems of perception and the foundations of necessary truths and judgments. Accordingly, we must be prepared for problems of equivocation, for conceptions which might be readily applicable in one paradigm which are not appropriate in the other. For example, the notion of "perspective," Which looms so large in the Gurwitsch interpretations of the perceptual noema, is not even a plausible candidate for clarifying the role of the noema in the foundations of arithmetic.

The dispute between the "orthodox" view of Gurwitsch, Cairns, et al. (what Hubert Dreyfus has called "the New School school") and the "heretical" view of Føllesdal and his students[9] can be seen largely in terms of their acceptance of one of these competing paradigms and their relative neglect of the other. Gurwitsch, who has also been a major contributor to the philosophical aspects of Gestalt psychology,[10] takes perception and its problems to be the proper setting for Husserl's noema. Føllesdal, a first-rate logician and student of W. V. O. Quine, sees in Husserl's conception of the noema an answer to certain puzzles in the Fregean theory of "indirect" or "opaque" intensional contexts.[11] Although Gurwitsch is agreeable to Husserl's characterization of the noema as "ideal" and "irreal" (as an "atemporal meaning"), he insists on casting the noema in strictly perceptual terms, as a "percept" and even as "perceptual phenomenon."[12] The concept of the noema is introduced to account for the identification of objects through changes and over time in different acts and different kinds of acts. Gurwitsch's examples, as well as his analysis, leave no doubt that the "objects" he has in mind are in virtually every case *material* (perceptual) objects.[13] Føllesdal, on the other hand, takes Husserl's noema to be very much like Frege's notion of the *Sinn* of a linguistic expression, generalized appropriately to nonlinguistic acts. Frege had sharply distinguished between an expression and its *meaning* (*Sinn*), and also between the meaning (*Sinn*) and the *reference* (*Bedeutung*) of an expression. Using this pair of Fregean distinctions, Føllesdal interprets Husserl's noema as the meaning or *Sinn* of an intentional act (or *noesis*)—as distinct from its reference (or intended object) as well as distinct from the act itself. Like the Gurwitsch interpretation, this view has a solid foundation in Husserl's writings.[14]

More enticing than the interpretation itself, however, is its consequences: the noema as a *Sinn* or meaning now falls into alignment with the various concepts of linguistic meaning that have been formulated and debated in the seventy years since Frege's pioneering efforts. And with this conceptual bridge between two initially different conceptions of meaning comes a bridge between two philosophical disciplines that have seemed to be mutually incomprehensible and irreconcilable.[15]

2. Noema and Intentionality

Husserl introduces the concept of the noema in his attempt to clarify his conception of intentionality, adapted from a similar notion in Brentano.[16] Along with the notion itself, Husserl adopts Brentano's celebrated doctrine of intentionality, which we may summarize as (1) "all consciousness is consciousness of something" and (2) one cannot infer from the fact that an act is directed toward something that that "something" exists. If it ever makes sense to say that "S sees y" when y does not exist, then it must be true that S sees something even if it is also true that there is not something which S sees. To resolve this apparent paradox, Brentano resurrected the scholastic concept of "intentional inexistence"—the idea that the "object" of a mental act need not be a "real" object. Husserl, according to Føllesdal's account, rejects this part of Brentano:

Husserl resolved this dilemma by holding that although every act is directed, this does not mean that there is always some object towards which it is directed. According to Husserl, there is associated with each act a *noema*, in virtue of which the act is directed towards its object, if it has any....To be directed is simply to have a noema.[17]

Husserl's modification can be summarized as a denial of the thesis that every act of consciousness has a (real) object; yet every act is directed by virtue of its noema, whether or not it in fact has an object. To be "directed" is simply, to have a noema. But what is this noema? And how does it "direct" the act toward its object? Husserl's claim that the noema is a meaning ("a generalization of linguistic meaning") is clearly an attempt to extend Frege's notion of the *Sinn*, by virtue of which linguistic expressions have reference, to mental acts in general. But Frege's notion, even in its more restricted context, raises notorious difficulties; how, then, does Husserl attempt to clarify that notion?

It is to clarify the conception of the noema as meaning that Gurwitsch and Føllesdal offer us their interpretations.

According to Gurwitsch and the "orthodox" view, the noema is nothing other than the "perceived as such," the object of perception (appropriately "bracketed" by the phenomenological epoche) from this particular viewpoint:

To each act there corresponds a noema— namely an object just, exactly and only just, as the subject is aware of it and has it in view, when he is experiencing the act in question.[18]

It is what Gurwitsch elsewhere calls a perceptual *Gestalt*,[19] a *percept*,[20] and a *theme*.[21]

The key to the orthodox view of the noema is the notion of "perspective," for it is through a perspective—or rather a variety of perspectives[22]—that one comes to know an object. There are dangers here, as Gurwitsch has been the first to point out: there is the danger of turning the noema into a sensory object with "real" status of its own, thus forcing the phenomenologist into the subjective idealist position that Husserl always opposed. (It is important to stress, even though it is not our topic, that the sensory matter or "hyletic data" of perception are not introduced on the noematic side of the act but rather in the noesis itself. The purpose of this move is precisely to avoid making the sensory into an object.)[23] The noema is not the object of an act of consciousness but, rather, its *meaning*. In Husserl as in Frege, meaning and reference must always be kept apart. But what, then, is this concept of meaning (*Sinn*) that plays such an important role here?

Gurwitsch, attempting to remain faithful to Husserl on this matter, insists that the noema is a *Sinn* ("belongs to the sphere of sense").[24] But it turns out that Gurwitsch's conception of *Sinn* is extremely emasculated; quoting from Husserl, he tells us that the noema is a *Sinn* because of its "atemporality":

i.e. in a certain independence of the concrete act by which they are actualized, in the sense that every one of them may correspond, as identically the same, to another act, and even to an indefinite number of acts.[25]

Gurwitsch, in other words, employs a

conception of *Sinn* which embodies the reference of an act as well as its meaning. (Both of these hide under the rubric of "the noematic correlate".) by extending the concept of *Sinn* to include both meaning and reference, Gurwitsch (and at times Husserl) makes it extremely difficult to provide an adequate analysis of the noema. If the noema is a *Sinn*, then of course it cannot be unique to any particular ("concrete") act; but neither can it be wholly "independent of any concrete act."[26] And however much Gurwitsch may insist upon following Husserl in his distinction between noema and object, that distinction, in Gurwitsch's interpretation, always seems to appear as a scholarly fine point when he describes the noema (of perception) as

the object just (exactly and only just) as the perceiving subject is aware of it,....the 'perceived tree as such' varies according to the standpoint, the orientation, the attitude, etc.[27]

Gurwitsch's "orthodox" interpretation has established its orthodoxy by virtue of the fact that it is a manageable interpretation of Husserl. But its onesidedness and inadequacy for the richness of Husserl's thought become obvious as soon as we ask, even with particular reference to perception, why Husserl should have thought the noema to be such an important conception. In Gurwitsch's view, the doctrine of the noema reduces to little more than a restatement of the epistemological platitude that we never simply "see" material objects, but only material objects from a certain perspective, within a certain context, and so on. Moreover, this conception of the noema leaves no room for an adequate analysis of the noemata of abstract judgments, arithmetical propositions, and the like. In the orthodox view, why should Husserl have introduced the concept of noema at all—or, for that matter, the concept of *Sinn*? If his concerns were limited to the Brentanesque problem of "intentional inexistence," would not his revolutionary conception of the epoche and phenomenological reductions have been sufficient? The epoche would allow the

phenomenologist, from an exclusively first-person viewpoint, to describe the various "objects" of his experience without asking any ontological questions and so without being forced to make any peculiar ontological claims about the "subsistence" ("*Sosein*," "*Aussersein*," "*Nichtsein*," or "*Quasi-sein*") of those objects which did not "exist." Why could Husserl not have rested with this early conception of intentionality with reference to intentional objects, without bothering himself with the intricacies of the very difficult theses concerning the noema and the *Sinn*? Gurwitsch's interpretation does not provide us with a satisfactory answer to these skeptical questions. In his view, the noema is simply the object viewed from a perspective and *Sinn* refers us only to the easily statable fact than an act has transnoetic reference. Nothing much would be lost if we deleted these concepts from Husserl's theory altogether. "Intentionality" alone would be sufficient.[28]

The importance of the concepts of noema and *Sinn* becomes evident only when we free ourselves from an exclusively perceptual paradigm and turn to "the higher level spheres of intentionality." It is worth noting that Husserl's protracted discussion of the noema in *Ideas*, although it begins with a brief consideration of the noema of perception, is devoted almost entirely to a discussion of the noema of judgment. *That* is where Husserl's primordial interests lie, and it is the noema of conceptual judgments, not the noema of perceptual judgments or perceptual acts, that occupies the center of his attention.

3. The Individuation Problem

According to Husserl, and according to both the Gurwitsch and the Føllesdal interpretations, it is by virtue of the noema that consciousness relates to objects, but the noema is not itself the object of consciousness.[29] This point is often obscured by Husserl's characterizations of the noema as the "noematic" or "objective content" and the ambiguous relationship between the noema, the noematic "correlate," and the intentional object. The noematic correlate is something more than the noema, yet less than the object. Furthermore, there is some confusion regarding the relationship between the noema, the object, and the noematic *Sinn*. At times it appears that the "full noema" (*das volle Noema*) is equivalent to the object; other times it is only equated with the *Sinn*. Sometimes the noema is said to *be* a *Sinn*; elsewhere it *has* a *Sinn*. Moreover, there is a general problem in Husserl's discussions, which I will call the Individuation Problem: Husserl continuously writes as if the various acts or noeses and the various noemata could be distinguished and counted like so many sneezes or marbles. Thus he insists that each act has its own noema (as well as its own intended object), that different acts may have the same noema, and that each "act phase" has its own "noematic phase."[30]

But it is not at all clear, for example, when I am observing an object before me—whether moving or stationary (and whether I am moving or stationary)—how many *acts* I am performing. There is a sense in which intentional acts (as Husserl tells us in *Logical Investigations*) are not to be construed as actions or events, and it is not clear that acts can be so easily distinguished as actions or events, whether in terms of their intentions or by appeal to temporality.[31] The same can be said of the noema; it is not at all clear that noemata can be individuated as simply as Husserl's discussion suggests. Of course, there are evident distinctions—between an object seen from the front and an object seen from the back, to pick the usual example, or looking once on Tuesday and again on Wednesday. Short of a criterion for the identity of noemata and noeses respectively, however, there is no substance to the frequent "one-many" and "one-one" correlations that appear in the writings of Husserl and his interpreters.[32]

This Individuation Problem makes an adequate analysis of the noema far more problematic than it appears to be in most discussions. The common model, made popular in Gurwitsch's commentaries, is that a single "view" constitutes a single noema, just as a single "viewing" constitutes a single noesis.[33] But this assumption turns wholly upon a "snapshot" paradigm that utterly dissolves upon reflection.[34] Why should we suppose that our experience is dissectible into such views and viewings? (Husserl's arguments, for example, in *The Phenomenology of Internal Time-Consciousness* have taught us better.) Should we not more accurately describe our experience in terms of flux and continuity? (These are the dynamic terms which Husserl, like William James, often uses.) But if we do, then the facile individuation of acts and noemata of acts is unwarranted. And if it is not clear how to distinguish a single act or a single noema, then the usual formulae for their "correlation" are inappropriate. But they are also unnecessary. Husserl's notion of an "act phase" and a "noematic phase" introduces a promising vagueness which the more static talk of "act" and "noema" leaves out.[35] How this more dynamic vagueness can be used to answer the Individuation Problem would take us far beyond our scope in this essay. But no discussion of the noema can be complete unless it can account for some of the confusion of identities that penetrates Husserl's theory: the convoluted relationship between the noema and the object, the complex relationship between the noema and the act, and the confused relationship between the noema and its *Sinn*. The Individuation Problem does not resolve these complexities and confusions for us, but it explains why they arise. Quantifiable relationships that hold between countables cannot be coherently described between uncountables. Until some criterion has been provided for the individuation of intentional acts and their noemata, all talk of "noetico-noematic correlations" ought to be suspended.

Although Husserl introduces the concept of the noema in the context of (and with an example from) perception, he soon makes it clear that *all* acts have noemata—acts of judgment and expres-

sion as well as acts of perceiving and imagining. A perceptual noema may well be
described as "the perceived as such,"[36]
but that formula is of little help when extended to the sphere of judgment. Husserl
speaks of "the judgment as such," of
course,[37] but it is not at all clear how that
phrase is to be clarified in comparison
with the perception case. What is clear is
that the judgmental noema is a *Sinn*, a
meaning, and here the connection between Husserl and Frege is most in evidence.

Husserl tells us repeatedly that it is
through the noema that we intend an object but that the noema itself is not the
object. What does this mean? In the Gurwitsch interpretation, taking perception
as its paradigm, the noema is the object
"viewed"[38] from a particular perspective
(e.g. the house viewed from this side; the
tree viewed from this angle). Thus we
"see" an object "through" its various
perspectives, yet no one of those
perspectives *is* the object. (Neither, of
course, is it *other than* the object; thus
Husserl does not say that the noema is
"unreal" in the sense of a mere "image"
or a "phantom," but only "irreal" in the
sense that it is not by itself the object. [We
might borrow Husserl's terms from
Cartesian Meditations[39] in this context:
"actual" and "quasi-actual" as opposed
to "actual" and "non-actual."])

In the Føllesdal interpretation it is not
perception but judgment that provides
the paradigm, even though Føllesdal begins his essay with a set of examples
drawn from perception. This is not an
inconsistency on his part, however, but
rather an important philosophical presupposition; the noema of perception—
an abstract and nonperceived *Sinn*—is
the *same* noema that one finds as the
noema of judgment. Thus Føllesdal
claims, against Gurwitsch and the "orthodox" view, that "noemata are not
perceived through the senses," that they
are abstract, and that they are intensional
entities: meanings, not objects viewed
from a perspective. Føllesdal's conception of *Sinn* seems to correspond with
what Husserl calls the *Bedeutung*—

"meaning on the conceptual level."[40]

Thus the phenomenological concept of
intentionality becomes the equivalent of
the neo-Fregean logical concept of intensionality. The first was introduced as the
characteristic of *acts* of consciousness;
the second was introduced as a characteristic of certain *sentences*. In Føllesdal's interpretation, the equivalence of
noema and *Sinn*, the meaning of mental
acts and the meaning of sentences, results
in the further equivalence of intentionality and intensionality.[41]

4. The Opacity of Perception: The Role of the *Sinn*

One of Husserl's spectacular insights
(contrary to the usual view of phenomenology as a primarily epistemological
[perceptual] investigation) is the reinterpretation of perception along lines of
analysis that are usually reserved for such
"conceptual" acts as asserting, believing, judging, doubting, and denying.
While Frege limited the notion of *Sinn* to
verbal expressions (and it was the expression, rather than the act, that had the
Sinn), Husserl attempted to extend the
notion of *Sinn* (through the noema) to all
acts. Thus Husserl says, in his introduction of the concept of the noematic *Sinn*,
that it is "an extension of *Sinn* to the field
of all acts."[42] (He makes the same claim
later regarding *Bedeutung*, but more of
this later.) Frege was concerned about
the nature of "opaque" contexts in
language-related acts ("indirect discourse"), but Husserl extended this concern to all acts, including perceptual acts.
Thus perception, even prior to all judgments, gives rise to a type of "opaque"
context. This general opacity of all conscious acts is clumsily captured in the
Gurwitsch analysis, which is well suited
to the concerns of the psychology of perception. But that is not *Husserl's* interest,
and Gurwitsch's "perspective" analysis
is far too narrow to do justice to Husserl's
interest in judgments and expression.

According to Husserl, "S sees y," like
"S believes that p" and unlike "S kicks
y", does not maintain its truth value or its

meaning for all substitutions for "y" and "p". (This is not only to say that a judgment *by* S about his perceptions gives rise to opaque contexts; it is also, and more radically, to say that a judgment about S's perceptions gives rise to such contexts.) By extending the notion of opacity beyond its usual narrowly linguistic context, we may say that perception itself is opaque. Underlying this extension, as in all of Husserl, is a claim that is old (Kantian) but still radical (e.g. in Quine and Sellars): that all acts (including the most rudimentary acts of perception) are judgment and concept-laden.[43] It is here, we may anticipate, that the conception of *Sinn* (and *Bedeutung*) will become of paramount importance. Not only acts of verbal expression but all acts, according to Husserl, display the "logic" that Frege and he had investigated in the more esoteric realms of intentionality.

Consider the act of asserting that-p. It is clear that one can perform that act although "p" is false. What, then, is the status of "that-p"? It is not a "fact" (for there is no such fact). One might say that it is a possible yet not an actual state of affairs. But this Leibnizian conception introduces a nightmare of ontological complications which Husserl's epoche wisely avoids. One might say, in line with many prominent philosophers in the analytic tradition, that that-p is a sentence, namely, the sentence that was asserted, p. Unfortunately, no particular sentence uttered has any such exclusive claim: the sentence p, in a different language, might also be an apt expression of that-p, and one might assert that-p without uttering any sentence at all (e.g. by nodding approval). This myriad of complications is too well known to bear repetition here. But the conclusion drawn from these problems by Frege is worth repeating: that-p is neither a sentence nor a set of sentences (no matter how complex); nor is that-p a state of affairs nor a mental image of any kind; that-p is an abstract entity, a *Sinn*, which is expressed by any number of sentences in any number of languages. It might also be expressed, we can add (going beyond Frege's interests),

in any number of semiverbal acts (e.g. grunting agreement) and nonverbal acts (a gesture or a signal).

This conception of *Sinn* need not be limited to these linguistic contexts (assertion, etc.); it was also applied by Frege to belief contexts ("doxic" contexts in Husserl), prior to verbal expression. Carrying the matter one step further, Husserl extends this notion of *Sinn* to all acts, including perception. It has long been obvious to linguistic philosophers that "S believes that p" cannot be successfully analyzed as a relationship between S and the fact that-p; it might not be the case that-p, even though "S believes that p" is true. *What* one believes is not a fact but that-p, whether or not p. In the same vein, "S sees y" cannot be construed as a relationship between S and y, for there might be no y.

Granted, it might be argued that "sees" is one of those verbs that has its veracity built into it, such that "S sees y" cannot be true unless there is a y that S sees. But of course this is not what Husserl has in mind, for the existence of y has already been "bracketed out" as a consideration in the phenomenological description of "seeing y." Although this problem has occupied an embarrassingly voluminous place in British philosophical journals, it is a strictly pedantic one. If "sees" is considered such a verb (a "success verb"), "seems to see" is surely not, and in each case the latter can be substituted above. Accordingly, what one sees—for example in cases of illusion and hallucination—is not y, but (y). It is this (y) that Husserl calls the noematic correlate. It is not the case that (y) has anything like the ontological status of y. In fact, (y) has *no* ontological status; rather, it is the *candidate* upon which ontological status is conferred. It is like the meaning of a sentence, which itself is neither asserted nor denied, true nor false, appropriate nor inappropriate, sincere nor prevaricating. Assertion and denial, or truth and falsity, arise only when a sentence with a meaning is put to some *use*—made the object of an act. Similarly, seeing (y), as described by the phenomenologist, precedes all judgments about the existence of y. But it must not therefore be supposed that seeing (y) precedes all judgments about (y), any more than the meaning of a sentence is without "meaning" until it is asserted or otherwise expressed in the language. (J. L. Austin's distinction between "locutionary" and "illocutionary act potential" comes to mind here.) Seeing (y) is already laden with conceptual judgments. It is not mere "experience" or "intuition" to which judgments are added subsequently. And so it is that *Sinn* (and *Bedeutung*) become essential to all acts.

5. The Noema as a Generalization of Meaning: Føllesdal's View

The main theme of Føllesdal's interpretation of the noema is that

the noema is an intensional entity, a generalization of the notion of meaning (Sinn, Bedeutung).[44]

It is worth noting from the outset that *Sinn* and *Bedeutung* are treated *in tandem*, and the remainder of Føllesdal's essay similarly treats these two different senses of "meaning" cooperatively, one reinforcing the other. Føllesdal's noema is a close relative to Frege's *Sinn*.[45] He takes Husserl like Frege: to be supporting an intimacy between "experience and judgment" in which language plays a central if perhaps silent role.

Føllesdal rightly comments that there is an ambiguity in Husserl's use of the term *Sinn*: sometimes he means the full noema; at other times just a part of it. For this reason Føllesdal asserts (thesis two) that the noema has two "components": one "common to all acts that have the same object," another that is different in acts with a different "thetic" (or positional) character.[46] Like Gurwitsch, Føllesdal fully agrees that it is the noema— particularly the noematic *Sinn*—that allows consciousness to be "directed" toward an object (thesis three). He also insists—again in full agreement with Gurwitsch—that the noema is not itself

the object (thesis four).[47] And, ignoring what we have called the Individuation Problem, Føllesdal also agrees that there is only one object per noema (thesis five) and one noema per act (thesis six), but any number of different noemata and noematic *Sinne* per object (thesis seven).[48] Of the utmost importance in distinguishing the Føllesdal interpretation from the "orthodox" view are the following two propositions:[49]

Noemata are abstract entities. (thesis 8)

Noemata are not perceived through the senses. (thesis 9)

In a famous passage Husserl claims that the noema of a tree, unlike the tree, cannot burn or suffer chemical decomposition.[50] In the unpublished manuscript "Noema and Sinn" Husserl adds that the "*Sinne* are unreal objects," and "a *Sinn* does not have Reality."[51] Husserl also tells us, however, that the noema of perception is the perceived as such,"[52] and an unquestionable absurdity seems to arise when one suggests that "the perceived as such" is not itself perceived.

This apparent paradox may be resolved in a variety of ways. We must note that, as Føllesdal insists, thesis 9 is "an immediate consequence" of thesis 8. This means, first of all, that the two stand or fall together (i.e. the falsity of 9 entails the falsity of 8). But this logical relationship gives us an important clue to the nature of Føllesdal's use of the term 'abstract' in thesis 8. 'Abstract' does not mean, as it often means, "conceptual"; neither does it mean, as it has often meant in German idealism, "separable in thought but not in Reality." 'Abstract' means, at least, "not perceived." And here we can see the source of the significant differences between Føllesdal's interpretation and the "orthodox" view. If it is judgment we are discussing, then clearly this conception of the noema ties in perfectly with Frege's characterization of the *Sinn* or meaning of a linguistic expression. Of course the *Sinn* of a *Satz* is not perceived through the senses; and of course, consequently, it is "abstract". If it is perception that concerns us, however, it is clear that the noema *must*, if it is what directs us to the object, be itself perceived. And though it might be called "abstract" in some other sense, it cannot be abstract in *this* sense. In perception, the noema must be perceived; yet Føllesdal's theses are intended for perception as well as for judgment. Like Husserl, Føllesdal would want to hold that all noemata belong intrinsically to a single supreme genus. How, then, can these difficulties be resolved?

It is important to note that, having distinguished between two "components" of the noema (his second thesis), Føllesdal proceeds to ignore this distinction. The quotes above do not argue for the abstractness of the noema but rather for the abstractness of the *Sinn*. And on the following page Føllesdal makes a casual remark that earmarks the confusion of his ultimate thesis: "Again, Husserl is here talking about the noematic *Sinn*, but, as noted above, the remark presumably applies to all components of the noema."[53] But Føllesdal had also sharply distinguished the *Sinn* as one "component" of the noema; it does not follow, then, that we can "presume" that Husserl's remarks about the noematic *Sinn* apply to the noema itself.

In his discussion of thesis 8 Føllesdal argues that the noema is abstract because it is "not a spacial object," and this because "spacial objects can be experienced only through perspectives (*Abschattungen*)." But here Gurwitsch's interpretation strikes full force against Føllesdal's "heretical" view; of course a noema cannot be viewed "through perspectives," because it is itself characterized *in terms of* the perspectives through which the object is viewed. To argue that the noema is not therefore a spacial object (with which all interpretations agree) does not permit the conclusion that it is therefore abstract. The equation that seems to be operating at the root of Føllesdal's theses 8 and 9 is that something can be perceived and is not abstract only if it is a spacial object. And

in this sense we might disinterestedly agree that the noema is not perceived and abstract, in some contentious sense of "perceived" and "abstract"; but we can continue to adhere to the Gurwitsch interpretation according to which the noema is indeed "the perceived as such."

It would seem that Føllesdal's interpretation of the noema leaves out something vital in the case of perception; but we have seen that Gurwitsch's interpretation leaves out something equally essential in cases of abstract judgment. But, returning to Føllesdal's second thesis about the "two components" of the noema, we can see our way out of this impasse. Although Føllesdal introduced the conception of a "thetic" component of the noema, he proceeds, once he has done so, to concentrate wholly on the noematic *Sinn*. Although Gurwitsch admits without concern the importance of the noematic *Sinn*, he focuses wholly upon the thetic components of the noema: those which change with different "perspectives" and acts and those which can be said, without contradicting Husserl, to be "perceived" in various acts of perception. In other words, the noema consists of both a *Sinn* and various changing "characters."[54] *Every* noema, we must insist—including the noemata of abstract judgments and ideal entities—consists of *both* of these components. In acts of perception the thetic component of the noema is partially determined by sensory data or *hyle* through which various "views" are constituted: "the tree viewed from this side" and "that side"; and the content of those views consists of colors, textures, and the like. (It is important to stress that the *hyle* or sensory data are not themselves perceived but rather determine what we perceive, namely, the thetic component of the noema. Yet the thetic component itself—colors, textures, etc.—surely can be said to be perceived through the senses. This point is a matter of some obscurity in Husserl and Gurwitsch, but surely goes against Føllesdal's thesis 9.) In imagination, the thetic component also consists of views—but in this case they are not perceived through but are still imagined on the basis of the senses. In judgment, the thetic component might be suggested to be the various sentences—in either the same language or in any number of languages—which express the same thought. Insofar as we concentrate on these latter examples, the Føllesdal interpretation is valid without qualification. But when perception is considered, Føllesdal must be augmented by Gurwitsch, who has given us an exemplary development and characterization of the thetic components of perception. But, accordingly, there is no serious disagreement between the interpretations. It is merely a difference in emphasis and interest, not a difference in the supposed nature of the noema.

6. Husserl's Radical Thesis

Brentano believed that all acts were directed toward objects; and in order to maintain this thesis he wavered between a Meinongian idealism and an unsatisfactory realism, populating his ontology with "unreal" entities on the one hand, denying the reality of unfulfilled acts on the other.[55] Husserl resolved this dilemma by denying the universality of intentionality in *this* sense. In place of the thesis that consciousness always takes an object, he substituted the thesis that consciousness is always directed. It need not have an object, but it always has a *noema*. But this noema, we have seen, is not only an apparent object or an "appearance." (At most this claim would be a misleading account of the "thetic" noematic phases of putative objects of perception.) The noema is also a *Sinn*, or rather it *has* a *Sinn*, and "separates off a certain '*noematic nucleus*' from the changing '*characters*' that belong to it."[56] Once again, there is a problem of precision here; just as Husserl was found to be ambiguous on the relationship between noema and *Sinn*, so he is imprecise on the relationship between *Sinn* and noematic nucleus. It is clear, however, that the nucleus is something less than the noema as a whole and that it is intimately related to that "component" of the noema which

remains common through various "thetic" changes, namely the *Sinn*. (The analogy with biology—the cell with its changing protoplasm and its unchanging nucleus—is not inappropriate here.) Moreover, the notion of the noematic nucleus warns us against taking the two "components" of the noema as independent and separate; rather they form an organic and inseparable unity, with the nucleus and the *Sinn* forming the common thread and organizing the indefinitely many noetic "characters" or "phases" that fulfill it. It is the noema—these indefinitely many noematic phases linked together and given meaning by the noematic *Sinn*—that allows our conscious acts to be directed toward object. But the familiar phrase "all consciousness is consciousness *of* something" no longer means that all consciousness is consciousness of a real object. It means, rather, that every act of consciousness is directed by virtue of its noema *toward* objects, and it is possible (though absurd to suppose) that our acts are *never* directed in fact toward a "real" world beyond our experience.[57]

Husserl is not simply offering us a modification of Brentano's thesis, he is giving us a radical alternative to it. That radical thesis is essentially a Kantian thesis:[58] the claim that concepts are basic not only to conceptual thought but to the most primitive perception and experience as well. Perception, like belief, judgment, and assertion, has "meaning" (*Sinn*), not simply reference (with which the meaning is often confused). All perception involves judgments, not simply "seeing" but always seeing-as, not simply a "this" but always a "what" as well. In Kantian terms, we would say that all our experience is concept-laden and *meaning*-full, that *what* we experience is "constituted" through our judgments. The Husserlian thesis is strikingly similar to this, except that he would speak of an "essence" where Kant spoke of "concept." But if all acts of perception are also (or are accompanied by—the Individuation Problem again) acts of *con*ception and judgment, then perception is subject to much the same "logic" as abstract thought, including in particular the characteristics of "opacity" that have been so celebrated in the Fregean tradition.

Every act, as also every act correlate, harbors—explicitly or implicitly—a 'logical' factor.[59] We said earlier that this argument carries with it a merger of intentionality and intensionality, *Sinn* and *Bedeutung*. Like *Sinn*, *Bedeutung* originates "in the sphere of speech" and "conceptual meaning," but is extended to "the whole noetico-noematic sphere."[60] Husserl restricts the concept of *Bedeutung* to the sphere of articulate judgment and expression—but this does not entail that *Bedeutungen* are involved only in *actual* expression.[61] *Sinn* is given wider scope, such that *all* acts involve *Sinn*. But it must not be thought that *Sinn* thereby dispenses with linguistic concepts and meanings. The relationship between *Sinn*, *Bedeutung*, and verbal expression (*Ausdruck*) is not at all clear in Husserl. He often writes as if the "phenomena" described by the phenomenologist are wholly independent of the language used to describe them.[62] Then he will claim that words "occasion" the phenomena.[63] At several points he indicates that it is language that "fixes" the essences they express.[64] The differences between these positions are enormously important: the difference between Husserl's phenomenology and the analytic tradition following Frege turns on them. Whether language conditions our experience through *its* meanings or whether language serves as a vehicle for the expression of already constituted meanings is the primary focus of the confrontation between phenomenology and "analytic" philosophy.[65] With particular concern for the noema, the question is this: Is the noematic *Sinn* a product of language (and therefore based on *Bedeutungen*) or is the *Sinn* constituted prior to our ability to express it (and therefore independently of *Bedeutungen*)?

In *Ideas* (sec. 124) Husserl tells us:

Whatever is "meant as such", every meaning

(*Meinung*) in the noematic sense . . .of any act whatsoever *can be expressed conceptually* (*durch 'Bedeutungen'*).

In this sentence, and many others like it, Husserl makes it clear that there is an essential connection between intentionality, noema, and conceptual expression. Contemporary analytic philosophy, following Wittgenstein in particular, would argue that the meanings we find in our experience are derivative of the language we use to describe that experience. Most phenomenologists, on the other hand, would argue that it is the pre-linguistic meanings which constitute the experiences which provide the meanings expressed in language. But "pre-linguistic" here is not the same as "pre-conceptual" or "pre-judgmental," and it is important to stress Husserl's insistence upon the role of concepts and judgments even apart from their expression in language. *Bedeutungen* may be expressed in language, but they do not exist only in their expression. Like *Sinne*, they exist preverbally in our experience and judgments.

In *Cartesian Meditations* (cf. *Ideas*, p. 126) Husserl mentions the possible divergence of *Bedeutung* and *Sinn*, the meanings of expressions and the meanings of experience. It is important to stress, in the face of the preceding quotation, that there is no guarantee in Husserl that language does or can accurately capture the pre-verbal meanings of experience.[66] If this were not so, there would be no need for a phenomenological inquiry which attempted to "cut below" the meanings of expression to seek the meanings of experience; nor would there be any need for the invention of a difficult new vocabulary. If the *Sinne* of experience were always captured by the *Bedeutungen* of language, then "ordinary language" philosophy would indeed be a far less difficult yet adequate approach to the meanings of our experience. As it stands, the meanings and structures of language provide at most a clue to the meanings and structures of experience—and it is important to stress, as above, that there is no guarantee that language and experiential meanings will be in agreement. This is why (as even Austin was forced to admit) philosophical investigation will always require a phenomenological component as well as an investigation of language. Yet we must also guard against the conclusion that, because *Sinn* and *Bedeutung* may disagree, they must therefore be wholly independent of each other.

It has now become virtually axiomatic among phenomenologists that the *Sinne* of experience stand independent of the *Bedeutungen* of linguistic expressions. It has become all but axiomatic among analytic philosophers that there is no meaning apart from language.[67] It is the concept of the noema that provides the link between them. The noema embodies both the changing phases of experience and the organizing sense of our experience. But these two "components" are not separable, for all experience requires meaning, not as an after-the-fact luxury in

reflective judgments but in order for it to be experience *of* anything. It is important to stress, along with Husserl, that meaning must be found in our experience, not only in the expressions we use to describe our experiences. But there is no ground for separating, on this account, the *Sinne* of experience from the *Bedeutungen* of expressions in the extreme way which is common to both phenomenologists and analysts. There is nothing in Husserl to support the all too frequent radical separation of nonlinguistic and Fregean conceptions of *Sinn*, and there is much to support their interrelationship. Husserl's radical thesis regarding the noema does not yield the severe segregation of phenomenology and the more formal Fregean enterprise; on the contrary, it provides the grounds for the integration of his "subjective" enterprise with the sophisticated logical investigations in which he, with Frege, played such a vital role.

NOTES

This essay is a much-revised version of my reply to Dagfin Føllesdal in an American Philosophical Association symposium on phenomenology Dec. 27, 1969, in New York. Føllesdal's paper, "Husserl's Notion of Noema," was first published in *The Journal of Philosophy*, 66, no. 20 (Oct. 16, 1969): 680-87. I have since benefited from private correspondence with Professor Føllesdal, from discussions with Hubert Dreyfus, and from extensive conversations with Izchak Miller, to whom I am deeply grateful.

1. *Ideen zu einer reinen Phänomenologie und phänomenologischen Philosophie*, vol. 1, translated into English as *Ideas* by W. R. Boyce Gibson and published in 1931 by Macmillan. I have used the Collier edition of 1962, and unless otherwise noted it is to this edition that I refer in parentheses.

2. Aron Gurwitsch, *The Field of Consciousness* (Pittsburgh: Duquesne University Press, 1964) and *Studies in Phenomenology and Psychology* (Evanston: Northwestern University Press, 1966).

3. "An Approach to Phenomenology," in *Essays in Memory of Edmund Husserl*, ed. M. Farber (Cambridge: Harvard University Press, 1940), and by widespread reputation in his now famous lectures at the New School for Social Research.

4. Føllesdal, op. cit. Also Hubert Dreyfus, "Husserl's Phenomenology of Perception" (Ph.D. dissertation, Harvard University, 1965).

5. Recently by Frederick Kersten, "Husserl's Doctrine of Noesis-Noema," in *Phenomenology:*

Continuation and Criticism, ed. F. Kersten and R. Zaner (The Hague: Nijhoff, 1973), pp. 114-44.

6. See "Husserl-Frege Correspondence," tr. J. N. Mohanty, *Southwestern Journal of Philosophy*, 5(1974): 83-96.

7. Although *Ideas*, together with *Cartesian Meditations*, are Husserl's best-known introduction to his phenomenology, *Logical Investigations*, trans. J. N. Findlay (New York: Humanities Press, 1970), *Experience and Judgement* (Prague: Academic, 1948), and *Formal and Transcendental Logic*, trans. D. Cairns (The Hague: Nijhoff, 1970), are far more representative of Husserl's interests in philosophy. The problems of perception have been given a far larger role in phenomenology than they received in Husserl's investigations.

8. I have yet to meet or read a philosopher, versed in phenomenology but "outside" the movement, who has not thought Husserl's *Logical Investigations* is his best work. To mention but two very diverse examples: J. N. Findlay's "Phenomenology," *Encyclopaedia Britannica*, 14 (1957), pp. 699-702, and Gustav Bergmann's *Logic and Reality* (Madison: University of Wisconsin Press, 1964), pp. 193ff. Even those who would not share this opinion would agree that his philosophy of logic is of far more enduring interest and its products far better developed than anything that might be called his "philosophy of perception."

9. Little has been published apart from Føllesdal's essay (op. cit.). His position has been well

developed and defended in dissertations by Dreyfus, op. cit., reprinted in part in Robert Solomon, ed., *Phenomenology and Existentialism* (New York: Harper & Row, 1972), pp. 196-210, and by David Smith and Ronald McIntyre of Stanford University and Izchak Miller of U.C.L.A. (no published versions yet available).

10. Gurwitsch, *The Field of Consciousness*, esp. chs. 1 and 2; idem, "The Phenomenology of Perception: Perceptual Implications," in *Studies*, esp. pp. 175-286; and idem, *Invitation to Phenomenology*, ed. J. Edie (Chicago: Quadrangle, 1965), pp. 17-30.

11. Føllesdal's doctoral dissertation was written on this topic under Quine's direction. See also Willard V. Quine, ed., "Reference and Modality" in *From a Logical Point of View* (Cambridge: Harvard University Press, 1964), esp. pp. 142-59.

12. *Studies*, p. 55.

13. Gurwitsch's short pieces on nonperceptual themes (e.g. "On Objects of Thought," *Studies*, pp. 141ff.; "Philosophical Presuppositions of Logic," *Studies*, pp. 350ff.; and "On the Conceptual Consciousness") are notably lacking in development and concrete illustrations compared to his more famous essays on perception. Gurwitsch clearly holds to the "primacy of perception"—to use an expression of one of Husserl's most famous students.

14. Føllesdal makes particular use of Husserl's essay "Noema und Sinn" and other unpublished manuscripts.

15. I have discussed this thesis in some detail in "Sense and Essence: Husserl and Frege," *International Philosophical Quarterly*, 10, no. 3 (1970): 378-401.

16. *Psychologie vom empirischen Standpunkt* (Leipzig: Felix Meiner, 1924), vol. 1, bk. 2, ch. 1. Brentano's views on intentionality changed considerably throughout his career. Husserl, through whom Brentano's concept is best known, often treated his teacher's views unfairly, in an unsympathetic if not misrepresentative way. Brentano's thesis and Husserl's adaptation of it are ably discussed in J. C. Morrison, "Husserl and Brentano on Intentionality," *Philosophy and Phenomenological Research*, 31 (1970): 27-46.

17. Føllesdal, op. cit., p. 680.

18. *Studies*, p. 132. C.f. Alfred Schutz, "Some Leading Concepts of Phenomenology," in M. Natanson, *Essays in Phenomenology* (The Hague: Nijhoff, 1966), p. 30.

19. "Phenomenology and Psychological Applications to Consciousness," in Natanson, op. cit., p. 41.

20. *Studies*, p. 55.

21. Ibid., p. 185.

22. It is characteristic of material objects that they involve any number of perspectives. The concept of "transcendence" in Husserl refers to the fact that an object is never "exhausted" in any number of acts. Husserl often seems to argue that ideal objects, by way of contrast, can be grasped "all at once." This is a dubious thesis, however, since Husserl recognized that "ideal" objects, e.g. the number 7, also involve any number of noemata: 2×3.5, $\sqrt{49}$, $14/2$, etc. "Perspective" is surely inappropriate here.

23. See Gurwitsch, "On the Intentionality of Consciousness," in *Studies*; A. Lingis, "Hyletic Data," in *Analecta Husserliana* (Dordrecht, Holland: D. Reidel, 1972), 2: 96-103. C.f. Frege, "On Sense and Reference" (trans. Black and Geach, [Oxford: Blackwell, 1960]), in which he compares the *Sinn* to the image of the moon on the glass of a telescope, contrasting it both with the moon itself (the object) and the sensory image.

24. Gurwitsch, "On the Intentionality of Consciousness."

25. Ibid.

26. See, e.g., Tugendhat, *Der Wahrheitbegriff bei Husserl und Heidegger* (Berlin: Gruyter, 1970), pp. 38ff.

27. *Studies*, p. 132.

28. It is worth considering the relative positions of *Sinn* and intentionality in *Logical Investigations* (vol. 2). *Sinn* is clearly the dominant conception. Despite the usual emphasis on intentionality, it is *Sinn* which dominates the discussion in *Ideas*, as well as in the later logical works. Intentionality provides the framework in which *Sinn* is the leading *analysandum*.

29. *Ideas*. pp. 128, 129. Føllesdal (op. cit., thesis 4) says that the noema of an act is not the object of the act (i.e. the object toward which the act is directed). Gurwitsch, *Studies*, pp. 116ff., 131ff. See also J. Mohanty, "Husserl's Concept of Intentionality," in *Analecta Husserliana* (New York: Humanities Press, 1971), 1: 108ff., and *Phenomenology and Ontology* (The Hague: Nijhoff, 1970), p. 141. Cf. also E. Levinas: "The object of perception of a tree is a tree, but the noema of this perception is its complete correlate, a tree with all the complexity of its predicates and especially of the modes in which it is given" (*The Theory of Intuition in Husserl's Phenomenology* [Evanston: Northwestern University Press, 1973], p. 54).

30. *Ideas*, sec. 93, p. 250.

31. *Ibid.*, sec. 35, pp. 105ff.

32. Cf. Gurwitsch, *Studies*, pp. 131-34; Føllesdal, op. cit., prop. 5, 6, 7; Mohanty, "Husserl's Concept of Intentionality," in *Analecta Husserliana*, 1: 108, and his "Note" in *Analecta Husserliana*, 2: 318.

33. Gurwitsch, *Studies*, p. 134.

34. Cf. Wittgenstein's puzzle in *Philosophical Investigations (trans. G. E. M. Anscombe* [Oxford: Blackwell, 1958]) concerning the picture of the man on the hill: "Is he going up or coming down?" At least the *Tractatus* was written before the advent of motion pictures.

35. Cf. Mohanty's criticism on his "Note," *Analecta Husserliana*, 2: 320.

36. *Ideas*, sec. 88-89, pp. 237ff.

37. Ibid., sec. 94, p. 251. The individuation of judgments is even more problematic than that of perceptual acts and noemata.

38. *Studies*, p. 133. The frequency of visual verbs in Husserl and Gurwitsch is noteworthy. But where Husserl often places such verbs in "inverted commas"—e.g. *"Sehen"* (*Ideas*, sec. 19, p. 75 et passim)—Gurwitsch, restricting himself to perception, takes them literally.

39. Third Cartesian Meditation, sec. 25, pp. 58ff.

40. Esp. *Ideas*, sec. 124, pp. 318ff. It is *very* important to warn ourselves about the difference between Husserl's use of *Bedeutung* and Frege's use. For Husserl, *Bedeutung* is conceptual meaning; for Frege, it means reference. Cf. "Über Sinn und Bedeutung," *Zeitschrift für Philosophie und philosophische Kritik* (1892).

41. Thus we find Roderick Chisholm, and many other recent philosophers, attempting to analyze Brentano's concept of intentionality in terms of intensional contexts. See, e.g., his *Perceiving* (Ithaca, N.Y.: Cornell University Press, 1957), the last chapter, and "On Some Psychological Concepts and the 'Logic' of Intentionality," in H.-N. Casteneda, ed., *Intention, Minds and Perception* (Detroit: Wayne State University Press, 1960), pp. 11-35.

42. *Ideen III*, p. 89 (quoted in Føllesdal, op. cit.); also *Ideas I*, ch. 9 et passim.

43. Husserl avoids the heavily psychologistic term 'concept' (*Begriff*). He prefers 'essence' (*Wesen*), but the point is the same. Cf. *Ideas*, ch. 1, sec. 2-5.

44. Føllesdal, op. cit., thesis 1.

45. Føllesdal makes only brief mention of Frege in this piece. The relationship is developed in Dreyfus, "*Sinn* and Intentional Object," in Solomon, *Phenomenology and Existentialism*, pp. 1-17.

46. Føllesdal, op. cit., thesis 2.

47. Ibid., theses 3, 4.

48. Ibid., theses 5, 6, 7.

49. Ibid., theses 8, 9.

50. *Ideas*, sec. 89, p. 240.

51. Quoted by Føllesdal, op. cit.

52. *Ideas*, sec. 89, 90.

53. Op. cit. (in defense of thesis 9).

54. *Ideas*, sec. 129, p. 333.

55. See Chisholm's discussion of Brentano, op. cit., and in Lee and Mandlebaum, eds., *Phenomenology and Existentialism* (Baltimore: Johns Hopkins Press, 1967).

56. *Ideas*, sec. 129, p. 333.

57. Ibid., sec. 48, p. 133.

58. It is worth remembering how much Brentano came to dislike Kant's philosophy in considering this affinity between his student and Kant.

59. *Ideas*, sec. 117, p. 306; cf. "the universality of the logical," ibid., p. 307.

60. Ibid., p. 307.

61. See the first of the *Logical Investigations*, vol. II.

62. *Ideas*, sec. 19, pp. 74f.

63. *Philosophy as a Rigorous Science*, trans. Q. Lauer (New York: Harper Torchbooks, 1965), p. 95.

64. E.g. *Ideas*, sec. 66, p. 176.

65. For an admirable attempt at such a synthesis, see J. N. Mohanty's essays "Language and Reality" in his *Phenomenology and Ontology* (The Hague: Nijhoff, 1970), esp. pp. 62f., 30-59. See also the last section of my "Frege and Husserl."

66. On the pessimistic side, it may be argued that there is no way to know if language can ever capture these prelinguistic meanings. This thought haunted Merleau-Ponty throughout his career and drove Heidegger beyond the attempts at metaphysics begun in *Sein und Zeit*, as it chased Mallarmé beyond the transcendental limits of his onetime devotion to poetry.

67. The violent reaction in analytic quarters to the notion of pre-linguistic meanings extends far beyond the limits of phenomenology. It has been evident in the reactions to structuralism and, closer to home, to Chomsky's recent theories of pre-linguistic structures of language.

The Horizon

CORNELIUS A. VAN PEURSEN

A. The Word 'Horizon'

The word 'horizon' comes from a Greek word which is related to the verb 'to delimit.' The horizon is the line which marks the extremity of the visual field. Yet from the outset this word has a fuller meaning. The verb indicates every delimitation, whether physical or mental. Hence other meanings arise: to demarcate, to set bounds to, to mark as one's property, to erect an altar, to give a definition, and to judge. 'Horizon' covers much ground, and it is probably not justified to make it bear distinct literal and figurative senses.

In general, the term 'horizon,' even in the strictest sense, means different things. It denotes the line which limits the visual field. Physical geography defines the horizon as the line of intersection between the celestial sphere and the level plane tangent to the earth at the point where the observer is situated. When the point of observation is situated at a certain distance above the level of the earth, the horizon as the extremity of the visual field is situated below this natural horizon. The line which ties the eyes of the observer to the limit of his visual field will be more oblique the more he rises above the level of the earth. He will always see even more sky and earth. This phenomenon is called the lowering of the horizon and it has to do with the horizon in its

most usual sense—namely, the line which divides the sky and the earth into two parts, one of which is visible and the other invisible. In physical geography this horizon is called the apparent horizon. The true horizon or the geocentric horizon is further distinguished. This line is a fixed line, whereas the natural horizon and the apparent horizon may be displaced. The true horizon is situated where a level plane stretching from the center of the earth intersects the sky.

These divergent meanings show that the horizon is not easily interpreted in terms of a purely spatial framework. There is something unreal in the horizon which induces talk about an apparent horizon. On the other hand, its reality cannot be denied, and so one tries to define a natural horizon and a true horizon. The really striking fact about the horizon is that it recedes.

All this makes the demarcation between the literal and the figurative senses of the word 'horizon' highly uncertain. There is a horizon everywhere man gazes. Even though it is not the extremity of the visual field, the geocentric horizon still limits a supposed plane, which is present to man's gaze. Language attests to this horizon which surrounds man in every domain. Every man has his own horizon; it may be very confined but it also may be quite extensive. One may even speak of a cultural horizon whereby one epoch may be distinguished from another.

Translated by F. Elliston and P. McCormick. © 1976 Elliston and McCormick.

At times the meaning changes imperceptibly from the literal (as far as we may use this expression) to the figurative. As he walks to his plane, the flyer sees the horizon around him. During his flight, too, he orients himself by the horizon. But when he finds himself fogbound, he uses an instrument called the artificial horizon. This horizon, for the pilot, is the set of readings his instrument board gives him.

The word 'horizon' connotes something fleeting and at the same time denotes, in the most disparate senses, a kind of reference point. The horizon is tied to an observer; there is something subjective about it. On the other hand, it seems that the horizon encompasses everything. The horizon has a problematic character. Prosaic space, which is encircled by the horizon, becomes mysterious. The horizon hides a secret, and the following sections will try to come to grips with this unattainable line which is so near us and yet all the while recedes from us.

B. The Horizon as the Expression of Man in the World

What is more external to man than the horizon? It is always far ahead of us; we cannot catch up with it—it eludes every effort to overtake it. But this characteristic of being external is, all the same, quite peculiar. This "outside," where the horizon is found, has something mysterious about it, something fleeting and unreal. When we see a wall, we can establish that it is situated outside us. Apart from all philosophical and especially epistemological problems, the wall is itself over there—given in perception. We can approach it, and each step and then each motion with which we grope toward it reveals aspects of this wall to us. It is the wall which manifests itself as being identically there, outside us. The horizon is altogether different: it is not a question of an "over there" which we can approach. The horizon is not in the world, among trees and walls. The "outside" of the horizon does not seem to function in the

world, and that raises a problem. Is not the concept of an "outside" uniquely applicable to the world's territory?

One might answer that the horizon does not exist if it is analyzed scientifically. It is an optical illusion. Man sees it outwardly, but in reality it does not exist. Perhaps someone of a scientific background might even denounce a parallelism with the colors we see and which would not exist in the world outside where there are only electro-magnetic waves. But it is not hard to see that the relation between the everyday image of the world and the scientific conception of it are entirely different in the case of the horizon and that of colors. Whatever the interpretation of colors and the scientific and epistemological abstractions concerning them, everyone can agree that in primordial experience the colors, as phenomena, indicate a real world outside man. They are not interior signs of a hidden and exterior reality. Rather, the colors themselves are given as outside, and it is the object itself which we perceive as immediately given in these colors. The relation between the scientific conception and everyday experience in the case of the horizon is distinguished from this relation in the case of colors by the fact that, in primordial experience, the horizon is not found in the midst of the world, as colors are. To be sure, there is a gap between scientific abstractions and the established facts of everyday life. The word 'unreality' has a different meaning at the two levels. But in the original experience the horizon is characterized by its unreality, that is, as a phenomenon that appears outside of man without being a real thing in the external world.

As a directly given phenomenon, the horizon presents itself as a line which recedes as we advance. One can imagine that chronologically (in the case of the child, for example) there is a period during which the horizon is seen as a fixed border of the known world. But soon one notices that the horizon is displaced. The horizon accompanies him in the course of long walks or during ocean voyages, whereby primitive man reaches unknown shores. The horizon as a phenomenon of daily life has a different degree of reality than, for example, a color. The "unreality" of the horizon does not derive from a scientific claim but is involved in primordial experience. Colors and sounds refer to a reality. Since the horizon is not found at the center of the world, it cannot be referred to as being outside. Its "unreality" does not allow it to be simply outside.

This strange character of the horizon also follows from the fact that the horizon adds nothing to the world. The world does not become fuller because something like a horizon exists. The horizon does not enrich the world. This does not mean that the horizon is nothing and that we could just as well not take it into account. On the contrary, that the horizon does not add anything to the world implies that it is not possible to remove the horizon the way we remove some object. Every object can be thought of as nonexisting, as removed from the framework of this world. The world would be a little poorer for the loss of certain colors, sounds, or objects—but it would remain the same. Without a horizon, the world would not be any poorer but it would not remain the same. The world without a horizon is unimaginable. The world would lose its framework, along with the horizon, thereby making it entirely different. The world, as a human world, is even impossible without the horizon. The horizon, in adding nothing to the world, is for that reason precisely all the more indispensable.

The horizon has something intangible, something inviolable about it. Man cannot remove it, not even in thought, nor can he reach it. Every fence can be removed, every limit can be reached, every frontier can be crossed. The horizon, nonetheless, is given as an absolute limit, an impassable boundary. Here again the horizon is shown as not entirely outside. What is outside in the world is accessible. Whatever does not belong to man's being, namely, the objects of the world, may be surpassed by man. Man cannot deny the horizon. To eliminate the horizon is to remove man. The horizon is in some manner tied to man. It is not, strictly speaking, outside him. Since the horizon is natural to the human point of view, man does not succeed in transcending it. For that reason it seems to be precisely so far outside; it is the absolute limit.

The horizon is related to the human body. Man's optical structure, his bodily height, his erect posture—his whole bodily organism is found to be involved in the sighting of the horizon. The horizon reflects the different aspects of man's corporality. To reach something means that man reaches it with his body. It is nonetheless impossible for man to reach the reflection of his own body. The body cannot overtake its own space. An accessible horizon would destroy bodily space. Man drives the horizon before him.

On the other hand, the horizon manifests man's scope. It is the human world which stretches as far as the eye can see, framed by the horizon. The horizon is beyond reach, and it is precisely for that reason that it ensures the scope of human space. The horizon denotes the zone of human actions. Undoubtedly, the horizon signifies the limit which man cannot reach, but equally it designates the region to which man reaches by means of his sight, his desires, his framed picture of the world. Man allows himself to be invited and intrigued by this horizon which he knows is mysteriously linked to himself.

Human beings lay out the path of their life; they discern a direction, they strain toward it, they project themselves. All this is possible only because of the scope of their actions, of their being; because of this scope of which the horizon is the sign. It is likewise in the figurative sense that man knows the horizon and that this horizon opens up to him the sphere of his mind and of his activities. The double aspect of the horizon—inaccessible border and space for advancing—is the presupposition for the realization of man: it is the initial condition which exists prior to every human act. The horizon invites and repels at the same time.

The world cannot be represented without a horizon. The horizon is related to being human. The horizon cannot be pictured without men. If the objects of the world are taken away, the horizon remains. If the men who inhabit the world are taken away, the horizon disappears.

Would it be justifiable to conclude that the horizon is not found outside man, but within him? The horizon is neither purely outside nor purely within. It accompanies man like his shadow. There is still a big difference between the horizon and man's shadow. Man's shadow accompanies him in the world amid the surrounding horizon. Man's shadow is thus more directly subject to man; it follows all his movements and does not possess this mysterious character of being "inviting-repelling." On the contrary, the horizon accentuates the outside world for man. It is in front of us, very far away.

The conclusion which follows from the preceding definitions is summed up by recognizing that the horizon cuts across the distinctions of inside-outside—belonging to man, exterior to man. In the horizon, exteriority merges with interiority; man merges with the world. It is even made evident that man is man only because of the extrahuman, because of the exterior world into which he finds himself introduced from the very beginning, encompassed by the horizon. The horizon shows him that. The horizon is the translation of man into the world.

Tied to man, the horizon involves an aspect of reflection. The horizon brings out the fact that the world, as man experiences it, reflects man. What is more, the horizon shows that this world itself is reflected by man. It is a totally unique characteristic of the horizon that it manifests an element of human reflection. This reflection is not detached from the world, but on the contrary is outlined on the world. The horizon is more than a simple physical line, a fixed border of the world. It is also more than a purely optical phenomenon. The "unreality" of the horizon is not discovered through scientific learning but is given immediately in everyday experience. With animals the horizon may be purely optical: a line out-

side of the animal which is displaced as the animal advances. Man, however, regains something of himself in the horizon facing him. For him the horizon is mysterious, tied to his being human, inciting him to reflection and, because of that, a phenomenon of the intellectual order.

And so it is that the horizon is man's translation into the world. Surrounded by the horizon, this world is reflected by man; reflected on by him. Through the horizon, the world becomes linked to man: it is his world, the human world, the inhabited world. It is not in the division of scientific concepts that man becomes aware of his participation in the image of the world but in the unity of lived experience. Man lives in the horizon, the horizon is himself, the horizon is the world, the horizon reflects back to him the human world, namely, the world as visible in the beam of human reflection.

This point could also be formulated as follows: the horizon shows the physical domain as a territory reflected upon. Certainly scientific or philosophical thought can endeavor to extract this lived world from its framework, in order to keep only a dehumanized, objective, and purely physical world. But the everyday world, where every mode of thought finds its point of departure, is the grounds of the horizon, the reflected world. The separation between the physical and psychical disappears here. It is a case of the human world, material and spiritual at once.

This comes back to saying that the horizon outlines the oriented space whose center is the body. By remaining out of reach, the horizon at the same time circumscribes the scope of man; it is the world insofar as man can approach it. The horizon shows the mental dimension of the human body. In the figurative sense, the horizon signifies the domain which is found in the range of human reflection and action. As will be established again, there is no fundamental difference between the two senses of horizon. The description of the horizon cuts across the dualisms of psychical and physical, interior and exterior, literal and figurative, human world and objective world.

There would be no horizon for a stationary, fixed being. The horizon is the border, the line which accompanies us. The horizon invites us to draw near. The horizon is there when we go toward it. "To go toward" is not just a motor or biological activity but, above all, a mental one. It implies that man considers the world, takes cognizance of the world. For man, the horizon reflects a certain notion of the world. To go toward this world, even if this is realized in a walk, implies a mental aspect.

The horizon is man's translation into the world—man as a creature who goes toward this world and who adheres to it. The horizon is the manifestation—physical, optical, psychical, spiritual—of man finding his way in the world. Corporal man is not a being isolated the way an object could be isolated in the midst of the world, but an adhesion to the world. On the other hand, the horizon shows a contrary trend: the world *qua* world manifested to man. The lived world of the horizon comes toward man, participates in man—two aspects which will be elaborated in the following sections and which are involved in the phenomenon called horizon.

C. Finitude and Transcendence

Man goes toward the world. This human character is revealed by the horizon. The horizon reveals thereby two aspects of man: his finitude and his transcendence.

The horizon confines man, it circumscribes him, it surrounds him with the image of the end, it de-fines (*de-limits*) him. It is impossible to flee the horizon. However far we go, it is always there. It accompanies man on all his travels. The human body occupies a very limited place in the vast world. When man touches things, he gets hold of only what is near him. Sight presupposes the limitations of the body as a physiological complex. But however extensive its domain, sight reaches to the limits. The horizon takes shape around sight. Bodily space is restricted: in his mind man goes beyond his confines. In his imagination he inhabits lofty worlds, and in his thought he soars above the imperceptible spaces of the microcosm and the macrocosm. But here again he meets limits. His mind knows of horizons which move but which do not disappear. Also, the mind has its own space, surrounded by horizons.

All human life exists thanks to the horizon. Logical thought, legal and social action, artistic creation—all this circumscribes, defines, com-prehends (*com-prends*), concludes, delimits, forms. Each of these activities proceeds in its own natural horizon. Man, in his cultural activity, interferes with nature in order to impound it. Nature undergoes the metamorphosis of being included in the restricting activity of culture. Nature there becomes human by receiving its horizon. The horizon is human finitude.

Does nature itself not represent precisely a progress without end? Take, for example, the idea of the sciences. It would be absurd to claim that there will be a limit to the development of scientific thought. Consciousness itself is defined by its own progress: without infinite possibilities of advancing, it would fade away.

In fact, culture does not know an ultimate end. But this progress is characterized by the transcending of frontiers which are forever new. The progress of human consciousness itself is preconditioned by the fact that the totality is never attained; possibilities remain to be realized. Progress, consciousness, and culture presuppose a visual field which is always limited. The impulse toward the infinite is defined by the finite.

This seems paradoxical, but it is not if we take note of the phenomenon of the horizon. The horizon does not frame a fixed terrain. The world which man encompasses is not an unchangeable datum. The horizon yields, it takes shape on a changing scene: the clouds, the sea, the meadows. Thus one speaks of successive horizons. Behind the horizon in front of us is found another. At bottom, it is the same horizon, which is displaced in the world around us and in the mental domain. The human range is forever changing: it is the rich panorama of the horizon, of culture, but it will always be a matter of human range, of the horizon of the human world.

The animal is not aware of a horizon in this sense. The world with which it is closely tied is a fixed setting. Man has a margin at his disposal. He draws near, he goes toward, he surpasses, he transcends. Man finds his bearings in the horizon in front of him. He is aware of the horizons of his existence. It is his finitude he is looking at, the visual field and its mental realization; everything reflects to him the possibilities of delineating his way, of transcending the demarcations of the world.

The horizon attracts. What is more characteristic of the horizon than this seductive trait which makes us advance, always farther, even though we can never reach the horizon? All the same, the receding horizon shows us our possibilities of continuing, of surpassing.

This brings to light the idea of finitude. Man knows his finitude. And this is because it is with him in all his acts of transcending. If we cannot speak of the transcendence of an animal, we cannot speak of its finitude either. Human finitude is situated on another plane. It is revealed in its transcendence, in the horizon which recedes toward the infinite. The horizon shows finitude from the infinite. The infinite, on the other hand, is revealed only in the finitude of the horizon. By restricting, the horizon shows the infinity of human possibilities; by confining, it conceals the open transcendence.

In opposition to a fixed line, the horizon encloses an appearance of movement, physical and mental. It is in the horizon that man knows what he is. The glance at the horizon is like a dialogue of man with himself. Culture offers a scene of action where there is dialogue of the history of human consciousness. It is an endless play of succeeding levels of scientific thought and of artistic activity. These are always limited, but by limitations which give way and which never exhaust human possibilities. Culture, essentially tied to man, throws the horizon into relief.

The horizon has a certain ambiguity. The aspects of finitude and of infinitude, of restriction and of openness are here joined. Each of these aspects indicates that the horizon is meaningful and that it gives a sense to the ground it encloses.

The horizon makes possible the localization of things. Everything is found somewhere. This means that wings are not lost in an infinite space but that they are found in delimited areas. Even man can locate himself, thanks to the horizon. Behind the mountains which we notice in the distance are found new valleys. The horizon is not the frontier of nothingness, but inhabitable areas follow one after another with the receding horizon.

This is equally valid in the mental domain. The canvas of the landscape painter of the seventeenth century has a painted horizon; but, at the same time, it has a mental horizon of the artist, whose work it permeates. This horizon was once a limited horizon; but it is thanks to these limitations, to this well-defined cultural ambience that the painter was able to finish his work. The landscape stops somewhere, the canvas has an edge, the colors have hues restricted by their relations to the technique of that period. The visual field of the landscape painter is likewise limited by his time—whatever. So it is that the artist can finish his work, thanks to a horizon in which he finds himself situated.

Every cultural work has limitations which locate it. A system of thought exists thanks to these restrictions. It aims to distinguish, to bring to light, to define, to make clear. It arranges, disposes, constructs. All this can be produced only in areas circumscribed by the horizon. The horizon prevents man from becoming lost and gives him the means of locating himself and of tracing the paths of his mind. The aspects of infinity and of openness mix also with the meaning-structure of the horizon. To man, the horizon represents the idea that there is more than what he sees. A walled-up world would be absurd. Every visual field is surrounded by the horizon, and this means that it is always part of the world. The horizon as a receding line gives meaning to the circumscribed domain. By its horizon, the visual field anticipates a world still invisible. The visible world becomes a ground of the possibilities of endless advancement.

This idea is likewise valid in the mental domain. Every inquiry aims at an end, every reasoning at a conclusion. This gives a sense to the inquiry, but solely because it is not a question of an ultimate end. The idea that the result of the discovery would make each further investigation or each subsequent theory superfluous would annihilate the meaning of such results or discoveries.

The sense of order in scientific thought consists in indicating new orders of possibilities. Scientific method is a procedural activity rather than an advance esteemed forever. Every accomplishment outlines a new horizon. Every end is a new, possible point of departure. The method of the intellectual life knows the clarity of horizons which lead to the infinite. Each new discovery breaks the demarcations already reached, and in manifesting a horizon further away it opens innumerable perspectives.

D. Perspective and Perspicuity

The man who finds himself facing the horizon could imagine himself fleeing from this horizon by rising above the earth. But however high he climbs, he again finds a horizon, everywhere. To soar above the world, id est, not to be surrounded by a horizon, would involve a point of view completely outside the world. But the words 'point of view' indicate a localization and thus a point within the world, which is projected against the horizon. Man stays tied to the world even if he takes flight toward a spiraled nebula. A human being can never escape the horizon.

Man is in the world; he finds himself put there at the start. This constraint is the expression of his being and it is represented to him by the horizon. The horizon constantly reminds him that he finds himself in the world.

All this is summed up by the word 'perspective.' Human life, its acts, its thoughts unfold in perspectives. To come "out of perspective" is incompatible with being human. Perspective locates man. Perspective is evidence for the fact that the plane of human existence is tied down to the horizon.

'Perspective' expresses the idea that a thing or a scene is not looked at from all sides at once. Things show a certain part of themselves, depending on the side from which we approach them. Ideas are likewise grasped in perspectives. This is not equivalent to a philosophy of perspectivism in the sense of a relativism which would not separate the false from the true, but it implies that a philosophy—whether true or false—takes hold of its ideas from a given side and arranges them in a given perspective.

Even if man succeeds in going beyond his normal confines, he finds perspectives again. A photo taken from outside inhabited areas of space—for example, by an instrument in a rocket sent to the moon—would show a perspective because its point of view remains localized in a horizon.

A world without perspectives would no longer be human and therefore would be unimaginable. Without perspectives, the observer would see each thing from all sides at once. He would even see all things at once. There would no longer be a limit or a horizon. To see all things "outside" a perspective implies that we see them without sides, front, rear. One could no longer determine whether one thing is farther than another. Everything would be situated at the same distance. And even this expression is not sufficient, for the notion of distance would have disappeared. Distance is related to position, to "station." Areas which we can point out are found in perspectives and are also oriented in space. Without spatial orientation, it is not possible to say that everything is located. Without perspectives, nothing is situated. To rise above the horizon and to lose perspective ends with the elimination of every means of orientation. Thus spatial indications would no longer be usable: 'here' and 'there' are stripped of meaning, and the word which would be substituted is 'everywhere'—which would, moreover, become identical with 'nowhere.'

The importance of perspective is that it clarifies the notion of horizon. It shows that the horizon is not found only at the edge of the oriented world but that it penetrates the visual field (in the figurative sense as well). The manner in which the world is structured internally manifests the presence of the horizon. The horizon situates man in the totality; it makes all positions outside the world impossible; it forces man to enter into perspectives. The horizon compels us to have a point of view, a meaningful expression that indicates the viewing, which is directed, and its necessary starting point—all of which is included by perspective. Every perspective—a notion which is at the same time a physical and a mental concept—renews this obligation, which no one, as a human being, can avoid.

Perspective offers different aspects. The totality as such is never grasped, but it is apprehended through aspects in perspective. Perspective contains a series of aspects, but a series which is easy to take in at a single glance. This process of perspective extends from the well-ordered impression of a landscape up to a system of thought and a synoptic table and makes the richness of impressions and of concepts manageable. The world thus becomes accessible. It reveals itself to man in the horizon by means of perspectives.

In its restrictive role, a perspective facilitates insights. These estimates are elicited in the general view profiled by the horizon. The perspectives point back to the horizon; they are tied to one another thanks to the horizon. The horizon sums up all possible perspectives. In the basic teaching of drawing we learn that the landscape must be projected according to the lines of perspective. One begins by drawing these lines in order to lay out the landscape. This is done by drawing the

line of the horizon on which the point of perspective is selected, where all the lines of perspective converge. The horizon could be defined as a line consisting of the collection of all possible points of perspective.

Thus in man's immediate surroundings and in the objects he sees and touches, perspective reflects the fact that man is situated in the horizon. By means of this, the world acquires human characteristics. Objects are found here or there; they "follow" one another. They show man one side and hide another. They show their faces and thus intrigue man. Man can go and meet objects. An object of the everday world is never purely a thing completely outside the human domain. Man would be lost among completely dehumanized things. But he meets them, he orients himself in respect to them, and he can take hold of them. The world, with its objects, manifests itself to man within the confines of the horizon as a world that is human and inhabitable. Orientation implies the possibility of knowledge in general. Knowledge is a mode of orientation preconditioned by an essential affinity between the subject and the object of the act of knowledge. This meeting place is prefigured in the horizon and in the perspectives which lead to it.

The visual field in perspective reflects the human structure. The limitations of aspects visible and invisible, of front and rear, of high and low, of left and right, of far and near, are the restrictions of embodied man. All the characteristics of the surrounding world are characteristics of our own body. They show that man draws near to the world by means of his body. This access is restricted and finite; body and mind are there joined: there the mental view likewise reveals its limitations in the mental perspectives which open up before man. Perspective is man as a body-mind in its finitude. But it means as well, as has just been explained, that the world in the reflection of this finitude becomes manipulable and known. And the word 'reflection' itself remains an image because it is not a question of two entities, one of which would be reflected in the other, but of a unity, a common ground. Hence a definition of the essence of one implies the other, as will be elaborated in one of the final sections.

The meaning of perspective in its relation to the horizon becomes clearer if one takes note of the etymology of the word. *Perspico* means to catch sight of, to have a glimpse of. Looking between the farmhouse and the barn, one sees a meadow. Each perspective has its contours. Even if the visual field is completely clear, it is inevitable that we look in a certain direction. Without a directed gaze, nothing is noticed. The direction is a limitation of the gaze, which is again manifested in the perspective.

In this way, man sees everything through a frame. To see, to catch sight of, to take cognizance of, are acts which proceed by limitation. These acts are inseparable from the fact that man penetrates into perspectives. Every human act (to look at, to understand) manifests an acceptance and a realization of finitude. Situated amid perspectives, man catches glimpses of things by means of his very body. He looks at the world, so to speak, through his own finitude. The world appears to him as a ground structured by this finitude, which is projected all the way into the horizon.

Perspective is not restrictive because it admits only certain aspects compatible with the human position and structure but also because it is not possible to continue without stopping in any perspective whatsoever. Every perspective has its ultimate frontier; perspectives follow from the horizon.

Perspective lends the world its perspicuity. Without perspective, the world would be opaque and obscure. For man, a pure mind without location is without meaning. Mental clarity and distinctness have their origin in the restrictions of perspective. Transparency is always transparency in respect to someone. Transparency is a notion of orientation and not a notion of an absolute view. The word 'view' implies, moreover, that something is grasped from a certain position. The body's or the mind's eye is, as

such, already involved in a perspective. Transparency implies relation, collaboration, synoptic function. Perspective is identifiable with perspicuity.

The orientation within perspective transforms chaos into a cosmos. The etymology of this last word indicates something about perspective: to arrange in ranks, to space out, to class. "Cosmos" is a dynamic concept. It is never immediately given or something always already there, but it comes about bit by bit. It is like a crystallization starting from an initial point.

The cosmos is human in its perspicuity. It was mentioned above that knowledge as a mode of orientation is based on an affinity between man and his object. Here again we notice the impossibility of a definitive separation between man and the world—the inside and the outside. The cosmos is the world bound up with man. It is the world surrounded by the horizon, which penetrates into the perspectives and which attests to the structural solidarity between the human and the territory of the world.

The horizon, then, situates man in the center of reality. A lofty point of view allows the spectator to take in at a glance the ground which stretches at his feet; he gets a better orientation. But this orientation would be annihilated if the spectator climbed so high that he succeeded in getting beyond the totality. It is, moreover, an impossible idea: the word 'outside' designating a position taken in a perspective. For man, the world becomes transparent within perspectives. The world becomes clear. The light from the finite and human position renders the world visible: clarity reveals the differences. In the horizon and its perspectives we catch sight of the world in the light of human reflection. Then, again, we catch sight of the horizon—not as the border of the world but as having penetrated the interior of the world.

The last paragraph sums up some ideas that were developed above but now are tied to the notion of perspective and perspicuity. This is also true of the idea of method. Method enlightens by going toward. Method implies perspective. Etymologically, "method" contains the word 'road.' It expresses the world's viability. The world, caught in the contours of human existence, is accessible. Method calls attention to the perspicuity of the reflected world.

This leads us to acknowledge that a fact does not exist: a brute fact or pure facticity is impossible. A brute fact would be a thing completely in itself, isolated. But such a fact would be neither perceptible nor conceivable. Each fact which we verify is located from a certain position and discovered within a perspective. Each fact is found within a coherence. Verified facts are linked to each other, and a fact cannot be found save within the horizon.

E. The Horizon as Meaningful Coherence

The horizon has an englobing function. A piece of interlaced work must be stretched out on a frame. What makes it hold together is the frame, whose effect can be noticed throughout the piece. The horizon is such a frame. Even if the horizon is not visible, the coherence within the world immediately surrounding man points to the horizon. Everything bears the mark of a relationship to the horizon. This is especially noticeable if one finds himself in an area surrounded by a visible horizon. The height of that house over there, or of those trees a little farther back, is evaluated by comparing them with one another, then with the surroundings, and lastly with the horizon. We judge the height of a hill, which we notice far in the distance on a plain, by judging the distance of this hill to the horizon. Even if the horizon is hidden by some woods, we trace in our thoughts the line where the horizon might be in order to have a point of reference so as to measure the height of things localized in front of us, the observer.

The horizon serves as much as an index for qualifying a thing's nearness or farness as for predicting a thing's speed. Thus localizations and movements in the sky (of an airplane or a bird) are measured thanks to the horizon. This also explains the indispensable use of the word 'horizon' for denoting a line conceived on the celestial sphere: it facilitates the situating of observed phenomena.

The horizon is a sign of reality. Something which would manifest itself to us without being found within the same horizon would seem to us phantasmagoric. Thus in art the phantasmagoric effects do not belong to the same horizon as the masterpiece itself. The same would hold for an apparition we see in front of us, without being able to indicate where this strange sight is situated—neither among the trees, nor in front of the house, nor on the ground. Such an apparition, which cannot be located within a ground surrounded by the horizon, would be unreal.

All this comes back to saying that each real object within the horizon is related to other things. Each object and each aspect refers back to other objects and aspects. They exist as such by a coherence with one another. Objects are not isolatable; nor are their properties. The thing is not a sum of properties. The world is not an agglomeration of things. The house which we see is not a totality which is composed of different qualities—red, low, an oblique roof, etc. But the rough and crumbly red of the stone walls is given as a whole and refers back to the low construction: and it is in this manner that the house shows itself as a house with a pointed roof, and as closely tied with the surroundings, with its spaces interlaced in the perspective. All this gives rise to the contours of the horizon.

Except in the case where we locate ourselves at a certain distance from reality, as immediately given in the horizon, it is impossible to speak of a certain isolated object which possesses such and such properties. In reality—namely, in the horizon—a thing does not exist, save in a perspective, by manifesting itself under a set of aspects.

The same point of view can be developed with respect to the mind's horizon. Ideas are never isolatable, but their meanings and their importance derive from their connections with and their distance from the mind's horizon. Every image, every symptom, every nervous disorder can be explained only by taking account of the horizon of human life. The human body likewise participates in this coherence. A simple stomach upset may be linked to a situation extending from the conflict which reveals the horizon of life.

Similarly, the sciences have a horizon. Theirs is evidently a horizon further removed than that of everyday life, but the level of the sciences is never situated in the infinite. Every scientific concept originates from a whole and is profiled on a horizon. This horizon is modified by the epoch, by the culture and its philosophical conceptions, by the structure of the scientific field itself. Even the concepts called "absolute" or "completely abstract" are still situated. The horizons of the sciences are like concentric circles around the primary horizon which surrounds man's visual field. They have sequences, a history. The scientific concepts belong to a chronological and especially a structural history. They are derived from a sequence, from a coherence.

Abstract concepts like pure qualities (isolated), quantities, substance, and properties verge upon the unreal because one conceives them as isolatable. In reality, these notions themselves have their coherence in a structural history. The electromagnetic waves function against the base of an isolated quality (such-and-such a color) and this quality is an abstraction of the colored aspect of an object involved in the coherence of the primordial horizon. For the physical sciences, laboratory experiments are the means for pushing back the horizon. The experimental method isolates a certain process or a few of its aspects. The experiment is still found in the field of everyday life, but the instruments are selective and are meant to put in relief only certain qualifying aspects which will be isolated by the scientific researcher's thought. As soon as the concepts thus gained (absolute space, wavelength) are interrelated in their new field, they acquire a certain reality which they do not possess in themselves—since they are now in a coherence defined by a horizon. The absolute and the abstract are replaced in the finitude of a concrete horizon from which they had come. Even absolute space becomes the limiting case of other spatial structures which all have their own frontiers. Mathematical abstractions can be inserted into the concrete world of astronomy. Thanks to the intermediary of verification, the abstract language of logic is situated within the horizon of the world. One could therefore conclude that each concept exists only by means of the coherence of a horizon, and that each horizon keeps something of the primordial horizon which it surrounds concentrically.

The etymology of the word 'absolute' indicates a state of detachment. Absolute refers to the absence of a relation to the horizon. A complete description of the absolute thing could be given, but it would be unreal. The thing tied up with other things is real, but it could not be given a limiting description because it always refers beyond and each aspect is derived from a coherence of innumerable other aspects. Nor are the sciences exhaustible. All science is conditioned by a coherence wherein each symbol refers to another. Scientific thought as such does not know the absolute in the sense of a detached-in-itself. A science that wishes to become absolute would destroy itself.

To summarize the conclusions reached, reality can be considered as a coherence. The collection of things links up references to all directions. The world shows itself in this way. In these referential sequences we catch only aspects. Objects show us one side. These limiting aspects express the inexhaustible riches of the reality manifesting itself: the coherence is meaningful.

The idea of the horizon is thus found to be related to the concept of reference, of direction, of sense. The horizon gives shape to a movement. Each thing or aspect indicates something more than itself.

Only in abstraction can we speak of an object which remains in itself. Absurdity indicates the senselessness of a situation where there are no longer any means of going further, of reaching further, and thus of penetrating into reality—no longer a means to disclose the world.

The truth which manifests something to us is not a finished idea but an uninterrupted chain of meaning. The sense of a glance is implied in the red patch of color we see and which indicates the roof, showing an aspect of the house, which in turn refers to the countryside circumscribed by the horizon. The propulsive movement is found again in the domains formed by the horizon in the figurative sense. The pure fact does not exist, for each fact is found in an impulse which is the expression of the horizon's attracting and inviting characteristics.

F. The Horizon and Time

The coherence of the world in the horizon exists thanks to anticipating. Through the action of anticipation, the position of man in the horizon is not solely that of finding himself in the world but, above all, that of entering deeper and deeper into the world. Man is situated there in time.

The perception of each thing or aspect of a thing is spread out in time (before and after). The rambler who approaches an isolated house always sees more aspects of this house. He already anticipates the sides which he does not yet see: in a moment he will see the back part of the house with all that is now hidden. From the first, however, he knows that the house has many sides, even if he does not see them. When an aspect is apprehended as an aspect of an object, anticipations and acquired experiences of the coherence of the world are implied. The perception of the world is based on time.

In one of the preceding sections the horizon was seen to outline the world as reflected upon by man. This idea has now perhaps been put in a better light. The horizon indicates that there is more than the instantaneous: there is time through

which man possesses the faculty of knowing the world around him. The horizon represents this movement of embracing the world, which is the human glance. The horizon reflects human consciousness which accedes to the world, even when consciousness seems to be stable—just as the rambler who stops anticipates at the same time the whole house, which will never be given to him otherwise than by fragmentary glimpses.

Human perception in general functions solely through time. Understanding is acquainted with method, an order, an access. The cosmos is perspicuous to human consciousness because it is temporal. If man encompassed a finished, absolute whole, there would be neither time nor the ceaseless evolution of human consciousness. If man discerned only the instantaneous, there would be neither time nor the coherence of human thought.

The notion of the world implies the manifestation of this world. The world is the terrain that one sees, could see, or thinks of as always existing. Even the ideal world of certain philosophies is a world which manifests itself, though hidden to rational thought or to metaphysical intuition. The abstract world of the physicist as the domain of mathematical equations is likewise concerned with an order of phenomena which are in fact phenomena for the human observer. The world is manifestation—namely, a connection of aspects, a connection of ideas which are interlinked within the time of the look of apperception and reflection.

The horizon marks the temporality of the world as manifestation. The supposition of a thing or of an aspect of the world as absolute entity (detached from the horizon and from its relations) would deny their temporal character and render their manifestation impossible. Every definition of a phenomenon in modern physics, however independent it may appear to be, is related to a temporal point of reference. Reality is located in the horizon of time. In Einstein's theory, by contrast, some schema or other of time that differs from our known time is always relative to this known time through the intermediary of complicated equations.

The fairy tale is located in another time. That is why it is unreal. All the same, it is imaginable—because it also is tied to our temporal horizon. The intermediary is found at the beginning of the tale: "Once upon a time," "A long long time ago."

The world's space which is revealed in the horizon is found therefore in time It is within the framework of the horizon that space possesses a future. The relation between space and the future seems strange at first sight. But "absolute" Euclidean space inserts its presence—as has been outlined in the preceding section—in the superstructures, the curved spaces of the astronomical world. By successive reliefs, reality manifests itself in space. The space of the real world is restrained by the horizon. It is nonetheless through this limitation that it always points farther. Space shows perspectives and becomes a field of possibilities. Beyond the horizon are found new avenues. Space is oriented by means of the future. It is there that one of the most essential characteristics of the horizon is discovered: by means of the horizon time is linked to space. Space is encircled by the horizon, but not confined. The circumscription of the horizon indicates the escape of time.

The future has therefore a special importance. This becomes clearer when we realize that the horizon is always found in front of us. The horizon is especially the stretched line, straight or slightly curved, and it is very seldom that one sees oneself surrounded by the horizon (on a "lookout," for example). It is evident that man knows that the horizon is all around him, even where he sees it only partially.

On the other hand, the motion of advancing always reveals to man the true character of the horizon as a receding line. We might, possibly, walk backward, knowing that we are going toward that part of the horizon which is behind us. In that case, it is still a way of getting closer.

The conclusion that space can be traversed in all possible directions is justified and it takes on its unique sense when the movement is confronted by the horizon. This reflects known time, which

has only one dimension and is irreversible. The man who advances comes from somewhere and can thus turn back. In the horizon space finds its future, and only by means of that, its past. Space is thus oriented by time, which implies one sense and one direction.

The horizon encircles space-time. The mystery of the horizon is derived above all from this penetration of time into space. It is not a question of a linear time-length which dissolves in the homogeneity of mathematical space but, on the contrary, of a space whose significative orientation is put into relief by time.

The elimination of time is another way artificially to isolate, to render an idea, object, or quality absolute. In this case there would no longer be anticipations either of possibilities, of sides, or of backs. The result would be the impossibility of advancing, of relating—therefore, an unknowable world. The elimination of time, then, amounts to extracting the world from its horizon. That would make the world unreal; it would no longer be a world for man, or a world related to human consciousness.

It might be asked whether it is possible to perpetuate something without eliminating the horizon. For example, if we take a photo of a countryside with a horizon, we get a view which escapes time's grasp. Is this not a symbol of human understanding, which takes, so to speak, a photo of a process situated within a horizon in order to fix it for all time? For this purpose we could think of scientific attempts to get a picture of the whole universe, a view consisting of the instantaneous conjunction of events in the universe, in order to deduce the past and future.

This method, all the while keeping hold of the horizon, makes no headway toward the eternal or the absolute. It is not a matter of a view which escapes time but, on the contrary, of an instantaneous photography. A cross-section of the universe, as done by the sciences, remains temporal and surrounded by the horizon. It can serve as point of departure for a systematic extension toward the future or toward the past, but this would only amount to a sequence of views situated in cosmic history and encircled by concentric horizons.

A view outside of time would be a conglomeration of all possible instantaneous photographs. Man would find himself confronted by the most complete and most opaque chaos. It would not be a matter of views, because a view of a totality presupposes intentionality—a direction, an orientation, and therefore a point of view in the space-time of a horizon.

Again, that the world does not manifest itself outside of time must be accepted as a fact. Man would not succeed in approaching the world. The process of human consciousness would be congealed. The conclusion which imposes itself here is that truth for man does not exist outside the framework of the horizon. Without time, there is no manifestation, no truth. Truth is revealed in the field of space-time formed by the horizon.

G. Reality Is Relative to Man

The themes of the preceding sections are repeated when reality is approached from the point of view of its relation to man. At the start, the secret of the horizon was brought to light by considering the horizon as man's expression of himself in the world. Now a more profound level is reached. The horizon relates the totality of the surroundings to man. It is no longer a matter solely of a reflection of man in the world, rather, this world, from its periphery to its center, is expressed in an impulse that goes toward man.

It is not only the transposition of man into the world which is indicated by the horizon but, equally, the world's transmission to man. The horizon is the human hold on the world. And even this expression is inadequate because this hold is not accidental but essential—namely, the world exists as such only through its relation to man. This is what was sketched out in the preceding sections: the world is a human domain, glimpsed through perspective, thought about within the restrictions of a method.

All this gives evidence of limitations.

But it is exactly through this structure of finitude and through these defining demarcations that reality becomes approachable for human intentionality. The world is reality par excellence—that is, reality within reach of man. As soon as a thing is real, it implies a relation to man; it manifests itself to man through his senses, his thought, or through entirely different means. Such a manifestation is brought about by perspectives, aspects, qualities. The ether which was once imagined as fine matter spread throughout the universe appeared to be nonexistent when scientific research proved that its qualities, one after another, had no value; it showed no relation to man.

It is time which is indispensable, as has just been explained, for the binding of reality to man. Here, more than elsewhere, is felt the impossibility of treating man and reality as two separate poles. Time seems to us the most intimate part of man. It is opposed to the exteriority of space. But even thinkers who clearly distinguish time as a form of the interior experience of space, and as a form of exterior experience, often refer to a more fundamental layer where time penetrates and marks the exterior world. The horizon, which shows space-time to man, roots him in the world in a unity which cuts across the radical separation between the interior and the exterior.

By means of time, reality turns toward man. Time is the act of reality whereby it comes within reach of man; or, rather, time is the actualization whereby the word 'reality' acquires a meaning.

The judgment that in the horizon nothing exists in itself is thus strongly emphasized. Everything exists relative to human beings—whereas, on the other hand, man does not exist except thanks to this open field before him, without which there would be no intentional life. The distinction between a world of appearances and a world more real, existing only in itself, is a familiar one in the history of philosophy. Moreover, it is the everyday world which is considered as the world of appearances—however real it may appear at first sight.

The world of the horizon does not know of such a distinction. Certainly it bears the mark of a horizon which is not real in the ordinary sense of that word. Everyday experience is aware of the fleetingness of the horizon which characterizes it as not being simply exterior to man—without, for all that, relegating it to the domain of the imagination. Surrounded by the horizon, the world does not appear simply real in the sense of an objective terrain which exists apart from man. On the contrary, it is shown to be related to man. On the other hand, it is not a matter of a world of appearances because in that case man would absorb the world, which would exist in its everyday form only in man. The two extremes of a naive realism and an idealism (here understood as transcendental realism) vanish as soon as the world and man regain the horizon.

The preceding paragraph can be summed up by defining the world in the horizon as a field of phenomena instead of appearances. The word 'phenomenon' indicates that the essential trait of the world, thus conceived, is dependent upon its relation to man—namely, upon its manifestation. As well, it is no longer a question of an absolutely objective world, nor of an apparent world which is in need of a support or of a cause in itself. In the horizon the human world of phenomena is revealed, making a world behind the scenes superfluous.

The idea of a world in itself, hidden behind an everyday world, is likewise found in a horizon of ideas. The in-itself is conceived by starting from an accessible plane. The in-itself is found in the domain of philosophic thought and thus remains related in a certain way to man. Even the concept of a metaphysical foundation that is inaccessible and unknowable symbolizes a confrontation, therefore a relation, with human thought. No indication, not even a privative one, would be forthcoming from an absolute in-itself. Here, negative predicates are still much too positive. The pure in-itself has no meaning for man, not even a negative one. The absolute in-itself is situated outside the human horizon and no longer functions in a field of reality: it is not possible to relate oneself to it. The in-itself is not predicable; it is stripped of meaning; there is no truth concerning it.

All this affirms the impossibility of a strict separation between the horizon in the literal and in the figurative senses, a separation which the first sections have already opposed. As a physical notion, the horizon is directly applicable to the domain of the mind. It is not a question of a poetic image but of a coherence and of a significative limitation which characterize the mind's field where real and embodied man is present. *Natura saltus non facit.* There exists a gradual sequence of steps, starting from the horizon of sight and climbing up to the horizon of ideas, through the horizon of astronomy, of aviation, and of laboratory experiments, of physical concepts, etc. The horizon opens the question whether mental space is not perhaps more physical than one thinks. But the visual field which is encircled by the horizon is thus more mental than one is sometimes inclined to suppose: it is the human and reflected domain. Every operation which isolates man or the world, the body or the mind, the interior and the exterior, the appearance and the in-itself, imparting to them for the most part a character of absoluteness, begins with the horizon. A transcendental investigation, concerning these concepts and their claims, would be carried out by bringing them into relation with the horizon. All transcendental elucidation throws into relief structures by means of which reality manifests itself. It is the horizon which throws them into relief.

Another aspect demands still further explanation. There is no meaningful reality without a horizon—namely, without a relation to man. It follows that a hidden world does not exist in the horizon. In the horizon there is undoubtedly a reference to the beyond. The horizon is a receding line which invites man to advance. The horizon indicates human transcendence (the act of surpassing). But this does not imply that here it is a question of a hidden reality. The horizon already indicates the territory on its other side. The beyond is not absolutely hidden: it is the territory which we do not yet see but which we can, in principle, reach. The receding horizon merely shows that the domain over there possesses no character different from the present field of vision. It can be said that there is a world hidden behind the horizon; but this judgment is accidental—it indicates only the present and provisional state, and not the permanent structure. The horizon opens into the future, and what is hidden shows itself as revealed in the temporal motion which characterizes the space circumscribed by the horizon.

When it is a question of a hidden reality, the existence of another world is claimed on a level different from that of the manifested world. In addition to what has been noted in relation to the idea of an in-itself—which is posited in confrontation with, and so by starting from, the reality of the horizon—it must now be added that the horizon denies such a difference of levels. The horizon shows that the hidden world is situated on the same plane. If it is hidden, it is so provisionally. A reality which is definitively hidden is a reduplication of the starting point in a world behind the scenes. However, this extrapolation is superfluous. The horizon mingles the hidden and the manifested by englobing them in its relation to man. The horizon hides the world in the sense that it hides and shows it at the same time. The plane of the world not yet reached is the extension of the terrain where we find ourselves—in sight, as well as in thought.

The hidden substance does not exist. It was once the vain hope of the physical sciences to discover the true substance behind phenomena: matter or mind. The sciences do not extend to the world behind the scenes. They proceed by enlarging their horizon. They are forever relating unknown worlds to man. They manifest only phenomena. Philosophy itself does not do otherwise.

In the horizon itself all is visible. Space is turned toward man in the limitations of perspective. These limitations do not fix man nor do they rob him of a consciousness of the world. Man roams the space-time continuum. He anticipates the perspectives in which he is not yet present. In the limitations he approaches the totality of the world as situated in the coherence of references.

The rambler who approaches a farm does not yet see the back end of the barn hidden behind the trees: he catches sight of only a small part of it. Yet he sees the farm in its totality, a farm with a back end, and not half of a farm. He sees the farm with its surroundings: among other things, the huge barn among the trees. He sees all this because his glance takes in more than the instantaneous. Framed by the horizon, the hidden aspects of the world are the hatchmarks which throw into relief the field of vision. Throwing something into relief in the domain of perception, as well as in the domain of thought, consists of a relation structured with respect to the observer.

Reality is related to man through bounded profiles. There is neither a world in itself nor a world absolutely hidden. The word 'reality' implies being bound to man. Every relation has something specific in the sense that it is a relation to somebody. Limitation manifests, the topographical structure makes accessible, and the hatchmarks clarify, what is hidden reveals the disclosure. Truth appears to man in successive stages, which extend toward man. Reality is shaped by the horizon. It is relative to man.

All these characteristics indicate the inexhaustible perspective of truth. It is never complete, never enclosed in a global view. It does not even congeal in a hidden and inaccessible absolute. It is found where man works out the temporal process of his perception, of his thought, of his subconscious history, of his whole life. Man is finite and he transcends; the horizon is impassable and receding. It is in this life that man knows the infinite riches of the restrictive reality which manifests itself in the horizon.

H. The Horizon and the Beyond

It might be asked whether a description

of the horizon necessarily leads to the conclusion that the finite and tangible world alone exists around man. The negative answer which will be given in this section will reveal a new element of what has been called the mysterious character of the horizon. The horizon—and this idea is to be developed—manifests the idea of a beyond, in spite of the fact that it denies the existence of a world behind the scenes.

At the summit of a mountain the tourist sees the mountain range, extending farther and farther back, and the valleys ensconced in the shelter of the mountains. In the summer mist the last range is vaguely outlined in the horizon. What is farther away is situated outside the horizon and is hidden. But we have just established that the words 'outside' and 'hidden' have only a relative meaning. The tourist knows that behind the last range is another valley. He can succumb to the lure of the horizon in order to get to these regions behind the horizon. The horizon itself moves away from other things and accompanies the traveler abroad.

The conclusion could be drawn that the beyond therefore does not exist. It is a provisional concept. However, an entirely different view of the beyond now appears: the voyage in the company of the horizon is not a voyage in this world. Such a voyage would have a goal which, once reached, would put an end to the voyage. The space of the world can be measured. Its distances go from here to there. The world's territory is always finite.

The voyage which has only the horizon as a point of reference in a sense transcends this finitude. It is never finished. From the first, the horizon has been described as unattainable. Here it becomes clear that this property is strongly felt especially in the case of the endless voyage. In the physical world, as in the world of the mind, the horizon hides something infinite.

One must still, however, return to the idea that the horizon encompasses a finite terrain and that everything acquires its relation to man solely through the limitations of the horizon. Man never reaches the outside of the horizon: he sees only in perspectives; he advances only in time. The horizon forever indicates to man the bounded region of his imagination and of his ideas. Man can range over reality without ever breaking away from the receding boundaries.

What is more, it is not even possible to understand successively the totality of reality. Whatever divergent directions they may take, however far they may go, the perspectives will never be exhausted and the same horizon will never be found again. Every horizon retains the newness of the unknown. The succession of horizons is endless.

Thus the horizon manifests the beyond in a concatenation of boundaries. The horizon does not indicate a world beyond. We never reach another plane—that of the infinite. Man does not play the role of a traveler of two worlds. It is a question of this reality, here. But that is more than is generally understood by this word. Finite reality is penetrated by the infinite. Space incessantly finds its future in the time which is inscribed in the receding horizon. Scientific thought becomes aware of the infinite impulse as it probes successive horizons without reaching the final term. All of human culture, in its closed forms and restricted stages of development, is penetrated by the infinite.

Totality is an idea which surpasses the human. It is never given as such nor is it realizable in human life. However, its presence is felt. The horizon does not show the existence of many panoramas but of their endless succession. This is no longer an empirical idea, though it enters into the experience of the horizon. No one succeeds in making this endless voyage. Every human voyage is situated in the finite distances of the world. But man knows it just the same: the horizon, beyond the reach of the traveler, gives him immediate assurance of this infinity. It is neither an infinity in the world beyond nor in an empirical world around man. One could speak of it as a synthetic *a priori* judgment. That is to say, it is a question of an evident structure and not of a factual determination.

In this way it happens that another plane is manifested in the finite plane. The succession of landscapes signifies more than a simple series. The horizons have a sense different from that of a series of concentric circles. Evidence is brought to light about an absolute transcendence, about finite domains. The word 'transcendence' indicates the surpassing of the stable finitude of this world and does not in any way imply the reduplication of this world. Rather, it represents the beyond which is manifested in the perspectives of the human world. The word 'absolute' signifies something different from this transcendence and does not accentuate a level detached from the human world but, instead, the beyond which constitutes the necessary condition which structures the world—(that is, the means of relating to man.

Would it perhaps be too speculative to claim that this world, here in its finitude, and that world beyond, in its absoluteness, are both abstractions from the lived world of man? The horizon recalls to man the inexhaustible secret of his existence. By enclosing himself in the concatenation of horizons, man follows the call of the beyond. He enters into the coherence of limited perspectives. Every fact is found in the impulses of referential reflections, depending upon where his glance may chance. As a traveler of horizons, man is aware of the possibility of the direction to follow in which even the simplest facts are more than facts since they are included in the aggregate of possibilities evinced by the horizon.

Thus the world differs from a conglomeration of elements, the sciences differ from a cohesion of facts, and history differs from an enumeration of events. Each thing or idea, instead of being an aggregate of more elementary parts, appears as the restriction of a totality which is itself situated outside the plane of the everyday. Common linguistic usage also distinguishes the totality from the parts—but here it is a question of magnitudes which are comparable within the same plane, whereas there it was a question of the beyond which in the horizon gives itself as totality, which does not reveal itself save through limitation.

Man must commit himself to the limited access which is presented to him by the horizon in order to affirm the possibilities of his proper being and the presence of a truth which surpasses him.

Thus the horizon refutes the theories of two worlds. But it is not denied that there is more than the world which we see, touch, and think of. Man rediscovers himself in the horizon because therein he recognizes the call toward this other order, whose essential characteristic consists in its relative manifestation to man. The same aspect could be expressed in less anthropocentric language by saying that the essence of man is to be related to this order of the infinite, whose stamp is borne by the finite structure of the human world.

I. The Anthropology of the Horizon

Man does not reach reality as a whole by fleeing the restrictions of the world toward a superhuman absolute but, instead, by rooting himself in the horizon. The horizon reveals the presence of the totality. The horizon circumscribes the human world—namely, the terrain which is characterized by man's connection with the world. The horizon points back to man.

The manifestation of the totality is thus realized in the human. This disclosure is not brought about in man as an isolated being but in the reality outlined by the horizon where man enters into the world. A description of man must include this order of the infinite which is met in the human plane, although such an inclusion never surmounts certain limited indications. This disclosure of what is more than man forms an essential characteristic of man.

In this way the horizon outlines an anthropology. The beyond enters there through its manifestation. The temporal field of man is the presence of the ultimate reality. The horizon shows this mysterious characteristic of the human being so that it is essential for man to surpass what is human. Man is not a *factum* of fact but an act of striking out, of being on his way. Man exists only by means of this field which the horizon forms before him. The words 'to dwell' could denote this human existence.

Man dwells in the world. These few words sum up what has been developed in the preceding sections. As an inhabitant of the world, man finds himself there from the start. He never gets a view of the outside, but he is brought into perspectives whereby he obtains his field of vision. He recognizes his finitude, all the while conscious of his possibilities for advancing. He is not situated in an abstract space but in a space-time where a coherent world is invested with meaning.

Man dwells in the world. This means that in eliminating the world, there is no more question about the human. The idea of the world blends with every anthropology. This must not be understood in a sense that would make man the product of the world, or of a certain aspect of this world (society, the spirit of an epoch, biological factors). Such a conception is always based on the duality of man and the world, whereas the considerations of the horizon have shown that neither man nor the world is an isolatable unity. The concept of man as a dweller in the world points back, moreover, to an order which is not found in such hard and fast distinctions as man in himself, separate space and time, and the like.

Man's inhabiting the world, then, is not a matter of an accidental quality but rather of an indispensable anthropological characteristic. Here man is fundamentally distinct from objects. Objects can be set apart. Many sciences isolate objects in order to study what they are in themselves. This is impossible with man. He would no longer be man if no account were taken of the fact that man exists and lives solely by inhabiting the world. The horizon reveals the need to approach the problem of man in the temporal act of dwelling.

Moreover, a complete isolation of an object is impossible. In section E, the reality of an object was shown to disappear if its coherence with the world is destroyed. The object in itself is a limiting concept. This differs considerably from the idea of man not conceived as man in himself, for this idea would annihilate what is most essential in man. One could progress by similarly establishing that the coherence of objects is the consequence of their relations to man. Reality manifests itself to man and everything acquires its meaning in this human field. And this again rests on the presence of an infinite order, precisely on the restriction of the horizon. This presence is felt in every anthropology and conditions the coherent reality of objects.

Man is thus much less amenable to a precise description than is an object. The essence of man is found when man, as a biological object or as a spatial localization, is no more. An example might illustrate this. When we want to know what the word 'painter' means, it is not enough to look at the man who calls himself a painter, however picturesque his appearance. It is necessary to turn our attention away from the painter toward his canvas in order to find out what the word 'painter' implies. Anthropology does not fix its attention on man; rather, it turns its back on him. Man is discovered on the field before him, outside of himself. What distinguishes the human is the horizon. The theory of man's essence becomes an anthropology of the horizon.

Man can be explained through the courses of action he envisages. He exists only through the acts which tend toward a goal. Man realizes himself in the intentionality of his life whereby the human field opens up. All his tendencies, aspirations, projects, activities—whether artistic or scientific, conscious or unconscious—are summed up in the words 'to dwell.' The human being concretizes himself by embracing the world, the horizon.

Anthropology is one of the most subtle disciplines, for the essence of man cannot be grasped: it cannot be analyzed in the laboratory. This essence consists, however, in the act of dwelling. Anthropology covers the whole world, so to speak. It deals with man, following the call of the horizon and answering the invitation of the infinite. This responsibility is fundamental to being human. Dwelling outlines an area of responsibility. Man as dweller in the world is aware of a duty and of courses of action which imply as many decisions. Anthropology is never occupied with a simple facticity. Thus the human being is constituted by the call of another order in the horizon.

A dwelling furnishes a shelter. Man, who dwells in the world, seeks there an abode; he is surrounded by it. The horizon shows this element of protection. Man would not be able to live in the infinite. A field of vision without limit would cause him anguish. Without boundaries for the imagination, thought, technical means, and sight, man would feel forsaken. He must be included within a whole in order not to be lost. The poet whose nascent images elude him undergoes anguish when the intended context of his poem begins to fail him and to take from him the perspective where words find their meanings. The airplane pilot also experiences something akin to this feeling. The horizon abandons him the moment he is caught in a spinning dive. Every man has felt such anguished moments, when circumstances have placed him outside his normal routine, as if pure nothingness opened up before him. But man will always seek a prop in a new boundary, and a more distant horizon which surges into view is evidence to him of the possibility of inhabiting the world even more, without losing himself in the emptiness.

The dialectic of the horizon has been stressed repeatedly—for example, in respect to the finitude and transcendence it evinces. Here, it appears under a new form. Man dwells in the world. Anthropology directs itself toward what is outside man by orienting itself toward the horizon. It describes the being which arises from all stable positions. On the other hand, man settles down in the world. By dwelling in the world, he feels at home. The horizon surrounds him and shelters him.

All this is understood in the essential relationship between man and the world, in the act of dwelling. The world is not a dwelling man can enter and leave at will. The human dwelling place manifests a presence whereby man establishes himself in his ceaseless activities. Acts of mind and body do not acquire an end by being situated in a horizon. Culture brings to light the human dwelling place.

The tie between man and his milieu (biological, etc.) is not fixed, as is that of the animal. Man penetrates his frontiers. He discovers new horizons in his social activities, in his artistic creations, in his scientific hypotheses, in his agricultural methods, etc. It may happen that in a certain epoch the cultural horizon bursts and man finds himself threatened by uncertainty. But the sciences and arts try to fill up this void, and new discoveries and hypotheses make the unknown terrain inhabitable. Human consciousness makes progress in the sense that man is always extending his hold upon the world by means of culture, without ever forsaking the horizon.

The religious man is aware of the divine presence in the human horizon. The word from beyond is framed in human language. It is a spoken word, asking for a course to follow. It does not insist on a flight toward a world beyond, but it gives a meaning to the human dwelling place. And the Word was made flesh and dwelt among us.

The horizon reveals man as a dweller in the world. The secret of the horizon is the mystery of man and of what transcends him. Man advances in time. He is situated within a coherent reality that is endowed with sense. There is a solidarity between man and the world because they are inseparable. The world is what is human outside of man and man is what is realized through the world. The two merge in the same activity of dwelling. Man is found in the cultural history of humanity, where the field of his responsibility is opened to him. Human life is thus framed by the horizon.

Husserl's Problematic Concept of the Life-World

DAVID CARR

As Herbert Spiegelberg notes in his historical study of the phenomenological movement, "the most influential and suggestive idea that has come out of the study and edition of Husserl's unpublished manuscripts thus far is that of the *Lebenswelt* or world of lived experience."[1] Because this fertile idea has inspired so many original and insightful contributions to phenomenology since Husserl's death, notably in the work of Maurice Merleau-Ponty and Alfred Schutz, and since the investigation of the life-world seems firmly established as an important subject for philosophical concern, it may seem a matter of only historical interest to return to Husserl's writings for a critical analysis of his own thoughts on the subject. But philosophy, as Husserl recognized and insisted at the end of his life, is like any other cultural activity in existing as a cumulative *tradition*; that is, it is able to proceed by being able to take its origins and its fundamental task for granted; it owes its ongoing mode of being to its capacity to move away from and in a certain sense forget its origins. But in exchange for this very capacity to move forward, it always runs the risk of not only forgetting but also being unable to reactivate and critically examine its

Reprinted with permission of the publisher and author from *American Philosophical Quarterly*, 7 (1970): 331-39.

origins. And if the origins are faulty, the heirs to the tradition may inherit such faults through too little critical awareness of what they owe to the past.

After working on a translation of *The Crisis of European Sciences*,[2] in which Husserl developed at length his notion of the *Lebenswelt*, I am convinced that there are many faults and confusions in his exposition which need to be sorted out and examined. This task seems especially important since I suspect that some of Husserl's confusions have been handed down to his successors along with his profoundest insights. This latter point is something I shall not try to establish here. But even the suspicion provides warrant enough for reopening the case, especially in this instance, since some have come to see the investigation of the life-world as either synonymous with phenomenology itself or as forming its most profound stratum. Husserl scholars point out, quite rightly, that the master himself did not see it this way, that he regarded this investigation of the *Lebenswelt* as merely a necessary preliminary stage on the way to transcendental subjectivity. "Original" phenomenologists reply, also quite rightly, that being true to Husserl is less important than being true to the "*Sachen selbst*," and it is precisely his move to transcendental idealism they object to. Nevertheless, they do credit Husserl with the discovery of the life-world and see themselves as continuing in the exploration of the terrain to which he led the way.

Husserl would have rejoiced in seeing himself thus characterized as a sort of Moses to the children of Thales, for he claimed the role for himself often enough. And he lived up to it all too well in one sense, as his readers know, at least in those works either published or meant for publication. He has a maddening tendency to describe in rough outline, as if discerned from the heights of Mount Nebo, the salient features of a new domain, confident that this will provide his successors with a reliable map with which to venture forth and fill in the details. More than any of his other books, the *Crisis* exhibits this character of outlining a program and issuing anticipatory directives. And this is true especially of the ninety-page section devoted to the life-world. There is evidence, in fact, that this section was the very last thing to be inserted in the plan of the *Crisis,* forming an innovation even over the Prague lecture on which the work is based. It was apparently written during the very last year of Husserl's active life, a year of feverish activity interrupted again and again, and finally interrupted for good, by illness. Husserl never claimed that it was more than a rough outline, of course, but as such it needs to be reexamined. For as explorers know, a faulty map of the terrain to be explored can cause grave difficulties to the exploration itself, setting it off on wrong paths and disorienting it from the start.

What I wish to argue in the following is that Husserl has assembled under one *title* a number of disparate and in some senses even incompatible *concepts*. Each of these concepts has some validity and importance, but Husserl does not seem to be fully aware of their separateness and thus does not concern himself with showing that or how they belong together. The question, then, is whether these notions can legitimately be combined under the title "life-world," and if so, whether the resulting clarified conception can play the role in phenomenology that Husserl thought it should play.

I

It is not actually in the *Crisis* that the term *Lebenswelt* makes its first appearance in Husserl's vocabulary; in fact, it appears in a manuscript meant as a supplementary text to *Ideas,* volume 2, dated by the Louvain archivists at 1917.[3] It appears there closely related to a term that is familiar to readers of Heidegger and Merleau-Ponty: *natürlicher Weltbegriff,* natural world-concept,[4] and it is linked to the investigations of part 3 of *Ideen II* concerning the construction of the personal, spiritual, or cultural world as opposed to the scientific or natural world. A comparison would reveal that many of the themes and descriptions of *Ideen II* and the *Crisis* are similar on this point, and that Husserl's later writings on the subject were thus able to draw on reflections initiated at a much earlier date. Nevertheless, it is only in the *Crisis* (1936) that Husserl self-consciously uses the term *Lebenswelt* with emphasis, employing it in the title of a major section of the projected book and according to the elaboration of the notion a decisive position in the phenomenological program. After a brief introductory section on "The Crisis of the Sciences as Expression of the Radical Life-Crisis of European Humanity" (part 1) and a longer historical section devoted to "The Clarification of the Origin of the Modern Opposition between Physicalistic Objectivism and Transcendental Subjectivism" (part 2), Husserl turns to the lengthy third part, "The Clarification of the Transcendental Problem, and the Related Function of Psychology," which was to be the central section of the projected but unfinished five-part work.[5] The first half of this third part bears the subheading "The Way into Phenomenological Transcendental Philosophy by Inquiring Back from the Pre-given Life-World," and it constitutes the longest single division of the book as it stands.

But by the time Husserl begins this section he has already prepared the way for the concept of the life-world; in fact the notion is introduced gradually in the framework of the historical discussions of part 2, beginning with the long section devoted to Galileo. If we look closely at the conception that emerges there, we shall be able to see clearly *one* of the several themes which are interwoven, as I claim rather confusedly, into the notion of the life-world later on.

According to Husserl, Galileo's great accomplishment, to which modern science owes its success, was the mathematization of nature. Husserl asks: "What is the meaning of this mathematization of nature?" and he rephrases the question as: "How do we reconstruct the train of thought which motivated it?"[6] This question sets the tone for the long, quasi-historical inquiry which follows, and Husserl's answer is prefigured in the next paragraph.

"Prescientifically, in every-day sense experience, the world is given in a subjectively relative way. Each of us has his own appearances," Husserl says, and points out that these may be at variance with one another, a fact with which we are all familiar. "But we do not think," he goes on, "that, because of this, there are many worlds. Necessarily, we believe in *the* world whose things only appear to us differently but are the same. [Now] have we nothing more than the empty, necessary idea of things which exist objectively in themselves? Is there not, in the appearances themselves, a content we must ascribe to true nature? Surely this includes everything which pure geometry, and in general the mathematics of the pure form of space-time, teaches us, with the self-evidence of absolute universal validity, about the pure shapes it can construct *idealiter*—and here I am describing," Husserl notes, "without taking a position, what was 'obvious' to Galileo and motivated his thinking."[7]

Here Husserl has described in a few words both the brilliant insight upon which modern science rests and the fateful mistake which has consistently misled the various attempts at its philosophical interpretation. Galileo inherits "pure geometry" from the Greeks as a science which affords exact, intersubjectively valid knowledge for its domain of objects. In our encounters with the real world we have the problem of the subjective relativity of what appears, and it is the task of a science of the world to overcome this relativity. Now pure geometry is not unrelated to the world; in fact, as a science it can be seen as originally arising out of the practical needs of accurately surveying land and the like, and its theoretical formulation has always found application back to the real world. Galileo sees that this is because the real world as it presents itself to us in experience contains, somehow embedded in it, examples of what is dealt with so successfully in geometry. Galileo's proposal is that exact and intersubjectively valid knowledge of the real world can be attained by treating *everything about this world* as an example of a geometrical object or relationship. If every physical shape, trajectory, vibration, etc., is seen, after being measured as accurately as possible, as a version of a pure geometrical shape, geometrical statements about the properties and relationships among these pure shapes will turn out to provide us with information about nature which shares in the exactness and universality of pure geometry. This leaves untouched, of course, certain properties which do not seem directly measurable in geometrical terms: color, warmth, weight, tone, smell, etc. Galileo notes, however, that changes in some of these properties correspond exactly to measurable changes in geometrical properties—even the Greeks had known of the relationship between the pitch of a tone emitted by a vibrating string and its length, thickness, and tension. In his boldest move of all, Galileo proposes to treat all such "secondary qualities," as they were later called, exclusively in terms of their measurable geometrical correlates with the idea that *all* will be accounted for thereby.

Thus is accomplished, according to Husserl, the mathematization of nature, and such is the origin of mathematical physics. It can be broken down into two steps, actually: Galileo's *geometrization* of nature, and the *arithmetization* of geometry accomplished by Descartes and Leibniz. Nature becomes a mathematical manifold and mathematical techniques provide the key to its inner workings. In mathematics we have access to an infinite domain, and if nature is identified with that domain we have access not only to what lies beyond the scope of our immediate experience, but to everything that could *ever* be experienced in nature, i.e., to nature as an infinite domain.

It is by contrast to the Galilean conception of nature that Husserl's first characterization of the life-world emerges. The philosophical interpretation of Galileo's mathematization becomes involved in a series of equivocations. To overcome the vagueness and relativity of ordinary experience, science performs a set of abstractions and interpretations upon the world as it originally presents itself. First it focuses upon the shape-aspect of the world, to the exclusion of so-called secondary qualities; then it interprets these shapes as pure geometrical shapes in order to deal with them in geometrical terms. But it forgets that its first move is an abstraction *from* something and its second an interpretation *of* something. Its first move is an abstraction because, no matter how successful we may be in correlating secondary with primary qualities, the world we are trying to explain still presents itself to us as having both kinds of properties, one of which we systematically ignore or declare "merely subjective." Its second move is an interpretation because, to treat the spatial relationships of the world with geometrical exactness, it must consider these relationships as the ideal ones with which pure geometry deals, whereas the real shape-aspect of the world, no matter how accurately measured, can never present us with anything but approximations to these ideal relationships.

Having forgotten the abstractive and idealizing role of scientific thought, the philosophical interpretation comes up with an ontological claim: *to be is to be measurable* in ideal terms as a geometrically determined configuration. Thus it happens, says Husserl, "that we take for *true being* what is actually a *method*."[8] Mathematical science is a method which considers the world *as if it were* exclusively a manifold of idealized shape-occurrences; the ontological interpretation simply states that it *is* such a manifold. The ontological claim then gives rise—and such is the course of modern philosophy—to a sequence of epistemological absurdities, the mathematical realism of the rationalists and the subjectivism and ultimately the skepticism of the empiricists. Rationalism treats the scientific method as if it were a kind of instrument, like the microscope, which allows us to *see* the world as it actually is, which pulls back the curtain of appearances and puts us into contact with reality. Empiricism recognizes that all we ever *see* is the causal effects of the real world upon the mind, and it raises the ultimately insoluble question of whether what we *see* accurately informs us of what *is*. The curtain of appearance is thus lowered again for good.

Husserl's critique is directed not so much against Galileo's methodical innovations as against those ontological and epistemological consequences drawn from it. The scientific method is not an instrument for improving our *sight*, something invented during the Renaissance which enables us once and for all to put aside the world of appearances. It was and remains an abstraction from and interpretation of what *is* seen, and what *is* seen remains ever the same whether or not we are scientists who operate with the method. This is the "world of sense experience,"[9] the "intuitively given surrounding world (*Umwelt*),"[10] as Husserl first calls it, or finally, the "prescientific life-world."[11] It is that *from* which science abstracts and *of* which it is the interpretation, the world of objects possessing both primary and secondary qualities, the world of spatial aspects belonging to vague and approximate types and not a world of geometrical idealities. On the other hand it is a *world* and not a mental representation of the world. It is "subjectively relative" by comparison to the intersubjective agreement the scientific interpretation affords, but it is not "merely subjective" in the sense that it belongs to the mind.[12] And most important, the life-world is the "meaning fundament,"[13] as Husserl says, of natural science, if natural science is correctly understood; for as an abstraction-interpretation, science would have no meaning, make no sense, without reference to that *of* which it is the abstraction-interpretation.

II

When he begins the section devoted directly to the notion of the life-world, Husserl picks up many of the themes that emerged from his critique of modern science and philosophy. Science operates with abstractions, the life-world is the concrete fullness from which this abstraction is derived; science constructs, the life-world provides the materials out of which the construction arises; the ideal character of scientific entities precludes their availability to sense intuition, while the life-world is the field of intuition itself, the "universe of what is intuitable in principle," the "realm of original self-evidence"[14] to which the scientist must return to verify his theories. Science interprets and explains what is given, the life-world is the locus of all givenness. The emphasis here is on the *immediacy* of life-world experience in contrast to the mediated character of scientific entities. The life-world is prior to science, prior to theory, not only historically but also epistemologically, even after the advent and rich development of the scientific tradition in the West.

It must be said that in the context we have been describing, the *Crisis* offers us little that is new. Much of Husserl's actual description of the life-world at this point is simply a recapitulation of the phenomenology of perception with which readers of the *Ideas* and the *Cartesian Meditations* are familiar. The life-world is primarily a world of perceived "things," "bodies." He speaks of the perspectival character of perception, of outer and inner horizons, placing more emphasis than before, perhaps, on the role of the living body and its kinesthetic functions and on the oriented character of the field of perception around the body. His descriptions correspond to those centered around the concept of the "world of pure experience" in the *Phenomenological Psychology*,[15] the analyses of passive synthesis and pre-predicative experience found in *Erfahrung und Urteil*.[16] The critique of the distinction between primary and secondary qualities, in which Husserl follows Berkeley, is of course not new, nor is his insistence on the ideal character of pure geometrical structures in opposition to the realities of the experienced world. Husserl's greatest innovation in this context, in fact, concerns not so much his characterization of the life-world as his assessment of the status of science. Mathematization is seen not merely as one interpretative way of dealing with the world, but as a historical phenomenon which involves an original establishment and a handed-down tradition. Galileo inherits the tradition of Greek geometry and combines it in a fruitful way with the need for a science of the world. His successors, in turn, take for granted his way of *interpreting* the world—which Husserl regards as a kind of methodological proposal or hypothesis[17]—and go on to make great discoveries and theoretical refinements. Philosophers, also taking for granted Galileo's proposal, absolutize it into an ontological claim which then makes experience and knowledge incomprehensible. It is to this historically determined, modern scientific *view* of the world that Husserl wishes to oppose the world as it really presents itself, the pre-scientific life-world in which we always *live* but to which our theoretical reflection has been blinded by our scientific prejudices. This historical characterization of scientific thought does reflect, by contrast, on the concept of the life-world, for it implies that the life-world is *not* historically relative phenomenon but the constant underlying ground of all such phenomena, the world from which the scientific interpretation takes its start and which it constantly presupposes.

III

It is against this background of explicit and implied characterizations of the life-world that many of Husserl's remarks appear puzzling and, in my view, point to a second notion of the life-world which differs radically from the first. Very early in the life-world section, attacking Kant for taking the world as the scientific world and ignoring the role of the life-world in scientific experience, Husserl writes: "Naturally, from the very start in the Kantian manner of posing questions, the everyday surrounding world of life is presupposed as existing—the surrounding world in which all of us (even I who am now philosophizing) consciously have our existence; and here are also the sciences, as cultural facts in this world, with their scientists and theories."[18] The sciences as theories, then, together with the scientists as creators of the theories, are part of the life-world. Again and again, but almost always in passing, Husserl refers to the sciences as cultural facts which belong, presumably along with other cultural facts, to the life-world. As they arise, he says, they "flow into"[19] the life-world, "add themselves to its own composition,"[20] and enrich its content.

At first Husserl might seem to be involved in a flat contradiction here, since he previously distinguished the life-world from the world of science and now seems to be putting them back together. Husserl is aware of this seeming contradiction when he writes: "the concrete life-world, then, is the grounding soil (*der gründende Boden*) of the 'scientifically true' world and at the same time encompasses it in its own universal concreteness. How is this to be understood? How are we to do justice systematically—that is, with appropriate scientific discipline—to the all-encompassing, so paradoxically demanding manner of being of the life-world?"[21] But Husserl seems to regard this particular paradox, at any rate, as being easily resolved. For it is not quite true that the

scientific world and the life-world, previously distinguished with great care, are now being merged.

What Husserl is adding to the life-world is not the world *as described* by scientific theories but rather the scientific theories themselves; and when he refers to them in this way he always adds: "as cultural facts" or "as spiritual (intellectual) accomplishments (*geistige Leistungen*)."[22] "[Science's] theories," he writes, "the logical constructs, are of course not things in the life-world like stones, houses, or trees. They are logical wholes and logical parts made up of ultimate logical elements.... But this-...ideality does not change in the least the fact that they are human formations, essentially related to human actualities and potentialities, and thus belong to this concrete unity of the life-world, whose concreteness thus extends further than that of 'things'."[23] There is a difference between engaging in science, i.e., interpreting the world according to its methods, and living in a cultural world of which science is a part. "If we cease being immersed in our scientific thinking," Husserl writes, "we become aware that we scientists are, after all, human beings and as such are among the components of the life-world which always exists for us, ever pre-given; and thus all of science is pulled, along with us, into the—merely 'subjective-relative'—life-world."[24] Here Husserl has accomplished a brilliant reversal. The scientist sees himself as overcoming the relativity of our "merely subjective" *pictures* of the world by finding the *objective* world, the world as it really is. Husserl shows that the scientist can just as easily be seen, by a shift in perspective, as a man who himself has a particular sort of *picture* of the world, and that as such both he and his picture belong *within* the "real" world, which Husserl calls the life-world.

Now with this Husserl may have resolved one paradox about the life-world, but he has left us with another. For in describing the life-world as a cultural world which can contain scientific theories as well as stones, houses, and trees, Husserl has moved into what by his own account is a very different phenomenological domain. As Husserl says, scientific theories are not things, and, what counts most for the phenomenologist, they are not *given* as things are; they are not objects of perception, they are not given in perspective, they are not, strictly speaking, even spatio-temporal. And the same thing is obviously true of other elements of the cultural world: institutions, such as the state, the university, the church, the Bureau of Internal Revenue, do not stand before us simply as objects to be perceived; nor do works of literature, protest movements, the generation gap. Elaborate and many-level constitutive analyses must be devoted to these phenomena if this world is to be understood, as Husserl himself insisted in *Ideen,* volume 2; and above all the role of language in structuring both the community and its world must be appreciated. How is this to be squared with the "world of immediate experience"? This cultural world may indeed be described as pre-theoretical, in the sense that it does not need to number among its constitutive elements a scientific theory of the world, much less the particular sort of mathematical-scientific theory developed in the modern West. But such terms as "pre-predicative," "immediate," "intuitively given" are clearly out of place. Least of all can the cultural world be described as historically and sociologically nonrelative, i.e., as something which does not change with the times and circumstances. How can the term "life-world" be used for such disparate concepts?[25]

Husserl is not unaware of one aspect of the paradox just described and seems to think he has taken it into account: this is the historical and possibly sociological relativity of the life-world considered as cultural world. In spite of the "subjective relativity" of the life-world by contrast to the objective scientific world, Husserl writes, "normally, in our experience and in the social group united with us in the community of life, we arrive at 'secure' facts; within a certain range this occurs of

its own accord, that is, undisturbed by any noticeable disagreement.... But when we are thrown into an alien social sphere, that of the Negroes in the Congo, Chinese peasants, etc., we discover that their truths, the facts that for them are fixed, generally verified or verifiable, are by no means the same as ours."[26] It is in this connection that Husserl often uses the term "life-world" in the plural, such that different historical periods and social groupings have different life-worlds. One way to over-come this "cultural relativity," of course, is to go the way of objective science itself, leaving the life-world behind to reach objective, i.e., mathematically determined truth. Husserl then asks if we are left with nothing else to say about the life-world other than that it is culturally relative. "But this embarassment disappears immediately," he writes, "when we consider that the life-world does have, in all its relative features, a *general structure.* This general structure, to which everything that exists relatively is bound, is not itself relative. We can regard it in its generality and, with sufficient care, fix it once and for all in a way equally accessible to all."[27] This structure is what Husserl calls the *a priori* of the life-world, the essence shared by all particular life-worlds, whatever their content, which makes them what they are.

Now these considerations, I maintain, important as they are, do not dispel the discrepancy described earlier between life-world as cultural world and life-world as world of immediate experience. It is quite correct to speak of the different "worlds" of different peoples and historical periods, and it is also quite correct, in my opinion, to seek the general or *a priori* structures belonging to any such world purely as such. But we should be clear on the fact that, in undertaking the latter task, we are seeking the general structures of the *cultural* world and not necessarily of the world of immediate experience. Several differences between the two types of inquiries suggest themselves immediately. First, phenomenological analysis of the cultural world will have to deal, and in fact must deal primarily, with the constitution of precisely those cultural entities whose mode of givenness was contrasted earlier with that of the perceptual world. Its first subject of concern must be the ontological status of the community as such and the conditions of the possibility of such phenomena as institutions, political organizations, literature, religion, and mores, whatever particular forms they may take. This is the farthest thing from a phenomenology of perception. Second, since the "life-world" in this cultural sense can change historically, its phenomenology must deal with the eidetic structures of such change, the essential conditions of any and all cultural transformations. The phenomenology of perception, at least on Husserl's own account, need not concern itself with such transformations, since perceptual structures do not change. Finally, the investigation of the cultural world must appreciate the structuring role of language and the communication based on it, while the world of immediate experience, according to Husserl, is distinguished by being pre-linguistic or pre-predicative in character.

Now this is not to say that the phenomenology of the cultural world is totally *unrelated* to the phenomenology of the perceived or immediately experienced world. In fact, it is of the utmost importance to show the dependence of the cultural world upon the perceived world for its constitution, and this again according to Husserl himself. The cultural community is not something perceived, like a thing or a body, but neither is it given to us independently of perceived bodies; we know the community because we perceive other persons as members, representatives, or authorities of the community and because we perceive physical objects such as tools and books, factories and monuments, as its artifacts and documents. But the cultural world is precisely *dependent* for its sense upon the perceived world and is not *identical* with it. It represents a higher and distinct level of constitution, just as, to go back to the first of the *Logical Investiga-*

tions, reading and understanding a sentence represents a higher level than simply perceiving the words as physical configurations on the page.[28] The former is *founded* upon the latter, as Husserl would say, but is by no means *reducible* to it. What is needed is a stratified constitutive analysis like the one in the fifth *Cartesian Meditation* leading from straightforward perception to the experience of persons and, from there, to the much more complicated constitution of the community.[29]

But notice that we have now placed the cultural world in the same position, relative to the so-called world of immediate experience, as the scientifically constructed world of mathematical physics. That is, the cultural world is a domain of entities and structures whose givenness is mediated by and founded on the spatio-temporal world of perception. No less than the scientific world, the cultural world has its meaning-fundament in the world of perception as the domain through which its structures are always mediated, in which its truths are always directly "verified" in our experience. To be sure, the character of the mediation and the mode of being of the entities that make up the two "worlds" are quite different. It could be said that the two types of "mediated" experience focus on different aspects of the concrete world. Both are historical in that a coherent development and transformation of truths about the world is essential to both. But the character of the historical development is different; as Husserl points out, especially in these later writings, the historical development of science is cumulative, at least ideally; our concept of what is true does not simply change from one time to the next but grows in a constant progression, with each new stage building upon the ones before it. In spite of these differences, however, the parallels are obvious: surely our degree of removal from the gold crisis, for example, or the "Establishment," is as great as our degree of removal from the electron, and our access to these two sorts of entities is in many ways similar, in any case necessitating simple perception at some stage.

IV

The argument I have developed thus far points to a serious ambiguity in Husserl's notion of the life-world and to a resulting structural mistake regarding its position on the phenomenological map. He begins by distinguishing the world of post-Galilean mathematical science from the world of everyday life or life-world. He tries to show the priority of the life-world, the way in which the scientific world is dependent on the life-world for its sense. But the phenomena ranged by Husserl under the term "life-world" turn out, as we have seen, to fall into two distinct strata, one of which is indeed prior to the scientific domain (the "world of immediate experience") but the other of which seems to be on the *same* phenomenological level as the scientific domain, in spite of its differences—that is, in respect to its derivative or mediated character. From this perspective it is confusing at best to use a single name for the two different concepts I have been discussing.

But we might ask how Husserl was able to fall prey to this confusion. Or, to put the question in a more flattering way: Do the world of immediate experience and the cultural world have something in common, something of which Husserl was aware in placing them together under one term? This question can be answered affirmatively in a way which partly justifies Husserl's use of the term "life-world" even though it does not exonerate him from the error of using it in a confusing way. But it complicates matters further, supporting my statement earlier in this paper that Husserl's term "life-world" involves not just two but several different concepts at once. A brief examination of how this is so reveals the great multiplicity of interests and directions of inquiry which motivate Husserl in *The Crisis of European Sciences*.

Three considerations point to elements that are common to the two types of world we found involved in Husserl's "life-world." First, we must remember that the touchstone of the *Crisis*, and the point to which it returns again and again,

is modern mathematical science, and, in general, the problem of the theoretical science of nature. Now something which emerges, not so much from the *Crisis* as from the important short paper on the "Origin of Geometry,"[30] is Husserl's claim that theoretical science depends for its possibility not only on the world of immediate experience, the perceived world, but *also* on the cultural and linguistic community and *its* world. To exist and construct its mathematically determined world, science must have at its disposal not only a whole system of language but also a system of culture in which certain truths can be shared and taken for granted as a basis for continued work. The cultural world and the world of immediate experience, then, whatever their differences, are alike in constituting the preconditions for the existence of science. This means that the phenomenological stratification developed earlier must be somewhat revised. It is not as if the world of immediate experience made up a primary level supporting a secondary level which can take the form *either* of culture *or* of the scientific domain. Rather, the scientific level constitutes a *tertiary* stratum built on the second or cultural level. This does not invalidate our point about the important differences between the first two levels, but it does justify their sharing the designation "pre-scientific" in the sense that together they form the foundation for the mathematized world.

A second point in Husserl's favor centers around a term that is used repeatedly in connection with the life-world, namely "pre-given" (*vorgegeben*): The pre-given is what is there in advance, that which is taken for granted, which is passively received by consciousness and forms the background for its activity in relation to the world and itself. In keeping with his growing emphasis on the cultural world in his later writings, Husserl in the *Crisis* and other late texts sees it as contributing to what is always and necessarily pre-given to consciousness. It is not only the world of pure experience, the *a priori* of the life-world in *this* sense, that consciousness takes for granted in its dealings with the world; it is also the cultural world and whatever prejudices and interpretations may derive from it. In conscious life, man may be without scientific upbringing and thus lack the scientific interpretation of the world. But he is never, Husserl means to say, without culture, and thus never without some view of the world which goes beyond its immediate givenness to perception. Thus the cultural world, like the world of pure experience, is a necessary ground (*Boden*) of conscious life; it is pre-given not only for the theoretical activity of the scientist but for any activity whatever.

Finally, cultural world and perceived world are united in the very important conception of the pre-theoretical. This is a slightly different point from the first in this series, which pointed to the priority of the life-world over the scientific world; for in using the term "pre-theoretical" Husserl refers primarily to consciousness and the different sorts of attitudes it can assume. He had come to stress much more than in his earlier writings that conscious life is not exclusively, not even primarily, a quest for objective truths about the world which could be combined into a coherent world theory. The "natural" attitude in this later period is rather different from the "natural attitude" of the *Ideas* which, when closely examined, turns out to be the philosophical theory of naive realism. "Original natural life," as Husserl calls it in the Vienna Lecture,[31] for example, is not theoretical at all, but rather practical. For consciousness at this level, the world is the domain of ends to be attained, projects to be carried out, materials to be used in carrying them out. It is not a mathematical manifold of entities to be known with theoretical exactness, but a pre-given horizon of the useful and the useless, the significant and the insignificant, the relevant and the irrelevant. There is no denying the Heideggerian flavor in these later considerations of Husserl, and the question of influence is properly raised. But in any case we can see that both the cultural world, with its instruments and socially determined projects, and the world of immediate experience must be seen as the

milieu in which the pre-theoretical, practical life of consciousness runs its course. In much of what Husserl says about the perceived world here, one is reminded of Merleau-Ponty's warning that perception must not be analyzed as if it were an "incipient science." The orientation of the perceived world around the lived body is a *practical* orientation of movement and accomplishment, not a theoretical orientation. Similarly, culture does not essentially present us with a "theory" of the world, but envelopes us in a domain articulated according to spheres of action, providing norms and directives for getting around. The cultural world may contain a scientific theory among its elements, but is not exhausted in the stock of objective truths the theory provides. Not that the concept of *truth* has no relevance here, for hand in hand with Husserl's new descriptions of consciousness and the world goes a new concept of truth. Here he refers to "situational" or "practical" truth,[32] which is properly characterized as "merely relative"—i.e., relative to the subject or the community, relative to the project under consideration—only by contrast to the notion of "objective" truth, truth-in-itself about the world-in-itself.

The cultural and the perceived worlds combined, then, form the horizon of "natural" or primordial conscious life with its pre-theoretical attitude. And as such they form the pre-given ground from which the theoretical attitude arises, the pre-scientific world underlying the scientific. As I have said, these considerations go some distance toward clearing up the confusions built into the celebrated concept of the life-world and offer some justification for Husserl's rather broad use of the term. But at the same time they indicate that much more work needs to be done. Moreover, I think that if taken seriously they raise profound problems for the whole phenomenological enterprise, at least as its founder originally conceived it. In any case we should be warned that Husserl's concept of the life-world is not something that phenomenologists can simply take for granted.[33]

NOTES

1. Herbert Spiegelberg, *The Phenomenological Movement: A Historical Introduction* (The Hague, Nijhoff, 1960), 1: 159.

2. *The Crisis of European Sciences and Transcendental Phenomenology*, trans. David Carr (Evanston, Northwestern University Press, 1970).

3. *Ideen zu einer reinen Phänomenologie und phänomenologischen Philosophie, Zweites Buch* (*Husserliana*, vol. 4), ed. Marly Biemel (The Hague: Nijhoff, 1952), p. 375. See the "textkritische Anmerkungen," p. 423.

4. This term apparently derives from Richard Avenarius' book *Der menschliche Weltbegriff* (first published in 1891; 3d ed.; Leipzig: O.R. Reisland, 1912), where it is the title of the first section. Heidegger implies that his *Sein und Zeit* (1927) provides the first adequate elaboration of this concept (8th ed.; Tübingen: Niemeyer, 1957 [p. 52]), but it was also discussed in detail by Husserl, not only in the manuscript mentioned but also, for example, in the *Phänomenologische Psychologie* lectures of 1925 (*Husserliana*, vol. 9, ed. Walter Biemel [The Hague: Nijhoff, 1962], p. 87). It is often claimed that the *Crisis* (1936) was influenced by Heidegger's book, and in some respects this is true. But it seems clear that Husserl's concern with the *natürlicher Weltbegriff* is at least as old as Heidegger's. See Merleau-Ponty, *Phénoménologie de la Perception* (Paris: Gallimard, 1945), p. i.

5. *Crisis*, p. 397ff.

6. Ibid., p. 23.

7. Ibid., p. 23f.

8. Ibid., p. 51.

9. Ibid., p. 24.

10. Ibid., p. 25.

11. Ibid., p. 43.

12. Ibid., p. 125.

13. Ibid., p. 48.

14. Ibid., p. 127.

15. *Phänomenologische Psychologie*, pp. 55ff.

16. *Experience and Judgment*, rev. and ed. Ludwig Landgrebe, trans. James S. Churchill and Karl Ameriks (Evanston: Northwestern University Press, 1973), pp. 71 ff.

17. *Crisis*, p. 38f.

18. Ibid., p. 104.

19. Ibid., p. 113.

20. Ibid., p. 131.

21. Ibid.

22. Ibid., p. 130.

23. Ibid.

24. Ibid., p. 130f.

25. I cannot agree with Kockelmans' claim that there is "a perfect correspondence" between the "life-world" of the *Crisis* and the "world of immediate experience" in *Phänomenologische Psychologie*, and that the *Crisis* formulation is simply "more comprehensive and desirable" (*Edmund Husserl's Phenomenological Psychology: A Historico-Critical Study* (Pittsburgh: Duquesne University Press, 1967) [p. 288]). It is true that the 1925 lectures deal with "the appearance of *das Geistige* in the world of experience" (*Phänomenologische Psychologie*, p. 110) and even refer to "die Erfahrungswelt als Kulturwelt" at one point (p. 113). But Husserl is quite clear that cultural objects and even persons, though they are "perceived" in a broad sense (p. 115), are not given in sense experience strictly speaking. Thus he finally proposes a reduction to the world of (strictly) perceived "things": "Offenbar ist diese Dingwelt gegenüber der Kulturwelt das an sich Frühere. Kultur setzt Menschen und Tiere voraus, wie diese ihrerseits Körperlichkeit voraussetzen" (p. 119). Actually the *Psychologie* is more "desirable" since it contains many of the distinctions so badly needed in the *Crisis*.

26. *Crisis*, p. 138f.

27. Ibid., p. 139.

28. *Logical Investigations II*, trans. J. N. Findlay, pp. 299ff.

29. *Cartesian Meditations*, pp. 120ff.

30. This paper appears as one of the appendices to *Crisis*, pp. 353ff.

31. *Crisis*, p. 281. The Vienna Lecture ("Die Krisis des europäischen Menschentums und die Philosophie") in another of the appendices, pp. 269 ff.

32. *Crisis*, p. 132.

33. For a more extensive treatment of the problems discussed in this paper, see "Ambiguities in the Concept of the Life-World," in David Carr, *Phenomenology and the Problem of History: A Study of Husserl's Transcendental Philosophy* (Evanston: Northwestern University Press, 1974), pp. 190-211.

Husserl's Phenomenology of Empathy

Frederick A. Elliston

Paul Ricoeur has termed the problem of the other "the touchstone of transcendental phenomenology."[1] The frequency and determination with which Husserl returns to it testify to his concurrence, but few of his interpreters or critics have been satisfied with his solution. In this paper my aim is to defend his account against their attacks. Contrary to what they contend, I shall argue that the account Husserl provides in the fifth chapter of *Cartesian Meditations* is both schematically sound and methodologically fruitful.[2]

A. Significance and Urgency of the Problem of Others

That other people are a problem is a notorious commonplace. That other people pose a philosophical problem is neither so notorious nor commonplace, for many critical thinkers do not deal with this problem explicitly and yet are not scandalized by this neglect. They picture philosophy as a number of disjointed problems and attribute no privileged position to this one. Not so with Husserl, who felt both its significance and urgency, and believed that his failure to solve it called into question nothing less than

the claim of transcendental phenomenology to be transcendental philosophy and thus...to be able to solve the transcendental problem of the objective world. [*CM*, p. 121]

The frequency with which the problem arises testifies to its importance. In the corpus of Husserl's published works it occurs in the following texts: *Husserliana I*, pp. 121-76; *III*, pp. 11, 61, 107, 113, 131, 172, 330, 344, 372-73; *IV*, pp. 76-89, 162-71, 190-200, 228-29, 311-14, 318-20, 347; *V*, pp. 109-29, 150; *VI*, pp. 185-89, 247-60; *VII*, pp. 110-15, 248-55; *VIII*, pp. 64-67, 169-80, 193-202, 394-95, 482-96; *IX*, pp. 110-129; and *XVII*, pp. 239-51. Recently an exhaustive three-volume study has been edited from manuscripts under the title *Zur Phänomenologie der Intersubjektivität*—parts 1 (1905-20), 2 (1921-28), and 3 (1929-35). An unsympathetic critic might dismiss this recurrence as an obsession. I shall try to justify it in terms of two basic concepts: objectivity and intersubjectivity.

For Husserl, something exists objectively if, and only if, it is "there for everyone" (*CM*, p. 124). Something which exists for me only would be private—the antithesis of "objective" in Husserl's precise sense. His philosophy is an attempt to explain how knowledge of what is objective is possible. To speak of *objective* knowledge is to refer to truths which hold not just for me but for others too. The truths of arithmetic are binding not just on the mathematician but on everyone who counts by using the conventional symbols; the principles of logic do not describe the ways some people happen to think but prescribe correct thinking for all; likewise, the results of science purport to hold not just for the scientist who has conducted a particular investigation but for everyone. Thus the objectivity of the truths of arithmetic, logic, and science—three domains of inquiry in which Husserl was especially interested—involves a reference to others for whom such truths are valid.

These remarks on the significance of the problem do not capture its full urgency. It is one thing to note that Husserl often raised the problem of intersubjectivity, but more serious is the charge of solipsism that he had to solve it, yet could not. This failure is no accident or oversight but stems from a device essential to this form of inquiry: the transcendental reduction.

> The transcendental reduction binds me to the stream of my pure conscious lived-experiences and to the unities constituted through its actualities and potentialities. Yet it seems obvious that such unities are inseparable from my ego and therefore belong to its very concretion. [*CM*, p. 121]

The philosophic problem of others is thus particularly acute for Husserl because the *aim* of his inquiry requires its solution yet the *procedure* he employs appears to preclude it.[3]

B. Husserl's Critique of Transcendental Realism

Husserl's first defense against the charge of solipsism is an offense against the standpoint from which it is launched: transcendental realism. His critique of transcendental realism serves to safeguard important phenomenological principles and to rebut an important line of criticism against his subsequent solution.

He characterizes transcendental realism as a general philosophy in the following terms:

> The nature and world which are constituted immanently within the ego have behind them first of all the world which exists *in itself* to which the way is first to be found. [*CM*, p. 122]

The philosophical position under attack advances two claims represented by each of its terms: it is *transcendental* in that it asserts that things are constituted by the ego within its own experience; it is

a *realism* in holding, naively, that beyond all the ego's actual or possible consciousness is a realm of things that are not apprehended. This brand of realism must be characterized as *naive* because the claim about things beyond actual or possible experience is a critical assumption which Husserl will try to prove is either unnecessary, false, or meaningless. The spirit of Husserl's philosophy is precisely to overcome the naivete of all such assumptions.[4]

His response to the charge of solipsism implicitly suggests two criticisms of transcendental realism:

> Before one decides . . . in favour of the "self-evident truths" (*Selbstverständlichkeiten*) employed in it and lets oneself in for dialectical argumentation and for self-termed "metaphysical" hypotheses whose reputed possibility perhaps turns out to be complete nonsense, it might be more appropriate first of all to take up the task indicated by the expression "alter ego" and to carry it through. [*CM*, p. 122]

His first criticism bears on the assumption that some things are self-evident or obvious (*selbstverständlich*). By making such an undefended assumption, the transcendental realist fails to measure up to the ideal of "radical" philosophy—to be free from all presuppositions.[5] He assumes that beyond all experience are things which exist in and of themselves, including, specifically, other minds. Husserl is implicitly faulting the realists for making this assumption without supporting arguments. A weak censure would be that this assumption is never defended. For example, in Bertrand Russell's classic statement of the argument from analogy[6] and in A. J. Ayer's inductive argument,[7] the presumption that another's thoughts and feelings exist, and exist independently of my experience, is never explicitly defended. Their logical devices do not *prove* this metaphysical hypothesis, but only *presume* it. Though the rationale for their deductive or inductive arguments is derived from it, no argument is given for the hypothesis itself.

Implicit in Husserl's remarks is a second criticism in the form of a stronger argument against this first assumption: It cannot be defended because it logically contradicts a second tenet. As a *transcendental* philosopher, this kind of realist subscribes to the doctrine of constitution and to the principle of meaningfulness. Briefly stated, the latter claims that

every sense which any entity has and can have for me... is a sense which is clarified and revealed for me *in* and *in terms of* my intentional life, in terms of its constitutive syntheses and in systems of harmonious verification. [*CM*, p. 123]

The incoherence of transcendental realism, and hence the reason why the presumption of things in themselves not only is not but cannot be defended, could be summarized in the following argument.

P_1: All things (or statements about them) are meaningful if and only if their meaning is derived from and located within my intentional life.

P_2: Things in themselves such as other minds (or statements about them) have a meaning that is neither derived from nor located within my intentional life.

C : Things in themselves (or statements about them) are not meaningful.

P_1 is a restatement of the phenomenological principle of meaningfulness and P_2 is just a way of giving force to the expression "in themselves." The argument is then a valid syllogism of the logical form *modus tolens*.

The transcendental realist is subject to a third criticism by making a second assumption which violates this same phenomenological ideal of presuppositionlessness: The phenomenologist cannot provide an adequate account of others within the domain of his inquiry. On this assumption, the transcendental realist is led to look elsewhere. But perhaps, Husserl suggests, he too precipitously forsakes the phenomenological realm of actual and possible consciousness. Closer inspection may reveal that within these confines an adequate ac-

count of others can be provided. At any rate, the transcendental realist has not given a sound argument why such an account might not be forthcoming, and his demand for an account of others, interpreted as things in themselves, involves an undefended, indefensible, or meaningless assumption.

By this critique of transcendental realism Husserl has rendered the assumption that others are things in themselves at least problematic, and he has transformed the *charge* of solipsism into a *challenge* to phenomenology to solve the problem of others. He takes up this challenge with the resolution to undertake a phenomenology of empathy.

C. Intentional Analysis of the Sense
Alter Ego

The philosophic problem of others is, for phenomenology, a problem about the philosopher's experience of others— what Husserl calls 'empathy' (*Einfühlung*)—using this term more inclusively than in ordinary discourse. The philosophic problem is egological, for all experiences belong to someone, namely, myself or the ego. But we must not be misled into thinking that others exist "in" this ego or its experiences—giving "in" a realistic interpretation on the paradigm of water's being *in* the glass.[8] Rather, the relationship between the ego and others is intentional: they appear within the field of my perception as things intended by me. This difference between real and intentional relationships will emerge through the subsequent exposition. Husserl's immediate task is to analyze the components of this form of intentionality, a procedure he calls "intentional analysis" (*CM*, p. 83).

To perceive others is to take something given, as another self, or to ascribe to this something the sense *alter ego*. What are the components of this sense and how is it formed? The first step which analyzes the sense of alter ego has its analogues within the British-American tradition in the linguistic or conceptual analysis of philosophers such as A. J. Ayer[9] and P.

F. Strawson.[10] The difficulty for each tradition is to avoid the intrusion of philosophic views into what is, or purports to be, simply a *description* about the way people use language (Ayer), conceptualize the world (Strawson), or experience things (Husserl).

Securing a vantage point from which we can analyze this sense turns out to be no problem at all, for it is simply a matter of avoiding the unwarranted distortion of theoretical concepts in order to let the thing reveal itself. We live in these experiences, as the German term *Erlebnis* emphasizes. This first moment in phenomenological analysis is therefore "histrionic"[11] (to invoke an expression Loewenberg uses to characterize Hegel's phenomenology): as philosophers, we abandon the distant and disinterested standpoint from which we criticize experience in order first to live it. This step parallels the earlier step in *Cartesian Meditations* whereby Husserl immersed himself in scientific activity to elicit its sense. Now we immerse ourselves in our everyday experiences of others in order to describe the meaning of what presents itself. The results of this procedure are summarized as follows:

In changeable harmonious multiplicities of experience I experience others as actually existing and on the one hand as world objects—not as mere physical things belonging to Nature (though indeed in one respect as that too). They are in effect experienced also as always governing psychically in their respective natural organisms. . . . On the other hand I experience them at the same time as subjects for this world, as experiencing it, this same world that I experience, and in so doing, they experience me too, even as I experience the world and others in it. [*CM*, p. 123]

Husserl claims, first, that "I experience others as actually existing." This component is not meant to deny that some people no longer exist. Nor does it exclude the possibility of a self which necessarily exists, such as God. There are many modalities of existence: possible, probable, doubtful, necessary, and actual. Husserl is simply reporting the familiar fact that others, as we typically encounter them in everyday life, are things that *actually* exist. How we can experience them in this way will be subsequently explained in terms of Husserl's doctrine of evidence (*Evidenz*),[12] to which the preceding expression, "changeable harmonious multiplicities of experience," alludes.

Second, others are experienced ordinarily "not as mere physical things belonging to nature." This denial is tantamount to an affirmation that others are in part *physical things*, bodies extended in space and locatable in time. Whatever else disembodied spirits may be, they are not other people in the ordinary sense. Though others are not just their bodies, they are at least this.

What "more" there is to others is suggested by the expression "governing psychically in their natural organism." In this third component Husserl points to that *mental life* which distinguishes others as more than mere material things. The preposition "in" suggests a somewhat closer connection between the psychic and the physical than the metaphor "governor" alone would: the mental is not one thing divorced from the body, like a captain and his ship; rather, it is through their physical behavior that I am witness to the nonphysical dimension to others.

Fourth and finally, I experience others "as subjects for this world, as experiencing it, this same world that I experience, and in so doing, they experience me too, even as I experience the world and others in it." Whereas the third component marked a connection between the psychic life of others and their bodies, this fourth component extends this connection to include the world. I experience others as experiencing the world: they see, hear, smell, touch, and taste the things I do, or can apprehend, in a similar way; they have thoughts and beliefs about things, and likes and dislikes too. But to be a *subject* is not just to have these different kinds of experiences. It is to be able to act through their body on the world as well, to transform it according to what they perceive, know, or desire.

Moreover, the world that others apprehend and shape includes me as well, so that the relation between self and others is reciprocal: we are simultaneously both subject and object for one another.

These four components form the *explanandum*. Though presented in philosophical language, these descriptions serve merely to report the content of everyday experiences that are familiar to all. In the course of my ordinary life I empathetically experience something which I take as another self. This empathy is now seen to mean (1) this other *actually exists*, (2) he is a *physical thing*, (3) he *controls his body*, and (4) he *has a world* to which he relates through sensory, cognitive, and affective experiences and upon which he acts. Given these four data, the philosophic task is to show how such empathetic experiences are possible. How does it come about that I ascribe to something a sense with these four constituents? What is the basis for this ascription? How can I know that I have correctly interpreted the data of experience?

Husserl answers these questions in two stages: first, a reduction to what he terms the "sphere of ownness"; second, a constitution in terms of this sphere of the sense *alter ego*.

D. The Peculiar Kind of Epoche

Husserl resolves to answer the questions just posed by "carrying out a peculiar kind of thematic epoche" (*CM*, p. 124). This new epoche is the negative moment in the reduction or return to (*reducere*) the sphere of ownness.[13] Husserl describes it in the following terms:

We disregard all constitutive achievements (*Leistungen*) of intentionality which relate either directly or indirectly to another subjectivity. [*CM*, p. 124]

What intentionality achieves is meaning or sense (*Sinn*).[14] Husserl is asking us to strip the world of all social meaning that is involved in the ascription of a mental life to someone other than myself.

Through this new epoche the face to face encounter is denuded of all thoughts, feelings, and actions which are not my own. In addition, we have already seen that objectivity is understood by Husserl to mean "there for everyone" (*CM*, p. 124). Consequently, by this new epoche the world loses its objectivity as well. Moreover, a similar indirect reference to others is built into the "spiritual predicates [of] all cultural objects" (*CM*, p. 124). Books, for example, must hereby lose their sense of being written by an author, produced by a manufacturer, sold by a clerk, and read by students—because author, manufacturer, clerk, and students are other people.

The way in which the world is deprived of all social meaning can be understood by contrasting it to social deprivation in a natural sense.

If I abstract from the other in the usual sense, then I am left behind *alone*. But such abstraction is not radical, such being alone does not change anything of the natural sense in which the world is there for everyone to experience. [*CM*, p. 125][15]

By this new epoche I do not physically absent myself from the company of others, for such a withdrawal is consistent with preserving all kinds of indirect references to them. I may continue to take the world as something which objectively exists and still give to the things which accompany me on my retreat their usual social significance. Physical withdrawal fails to be radical because the presuppositions about the social dimension of the world are not suspended and the roots of these presuppositions are not revealed.

This new epoche also stands in contrast to the phenomenological epoche.[16] Husserl relates the two as follows:

The thematic exclusion of the constitutive achievements of experiences of others and along with them all ways of being conscious which refer to others does not now mean merely the phenomenological *epoche* with respect to the naive way in which we take others, like all objects which we naively take straightforwardly as existing for us. The transcendental attitude always is and remains presupposed as that according to which everything which previously existed straightforwardly for us is taken exclusively as *phenomenon*—something whose sense is supposed and is to be confirmed, purely as it secures and has secured the sense of being for us as the correlate of constitutive systems which are to be disclosed. [*CM*, p. 126]

Husserl seems in danger of presupposing the phenomenological epoche so as to make his subsequent solution to the problem of others circular: his formulation of the problem would then be infected by the techniques subsequently used to solve it. How can we avoid begging the question in this way?

The phenomenological epoche marks a *general* movement from the naive belief in an independently existing real world to a critical standpoint which questions all such naiveté. Husserl's earlier critique of transcendental realism discredited such ontological naiveté. But for the specific problem at hand it is necessary to question not just this general ontological faith in things—which includes others—but to question more particularly the sense or meaning which refers both directly and indirectly to others. As a critique of naive realism, the phenomenological epoche alone is not adequate for this second task. Hence a new, more specific kind of reduction must be carried out. This new epoche is a selection of phenomena from the field of philosophical inquiry uncovered earlier by the phenomenological reduction in order to solve a particular problem. But because of the peculiar status of the problem of intersubjectivity, it serves as a methodological reflection on the very nature of the reduction and hence on the limits of phenomenological inquiry.

How can such claims be verified? According to Husserl, the answer lies in what remains—the sphere of ownness, or, as he terms it, *Eigenheitssphäre*.

E. The Sphere of Ownness

Nothing in Husserl's procedure does or can guarantee in advance that this peculiar kind of epoche can be successfully executed. It may very well turn out that when the world has been stripped of all reference to others, nothing coherent survives. To deny this possibility at the outset would be to beg the question at hand. Failure to disclose a harmonious level of experience would demonstrate the irreducibly social character of all experience. The philosophic question about the *basis* for our knowledge of others would thereby be unmasked as a pseudo problem. If every level of experience to which we can abstract involves a reference to others as part of its sense, the transcendental problem about the conditions for the possibility of my experience of others is thereby dissolved rather than solved.

The sphere of ownness which Husserl purports to discover after the new epoche has both a noetic and noematic side which illustrates the general structure of all consciousness (outlined earlier in section 17). On the one hand, there is the ego as an animate organism (*Leib*), along with its mental acts and processes; on the other is the world of nature as intentional correlate.

The self, as one component of this stratum to which experience has been reduced, is described as follows:

Among the bodies belonging to this "Nature" ... I then find my *animate organism* as *uniquely* singled out—namely as the only one of them that is not just a body (*Körper*) but precisely an *animate organism* (*Leib*): the sole object within my abstract world-stratum to which I ascribe fields of sensation ... the only object *in* which I *rule and govern* immediately.... Meanwhile the *kinesthesias* pertaining to the organs flow in the mode "I am doing" and are subject to my "I can". Furthermore by calling these kinesthesias into play, I can push, thrust and so forth, and can thereby "act" somatically—immediately and then mediately. As perceptively active, I experience (or can experience) all of Nature including my own animate organism, which therefore in the process is reflexively related to itself.... And it is the same in the case of my generally possible original dealing with *nature* and with my animate organism itself by means of this organism—which is therefore reflexively related to itself in practice too. [*CM*, p. 128]

This self is first of all a physical thing among a totality of physical things which are extended spatially and which endure through time. This first component of the reduced self corresponds to the second component of the alter ego, which was analyzed earlier. This correlation between the self and other is essential if the sense *alter ego* is to be constituted out of the reduced sphere: the other self will be a self like me, and if I am not physical, it will be inexplicable how the other can acquire this sense from me.

Husserl claims, secondly, that my physical body is distinct among all "Nature" in that it is the only one which has a field of sensations. When I hit a nail I do not feel pain, but when I hit my thumb the subsequent sensation of pain is something I feel directly and unquestionably. Similarly, when I close my eyes I cease to see, but when I close your eyes the world does not undergo a similar visual transformation. And when I plug my ears the world ceases to make sounds, but nothing similar happens when I do the same to any other physical thing. Such observations, which are available to all, support Husserl's contention that there is an intimate connection between my body and visual, tactile, auditory, taste, and olfactory sensations: it is my body to which such sensory fields directly belong. He marks this distinction between my body and all others terminologically, by calling mine an "animate organism" (*Leib*) and all others "bodies" (*Körper*).

Husserl claims that my body is "the only object *in* which I *rule and govern immediately*" (*CM*, p. 128). For example, when I want to raise your arm I must reach out and lift it, but when I want to raise my arm I do not have to perform any such intervening operation.[17] This descriptive claim need not be taken to deny that mastery over my body is acquired: as a child I gradually discovered this connection between me and my body, which is originally more intimate than that between me and any other thing. Nor need Husserl be taken to exclude the possibility of extending this intimacy, so that, for example, a driver and his car can become one. Rather, he is claiming simply that

ordinarily (and perhaps paradigmatically) I control my body in a way which is different from the way in which I control other things. Within this reduced sphere, he must secure this third component of the sense *self as animate organism* in order to prepare for its appearance in others as the third component of the sense *alter ego*.

Fourth and finally, Husserl establishes the duality of the self as both subject and object by noting that I not only experience things in the world (self as subject) but that I can experience myself as well (self as object): "As perceptively active, I experience (or can experience) all of Nature including my own animate organism" (*CM*, p. 128). This "Nature" was carefully put in quotation marks earlier to distinguish it from the "nature" of the natural scientist; the latter is eliminated by the reduction insofar as it has the sense of existing for other scientists too. Not only can I touch other things, I can touch myself as well. So, too, I can see, smell, taste, and hear my body. As an incarnate body-subject, I can be reflexively aware of myself. Again, without this duality of the self as animate organism it would be impossible to account for the sense of others, which was analyzed earlier as "world objects [and] subjects for this world" (*CM*, p. 123).

It is important not to reify these four components of the sense *self as animate organism*: the self as subject is not one thing distinct from some second thing— the self as object. Rather, these two dimensions of the self are analogous to the different roles one person plays. Similarly, the self as animate organism is not literally a thing apart from the philosophizing self. The philosopher who carries out this new epoche thereby achieves an insight into himself. As Husserl makes clear in section 45, I, the philosopher, am aware of myself through reflection as an animate organism. What I thereby confront is distinct but not separate, an aspect of myself—and not a second, independently existing thing.

To account for the animate organism as a totality, its temporal horizon must be included.[18] The new epoche has reduced the self to what is actual within the sphere of ownness. But as section 19 demonstrated, all such actualities are situated within their temporal horizon of potentialities. Whereas the former are given perceptually, these latter are apprehended through recollections and expectations:

Although I am continually given to myself originally and can experience progressively what is included in my own essence, this explication is carried out largely in acts of consciousness that are not perceptions.... All possibilities subsumed under the "I can" or "could have" set this or that series of subjective experiences going (including in particular I can look ahead or look back, I can penetrate and uncover the horizon of my temporal being)—all such possibilities manifestly belong to me as moments of my own essence. [CM, p. 133]

This self as animate organism, with its actual and potential sensory experiences, forms the noetic component of the sphere of ownness. But there is more to the latter than just this self. According to Husserl's general thesis of intentionality, each mental act or process should have an intentional object as its correlate. In this specific case the sphere of ownness includes things which transcend the sensory experiences of the animate organism. As objects on the noematic side they go beyond the noetic acts and processes which intend them. But insofar as they are objects within the sphere of ownness, they remain "immanent." For this reason Husserl speaks of an "immanent transcendence" (CM, p. 134).

What properly belongs to my ego as something essential to it ... evidently extends ... to the constituted unities ... where and insofar as the constituted unity is inseparable from the original constitution itself... that is, just like the constituting perception, the perceived entity belongs to the ownness of my concrete self. [CM, p. 134]

Though these objects belong to a "transcendent world" (CM, p. 135), they do not belong to the objective world, which is a higher level of transcendence, since its sense refers indirectly to those others yet to be constituted. These objects

within the sphere of ownness are unities of the different aspects (Abschattungen)—the varying shapes, tones, textures, and smells which things emit and which the animate organism passively synthesizes in sensory perception.

This progression to the noematic parallels the movement of Husserl's Fourth Meditation and marks the expanded and full concept of the self. In section 31 Husserl first identified a limited notion of the self as the empty pole of identity for lived experiences: all the mental acts and processes which are performed or occur within one stream of experience form a unity in that all refer back to a single self to which each belongs. At this juncture the self is empty in that it is a purely formal concept, like Kant's "I think," which must accompany all my representations.[19] In section 32 he expanded this concept of the self to include a substrate of habitualities. The self becomes more delineated in its content as that which persists in holding certain beliefs, values, or desires. Finally, in section 33, he enlarges this second notion to self in the full sense, which includes its world of objects, and calls this complete self "the monad."[20]

These three distinctions are important. If the concept of self is taken too narrowly—in the sense of self as empty pole of identity or as substrate of habitualities—Husserl's doctrine of constitution is made to appear absurd: subjectivity (self in the first two senses) reaches out through its mental life to create its object ex nihilo.

As applied to the problem at hand, it is important to recall that the sphere of ownness out of which the sense alter ego will be constituted includes its world of objects. Husserl never encapsulates the self within its mental life so as to create an abyss it must mysteriously bridge in getting to know others. His doctrine of intentionality, which is operative in the noetic-noematic correlation just drawn, refutes this formulation of the problem. For Husserl, the problem is hermeneutical: How do I come to interpret something within the sphere of immediate experience as another self?

The sphere of ownness with its noetic (animate organism) and noematic (sensory objects) components is to function as that out of which the sense *alter ego* will be constituted. It therefore serves as the foundation of "empathy" in Husserl's broadened sense.

This unitary stratum, furthermore, is distinguished by being essentially the *founding* stratum—that is to say: I obviously cannot have the "other" as an experience, and hence cannot have the sense "objective world" as a sense of experience, without having this level in actual experience; while the opposite is not the case. [*CM*, p. 127]

I could not relate to others either directly or indirectly except insofar as I have the sensory experiences Husserl has just described. Hence the sphere of ownness is logically prior to empathy and all higher forms of social consciousness.

Husserl's task is now to explain how such higher modes of consciousness can occur. The first step is the constitution of the sense *alter ego* in terms of the elements of this sphere.

F. Constitution of the Sense *Alter Ego*

The intentional analysis has furnished the *explanandum* and the sphere of ownness provides the first part of the *explanans*. Husserl's doctrine of constitution is an advance beyond description into a theoretical explanation, couched in such technical expressions as 'analogical apperception', 'assimilative apprehension', 'apperceptive transfer', and 'pairing'. For simplicity I will take 'analogical', 'analogizing', and 'assimilative' as approximately synonymous and I will use 'appresentation' and 'apperception' interchangeably. These expressions distinguish what is directly and immediately present from what is only indirectly or mediately present. The former are to provide the basis upon which the latter is founded.

Since others are not directly present in the sphere of ownness, it is necessary to locate within this sphere the basis for an indirect awareness of them.

A certain *mediation of intentionality* must here be present extending from the substratum *primordial world* which is the constant underlying basis in every case. This mediation makes present to consciousness an "also there" which nevertheless is not itself there and which can never become an itself there. Thus it is a matter of a kind of making-*copresent*, a kind of *appresentation*. [*CM*, p. 139]

This passage raises a series of questions. Why can the other not be himself there? In what sense is he "copresent"? How does this "making-copresent" come about?

Husserl discounts the possibility of my being directly and immediately aware of the mental life of another.[21] This limitation to my abilities is not contingent, to be overcome by improved communication. Husserl would agree with Ayer that, as an attempt to bridge the gap between myself and others, "telepathy is no better than the telephone."[22] Rather, the impossibility of my having your thoughts arises on logical or, more precisely, intentional grounds.[23]

If what properly belongs to the essence of the other were accessible in a direct way, then it would be a mere moment of my own proper essence, and ultimately he himself and I myself would be one and the same (*einerlei*). [*CM*, p. 139]

To understand Husserl's claim here, we must recall sections 31 and 32, where he proved that the self is defined in part by its own lived experiences. Hence for me to have your thoughts is for me to be you. But it is impossible for me to be both me and you—any more than any one thing can be some other. As Butler noted and Moore reiterated, everything is what it is and not another thing.[24] The sense of the experiences (intentionality)—not of the words (intensionality)—precludes my having your lived experiences. I cannot directly perceive your thoughts the way I directly perceive, for example, the front of a book. Success in carrying out the new epoche and in describing the sphere of ownness without reference to others proves that their mental life is not a component of my immediate experience. The problem, then, is to delineate a mediated form of intentionality which accounts for my experience of others.

Husserl calls this mediated consciousness "appresentation" (or "apperception"). This term is not introduced arbitrarily, as an *ad hoc* solution; rather, as Schutz pointed out, it has a venerable history.[25] For example, when I look at a book from the front, its back is "appresented": it is made copresent with the front, which is directly given. Analogical appresentation (or assimilative apperception) occurs when I apprehend this thing as analogous (or similar) to other books I have seen. Without this component to experience it would be impossible to link one thing to another under the heading 'book'. Without analogical appresentation it would be impossible to understand the word 'book' or to develop the concept "book."

To appreciate Husserl's divergence from those who advance an *argument* from analogy it is important to note that the expressions "assimilative apperception" and "analogizing appresentation" refer to a *single* complex act of apprehending one thing as like or unlike another. He gives the following illustration:

The child who already sees things understands for the first time the purpose of scissors and from then on he sees them as scissors in the first glance—but of course not in explicit reproduction, comparison and in drawing a conclusion. [*CM*, p. 141]

In a similar fashion within the unity of one complex act, I apprehend the other's thoughts as similar or analogous to what I might experience in his situation. Husserl does not appeal to a series of comparisons, formulated in propositions, from which one infers inductively or deductively the similarity or analogy between self and others: "Apperception is not an inference, not an act of thinking" (*CM*, p. 141).

Many philosophers in the "analytic" tradition, perhaps misled by a scientific paradigm, invoke inductive and deductive arguments in place of Husserl's analogizing apprehension.[26] These two forms of rationality serve as paths that lead them into the nonsense Husserl earlier critized in transcendental realism. According to them, when I observe someone else in pain I am supposed to reason somewhat as follows:

P_1: When I moan, hold my jaw, and cry out in pain, I have a toothache.

C_1: Whenever anyone moans..., he has a toothache.

P_2: S is moaning...

C_2: S has a toothache.

Children who recognize the feelings of their parents must be capable of inductive generalizations to infer C_1 from P_1, as well as, *modus ponens,* to infer C_2 from C_1 and P_2. To offer this argument from analogy as a description is to misdescribe what actually goes on in our head. To offer it as a justification for knowledge of others is to introduce an abyss between philosophical explanation and everyday life. Moreover, as the conclusion of an inductive generalization, C_1 succumbs to the fallacy of hasty generalization, and leaves one wondering with Wittgenstein: "And how can I generalize the *one* case so irresponsibly?"[27] By contrast, Husserl's account is simpler and more faithfully reports the content of everyday experience.

Admittedly, the use of these expressions in the context of the present problem is contentious. Husserl is suggesting that the thoughts and feelings of others are made copresent with something directly given to me of others within my sphere of ownness. This line of reasoning is subject to an obvious objection, which Husserl immediately raises. What is appresented in the case of the book can be presented: the "empty" intention can be fulfilled when I turn the book over and intuit the back of the book in the original (*originaliter*). But the mental life of others can never be directly present to me:

Appresentation [sc. in the constitution of primordial nature] involves the possibility of confirmation through the corresponding fulfilling presentation (the back becomes the front); whereas for the appresentation which is supposed to lead into another original sphere, such confirmation must be excluded a priori. [CM, p. 139]

Does this limitation preclude the use of appresentation and apperception within an account of others?

Husserl does not abandon the analogy between apperceiving others and apperceiving the back of things. Rather, he transforms this disanalogy into a new problem: "How can the appresentation of another and thereby the sense 'other' be motivated in the sphere which is mine?" (CM, p. 139). What makes me anticipate the back of a book when I see its front is my past experiences with books and their backs, or the backs of similar things. Related past experiences motivate the appresentation. The disanalogy between the backs of books and the inner life of others simply brings this question of motivation into focus.[28]

Husserl answers this question in terms of the physical appearance and bodily movement of others and introduces the term "pairing" to mark more specifically the kind of analogizing appresentation which constitutes this type of awareness:

If a body appears in my primordial sphere as something outstanding, a body which is *similar* to mine, i.e. so created that he must enter into a phenomenal pairing with my own, then it seems clear without further ado that in the sense-transfer, it must take over the sense animate organism from my body. [CM., p. 143]

The experienced animate organism of the other continues to prove it actually exists as an animate organism only in its changing but continuously harmonious *behaviour* (*Gebaren*). [CM, p. 144]

What motivates the apperceptive transfer whereby something acquires the sense of being an animate organism like me (the only animate organism in the sphere of ownness up to this point) is our similarity in appearance and behavior. Of course the other is not given to me in exactly the same way I appear to myself—as the previous distinction between the animate organism and other bodies in the sphere of ownness makes clear. Rather, the similarity is mediated by a kind of *indirect* and counterfactual "comparison": the other looks not the way I in fact look here but the way I would look if I were there.

The body belonging to my primordial world (of what subsequently becomes the other) is a body for me in the mode *there*. Its ways of appearing are not paired in direct association with the ways in which my body actually appears (in the mode *here*). . . . It brings to mind the way my body would look *if I were there*. [CM, p. 147]

The given similarities between my actual bodily appearance and movements and those of the others are what lead me to ascribe subjectivity to something within this reduced sphere. By themselves, though, these two kinds of data are not sufficient to generate the sense "*alter ego*". As transcendental subject, I too contribute something to the experience of empathy. This "contribution" occurs through imagination.[29] I try to picture to myself, standing *here*, how I would look, what I would feel, and how the world would appear if I were *there*—in the place of that body which resembles mine and acts as I might. My imaginative projection into the place of another, conjoined with the two types of data given by the senses, makes empathy possible.

As a type of analogizing apprehension, being paired with the other has two defining characteristics:

First, that the instituting original is continuously present as something alive . . . and second . . . that what is appresented through that analogizing can never actually become present, thus be actually perceived. [CM, p. 142]

The pairing which constitutes empathy can occur only in the face to face encounter: as the original source of the sense *self*, I must always be there—unlike other paired relations in which the original no longer need be present. Also, what distinguishes other people (as something paired with me) from other things (which may be paired with me) is that their mental life remains forever beyond my immediate grasp. This pairing establishes an intentional overreaching (*intentionales Übergreifen* [*CM*, p. 142]) which Husserl characterizes as "a living mutual awakening, a mutual give and take and overlaying of each with the objective sense of the other" (*CM*, p. 142). This use of analogy differs from the usual argument from analogy, not only in that it is noninferential but in that I do not need to acquire knowledge from my own case and then extend it to others. The *reciprocal* character of pairing enables me to learn from another truths which I only subsequently discover hold for me. Consequently, Husserl is not committed to a type of self-knowledge that is logically and temporally prior to others, and his account is not subject to the objections that are raised against accounts which rely on this type of self-knowledge.

This point is important, for many critics have seized on this assumption of the priority of self-knowledge. Malcolm and Strawson, for example, have tried to rebut the use of analogy by contending that to know something about myself requires that I have a concept of self which—in principle, at any rate—I am prepared to ascribe to others as well.[30] Once this general character of concepts or terms—and hence of knowledge—is recognized, both the need for and possibility of an exclusive self-awareness collapses. Self-knowledge can never exclude others in principle, as Husserl's sphere of ownness seems to do, and hence the argument which begins with the self cannot even be formulated.

I raise this possible line of objection (though it was not directed at Husserl) primarily to clarify Husserl's position. First, for him, it is not a matter of concepts or language but of experiences and, more precisely, an abstract stratum of a particular type of experience. Language and concepts would not be possible if the animate organism within the sphere of ownness did not pair itself with things that indirectly resemble it; but the converse is not true: before I can have words with which to talk meaningfully about others, or before I can conceive of them, I must have experienced them. Without this sensory contact, which logically—though not necessarily temporally—precedes others, the terms and concepts which apply to others would signify nothing for me. And second—contrary to what this line of attack assumes—all use of analogy does not entail that I first have knowledge of myself which I subsequently extend to others. Husserl's intentional overreaching is logically compatible with my learning through other truths which I only later apply to myself.

Husserl's theory of verification challenges the connection such critics make between knowledge on the one hand and language or concepts on the other. If they are right that the former requires the latter, I will be unable to know anything about others without the language or concepts which refer to them as part of their sense. For words have a meaning that is binding on all speakers of that language and conceptual truths are similarly held to be valid for all—for myself and every other. If knowledge is indeed intersubjective, there can be no self-knowledge independent of others, and the foundation for my knowledge of others cannot itself be a form of knowledge. Knowledge within the sphere of ownness would then be impossible.

Husserl deals with this issue in sections 52 to 54. He treats knowledge in terms of *Evidenz*, which I shall translate as evidential experiences or the process of making evident. Earlier, in section 6, he distinguished two types of evidential experiences: adequate and apodictic. He defined inadequacy as an

incompleteness, a one-sidedness and relative unclarity and indistinctness in the way in which the thing or state of affairs is given. The experience is laden with components of *unfulfilled expectant* and *attendant* intentions. [*CM*, p. 55]

On the other hand, apodicticity was defined as

an absolute indubitability in a quite definite

and peculiar sense, that which the scientist expects of all *principles*.... An apodictic evidential experience... has the distinctive peculiarity that it is not merely certain of any thing or state of affairs evident in it; rather through a critical reflection it is disclosed at the same time that their non-being is completely unthinkable. [*CM*, pp. 56-7]

As a *principle* which explains how empathy is possible, pairing could be taken as apodictic—even though Husserl never explicitly does so. The content of my paired experiences of others, like all "outer" experiences, is inadequate in Husserl's sense. Furthermore, they must remain inadequate since the appresented inner life can never be given. From this inadequacy the skeptic concludes that knowledge of others is impossible. Husserl rejects such skepticism, employing his general principle of verification:

Every experience points to further experiences which fulfill and confirm the appresented horizon. They include potentially confirmable syntheses of harmonious further experiences and include them in the form of unintuitive anticipations. [*CM*, p. 144]

Each experience has, as part of its sense, a reference to further experiences which I anticipate emptily, though the content is more or less predelineated according to relevant past experiences. When these expectations are fulfilled in an intuition, the sense of the experience is confirmed. What is troublesome in the case of others is that direct confirmation is impossible in principle. How, then, can the meaning that is built into the horizon of such experiences ever be sufficiently verified to justify a claim to know? Husserl provides the following schema as an answer.

The experienced animate organism of the other continues to prove that it actually exists as animate organism only in its changing but continuously harmonious *behaviour,* in such a way that this behaviour has its physical side which indicates the psychic as something appresented. This harmonious behaviour must now emerge as something fulfilled in original experience. It does so in the constant change of behaviour from phase to phase. The animate organism is experienced as a pseudo-animate organism if this behaviour is discordant. [*CM*, p. 144]

Once the intimate connection between the mental life of another and his physical behavior is established by analogizing apprehension, the harmony (or lack of it) in his behavior provides the basis for confirming (or disconfirming) my understanding of the other's mental life. For example, I know that a child feels the heat of the stove because he removes his hand when he gets too close—just as I would if I were in his situation. If he does not pull his hand back as I would, I begin to suspect that he does not feel pain as I do. And if, for example, on a later occasion his accidentally striking his hand with a hammer is not followed by the kinds of sounds I might utter, I have further evidence to confirm my tentative belief that he does not feel pain in typical situations. Fulfillment of my expectations about anticipated behavior is confirmation of my ascription to another of a mental life, and nonfulfillment is disconfirmation.

The skeptic will insist that we can always be wrong about others. In a sense, Husserl grants this point by recognizing that the horizon is open, the future is never exhausted, and the process of making evident is never complete. These concessions, however, do not discount those expectations which have been fulfilled and render such evidence worthless. To admit the possibility of being wrong about others because our evidence is always inadequate is not to say that we *are* wrong or that we cannot tell what is most likely accurate or true. Each experience provides evidence which confirms and/or disconfirms, and the rational person will side with the stronger evidence. Skepticism is bought at the expense of rationality.

Is this evidence knowledge? Certainly the harmonious fulfillment of expectations about others can reach a point where doubt becomes irrational. Such experiences provide the basis for knowledge of others by justifying my claims to know things about them. Are such experiences a form of knowledge? Traditionally, knowledge is defined as jus- tified true belief. If belief is defined in terms of language which refers to others, then the answer is no. If belief is defined in terms of mental acts or processes, the answer is yes. But, in either case, Hus- serl's focal point is more the nature of justification than the nature of knowl- edge. He is satisfied to delineate a stratum of experience which has cogni- tive worth in getting to know others.

Husserl approximates a coherence theory of truth in his use of harmony. Clearly, however, the harmony does not hold among propositions; so it must not be identified with logical consistency. Rather, this harmony is a primitive con- cept in Husserl's philosophy, which is to be understood here in terms of a pattern in the fulfillment of expectations about the behavior of others—both what they will do and what they will not do. Nonful- fillment signifies a discordant element which requires the ascription of a new sense or the retraction of an old one.

In the process of confirmation, the confirma- tion can be turned into its negative. Instead of what was supposed (*Vermeinten*), *something else* can emerge, in the mode of *it itself*. The position taken on what was meant founders on this and what was meant in turn takes on the character of nullity. [*CM*, p. 93]

In its final form, Husserl's account avoids two extremes. Though the be- havior of another motivates the ascrip- tion of phenomenological sense, this sense is not identified with the behavior. Husserl's account is not committed to behaviorism, of either a philosophical or methodological sort.[31] But, on the other hand, Husserl nowhere claims that the mental life of either myself or others exists or can exist independently of our bodies as material things (*Körper*). Hence he is not committed to an irreducible Cartesian dualism in which the mental and the physical are two autonomous realities. Even at the abstract level of the sphere of ownness my body was not only physical but had a mental (i.e. sensory) life as well. And in the case of the other, appresentation as a relation between his

corporeal and sensory life entails that his conscious self is not an *autonomously* existing substance—any more than the back of a thing can exist without the front. Though Husserl's account is therefore immune to the objections usually raised against behaviorism and Cartesianism, it has been severely criticized by many phenomenologists. I turn now to their criticisms.

G. Criticisms and Assessments

In the main, Husserl has provided what I regard as an adequate rebuttal to the charge of solipsism. Once we grant that the transcendental realist's formulation of the problem of others generates a pseudo problem, the way is cleared for Husserl's phenomenological account. His analysis of the sense *alter ego* accu- rately reports the content of everyday experiences, and his sphere of ownness and theory of analogical appresentation provide the schema for the constitution of this sense. If Husserl is to be faulted, it is primarily because his account is incomplete—rather than because it is mistaken.

Few critics accept this positive as- sessment. I shall not examine the more radical charges of such "external" critics as Heidegger[32] and Sartre[33]: by adopting a perspective outside it they claim to un- cover faulty assumptions in the roots of Husserl's philosophy. Rather, I shall limit myself to those "internal" critics who work within the framework of Hus- serl's phenomenology. Schutz[34] claims the analogy fails; Ballard has doubts that the new epoche can be carried out;[35] and Sallis[36] contends (more strongly) that it is impossible.

The main difficulty is posed by lan- guage and is formulated by Ballard as fol- lows:

In particular, one would be disposed to won- der, for example, how communication could go on within this "reduced" world of my own consciousness, especially such communica- tion as is required to practice philosophy.[37]

The elements of language which provide the medium for philosophizing have a shared meaning, and are used according to common convention. Yet this intersubjectivity is ruled out by the new epoche. Within the sphere of ownness, words are reduced to shaped, colored configurations or to auditory stimuli which impinge on my senses.[38] This transformation would seem to preclude communication as it is ordinarily understood. Hence philosophizing about this reduced sphere is impossible: the new epoche cannot be carried out because the linguistic means essential to it are denied the philosopher.

This objection rests on a confusion between the ego of the philosopher, which of course speaks, and the ego of the sphere of ownness (the animate organism), which is made dumb by the new epoche. In somewhat more general terms, it conflates the distinction between the process of philosophizing and the object upon which one philosophizes—the well-established phenomenlogical distinction between the noetic and noematic. The fallacy behind this objection can be elicited by an analogy.

If I now report the date of my birth, my statement employs language: it uses terms I take to be meaningful to others and it accords with the grammatical and semantic conventions that are binding on all speakers of English. But according to the reasoning behind the objection, as a child (cf. animate organism) in my childhood (cf. sphere of ownness) I must have been able to speak, in order to offer this report now. This inference equivocates on the different senses of "I." Perhaps as a child I was too young to speak: I, who can now speak, say this of myself, who could not speak then. Similarly, for the philosopher to describe himself as an animate organism does not require that the animate organism speak or be able to speak.

The confusion behind this objection turns on three types of sameness. I am the same as the child inasmuch as a *temporal* continuity links my life at present to my childhood. This sense of sameness does not logically entail the stronger *epistemological* sense, that whatever is true of one is true of the other: as a young child I could not speak yet as an adult I can, even though each person is the same. In the case of the philosopher and the animate organism this continuity of sameness is *methodological* rather than temporal. In the new epoche I reflectively adopt a disinterested standpoint on myself, from which I can abstract my features until I have disclosed myself as an animate organism. The latter is the same as the philosopher inasmuch as the two are joined along a procedural continuum of increasing abstractness. Again, though, this methodological sense of sameness does not entail that whatever is true of the one is true of the other: the philosopher speaks; the animate organism is dumb; and yet they are the same.

Both Ballard and Schutz challenge Husserl on a second important issue: the question of similarities. A standard objection against all use of analogies is that they do not hold: purported similarities turn into dissimilarities.

May one not, on phenomenal grounds, doubt that this similarity of another's body to my own is perceived...? I know my own body through internal visceral and kinaesthetic sensations, but I become aware of the other's body in a radically different manner, usually through the sense of sight. This recognition that the two bodies, presented in these two quite different fashions, are nevertheless similar would seem to be a complex recognition not reducible to "appresentation".

It [sc. my living body] is thus present precisely in a way which is as dissimilar as possible from the external perception of an animate body other than mine and therefore can never lead to an analogical apperception.[39]

In defense of Husserl, let me point to a logical fallacy behind this line of reasoning. Ballard and Schutz contend that because I am aware of myself in a way that is radically different from the way I am aware of others, I cannot share similarities with them to provide a basis for apperception. More generally, their objection assumes that if two things are apprehended in different *ways*, then those two *things* must be different. But consider this counterexample: Remembering is different from seeing, yet I often see persons I remember and remember persons I see. That remembering and seeing are different ways of experiencing things does not entail that the things experienced cannot be similar—even to the point of being the same. That I apprehend myself "internally" and the other "externally" does not, of itself, entail disanalogies between us. Husserl not only grants that I apprehend myself and others differently but insists on this distinction to account for the otherness of the "alter ego." My body is here; I directly ascribe to it a field of sensations. The other's body is there, and his mental life is never directly presented but only indirectly appresented.[40] Imagination enters into pairing to place me in the other's situation. I "compare" (or apprehend analogously) the way the other looks and the way I would look in his place. The counterfactual conditional is essential here. I must picture to myself what is not—and indeed what cannot be the case—namely, that I am not myself but the other. The form of this imagination ranges along a continuum from the concrete to the abstract and is perhaps most fully explored in dramatic contexts: at one extreme is an immediate shudder as Rod Steiger's pawnbroker thrusts his hand onto the spike of a paperholder; at the other is the indirect and complex re-construction of the emotional life of two women in love. Once both the indirect character and the hypothetical character of this paired association of the self and others are appreciated, the denial of similarities turns out to be false.

Husserl's account is still rather formal since he does not specify the relevant similarities concretely. This lacuna makes the range of application of his model problematic. Schutz and Fink claim that Husserl's model is too limited: it fails to account for some ordinary social encounters. I shall deal with their objections in some detail to elicit an important

but unappreciated feature of Husserl's account.

Fink raises the following objection:

> The character of the Other encountered in the mode of the opposite, complementary sex cannot be understood by virtue of an appresentation which extends, analogically, the ways and the functioning (*das Walten*) of my body to the body of the Other.

> In a certain way, Husserl's analysis remains caught in the reduplication of the ego. Even though he sees this danger he does not succeed in overcoming it methodically.[41]

Ortega y Gasset has made much of this same point in *Man and People*.[42] It is significant because it touches on many contemporary issues regarding sexual equality, and therefore invites elaboration.[43]

Obviously the sexes are different, and these differences are in part physical but extend to behavior as well. Not only do women undertake uniquely female activities, such as bearing children, they frequently perform the same activities as men, with their own distinctive style: compare, for example, the different roles of a mother and a father in raising children. Fink argues that Husserl's analogical appresentation requires similarities but that in the opposite sex we find pronounced and irreducible differences. Consequently, the objection runs, the analogy lacks a basis, and this failure points to a more general failure: Husserl has not accounted for the otherness of the "alter ego" but simply constructed the others as a mirror image of myself.

Do these objections point to a genuine or to a pseudo problem? The differences between the sexes cannot (and should not) be denied. But Fink overemphasizes these differences by ignoring certain similarities. Though women are physically different from men, the two sexes share some traits. Men seldom mistake a tree for a member of the opposite sex (Twiggy notwithstanding)—simply because the gross similarities in appearance and behavior are not there. What distinguishes women from inanimate things is, in part, what they have in common with men. These shared similarities in the ways men and women look and act are given at the level of reduced experience. They suffice to motivate the apperceptive transfer.

At the same time they serve a second, so far unappreciated function: they mark the limits of empathy between the sexes. The notorious inability of men to "understand" women is rooted in just these differences. More generally, my ability to understand others is restricted by and to the things we share in actual or imagined experiences. Husserl's account is to be recommended because he explains not only what I can and do understand of others but what I fail to understand as well.[44]

His theory of apperceptive transfer and analogizing appresentation has a second unappreciated advantage: it provides a useful model for the social scientist. Here I will simply provide three illustrations to suggest (but not prove) its value.

If something is black and I am white, I may for that reason—despite various similarities—decide that this thing is not another person. Some people believe that to be human is to be white—or, conversely, not to be white is not to be (fully) human. Blacks are sometimes regarded as less than fully human because they lack this one feature that some people consider essential to their humanity. A phenomenological analysis of prejudice could use Husserl's model to demarcate the relevant similarities between groups. Husserl's formal schema could thereby provide the sociologist with a valuable

explanatory mechanism. As a second example, babies have been known to respond enthusiastically to a smile—whether it be on a teddy bear, a balloon, or a piece of cardboard. For them, the relevant similarity which motivates their apperceptive transfer is simply this smiling figure. Adults have a much more rigorous conception of the self (and perhaps their world is much poorer as a result).[45] Thus child psychologists might find Husserl's model useful. Third and finally, anthropologists might employ this schema to understand primitive cultures. In some mythologies the wind is taken as a self because it seems to move of its own accord. In such cultures the relevant similarity for the ascription of the sense "self" is autonomous movement.

To suggest the fruitfulness of Husserl's account for the sociologist, psychologist, and anthropologist is also to warn of a danger. If Husserl were to specify the relevant similarities, such as color or shape, he might be committing himself on a scientific rather than a philosophic issue. Empirical investigations could then refute his philosophic claim. The result of Husserl's "abstention" or bracketing of these contingent issues is a purely formal account, which is not to be faulted as vacuous because of this formality. Rather, this characteristic extends the range of application of the model and makes it a useful scientific tool. Whatever the content of empathy, Husserl has reached his philosophic goal: to disclose its foundation and to articulate its invariant eidetic structure.

NOTES

1. Paul Ricoeur, *Husserl: An Analysis of His Phenomenology* (Evanston: Northwestern University Press, 1967), p. 115.

2. References to the original German, published by Nijhoff in its Husserliana series, will be abbreviated *CM.* Unless otherwise noted, English translations are my own.

3. Husserl's preoccupation with the problem of others can be justified not only as a means to an end but as an investigation that is intrinsically worthwhile as part of a phenomenology of the social world. For an examination of the problem from this perspective, see René Toulemont's *L'Essence de la Société selon Husserl* (Paris: Paris University Press, 1962).

4. See Eugen Fink's "Philosophie als Überwindung der Naivetät," *Lexis* (1948), pp. 107-27.

5. See Marvin Farber's "The Ideal of Presuppositionless Philosophy" in M. Farber (ed.), *Philosophical Essays in Memory of Edmund Husserl* (Cambridge, Mass., Harvard University Press), pp. 44-64.

6. See Bertrand Russell's *Human Knowledge: Its Scope and Limits* (New York: Simon & Schuster, 1948), pp. 482-86.

7. See A. J. Ayer's "One's Knowledge of Other

Minds" in his *Philosophical Essays* (London: Macmillan, 1954), pp. 191-214.

8. In contrast to real relations, intentional relations do not require the existence of both relata: I can think about a unicorn, though none exists, but real water cannot be contained in a nonexistent glass. And real relations are not altered by the substitution of one relata for another. Containedness, for example, is a real relation which still obtains when I substitute milk for water in the glass. But the intentional relation of thinking is changed when I substitute an angel for a unicorn.

9. See Ayer, "One's Knowledge of Other Minds."

10. See P. F. Strawson's "Persons" in *Individuals* (London: Methuen, 1959), pp. 87-116.

11. See Jacob Loewenberg's *Hegel's Phenomenology: Dialogues on the Life of the Mind* (LaSalle, Ill.: Open Court, 1965), pp. 77ff.

12. For a more extensive discussion of this concept, see Henry Pietersma's "The Evident and the True" in this volume.

13. Some critics distinguish between the epoche and reduction. The former is the suspension of our naive beliefs about the existence and nature of the world; the latter is the return to (*re-ducere*) the foundation for this belief. The distinction is an abstraction: in drawing a circle I not only exclude some area as outside (negative moment of suspension), I include another area as inside (positive moment of return). See Richard Schmitt, "Husserl's Transcendental Phenomenological Reduction," *Philosophy and Phenomenological Research*, 20 (1960): 238-45.

14. For a discussion of the phenomenological concept of meaning, see the contributions by Mohanty and Welton to this volume: J. N. Mohanty, "Husserl's Theory of Meaning," and D. Welton, "Structure and Genesis in Husserl's Phenomenology."

15. This remark makes clear that solipsism is not to be understood in natural or physical terms as solitude. For a phenomenology of solitude see R. Gotesky, "Aloneness, Loneliness, Isolation and Solitude," in J. Edie (ed.), *Invitation to Phenomenology* (Chicago: Quadrangle, 1965), pp. 211-39.

16. Alfred Schutz and E. G. Ballard have difficulty understanding the sense in which this epoche is second—that is, the sense in which the transcendental attitude is already "presupposed" (*CM*, p. 126). See Schutz's "The Problem of Transcendental Intersubjectivity in Husserl" in Schutz's *Collected Papers*, vol. 3, esp. pp. 57-61; see also E. G. Ballard's "Husserl's Philosophy of Intersubjectivity in Relation to His Rational Ideal" in *Tulane Studies in Philosophy*, 2 (1962): 3-38, 23 and 24. In his paper "On the Limitation of Transcendental Reflection or Is Intersubjectivity Transcendental?" *Monist* (1971), pp. 312-33, Sallis rejects the very possibility of this new epoche.

17. These are what Arthur Danto has termed "basic actions." See his "Basic Actions," *American Philosophical Quarterly*, 2 (1965): 141-48.

18. For a fuller discussion of Husserl's notion of horizon, see the contributions to this volume by D. Welton and C. van Peursen.

19. In *The Transcendence of the Ego*, Sartre tries to destroy Husserl's egological conception of consciousness by arguing that the self in this sense (as an empty pole of identity) is superfluous. It is redundant as an explanatory principle because consciousness is already unified through its relation to objects in the world. But I think Sartre wrongly takes Husserl to be advancing an explanation, rather than a description. Husserl is describing a feature of my mental life which I can become aware of through reflection. Consequently, Sartre's objection fails.

20. L. Landgrebe discusses the significance of Husserl's introduction of the Leibnizian term in his contribution to this volume "Phenomenology as Transcendental Theory of History." Like Held and others, he is critical of Husserl's solution to the problem of intersubjectivity.

21. Like several analytic philosophers, Husserl recognized that experiencing others is not unique in this respect, and that in recollection what is intended is not and cannot be immediately given.

22. Ayer, "One's knowledge of other minds," p. 196. The point to his example is that if the gap between the self and others were only empirical (rather than logical), it could be solved by some technological innovations. Since all improved communications would still have room for doubt about whose thoughts I am thereby directly apprehending, he concludes that the gap cannot be of this contingent sort.

23. The term 'intentional' is preferable to 'logical' (or 'intensional') because a form of experience is at issue, rather than a relation among propositions. Husserl denies the priority of language on many occasions—a claim I shall discuss in section G. Cf. the following remark: "The eidos...is *prior to all concepts* in the sense of meanings of words; as pure concepts these meanings are to be made to fit the eidos" (*CM*, p. 105).

24. Cited by G. E. Moore as his inscription to *Principia Ethica* (Cambridge: Cambridge University Press, 1903).

25. See Schutz, p. 63, "The Problem of Transcendental Intersubjectivity in Husserl," and his "Symbol, Reality and Society" in *Collected Papers* (The Hague: Nijhoff, 1962), vol. 1, pp. 287-356.

26. The classic inductive argument is formulated by J. S. Mill in *An Examination of Sir William Hamilton's Philosophy* (6th ed.; New York: Longman Green, 1889), pp. 243-44. For more recent discussions, see Alvin Plantinga's "Induction and Other Minds" in *Review of Metaphysics*, 19 (1966): 441-61, and Michael Slote's "Induction and Other Minds" in *Review of Metaphysics*, 20 (1966): 341-60. A. J. Ayer uses similar inductive logic but tries to destroy its analogical character in order to transform it into a straightforward inductive argument. H. H. Price tries to strengthen the argument by appealing to linguistic behavior, but its logical form remains intact. See "Our Evidence for the Exis-

tence of Other Minds," *Philosophy*, 13 (1938): 425-56.

27. Ludwig Wittgenstein, *Philosophical Investigations* (Oxford: Blackwell, 1963), para. 293.

28. I shall not discuss the term 'motivation', though it is an important technical expression which Husserl uses to characterize "causality in the transcendental sphere" (*CM*, p. 109).

29. For a more extensive discussion of the general role of imagination in phenomenology, see Ed Casey's "Imagination and Phenomenological Method" in this volume.

30. See Norman Malcolm's "Knowledge of Other Minds" in his *Knowledge and Certainty* (New York: Prentice-Hall, 1963), pp. 130-40, and Peter F. Strawson's "Persons" in *Individuals* (London: Methuen, 1959), pp. 87-117.

31. For an explanation of this distinction, see section XVI of Wilfred Sellars, "Empiricism and the Philosophy of Mind," in *Science Perception and Reality* (London: Routledge & Kegan Paul, 1963), pp. 183-86.

32. Heidegger's criticisms are implicit in his discussion of empathy. See *Sein und Zeit*, pp. 124-25 (*Being and Time*, pp. 161-63).

33. Sartre discusses Husserl's account in *L'Etre et le Neant*, pp. 288-91. (*Being and Nothingness*, pp. 233-35 [part 3, chap. 1, sec. 3]).

34. Schutz, "The Problem of Transcendental Intersubjectivity in Husserl," pp. 63-64.

35. Ballard, "Husserl's Philosophy of Intersubjectivity in Relation to His Rational Ideal," p. 31.

36. John Sallis, "On the Limitations of Transcendental Reflection or Is Intersubjectivity Transcendental," pp. 312-33.

37. Ballard, "Husserl's Philosophy of Intersubjectivity," p. 31.

38. In the language of linguistic analysts, they are reduced to what Max Black calls "phonemes." See *The Labyrinth of Language* (New York: Praeger, 1968), pp. 20-42. This terminology was developed earlier by J. L. Austin in *How to Do Things with Words* (Oxford: Oxford University Press, 1962 [pp. 93-120]), who regarded himself as a linguistic phenomenologist. For a comparison of Husserl and Austin, see John Wheatley's "Phenomenology: English and Continental" in David Carr and Edward S. Casey (ed.), *Dialogues in Phenomenology* (The Hague: Nijhoff, 1973), pp. 230-42.

39. Ballard, "Husserl's Philosophy of Intersubjectivity," p. 30; Schutz, "The Problem of Transcendental Intersubjectivity in Husserl," p. 63.

40. See *CM*, p. 147.

41. Cited from Schutz, "The Problem of Transcendental Intersubjectivity in Husserl," p. 84.

42. See Ortega y Gasset, *Man and People*, tr. William R. Trask (New York: Norton, 1957), pp. 127-38.

43. Some of these issues are explored in Robert Baker and Frederick Elliston, (eds.), *Philosophy and Sex* (Buffalo: Prometheus Books, 1975).

44. This account is somewhat oversimplified because the role of imagination is ignored. My ability to place myself in someone else's situation is affected by psychological factors (e.g. intelligence, feelings) and philosophical factors (e.g. the role of past experience), but the distinction between these two types of factors cannot be fully defined for each individual. What is ambiguous is the role these apprehended similarities play.

45. On the topic of children and teddy bears, see E. V. Kohak's entertaining and perceptive discussion "I, Thou and It: A Contribution to the Phenomenology of Being-in-the-World," *Philosophical Forum*, 1 (1968): 38-72.

Further References

Phenomenological Reduction

Aguirre, Antonio. *Genetische Phänom-enologie und Reduktion: Zur Letzbeg-rundung der Wissenschaft aus der radika-len Skepsis im Denken E. Husserls.* Hague: Nijhoff, 1970.

Ballard, Edward G. "On the Method of Phenomenological Reduction, Its Pre-suppositions and Its Future" in *Life-World and Consciousness,* ed. Lester E. Embree. Evanston: Northwestern Uni-versity Press, 1972, pp. 101-24.

Bednarski, Juliusz. "Two Aspects of Hus-serl's Reduction: Bracketing and Reflec-tion." *Philosophy Today,* 4 (1960), 208-22.

Boehm, Rudolf. "Basic Reflections on Hus-serl's Phenomenological Reduction." *In-ternational Philosophical Quarterly,* 5 (1965), 183-202.

Bossert, Phillip J. "The Sense of the 'Epoché' and 'Reduction' in Husserl's Philoso-phy." *Journal of the British Society for Phenomenology,* 5 (1974), 243-55.

Fink, Eugen. "Reflexionen zu Husserls phänomenologischer Reduktion." *Tijdschrift voor Filosofie,* 33 (1971), 540-58.

Kockelmans, Joseph J. "Phenomenologico-Psychological and Transcendental Re-ductions in Husserl's 'Crisis' " *Analecta Husserliana,* 2 (1972), 78-89.

Lowitt, Alexandre. "l' 'epoche' de Husserl et le doute de Descartes." *Revue de Métaphysique et de Morale,* 62 (1957), 399-415.

Macann, Christopher. "Genetic Production and the Transcendental Reduction." *Journal of the British Society for Phenomenology,* 2 (1971), 28-34.

Prufer, Thomas. "Reduction and Constitu-tion" in *Ancients and Moderns,* ed. John K. Ryan. Washington: The Catholic Uni-versity of America Press, 1970, pp. 341-43.

Scanlon, John. "The Epoché and Phenomenological Anthropology." *Re-search in Phenomenology,* 2 (1972), 95-109.

Schmitt, Richard. "Husserl's Transcen-dental-Phenomenological Reduction." *Philosophy and Phenomenological Re-search,* 20 (1959-60), 238-45.

Spiegelberg, Herbert. "Epoché without Re-duction: Some Replies to My Critics." *Journal of the British Society for Phenomenology,* 5 (1974), 256-61.

Ströker, Elisabeth. "Das Problem der 'epoche' in der Philosophie Edmund Husserls." *Analecta Husserliana,* 1 (1971), 170-85.

Tran-Duc-Thao. "Les origines de la réduction phénoménologique chez Husserl." *Deucalion,* 3 (1950), 128-42.

Eidetic Intuition

Bruzina, Ronald C. *Logos and Eidos: The Concept in Phenomenology.* The Hague: Mouton, 1970.

De Marneffe, J. "Bergson's and Husserl's Concepts of Intuition." *Philosophical Quarterly* (Axsualner, India), 33(1960), 169-80.

Henry, Michel. *L'essence de la manifesta-tion.* Paris: Presses Universitaires de France, 1963.

Kersten, Frederick. "On Understanding Idea and Essence in Husserl and Ingarden." *Analecta Husserliana,* 2 (1972), 55-63.

Levin, David Michael. "Induction and Hus-serl's Method of Eidetic Variation." *Phi-losophy and Phenomenological Re-search,* 29 (1968-69), 1-15.

———. "Husserlian Essences Reconsid-ered" in *Explorations in Phe-nomenology,* ed. David Carr and

Edward S. Casey. The Hague: Nijhoff, 1973, pp. 169-83.

Levinas, Emmanuel. *The Theory of Intuition in Husserl's Phenomenology,* tr. André Orianne. Evanston: Northwestern University Press, 1973.

Linke, Paul. "Beobachten und Schauen." *Vierteljahrsschrift für philosophische Pedagogik,* 2, pp. 44-57.

Pietersma, Henry. "Intuition and Horizon in the Philosophy of Husserl." *Philosophy and Phenomenological Research,* 34 (1973-74), 95-101.

Sinha, Debabrata. "Phenomenology: A Break-Through to a New Intuitionism" in *Phänomenologie Heute: Festschrift für Ludwig Landgrebe.* The Hague: Nijhoff, 1972, pp. 27-48.

Strasser, Stephan. "Intuition und Dialektik in der Philosophie Edmund Husserls" in *Edmund Husserl 1859-1959.* The Hague: Nijhoff, 1959, pp. 148-53.

Intentionality

Anzembacher, Arno. *Die Intentionalität bei Thomas von Aquin und Edmund Husserl.* Munich: Oldenbourg, 1972.

Brand, Gerd. "Intentionality, Reduction and Intentional Analysis in Husserl's Later Manuscripts" in *Phenomenology: The Philosophy of Edmund Husserl and Its Interpretation,* ed. Joseph J. Kochelmans. New York: Doubleday, 1967, pp. 197-220.

Breton, Stanislaus. *Conscience et intentionalité.* Lyon: Vitte, 1956.

Carr, David. "Intentionality" in *Phenomenology and Philosophical Understanding,* ed. Edo Pivcevic. New York: Cambridge University Press, 1975, pp. 17-36.

Chisholm, Roderick M. "Intentionality" in *Encyclopedia of Philosophy,* IV. New York: Macmillan, 1970, pp. 201-4.

Claesges, Ulrich. "Intentionality and Transcendence: on the Constitution of Material Nature." *Analecta Husserliana,* 2 (1972), 283-91.

De Murault, André. "Les deux dimensions de l'intentionnalité husserlienne." *Revue de Theologie et de Philosophie,* 8 (1958), 188-202.

De Waelhens, Alphonse. "The Phenomenological Concept of Intentionality," tr. A. Fisher. *Philosophy Today,* 6 (1962), 3-13.

Gurwitsch, Aron. "Towards a Theory of Intentionality." *Philosophy and Phenomenological Research,* 30 (1969-70), 354-67.

Levinas, Emmanuel. "Intentionalité et sensation." *Revue Internationale de Philosophie,* 71(1965), 34-54.

Mohanty, Jitendranath. *The Concept of Intentionality.* St. Louis: W. H. Green, 1972.

Moreau, J. "The Problem of Intentionality and Classical Thought." *International Philosophical Quarterly,* 1 (1961), 215-34.

Morrison, James. "Husserl and Brentano on Intentionality." *Philosophy and Phenomenological Research,* 31 (1970-71), 27-46.

Sartre, Jean-Paul. "Intentionality: A Fundamental Idea of Husserl's Phenomenology," tr. Joseph P. Fell. *Journal of the British Society for Phenomenology,* 1 (1970), 4-5.

Souche-Dagues, D. *Le developpement de l'intentionalité dans la phénoménologie husserlienne.* The Hague: Nijhoff, 1972.

Spiegelberg, Herbert. "Der Begriff der Intentionalität in der Scholastik, bei Brentano und bei Husserl." *Philosophische Hefte,* 5 (1936), 75-91.

Noema

Dreyfus, Hubert. "The Perceptual Noema: Gurwitsch's Crucial Contribution" in *Life-World and Consciousness,* ed. Lester E. Embree. Evanston: Northwestern University Press, 1972, pp. 135-70.

Funke, Gerhard. "A Crucial Question in Transcendental Phenomenology: What Is Appearance in Its Appearing?" *Journal of the British Society for Phenomenology,* 4 (1973), 47-60.

Gurwitsch, Aron. "On the Intentionality of Consciousness" in *Philosophical Essays in Memory of Edmund Husserl,* ed. Marvin Farber. Cambridge: Harvard University Press, 1940, pp. 65-83.

Holmes, Richard. "An Explication of Husserl's Theory of Noema." *Research in Phenomenology,* 5 (1975), pp. 143-53.

Kersten, Frederick. "Husserl's Doctrine of Noesis-Noema" in *Phenomenology: Continuation and Criticism,* ed. F. Kersten and R. Zaner. The Hague: Nijhoff, 1973, pp. 114-44.

Küng, Guido. "World as Noema and as Referent." *Journal of the British Society for Phenomenology,* 3 (1972), 15-26.

Mohanty, Jitendranath. "A Note on the Doctrine of Noetic-Noematic Correlation." *Analecta Husserliana,* 2 (1972), 317-21.

Horizon

Kuhn, Helmut. "The Phenomenological Concept of 'Horizon' " in *Philosophical Essays in Memory of Edmund Husserl*, ed. Marvin Farber. Cambridge: Harvard University Press, 1940, 106-23.

Pietersma, Henry. "The Concept of Horizon." *Analecta Husserliana*, 2 (1972), 278-82.

Schmidt, Helmut. "Der Horizontbegriff Husserls in Anwendung auf die ästhetische Erfahrung." *Zeitschrift für philosophische Forschung*, 21 (1967), 499-511.

Schrag, Calvin O. "The Life-World and Its Historical Horizon" in *Patterns of the Life-World*, ed. James M. Edie *et al.* Evanston: Northwestern University Press, 1970, pp. 107-22.

Schuhmann, Karl. *Die Fundamentalbetrachtung der Phänomenologie. Zum Weltproblem in der Philosophie Edmund Husserls*. The Hague: Nijhoff, 1971.

Life-World

Biemel, Walter. "Réflexions à propos des recherches husserliennes de la Lebenswelt." *Tijdschrift voor Filosofie*, 33 (1971), 659-83.

Brand, Gerd. *Die Lebenswelt: Eine Philosophie des konkreten Apriori*. Berlin: de Gruyter, 1971.

Claesges, Ulrich. "Zweideutigkeiten in Husserls Lebenswelt Begriff" in *Perspektiven Transzendental Phänomenologischer Forschung*. The Hague: Nijhoff 1972, pp. 85-101.

Décleve, Henri, "La Lebenswelt selon Husserl." *Laval Théologique et Philosophique*, 27 (1971), 151-61.

De Laguna, Grace A. "The Lebenswelt and the Cultural World." *Journal of Philosophy*, 57 (1960), 777-91.

Embree, Lester E. (ed.). *Life-World and Consciousness*. Evanston: Northwestern University Press, 1972.

Gadamer, Hans-Georg. "The Science of the Life-World." *Analecta Husserliana*, 2 (1972), 173-85.

Gurwitsch, Aron. "Problems of the Life-World" in *Phenomenology and Social Reality*, ed. Maurice Natanson. The Hague: Nijhoff, 1970, pp. 35-61.

Kersten, Frederick. "The Life-World Revisited." *Research in Phenomenology*, 1 (1971), 33-62.

Marx, Werner. "The Life-World and Its Particular Substructures" in *Reason and World*, ed. Marx Werner. The Hague: Nijhoff, 1971, pp. 62-76.

Misch, Georg. *Lebensphilosophie und Phänomenologie*. Stuttgart: Teubner, 1967.

Natanson, Maurice. "The 'Lebenswelt' " in *Phenomenology: Pure and Applied*, ed. Erwin W. Strauss. Pittsburgh: Duquesne University Press, 1964, pp. 75-93.

Wild, John. "Husserl's Life-World and the Lived-Body" in *Phenomenology: Pure and Applied*, ed. Erwin W. Strauss. Pittsburgh: Duquesne University Press, 1964, pp. 10-28.

Intersubjectivity

Carr, David. "The 'Fifth Meditation' and Husserl's Cartesianism." *Philosophy and Phenomenological Research*, 34 (1973-74), 14-35.

Danek, Jaromir. "Meditation Husserlienne sur l''Alter Ego.' " *Laval Théologique et Philosophique*, 31 (1975), 175-91.

Held, Klaus. "Das Problem der Intersubjektivität und die Idee einer phänomenologischen Transcendentalphilosophie" in *Perspectiven transcendental-phänomenologischer Forschung*, ed. Ulrich Claesges and Klaus Held. The Hague: Nijhoff, 1972, pp. 3-60.

Hyppolite, Jean. "L'Intersubjectivité chez Husserl" in *Figures de la pensée philosophique*. Paris: Presses universitaires de France, 1971, pp. 499-512.

Kelkel, Lothar. "Le problème de l'autre dans la phénoménologie transcendentale de Husserl." *Revue de la Métaphysique et de Morale*, 61 (1956), 40-52.

Kern, Iso. "Einleitung des Herausgebers" in Edmund Husserl, *Zur Phänomenologie der Intersubjektivität* in *Husserliana* 13: xvii-xlviii; *Husserliana*, 14: xvii-xxxv; *Husserliana*, 15: xv-lxx.

Lambert, Frank. "Husserl's Constitution of the Other in the Fifth Cartesian Meditation." *Dialogue*, 17 (1975), 44-51.

Lingis, Alphonso. "The Perception of Others." *Research in Phenomenology*, 2 (1972), 47-62.

McCormick, Peter. "Husserl and the Intersubjectivity Materials." *Research in Phenomenology*, 6 (1976).

Owens, Thomas J. *Phenomenology and Intersubjectivity Contemporary Interpreta-*

tions of the Interpersonal Situation. The Hague: Nijhoff, 1970.

Scheler, Max. *The Nature of Sympathy,* tr. Peter Heath. London: Routledge and Kegan Paul Ltd., 1954.

Sinn, Dieter. *Die transzendentale Intersubjektivität bei Edmund Husserl mit ihren Seinshorizonten.* Heidelberg, 1958. (Dissertation)

Stein, Edith. *On the Problem of Empathy.* The Hague: Nijhoff, 1970.

Waldenfels, Bernhard. *Das Zwischenreich des Dialogs. Sozialphilosophische Untersuchungen in Anschluss an Edmund Husserl.* The Hague: Nijhoff, 1971.

Zeltner, Hermann. "Das Ich und die Andern." *Zeitschrift für philosophische Forschung,* 13 (1959), 288-315.

PART THREE

Comparisons and Contrasts

Introduction

The articles in Part One ("Philosophical Themes") dealt mainly with reflections on familiar themes in the philosophical tradition. Part Two, "Phenomenological Concepts," presented a series of articles chosen to explicate themes peculiar to the detail of Husserl's phenomenology. The articles in this third and final part shift the emphasis from description to appraisal by attempting to mark out boundaries for some important comparisons and contrasts.

These articles can be grouped into three sets. The first set traces some of the interrelations between Husserl's phenomenology and such major traditions as Kantian philosophy, Idealism, Existentialism, Marxism, and Heidegger's philosophy. The second set, more narrow in its contemporary scope and mainly analytical, is concerned (respectively) with phenomenology and the philosophy of logic, linguistic analysis, and formal semantics. The third set consists of only one article, which attempts to focus several general issues which follow from the attempts to appraise phenomenological claims.

I

G.B. Madison's "Phenomenology and Existentialism: Husserl and the End of Idealism" tries to expose the incompatibility between phenomenology and Existentialism and the reasons for and consequences of this incompatibility.

Idealism, in Madison's sense, refers to the major tradition in philosophy which, since Plato, has construed philosophy in terms of the scientific ideal of rationality. This tradition interprets being preeminently as sense or essence and objects as nothing more than correlates of different acts of consciousness.

Madison takes up Husserl's intellectual context, the Greek rationalist tradition, which overcomes radical epistemological skepticism. The Greek ideal made reason conform to the natural order of things—an ideal which takes forms as diverse as Parmenidean metaphysics and Democritean atomism. Philosophy is a system, a strictly rigorous science. Husserl sees himself as part of that tradition, which since Descartes has taken the turn toward pure subjectivity. Hence, while maintaining the Greek view of philosophy as science, Husserl situates the task of constructing such a science in the domain of pure consciousness.

For Husserl, this concept of science is grounded in the presence of things to consciousness—what Husserl continually has in mind when he speaks of evidence as apodictic. And it is this apodictic evidence which is the basis of science (see Pietersma's article, above). The concept of epoche or reduction is designed to discover apodictic evidence in transcendental subjectivity. Husserl adds to the idea of the ground of science the Leibnizian idea of a *philosophical* science "as the systematic unity of all conceivable *a priori sciences*." Ironically, some contemporary analytic critics of Husserl, Madison suggests, fail to see the common ancestry and goal they share with phenomenologists: Leibniz and the goal of a unified science. Phenomenology is to be a science of all science—what Husserl ultimately will construe as a science of transcendental subjectivity.

How could Husserl inspire the Existentialists, given that his orientation was so much that of "a rationalist idealist, a scientific dogmatist"? According to Madison, the answer lies in the Existentialist exploitation of four ambiguities in Husserl's thought. First, Husserl hesitates between a view of science as a closed system and as infinitely open. Second, he combines an openness to phenomenological description with a rigidness about conceptual and linguistic apparatus. Third, he views experience two-sidedly; he is concerned about both the prepredicative domain of lived experience and the dominant role of sense perception. Finally, wonder is viewed, on the one hand, as both the beginning and the end of phenomenology, and on the other hand as only the beginning, with science as the end.

On the basis of these four ambiguities, Madison claims that the Husserl of Existentialism is far removed from the real Husserl. His world remains the idealist world, constituted by the transcendental ego in the endless streaming of time consciousness, a world of intuition, which of course not only the Existentialists but Heidegger too has repeatedly called into question. Madison thematizes this deeper opposition between Husserl and Heidegger in terms of a tension between Husserl's optimistic expectations of reason and Heidegger's tragic emphasis on contingency.

Does the existential rejection of Idealism in its Husserlian form involve irrationalism, and does the rejection of the idealist tradition in general involve the rejection of philosophy? Madison claims that "irrationalism is not a viable alternative to rationalism," and emphasizes the countertradition of philosophy as wisdom—a tradition which is still philosophy although it rejects the scientific ideal of philosophy. Philosophy, he concludes, can also be understood as a Socratic type of discipline which works at the continual criticism of the presuppositions and pretensions of science.

In "Husserl and Kant on the Pure Ego," J.J. Kockelmans examines Kant as a major influence on Husserl's ideal of philosophy. Husserl's move from a secondhand, negative view of Kant's philosophy as a form of skepticism to a firsthand, positive view of that philosophy as transcendental philosophy enabled him to develop twelve important criticisms of Kant, which Kockelmans outlines in detail. One of them, the criticism of Kant's conception of the ego, is the major theme of Kockelmans' paper.

Kockelmans describes four stages in the development of Husserl's mature view of the ego. First, in his early philosophy, before the *Logical Investigations*, Husserl hesitated over the physiological and psychological conception of the ego which Brentano and Helmholtz had advanced. Then, rejecting Natorp's neo-Kantian view that there is something more than the empirical ego, in the second of *Logical Investigations* (1913) Husserl opted for some kind of nonempirical ego. Third, he changed his position between 1912 and 1915 on whether the ego can be made into an object; and he claims, against Natorp, that the pure ego can be grasped intuitively and that its presence in the different modes of experience can be described phenomenologically. Finally, between 1916 and 1922 Husserl developed his mature account more closely by examining Kant's views on the ego in light of the fourfold distinction arrived at in *Ideen II*: between the everyday ego, the pure ego, the psychic subject, and the personal or cultural ego.

Kockelmans cites passages from the *Critique of Pure Reason* as backdrop for appreciating Husserl's views, especially on Kant's distinction in the deduction of the pure concept of the understanding between the combination of the manifold of representations and the synthetic unity of the manifold. The former is the work of the subject, representing the synthetic unity of the manifold. But this representation presupposes an original unity of pure apperception, already given in intuition, that Kant also calls the transcendental unity of self-consciousness. In other words, as Kockelmans puts it, "all my representations in any given intuition must be subject to that condition under which alone I can ascribe them to the identical self as *my* representations." The second passage from the *Critique* is Kant's discussion of the paralogism of pure reason, where Kant speaks of the "I" as the simple form of consciousness that is presupposed in all thought prior to experience, a mere presence which accompanies all concepts. The ego is not a representation but the form of representation in general.

Kockelmans goes on to show Kantian elements in Husserl's later (1916-28) conception of the ego—Kant's doctrine of transcendental unity of apperception whereby the ego as a thinking entity is necessarily present to itself, and the idea that the identity of the ego has a necessary correlate in the necessary uniformity in the world of objects. Here as elsewhere, however, Husserl rejects Kant's continuing commitment to the idea of the thing-in-itself, as well as Kant's view of the ego as purely psychological. Nonetheless, Husserl credits Kant with the intention of developing a transcendental theory of the ego with the help of Leibniz's theory of monads (see Landgrebe's paper, above). But for Husserl, like Kant, the relation between the unity of the pure ego and the constitution of the world remained puzzling.

In part V Kockelmans shows an extremely important development: from the transcendental view of *Cartesian Meditations* (1931) to what we might call, in Husserl's special sense, the teleological view of *Crisis* (ca. 1936). He concludes by showing how Husserl's return to the Cartesian ideal of an absolutely radical philosophy departed from both the modified empiricism of his many years under Brentano's influence and from his later concern for Kant's failure to eliminate the split between the phenomenon and the noumenon. Husserl sees the transcendental subject-object *correlation* as prior to the mundane subject-object correlation. This transcendental correlation is a kind of horizon, the subjectivity of the

subject (see Van Peursen's article, above).

The well-foundedness of this view is precisely what Heidegger was to call into question (see Biemel's article, below). Heidegger insisted on the distinction between the ego as a subject and the ego as a self. The former was to be characterized in terms of consciousness whereas the latter was to be viewed in terms of its finite transcendence. And, for Heidegger, the ego as self is fundamental—not the ego as subject. One might say that Heidegger's view of the ego as self is largely a development of Husserl's somewhat neglected theme of the material a priori and his renewed effort (in the thirties) to deal with the ego and temporalization.

Such relations between Husserl's phenomenology and Heidegger's are the subject of Walter Biemel's "Husserl's *Encyclopaedia Britannica* Article and Heidegger's Remarks Thereon." Noting the division of this article into three sections—the idea of a pure psychology, the relation of psychology to transcendental phenomenology, and the essence of transcendental phenomenology—Biemel asks why Husserl begins with pure psychology. Unlike general psychology, pure psychology is not concerned with physical presuppositions of mind, such as psychophysical causality, because Husserl thought that such presuppositions could not explain what is essential in the psychic. Rather, it is opposed to empirical psychology in the way geometry is opposed to surveying, in the way the essential is opposed to the factual. Hence the task of pure psychology is to describe "the a priori set of types without which the I, and respectively the we, consciousness, the objectivity of consciousness, and thereby mental being in general would be unthinkable."

But why does Husserl call pure psychology 'phenomenological' psychology? After examining Husserl's concepts of the natural versus the reflexive attitude, intentionality, and the Husserlian senses of "phenomenon," Biemel says that this kind of description involves the work of the reductions, which bracket the world of objects and reveal the essential character of each experience. These moves correspond, respectively, to the phenomenological and the eidetic reductions; the first accents the psychical as phenomenon, the second the "invariant essential forms" of the lived experiences.

But how does pure or phenomenological psychology serve as a propaedeutic to transcendental phenomenology? By "transcendental" Husserl understands the kind of consciousness which constitutes what is objective—and the problem of a transcendental phenomenology is to show just how any category, objectivity, or experience whatsoever arises from specific modes of consciousness. The world is no longer the horizon but is constituted as the world by transcendental subjectivity. Transcendental phenomenology aims at exhibiting how the world is constituted by the transcendental "I", preeminently by means of temporalization (see Brough's article, above).

In the last section of the *Encyclopaedia Britannica* draft Husserl deals with the relation between phenomenology and ontology. The problem, as Biemel sees it, is whether ontology—for Husserl—is only a formal discipline which is concerned exclusively with the structures of constitution. Husserl never provided the developed ontology he thought essential. He continued to take universal ontology (quite sketchily) to be the work of an eidetic phenomenology which ultimately strives to unveil a new view of mankind. This belief in the progress of rational self-reflection sounded the theme of the historicity of mankind, which was to preoccupy Heidegger in such a different way.

Heidegger's remarks on the early draft of the *Encyclopaedia Britannica* article, which were made in the same year that *Sein und Zeit* was published, contest Husserl's view that no entity can constitute the domain of the transcendental and propose, instead, that such an entity exists and can be construed as *Dasein*. Heidegger writes: "The constitution of the existence of *Dasein* makes possible the transcendental constitution of all which is positive." He agrees with Husserl that the nature of entities as such must be investigated, but claims that such an investigation must not take the form of a theory of the transcendental ego but of an existential analytic of *Dasein*. Husserl's theory involves the problematic doctrine of the reduction; Heidegger's does not. The key difference, as Biemel sees it, lies in Husserl's separating the transcendental ego from the world, whereas Heidegger's *Dasein* is already and always in the world. Heidegger's marginal notes on Husserl's draft frequently return to the point that man is not just "pure ego" but "being-in-the-world." Heidegger insists that Husserl's version of the transcendental ego relies on an insufficiently differentiated sense of "is," whereby everything is construed as really existing in terms of the one spatio-temporal world. Heidegger wants to enlarge this restricted sense of "is" by stressing facticity, time, different senses of "world," concrete existence—themes he was to develop later in his own philosophy until the famous turnabout (*die Kehre*) of the thirties.

The final article in this first section turns aside from any immanent critique of phenomenology, such as Heidegger's, and instead juxtaposes phenomenology with an external point of view. Marx Wartofsky's "Consciousness, Praxis, and Reality: Marxism versus Phenomenology," after showing a common point of departure for the two philosophies, examines the viability of phenomenology given the Marxist critique. This examination proceeds in terms of three points of reference: the initial problem of each philosophy, then the sharpest form of their antithesis, and finally what Wartofsky calls the mediations each introduces into its initial formulation. The pervasive question is how consciousness is related to reality. And the general conclusion is that phenomenology fails "to give consciousness a social or nonsubjective character."

What set of problems generates both
Marxism and phenomenology? The latter
begins, for Wartofsky, with the problem
of reappropriating the object. Objectivity
is the work, finally, of the subject, and
begins with the critique of the constitutive activity of the ego, which is seen as a
construction of the world rather than the
other way round. In short, the issue at the
outset is whether the ego or the world is
primordial. For the Marxist, the world is
primordial, whereas for the phenomenologist the ego is primordial. For the
Marxist, consciousness rises from the activity of production, whereas for the
phenomenologist both production relations and family relations arise from consciousness. "It is only in social practice
that the Ego becomes an Ego, namely,
becomes capable of the actual production
of a world in its own image: not in reflection merely, but in the world itself."
Phenomenology, on the contrary, imposes consciousness on the body, the
world, and history itself.

Wartofsky proposes three mediations
of these dichotomies. First, phenomenologists attempt to save Marx from the
Marxists by showing that the self-activity
and interiority of the ego are part of
Marx's doctrine, despite Marxists' attempts to deal with consciousness as an
epiphenomenon. The second mediation
shows that the phenomenological primacy of the subjective leads ultimately to
the closedness of the ego. The third mediation thereby becomes the problem of rescuing subjectivity from solipsism without rendering subjectivity redundant by
adopting the standpoint of a "theorized
praxis." "Theorized praxis" comes to
the view that such a problem can be
solved only outside philosophy, in practical rather than purely theoretical intervention.

There is fault or error in phenomenology's divorce from historical
praxis, in its "passivity and a-historicity"
when seen from Marx's perspective on
man as a social, historical being. This is
the viewpoint Wartofsky himself adopts
in his conclusion.

II

Whereas the first set of articles takes a
largely historical approach to appraising
Husserl's phenomenology, the second
employs argumentative strategies; it focuses on the single domain of language
and meaning as surveyed from an analytic
standpoint.

Frege's 1894 review of Husserl's *Philosophy of Arithmetic* is mainly critical of
Husserl's distinctions between number
and multiplicity (which he finds not sharp
enough) and between the relations of difference and connection (which he finds
lacking). Frege's basic contention is that
Husserl's treatment of number is naive in
that it considers number-statements as
assertions about neither concepts nor the
extension of concepts. Though Husserl
rejects the view that a number is like a
heap and is a property of something like a
heap, he loses himself in a psychologism
which construes both objects and concepts as presentations. Frege acknowledges Husserl's concern with the nature
of the act of presentation but claims that
he blurs the distinctions between presentation and concept, presenting and thinking, the subjective and the objective.
Husserl's subsequent treatment of multiplicity is thereby equivocal, depending
on whether multiplicity is seen as a presentation or as something objective.

In light of this criticism of what he calls
Husserl's "psychological-logical mode of
thought," Frege turns to Husserl's
treatment of definitions. He contends
that Husserl has neglected the distinction
between a concept's content and its extension, so that Husserl's definitions become extensional ones only. Frege dissociates himself from this kind of procedure, where words and their combinations refer to presentations only. He
characterizes "psychological logicians"
as concerned with the sense of words
(their presentations), whereas "mathematicians" are concerned with the reference of the words, "the matter itself."
Frege grants that the definitions of mathematics are extensional, but he claims

that a concept and its extension are not identical.

Turning to a number of details, Frege first scrutinizes Husserl's view that a number-statement refers to the totality of objects counted and that number belongs to the extension of the concept. The problem is that Husserl refuses to identify the totality with the extension of a concept, so that he is forced to hold the unfounded view that a concept under which either no object falls or infinitely many objects fall involves no totality. Frege criticizes Husserl's view of the genesis of a totality. He claims that following Husserl's instructions does not enable him to form a totality, for—Husserl's doctrine notwithstanding—both contents and their connections must be presented together. Frege's doctrine is that an assertion about a concept is contained in the number-statement itself.

Frege then turns to three basic issues about the nature of numbers: (1) reconciling the sameness of numbers with their distinguishability, (2) the numbers zero and one, and (3) the large numbers. On all three issues he criticizes Husserl sharply: first by replying to Husserl's criticisms of Frege's *Foundations of Arithmetic*, then by showing how Husserl's construal of zero and one as negative answers to the question "How many?" is inadequate, and finally by demonstrating how construing numbers as presentations which are always finite entails that there cannot be infinitely many numbers.

Frege has shown the first part of Husserl's book to be psychologistic, whereas (for Frege) the second part represents the beginning of some attempt to overcome the difficulties of logical psychologism. The second part is concerned to focus attention on what we have presentations of rather than exclusively on the presentations. Concepts are taken as largely objective when Husserl talks of the *species* of the concept number or numbers in themselves. But even here, as throughout the book, Frege is dissatisfied with Husserl's apparently unclear grasp of the basic distinctions between real and objec-

tive entities. A number is not real, but it is, Frege claims, objective. This objectivity of number is what logical psychologism has neglected.

Although this review is extremely critical of Husserl, it does not do justice to some of the fruitful areas of agreement between Husserl and Frege. The recently published Husserl-Frege correspondence corrects the mistaken one-sided view of Husserl as simply Frege's follower in one area of the philosophy of logic.

Other substantive issues that separate Husserl from the largely Fregean-inspired contemporary views on the philosophy of logic emerge in Ernst Tugendhat's article, "Phenomenology and Linguistic Analysis." Tugendhat begins by underlining his view that philosophical positions either complement or exclude one another but cannot coexist, since each makes truth claims. Since he holds that phenomenology and linguistic analysis differ only in method, to the degree that each makes different truth claims they cannot coexist. He proposes then an examination of the opposition between phenomenology and linguistic analysis with a view to the possibility of a later examination of the "more important confrontation" between linguistic analysis and hermeneutics. He limits himself to Husserl, and the issue he explores is whether starting with intuitional acts which refer to objects is, in the end, a viable procedure for dealing adequately with meanings. (See Patocka's article, above, as well.)

Husserl holds that an expression is meaningful to the extent that it has received meaning from a "meaning-conferring act" (see Welton's article, above). The key concept here is act, and this concept derives from an intuitive analysis of consciousness as essentially intuitional. Hence meaning for Husserl is first construed with the help of concepts from different areas of the analysis of consciousness.

The result of this borrowing for Husserl's theory of meaning is "that nominal expressions become the model for all expressions." However, how are nominal expressions to be understood? A nominal meaning and the essence of its related act, Husserl holds, are not identical. He changes his view of nominal expressions later (in *Ideas*) and posits a connection between differentiation on one side and the act (*noesis*) and those on the side of the object (*noema*). But there are problems here also, since the *new* identity between the meaning of the expression and the ways in which the object is given (*Gegenstand-im-Wie*) seems just as questionable as the old. Moreover, the noematic interpretation of *non*naming expressions seems faulty, because Tugendhat raises the objection: "When an expression does not signify an object, ...there is no object there for which the meaning could be understood as its mode of givenness."

Can the phenomenological attempt to assimilate all meanings to nominal ones be carried through? Tugendhat begins by considering which of the two alternative accounts of the object of a declarative sentence is correct: the object the subject refers to or the state of affairs to which the sentence as a whole refers. Husserl holds that both accounts are correct because, in different ways, an expression functions as the subject of true predications in each view and hence stands for an object. After criticizing Husserl's hesitation between these two views, Tugendhat maintains that Husserl's attempt fails because statements have been considered too much as wholes and not enough in terms of their minor structure. He points out, for example, that Husserl's attempts to understand a predicative sentence in terms of a theory of categorical acts does not work. But this failure concerns something so central to the nature of the predicative sentence that any starting point which leads to such a failure must simply be abandoned. Hence, construing acts in terms of a doctrine of intentionality as a "referring directedness" must be rejected because it forces on us, finally, a misunderstanding of both predicative sentences and predicates. A similar conclusion follows from a consideration of

Husserl's treatment of conjunction and disjunction in terms of the same doctrine of categorical acts. Tugendhat concludes that the theory of categorical acts as a means of explaining different levels of statements breaks down completely because of "a hopelessly inadequate starting point." He suggests that the derivative objectification expressed in nominalization could be better explained in terms of viewing an "ideal" object as the result not of syntheses but of abstractions "based on linguistic utterances in accordance with their conditions of use."

In a final section Tugendhat turns from meanings to references to objects. Again, his claim is that "starting with references to objects prevents not only a satisfactory clarification of meanings but a satisfactory clarification of the reference to objects." This problem arises from the discrepancy between Husserl's linguistic orientation in the first edition of *Logical Investigations* and the psychological orientation of the fifth edition. The result is an untenable view of objects which fatally hesitates between understanding objects as subjects of true predications (a linguistic view) and representations of a representation (a psychological view). Husserl's advocating the second view entailed the primacy of a psychological account and, with it, commitment to the primacy of names in sentences (instead of vice versa).

Some of the controversial background for Tugendhat's critique can be found in Guido Küng's article, "The Phenomenological Reduction as Epoche and Explication." Küng's purpose is to scrutinize the different notions of the phenomenological reduction in light of work in contemporary semantic theory on concepts such as sense, referent, and explication. He claims that the key to evaluating Husserl's transcendental phenomenology is the coherence of the analogical transposition from ordinary to metaphysical semantics. His attempt to detail and substantiate his claim follows what is largely a developmental approach.

Küng begins with an account of Husserl's early views on a descriptive psychology, based on the reflective, indeed intuitive grasp of immanently given mental acts—what Husserl called 'inner perception'. Husserl developed these views by elaborating on what he had learned from Brentano and Brentano's critics (both Natorp and Frege). By 1900 or 1901 Husserl's phenomenology, as descriptive phenomenology, turned on two doctrines: "the perception of real mental particulars and . . .the intuitive grasp of ideal universals." The first doctrine, however, involved the exclusion of the object of external perception. Husserl now began to revise this anti-Brentano view, since he found that describing the acts of external perception seemed to entail describing their objects as well. Moreover, both the Munich group (Lipp's students) and the Graz group (Meinong's students) were dissatisfied with construing the aims of such a descriptive psychology only in terms of essences of mental particulars. Finally, Husserl discovered that the domain of inner perception, to which he was restricting descriptive psychology, was as problematic as that of external perception. Husserl therefore tried to find a way to admit into the phenomenological domain "the intentional correlation of all mental acts," first by turning to the concept of Cartesian doubt and then by the skeptical concept of epoche. The latter enabled Husserl to avoid all questions about the actual existence of the objects whose appearance was the concern of phenomenological description.

The epoche had brought into phenomenology the distinction between the external object as an actual entity and as an intentional object. Since neither the causal nor the representationalist account of this interrelation between reality and appearance had proved satisfactory, Husserl turned to Frege's account of sense-reference. The result was twofold. Husserl rejected his earlier view that meaning is a sort of universal kind (*species*) in favor of the view that meaning is *sui generis*. But he failed to appreciate the role of the referent in Frege's theory. Hence the epoche was taken too broadly as excluding consideration both of factual questions about the actual existence of the referent of external perception *and* questions concerning the notion of the referent itself.

This notion of referent, however, is not the current notion of a universe of discourse, but a metaphysical notion about a particular kind of appearance which is already a conceptualization of reality and not reality itself. Unlike Russellian semantics, therefore, contemporary possible-world semantics allows for metaphysical illusion: the possibility that an entire ontology may be mistaken. This shift from the ordinary to the metaphysical relation between sense and referent involves a shift from taking the ordinary referent metaphysically as "a kind of noematic pole."

Including the noema or intentional object as such in phenomenology inclined Husserl to stress the noematic aspect of description over the noetic. Both aspects involve analysis of the infinite hierarchies of sense. Phenomenology becomes the analysis of the correlation between *noesis* and *noema*, the constitution of sense. This descriptive work of transcendental phenomenology can be viewed in terms of the notion of "explication," which is one of the forms of meaning analysis analytic philosophers practice.

Explication involves the move from expressions of ordinary language to explicitly defined expressions "of a language with an explicit system of exact definitions." Küng believes that construing the aims of transcendental phenomenology as explication enables us to drop the problematic talk about epoche for simpler talk about "translating all our knowledge claims into a most accurate scientific language." This ontological or Kantian way into phenomenology, as opposed to the Cartesian and the psychological way, views phenomenology as explaining the necessary features of our conceptual schemes (see Kern, above). Phenomenological explication, unlike ordinary explication, however, does not translate terms into exact places in an explicitly stated system of definitions, but into inexact places in the process of transcendental constitution.

Transcendental phenomenology can be distinguished from epistemology by insisting on the distinction between a descriptive and an evaluative discipline. Husserl was increasingly discontent with the Cartesian epistemological entry to phenomenology because of the necessity of raising evaluative questions prematurely—that is, before, and often in place of, the descriptive issues. Küng then shows the connections between Husserl's dissatisfaction with the Cartesian approach and contemporary attacks on the myth of the given. Küng opts for a modified Cartesian program which abandons the notion of the absolute certainty of inner experience but retains the importance of the unique kind of certainty that is characteristic of inner experience.

III

The last article, P. McCormick's "Phenomenology and Metaphilosophy," stands outside both the historical and the analytic concerns of the first two groups. Its aim is to articulate, if only in a provisional way, several metaphilosophical issues which seem to obscure the confrontations between phenomenology and other traditions.

Using Rorty's classification of three groups of philosophers in terms of the methodological issue and the criteriological issue, McCormick examines the first two categories, Husserl and Heidegger. The criteriological issue is construed more broadly in terms of a metaphilosophical issue, and the general concern of the paper is whether phenomenological claims can be criticized from non-phenomenological standpoints.

After detailing particular senses of the terms 'metaphilosophy' and 'phenomenology', McCormick examines Heidegger and Husserl in light of the methodological and criteriological issues. He isolates an example of Heidegger's later thinking about language in *Unterwegs zur Sprache* and calls attention to both the terminological and argumentative problems in appraising such claims. The result shows that Heidegger rejects both the kind of nominalism that follows upon the methodological issue Rorty defines and the nature of the criteria in the criteriological issue. McCormick then examines, in similar detail, an instance of the early Husserl's reflections on problems of logical psychologism. Here the criteriological issue is seen to be pertinent, but the methodological issue is rejected, as in Heidegger's case (though for different reasons).

With these two detailed analyses available, McCormick isolates the general features that both issues seem to presuppose in a confrontation between phenomenology and linguistic analysis. The opposition between them is interpreted in terms of a "metaphilosophical difference." After detailing one of Husserl's later claims about logic in *Formal and Transcendental Logic* (1929), the article contrasts such claims with those in Heidegger's *What Is Called Thinking*. What becomes clear is the different kind of problem involved in adjudicating disputes between analytic philosophers and phenomenologists on the one hand, and such different phenomenologists as Husserl and Heidegger on the other. The former set of problems is qualitatively different from the latter. And this difference is termed a 'metaphilosophical difference' in the sense that resolving it does not entail argument *with* common paradigms of philosophy so much as *between* paradigms. A final section of the paper explores several questions about the consequences of such a difference for appraising the claims of phenomenology.

Phenomenology and Existentialism: Husserl and the End of Idealism

GARY B. MADISON

Phenomenology and existentialism—these two terms which are so often uttered together in one breath—are just as often taken to designate a single, coherent school of philosophy. What, however, is the relation between phenomenology and existentialism? Just what relation obtains between the philosophy of Husserl, the originator of contemporary phenomenology, and that of modern "existentialists" such as Heidegger, Sartre, and Merleau-Ponty? Historically, Husserl was introduced to the general public through the work of the "existentialists" in Germany, France, and America, and this fact served to generate a widespread belief that contemporary existentialism represents the proper culimination of Husserlian phenomenology. In recent years, however, a number of Husserl scholars have attempted to present a view of Husserl which completely bypasses existentialism;[1] many such scholars would even want to maintain that existentialism, far from being the legitimate heir to Husserlian phenomenology, is instead but a deviant offshoot of the former. Thus the marriage between phenomenology and existentialism is turning out to be increasingly unstable and may even end in an official divorce in the near future—for reasons of incompatibility between the partners. It is the aim of my paper to expose this incompatibility and to explore some of the reasons for it, as well as some of the consequences which follow from it.

1. Idealism and the Ideal of Science

"Philosophy as science, as serious, rigorous, indeed apodictically rigorous, science—the dream is over."[2] This statement of Husserl, written not long before his death, has been interpreted by certain commentators, Roman Ingarden among them,[3] as a confession on Husserl's part of a loss of faith in what had been his life-long goal: the ideal of an absolutely fundamental science. The evidence—and the context of the statement—indicate, on the contrary, that Husserl never faltered in his faith in science, although he did at times, earlier on, undergo crises of doubt, crises from which nonetheless his faith emerged stronger and purer than ever.[4] Rather, Husserl in this notorious statement was expressing his profound disappointment over the direction the philosophy he had labored all his life to set up on a firm footing—phenomenology—was taking in the hands of students and disciples in whom he had formerly placed his full confidence and highest hopes. Above all, Husserl saw himself as deserted by that student in whom he had placed his greatest trust and who, in fact, upon his request, had succeeded him in his chair at Freiburg: Martin Heidegger. Husserl viewed Heidegger's "existentialism" as

247

an unfortunate resurgence of "irrationalism," and Husserl's last work, the *Crisis*, can in fact be read as a last attempt to reassert, against the current trend toward "irrationalism," the infinite power of reason and the ideal of a perfect, all-embracing science.[5]

Phenomenology for Husserl was

a method by which I want to establish, against mysticism and irrationalism, a kind of superrationalism which transcends the old rationalism as inadequate and yet vindicates its inmost objectives.[6]

The only solution Husserl could see to the contemporary, existential crisis of Western man—and which he attempted to set forth in the *Crisis*—lay in the reassertion of the ancient Greek ideal of pure science:

The universally, apodictically grounded and grounding science arises now as the necessarily highest function of mankind, as I said, namely, as making possible mankind's development into a personal autonomy and into an all-encompassing autonomy for mankind—the idea which represents the driving force of life for the highest stage of mankind.

...Reason is precisely that which man *qua* man, in his innermost being, is aiming for, that which alone can satisfy him, make him "blessed".[7]

Now *the idea of an absolute science is the ultimate expression of the idealist/rationalist spirit*. Idealism tends toward science as toward its natural fulfillment. It postulates, with Hegel, the identity of the rational and the real, for to say that reality is supremely knowable—that is, is the fitting object of a science—is to say that it is thoroughly rational. But if the real is rational, it is also ideal. To say that the real is essentially knowable is to say that it is indeed nothing but essence or meaning. Idealism reduces being to meaning. Thus in this paper I shall use the terms *rationalism* and *idealism* interchangeably and shall, moreover, use them to refer to that tradition in philosophy—"the" tradition—which from Plato to our days has sought to identify philosophy with science and which has viewed science as the highest and most noble goal of

mankind (to paraphrase Husserl). This is the tradition Heidegger labeled "metaphysics" and within which I wish to situate Husserl. I wish thereby to suggest that the existential revolt against idealism necessarily entails a break between existentialism and phenomenology.

If the mark of idealism is that in attempting to achieve a science of reality it reduces being to meaning, namely, "idealizes" reality, the philosophy of Husserl is a thoroughgoing idealism. A perfect example of this idealism is to be found in *Ideas*, chapters 11 and 12, where Husserl attempts to give a phenomenological account of the "object."

The object itself, the "real" object, the object *simpliciter*, Husserl says, cannot be reduced to the noema—to, that is, any given *appearance* of the object. This is to say that in the case of sensuous objects we can never achieve adequate evidence: there are always possible appearances which are not now given, which transcend the consciousness of the moment. But the Husserlian phenomenologist cannot, methodologically, permit himself to make any statements about that for which he does not have sufficient evidence; he cannot say anything about non-reduced transcendencies. What then does Husserl do? He must either simply refuse to give a phenomenological account of the "real" object—and thereby admit limits to the scope of phenomenology, the supposedly all-embracing science—or he must somehow circumvent the difficulty by transforming the very *being* of the object into its *meaning* for consciousness. It is this latter course which Husserl, none to our surprise, takes. Since true being is defined as that which is the correlate of a consciousness which intends or intuits it in an original and perfectly adequate manner,[8] and since, as we have seen, the object cannot show itself completely in any given series of appearances, the true being of the object can only be an *idea* in the Kantian sense, that is, the idea of the totality of all its possible appearances. We *can* have an adequate intuition of an idea, and so if the "real" object is to have meaning this can only be as idea. As Husserl says:

Where the dator intuition is of a *transcending* character, the objective factor cannot come to be adequately given; what can alone be given here is the *Idea* of such a factor. . . .

But *as "Idea"* (in the Kantian sense), *the complete givenness is nevertheless prescribed*—as a connexion of endless processes of continuous appearing, absolutely fixed in its essential type, or, as the field for these processes, *a continuum of appearances* determined *a priori*, possessing different but determinate dimensions, governed by an established dispensation of essential order.[9]

This is why, of course, *vision* (of the object) in Husserl's philosophy is basically *constitution* (of the object). The ineterpreter of Husserl should, in the last analysis, experience no difficulty in reconciling the seemingly opposed notions of intuition (and description) and constitution for Husserlian intuitionism, phenomenological description, far from being the mark of a realist philosophy, is the most perfect expression of a thoroughgoing idealism. As Ricoeur has remarked, "Husserl would be understood if the intentionality which culminates in seeing were recognized to be a creative vision."[10]

This is why A. Dondeyne is perfectly justified in speaking of an "idealism of meaning" in phenomenology.[11] We would only add, for our part, that an Idealism of meaning is not a lesser form of idealism (weaker than, say, an idealism which simply denies the real existence of the object altogether) but the highest and most sophisticated form of idealism.[12] This is to say that Husserl's "transcendental idealism" is not a watered-down or deviant version of idealism but the very epitome of the idealist mentality and the culmination of a long tradition which is in fact the dominant, orthodox tradition in philosophy, almost (but not entirely, as we shall see) coextensive with philosophy. This is the tradition which has conceived of philosophy as the search for the Truth, for Knowledge, for, in a

word, *Science*. This is the tradition, it might be added, which Nietzsche was attacking single-handedly when he dared to question the most fundamental of all the values of our rationalist/idealist tradition, the metaphysical value *par excellence*, the intrinsic value of *Truth*.[13]

If, then, post-Husserlian existential phenomenology has rejected idealism, it is because it has renounced the ideal of science (as the highest and noblest goal of mankind). The end of this ideal spells the end of idealism and, in fact—even though many latter-day "phenomenologists" prefer not to go so far as to recognize this further consequence[14]—the end of a long tradition in philosophy—the end, some might even say, of philosophy itself. An event as portentous as the "death of idealism" merits serious reflection, for, as is always the case when we have experienced the death of one we have known long and well, it is the meaning of our own lives which is unmistakably called into question.

2. Husserl and the Tradition

To properly understand Husserl and the true import of his philosophizing it is necessary—absolutely indispensable—to view him in the proper setting, in the context of the tradition of which he is the rightful heir and one of the most outstanding embodiments. Husserl was essentially—down to the very marrow of his intellectual bones, so to speak—a "Greek." One has only to reread his famous "Crisis" (Vienna) lecture[15] to become vividly aware of this. Husserl explicitly viewed himself as carrying on and in fact reasserting, in the face of the contemporary "skepticism" and "spiritual sickness"—typified for him by existentialism[16]—the ancient Greek ideal of pure science.

Spiritual Europe has a birthplace. . . .It is the ancient Greek nation in the seventh and sixth centuries B.C. Here there arises a *new sort of attitude* of individuals toward their surrounding world. And its consequence is the breakthrough of a completely new sort of spiritual structure, rapidly growing into a systematically self-enclosed cultural form; the Greeks called it *philosophy*. Correctly translated, in the original sense, that means nothing other than universal science, science of the universe, of the all-encompassing unity of all that is.[17]

For Husserl, phenomenology was to be the actual working out of the universal science, the science of the Totality, of "the all-encompassing unity of all that is." One does not, therefore, have to do hermeneutical violence to Husserl but only acquiesce in his self-interpretation in order to situate him in the rationalist tradition inaugurated by the Greeks in general and Plato in particular. Husserl in effect claims for himself the title "super-rationalist."[18] Husserl's great *optimism* in the powers of reason is the perfect echo to the optimism of the great Greek rationalists. This optimism justifies itself through its belief that the world is a perfectly ordered *totality*. The great Greek discovery—or rather the conceptual innovation wrought by the Greeks, which alone permitted the outburst of philosophy and science—was that the world is a *cosmos*. The world was interpreted as a *universe:* an intelligible, because perfectly articulated, whole. Now if the world is a cosmos, the "presumption of reason" (to borrow a term from Merleau-Ponty) is fully vindicated, for in this case reason or consciousness has only to discover and conform itself to the reason in things to achieve a total science that perfectly mirrors the totality of beings. Language has only to articulate the *natural* articulations of the world.

The idea of science is necessarily, therefore—when it is fully self-conscious of itself—the idea of a total *system* of all knowledge. The meaning of philosophy, as Husserl says, "implies the ideal possibility of a systematic philosophy as a strict science."[19] Universal science, as we have heard Husserl say, is the "science of the universe, of the all-encompassing unity of all that is." It is, as Husserl says of his own sought-after phenomenological science, knowledge of "the complete universe of the *a priori*."[20] Husserl speaks of "the chaos that

genuine science wants to transform into a cosmos, into a simple, completely clear, lucid order."[21]

It is not difficult, therefore, to situate Husserl historically. He comes at the end of a long, unbroken spiritual line stemming from Plato, who, in his disputations with the Sophists, first clearly articulated the idea of *episteme*. Other stages in the unfolding of the tradition need only be mentioned: the summas of the medieval Christian rationalists; Descartes' philosophical tree (the organic unity of the sciences, grounded in metaphysics); Leibniz's *mathesis universalis*; the grandiose Enlightenment project of the *Encyclopédie*; the Hegelian System. Of course, for Husserl the cosmos, the rational totality, the object of a universal science, is no longer the objective world of the Greeks or Medievals but the world subsequent to the "Copernican revolution" in philosophy, namely, the world after the "turn to subjectivity" that was inaugurated by Descartes: the transcendentally purified world which is nothing other than the field of *pure consciousness*—consciousness being conceived of by Husserl as *omnitudo realitatis*.

It is, then, within this "remarkable teleology"[22] of the Western spirit that Husserl explicitly situates himself. One can object neither to Husserl's reading of history—for the history of the West is indeed, in a very basic sense, the history of the scientific project—nor to Husserl's estimation of his own place in this history as the self-conscious realization of its "inner entelechy"; but one can wonder if this teleology has not simply reached its *telos* or end, if the ideal has not lost its value as an unquestionably accepted goal for the human spirit. Philosophy as a rigorous science—was this not perhaps a dream, and so, like all dreams, destined to end at one time or another? It is, in any event, a curious state of affairs that while Husserl possessed such an uncanny sensitivity for the spiritual history of Western consciousness, he yet failed so completely to see that if (precisely as he says) the notions of science and cosmos were conceptual innovations effected in the history of our culture, they cannot, for that very reason, be accorded a transcultural or supratemporal (i.e., ontological) value and be accepted unquestioningly. Husserl, it might be said, while fully aware of the history of consciousness, totally ignored its *historicity*.

3. The Guiding Idea of an Absolute Science

If, to understand Husserl, it is necessary to situate him in the tradition, to properly appreciate his work it is necessary to lay bare its conceptual make-up. Now were one to attempt a "conceptual analysis" of Husserl's writings one would soon discover that the key concept which, in the process of working itself out, determines the subject matter, the approach, and the style of argumentation is the concept of *science*. Husserl's 1911 *Logos* article, "Philosophy as Rigorous Science," is a perfect statement of the theme of his life's work, a theme which finds expression in all of his major published works. From the *Logical Investigations* to the end, Husserl is constantly at pains to reassert the phenomenological "principle of principles," namely that intuition or evidence (the presence of the things themselves) is the ultimate source of justification for all rational statements. Why does Husserl devote so much attention to the notion of *evidence*? The reason is, quite simply, that Husserl's goal is to set up philosophy as the all-embracing *science*, and science is possible only on the basis of evidence. As S. Bachelard has observed:

The notion of apodictic evidence is brought to light everywhere in Husserl's works, from the earliest to the latest. And it goes without saying that since the principal theme of Husserl's researches is the problem-set of logic and science, apodictic evidence plays a role of the first order.[23]

It is thus that Husserl turns to Descartes as to a model, for the *ego cogito* furnishes him a *fundamentum inconcusum*, "an absolute foundation,"[24] on which to erect the edifice of science. The notion of the phenomenological reduction or epoche is accordingly, in Husserl, conceptually subordinate to the notion of science, for it permits Husserl to isolate transcendental subjectivity and to discover in this subjectivity a realm of apodictic evidence. The reduction

makes possible an *apodictic* evidence of the being of transcendental subjectivity. Only if my experiencing of my transcendental self is apodictic can it serve as ground and basis for apodictic judgments; only then is there accordingly the prospect of a philosophy, a systematic structure made up of apodictic cognitions, starting with the intrinsically first field of experience and judgment.[25]

Husserl explicitly makes his own "the Cartesian idea of a science that shall be established as radically genuine, ultimately an all-embracing science."[26] He is constantly at pains to restore "the most primordial concept of philosophy—as all-embracing science which is alone [truly] science in the ancient Platonic and again in the Cartesian sense."[27] He sees transcendental phenomenology as bringing "to realization the Leibnizian idea of a universal ontology as the systematic unity of all conceivable *a priori* sciences."[28] He in fact defines phenomenology as " the *a priori* science of all conceivable existent beings, . . .the truly universal ontology."[29]

It is assuredly rather ironical, therefore, that Anglo-Saxon positivists have so little knowledge of and/or sympathy with Husserl, for their ancestry is a common one and their goal, in many ways, is the same. The ancestry is Leibnizian and the goal is unified science.[30] Like the movement associated with the Vienna circle, Husserl's phenomenology was an attempt to achieve a fundamental clarification and thereby an all-embracing unity of the sciences. Phenomenology, in fact, was to be the "true positivism."[31] And as Husserl attempted to show with regard to logic (*Formal and Transcendental Logic*), this could only be achieved if a sound grounding could be given to the sciences. [This grounding would have to come from a science which depended on no other, which was truly ultimate and "presuppositionless"—and this, as Husserl defined it, was phenomenology, the science of *transcendental subjectivity*, itself the ultimate source of all ideal objects (and for Husserl, the idealist, all objects are essentially ideal in that their meaning is constituted through active and passive synthesis).] Husserl's conception of the scientific corpus was strictly traditional; science was pyramidal, hierarchically organized knowledge. The purpose of phenomenology is, accordingly, to transform all the historical sciences

into true, methodical, fully self-justifying sciences. But precisely by this they will cease to be positive (dogmatic) sciences and become dependent branches of the one phenomenology as all-encompassing eidetic entology.[32]

It is only by being grounded in the absolute science of phenomenology that the particular sciences become *genuine* sciences and cease to be what they are now, mere *techniques*.[33] Husserl thus saw all the particular sciences as forming a totality—or as having to form such a totality if the idea of science is to be fully realized—organized in a hierarchical order with phenomenology, the ultimate, self-grounding science, at its head. "In other words, *there is only one philosophy, one actual and genuine science;* and particular genuine sciences are only non-selfsufficient members within it."[34]

Phenomenology is thus to be the "*a priori* science of all conceivable existent beings,"[35] the exploration and clarification of the cosmos, "the complete universe of the *a priori*." But, of course, the only sense existing beings can conceivably have is their sense as constituted in and by transcendental subjectivity. This means that phenomenology must consist in the discovery and mapping out of the essential intentional networks, running through consciousness, which prescribe, a priori, the sense of all possible objects. And this in turn means that consciousness must be conceived as a kind of closed-off "*self-contained system of being*, into which nothing can penetrate, and from which nothing can escape;

which has no spatio-temporal exterior."[36] *Consciousness for Husserl has no context;* it is itself *omnitudo realitatis*, the world as cosmos, as a perfectly determined and intelligible Whole. Just as scientific experiments are possible only when the scientist abstracts from the great wealth of natural interconnections, so as to set up an isolated system with as few extrinsic factors operative as possible, so, more generally, science itself is possible only in regard to closed-off, isolated systems that form a totality in themselves. This is why Husserl insists on the *teleological* coherence of consciousness.[37] As he says in *Ideas*:

All treatment of detail is governed by the "teleological" view of its function in making "synthetic unity" possible. The treatment considers from the standpoint of the essence of the various conscious groupings which in the experiences themselves, in their dispensings of meaning, in their noeses generally, are as it were *prefigured*, needing to be just drawn out from them.[38]

Consciousness is not a chaos but a cosmos, a system, and phenomenology, as constitutional investigation, is the exploration of the egological monad and the discovery of its immanent and invariant structures.[39]

In reading Husserl as he insists on the determinable eidetic laws of consciousness which prescribe in advance the various ways in which consciousness can intend objects—which, therefore, prescribe the conditions of objectivity of the object—when he says that "everything, however far we stretch the framework, and on whatever level of generality and particularity we may also be moving— even down to the lowest concreta—is essentially prefigured,"[40] and that "all of existence...is one universal synthetic unity"[41]—one is reminded of nothing so much as the Thomist intellectualist God who orders the world and himself acts in obedience to an order of divine Ideas, fixed from all eternity, and his creation product: a perfectly ordered and hierarchically structured world wherein everything has its specified place. This is of course no accidental analogy since medieval rationalist theology was an apt expression of the Greek idealist ideal of absolute science.

4. Scientific Dogmatism

There is an essential if often unsuspected conceptual interrelatedness of idealism, science, and dogmatism. Science is often spoken of as an open-minded search for the truth and as the diametrical opposite of dogmatism, but this is due to an oversight of the true nature of dogmatism as well as science. There is certainly a kind of dogmatism— and here the term is properly used in its pejorative sense—to which science is from the outset opposed; this is the dogmatism of blind opinion (*doxa*) which refuses to subject itself to scrutiny and to revision in the light of experience and rational argument. Science indeed liberates us from this kind of closed, stubborn mentality. But science results in a higher-order dogmatism, for science is possible only on the dogmatic (i.e., unquestioned) assumption that the truth is attainable, that man can, at least in principle, attain *certainty*, that reality is intelligible. Thus Husserl's philosophy is a form of (scientific) dogmatism since its goal is none other than the definitive overcoming of skepticism through the attainment of an unshakable certainty and absolute indubitability. Far from being an open-mindedness, science is—in the end, as regards its goal—the epitome of closed-mindedness, for it postulates the total determinancy and fixity of what is, and—corresponding to this (as an infinite *telos* perhaps)—invariant, exhaustive, systematic knowledge that is immune to further doubt and revision. To conceive, for instance, of history as Husserl does, as the progressive unfolding of the Idea of Reason, is, *eo ipso*, to take up a dogmatic position, for, as Ricoeur remarks, "the rationality of history implies a nascent dogmatism for which history is an Idea and an Idea thinkable by me."[42]

How is it, then, it might be objected, that if Husserl is as thorough a rationalist, idealist, and scientific dogmatist as I have been making him out to be, he was yet able to serve as the inspiration source for the "existentialists" and their anti-intellectualistic, anti-scientific, and anti-dogmatic philosophies? For it is incontestable that Husserl furnished both the method and, to a considerable extent, the themes for later existential phenomenology. Does this militate against situating Husserl solidly in the Platonic-Idealist tradition? I do not believe it does, for it seems to me that there are deep ambiguities in Husserl's work and that it is precisely because of these ambiguities that the "existentialists" were able to interpret Husserl in a manner compatible with their own anti-rationalism. If, however, we do not simply play on these ambiguities but become expressly aware of them, we will, I think, have no difficulty in perceiving the ultimately rationalist character of Husserl's philosophy and, thereby, its incompatibility with "existentialism." The ambiguities I have in mind are four in number.

(1) The first ambiguity concerns Husserl's conception of science itself. It will be objected that Husserl definitely is not a dogmatist, for he explicitly conceives of himself as but a "perpetual beginner" in philosophy, and, in the *Crisis*, he characterizes the sought-after science as "an eternal pole,"[43] the realization of which lies in infinity. The pure science is an infinite telos, which means that science at any given moment is necessarily only "on the way." Husserl never claimed to have realized this science but, on the contrary, explicitly saw himself as merely on its threshold: "The author sees the infinite open country of the true philosophy, the 'promised land' on which he himself will never set foot."[44] It is known, however, that Husserl, like scientists in general, hoped his work would be carried on after him by a dedicated group of researchers who would, in concentrated teamwork, penetrate ever deeper into the field of pure subjectivity, mapping ever more completely its essential, a priori, necessarily determined configurations. Husserl stands in stark contrast, therefore, to

Hegel (as the latter is usually viewed), as claiming effective possession of the absolute science. Scholars (e.g., Lewis White Beck) have recently, however, called into question this usual picture and have attempted to interpret Hegel in a way which brings him much closer to Husserl and his notion of science as an infinite goal. And the father of idealism himself, Plato, is easily viewed as "open minded," as ever ready to consider objections to the very basis of science as he saw it, the theory of forms.

The fact remains, nonetheless, that none of these thinkers ever seriously questions the value of science itself or the belief that reality is intrinsically intelligible. At the beginning of *Cartesian Meditations* Husserl says that whether or not an absolute science is possible and, if possible, what its exact nature must be, these questions are not presupposed. The possibility of this science can only be proved by being concretely worked out. "At first we must not presuppose even its possibility."[45] But, as he makes quite clear, this has nothing to do with the value or the desirability of the ideal itself; this indeed he does presuppose: "this does not imply that we renounce the general aim of grounding science absolutely."[46] In the midst of the contemporary crisis, in the barbarian decadence of Nazi Germany, Husserl could see no other solution than that of reaffirming the ancient Greek optimism in the infinite power of reason, the optimism of the Enlightenment, and the nineteenth-century dogma of unending progress. It is to this goal that Husserl summoned mankind; it seems never to have occurred to him that the present crisis might not perhaps be due so much to a faltering of the ideal as to the ideal itself. Husserl seems never to have been able to reconcile the contrary demands of what he termed—in a rather positivistic fashion—wisdom (*Weltanschauung* philosophy) and science. In his 1911 *Logos* article he presented the former as an attempt to enable man to live in the finite, in the present; the latter projected man into the future, the infinite, the transfinite.[47] Even though, Husserl ad-

mits, "it is certain that we cannot wait," even though we must take a position here and now, in the present moment of distress, still, he says, "it must be insisted that we remain aware of the responsibility we have in regard to humanity. For the sake of time we must not sacrifice eternity."[48] For Husserl, no choice was ultimately possible; he had to sacrifice "profundity" for "clarity," personal "wisdom" for impersonal "science." As Gadamer has observed: "Nobody can doubt that here the tension between the running flux of time and life and the philosophical claim of eternal truth remains."[49] Husserl's "presuppositionless" science is actually dominated by one great unclarified presupposition: the cultural presupposition of the tradition—the absolute, all-redeeming value of science as that which alone can make man "blessed."

Husserl is what one might call a "sophisticated absolutist."[50] Such a person wishes to maintain the absolute while rejecting dogmatism; he accordingly locates the absolute in infinity and characterizes it as an infinite goal. All finite knowledge is then only "on the way." *Science* is the name for the perfect system, immune to further revision, the true understanding which will genuinely exist only at the "end of time." Such a view can be very appealing for it offers people an assurance that Meaning, Truth, and Value do exist (as infinite Telos), and at the same time it also respects what they nonetheless know to be a fact, namely, the *relativity* of all factual, finite knowledge. It does this by *de-actualizing* the absolute, by defining the really real as the *ideal*, the "idea in the Kantian sense" (which is not to be confounded with any real [actual, given] manifestation or expression). But what is the consequence of this position? It results in a radical dissociation of *contemplation* (the true, final understanding) from *action* (the present, here and now existential situation in which man finds himself). This is to say that it *devalorizes* the here and now; that is, it denies to man in the present moment of his life any genuine access to the absolute (since the absolute is precisely not the actual but the ideal). It devalorizes the present for the sake of the future ("For the sake of time we must not sacrifice eternity").[51] Nietzsche's critique of Platonism therefore applies to Husserlianism as well, for the latter, too, is an idealism; it places true being beyond the reach of finite man; it disparages human life.

(2) The second ambiguity concerns language and terminology. Husserl is often praised for his open-mindedness in regard to his phenomenological descriptions and technical terms. And it is quite true that he attempts to preserve a certain openness to conceptual and linguistic formulations. Reference is often made to the following text:

Our procedure is that of a scientific traveller in an unknown part of the world who carefully describes what he finds on the trackless ways he takes—ways that will not always be the shortest. He should be full of the sure consciousness of bringing to expression what in relation to time and circumstances is the thing that *must* be said, which, because it faithfully expresses what has been seen, preserves its value always—even when further research calls for new descriptions with manifold improvements. In a similar temper we wish in what further lies before us to be loyal expounders of phenomenological formations, and for the rest to preserve the habit of inner freedom even in regard to our own descriptions.[52]

But just as in the case of the scientific ideal, where Husserl's self-accorded status of perpetual beginner did not prevent him from according an absolute and unquestioned value to the ideal itself, so also here: Husserl's seeming openness to any given phenomenological description—an openness which has greatly appealed to the "existentialists"[53]—hides within itself a firm conviction in the need for just the opposite of openness: a rigidly *fixed* conceptual and linguistic apparatus. This conviction is itself a consequence of Husserl's desire to make philosophy into a science. Thus when again in *Ideas* he makes a remark similar to the one just quoted—"in the beginnings of phenomenology all concepts or terms must in a

certain sense remain fluid"[54]—he immediately qualifies it and reveals his veritable intentions by stating: "it is not until a very highly developed stage of science has been reached that we can count on terminologies being definitely fixed." A phenomenology which has gone beyond its "beginnings," which has achieved the status of science, *will* have a definitely fixed terminology. Husserl thus speaks of "the requirement that the same words and propositions shall be unambiguously correlated with certain essences that can be intuitively apprehended and constitute their completed 'meaning'."[55]

Husserl's conception of language therefore resembles not so much that of the existential phenomenologists—for whom language is much more than the mere reproduction of ideal meanings; is in fact to a considerable extent productive of meaning—as that of the logical positivists—for whom the prime function of language is referential and whose ideal is, accordingly, a formal language of univocal meanings, wherein each term refers to but one object and no two objects are designated by the same term.[56] As Husserl would say, the essential function of language is *expression*; the role of language is merely to articulate a preexistent meaning: "The stratum of expression—and this constitutes its peculiarity—...is not productive."[57]

(3) It is of course difficult to imagine "existentialism" as able to have had logical positivism for a philosophical parent (Husserl is "existentialism's" paternal parent, so to speak—not in any event its maternal parent, this latter being the long tradition [the "countertradition," as I shall later call it] of moral, anti-scientific philosophy from Socrates through Pascal and Kierkegaard). There is an important difference between Husserl and the more common and crass type of rationalists and positivists, and this has to do with his conception of lived *experience*. But, as we shall see, this attractive side of Husserl's thought can be highly misleading. There are many themes in Husserl which require only a slight shift in meaning to

become the subject matter for an existential reflection, but this shift always involves an important change of context, an obfuscation of the original context; it involves substituting a different basic conceptual framework for that of Husserl, which, as we saw, rests on the guiding concept of science. This is especially true in regard to Husserl's emphasis on such "existential" themes as freedom, self-responsibility, perception, the body, pre-predicative lived experience, the life-world, and so on. A great many interpreters, it seems to me, have been guilty of reading their own desires into Husserl. And it must be admitted that what Husserl says about subjective, personal, "lived" experience permits them to do so without too much overt violence to the texts, even though it involves leaving out other important texts. The prime example of an existential reading of Husserl—its feasibility but also its limits—is probably best afforded by Merleau-Ponty. It does not seem to me, though, that in the last analysis there is the slightest justification for holding that Husserl ever abandoned his rationalism and conception of philosophy as rigorous science, and even Merleau-Ponty, who probably more than anyone else made a sustained attempt to remain faithful to Husserl, more or less confessed that Husserl remained an intransigent idealist.[58]

Albert Camus, however, was much more straightforward and did not hesitate to accuse Husserl of outright rationalism. In *The Myth of Sisyphus*, in the section entitled "Philosophical Suicide," Camus says that the first effect of Husserl's phenomenology is liberating in that it restores to the concrete world of our immediate experience its rich diversity, but he goes on to say that this attitude is in turn negated by Husserl himself, who repudiates lived experience in favor of an eternal Reason: "after having denied the integrating power of human reason, he [Husserl] proceeds to leap into eternal Reason. . . .It is not the taste for the concrete that I find here but an intellectualism sufficiently unbridled to generalize the concrete itself."

Contrary to the logical positivists, Husserl, it must be admitted, does not remain blind and insensitive to the corporeal side of human being and to the world of lived, personal experience, which are irreducible to the abstract logic of the physico-mathematical sciences. Indeed Husserl expressly says that all intellectual activity is based upon and presupposes the original life-world, and he accordingly makes this more and more a prime theme of his investigations. So as not to be misled, however, it is important to keep in mind the reason for Husserl's discovery and exploration of the human life-world. If one's goal is the achievement of a final, presuppositionless science, and if all the given sciences presuppose the life-world, then it is necessary to show how the life-world, the ground of all scientific activity, is itself grounded in and constituted by pure transcendental subjectivity. Gadamer writes:

Without any doubt the new way [through the *Lebenswelt*] leads to the old end of transcendental phenomenology, which is based in the transcendental ego. . . .This alone is rigorous science. . . .One hears there the old tones. The world of life in all its flexibility and relativity can be the theme of a universal science.[59]

Like the Hegelian dialectic of *Phenomenology of Mind*, which fully recognizes the existence and the power of the negative but which subsumes it in the Absolute, so in Husserl, the life-world is itself destined to be *aufgehoben* into the final science by being explained as a constituted product of the transcendental Ego.[60] The difference between, on the one side, the positivists and the contemporary cyberneticians of consciousness who attempt to construct an *objective* science of man and experience and, on the other side, Husserl, whose goal was, so to speak, a *subjective* science of experience[61]—and against both of these positions taken together: the "existentialists" for whom experience is quite simply recalcitrant to treatment by *any* science, objective or "subjective"—this overall difference is irreducible. Or, to express the matter in a slightly different way, the differences between the "existentialists" and Husserl are, when everything is taken into account, of a much more fundamental sort than those between Husserl and the positivists. For both Husserl and the positivists are fully within the mainstream of traditional philosophy, whereas it is an open question whether "existentialism" does not represent a radical break with this tradition.

(4) Finally, reference might be made to the ambiguous role that *wonder* plays in Husserl's philosophy. For Merleau-Ponty, who is typical of the "existentialists" in this regard, wonder is the beginning *and the end* of philosophy. As he saw it, the principal lesson of the phenomenological reduction is the impossibility of a complete reduction, for the reduction reveals the "unmotivated upsurge of the world"; it makes us intensely aware of the world as something forever "strange and paradoxical."[62] Merleau-Ponty appeals to Fink for support, and it is true that Fink in his famous *Kant-Studien* article, which was formally endorsed by Husserl, said that "what is of decisive importance is the awakening of an immeasurable astonishment over the mysteriousness" of the existence of the world and spoke of "the greatest mystery of all, the mystery of the being of the world itself."[63] Fink's emphasis on the existential themes of wonder, strangeness, paradoxicality and mystery, however, can be highly misleading. For as S. Bachelard, herself no existentialist, has pointed out, the experience of wonder and strangeness is for Husserl but the *beginning* of the philosophical quest.[64] It is necessary to have experienced wonder in order to set forth on the path to science, but science must in the end replace wonder and dispel all mystery.

On this score Husserl, once again, proves himself to be a true "Greek," for the wonder experienced by a rationalist is qualitatively different from that experienced by an "existentialist." The Greek—the idealist—is struck with awe when he contemplates the magnificent order of the world. This wonder is provoked by an experience of the world as *cosmos*, a marvelously ordered Totality. This type of wonder naturally culminates in *science*, for the question it evokes concerns the workings of nature. The idealist is provoked to ask: What is the secret of this wondrous order, what are the intelligible laws at work here? When, however, the "existentialist" asks, with Heidegger: "Why is there something rather than simply nothing at all?" he is experiencing the world in a radically different manner. For what awes him is not the *order* of the world but, more radically still, the fact that there *is* a world and not just *nothing*. This is an experience of the very real possibility of the *not-being* of the world, an experience not of its intrinsic rationality but of its utter contingency. It is an experience not of something but of nothing, not of hidden meaning but of fundamental, menacing absurdity. *It culminates not in science but in a heightened awareness of the final impossibility of all science.*

What the "existentialist" experiences in wonder is the *fact* of the world's being, the world's *facticity*, and he experiences this fact as something fundamentally *opaque*.[65] For Husserl, however, as for rationalism in general, the fact is essentially *transparent;* the fact is but an *instance*, an exemplification of a universal law or *essence* which it is the task of reason to uncover and lay bare. It is impossible for a rationalist, for one looking for the *essence* or nature of something, ever to fully recognize what an "existentialist" calls the "facticity of the fact," for to do so would require abandoning the goal of science, which can exist only so long as one presupposes the intelligibility, the "essentiality," of what-is. Husserl thus naturally maintains that "all the rationality of the fact lies, after all, in the apriori."[66] He says: " *'Fact'*, with its *'irrationality'*, is itself a structural concept within the system of the concrete apriori."[67] Or, as Berger said in his exposition of Husserl's philosophy: "*Fact* in its very opacity and in its historicity is still—just like nothingness or the absurd—a constituted reality."[68] And even more concisely: "There is no radical unintelligible."[69]

Like Leibniz, Husserl recognizes that innumerable worlds are possible: " 'The real world' . . .presents itself as *a special case of various possible worlds and non-worlds*.[70] But, like Leibniz also, Husserl in the end maintains that not all possibilities are compossible:[71] "There can *exist only one objective world*."[72] Husserl thus attempts to prove that this factually existing world exists necessarily (for reasons of essence). This rationalist insistence on necessity stands in stark contrast to the "existentialist" insistence on irreducible contingency as stated by Sartre:

being can neither be derived from the possible nor reduced to the necessary. Necessity concerns the connection between ideal propositions but not that of existents. An existing phenomenon can never be derived from another existent qua existent. This is what we shall call the *contingency* of being-in-itself. But neither can being-in-itself be derived from a *possibility*. The possible is a structure of the *for-itself* [i.e., consciousness]; that is, it belongs to the other region of being. This is what consciousness expresses in anthropomorphic terms by saying that being is superfluous (*de trop*)—that is, that consciousness absolutely cannot derive being from anything, either from another being, or from a possibility, or from a necessary law. Uncreated, without reason for being, without any connection with another being, being-in-itself is *de trop* for eternity.[73]

Philosophy, for Husserl, is explanation in terms of ultimate reasons,[74] and thus he attempts to demonstrate concretely the world's necessity. Only if there is an intrinsic, necessary order of possibilities, "*a system of apriori incompossibility*,"[75] is systematic philosophy, science, possible.[76] In spite of his aversion to speculative metaphysics, Husserl's conclusions perfectly rejoin those of traditional metaphysics; the only difference is that Husserl claims to be the first to have achieved scientific status for his metaphysical pronouncements.[77] For Husserl, just as for Leibniz, this world is the best of all possible worlds, best because necessary.

5. The Neglect of the Negative

The world of Husserl is thus quite simply *another* world than that of the "existentialists." It is a world of complete positivity, a firmly grounded world, perfectly ordered with no cracks or crevasses through which Nothing (the *Nihil*) could ever intrude in such a way as to menace the world in its very being, not to speak of its meaning. Husserl, the inveterate optimist, never gives serious consideration to the power and the threat of Nothing.[78] As with the medieval rationalists, evil for Husserl, one might say, is nothing more than the mere privation of the good. For him, "non-being is only a *modality* of simple being, of certain being (which is the primal mode)"; "nonsense is always a mode of sense."[79] As one existential phenomenologist, Emmanuel Lévinas, points out, Husserl quite simply denies "the existence of the irrational."[80] This *positivity* of spirit is reflected in Husserl's habitual terminology and key concepts. As J. Derrida has aptly pointed out, the root metaphor in Husserl is "*life*."[81] The reduction reveals "my pure living,"[82] the absolute life of the pure Ego.

When empirical life or even the region of the pure psychical are put in parentheses, it is still a transcendental *life* or, in the last analysis, the transcendentality of a *living* present that Husserl discovers.[83]

It is in the "living present," the basic Now moment of the Ego's transcendental life, that the world as well as the Ego itself are generated. The basic category for Husserl is, accordingly, that of *presence*: the presence of the Ego to itself in the absolute present. This is why Husserl cannot really conceive of anything like the *death* of consciousness. How, indeed, could a consciousness, which has no spatio-temporal exterior, ever experience something like a *threat* to its existence? The sting of death exists only for the empirical ego which still ignores its pure, transcendental essence. Because the Ego is pure presence, it is *eternally* present, absolute, indestructible *Life*, a kind of *nunc stans* which, while generative of time, is itself without time. The living stream of pure consciousness is "without end"; it "can neither begin nor end";[84] it is "an infinite unity."[85] Consciousness is eternal life because, as Husserl says in his time-book, it is impossible to conceive of "a now which nothing proceeded."[86] This is indeed impossible for a philosophy for which the basic concept is presence and which therefore has no means for thinking absence. Idealism is the philosophy of the identity of the ideal and the real; only that is real which is ideal, which is to say: only that which can be experienced in its full *presence* to consciousness. For Husserl as for Plato, the really real is the *eidos* which is seen face to face. What cannot be *intuited* is not real.

It would be extremely worthwhile to constrast Husserl with Heidegger on this score. For already in *Being and Time* Heidegger takes up in all seriousness those themes which find no proper place in Husserl's intuitionist, idealist philosophy. One has only to think of the phenomenon of death, which is absolutely central in this early book of Heidegger. And it is here, too, that being is defined as that which proximally and for the most part does *not* appear. This is of course why, for Heidegger, phenomenology cannot rely on intuition (evidence) but— since being is always more than its actual presence—must become a hermeneutics, an *interpretation*, an unearthing of what is proximally and for the most part covered over. The root metaphors of Heidegger are entirely un-Husserlian, and become even more so as Heidegger, similar to Aristotle, realizes philosophical adulthood in his own right; Heidegger speaks to us of death, nothing, meaninglessness, fate, absence, abysses, untruth, mystery, etc.

The Husserl/Heidegger relationship and the history of their unhappy collaboration could perhaps be best characterized as a case of "pseudomorphosis." This is the term, borrowed from mineral-ogy, which Spengler used to designate certain kinds of intercultural relationships. In mineralogy the term refers to the formation of a new crystalline substance in the hollow left in a rock by crystals which had in the meantime disappeared; the new crystal is forced to take the shape of the alien mold and thereby assume a form incongruous with its inner structure, such that, in the absence of careful chemical analysis, one will easily be misled and mistake it for a crystal of the original type. The self-articulation of Christianity in terms of the alien Greek rationalism would be an instance of this type of distortion phenomenon. Now, without a careful investigation of the inner structures of their thought, it is relatively easy to be deceived by surface resemblances and overlook the profound differences separating Husserl and Heidegger (these differences are basically those which separate Husserlian phenomenology and existential phenomenology). It is also easy, it might be added, to be misled by appearances and attribute to the two philosophers differences which do not exist—except, precisely, in appearance, as when certain commentators say that Husserl is an "essentialist" whereas Heidegger is an "existentialist" (taking this to be the last word) or that Heidegger rejects Husserl's phenomenological reduction.[87] The difference between the two is a difference—totally irremediable—of goals and outlooks.

An interesting pseudomorphosis occurs, however, when Heidegger in *Being and Time* attempts to pour his existential preoccupations into a Husserlian mold, for while Heidegger's philosophical orientation precludes the possibility of philosophy's ever becoming a science, he nonetheless continues to speak of philosophy as *aprioristic* and *scientific*. These are terms with which Heidegger would soon feel uncomfortable and drop altogether. Similarly, Husserl, most notably in the *Crisis*, tries to fit into his idealist mold certain "Heideggerian," existential themes. Certainly it can be no mere accident that the topics which at the end of

Cartesian Meditations (dating from 1929) Husserl singles out for eventual transcendental, eidetic analysis—the "higher" problems of constitutive investigation—are *precisely* those existential topics which occupy such a prominent place in Heidegger's existential analytic in *Being and Time* (published in 1927); as Husserl lists them, they are "*the problems of accidental factualness, of death, of fate,* of the possibility of a '*genuine*' human life,...of the 'meaning' of history."[88] The Husserl/Heidegger pseudomorphosis leads the interpreter into error when, becoming aware of the many existential concerns in Husserl's thought, he is led to conclude from this significant difference in appearance from what is usually called idealism that Husserl's philosophy is not really idealist and rationalist at all.[89]

More interesting still is that the Heidegger/Husserl pseudomorphosis very closely parallels the Christian/Greek pseudomorphosis. The Christian view of life and the world, as Hans Jonas (among others) has pointed out,[90] is radically at odds with the classical Greek outlook. The latter exalts reason and is optimistic; the former lays the emphasis on faith and is tragic (the tragedy of the Cross).[91] Husserl came to philosophy from the eminently Greek disciplines of mathematics and logic. Heidegger's early and formative interests were, as Pöggeler has shown,[92] of an essentially Christian nature. The question of basic import for the early Heidegger was What type of human self-understanding is contained in the early Christian experience and way of life? It is this Christian experience of man's thrownness, his radical finitude, alienage, and his being a stranger in the world, as well as the insignificance of the world itself (and all worldly science), which are articulated in Heidegger's "existialism," and it is this interest in an experience alien to Greek rationalism which eventually provoked Heidegger's rupture with the tradition and, consequently, with Husserl.

6. Unhappy Consciousness and Beyond

Does the end of the tradition spell the end of philosophy? Does the existential rejection of idealism and the ideal of science mean the renunciation of all claims to knowledge whatsoever in favor of some kind of blind irrationalism? The charge of irrationalism is often levied against the "existentialists"—by Husserl himself, apparently—and so it seems to me most important that this charge be confronted. Irrationalism is possible only within the conceptual framework of rationalism; in its destructive negativity it affirms, in spite of itself, the power of that which it refuses: the idealist notion of a cosmos and the ideal of science. In this it does not overcome but merely perpetuates the tradition. Now it is certainly true that one can find an inordinate amount of sheer irrationalism in much of what goes under the name of "existentialism." This is why I have in this paper used the term "existentialism" reluctantly and almost always in inverted commas. There is, however, in the best of "existentialism" an inner dynamics which tends to propel it beyond *mere* "existentialism," beyond, that is, a sterile protest against the pretensions of reason.

What must be overcome in "existentialism" if the tradition itself is to be genuinely overcome is the Kierkegaardian type of revolt against reason which merely exhausts itself in a passionately lyrical exaltation of irrational subjectivity. Kierkegaard's anti-idealism results, in the end, in nothing more than a morose embrace of *one* of the moments of the Hegelian rationalist dialectic: unhappy consciousness. Kierkegaard positively delights in what he takes to be the spirit's inability ever to reconcile its inner contradictions and achieve final knowledge (*Wissenschaft*). Kierkegaard wishes to accentuate to the maximum the suffering of the spirit that is thirsty for knowledge so that, precisely, it may perceive all the more acutely and painfully its utter impotence in the face of an Absolute which it can never *know*. Kierkegaard empties his whole being in an anguished protest against idealistic hope, in a romantic revolt against reason, so that, in the utter misery of defeat and despair, the spirit may perchance be accorded an unhoped-for and totally unmerited *grace*. Kierkegaard, one might say, is a philosophical masochist. Sartre, too, shares this kind of romantic irrationalism; he too is obsessed with the Hegelian unhappy consciousness—with, that is, the spirit's inability to reconcile the contradictions it perceives within itself. Only, unlike Kierkegaard, he does not hold out hope for a final salvation. Man, he says, is the impossible desire to be God; this is why he is a "useless passion."[93] The human reality "therefore is by nature an unhappy consciousness with no possibility of surpassing its unhappy state."[94] In a like vein, Camus attempted to work out a philosophy of the absurd, of the senselessness of man's existence, where all hope and all idealistic optimism were resolutely banished.[95] The early Merleau-Ponty is also a good example of this type of philosophical position, which exhausts itself in protest against the excesses of rationalism.

But the example of Merleau-Ponty may perhaps also serve as an indication or hint of how the tradition may not only be opposed but actually overcome. For his thought undergoes a decided evolution—having as one of its consequences the rupture of his relations with Sartre—whereby he comes to abandon and transcend the unhappy consciousness of irrationalistic existentialism. While at the time of *Phenomenology of Perception* Merleau-Ponty got no further than a critique of the "presumption of reason" and of idealism in general, and does no more than point out the insurmountable *contingency* of the world, which underlies all truth—a contingency which serves as an effective frustration to all attempts at absolute science—while, in other words, the early Merleau-Ponty, like Sartre and Camus, essentially does

no more than revive the romantic theme of the unhappy consciousness, in his later work he gropingly advances beyond this merely negative stance and, while not retracting his critique of idealism, nonetheless discovers, with the aid of the notion of "Being," that contingency, while very real, is not (for all that) the last word but that beyond the *adversity* of the world— the last word in his earlier thought—there is at the bottom of things a kind of "*generosity* which is not a compromise with the adversity of the world and which is on his [man's] side against it."[96] It did not escape Sartre's attention, although it caused him some dismay, that an important change had occurred in his erstwhile friend, for he saw that Merleau-Ponty had left romantic anti-rationalism behind and had embarked on a new philosophical adventure, had "plunged himself into the night of non-knowledge in search for what he now calls the 'fundamental'."[97]

It would be interesting to compare both Heidegger and Merleau-Ponty in their struggle against the tradition, in their attempt to overcome idealism. For, as with Heidegger, there is an early and a late Merleau-Ponty and, what is more, Merleau-Ponty is heavily influenced at each stage by his reading of the work of the corresponding Heidegger. The notion of "Being" in Merleau-Ponty's last, unfinished work, *The Visible and the Invisible*, is of late Heideggerian inspiration, but there is nonetheless a significant difference between these two great anti-idealists. For Merleau-Ponty believed he could overcome both idealism and the unhappy consciousness, both rationalism and irrationalism, while not—for all that—abandoning, like Heidegger, philosophy itself, although he recognized that the role and conception of philosophy—and phenomenology— could no longer be the traditional ones. Whereas Heidegger tends simply to leave traditional philosophy and phenomenology behind, Merleau-Ponty sought to overcome phenomenology and idealism "from within," so to speak. That is, he did not want, like Heidegger, simply to *abandon* traditional philosophy and Husserl in particular but to *transcend* them by showing how a philosophy of consciousness, if radical enough, leads to the recognition of its own limits (the limits of consciousness) and, in this way, to the recognition of a Being irreducible to consciousness. Thus in the case of Merleau-Ponty philosophy does not come to an "end" (to use a Heideggerian expression) but rather undergoes a radical *inner* transformation.[98] In this he differs from Sartre as well, who in his *Critique de la raison dialectique* (1960) simply repudiates his earlier existentialism as so much "ideology" and as a "parasitical system." Unlike both Heidegger and Merleau-Ponty, Sartre in no way overcomes the rationalist tradition; he in fact falls back into rationalism when he subscribes without reserve to Marxism, which, significantly, he refers to as "*le Savoir*."[99] The examples of Heidegger, Sartre, and Merleau-Ponty retrospectively point out the fittingness of a remark Gabriel Marcel made in 1946: "Existentialism stands to-day at a parting of the ways: it is, in the last analysis, obliged to deny or to transcend itself."[100]

By way of conclusion, let us consider, in only the most cursory way, this urgent question raised by the existential protest against idealism: Is there any future to philosophy beyond the tradition, after the "end" of idealism?

7. Philosophy or Antiphilosophy?

Does, then, the rejection of the tradition, of idealism, entail a rejection of philosophy itself? I have tried to indicate in the previous section that irrationalism is not a viable alternative to rationalism, for far from overcoming the tradition, it merely perpetuates it (in the same way, for instance, that a vehement atheism merely perpetuates, albeit unwittingly, the conceptual framework of theism on which it depends for its meaning). However, it is also a fact that the late Heidegger has advanced beyond mere irrationalism and has in the process abandoned the term "philosophy" in favor of "thought." Merleau-Ponty, for his part, prefers to speak of "negative philosophy." The term "antiphilosophy" has come into use to designate the thought of thinkers such as Heidegger and Merleau-Ponty and, in general, post-idealist thought. Whatever term we may use to designate postidealism, it will be useful to remember that it is not without its own history. It has its own tradition—although Heidegger seems to ignore this fact—which might properly be called the anti- or countertradition. This countertradition includes thinkers who are simply against the tradition as well as those who have attempted to forge a new path; it is as old as the tradition itself and has often disputed a legitimate claim to the term "philosophy." After his victorious battle with the rhetoricians, Plato, it is true, fairly well secured the term for the tradition. But the countertradition which refuses to identify philosophy and science goes back at least to Socrates if not to Protagoras, and can be traced through thinkers such as Pyrrho, Sextus, Pseudo-Dionysus, Tertullian, Montaigne, Charron, Pascal, Kierkegaard, and Nietzsche.

For the countertradition philosophy is wisdom, not science; but it is not simply or not always a rejection of science altogether, mere antiscience. Rather, when the countertradition is at its best it takes philosophy to be the recognition (recognition) of the limits of all science and in this way a kind of negative knowledge of what lies beyond the limits. As one postidealist expresses the matter:

Philosophical thinking is not science at all. . . .There is no claim of definitive knowledge with the exception of one: the acknowledgement of the finitude of human being in itself.[101]

A critique of Husserl such as the one undertaken here should not, therefore, be interpreted as an attempt to disparage him or to deny his historical greatness. Husserl is without doubt one of the greatest philosophers of all time, philosophy being understood in the traditional sense, as idealism. Even if with the "existentialists" we should feel obliged in the end to reject idealism, we cannot for all that deny its greatness—nor its necessity. For only through science can science be truly overcome; only when one has entertained the ideal of pure, absolute science can one become truly and *knowingly* aware of the insurmountable limits of science, and only then can one truly discern the infinite, open realm of being which transcends all possible scientific determinations.

Perhaps, therefore, it is not so odd after all that Husserl should have given rise to "existentialism" and, beyond that, to the movement toward negative philosophy. In the final analysis we might not even want to dispute the substance of an "existentializing" reading of Husserl. For one may no doubt view Husserl in two different but equally legitimate ways. We may, that is, say of Husserl (as we have said here) that in spite of everything he has to say of personal, lived experience, in the end and at bottom he is, and remains, a staunch idealist and thus fully a part of the tradition. Husserl certainly viewed himself as a rationalist; this at least is beyond dispute. Be we might, on the other hand, want to say something else. We might want to say that, in spite of Husserl's unquestioned allegiance to the tradition, there are elements in his thought which tend to propel him beyond it and which, if fully developed, would require a different philosophical context and the abandonment of the ideal of scientific philosophy. This latter interpretation is espoused by L. Landgrebe, Husserl's former assistant, who writes:

Husserl had wished to complete and fulfill this {idealist] tradition without knowing to what extent his attempt served to break up this tradition. It is therefore a moving document of an unprecedented struggle to express a content within the terminology of the traditions of modern thought that already forsakes this tradition and its alternatives and perspectives.[102]

Although any reading of Husserl of this latter sort must be undertaken with the greatest caution, so as not to read "existentialism" back into Husserl, it is not without philosophical or hermeneutical merits. For in this way negative philosophy, if we may call it that, would be seen as not merely antithetical and hostile to the tradition but as a kind of necessary outcome of it whereby the tradition is overcome by the very spirit of uncompromising, thoroughgoing "radicality" which motivates all of Husserl's work as he strives to realize an ultimate and presuppositionless science. Negative philosophy would achieve a far-reaching radicality of its own through its realization that a science is always the science of a given region of being, such that an all-encompassing, total science is impossible in that there is and can be no region which includes all the others—no *Ur region*, no horizon of all horizons (a "horizon" is precisely that beyond which there is something more), no class of all classes. A transcendental science is a contradiction in terms, for the true transcendental is precisely that which transcends all specific domains and thus all specialities, that is, all sciences. The transcendental can be known, on the contrary, only negatively, when we know the limits of the knowledge (science) of those who claim to know (scientists). Negative philosophy is indeed an antiphilosophy if philosophy means a definitive *system* of propositions and truths about man, the world, being, in short, a *science*. Husserl's idealist phenomenology actually leads idealism to its end and overcoming, for the culmination of the idealist ideal of absolute science is the realization of its utter impossibility.[103] The tradition is genuinely overcome only when its "shipwreck" has been fully experienced. We make contact with being when we founder in our attempt to grasp it knowingly. And in Husserl it is the inner drive of modern philosophy, of the tradition itself, which founders on the rocks.

It could thus be argued that negative philosophy is not genuinely possible at all, except on the basis of science, as science's "other." For before science, man has no choice; the only possibility open to him, when he thinks, is to construct *myths*. The only immediate, direct alternative to myth is science. But on a higher level it can be seen that the myth/science duality does not exhaust the possibilities of thought. Over and against both of these ways of expressing being is the indirect discourse of negative philosophy (negative science) which expresses being only indirectly and thus never in any determinate (scientific) fashion. It expresses an understanding of being which, because it rejects the idealist identity of being/presence/determinateness/essentiality/science, cannot issue in a determiniate terminology and conceptual system, which is therefore *arrheton*, "speechless." This "speechlessness" or impossibility of communication is not, however, the sheer *absence* of discourse and communication-mineffable mysticism, as Wittgenstein would have it—but discourse and communication *of a particular kind*. Negative philosophical utterances are not constatives but performatives; they are not pictures but metaphors of being. As Merleau-Ponty wrote shortly before his death:

Hence it is a question whether philosophy as the reconquest of brute or wild being can be accomplished by the resources of eloquent language, or whether it would not be necessary for philosophy to use language in a way that takes from it its power of immediate or direct signification in order to equal it with what it wishes all the same to say.[104]

Or again, as Heidegger said by way of a preface to a talk given in 1962: "The point is not to listen to a series of propositions, but rather to follow the movement of showing."[105]

The countertradition retains a non-Platonic, Socratic notion of *dialectic* and conceives of philosophy as a perpetual *critique* of the pretensions of science, a critique which culminates not in a new positivity but in the heightened awareness of one's own ignorance. The countertradition is, to paraphrase Nietzsche, the bad conscience of the tradition and is, as such, a constant reminder of the infinite openness lurking behind and encompassing the closed-off world of science. Negative philosophy's basic function is to remind us of that which we are forever forgetting and which we must necessarily tend to forget, since it is that which lies beyond the totality, beyond the cosmos. And what *that* is cannot be known scientifically, only negatively, for it can never in principle be brought to presence and be seen but is always experienced only in its irremediable absence and can be heard only in the silence of the spoken word.

Words move, music moves
Only in time; but that which is only living
Can only die. Words, after speech, reach
Into the silence. Only by the form, the
    pattern
Can words or music reach
The stillness, as a Chinese jar still
Moves perpetually in its stillness.[106]

NOTES

1. Cf., for instance, D. Føllesdal, *Husserl und Frege*, (Oslo: I Kommisjon Hoe H. Aschehoug, 1958); S. Bachelard, *A Study of Husserl's "Formal and Transcendental Logic"* (Evanston: Northwestern University Press, 1968); E. Holenstein, *Phänomenologie der Assoziation* (The Hague: Nijhoff, 1972); R. Sokolowski, *The Formation of Husserl's Concept of Constitution* (The Hague: Nijhoff, 1970) and *Husserlian Meditations* (Evanston: Northwestern University Press, 1974). In a 1971 review of Findlay's translation of Husserl's *Logical Investigations* (*Inquiry*, 14: 318-50), Sokolowski says: "With the decline of existential phenomenology, there has also been a sharper awareness of the logical and formal elements in Husserl's philosophy, and its affinity to and influence upon logic and the philosophy of language." Sokolowski here expresses the hope that the return to Husserl may be "a second journey to find the historical function phenomenology *might have had* under its own force."

In general, one may also refer to the work of the current generation of scholars trained at the New School for Social Research in New York; here the continuity between Husserlian phenomenology and existential philosophy which persisted in France and Germany was broken due to the fact that most of the phenomenologists teaching at the New School in the postwar years were emigrés from Nazi Germany who tended to associate existentialism

with Heidegger and who consequently tended to
view it with distrust if not outright antipathy, given
Heidegger's political activities in the '30s and their
own racial background.

2. Edmund Husserl, *The Crisis of European Sci-
ences and Transcendental Phenomenology*, trans.
David Carr (Evanston: Northwestern University
Press, 1970), p. 389.

3. As David Carr points out; see his Introduction
to *Crisis*, p. xxxi, n. 21.

4. Herbert Spiegelberg quotes the following entry
in Husserl's diary from the year 1906: "I have been
through enough torments from lack of clarity and
from doubt that wavers back and forth. . . .Only one
need absorbs me: I must win clarity, else I cannot
live; I cannot bear life unless I can believe that I
shall achieve it." *The Phenomenological Movement* (The Hague: Nijhoff, 1960), 1: 82.

5. Cf. Carr's Introduction to *Crisis*, pp. xxv-xxvi.

6. In a letter of 11 March 1935 to L. Lévy-Bruhl,
quoted by Spiegelberg, op. cit., p. 84.

7. *Crisis*, app. IV ("Philosophy as Mankind's
Self-Reflection; the Self-Realization of Reason"),
pp. 338, 341.

8. Cf. Husserl, *Ideas*, trans. W. R. Boyce Gibson
(New York: Collier Books, 1962), sec. 142, p. 365.

9. Ibid., sec. 144, p. 367, and sec. 143, p. 366.

10. Paul Ricoeur, "Husserl and the Sense of History," in *Husserl: An Analysis of His
Phenomenology* (EvanstonG Northwestern University Press, 1967), p. 147.

11. Albert Dondeyne, *Contemporary European
Thought and Christian Faith* (Pittsburgh: Duquesne
University Press, 1963), p. 112. Dondeyne is actually speaking of Merleau-Ponty but the characterization applies to Husserl as well, since it was precisely this "idealism of meaning" which the early
Merleau-Ponty inherited from Husserl and which in
his later years he was striving to overcome.

12. Emmanuel Lévinas, a pupil of both Husserl
and Heidegger, but more Heideggerian than Husserlian in his philosophical orientation, writes:
"L'idéalisme de Husserl qui s'exprime le mieux par
cette position du sujet en tant que monade ne con-
siste pas simplement à dire que le monde de notre
perception se réduit à des contenus psychologiques
comme le voudrai l'idéalisme berkeleyen. Car
l'idéalisme berkeleyen n'explique pas au fond en
quoi les contenus psychologiques sont plus subjec-
tifs que le monde extérieur qui s'y ramène.
L'idéalisme de Husserl essaie de définir le sujet en
tant qu'origine, en tant que lieu où toute chose ré-
pond d'elle-même." *En découvrant l'existence avec
Husserl et Heidegger* (Paris: Librairie Vrin, 1967),
p. 47.

13. Friedrich Nietzsche, *On the Geneology of
Morals/Ecce Homo*, trans. W. Kaufmann and R. J.
Hollindale (New York: Vintage Books, 1967), p. 153
(sec. 24).

14. I am thinking in particular of Paul Ricoeur.
While Ricoeur has objected to what he calls "Husserlian idealism" and wishes to substitute for this a
"hermeneutical phenomenology," and while he rejects the ideal of a philosophical *science*, he has not
gone so far as to call into question Husserl's under-

lying *idealism of meaning*. He says that he wishes to
disengage the wager for meaningfulness from
idealist presuppositions, but he finds it difficult to
abandon the idealist presupposition that experience
is essentially meaningful. "Il faut," he says, "sup-
poser que l'expérience dans toute son ampleur . . .a
une dicibilité de principe." While Ricoeur continues, therefore, to accept "la présupposition du
'sens'," he at least recognizes that "il est difficile, il
est vrai, de formuler cette présupposition dans un
langage non-idéaliste." Cf. his "Phénoménologie et
herméneutique" (Paris: Centre de recherches
phénoménologiques).

15. "Philosophy and the Crisis of European Humanity," app. I in Carr's translation of *Crisis* and
published also in E. Husserl, *Phenomenology and
the Crisis of Philosophy*, ed. Q. Lauer (New York:
Harper Torchbooks, 1965).

16. Cf. n. 5 above.

17. *Crisis*, p. 276.

18. See n. 6 above.

19. "Philosophy as Rigorous Science," in
Phenomenology and the Crisis of Philosophy, p.
127.

20. Husserl, "Phenomenology" (*Encyclopaedia
Britannica* article), reprinted in R. Zaner and D.
Ihde, eds., *Phenomenology and Existentialism*
(New York: G. P. Putnam's Sons, 1973), p. 67.

21. "Philosophy as Rigorous Science," p. 144.

22. *Crisis*, p. 273.

23. Suzanne Bachelard, *A Study of Husserl's
"Formal and Transcendental Logic*," trans. L.
Embree (Evanston: Northwestern University
Press, 1968), p. 106.

24. Husserl, *The Idea of Phenomenology*, trans.
W. Alton and G. Naknikian (The Hague: Nijhoff,
1964), p. 24.

25. Husserl, *Cartesian Meditations*, trans. Dorion Cairns (The Hague: Nijhoff, 1960), sec. 9, p. 22.

26. Ibid., sec. 3, p. 7.

27. "Phenomenology," p. 68.

28. Ibid., p. 66.

29. Ibid.

30. Besides the common rationalist ancestry
(Leibniz in particular, including, more recently,
Frege), which alone interests us here, both
positivism and Husserlian phenomenology are heirs
as well to British empiricism. Spiegelberg points out
that "the British empiricists from Locke to Hume
were Husserl's introductory readings in philosophy
and remained of basic importance to him all through
his later development. Often he gave them credit for
having developed a first though inadequate type of
phenomenology. He even kept recommending them
to his students, as I know from personal experience,
as one of the best approaches to phenomenology"
(*The Phenomenological Movement*, 1: 92-93). It
might be noted in this context that it was precisely
from empiricism that Husserl inherited his problem
of sense data ("hyletic" data) which French existential phenomenologists such as Sartre, Merleau-
Ponty, and Ricoeur were to find exceedingly embar-
rassing and even "unphenomenological." For if, as
Sartre says ("Une idée fondamentale de la
phénoménologie de Husserl: l'intentionalité"),

consciousness is essentially intentional, then "tout est dehors, tout, jusqu'à nous mêmes." Sense data cannot be really (genuinely) immanent to consciousness and there cannot even be things like sense data, since consciousness, being intentional, has no "inside" at all. (For Sartre's reaction to Husserl's notion of *hyle*, see *Being and Nothingness* [New York: Philosophical Library, 1956], p. lix. On p. 109 of this work Sartre says that Husserl's intentionality is only the "caricature" of genuine transcendence.) Husserl himself remarked in 1932: "Is not my original conception of the immanent sphere with immanent data which ultimately come to 'apprehension' only through the passive execution of association, still a remnant of the old psychology and its sensualistic empiricism?" (cited by Sokolowski, *The Formation of Husserl's Concept of Constitution*, pp. 179-80).

31. "Philosophy as Rigorous Science," p. 145. Cf. *Ideas*, sec. 20, p. 78: "If by *'positivism'* we are to mean the absolute unbiased grounding of all science on what is 'positive,' i.e., on what can be primordially apprehended, then it is *we* who are the genuine positivists." While Husserl credited logical positivism with being something of a "bulwark" against irrationalism, he did not think that it was at all adequate *qua* philosophy: "The bulwark of mathematical positivism will not help for long, since people will ultimately discover that it is a sham philosophy and not a true philosophy." Cited by Carr, *Crisis*, p. xxvi, n. 14.

32. "Phenomenology," p. 67.

33. Cf. *Cartesian Meditations*, sec. 64, p. 153.

34. Husserl, *Formal and Transcendental Logic*, trans. Dorion Cairns (The Hague: Nijhoff, 1969), sec. 103, p. 272.

35. "Phenomenology," p. 66.

36. *Ideas*, sec. 49, p. 139.

37. *The Idea of Phenomenology*, p. 60.

38. *Ideas*, sec. 86, p. 231.

39. Cf. *Cartesian Meditations,* sec. 21, 22.

40. Ibid., sec. 135, p. 347.

41. Husserl, *The Paris Lectures*, trans. P. Koestenbaum (The Hague: Nijhoff, 1967), p. 18.

42. Ricoeur, op. cit., p. 171.

43. *Crisis*, p. 275.

44. *Ideas, p. 21 ("Author's Preface to the English Edition")*.

45. *Cartesian Meditations*, sec. 3, p. 8.

46. Ibid. Quentin Lauer in his *Phénoménologie de Husserl* (Paris: Presses Universitaires de France, 1954) writes (p. 394): "Mais que l'idée d'une telle science supérieure, absolue, ainsi impliquée, soit une idée valable, cela, Husserl ne le soumet jamais réellement à la critique qu'il avait promise dans la *Première Méditation cartésienne.*"

47. "Philosophy as Rigorous Science," pp. 135ff.

48. Ibid., p. 141.

49. H.-G. Gadamer, "The Science of the Life-World," in Tymieniecka, ed., *Analecta Husserliana* (Dordrecht: D. Reidel, 1972), 2:184.

50. I borrow the term from W. T. Jones, *The Sciences and the Humanities* (Berkeley: University of California Press, 1967), p. 249, and my remarks that follow parallel—in part and up to a point only—those of Jones.

51. There is a remarkable convergence of the positions of the sophisticated absolutist and the sophisticated relativist, e.g., the pragmatist. Peirce and Husserl are first cousins in the contemporary idealist family. They tend to converge in their attempts to draw out the metaphysical implications of a radical philosophy of pure experience. "Philosophy of experience" is a modern incarnation of the idealist spirit.

52. *Ideas*, p. 259.

53. The following remarks of Gaston Berger are typical in this regard: "We would run into numerous contradictions if we were to apply Husserlian expressions strictly. Contrary to general opinion, nothing less resembles a scholasticism in which each term would have, once and for all, a perfectly determined meaning than does phenomenology. It is dogmatism that appears so sure of the future and does not hesitate to bind it with irrevocable definitions. Husserl wants to limit himself to describing what he sees." *The Cogito in Husserl's Philosophy*, trans. K. McLaughlin (Evanston: Northwestern University Press, 1972), pp. 53-54.

54. Ibid., sec. 84, p. 224.

55. Ibid., sec. 66, p. 176.

56. "The meanings of words are constantly shifting within the limits of immediate logical equivalence. But our business is to set out the equivalences everywhere, and to prune off sharply whatever reference to phenomena of an essentially different nature may lurk behind the equivalent concepts." *Ideas*, sec. 104, p. 276.

57. *Ideas*, sec. 124, p. 321. J. Derrida, in his translation of Husserl's *L'origine de géométrie* (Paris: Presses Universitaires de France, 1962), writes (P. 61): "Aux yeux de Husserl, il serait absurde que le sens ne précède pas . . .l'acte de langage dont la valeur propre sera toujours celle de l'*expression.*"

58. Cf. M. Merleau-Ponty, "Husserl et la notion de Nature," *Revue de métaphysique et morale* (July-September 1965), p. 264.

59. Gadamer, op. cit., pp. 183-84.

60. Cf. *Cartesian Meditations*, sec. 59.

61. "Among the objective sciences there is indeed a science of subjectivity; but it is precisely the science of objective subjectivity, the subjectivity of men and other animals, a subjectivity that is part of the world. Now, however, we are envisaging a science that is, so to speak, absolutely subjective, whose thematic object exists whether or not the world exists." *Cartesian Meditations*, sec. 13, p. 30.

62. Merleau-Ponty, *Phénoménologie de la perception* (Paris: Gallimard, 1945), p. viii.

63. Eugen Fink, "The Phenomenological Philosophy of Edmund Husserl and Contemporary Criticism," in R. O. Elveton, ed., *The Phenomenology of Husserl* (Chicago: Quadrangle Books, 1970), p. 109.

64. S. Bachelard, op. cit., p. 213.

65. Cf., for instance, Heidegger, *Being and Time,*

sec. 29, and Sartre, *Being and Nothingness*, p. lxvi.

66. *Cartesian Meditations*, sec. 64, p. 155.

67. Ibid., sec. 39, p. 81.

68. Gaston Berger, op. cit., p. 85.

69. Ibid., p. 82.

70. *Ideas*, sec. 47, p. 134.

71. *Cartesian Meditations*, sec. 60, pp. 140-141.

72. Ibid.

73. *Being and Nothingness*, p. lxvi. Sartre expresses the same points in more dramatic fashion in his novel *Nausea*.

74. Cf. ibid., sec. 59, p. 137.

75. Ibid., sec. 60, p. 141.

76. "Consequently, this system of the universal a priori must also be defined as the systematic development of the universal a priori which is inborn in the nature of transcendental subjectivity and intersubjectivity. It may further be defined as the systematic development of *the universal logos of all conceivable being*. In other words, a systematically and fully developed transcendental phenomenology is *ipso facto the true and genuine ontology*. It is not a vacuous and formal ontology, but one which includes all the regional possibilities of being and all their corresponding correlations. Thus universal and concrete ontology (also the universal logic of being) is therefore the first universe of science based on absolute proof." *Idea of Phenomenology*, p. 38. Cf. also *Cartesian Meditations*, sec. 64, p. 55.

77. "Such results and the course of the investigations leading to them enable us to understand how questions that, for traditional philosophy, had to lie beyond all the limits of science can acquire sense." *Cartesian Meditations*, sec. 60, p. 141.

78. It is perhaps worthwhile nothing in this regard that, as Lauer has observed (*Phénoménologie de Husserl*, p. 395), Husserl, in spite of his enormous indebtedness to Descartes, passes over in utter silence one of the key concepts in the latter's meditations, that of the *malin génie*.

79. Cf., respectively, *Cartesian Meditations*, sec. 24, p. 58, and sec. 41, p. 84.

80. Lévinas, op. cit., p. 47.

81. J. Derrida, *La voix et le phénomène* (Paris: Presses Universitaires de France, 1967), p. 9.

82. *Cartesian Meditations*, sec. 8, p. 20.

83. Derrida, *La voix*, p. 9.

84. *Ideas*, sec. 81, p. 217.

85. Ibid., sec. 82, p. 219.

86. Husserl, *The Phenomenology of Internal Time Consciousness*, trans. J. Churchill (The Hague: Nijhoff, 1964), p. 95.

87. Merleau-Ponty, it seems to me, was basically right in many respects when he wrote: "L' 'In-der-Welt-Sein' de Heidegger n'apparait que sur le fond de la réduction phénoménologique" (*Phénoménologie de la perception*, p. ix). It should not be said, however, as Merleau-Ponty nevertheless does, that Husserl's philosophy is not an idealism but rather that in being an idealism it is nonetheless concerned with the question of the being of the world. It is the existence of things that the reduction has as its essential function to make us aware of. In this respect Heidegger, far from reject-ing the reduction, can be said to presuppose it. Husserl's idealism has for its theme the existence of the world, and it is for this reason that Heidegger's anti-idealism can find in transcendental idealism a convenient point of departure. Heidegger writes in *Being and Time*: "As compared with realism, *idealism*, no matter how contrary and untenable it may be in its results, has an advantage in principle, provided that it does not misunderstand itself as 'psychological' idealism" (p. 251). Heidegger goes on to say that even more basic than the idealist attempt to explain being through consciousness, rather than just through entities, is the need to inquire into the being of consciousness itself.

88. *Cartesian Meditations*, sec. 64, p. 156. On the question of the life-world, cf. ibid., sec. 59, p. 138, for an interesting text wherein Husserl seems to be saying in effect that nothing prevents one from approaching the Husserlian problem of transcendental constitution by starting out from the type of analysis of being-in-the-world which Heidegger gives us in *Being and Time*. Husserl seems to be attempting to find a place for Heidegger in the context of his own transcendental phenomenology.

89. It seems to me that Maurice Natanson in his attractive study, *Edmund Husserl: Philosopher of Infinite Tasks* (Evanston: Northwestern University Press, 1973), has not sufficiently taken into account the "pseudomorphic factor."

90. Hans Jonas, *The Gnostic Religion* (Boston: Beacon Press, 1963).

91. I am speaking here, of course, of the *philosophical* world-view of the Greeks. As Nietzsche had the merit to point out, there is much in the Greek mentality which does not filter through into its philosophy.

92. Otto Pöggeler, *Der Denkweg Martin Heideggers* (Pfüllingen: Gunther Neske, 1963). Cf. also the following articles of H. Jonas: "Gnosticism, Existentialism, and Nihilism" and "Heidegger and Theology," both reprinted in Jonas, *The Phenomenon of Life* (New York: Delta Books, 1966).

93. *Being and Nothingness*, p. 615.

94. Ibid., p. 90.

95. Cf. esp. his *The Myth of Sisyphus*.

96. Merleau-Ponty, *In Praise of Philosophy* (Evanston: Northwestern Univeristy Press, 1963), p. 26, italics mine. In the text quoted, Merleau-Ponty is actually referring to Bergson, but the remark could be taken to be self-referential. For a detailed treatment of Merleau-Ponty's philosophical development, see my *La phénoménologie de Merleau-Ponty: une recherche des limites de la conscience* (Paris: Editions Klincksieck, 1973).

97. J.-P. Sartre, "Merleau-Ponty," in *Situations IV* (Paris: Gallimard, 1964), p. 266. In this essay Sartre reflects on his life-long relationship with Merleau-Ponty.

98. For the relations of the late Merleau-Ponty to Husserl and Heidegger, see my remarks in the joint Geraets/Madison symposium, "Autour de Merleau-Ponty: deux lectures de son oeuvre," *Philosophiques*, vol. 2, no. 1 (April 1975): 103-30.

99. Sartre, *Search for a Method* (New York: Knopf, 1963), p. 8.

100. G. Marcel, *The Philosophy of Existentialism* (New York: Citadel Press, 1961), p. 88. See my article "The Ambiguous Philosophy of Merleau-Ponty," *Philosophical Studies* (Ireland), 22: 63-77.

101. Gadamer, op. cit., p. 185.

102. Ludwig Landgrebe, "Husserl's Departure from Cartesianism," in Elveton, ed., *The Phenomenology of Husserl*, p. 260. Landgrebe goes on to write (p. 261): "Today, primarily as a result of Heidegger's work, the 'end of metaphysics' is spoken of as if with a certain obviousness. We shall first properly understand the sense of such language if we follow closely how, in this work [*Ideas*], metaphysics takes its departure behind Husserl's back. One can state quite frankly that this work *is* the end of metaphysics in the sense that after it any further advance along the concepts and paths of thought from which metaphysics seeks forcefully to extract the most extreme possibilities is no longer possible. To be sure, neither Husserl nor those who were his students at that time were explicitly aware of this, and it will still require a long and intensive struggle of interpretation and continuing thoughtful deliberation until we have experienced everything that here comes to an end." Cf. also Landgrebe's *Major Problems in Contemporary European Philosophy* (New York: F. Ungar, 1966), p. 28.

103. As a "philosopher of infinite tasks," Husserl concedes that a "total science" is a de facto impossibility, but he nonetheless would want to say that this does not invalidate the quest for such a science. What Husserl and the "sophisticated absolutist" do not see is that if the ideal of Science is not *actually* attainable, the search for it can only be, when all is said and done, a senseless pursuit after a meaningless will-o'-the-wisp.

104. Merleau-Ponty, *The Visible and the Invisible*, trans. A. Lingis (Evanston: Northwestern University Press, 1968), p. 102.

105. Heidegger, *On Time and Being*, trans. Joan Stambaugh (New York: Harper & Row, 1972), p. 2.

106. T. S. Eliot, *Four Quartets* ("Burnt Norton").

Husserl and Kant on the Pure Ego

JOSEPH J. KOCKELMANS

1. Husserl's Development in Relation to Kant and the Neo-Kantians

In a remarkable book, Iso Kern has given us a detailed account of the development of Husserl's thought in regard to the philosophy of Kant and neo-Kantianism.[1] In this book Kern explains that although Husserl attended lectures by Friedrich Paulsen, who in his epistemology took his point of departure in Kant but, in the manner of Helmholtz, interpreted Kant in a physico-psychological sense, Husserl did not really come in contact with Kant's philosophy before he met Franz Brentano. The latter, who was equally influenced by Helmholtz in his understanding of Kant's philosophy, had come to a very negative attitude toward Kant and was probably the leading Kant critic in the last two decades of the nineteenth century. Husserl adopted Brentano's views on Kant without personal study of Kant's works and those of his great commentators and turned his attention mainly to the leading empiricist philosophers (Locke, Berkeley, Hume, Stuart Mill) and to Leibniz, Bolzano, Lotze, and Herbart.[2]

After the publication of his *Philosophie der Arithmetik* (1891),[3] Husserl began to change his opinion about the value of Kant's epistemology. The change was influenced by two major events. On the one hand there was Frege's criticism of Husserl's *Philosophie der Arithmetik*.[4] On the other there was Natorp's critique of psychologism, formulated in his review of Lipps' *Grundtatsachen des Seelenlebens* and his article "Über objektive and subjektive Begründung der Erkenntnis."[5] Accordingly, in the period between 1894 and 1901 Husserl began for the first time to make a personal study of some of Kant's works and the publications of some of Kant's commentators, including Vaihinger, Natorp, and Cohen.[6]

However, Husserl was not involved in a thorough study of Kant's philosophy before 1907. Between 1907 and 1913 he examined Kant's epistemology more carefully,[7] and during that period he grew closer to several leading neo-Kantians (Natorp, Rickert, Cassirer).[8] Also in this period he read Wernicke's *Die Theorie des Gegenstandes und die Lehre vom Dinge-an-sich bei Immanuel Kant*[9] and Ewald's *Kants Methodologie in ihren Grundzügen*,[10] both of which had a great influence on Husserl's later interpretation of Kant's epistemology.[11]

According to his own view, the turn from his original conception of phenomenology (as found in the second volume of *Logical Investigations*) to transcendental phenomenology, first explained in a series of lectures in 1907 and later systematically developed in the first volume of *Ideas* in 1913, had come about under the influence of Descartes and the pre-Kantian philosophy after Descartes, rather than through the philosophy of Kant.[12] In 1917 Husserl turned again to Kant's philosophy, and this time the renewed contact with Kant and the neo-

Kantian tradition was to begin to influence Husserl's own thought, in that it would lead him gradually from his original static conception of phenomenology to genetic phenomenology.[13] The direct influence of Kant and the neo-Kantians became, from then on, more and more perspicuous in Husserl's work particularly in *Erste Philosophie*,[14] *Formal and Transcendental Logic*,[15] and notably in *Crisis*.[16]

During this long development Husserl's view on the value of Kant's philosophy changed from a very negative and critical attitude to one of great admiration and affiliation. In 1887 Husserl shared Brentano's view that Kant's philosophy represents a phase of skepsis and radical decline in philosophy.[17] In *Logical Investigations* Husserl calls Kant one of the great thinkers,[18] whereas in a note of the same period he writes that in his view Kant contributed more to the solution of the basic epistemological problem than any of his predecessors, including Descartes.[19] In the *Logos* article Husserl writes that a fully conscious will toward rigorous science, which dominated the Socratic-Platonic revolution in philosophy as well as the Cartesian revolution, "renews itself with most radical vigor in Kant's critique of reason."[20] In the first volume of *Ideas* Husserl speaks of an affinity between Kant's epistemology and transcendental phenomenology,[21] and states that in some of his reflections in the *Critique of Pure Reason* Kant "already moves strictly on phenomenological grounds."[22] Similar ideas are repeated in *Erste Philosophie*.[23] The most positive evaluation of Kant's philosophy is found in Husserl's essay "Kant und die Idee der Transzendentalphilosophie."[24] This positive attitude toward Kant's work is maintained in all of Husserl's later works. In *Crisis* Husserl argues that Kant was on the way to a genuine transcendental philosophy in Husserl's conception of this expression. He writes:

It is a philosophy which, in opposition to prescientific and scientific objectivism, goes back to the knowing subjectivity as the primal locus of all objective formations of sense and ontic

validities, undertakes to understand the existing world as a structure of sense and validity, and in this way seeks to set in motion an essentially new type of scientific attitude and a new type of philosophy. In fact . . .the Kantian system is the first attempt, and one carried out with impressive scientific seriousness, at a truly universal transcendental philosophy meant to be a *rigorous science* in a sense of scientific rigor which has only now been discovered and which is the only genuine sense.[25]

Yet, although it is true that Husserl gradually learned to appreciate the greatness of Kant's work and began to realize that there was a great affinity between Kant's transcendental philosophy and his own transcendental phenomenology, he always tried to avoid giving the impression that his own philosophy originated from Kant's philosophy or even should be understood from the perspective of the entire Kantian tradition.[26] In addition, all positive evaluation of Kant's philosophy notwithstanding, Husserl never refrained from severely criticizing Kant's philosophy with respect to a number of issues which are essential to Kant's critical philosophy taken as a whole. Among these issues the following are the most important.

(1) Kant misconceived the real meaning of the concept of *a priori* and thus did not see the necessity of introducing a nonformal or material a priori in the sense of Bolzano (the *eide*) in addition to the formal a priori employed by Kant himself. (2) Kant too rigorously separated sensibility and reason. (3) Kant did not make a distinction between *noesis* and *noema*, and neglected making a careful study of the noetic side of consciousness.

(4) Kant did not really push forward to the genuine root of the epistemological problem, and maintained a number of unexamined dogmatic presuppositions in his own philosophy. (5) Kant did not realize the necessity of the transcendental reduction. (6) Kant's thing-in-itself is to be rejected and his concept of phenomenon to be reinterpreted.

(7) Kant maintained a natural, psychological conception of the subject

and failed to see the need of thrusting forward to the transcendental subjectivity. (8) Kant did not yet realize the possibility of a genuinely transcendental experience.

(9) Kant failed to see that the constitution of inner time consciousness forms the deepest level, as far as all constitutive problems are concerned. (10) Kant did not realize that the problem concerning the constitution of scientific objects presupposes the problem concerning the original constitution of the life-world.

(11) Kant never developed a transcendental study of formal logic. (12) Kant's regressive-constructive methodology is totally inadequate for dealing with transcendental problems; his method must be replaced by one which discovers and shows what is given primordially, on the basis of immediate intuition.

Iso Kern has developed Husserl's critique of Kant concerning these and other issues in great detail.[27] In the pages to follow I wish to focus on some aspects of Husserl's criticism of Kant's conception of the pure ego. Both Marbach[28] and Kern[29] have stressed that, particularly with respect to the pure ego, Husserl was at first more directly influenced by Natorp than by Kant. This is particularly true for the first phase of Husserl's contact with critical philosophy. Both in the first and the second edition of *Logical Investigations* Husserl tried explicitly to establish his own position in regard to Natorp's conception of the pure ego—not directly to Kant's view on the relevant issues. And still, in the second volume of *Ideas*, it is Natorp and not directly Kant with whom Husserl engages in a dialogue concerning the pure ego. Yet it should be noted that in the latter case Natorp is no longer mentioned explicitly. From 1916 on, however, Husserl began to focus more directly on Kant's conception of the ego, as we shall see.[30]

2. Development in Husserl's Conception of the Ego (1887-1915)

The problematic connected with the ego originally occupied a very unimportant place in Husserl's reflections. Between 1887 and 1895 it appears that Husserl was acquainted with Kant's conception of subjectivity through the lectures and publications of Brentano and the works of Helmholtz. Both Helmholtz and Brentano interpreted the Kantian ego in a physiologico-psychological manner. From 1895 on, Husserl rejected this conception of the ego as part of an unacceptable form of psychologism. In 1900 Husserl appears still to have been convinced that Kant's idealism is a form of psychologism, but meanwhile had begun to realize that Kant's epistemology contains a number of elements which go beyond psychologism.[31] Gradually Husserl began to realize that Kant's subjective concepts cannot be explained, simply and solely, psychologically. Yet he maintained at that time that one does not find in Kant a methodical investigation nor an acceptable explanation of the deeper meaning of these concepts. Kant's approach to epistemological issues is affected he said, by a "mythical unintelligibility."[32]

In the second volume of *Logical Investigations* (1901) Husserl describes Natorp's conception of the pure ego or the ego of pure apperception—which is supposed to provide the unitary center of relation, to which all conscious content is as such referred in a very peculiar fashion. According to this view, the pure ego pertains essentially to the fact of subjective experience; being-in-consciousness is relation-to-the-ego, and whatever stands in this relation is a content of consciousness. This relation is always one and the same despite the manifold variations of content. The ego cannot itself be a content of consciousness, and it resembles nothing that could be a content of consciousness. For this reason, it cannot be further described. Concerning this view, Husserl says he must frankly confess that he is quite unable to find such an ego. "The only things I can take note of, and therefore perceive, are the empirical ego and its empirical relations to its own experiences...."[33]

In the second edition of *Logical Inves-*

tigations Husserl changed his conception of the ego. This change was influenced by (among other things) a more careful study of Natorp's publications. In a footnote found in the second edition Husserl remarks: "I have since managed to find it [the pure ego], i.e. have learned not to be led astray from a pure grasp of the given through corrupt forms of metaphysics."[34] In another footnote Husserl points to the fact that the empirical ego is as much a case of transcendence as the physical things. If the elimination of all transcendence, through the reduction, leaves us with no residual pure ego, there can be no real and adequate self-evidence attached to the *I am*. "But if there is really such an adequate self-evidence, how can one avoid assuming a pure ego?"[35]

The new insights concerning the pure ego to which Husserl had come between 1900 and 1913, and to which he merely alluded in the second edition of *Logical Investigations*, are developed in greater detail in the first volume of *Ideas*.[36] Husserl there states, in agreement with Natorp, that the pure ego belongs necessarily to every actual experience insofar as the ego's "glance" goes through every actual experience toward the object. In that sense one can say that the "I think" must be able to accompany all my presentations. Yet, Husserl continues, although every *cogito* is characterized as an act of the ego, the experiencing ego, taken in and for itself, cannot be made into an object of its own account. The ego is completely empty of essential components; it has no content that could be unraveled; it is pure ego and nothing further.[37]

Between 1912 and 1915 Husserl changed his view about the latter point, which was stressed in the first volume of *Ideas*. It is not true that the pure ego cannot be made into an object, as Natorp held. On the contrary, the pure ego can be grasped intuitively; the ego lives in the different types and modes of our experiences in different manners. Thus these modes of being can and must be described phenomenologically in constitutive analyses. Furthermore, Husserl argued, the pure ego is something that is inherently part of an intersubjective community, and not, as in Natorp's view, just an ego (*nur ein Ich überhaupt*).[38]

These new insights were formulated in systematic fashion for the first time in the second volume of *Ideas*. This work originated in 1912 and was reworked several times between 1912 and 1928, but it did not appear before Husserl's death. The book treats some very important groups of constitutive problems whose formulation and solution are a necessary condition to establish the relationship between phenomenology and the natural sciences, psychology, and the cultural sciences. The book consists of three major parts, devoted to the constitution of material nature, the constitution of psychic nature, and the constitution of cultural phenomena.[39]

In the second part of this work (which was probably added in 1915)[40] Husserl carefully distinguishes different concepts of the ego: (1) our everyday conception of the ego as this human being in the real world, (2) the pure ego, (3) the real psychic subject to be dealt with in psychology, and (4) the personal ego which plays the predominant role in the study of cultural phenomena. If we systematically order the various theses concerning the *pure* ego as found in the second volume of *Ideas*, we get the following picture.

The unity of the stream of conscious experiences presupposes that the stream is polarized by the ego; thus the pure ego is the individual ego-pole of all conscious acts on the ground of which they all have the form "*cogito*". This pole can be grasped intuitively as identical in each act of consciousness. The ego lives in its acts; it is active in them, but it can also be passively affected (*leidet*). The pure ego is not a real part of any act; it constitutes something "transcendent" in regard to the stream of experiences. The pure ego is unchangeable, absolutely simple, and empty of all content. It cannot be thought of as separated or distinct from its own life. Taken in and for itself, the pure ego is the functional center of the stream of experiences. The stream of experiences cannot be without the ego-polarization; all experiences can be changed into *cogitationes*. The pure ego is temporally enduring but its duration is of a different nature than the duration of the experiences themselves. The pure ego, however, is not the ground of the unity of consciousness; this unity is constituted by immanent time. The pure ego does not maintain its self-identity the way the real ego does; it has no character traits, abilities, or changeable properties. The ego, taken as I, this man in the real world, is a self-objectification of the pure ego. The real ego, taken as transcendent object, is constituted; the pure ego is given immanently. Finally, the pure ego is a substrate of habitualities in the sense that, once a position has been taken, the ego is henceforth as the ego that took that stand.[41]

These theses concerning the ego show clearly that Husserl's conception of the ego had come closer to Kant's ideas. Yet Husserl explicitly defends the view that the pure ego can grasp itself as that which it is and how it functions; thus the pure ego is not a subject that can never become an object.[42] Husserl acknowledges parallels between his own view and the basic ideas of Kant, but at that time he was not yet able positively to interpret Kant's conception of the transcendental apperception as the foundation for the unity of the objects of consciousness.[43]

Concerning the preceding reflections, three remarks seem to be in order. We have just seen that in *Ideen II*[44] Husserl mentions for the first time the idea that the unity of the pure ego is conditioned (or perhaps constituted) by its habitualities. He says there, explicitly, that the identity of the pure ego can be explained by the fact that (1) in regard to each *cogito* the ego can grasp itself as the identical ego of this *cogito*, and—more importantly—(2) I appear to myself a priori as the *same* ego insofar as every position I take necessarily leaves its consequence; it establishes a conviction that will remain. However, Husserl here limits himself to habitualities in regard to

individual position-takings; he does not yet mention the most fundamental thesis concerning the ego: its positing the world as universal horizon and the relation of primordially posited world to the identity of the ego.[45]

Secondly, the assertion that the pure ego is a pole of habitualities seems to be in conflict with the thesis that the pure ego is unchangeable. In the second volume of *Ideas*[46] Husserl specifies the latter thesis by claiming that the pure ego is not changeable in the common sense of the term. The pure ego, reflecting on the various experiences of the concrete ego, changes in the sense that it is the pole of ever increasing habitualities; but these changes are of a totally different nature than those to which the concrete subject in the world is continuously subject. This is ultimately due to the fact that inner time is basically different from mundane time.

Thirdly, according to Husserl the pure ego can be made into an object; and this is done by the identical, the same pure ego.[47] The pure ego can do this by reflecting on a preceding *cogito* which is still present in retention, or which can be made present again in recollection. In both cases there is an "original" *reflecting* ego and an *objectified* pure ego. Yet, from the perspective of a higher reflection, both egos appear as truly the same, identical ego. That the pure ego can be objectified is possible through the fact that the pure ego is inherently enduring; namely, it is in inner time; it is a unity which is constituted in inner time consciousness. In the Time lecture of 1905, and even in the first volume of *Ideas* (1913), Husserl had claimed that time consciousness is without ego-polarization.[48] From 1915 on, Husserl began to defend the view that in these instances, too, an ego-polarization is to be found; however, he then thought that the ego, taken as constituted in inner time consciousness, cannot be grasped intuitively; it can only be reconstructed. In his development of this point Husserl was again influenced by Natorp.[49]

In the next phase of the development of his conception of the ego (1916-28), Husserl began to concentrate more explicitly on Kant's idea concerning the ego. In these reflections Husserl very seldom quotes Kant directly; he seems to assume that his audience is familiar with Kant's philosophy.

To make the present discussion more readily understandable, I wish to interrupt my explanation of Husserl's development at this point to focus briefly on a few sections of Kant's *Critique of Pure Reason* which are immediately pertinent to the issue under consideration.

3. Kant's Conception of the Ego

In the *Critique of Pure Reason* Kant speaks about the ego in two different contexts; the first is titled "The Deduction of the Pure Concepts of the Understanding"[50] whereas the second is found in the transcendental dialectic under the heading "The Paralogisms of Pure Reason."[51]

In the deduction of the pure concepts of the understanding, Kant is concerned first with the unity of our representations. Although the *manifold* of representations can be given in intuition, the *combination* of a manifold into a unity can never come to us through the senses, for this combination is an act of spontaneity of the faculty of representation, namely, our understanding. Thus all combination, whatever nature it may be, is an act of the understanding, and to this act the general title of synthesis may be assigned. Synthesis cannot be executed except by the subject itself. The concept of combination now includes, besides the concept of the manifold and its synthesis, the concept of the unity of the manifold. Combination is representation of the synthetic unity of the manifold. Thus the representation of this unity cannot arise out of the combination. On the contrary, it is that which, by adding itself to the representation of the manifold, first makes possible the concept of the combination. Since this unity precedes, a priori, all concepts of combination, it cannot be the category of unity. Thus we must look elsewhere for this unity, namely in that which itself contains the ground of the

unity of diverse concepts in judgment. In Kant's view this unity is to be found in the original synthetic unity of apperception. He explains this view as follows.

It must be possible for the "I think" to accompany all my representations; otherwise something would be represented in me which could not be thought at all. That representation which can be given prior to all thought is called intuition. Thus all the manifolds of intuition have a necessary relation to the "I think" in that subject in which this manifold is found. But this representation is an act of spontaneity and, thus, cannot be regarded as belonging to sensibility. Kant calls it *pure* apperception to distinguish it from empirical apperception, and also *original* apperception because it is that self-consciousness which, while generating the representation "I think," which must be capable of accompanying all other representations and in all consciousness is one and the same, cannot itself be accompanied by any further representation. The unity of this apperception is likewise called the *transcendental* unity of self-consciousness in order to indicate the possibility of a priori knowledge arising from it. For the manifold representations, which are given in intuition, would not be one, and constitute all *my* representations, if they did not all belong to one self-consciousness.

Thus the thoroughgoing identity of the apperception of a manifold which is given in intuition contains a synthesis of representations, and is possible only through the consciousness of this synthesis. For empirical consciousness, which accompanies different representations, is in itself diverse and without relation to the identity of the subject. The relation to the identity of the subject comes about not simply through my accompanying each representation with consciousness, but only insofar as *I conjoin* the one representation with the other and am conscious of the synthesis of them. Thus only insofar as I can unite a manifold of given representations in one consciousness is it possible for me to represent to myself the identity of the consciousness in and through these representations The principle of the synthetic unity of apperception therefore states that all my representations in any given intuition must be subject to that condition under which alone I can ascribe them to the identical self as *my* representations and so can comprehend them as synthetically combined in one apperception through the universal expression "I think."[52]

In the paralogisms of pure reason Kant shows that the subjectivity of the subject cannot be further determined by claiming that the I of the "I think" is a soul and thus a substance characterized by simplicity, and personality. At the conclusion of his reflections on this issue Kant states that, in what we call soul, everything is in continual flux and there is nothing abiding except the "I", which is simple solely because its representation has no content, and therefore no manifold, and for this reason *seems* to denote a simple object. In order for it to be possible, by pure reason, to obtain knowledge of the nature of a thinking being, this "I" would have to be an intuition which, in being presupposed in all thought prior to all experience, might as intuition yield a priori synthetic propositions. However, this "I" is as little an intuition as it is a concept of an object. It is the mere form of consciousness, which can accompany our representations and which is in a position to elevate them to the rank of knowledge only insofar as something else is given in intuition which provides material for a representation of an object.[53]

One sees that Kant is the first in the modern era to realize that, on the basis of the phenomenal content found in saying "I" one can show that the classical theses about the soul which were inferred from the characteristics of substantiality, simplicity, and personality are without justification. In an attempt to do full justice to the phenomenal content of saying "I" Kant describes the ego as a bare consciousness which accompanies all concepts. In the ego, nothing more is represented than the transcendental subject of all thought. Consciousness in itself is not so much a representation as *the form* of

representation in general. The "I think" is the form of apperception, which clings to every experience and precedes it.[54] In other words, the "I think" is not something represented but is the formal structure of representing as such. The "I" is the subject of all our logical activities whose basic function it is to combine. "I think" thus means "I combine," "I bind together," and all binding-together is an "*I* bind together. The subject, or ego, is therefore consciousness in itself—not a representation but the form of representation in general. It is the formal structure which alone makes it possible for anything to have been represented. It is the necessary condition that makes every representation and everything represented be what it is.[55]

From the manner in which Kant introduces the problematic concerning the ego, it is clear that his major concern in the *Critique* was to determine the objectivity of the object. According to Kant, there must be a transcendental condition for the unity of consciousness in the synthesis of the manifold of all our intuitions. This condition cannot be found in the object; thus this original and transcendental condition is no other than transcendental apperception, namely, the pure original and unchangeable consciousness, the original and necessary consciousness of the identity of the self. When Kant later asks whether the mode of Being of the ego or self can be determined by claiming that it is a soul-substance, having certain characteristics, the answer has to be no because the consciousness of the identity of the self is a necessary condition for the application of the categories, and thus it itself can never be determined by means of the categories. All we can say about the ego is that it is the form of our representations in the sense indicated above.

4. Kantian Elements in Husserl's Conception of the Ego (1916-28)

From 1916 on, Husserl gradually came to a more positive evaluation of the philosophy of Kant, and this development would leave its marks on Husserl's final conception of the ego. In a 1916 lecture (from the series *Kant und die Philosophie der Neuzeit*) Husserl interpreted Kant's doctrine of the transcendental apperception by claiming that, in Kant's view, the ego is present to itself as ego necessarily insofar as it is thinking ego, but as thinking it necessarily thinks objects; to thinking, it relates itself necessarily to a world of existing objects (*eine seiende Objektwelt*).[56] The pure subject is such that it can maintain itself as identical with itself only insofar as it can maintain the world of objects as continuously identical with itself in all of its thinking activities. In the years to follow, Husserl returned to this idea on many occasions. Maintaining the Kantian title "transcendental apperception" Husserl no longer suggested this view as an interpretation of Kant's *Critique* but, rather, began to consider this insight as a new element of his own philosophical conception of the pure ego.[57]

At the same time, Husserl began to reject the idea of the pure ego as mere ego-pole. "I-pole is not I. I am in my habitual convictions. I maintain my own identical I, my ideal *Verstandesich*, when continuously and assuredly I can strive for the unity of an all-encompassing conviction and continuously one and the same world of objects maintains itself for me."[58] A uniform world, therefore, is the necessary correlate of the noetic identity of the ego, which maintains itself throughout the entire "life" of the pure ego, all changing of position in regard to details notwithstanding.[59] Thus, in Husserl's view, the constitution of a world as a uniform "cosmos" has a double but related function in regard to the constitution of the unity of the ego. First, the conviction of the consistency of the world is a condition for the consistency of the "life" of the pure ego as a whole, but, second, this conviction is also the foundation (horizon) of all individual convictions concerning transcendent things and events.[60]

However, Husserl does not yet draw the conclusion from this that it should be possible to derive a definitive, general on-tology of the world that is valid for all conceptions of world, or (as Kant did) derive a limited set of categories and axioms or principles that is valid for all theoretical knowledge of the world.[61] The only thing Husserl maintains here is that the realization of the ego is conditioned by the realization of the world as uniform in principle. The ego is not just a pure ego-pole but a subject that has convictions concerning what is transcendent. In other words, Husserl subscribes to "Kant's thesis" that the uniformity of the world of objects is a "necessary condition" for the unity of the pure ego, but adds to this thesis the idea that the pure ego is to be characterized by its convictions and specific egological habitualities. In addition, he explicitly rejects Kant's conception of the *metaphysical* relation between the pure ego and the possibility of its self-realization through the constitution of a uniform world that has validity for it.[62] Finally, Husserl claims that in the *Critique* Kant did not thrust forward to the *radical* epistemological problem, because he maintained *transcendent* elements in a reflection that was meant to be *transcendental*, namely, the thing-in-itself and a purely psychological ego.

Concerning the latter, Husserl says that in the *Critique* the faculties of the ego and all the functional laws are derived from the natural reality of the subject taken as this human person; thus Kant failed to make a distinction between the ego as this real man in the world and the pure ego.[63]

In 1917, in his lectures on Fichte, Husserl slightly reevaluated his judgment of Kant's *Critique*. He admits that Kant's epistemology can be interpreted in different ways. He rejects the physiological as well as the psychological interpretations, seeing them as conflicting with Kant's deepest intention. Kant really intended to develop a strictly transcendental theory of man's theoretical knowledge. In the framework of this endeavor, the pure ego of Kant must be understood from the viewpoint of Leibniz' monad, which, in turn, is to be comprehended in the sense of Descartes' pure ego.[64] It is true that in the *Critique* Kant keeps making use of elements of the pre-given world; and yet at the same time he *constructs* a subjectivity through whose *concealed*, transcendental functions the entire world of experience is formed with necessity. The problem here is that a particular quality of the human soul (which itself belongs to the world) is supposed to accomplish the formative process which constitutes the entire world of objects. In the *Critique*, as soon as one tries to distinguish between the soul and the subjectivity as constituting, one is confronted with something incomprehensibly mythical.[65]

Husserl's new interpretation of Kant's conception of the pure ego can perhaps be formulated as follows. According to Husserl, Kant's conception of the ego can be interpreted psychologically and phenomenologically. Kant aims at the transcendental-phenomenological dimension and his investigations move on a transcendental-phenomenological level. Yet Kant was unable to examine this dimension *methodically*, and appears to have been unable to follow the correct road systematically. The consequence was that the essence of the transcendental dimension remained partly unclarified and that several remnants of psychologism were left. Yet, Husserl adds to this—with an intuitive power which has no equal—Kant has seen essential structures of the subjectivity which are of extreme importance.[66]

It should be noted that when Husserl, under Kant's influence, came to the conclusion that the conviction concerning the consistency of the world is a necessary condition for the unity of the pure ego's life, he fully realized that this thesis was in conflict with his view (developed after 1908) that, in principle, it always remains possible for the entire world to be dissolved into chaos (*ein sinnloses Gewühl*). Between 1918 and 1926 Husserl returned several times to the thesis that the pure ego of the transcendental apperception which constitutes itself through the constitution of the world is and remains *a mere fact*, if seen from the viewpoint of the transcendental dimen-

sion. This thesis could perhaps be explained by pointing to the fact that although the pure ego, as this self-same ego, cannot maintain itself except on the basis of a world which has at least some consistency, this world itself need not necessarily be *our* world and need not be in harmony with the conception of world as developed in our empirical sciences. From the context it is indeed clear that Husserl tried to avoid establishing a too rigorous relationship between the self-realization of the pure ego and the constitution of the world as we find it in Kant, who had claimed that the categorial form of the world has its sufficient ground in the very being of the pure ego, or in Fichte, who had defended the thesis that the (absolute) ego posits the world on the basis of its own power alone in necessity.[67]

Yet in 1926 Husserl goes so far as to say that even such a minimally consistent world is not necessary for the unity of the pure ego. For although the pure ego, under the supposition that it were to reject every conceivable consistent world for some reason or other, would no longer have a world as objective and intersubjectively ratified, there would still be the unity of its own life in the unity of immanent time. In that supposition, Husserl continues, the pure ego would still be the self-same, but it would no longer be the self-same in regard to the world and to nature. It would no longer be in a world; it would be strictly without world.[68]

This text, which I think cannot be taken literally, because such an ego would no longer be a *finite subject*, shows clearly that the relationship between the constitution of the world and the pure ego continued to remain enigmatic for Husserl.

5. Systematic Explanation of Husserl's Final Conception of the Ego

Husserl has given us an idea of his final conception of the ego in several of his last publications. The most elaborate description of the ego is found in *Cartesian Meditations*;[69] shorter versions of this description are found in *Formal and Transcendental Logic*[70] and in *Crisis*.[71] It is well known that Husserl was dissatisfied with certain passages of the *Cartesian Meditations* because of difficulties encountered in the last Meditation, which showed the problematic character of the entire approach employed in that work. Later he tried to solve these difficulties by following another road to phenomenology; the insights gained from this endeavor were then systematically developed in *Crisis*. In the pages to follow I shall attempt to give a survey of Husserl's final view, using ideas from the three works mentioned. Where the explanation given in the *Cartesian Meditations* is in conflict with those found in the other two works, I shall follow the description presented in *Crisis*. But before we turn to these texts we must briefly deal with the introduction of the distinction between *pure* and *transcendental* ego, a distinction Husserl had not made in his earlier publications.

In the first and second volumes of *Ideen* Husserl does not use the expression "transcendental ego," nor does he attribute to the pure ego the function later attributed to the transcendental ego or subject. In the first volume of that work, discussing the phenomenological reduction, Husserl asks whether the pure ego is also affected by the reduction. Husserl explains that what is left after the reduction is the stream of pure consciousness, but he immediately adds that the pure ego is "permanently, even necessarily, there" in each experience of the stream. The pure ego "belongs to every experience that comes and streams past; its 'glance' goes 'through' every actual *coglto*, and towards the object....But the ego remains self-identical...the pure ego appears to be *necessary* in principle, and as that which remains absolutely self-identical in all real and possible changes of experience." In every actual *cogito* the ego lives its life in a special sense, but all experiences belong to it and it to them. And all of them, as belonging to *one* single stream of experience—that, namely, which is *mine*—must permit of

being transformed into actual *cogitationes*: the "I think" of Kant must be able to accompany all my presentations.[72] In the description of the general structures of pure consciousness he repeats that in the transcendentally purified field of experience the relation of that experience to the pure ego is maintained. Every *cogito* is characterized as an act of the ego, proceeding from the ego. The reduction cannot affect this. On the other hand, Husserl continues, the experiencing ego cannot be taken *for itself* and made into an object on its *own* account. Apart from its ways of being related or ways of behaving, it is completely empty of essential components: it has no content that could be unraveled and, taken in and for itself, it is indescribable; it is pure ego and nothing further.[73] Finally, where Husserl describes the transcendental constitution which is found on different levels, the expression "the originally giving consciousness" is used to refer to the "subject" of the deepest layer of constitution, and the expressions "transcendental ego or transcendental subject" are not yet used.[74]

The distinction between the pure and the transcendental ego was introduced by Husserl when he became aware of the possibility of a phenomenological psychology in addition to transcendental phenomenology. At that time it became clear that a distinction had to be made between the phenomenologico-psychological reduction and the transcendental reductions and, correspondingly, between the pure and transcendental egos.[75] In Husserl's works these distinctions were introduced for the first time in *Erste Philosophie* (1923-24)[76] and in *Phänomenologische Psychologie* (1925-26).[77] From then on the expressions came to belong to the basic terminology of Husserl's phenomenology.

These brief remarks, together with the reminder that between 1915 and 1923 Husserl gradually began to attribute a much more important role to the ego in his phenomenology than he had between 1907 and 1915, will help us understand

Husserl's final conception of the ego, to which we will now return.

In *Cartesian Meditations*[78] Husserl states that the transcendental ego is what it is solely in relation to intentional objectivities. These objectivities are of a twofold nature: (a) objects within the ego's own adequately verifiable sphere of immanent time and (b) world objects which can be shown to be existent only in inadequate and presumptive external experience. Thus it is an essential property of the transcendental ego to have systems of intentionality which are going on within it, as well as to have predelineating horizons as fixed potentialities which can be uncovered.

The transcendental ego exist for itself in continuous evidence; in itself it constitutes itself continuously as existing. The ego grasps itself not only as a flowing life and stream of experiences but also as I, who lives through this or that *cogito* as the same I. The ego polarizes the multiplicity of actual and possible consciousnesses toward identical objects or synthetic unities. In addition, in a second kind of synthesis the ego polarizes all the individual multiplicities of the *cogitationes* collectively as belonging to one and the same identical ego—that, as the active as well as the undergoing subject of consciousness, lives in all experiences of consciousness and is related through them to all object-poles.[79]

This polarizing ego, however, is not an empty pole of identity. Rather, according to a law of transcendental genesis, it acquires a new abiding property with every new act emanating from it and having a new objective meaning. After a decision has been made, I am (at least for some time) abidingly of this conviction; I am abidingly the ego who has made this decision. In this way the ego manifests itself as the identical substrate of ego properties which it constitutes itself in and through its own active genesis; it constitutes itself as a fixed and abiding *personal* ego. (The latter term is to be taken here in a maximally broad sense.)[80]

From the transcendental ego taken as identical pole (to be taken in the double

sense mentioned) and as substrate of habitualities, we must distinguish the ego taken in its full concreteness, that is, the ego taken together with the flowing multiformities of its intentional life along with all the objects meant in that life. This latter ego will be called *monad*. Since the monadically concrete ego includes the entire whole of my actual and potential conscious life, the explanation of the monadic ego in phenomenology includes all constitutional problems without exception.[81]

By the method of transcendental reduction, each transcendental meditator is led back to *his* transcendental ego, to be taken here together with its concrete monadic contents as this *de facto* ego, that is, as the one and *absolute* ego. If I reflect on the life of this (my) ego, I shall discover types of *de facto* occurrences in the *de facto* transcendental ego which, as such, still has an empirical significance. Since phenomenology is concerned with insights marked by essential universality and essential necessity, the transcendental meditator, in addition to performing the transcendental reduction, must also perform the eidetic reduction. This will lead him to the *eidos ego*. Thus phenomenology becomes nothing but the uncovering of the all-embracing *eidos*, transcendental ego, or *transcendental subjectivity* as such, which comprises all purely possible variants of my *de facto* ego and this ego itself as possible. Transcendental phenomenology thus explores the universal a priori without which neither I nor any other transcendental ego whatever is imaginable. After the transcendental reduction, my genuine interest is directed toward my pure ego, to uncovering this *de facto* ego. But this uncovering becomes scientific only if I go back to the apodictic principles that pertain to this ego as exemplifying the *eidos* ego. It should be noted that, in the transition from my *de facto* ego to the *eidos* ego as such, neither the actuality nor the possibility of other egos is presupposed.[82]

Husserl explicitly admits that a genuine eidetic phenomenology that concerns itself with a systematic discovery of the essential components belonging to the concrete ego, as such, involves enormous difficulties. "Only in the last decade has such a system begun to make itself clear and have new approaches to the specifically universal problems of the transcendental ego's constitution been discovered." The universal a priori pertaining to the transcendental ego as such is an eidetic form which contains *an infinity* of a priori types of actuality and potentiality of life, together with the objects that can be constituted as objects actually existing in that life. But in a unitary possible ego, not all types that are possible, taken individually, are compossible and not all compossible ones are compossible in just any order. One has only to compare the concrete ego of a small child, a man, woman, primitive, educated man, etc., to realize this. However, Husserl feels these difficulties can be met in principle by paying attention to the inherent temporality of the ego and by realizing that each concrete ego constitutes himself for himself in the unity of a "history." By uncovering eidetic laws of coexistence and succession as laws of compossibility, universal laws of genesis can be established in principle. It is in this context that the distinction between active and passive genesis is of prime importance for transcendental phenomenology.[83]

In *Cartesian Meditations* Husserl concludes these reflections with the following observation. We have seen that the access to the transcendental ego is formed by the transcendental reduction. After the reduction has been performed properly, I am confronted with the pure ego and its entire field of actual and possible consciousness. All that exists for the pure ego becomes constituted in itself according to its own particular manner of constitution. Every imaginable meaning and every imaginable being (whether the latter is called immanent or transcendent) falls within the domain of transcendental subjectivity as the subjectivity that constitutes all meaning and being (*Sein*). The universe of true being (*Sein*) and the universe of possible consciousness belong together essentially and they are con-cretely one in the only absolute concretion, called transcendental subjectivity. Transcendental subjectivity *is* the universe of all possible meaning.[84]

In *Crisis* Husserl rejects the view that transcendental subjectivity *is* the universe of all possible meaning. In this work he argues that the transcendental reduction discloses the universal, absolutely self-enclosed and absolutely self-sufficient *correlation* between the world itself and world-consciousness, namely, the conscious life of the transcendental subjectivity which affects the validity of the world. Through the reduction there results, finally, the absolute correlation between all meaning and being, (*Sein*) on the one hand, and absolute subjectivity as constituting all meaning.[85]

He explains his view as follows. The transcendental reduction reduces the world to the transcendental *phenomenon* "world" and the mundane ego to the transcendental subjectivity in and through whose conscious "life" the world attains its entire validity. In the reduction of the world, the reduction of *mankind* to the *phenomenon* "*mankind*" is included. Thus we must explain how mankind can be recognized as a self-objectification of the transcendental intersubjectivity which itself is constituted in transcendental subjectivity that is always functioning ultimately and thus is "absolute." In other words, one still must show how mankind becomes constituted as the necessary correlate of *the* world that is valid for everybody.[86] It is important to note that Husserl explicitly states that the self-objectification of the immediate subject of *the* world is to be found in historical mankind and not (as previously) in the I, this concrete man in the world.

In the next section Husserl explains that the Cartesian approach to the transcendental reduction has a great shortcoming: while it leads to the transcendental ego in one step, it brings this ego into view only as apparently empty of content. The introduction of the reduction from the viewpoint of the ontology of the life-world (developed in *Crisis* in outline) shows, on the other hand, that the reduction opens an extremely complicated domain for investigation.[87] This domain includes (1) an ego-pole, as well as a universe of ego-poles, (2) multiplicities of appearance, and (3) a universe of object-poles. It appears, then, that *the* world, as the world that is valid for all of us, is constituted primarily by a transcendental intersubjectivity and that the transcendental intersubjectivity is found here in two different modes: first as objectified in historical mankind and then as the transcendental ground of *the* world as the world that is valid for all of us.[88] Thus just as each human being bears within himself a transcendental ego (not as part or as a stratum of his soul or psyche but rather insofar as he is the self-objectification of the *corresponding* transcendental ego), so mankind as a whole is the self-objectification of the transcendental intersubjectivity as the transcendental ground of the world that is valid for all of us.[89]

Yet Husserl adds to this that the transcendental intersubjectivity is constituted primordially in the transcendental subjectivity to which each transcendental meditator is led by the reduction. It is for this reason that he calls the transcendental subjectivity "the absolute ego as the ultimate unique center or function of all constitution." Of this absolute ego one can say only that it is, functions, and constitutes in an absolute sense of the word. In other words, taken as such, it is world-less.[90]

6. Conclusion

From the preceding reflections it is clear that Husserl's thinking gradually developed from a moderate empiricist conception (as found in Locke or Hume), which he derived from Brentano, to a view that in concern, terminology, and results would come ever closer to the Kantian conception of the pure ego and to Natorp's interpretation of Kant's view. This is particularly clear for what Husserl calls the "absolute, transcendental subjectivity," which in the final analysis has in fact those "qualities" which Kant attributed to the pure ego. There are obviously important differences between the conceptions of Kant, Natorp, and Husserl, but according to Husserl's testimony these differences are mainly the result of the fact that Kant in many instances, with the flair of the genius, intuitively anticipated certain basic insights concerning the ego for which he could not account methodically, whereas Husserl was able to achieve similar insights on the basis of a rigorously applied method.

The preceding reflections also show that Husserl's concern about the pure ego remains within the framework of the modern problematic concerning the subjectivity of the subject. At no point has Husserl tried radically to overcome this problematic; he has merely attempted to radicalize the problems as well as their possible solutions. In harmony with this, it is also clear that whereas Kant's basic concern in the *Critique of Pure Reason* had been to account for the *finitude* of man's reason and set limitations to its theoretical employment, Husserl, returning to the Cartesian ideal, always believed in the possibility of an absolutely radical philosophy that genuinely deserves the name of a rigorous science. Let us briefly reflect on these two claims.

As we have seen, Husserl states in the *Cartesian Meditations* that every imaginable meaning and every imaginable being (*Sein*), whether the latter be called immanent or transcendent, falls within the domain of the transcendental subjectivity, as the subjectivity that constitutes meaning and being (*Sein*). Any attempt to conceive of the universe of true being (*Sein*) as something lying outside the universe of possible consciousness, the two being related to one another merely externally by some law, is *nonsensical*. They belong together essentially; and, as belonging together essentially, they are also concretely one, one in the only absolute concretion: transcendental subjectivity. If transcendental subjectivity is the universe of all possible meaning, then an outside is precisely nonsense.[91] From this we can derive that in Husserl's view the transcendental subjectivity itself precedes the common subject-object opposition and that it is the source from which both ultimately flow.

This interpretation is confirmed by a similar passage in *Crisis*, where Husserl slightly reformulates the same idea in order to make room for the transcendental intersubjectivity and the world that is valid for everybody. He writes that the transcendental reduction

in giving us the attitude *above* the subject-object correlation which belongs to the world and thus the attitude of focus upon the *transcendental subject-object correlation*, leads us to recognize, in self-reflection, that the world that exists for us, that is, our world in its being and being-such, takes its ontic meaning entirely from our intentional life through a priori types of accomplishments that can be exhibited rather than argumentatively constructed or conceived through mythical thinking.[92]

It is particularly important to note that the function Husserl attributes to the transcendental subjectivity is the same as the one Kant (in the first edition of the *Critique*) attributed to the transcendental imagination.[93] For according to Kant the transcendental imagination is not a mere subject of knowledge, it must institute the horizon within which two "entities", the knower and that which is to be known, can encounter each other and become opposed to one another as subject and object. Thus the transcendental imagination renders the mundane subject-object correlation possible. This horizon, in addition, implies a self-orientation of the knowing subject toward the being to be known as object; thus it renders it possible for the knower to be a subject. In other words, it constitutes the subjectivity of the subject. On the other hand, the horizon renders it possible for the being-to-be-known to reveal itself as opposed to the knower, id est, to be an object. In this way the horizon also constitutes the objectivity of the object. Thus the horizon instituted by the transcendental imagination simultaneously enables the "natural" subject to be subject and the

"natural" object to be object. Yet the horizon, enabling subject and object to be what they are, lies—as it were—between them, antecedes both, and renders it possible for the relation between them to come about.[94]

Yet in the passage of *Crisis* just quoted, Husserl again implicitly formulates his criticism of Kant's philosophy as a whole: (1) the distinction between the transcendental and the mundane is not always sharply maintained; and (2) many of Kant's valuable insights were "argumentatively constructed" or were the result of "mythical thinking"—not disclosed methodically and developed systematically.

Husserl was convinced that his phenomenology had made a great contribution to philosophy and that he had been able to solve a number of important problems which had been only vaguely anticipated in the works of great philosophers of the past. If one compares his works with those of Descartes, Hume, Leibniz, or Kant, I think one has to agree with Husserl's evaluation of his work. Yet we must add that Husserl never clearly realized that the entire problematic concerning the subjectivity of the subject perhaps rests upon a basic misunderstanding. It seems to me one of the greatest contributions of Heidegger to have focused on this possibility.[95] The reflections that follow may be helpful in clarifying my view in this regard.

In the preceding pages we have seen that during the last two decades on his life Husserl became more and more convinced that there is no essential difference between his phenomenology and Kant's critical philosophy as far as content and basic intention are concerned; the difference between these two philosophies consists mainly in methodology and rigor. In his phenomenology Husserl attempted to bring to original givenness the *life of transcendental subjectivity* in all of its intentional structures and implications by means of constitutive analyses, in order to thrust forward to the very *principles of consciousness*.[96]

For Heidegger, on the other hand, phenomenology is not concerned primarily with the life of transcendental subjectivity but with the question concerning the *meaning of being (Sein)*. In his letter to Richardson, Heidegger writes that he gradually began to doubt whether the "thing itself" with which phenomenology is concerned is to be characterized as intentional consciousness, or even the transcendental ego. Gradually it became clear to him that the being *(Sein)* of beings "had to remain the first and last thing-itself of thought." In addition, Heidegger began to realize that Husserl's phenomenology was elaborated "into a distinctive philosophical position according to a pattern set by Descartes, Kant, and Fichte." In *Being and Time*, Heidegger says, "I parted company with this philosophical position, and that on the basis of what to this day I still consider a more faithful adherence to the principle of phenomenology."[97] Finally, Heidegger remarks in the same letter that the philosophical problematic developed in *Being and Time* "is set up outside the sphere of subjectivism," and that the being *(Sein)* into which this work inquires cannot remain something that the human subject posits or constitutes.[98]

In Husserl's phenomenology the human reality is determined exclusively in terms of subjectivity. Furthermore, in view of the fact that the very mode of being of the subject is to be *Bewusst-sein*, consciousness, the expression "subjectivity" is taken to be interchangeable with the expression "consciousness." Like Kant, Husserl believed that from this perspective there is no need for making an explicit distinction between the subject and the self on the level of phenomenological reflection. For Heidegger, on the other hand, man, taken as *Dasein*, is not to be understood as a subject, although he most certainly is a self. Primordially, he is a self that is not yet a subject, but precedes the dichotomy of subject and object and makes this dichotomy possible. Heidegger agrees with both Kant and Husserl that the essence of the *subject* or the ego is to be

determined by self-consciousness; yet he disagrees with them when they claim that self-consciousness equally characterizes the being *(Sein)* of the *self*. In Heidegger's view, it is necessary to make a clear distinction between the knower taken as a self and taken as a subject. Whereas the knower as a self is to be characterized by finite transcendence, namely, by his being *(Sein)*-in-the-world, the knower taken as a subject is to be defined by self-consciousness. Commenting on Kant's thesis that the "I think ..." accompanies every act of synthesis, Heidegger observes that insofar as the ego is what it is only and exclusively in this "I think ...," the essence of the ego lies in pure self-consciousness. However, in his view this consciousness of the self is still to be illuminated by the being of the self, and not vice versa. For if one attempts (as Kant did) to illuminate the being of the self by consciousness, the self is made superfluous. In other words, if one fails to explore the self in terms of its finite transcendence, one interprets it implicitly as a mere being present-at-hand by understanding its being simply in terms of the reality of the *res cogitans*. If, on the other hand, one explores the self in terms of finite transcendence, it becomes clear that the self taken as a subject, namely, as made manifest by the transcendental unity of consciousness, is ontologically subsequent to and made possible by the self as transcendence, whose ultimate meaning is time.[99]

In the preceding reflections I have limited myself to describing Husserl's conception of the pure ego insofar as it can be documented by material from his published works. Marbach, in his previously mentioned work,[100] has made accessible to us a great number of ideas stemming from manuscripts which shed additional light on the development in Husserl's conception of the pure ego between the first edition of *Logical Investigations* and the completion of the text of the second volume of *Ideen* (1900-1916). In addition, Klaus Held, in his book *Lebendige Gegenwart*,[101] has stated—again largely

on the basis of unpublished manuscripts—that during the last decade of his
life Husserl made a systematic effort to
further determine the mode of being of
the transcendental subjectivity. In the
thirties Husserl gradually began to realize
that all constitutive problems of transcendental phenomenology must be understood in terms of temporalization. In
his view the primordial form of temporalization is to be found in the presentification, namely, in letting something be
encountered *as present*, whereas the
most primordial form of presentification
consists in the self-presentification of the
transcendental ego. The *locus* of the taking place of this process of self-
presentification is the living present
(*lebendige Gegenwart*). From this line of
thinking Husserl came to determine the
being of the ego as the living present of all

presentification. It was Husserl's contention that all of this can be shown *in immediate intuition* on the basis of reduction and analysis. Yet the analyses that
were developed to substantiate this conception did not lead to the desired result.
It appeared that the living present cannot
be made accessible to immediate intuition
in that the primordial present manifests
itself, on the one hand, as something
permanently flowing and streaming
whereas, on the other hand, it appears to
have the character of a *nunc stans*.

It is well-known by now that in interpretative phenomenology, where the
being of the ego is understood in terms of
finite transcendence, Husserl's dilemma
can be resolved by the realization that the
present of the finite self *is* the coming to
its own self (*Zu-kunft*, future) on the basis
of its own having-been.[102]

NOTES

1. Iso Kern, *Husserl und Kant. Eine Unter-suchung über Husserls Verhältnis zu Kant und zum Neukantianismus* (The Hague: Nijhoff, 1964).
2. Ibid., pp. 3-5, 11-12.
3. Edmund Husserl, *Philosophie der Arithmetik. Psychologische und logische Untersuchungen* (Halle: Pfeffer, 1891).
4. *Zeitschrift für Philosophie und philosophische Kritik*, 103 (1949): 27.
5. Theodor Lipps, *Grundtatsachen des Seelenlebens* (Bonn: Bouvier, 1883); Paul Natorp, "Über objektive und subjektive Begründung der Erkenntnis," *Philosophische Monathefte,* 23 (1887): 256-85.
6. Kern, op cit., pp. 13, 21-22.
7. Ibid., pp. 28-33.
8. Ibid., pp. 27, 31-33.
9. Braunschweig: Meyer, 1904.
10. Berlin: Hofmann, 1906.
11. Kern, op. cit., p. 30.
12. Ibid., p. 29.
13. Ibid., pp. 34-39.
14. Edmund Husserl, *Erste Philosophie*, 2 vols., ed. Rudolf Boehm (The Hague: Nijhoff, 1956-59).
15. Edmund Husserl, *Formale und transzendentale Logik. Versuch einer Kritik der logischen Vernunft* (Halle: Niemeyer, 1929). English: *Formal and Transcendental Logic*, trans. Dorion Cairns (The Hague: Nijhoff, 1969).
16. Edmund Husserl, *Die Krisis der europäischen Wissenschaften und die transzendentale Phänomenologie. Eine Einleitung in die phänomenologische Philosophie*, ed. Walter Biemel (The Hague: Nijhoff, 1954). English: *The*

Crisis of European Sciences and Transcendental Phenomenology: An Introduction to Phenomenological Philosophy, trans. David Carr (Evanston: Northwestern University Press, 1970).
17. Kern, op. cit., pp. 5, 9-11.
18. Edmund Husserl, *Logische Untersuchungen*, 3 vols. (Halle: Niemeyer, 1921-22). English: *Logical Investigations*, 2 vols., trans. J. N. Findlay (New York: Humanities Press, 1970), I: 214.
19. Kern, op. cit., p. 17.
20. Edmund Husserl, "Philosophie als strenge Wissenschaft," *Logos*, 1 (1910-11): 289-341. English: "Philosophy as Rigorous Science," in Quentin Lauer, *Edmund Husserl: Phenomenology and the Crisis of Philosophy* (New York: Harper and Row, 1965), pp. 69-147, 76.
21. Edmund Husserl, *Ideen zu einer reinen Phänomenologie und phänomenologischen Philosophie*, 3 vols., ed. Walter and Marly Biemel (The Hague: Nijhoff, 1950-52). English tr. of vol. 1: *Ideas: General Introduction to Pure Phenomenology*, trans. W. R. Boyce Gibson (New York: Collier Books, 1962), p. 70.
22. Ibid., p. 166.
23. Husserl, *Erste Philosophie*, I: 197.
24. Ibid., pp. 230-87; cf. pp. 440-41.
25. Husserl, *Crisis*, p. 99.
26. Kern, op. cit., p. 41.
27. Ibid., pp. 55-134 and passim.
28. Eduard Marbach, *Das Problem des Ich in der Phänomenologie Husserls* (The Hague: Nijhoff, 1974).
29. Kern, op. cit., pp. 12ff., 286ff., 356-66.
30. Ibid., pp. 286-93.

31. Ibid., pp. 11, 16, 72-73.

32. Ibid., p. 74.

33. Husserl, *Logical Investigations*, II: 548-50.

34. Ibid., p. 549, n. 1.

35. Ibid., p. 544, n. 1.

36. Husserl, *Ideas*, sec. 46, 57, 78, 80, 82, 92, 115, 122, and passim.

37. Ibid., sec. 57, 80. Cf. Jean-Paul Sartre, "La transcendence de l'ego," *Recherches philosophiques*, 6 (1936): 85-123; Aron Gurwitsch, "A Non-egological Conception of Consciousness," in *Studies in Phenomenology and Psychology* (Evanston: Northwestern University Press, 1966), pp. 287-300.

38. Kern, op. cit., pp. 359-63; cf. Husserl, *Ideen*, II: 101ff.

39. Husserl, *Ideen*, II: xiv-xvi.

40. Ibid., p. xvi.

41. Kern, op. cit., pp. 287-89.

42. Cf. Immanuel Kant, *Critique of Pure Reason*, trans. Norman Kemp Smith (New York: St. Martin's Press, 1965), pp. 352-67 (A 381-405), 381-83 (B 428-32); Paul Natorp, *Allgemeine Psychologie* (Tübingen: Mohr, 1912), pp. 207ff.; Husserl, *Ideen*, II: pp. 101-14.

43. Kern, op. cit., pp. 286-87.

44. Sec. 29.

45. Kern, op. cit., p. 288.

46. Husserl, *Ideen*, II: 104-5.

47. Ibid., p. 101.

48. Edmund Husserl, *Zur Phänomenologie des inneren Zeitbewusstseins* (1893-1917), ed. Rudolf Boehm (The Hague: Nijhoff, 1966), pp. 111ff., 116ff., and passim, and *Ideas*, vol. I, sec. 81.

49. Kern, op. cit., pp. 363, 371-72.

50. Kant, op. cit., pp. 129-50 (A 95-130), 151-175 (B 129-69).

51. Ibid., pp. 328-67 (A 341-405), 368-83 (B 399-432).

52. Ibid., pp. 151-58 (B 129-40).

53. Ibid., pp. 352ff. (A 381ff.), 381-83 (B 428-32).

54. Ibid., pp. 336-37 (A 354), 331-32 (B 404).

55. Aron Gurwitsch, "The Kantian and Husserlian Conceptions of Consciousness," in *Studies in Phenomenology and Psychology*, pp. 148-74; Martin Heidegger, *Being and Time*, trans. John Macquarrie and Edward Robinson (London: SCM Press, 1962), sec. 64.

56. It should be noted that although Kant recognizes the "intentionality" of consciousness, he does not realize that a *definite* conception of "world" (in addition to that of "world of objects") is preunderstood in his idea of the pure ego. Heidegger, op. cit., sec. 64.

57. Kern, op. cit., pp. 288-89, 289 n. 2.

58. Ibid., p. 289, n. 3.

59. Ibid., p. 290, n. 3.

60. Ibid., p. 291, nn. 1, 2, 3.

61. Ibid., pp. 291-92.

62. Ibid., p. 293.

63. Ibid., pp. 69-70, 72-73.

64. Cf. *Erste Philosophie*, I: 71.

65. Cf. *Crisis*, sec. 31.

66. Kern, op. cit., pp. 75-76, 246-47.

67. Ibid., p. 297.

68. Ibid., pp. 293-94.

69. Edmund Husserl, *Cartesianische Meditationen und Pariser Vorträge*, ed. S. Strasser (The Hague: Nijhoff, 1950). English: *Cartesian Meditations: An Introduction to Phenomenology*, trans. Dorion Cairns (The Hague: Nijhoff, 1954), pp. 65-151 (fourth and fifth meditations).

70. Husserl, *Formal and Transcendental Logic*, pp. 234-66.

71. Husserl, *Crisis*, pp. 174-89, 244-65.

72. Husserl, *Ideas*, I: 156.

73. Ibid., pp. 213-14.

74. Ibid., pp. 373-94.

75. Cf. Joseph J. Kockelmans, *A First Introduction to Husserl's Phenomenology*. (Pittsburgh: Duquesne University Press, 1967), pp. 281-314; idem, *Edmund Husserl's Phenomenological Psychology* (Pittsburgh: Duquesne University Press, 1967), pp. 232-63 and passim.

76. Husserl, *Erste Philosophie*, II: 164ff.

77. Edmund Husserl, *Phänomenologische Psychologie* (1925), ed. Walter Biemel (The Hague: Nijhoff, 1962), pp. 287-97, 328-49.

78. Husserl, *Cartesian Meditations*, sec. 30.

79. Ibid., sec. 31.

80. Ibid., sec. 32.

81. Ibid., sec. 33.

82. Ibid., sec. 34.

83. Ibid., sec. 36-39.

84. Ibid., sec. 41.

85. Husserl, *Crisis*, sec. 41.

86. Ibid., sec. 42.

87. Ibid., pp. 167-8, 168-70.

88. Ibid., pp. 176-86.

89. Ibid., pp. 186-87.

90. Ibid., p. 186.

91. Husserl, *Cartesian Meditations*, sec. 41.

92. Husserl, *Crisis*, p. 181.

93. Kant, op. cit., pp. 141-49 (A 113-128).

94. Cf. William J. Richardson, *Heidegger: Through Phenomenology to Thought* (The Hague: Nijhoff, 1963), 154-58.

95. Martin Heidegger, *Holzwege* (Frankfurt: Kostermann, 1963), pp. 69-104.

96. Kern, op. cit., p. 423.

97. Richardson, op. cit., pp. xii-xiv.

98. Ibid., p. xviii.

99. Martin Heidegger, *Kant und das Problem der Metaphysik* (Bonn: Cohen, 1929), pp. 137-38; 171-78; *Being and Time*, sec. 64; Richardson, op. cit., idem, pp. 154-59.

100. Cf. n. 28.

101. Klaus Held, *Lebendige Gegenwart, Die Frage nach der Seinsweise des transzendentalen Ich bei Edmund Husserl entwickelt am Leitfaden der Zeitproblematik* (The Hague: Nijhoff, 1966).

102. Heidegger, *Being and Time*, sec. 64.

Husserl's *Encyclopaedia Britannica* Article and Heidegger's Remarks Thereon

WALTER BIEMEL

In what follows I shall discuss several fundamental concepts of Husserl's phenomenology above all on the basis of the various drafts for the *Encyclopaedia Britannica* article he prepared in the autumn of 1927. In these drafts Husserl attempts concisely to define the essence of phenomenology. The Husserl Archive possesses the various drafts, as well as Heidegger's critical comments on them, which will be discussed in the conclusion.[1]

After various beginnings, Husserl chose a structure for his article which can be outlined as follows. In the first section he deals with the idea of a pure psychology; in the second section with the relation of psychology to transcendental phenomenology; and in the third section with a determination of the essence of transcendental phenomenology. Each section may be analyzed in somewhat more detail.

The first question that arises when we first look at the structure of the draft in a purely external way is this: Why does Husserl begin his discussion with an exposition of "pure psychology"? Even before this question is answered, however, we must explain what Husserl under-

This article originally appeared in *Tijdschrift voor Filosofie*, 12 (1950: 246-80. Translated by permission of the publisher and author. Translated by P. McCormick and F. Elliston. © 1976 McCormick and Elliston.

stands by the expression 'pure psychology'.

In the second version of the article, the first eleven pages of which were written by Heidegger on the basis of the first draft, which was at hand, the question about pure psychology was divided into three questions:

Clarifying the comprehension of the idea of a pure psychology requires answering three question: 1. What belongs to the object of pure psychology; 2. What access to and method of treatment does this object require according to its own constitution; 3. What is the fundamental function of pure psychology? [III, 3, p. 4]

The object of general psychology is the investigation of the totality of man's modes of consciousness (thinking, feeling, willing). The study of the modes of consciousness, however, does not exhaust the knowledge about man which can be subsumed under the term anthropology. "Psychology is *a branch* of concrete Anthropology" (I, 1, pp. 1ff., my italics). The comprehension of the "physical" aspect of man also belongs to anthropology. Insofar as psychology deals with the psychical purely as such, it is called *pure* psychology, as opposed to all psycho-physical studies. Consequently, pure psychology is not concerned with the physical presuppositions of the life of the mind. However, this negative definition is insufficient. What must immediately be added is that pure psychology in no way denies that in order to occur psychical experiences necessarily presuppose a body. But as pure psychology it consciously disregards that. Why?

In his encyclopaedia drafts, Husserl does not give an immediate answer to this question, but from some of his other writings I believe we can infer the following. Pure psychology disregards psychophysical relations not because they do not exist but because they cannot explain what is essential to the psychic. When we know with what speed a stimulus impulse is transmitted along the nerve paths, we have an observation that is exactly measurable and testable, an observation which can hardly be doubted. But by no means do we have an explanation of what a stimulus sensation itself is. Husserl clearly saw that, as indispensable as all physiological processes are for the life of the mind, they are incapable of explaining this life. In order not to make the mistake of understanding the life of the mind as a "causal" effect of physiological processes (somewhat in the sense of the causality of natural science), pure psychology excludes psycho-physical considerations. Pure psychology wants to comprehend what is essential to the "mind." Thus just as physiology disregards all mental processes in order to grasp what is essential to the life processes of bodies, so pure psychology, for its part, excludes relations to the corporeal.

Husserl refers explicitly to this parallel:

Psychology is...a branch of concrete Anthropology or Zoology. Animal realities are first of all, at the most basic stratum, physical realities. As such, they belong in the closed context of physical nature, of nature in its first and pregnant sense as the universal theme of a pure natural science, i.e. of an objective science of nature which in persistent one-sidedness disregards all non-physical determinations of reality. The scientific experience of animal bodies comes under this science. In contrast to this, however, if the psychical element of the animal world is now to become the theme, then the first question to be posed

is: To what extent, in parallel with pure natural science, is a pure psychology possible? [I, 1, pp. 1ff.]

From this quotation it is also clear that the concept of the purity of psychology is conceived with respect to the purity of the *pure natural sciences*. Consequently, just as there is a pure natural science, there must also be a pure psychology. The expression "just as" must be defined more precisely; it does not mean that a pure psychology must be created as a pure natural science. We saw how that is not possible, since pure natural science disregards the mental and looks at the animal as a physical entity, while on the other hand pure psychology disregards all physical processes. "Just as" here means "corresponding to." Corresponding to pure natural science there would really have to be, according to Husserl, a pure psychology as well. To grasp more firmly the essence of this correspondence, we must see what the determinative factor of pure natural science is for Husserl. In other words, we need to see in what its purity consists and which meaning of purity is proper to it.

Not all natural sciences are pure. The opposite of pure natural science is *empirical* natural science. Husserl thus takes over, *cum grano salis*, the Kantian opposition between *pure* and *empirical*. Depending on their specific intention, the empirical natural sciences are concerned with the respective natural *givens* of their domain, the natural *objects* or *events* that can be factually encountered. Pure natural sciences are not interested in factual givens; they are a priori disciplines. Husserl refers explicitly to pure geometry, pure theory of time, pure theory of motion. None of these disciplines is related to factually given nature. Rather, they make up a "form-system of a nature in general which is capable of being thought" (I, 1, p. 10). "Vaguely inductive empiricism gains a share in the necessity of essence by using these a priori form-systems for factual nature. And empirical natural science itself gains a share in new methodological senses for all the vague concepts and rules which are to be worked through to the rational concepts and laws which necessarily underlie them" (ibid.).

The purity of the pure natural sciences thus consists in disregarding all *factual* givens and in looking toward *possible* givens, that is, toward the possibly thinkable as such. This "thinkable" is in no way something arbitrary. Rather, it must obey the laws of the corresponding discipline. The expression "the possible" is merely meant to show that the laws of a pure discipline do not stem from experience and are not read off from the facts at hand but, rather, are prescribed a priori. To cite a well-known example, whether a geometrical right angle ever actually occurs in nature does not interest the geometer; he does not have to be guided by the laws of what can be discovered as a fact but merely by the laws or rules which are prescribed by the axioms of his discipline.

The opposition of *pure* and *empirical* is at the same time an opposition between essentiality and factuality. Coming from a mathematical background, Husserl was fascinated by the results of the pure natural sciences and their significance for the empirical natural sciences. The thought of creating something analogous for the domain of the psychical, of the mental in general, motivated him throughout his lifetime. Obviously, he did not think of this domain as a pure imitation of the relationships which exist in the natural sciences. Repeatedly, he struggles quite firmly against all attempts to determine the domain of the "psychical" by exact, natural scientific research, in *The Idea of Phenomenology*[2] (1907) as well as in *Ideas* (1913) and the later writings, particularly in the *Crisis* (1936-37). Yet, despite this, he held that for the domain of the mental, an a priori pure psychology, which should constitute the foundation for empirical research in psychology, would also have to be created.

"As essential as it is that the methods of natural science and those of psychology be distinguished", he says in the quoted encyclopaedia draft, "their necessary common ground lies in the fact that even psychology, like any science, can only create its 'rigor' ('exactness') out of the rationality of the 'essential' (I, 1, p. 11). We are thus brought suddenly to the basic distinction between the factual and the essential, a distinction which forms the prerequisite for phenomenology which Husserl explicitly represented as a science of essences (see especially chap. 1 of the first division of *Ideas I*). At the same time, it becomes clear how Husserl came to this basic distinction and what essential role the model of the natural sciences, the relation between pure and empirical research (which was predominant for him), played. Thus it is by no means accidental that Husserl introduces as his first example something taken from the domain of the natural sciences:

Sciences of experience are *sciences of "facts."* Experience's founding acts of cognition posit a real thing as an individual. They posit it as a spatio-temporally existing entity, as something which is at *this* place in time, which has its duration and a reality-content which, according to its essence, it could have had just as well at any other place in time. And furthermore, they posit it as something which is in this physical form at this location (with the corporeal [*Leiblichem*]—which has this form, both are given together) whereas the real when regarded according to its own essence, could just as well be at any arbitrary location with any arbitrary form. Its location could be changed while it remains factually unchanged, or it could be changed in other ways than as it is factually changed [*Ideen*, I: 8].

Nevertheless, the problem of *pure psychology* must, first of all, be explained. At first it was shown that it is called pure because it disregards all physical considerations of natural science. Then it became clear that its purity must be understood as corresponding to the purity of the natural sciences. Thus, on the one hand, the considerations of the natural sciences are supposed to be disregarded while, on the other hand, they are supposed to serve precisely as the model. The contradiction is overcome by explaining that in the first case it is a matter of an empirical natural science and in the second case of a pure natural science. To be more precise, the consideration of man's physical givens individualizes him in this particular body which exists at one particular place in space. Thus man is necessarily observed as a factual givenness. This is exactly what must be prevented, Husserl thinks, if we want to grasp the essence of the psychical.

Thus, according to Husserl, the task of pure psychology is "the unveiling of the *a priori* types without which the I and respectively the We, consciousness, the objectivity of consciousness, and thereby mental being in general would be unthinkable—with all the essentially necessary and essentially possible forms of syntheses which are inseparable from the idea of a totality of the single mind and the community of minds. This unveiling creates an enormous field of exactness which carries over (and here even immediately) into empirical research into the mind" (loc. cit.). On the basis of the unveiling of the a priori structures of the life of the mind—a priori is here always to be understood as that which belongs necessarily to the life of the mind, something without which there can be no life of the mind—it is possible to comprehend purely the essence of the life of the mind. This essence is what finds its respective factual individualization in concrete singular individuals and what gives us access to the concrete understanding of the empirico-psychological. The correspondence to the pure natural sciences, for example, to pure geometry, consists then in that neither starts with factual data but rather with the knowledge of the essence. Whether the knowledge of essence can be the same in the two domains is nevertheless rather questionable; but, of course, not for Husserl. It should be pointed out that in pure natural sciences the project of the natural scientist is to establish the fundamental axioms. This determines the respective domain in its structure from the outset. However, the procedure of the psychologist cannot be the same, since he does not construct the objects of his research.

In other words, both the geometer and the psychologist must adhere to the essential laws of their domains. But these essential laws are in the first case determined by the constructive project of the scientist, while in the second no fundamental axioms can be established from which everything lawful would be derivable. Husserl does not seem to take this distinction sufficiently into consideration.

But even with the conception of the purely mental, namely, the a priori of consciousness, man is not yet comprehended as a whole. Husserl points out that pure psychology does not exhaust the science of the mental. The knowledge of the psycho-physical a priori, namely, the mind-body interconnection, belongs to it also. To be sure, this is only possible after the working out of the genuine psychical a priori. Pure psychology therefore has a certain priority. It must, however, be completed by the purely physical a priori, namely, the essential lawfulness of the organic body. "To be sure, the phenomenological *a priori* is not the complete one of psychology insofar as the psycho-physical interconnection as such has its own *a priori*. It is, however, clear that this *a priori* presupposes that of pure phenomenological psychology, as well as on the other hand the pure *a priori* of a physical (and especially organic) nature in general" (I, 1, p. 11).

In the encyclopaedia drafts Husserl does not pursue the psycho-physical a priori any further. Rather, he dedicates his considerations in the first section, as was mentioned, to *pure psychology*, and thus to the psychology which grasps what is properly essential to the life of the mind, and which is not to be found in the same way in any other realm (region) of entities, and which completely determines every psychical entity.

Before we attempt, as it were, to articulate the content of pure psychology, a concept which Husserl identifies with that of pure psychology should be explained in more detail, namely, the concept of phenomenological psychology. For what reason does Husserl also call pure psychology phenomenological psychology? What does phenomenological mean here? How is phenomenological psychology differentiated from plain psychology?

With the attempt to answer these questions we accomplish, at the same time, the transition from the first problem raised, about the *object* of pure psychology to the problem of *method*. Here it becomes clear how the first point can only be dealt with in connection with the second.

All psychical experiences are a kind of "consciousness" of.... The subject which experiences them is, in the experience, directed "toward...." This is the natural attitude in which every man always finds himself. Thus it belongs to his nature, to the essence of the psychic in general. Husserl normally tends to begin his expositions with the characterization of the natural attitude. For instance, he says at the beginning of the first lecture in *The Idea of Phenomenology:* "In the natural mode of reflection we, in intuiting and in thinking, turned towards *the things* which are given to us at any one time, even if they are given to us in various ways and in various kinds of being, depending on the source and the level of knowledge."[3] The natural attitude he also calls the straightforward attitude ("*intentio recta*"), because it runs straight from the subject to the object.

"Insofar as we are actively concious in a straightforward way (*geradehin*), the very things, thoughts, values, goals and means are then exclusively in our view" (I, 1, p. 3).

To the extent that Husserl's motto, which today evokes great and worldwide response, is "To the things themselves!" it would have to be accepted that this attitude which is turned immediately to things is the authentic phenomenological one. But this is by no means so. The natural attitude must be overcome if we want to press forward to phenomenology. For just this reason, Husserl always begins to delineate the natural attitude because it is the one which is immediately given and which must be *relinquished*. This overcoming of the natural attitude,

or relinquishing, by no means entails that men in *everyday* life must give up being oriented to things; that is totally impossible. The "things" (*Sachen*), in the sense of physical things (*Dinge*), are just what men always run up against at first. What accounts for the fact that this occurs is the structure of the psychical, what Husserl calls *intentionality*. He says:

The terminological expression which comes from the scholastics for that basic character of being as consciousness of something is '*intentionality*'. When we are unreflectively conscious of any objects at all, we are "directed" to them, our "*intentio*" goes toward them....This directedness is an essential trait immanent in the respective lived-experiences; they are "intentional" lived-experiences. [I, 1, pp. 3ff.]

In another draft the corresponding passage reads:

In all pure mental lived-experiences (in perceiving something, in remembering something, in imagining something, in judging something, in willing something, in being pleased about something, in hoping for something, etc.) there is throughout a being directed to....The lived-experiences are intentional. This being related to...is not added to the psychical afterwards and occasionally as an accidental relation as if the lived-experiences could be what they are without the intentional relation. Rather, the *essential structure* of the pure psychical is revealed in the intentionality of the lived experiences. (III, 3, p. 4)

Husserl often presents intentionality with the image of the ray of consciousness whose original direction is precisely straight ahead to the objects (*Objekte*).

Psychology must attempt to comprehend the varied forms of intentionality which characterize the various acts of consciousness. But to be able to do that, it must put the straightforward attitude in question and make it the object of research. This happens when the researcher deflects the beam from its straight path and bends it back on itself, id est, reflects it (*reflexio*). Instead of the things of the environment, of the various objects which otherwise are given to him, he grasps in the "*intentio*" the "*intentio*" itself. In place of the straightforward attitude, we thus have *reflection* on the striaghtforward attitude. In this reflection, intentionality itself can first become the problem. Of course, intentionality does not create the reflection. It was already there before reflection, but without having been known as such. Reflection makes possible intentionality's becoming clear about itself.

For Husserl, the significance of reflection is enormous since by means of reflection we first secure the philosophical attitude which Husserl also calls the "reflexive" attitude. In my opinion, the decisive factor for Husserl was reading Fichte. The following paragraph from the *Wissenschaftslehre* (1801) could be viewed as an introduction to phenomenology and taken over word by word by Husserl:

In all mere knowing of the drawing of a line, of the relationships of the parts of a triangle, and whatever knowing there might otherwise be, knowing in its absolute identity precisely *as knowing* would be the actual middle point and place of the *knowing of* drawing lines, of the relationships of the parts of the triangle, etc. Precisely in the knowing and its unity, everything is *known* in one way in the sense we have shown, no matter how different the things may be. In no way is there cognition of knowing as such, because the cognition is not of knowing but of drawing lines and the like. Knowing *would be* as knowing, and would know because it was; but it would not know of itself merely because it was. In the *knowing* of *knowing*, however, this knowing itself would be thoroughly comprehended as such at a glance, and thus as the (self-equalizing) unity (of) itself, just as in knowing, drawing lines, etc. a (self-equal) unity was grasped. In the knowing of knowing, the knowing expresses itself and places itself before itself in order to grasp itself. [*Wissenschaftslehre*, IV: 7ff.]

Of course the comparison should not be pushed too far. The point of the comparison is in the recognition of reflection as the essential method of philosophy, while the nature of the Husserlian and the Fichtean "I" is different.

Through reflection, the lived experiences of consciousness themselves become "objects" and as such they can be investigated. Through them, as was said, the beam of the *intentio* is bent back on itself; it is turned toward itself. This turning back is at the same time a *leading back* from what is given as the usual object to a new "object," the lived experiences themselves. This leading back is a reduction. The earlier object is left out of the question, is put in brackets, in order to direct attention to the new one. For this reason we read in the draft which Heidegger wrote:

The about turn of the glance away from the unreflected perception, e.g. of a thing of nature, to this perceiving itself has as its essential peculiarity the fact that in it the tendency to comprehend, which previously was directed to the thing, is withdrawn from the unreflected perception in order to direct itself to the perceiving as such. This leading back (reduction) of the tendency to apprehend from the perception, and the adaption of apprehending to the perceiving is changed so little in the perception, that it is just the reduction which makes the perception accessible as what it is, namely as perception *of* the thing. [III, 3, p. 7]

The authentic "things" (*Sachen*) which phenomenology strives to advance to are thus in no way the immediately given things (*Dinge*) and objects of the natural attitude but, rather, the "lived experiences" in which these are given.

But the question remains unanswered as to why these considerations and researches are called "phenomenological." To be more precise: For what reason does an observation, which instead of being turned to "things" (*Dingen*) is turned to "lived experiences," thereby become phenomenological?

The expression 'phenomenological' shows that here it is a matter of "phenomena." The original Greek meaning of *phainesthai* is "showing itself," "coming to light." This sense is still preserved even in ordinary speech; we call a phenomenon an 'appearance'. In an appearance something comes to the fore, shows itself in a particular way. The Husserlian concept of phenomenon should not be in any way confused with that of Kant. For Husserl, there is no opposition between*phainomenon* and *noumenon*. In the phenomenon, that which is and that which we call an entity, appears, comes to light. Since, according to Husserl, the essence of man lies in being a subject, man can only have knowledge of entities through acts of consciousness (perception, remembering, feeling, willing, etc.) in which he is directed to the entity. In consciousness, in the various ways of "being directed to . . . ," the entity comes to light. This way of appearing through a form of consciousness is the only possible one for the subject. The investigation of the forms of appearance, and at the same time of the ways of givenness of the objects, is therefore necessarily phenomenological. In a manuscript from 1907 (B II 1) Husserl gives the following explanation of the concept of phenomenon, which has a twofold meaning: (1) phenomenon "in the sense of the appearance in which objectivity appears, and on the other hand . . . (2) phenomenon in the sense of objectivity considered merely insofar as it appears precisely in the appearances and even 'transcendentally' when everything posited empirically has been excluded" (B11 1, B1.25b).

In this study, the apprehension and description of kinds of consciousness and the modes of lived experiences are a matter of *phenomenological psychology*.

The first step which must be taken is thus to make the reflection effective. Reflection provides the possibility of grasping the lived experiences purely as such in the sense of an adequate description. However, the lived experiences, so grasped, are pure only in the first sense (see above); namely, they are not "contaminated" through "physical" observations. But they are not yet pure in the sense that was later explained (purity as essential lawfulness). For insofar as we limit ourselves to the description of the lived experiences just given, we have not yet gone beyond the domain of facticity. To this end, the return, the reduction, must be carried further.

The first step consisted of a bracketing of the immediately given objective world of entities which had precisely the func-

tion of throwing our glance back to the lived experiences themselves. Or, as Husserl said:

The universal epoché with regard to the world becoming conscious (its "bracketing") excludes from the phenomenological field the world which simply exists for the respective subject. In place of this world comes forth the world which is *conscious* in various ways (perceived, remembered, judged, thought, valued, etc.) exactly "*as such*", as the "*world in brackets*." Put differently, in place of the world, or of the individual things in the world, there comes forth the respective sense (*Sinn*) of consciousness in its various modes (sense of perception, sense of rememberance, etc.). [I, 1, p. 7]

The next step consists *not* in remaining with even the very precise description of the intuitively given lived experiences but, rather, in exhibiting the essential lawfulness of each form of experience—"what, for example, belongs to a perception in general, to a willing in general, depending on their full intentional structural constitution. Thus the reductive attitude to the pure psychical, which at first is given as an individual factual complex of lived-experiences, must disregard all psychical facticity" (III, 3, p. 8). The disregarding facticity and the looking to the respective essential laws of the kinds of lived experience are the result of the *eidetic reduction* which is constructed on the previously explained phenomenological-psychological reduction. The qualifications on the expression "reduction" never say what is placed in brackets but always that to which we return. In the phenomenological-psychological reduction this is the psychic as phenomenon; in the eidetic reduction it is the essence of the lived experiences; in the intersubjective reduction it is intersubjectivity (community of subjects).

The method of variation necessarily belongs to the eidetic reduction. This means that to apprehend what in the factually given lived experience belongs to the structure of the lived experience as such, we must try to vary the lived experience in question, to compare it with other similar lived experiences, and to see what they have in common. This common element (the identical) which in all variation remains invariant is the *eidos* or essence.

If phenomenological facticity becomes irrelevant, serving *only* as an example and as the support for a free but intuitive variation of the factually individual minds and communities of minds into an *a priori* possible (conceivable) one, and if now the thematic view is directed to what necessarily persists as invariant in the variation; then by this systematic procedure a peculiar realm of the *"a priori"* arises. With this the essential necessary form-style (the *Eidos*) arises, which must permeate all possible mental existence throughout its particularities, its synthetic assemblages and self-enclosed totalities. Psychological phenomenology is undoubtedly to be grounded in this way as "eidetic phenomenology." It is then exclusively directed to the invariant form of the essence. [I, 1, pp. 9ff.]

A "classical" argument, however, can be brought against the variation. In order to carry out the variation we must have a prior concept of what should be varied. For otherwise it could be that we are trying to bring totally different lived experiences under one category. In this case, then, the variation must necessarily fail. Husserl does not discuss the possibility of this criticism.

The exposition of the eidetic reduction is concluded with the following words. "If the phenomenological reduction created access to the 'phenomenon' of an actual and also therefore a possible inner experience, then the method of the 'eidetic reduction' which is founded on it secures access to the variant essential forms of the entire sphere of the purely mental" (op. cit., p. 10).

Before we go into the third question we mentioned at the beginning, the question of the functions of pure psychology, we shall summarize the discussions of its object; namely, we shall quote from the draft (I, 1) where Husserl himself gives a summary.

The systematic construction of a phenomenological pure psychology requires:

(1) the description of the peculiarities which universally belong to the essence of an intentional lived-experience in general, and to which the most general law of synthesis also belongs: every combination of consciousness with consciousness yields consciousness.

(2) the investigation of the individual forms of intentional lived-experiences, which must occur or be able to occur in any mind whatsoever with essential necessity: and along with that, the investigation of the essential types of syntheses which belong to it, of the continuous and the discrete, of the finitely closed or of those which continue in an open infinity.

(3) the exhibiting and description of the essence of the total form of mental life in general, and thus the kind of essence of a universal "stream of consciousness."

(4) a new direction for investigation is characterized by the term 'I' (still in abstraction from the social sense of this word) with regard to the essential forms of "habitualness" which belong to it, i.e. the I as the subject of abiding "convictions" (convictions of being, of value, decisions of will, etc.), as personal subject of habits, of well formed knowledge, of traits of character.

From all sides, this "static" description of essence leads finally to the problems of genesis and to a universal genesis which rules the entire life and the development of the personal I according to eidetic laws. Thus above this first "static phenomenology" a dynamic or genetic phenomenology is constructed at a higher level (I, 1, p. 11a).

The function of pure psychology is twofold: it should provide empirical psychology with a basis, an a priori foundation analogous to the way pure natural sciences provide a foundation for the empirical natural sciences.

Out of reductive eidetic investigation of what is purely psychical arises the determinatives which belong to the purely psychic as such,— i.e. the basic concepts of psychology so far as psychology, as an empirical science of the psycho-physical whole of concrete man, has its central domain in the pure mental life as such. Pure psychology provides the necessary *a priori* foundation for empirical psychology with respect to the purely mental as such. [III, 3, p. 10]

In addition, it should serve as a propaedeutic for authentic phenomenology. For this reason, Husserl begins answering the question "What is phenomenology?" with an explication of pure psychology.

The description of this psychological phenomenology (more precisely, it should be called phenomenological psychology) which stands nearer to natural thinking is quite suitable for a propaedeutical preliminary stage in order to ascend to the understanding of philosophical phenomenology. [I, 1, p. 1]

The next section (II) we find in the later versions of the encyclopaedia article is dedicated to just this problem: to show how phenomenological psychology can serve as a propaedeutic for phenomenology. The problems discussed up to now were psychological phenomenology, but not yet pure phenomenological ones; more precisely, they were not yet "transcendental - phenomenological ones." It is a matter of seeing what differentiates two ways of observing.

First of all, the concept of the *transcendental* should be discussed. At the very beginning of draft III (3) Husserl points out the necessity of the return to the transcendental, and he characterizes this as *the consciousness* which constitutes the transcendent (objective). "The return to consciousness, which all philosophy seeks with varying certainty and clarity, stretches over the domain of the pure psychical back into the field of pure subjectivity. This is called transcendental subjectivity because in it the being of everything which in various ways can be experienced by the subject, i.e. the being of the transcendent in the widest sense, is constituted" (III, 3, p. 2). Since this definition comes so immediately, as if "shot from a gun," and really cannot yet be grasped, Husserl did not retain this initial part of III (3) in the later version.

For the development of Husserl's thought it is interesting to point out that he had formulated the concept of transcendental consciousness twenty years earlier. The way to grasp it more clearly,

however, only became apparent to him step by step with the deepening of the idea of the reduction—more precisely, with the working out of the various reductions. Here is a text from the manuscript B II 1, which was written in September 1907.[4]

The *Logical Investigations* takes phenomenology as a descriptive psychology (although the interest in epistemology was the normative interest in it). However, this decriptive psychology understood as empirical phenomenology must be separated from transcendental phenomenology.... In this transcendental phenomenology we are not now concerned with an *a priori* ontology, nor with formal logic and formal mathematics, nor with geometry as an *a priori* theory of space, nor with *a priori* chronometry and kinematics, nor with an *a priori* real ontology of any kind (thing, change, etc.). Transcendental phenomenology is the phenomenology of *constituting consciousness*. Hence, no single objective axiom (relating to objects which are not consciousness) belongs in it. [BII, 1 Bl. 25a ff.]

In *The Crisis of the European Sciences and Transcendental Phenomenology* (*Husserliana*, vol. VI, ed. W. Biemel [The Hague, 1954] he gives—almost thirty years after the manuscript just quoted—the following definition of the "transcendental theme." "It is the theme of questioning back to the final source of all formations of knowledge, of the knower's reflecting upon himself and upon his cognitive life, in which all scientific formations which are valid for him occur purposively, are preserved as an acquisition, and become freely available." Husserl said of Kant that he was on the way to the authentic transcendental problematic. His philosophy was such that "as opposed to prescientific and even scientific objectivism, it goes back to *knowing subjectivity as the original place of all objective sense formations and validity of being*" (*Philosophia*, I: 174).

In the transcendental attitude we are thus directed to consciousness as the "place" in which any entity whatsoever can manifest itself. In the encyclopaedia's draft I (1) Husserl says: "As soon as theoretical interest in... is directed in a general turning of one's glance toward the life of consciousness, in which the world for us is just 'the' world which is present to us, then we are in a new cognitive situation" (I, 1, p. 13). For the most part, this does not tell us anything new. In the context of phenomenological psychology, the reflexive turning of one's glance was required in order to apprehend the lived experiences of consciousness as such. These, however, were always viewed as lived experiences of ...; namely, the lived experience as such is still grasped in a more passive, receptive way. With the transcendental attitude this changes. In the relation between I and object, the I is no mere *receptaculum* but rather the authentic pole of the relation since the sense of every entity is formed in it. "Every sense which it (the world in which we now reside) has for us—the sense which for the world is indefinite and general as well as the sense which is determined in every particularity—is in the inwardness of our own perceiving, representing, thinking, valuing life as conscious and, in our subjective genesis, a formative sense" (loc. cit.). With the statement of this theory, a wide field of research is opened up, namely, investigation of every way for entities to be constituted in modes of consciousness, beginning with their "being in and for themselves." "Once the world in this complete universality has been tied to the subjectivity of consciousness in whose life it steps forth precisely as 'the' world of the appropriate sense, then its whole mode of being receives a dimension of unintelligibility, or questionableness" (op. cit., p. 14).

But at the same time, it follows from what has been said that the thesis of the connection of entities to consciousness does not present a solution to the problem but merely provides a basis on which the genuine problems of constitution must be unraveled. Husserl himself says that "the first awareness of the world's connection to consciousness in its empty generality does not explain *how* the manifold life of consciousness, which is barely glimpsed as it sinks back into the darkness, brings itself to such [achievements], how it, so to speak, arranges it so that in its immanence anything can step forth *as* being in itself" (loc. cit.).

By the transcendental mode of inquiry it can be shown how all categories, in which we understand, conceive, or, in a word, represent wordly entities, spring from determined modes of consciousness and correspond to them. That is the real problem of constitution which kept Husserl in suspense, particularly after 1910—the reason why, for example, he changed the structure of *Ideen II*, in which the problem of constitution now played the main role.[5] Here we are only pointing to the fundamentals of the constitution problematic. In a separate article we will attempt to give a more exact analysis of this basic concept, as well as Husserl's work on constitution.

One question must, however, be discussed. How is it possible that I who am a subject *in the* world (the expression here is understood in Husserl's sense, as occurring along with other worldly entities) at the same time constitutes the world? Is that not a mad attempt to pull oneself out of the morass by one's own bootstraps?

Husserl answers by distinguishing the transcendental I from the psychological I. The I which occurs in the world with other I's and other entities is a psychological I. That means it is looked on as the soul of a body which belongs thus to the corporeal world. But even the pure I, the object of pure psychology, is a worldly one, says Husserl. "The psychologist even as an eidetic phenomenologist is transcendentally naive; he takes the possible 'souls' totally in accordance with the relative sense of the word, hence simply men and animals thought of as being on hand in a possible spatial world" (I, 1, p. 18). Husserl calls the phenomenological-psychological attitude 'transcendentally naive'—an expression which is to be equated with "positive."

In what does the positiveness of the phenomenological-psychological attitude fundamentally consist? What does positiveness mean here, and in general what does it always mean for Husserl? For Husserl "positive" means "posited." The opposite of positive is not negative but rather "posing" (in the sense of positing or placing)—if I may be permitted to use the word. But what distinction can be made between positing and posited? They are surely one and the same word, merely in two different grammatical forms. To look at something as posited means to consider it as standing there finished, as occurring independently of the observer. To understand something as positing means to grasp it in its proper relation to the observer, and thus not as detached from him and independent but, on the contrary, as—so to say—brought forth by him. In the posited, the act of positing disappears; in the positing, the act as such is actualized. For Husserl, a science is positive when it regards entities as posited once and for all. Insofar as every science does that, from the natural sciences up to the human sciences (psychology, literary scholarship, historical scholarship, etc.), all sciences are positive sciences for Husserl, who in no way limits this expression to the so-called natural sciences. The only nonpositive science is phenomenology, because it puts into question the existence of an entity with regard to its relation to actually functioning subjectivity. Thus phenomenology questions from what is posited (entities) to the positing. For the positive sciences, the world is the foundation; for phenomenology, the transcendental I is authentic foundation. Since phenomenological psychology has not yet comprehended this (although in the reflective attitude it is already directed to the lived experiences), it must itself also fall under the objection to positivity. For scientific psychology, "the world, which is presupposed by it as being obviously real, is the foundation; for us, it is just this foundation that has been taken away by the epoche. And in the pure correlative attitude which it creates, the objective world becomes a particular kind of subjective one" (*Crisis* ms., para. 52, p. 108).

What makes access to the transcendental possible? Once again, a reduction. Just as the phenomenological reduction leads to the phenomenon and the eidetic reduction leads to the essential structure of consciousness, so the transcendental reduction leads to the uncovering of transcendental subjectivity, and thus to the subjectivity in which all transcendental objectivity is constituted. The parallelism of the reductions does not, however, remove the task of explaining in what the peculiarities of each reduction consist, namely, of showing how the transcendental reduction differs from the others and to what degree it leads beyond the others.

Husserl says: "While thus the psychologist within the world, which is taken as natural for him, reduces the subjectivity which naturally occurs to purely mental subjectivity—in the world—, through his absolute and universal epoche, the transcendental phenomenologist reduces this psychological pure subjectivity to transcendentally pure subjectivity—to that subjectivity which apperception of the world and therein the objectifying apperception of the 'minds in animal realities' carries out and which posits its own validity" (I, 1, p. 21).

The transcendental epoche is characterized by *universality;* it is an absolute bracketing. But, taken as universal, did not the phenomenological-psychological epoche of the world, the universe of entities, already place the world in brackets? What makes up the higher level of the universality of the transcendental reduction?

In the phenomenological-psychological reduction we were led back to the modes of consciousness which corresponded to the various kinds of objectivities. But the actual conscious I was itself apprehended as worldly, namely, as something which belongs to the world. In the transcendental problematic this belonging to the world is now placed in brackets. By suspension of this characteristic of belonging to the world of consciousness, this reduction is therefore more universal than the previous ones. In place of the characteristic of belonging to the world, the constitution of the world emerges. Every comportment of consciousness is considered to be constitutive. In the referential relationship of world-I, the whole weight of the world is shifted onto the transcendental I. For this reason Husserl consciously called his philosophy 'transcendental idealism'. Through the act of the transcendental reduction we raise ourselves beyond the pure I and conceive its functioning as the formation of sense.

As mentioned before (see n. 1), the critical remarks of Heidegger are in manuscript III (3). One of these remarks refers directly to the difficulty of differentiating between the factual I and the absolute ego. Heidegger asks: "What is the mode of being of this absolute ego—in what sense is it *the same* as the factual I and in what sense is it *not* the same?"

Husserl answers this in the subsequent draft:

My transcendental I is therefore evidently "different" from the natural I, but by no means as a second I which is "separate," in the natural sense of the word, from the natural ego. Nor conversely is it in any way an I which is "bound" (in the natural sense) to the natural ego or intertwined with it. It is precisely the field (taken in full concreteness) of transcendental self-experience which can, at any time, be changed into the psychological self-experience by a mere shift of attitude. In this shift an identity of the I is necessarily produced; in transcendental reflection on the shift, the psychological objectification becomes visible as self-objectification of the transcendental I, and so it turns out as if it had in every moment of the natural attitude imposed an apperception upon itself." [I, 1, p. 22]

In other words, the I is always at the same time factual (psychological) and transcendental. In the natural attitude it lives directed to the objects, so that its transcendental function remains concealed from it, and we must push through to it by means of the various processes of the reduction. Because the function— more precisely, the functioning of the transcendental I—remains hidden from the respective factual I, Husserl also calls

the transcendental I the anonymous I. That it exists at all is to be inferred from the formations of sense which are its work. This transcendental I is for Husserl the absolute fundament beyond which one cannot go. The task of transcendental phenomenology consists in uncovering the various modes of functioning, in order to allow the constitution of the world to become visible.

Let us return to the problem of the paradox of human subjectivity that was posed above, namely, the opposition between "being a subject for the world and at the same time being an object *in* the world. According to Husserl's solution, this means that the true subject is never an object *in* the world but, rather, is constantly merely a subject for the world which it constitutes. Only as long as it has not apprehended itself as a transcendental subject can it understand itself as an object in the world. Already, in the psychological-phenomenological attitude, the world becomes a phenomenon, but here (we repeat) the being of the world is not called into question; rather, the psychological acts are merely observed, whereas in the transcendental attitude the world as foundation is abrogated.

We will not discuss further how the transcendental ego through the original process of temporalization (*Zeitigung*) begins the original constitution on which all other constitutions are constructed.

Earlier we quoted the statement: "The return to consciousness, which all philosophy seeks with certainty and clarity, stretches over the domain of the purely psychical back into the field of pure subjectivity." Husserl attempts (at the beginning of the second section) to pursue this return historically. "With Locke the limitation to the subjective was already determined by non-psychological interests. Psychology stood in the service of the transcendental problem which was awakened by Descartes" (I, 1, p. 12). Husserl was accustomed to construe the history of modern philosophy—we must add, in a very naive way—as a propaedeutic to phenomenology. Descartes was the first to see the transcendental problem, although he could not grasp it.

Descartes *discovers the pure I* of the pure life of consciousness, of the pure *cogitationes*—at least he stood in this discovery without himself working it out purely and without having protected it from unclear deformations. He discovers it while he is on the way to a *fundamentum inconcussum* on which all genuine knowledge, or better on which a universal science, a philosophy, a systematical universal knowledge of the world as universe of objective entities is to be grounded." [K III 21, MS B1. 13a-b; transcription p. 25]

From Descartes, Locke takes over the direction of the investigation, which then passes from him to Berkeley and Hume and finally is radically carried through by Kant.

In the third and last section of the encyclopedia draft, which I take as the final one (I, 1), Husserl deals in a very brief way with the relationship of phenomenology to the sciences—with its essential determination "as universal science in absolute grounding." He had dealt in detail with this theme fifteen years earlier in the third volume of the *Ideas for a Pure Phenomenology and Phenomenological Philosophy*, to which we therefore refer explicitly.[6]

The section begins with a short explanation of phenomenology's position on ontology:

Phenomenology is the science of all conceivable transcendental phenomena, in their synthetic total configurations in which alone they are concretely possible,—that is in the forms of the transcendental individual subjects bound to the communities of subjects. As such it is *eo ipso* an *a priori* science of all conceivable entities. But it is not merely *a priori* science of the totality of objective entities, nor is its attitude one of natural positivity. Rather it is such a science in full concretion of the entity in general, the way in which this entity creates its sense of being and its validity out of the correlative intentional constitution. This includes as well the being of transcendental subjectivity itself, whose demonstrable essence is to be transcendentally constituted in itself and for itself. [I, 1, p. 26]

Of course, we must ask whether an ontology, understood in this way, is not necessarily a merely formal one, namely, one which considers only the forms of constituting. In this section Husserl gives what are more like claims than demonstrative analyses. This point is even more thought provoking since he never carried through the attempt to provide a universal ontology. The expositions in this part of the work are aimed at defining the goal of phenomenology. Read without commentary, they could give the impression of summarizing what has already been achieved. This, however, is not the case.

Moreover, according to Husserl, it is through phenomenology that the crisis in the foundations of the exact sciences is to be resolved, since it understands the actual a priori of the exact sciences as the accomplishment of the transcendental ego and thereby the accomplishments it presupposes. Precisely because such conceiving does not grasp that a priori as given once and for all, but rather in its particular and limited function, it is doubtlessly a necessary element for overcoming the foundational crisis. But it is questionable whether it is also a sufficient element which explains everything.

According to Husserl, the a priori sciences, insofar as they conceptualize themselves, become branches of phenomenology.

With regard to the historically developed *a priori* sciences, the result of their developing in a transcendental naivety is that only a radical phenomenological grounding can transform them into genuine sciences which fully justify themselves. But precisely thereby, they cease to be positive (dogmatic) sciences and become dependent branches of the one phenomenology as universal eidetic ontology. [I, 1, p. 27]

In addition, through phenomenology the real grounding of the empirical sciences is supposed to ensue, too—just because the a priori sciences, which are their very foundations, have received through phenomenology the reference back to themselves, namely, become transparent in their own a priori content.

In my view, what has just been said is decisive for the mathematical sciences and for the foundation of the empirical sciences in the a priori sciences. It remains questionable, however, to what extent the parallel Husserl pointed to between a priori psychology and empirical psychology really is a parallel, and to what extent the so-called human sciences can be founded at all according to the model of the "exact" sciences.

Phenomenology, so understood, attains, according to Husserl, the ideal of the universal philosophy which has always hovered before philosophers.

Rigorous, systematically carried out, phenomenology...is identical with this philosophy which encompasses *all* genuine knowledge. It is divided into eidetic phenomenology (as universal ontology) as *first philosophy*, and into *second philosophy*, the science of the universe of facts or of transcendental intersubjectivity which comprises all syntheses. First philosophy is the totality of methods for second philosophy and is referred back to itself in its methodical grounding. [I, 1, p. 28]

Finally, according to Husserl, phenomenology is the instrument through which humanity attains absolute self-reflection: the actualizing of the authentic ideal of humanity. As the function of humanity's universal self-reflection, phenomenology recognizes itself in the service of a universal *praxis* of reason, namely, in the service of the striving which becomes free through the unveiling and which is directed to the idea—which lies in infinity—of a humanity, which truly and thoroughly would exist and live in truth and genuineness" (I, 1, p. 29).

In these words we hear a rationalistic belief in humanity's progress through rational self-reflection, a belief which commanded respect. It is, however, a confession of faith that Husserl lays down as a philosophical argumentation. Thus, for example, the essence of man's historicity is not properly conceived or even made a theme. It must be asked: What does it mean here to exist and live in truth and genuineness? In what are veracity and genuineness grounded?

Husserl says what phenomenology should be without investigating sufficiently whether it is in a position to be-

come that. Actually, Husserl left only a few manuscripts on this problem of the final definition of phenomenology (cf. X III 4, K III 6), and they have more of a prophetic than a "rigorous scientific" tone. Certainly it must not be forgotten that when he was working out these manuscripts Husserl was in his seventies. He attempted to work out a kind of program which was no longer really valid for him but was thought out for the benefit of those to come who were supposed to advance his work. That becomes clear from the last sentence of draft I (1): "For this reason phenomenology requires the phenomenologist to renounce for himself the ideal of a philosophical system and to live as a modest worker in community with others for a *philosophia perennis*" (I, 1, p. 34).

In conclusion, I want briefly to discuss the remarks Heidegger made on the continuation of an earlier draft (III, 3). That Husserl attributed a particular meaning to these remarks follows from the fact that he preserved not only Heidegger's letter but the remarks, also. He had all of it stenographically copied and, moreover, inserted this copy in a carbon copy of the manuscript. Perhaps, also, a few essential points could be made clear about the relationship between the two thinkers. The year of the encyclopaedia drafts was also the year of the publication of Heidegger's main work, *Being and Time*, which is dedicated to Husserl. In a letter to Husserl (October 22, 1927) Heidegger writes: "On the enclosed sheets I attempt once more to fix the essential points. This also gives me the opportunity to characterize the fundamental tendency of *Being and Time* within the transcendental problem."

Outline I from Heidegger's letter to Husserl runs as follows.

There is agreement that the entity in the sense of what you call "world" cannot be explained in its transcendental constitution by a return to an entity with the very same kind of being. However, this does not mean that what makes up the place of the transcendental is not an entity at all. Rather, just this *problem* arises:

what is the kind of being of the entity in which the "world" is constituted? That is the central problem of *Being and Time*—i.e., a fundamental ontology of Dasein. It is a matter of showing that the kind of being of human Dasein is totally different from that of all other entities, and that the kind of being, which it is, shelters right within it the possibility of transcendental constitution.

Transcendental consitution is a central possibility for the existence of the factual self. This self, the concrete man (is as such,—) as an entity which is never a worldly real fact, because man is never only present at hand but rather man exists. And the "wondrous" thing to be marvelled at is that the constitution of the existence of Dasein makes possible the transcendental constitution of all that is positive.

The "one-sided" observations of somatology and pure psychology are only possible on the ground of the concrete totality of man which as such primarily determines the kind of being of man.

The "pure psychic" has precisely not arisen with a view to the ontology of the whole man—i.e. not with an aim to psychology, but rather it originates basically from epistemological considerations since the time of Descartes.

What constitutes is not nothing; thus it is something and exists—though not in the sense of the positive.

The question about the kind of being of what does the constituting itself cannot be circumvented.

Thus the problem of being is universally tied to what constitutes and what is constituted.

In the first paragraph Heidegger points to the common ground between Husserl's thought and his own. But the expression 'common ground' really is too strong since it presupposes a common point of departure; Heidegger says, more cautiously, "agreement" (*Übereinstimmung*). Even from two different points of departure one can come to an agreement in reference to particular questions; that is what is really meant here.

What you call 'world'," it says—and thereby Heidegger is already pointing to the fact that the concept of world in *Being and Time* is a totally different one. The Husserlian concept of world means the "totality of entities" (universe). What the entities are cannot be clarified by a return

to an entity. On that there is agreement, and that means, at the same time, that there is agreement on the necessity of calling entities into question. This calling into question is not like that of the sciences which investigate particular realms of entities but never ask what entities *as* entities are. On that Heidegger and Husserl share the same opinion. Their ways part, however, as soon as it is determined more precisely what one must inquire back to in order to think of entities as entities? This appears at first to be exaggerated. Do not both thinkers make being human the problem—Husserl through the exposition of the transcendental ego, Heidegger through the existential analytic of *Dasein?* However, they differ in principle on the way they attempt to comprehend man.

For Heidegger *Dasein*[7] denotes an entity's way of being. For this reason he immediately adds "this does not mean that what makes up the place of the transcendental is not an entity at all." And he explains that in more detail "the problem arises at once: What is the kind of being of the entity in which 'world' is constituted?" This question leads him to carry through the analytic of *Dasein* and to the question about *being*—the basic question of his thinking and of any thinking whatsoever.

For Husserl, the problematic unfolds quite differently, insofar as I understand him correctly. That every entity must be called into question means that one must seek the unquestionable, which is the ground of all entities. Husserl finds this in the transcendental ego. If this is supposed to be the final ground, beyond which one cannot go further, then it must follow that everything is constituted in it. As Husserl says, every entity must be resolved in consciousness so that transcendental consciousness becomes quite simply being. On the other hand, Heidegger's concept of *Dasein* is in no way identified with that of being—something which, unfortunately, was often claimed.

Since Husserl's questioning leads back to the ego, his total method stands under the imprint of the reduction through which even the universe of entities is bracketed in order to obtain the pure ego. In Heidegger the reduction is totally missing. The relation between the entity called *Dasein* and the entity which is not called *Dasein* belongs directly to the essence of *Dasein*. *Dasein* is unfolded as a self in this relation since it is always a relation to itself. To bracket this relation (he usually avoids the expression "relation" because it points to a radical separation and creates a kind of abyss in the usual form of opposition between subject and object which cannot be bridged anymore) means to grasp man merely as a truncated subject. Moreover, *Dasein's* openness to entities in no way means a merging of man with nonhuman entities. In the criticism already cited, Heidegger said quite directly: "It is a matter of showing that the kind of being of human Dasein is totally different from that of all other entities, and that its kind of being, as the very kind that it is, shelters right in itself the possibility of transcendental constitution."[8] This distinction is brought to light in the existential analytic in which the essence of being open is really explained. To be sure, Husserl speaks constantly of the transcendental ego. However, he repeatedly views man, on the other hand, as a body among bodies, as something that belongs to the domain of being proper to things because of his body. For this reason Husserl occupied himself to the end of his life with the question: How is it possible that man, a thing of the world, constitutes the world and all things? This way of viewing is particularly evident in the discussion of the experience of other. The other is experienced first as a "body" which moves itself. Then I see that the movements are not arbitrary but mean something. Hence I finally come to the conclusion that the self-moving body is a man.

At the very beginning of *Being and Time* Heidegger separates the form of *Dasein's* being from that kind of being which is not like *Dasein* (readiness-to-hand, presence-at-hand). Man is never grasped as merely something present-at-hand. Rather, he is that entity which first

opens up the realm of entities in that he breaks into it and thereby breaks it open. In draft III (p. 24) Heidegger made the remark: "See our Todtnauberg talk on 'Being-in-the-World' [*Being and Time*, sec. 12-69] and the essential distinction about being present-at-hand 'within' such a world." For when man is grasped in Heidegger's sense as *Dasein*, he can no longer be understood simply as a "body among bodies"—what is called mere 'existence' ('*Dasein*').

While Husserl thus separates the transcendental ego from the world in order to keep it pure of everything worldly, for Heidegger *Dasein* is that entity which first discloses the world precisely in that it brings—or forces—every entity into the realm of openness. This relation to the world, which unfortunately we cannot discuss in more detail here,[9] is so essential that Heidegger even defines *Dasein* as "Being-in-the-World." However, "Being-in-the-World" never means the mere occurrence among other entities (which is what the term normally means for Husserl). For this reason Heidegger also noted on the Husserl text: "Does not any world whatsoever belong to the essence of the pure ego?" For him that is a necessity, since in the opening up of the world *Dasein* for the first time in fact begins to exist.

If one lets *Dasein's* reference to entities go by the way, then *Dasein* as such could no longer be grasped. Thus the "pure I" must, for Heidegger, be (to a certain extent) a nonconcept, an artificial abstraction which hinders grasping man in his totality and in his concrete existence. The existential analytic is aimed at grasping man as a whole—not an arbitrary idea of man but man in his existence. To be sure, it does so not in a descriptive way, through mere delineation of ways of behavior, but directly through the exhibition of the conditions for the possibility of his existence.

These conditions—or, better, structures—are not established a priori but are supposed to be elicited by means of an analysis of concrete *Dasein*. That the entire analytic of *Dasein* is no final aim (like Husserl's apprehension of the pure ego) but merely the preparation for raising the question of being should only be indicated briefly here, although for Heidegger it is of basic significance.

We repeatedly find marginal notes by Heidegger which point to the fact that man is never an entity which is merely present-at-hand and that he should not be grasped as such: "Human Dasein 'is' in such a way that, although an entity, it is never simply present-at-hand" (p. 25). Because Husserl did not really bring the form of man's being into question, and since for him an entity always somehow means the same as "what is present-at-hand" and thus is something within the world, he tries to exclude every worldly element in order to retain what is peculiar to "pure I". Thus he opposes the "pure ego" and the human I, that is, the I which still stands in relation to the world and is somehow related to entities. Discussing the transcendental reduction, Husserl says: "This [the transcendental reduction] will require that no transcendent apperception, no transcendent validity whatever be verified. It should be 'bracketed' and is only to be taken as what it is in itself—as pure subjective apperceiving, intending, taking as valid, etc. If I act in this way for myself, then I am not a human I" (III, 3, p. 25).

In this sentence Heidegger double-underlined "I am" and "not," and added: "Or perhaps *exactly* such, in its peculiar 'wondrous' possibility of existence." In the margin he remarked: "Why not? Is this action not a possibility for man? But just because he is never merely present-at-hand, is it not a *comporting*, i.e. a kind of being which precisely secures itself for itself and thus never belongs to the positivity of the merely present-at-hand?" (loc. cit.). He wanted to make Husserl understand that being, in the sense of the *being of man*, does *not* have to be *a positive being* which drops out in the reduction. He points to the fact that Husserl two sentences later—after he said that the reducing I is not a human one—wrote: "The ego reduced in this way is surely my I, in the

entire concreteness of its life." This difficulty of the separation between the pure I and the human I, and its questionableness, is emphasized by Heidegger.

Husserl said of the "transcendental ego": "Evidently, it can in fact be posited exclusively in its reduced peculiarity with all its intentional correlates and thus offers for me the most basic foundation, the first foundation for experience for a transcendental investigation" (III: 26).

Heidegger underlined "can be posited" and wrote instead "*positum*." Something positive! But what kind of *positing* is that? "In what sense is this a posited entity, if it is not nothing, but rather in a certain way is supposed to be everything?" And in another place he says: "What is the character of the positing in which the absolute ego is a posited? To what extent is there no positivity (positedness) present here?"

We see clearly how everything revolves around the concept of the "is." For Husserl "is" is synonymous with being worldly. And since all that is worldly must be bracketed, the concept of the *is* must also be bracketed. Heidegger, on the contrary, shows how in the positing of the transcendental ego an "*is*" is presupposed which would have to be bracketed insofar as everything positive (posited) is to be suspended.

Basically, Heidegger criticizes the undifferentiatedness of the "is" in Husserl (everything which is is present-at-hand in the world and must be bracketed with the worldly). To that he opposes the division between *Dasein* and being present-at-hand, as well as the separation of the transcendental ego from the factual I. For Heidegger, facticity belongs necessarily to concrete existence. Man never exists in any other way than is factually thrown into the *world*. "Transcendental constitution"—says Heidegger—"is a central possibility for the existence of the *factual self*. This, the *concrete man*, is as such, as an entity (*Seiendes*)—never a 'worldly real fact' because man is never merely present-at-hand but rather exists."[10] In other words, we may not suspend the concrete being of man and place it in brackets in order to find what Husserl calls constitution and Heidegger the unconcealment of entities. This can only be exhibited in concrete existence.

The task of philosophy is just this, to grasp the essence of man in such a way that it becomes transparent in his concrete total existence. According to Heidegger, this grasping is only possible in that one does not remain with man (be it as transcendental ego, as subject, as person), but rather goes back to the very place where man receives the determination of his essence—to *being*. Since for Husserl, in the perspective of transcendental idealism, the transcendental ego is the absolute final-certain ground of being, the problem of going beyond this does not arise. Consequently the authentic problematic of being which rules Heidegger's thought is missing in Husserl. Thus the paths of the two thinkers necessarily diverge. Husserl remains on the Cartesian-rationalistic line of modern metaphysics, while Heidegger attempts to comprehend the fate of Western metaphysics as a whole—in going back to the original premetaphysical thinkers.[11]

NOTES

1. The following drafts (in typescript) for the encyclopaedia article are in the Husserl Archive in Louvain: M III 10 I, 1; M III 10 I, 2; M III 10 III 1, 2, 3, 4, 5, 6. Since the basic catalogue number, M III '10, is always the same, I will cite the distinguishing numbers only (I, 1; III, 1; etc.). Landgrebe made the transcriptions, and in various texts there are also notes by him.

The various drafts come from the autumn of 1927. The order of their composition is, as I see it, the following. Husserl first wrote III, 1 (III, 2 is a copy of this). Presumably, Husserl wrote the first twenty pages of this draft during Heidegger's visit. He added the last ten pages of this text later and sent them to Heidegger in Messkirch.

On the basis of the first draft, Heidegger wrote the beginning of a new version (which is in folder III, 3), which Husserl continued (III, 3).

The subsequent composition, III, 4 (5 and 6 are carbon copies of it), is the most detailed of all; Husserl himself noted on it "final draft." Since this version presumably seemed to him too long (forty-five pages) for the *Encyclopaedia Britannica*, he wrote a new version, or rather he put together a new version on the basis of the one he had already written (I, 1). Its first section corresponds to III, 4, except the first four pages. The rest, however, is much more concise. While the text III, 4 is written continuously without paragraphing, Husserl used paragraphs in the final draft. Moreover, in composition I, 1 pages are taken from III, 4. This also leads to the erroneous conclusion that I, 1 is the final draft.

Heidegger's letter to Husserl is in folder III, 3, together with his remarks on the text of the first draft. In the second half of III, 3 are various marginal notes by Heidegger on the text.

The encyclopaedia text is published in *Husserliana*, vol. IX: *Phänomenologische Psychologie*, ed. S. Strasser (The Hague: Nijhoff, 1968).

(Translators' note: This volume appeared under the title indicated, but was edited by the author as *Husserliana*, vol. IX [The Hague: Nijhoff, 1968]).

2. The Hague: Nijhoff, 1950.

3. Op. cit., p. 17.

4. Op. cit., pp. ix ff.

5. Compare the foreword to the fourth volume of *Husserliana*, ed. Marly Wetzel-Biemel (The Hague: Nijhoff, 1952).

6. *Ideen zu einer reinen Phänomenologie und phänomenologischen Philosophie*, vols. II and III, ed. Marly Wetzel-Biemel as *Husserliana*, vols. IV and V (The Hague: Nijhoff, 1950).

7. See my article "Heideggers Begriff des Daseins," *Studia Catholica*, 24 (1949): 113-29.

8. When Heidegger, as here, uses the expression "transcendental constitution," he is doing so as a favor to Husserl. In *Being and Time*, as well as in his other writings, this term is not found because Heidegger looks on the constitution problematic as an idealistic residue that must be overcome.

9. An explanation of the Heideggerian concept of world is attempted by the author in *Le concept du monde chez Heidegger* (Louvain: Nauwelaerts, 1950).

10. My italics.

11. See Martin Heidegger: *Holzwege* (Frankfurt: Klostermann, 1950), as well as the preface to the fifth edition of *What Is Metaphysics?* and the *Letter on Humanism*.

Consciousness, Praxis, and Reality:
Marxism vs. Phenomenology

MARX W. WARTOFSKY

The beginning of phenomenology is the reassertion of subjectivity. The beginning of Marxism is the attack upon subjectivity. To contrast Marxism and phenomenology is to find, in the first place, the common point of departure for each, the common *Problematik* to which each addresses itself. Otherwise we are in the strange position of counterposing two indifferent world views or two incommensurable methodologies, without mediation. It is clear from the history of the subject that Marxism and phenomenology are not alien to each other. First, phenomenological themes lie at the heart of the origins of Marxism in Hegel and Feuerbach.[1] Second, there is a major current within Marxist theory which engages phenomenology, if it does not in fact adopt its stance. I refer here to Lukács and to an East-European Marxism, usually characterized as Marxist humanism, as well as to contemporary neo-Marxism of the Frankfurt or Italian variety.[2] Third, a major accommodation as well as critique of Marxism characterizes the problematic Marxism of the French phenomenologists, such as Sartre and Merleau-Ponty.[3]

I do not plan to enter into either a reconstruction of the Marxism of the

Read at the Symposium on Marxism and Phenomenology at the Annual Meeting of the Society for Phenomenology and Existential Philosophy, Duquesne University, Pittsburgh, Oct. 19, 1972.

phenomenologists or the phenomenology of the Marxists, or into the specific jargon of the schools. Just as "ordinary-language philosophy" at one point became a cottage industry in England (with branches abroad), this Marxism-phenomenology interaction has become a massive production enterprise of the word mills of Europe and America. The product is recognizable by its union labels: it is stitched with a plethora of philosophical neologisms, sometimes to the extent that the garment is hidden by the labels. These range from Hegelisms of the *pour-soi-en-soi* sort to Hellenisms of the *noema-noesis* sort to plain old Teutonisms of the *Vorhanden-Verfallen* sort. Nor do I mean to be snide with respect to philosophy's right and need to re-create language and to neologize. We pursue our human inquiry through language and in language, and the shape and forms of expression are not simply images of our thought but its structures as well. Still I will try not to ignore but to neutralize some of the divergence of expression in the service of an analysis and critique.

The question to which I address myself is the viability of phenomenology, given the Marxist critique. Its emphasis is, therefore, the reverse of the more common question: the viability of Marxism, given the phenomenological critique. I want to raise the question, first, in terms of the genesis of Marxism and of phenomenology—that is, with respect to the problem which each finds as its originating matrix; second, with respect to the sharpest (and perhaps most one-sided and abstract) form of their antithesis; and, finally, with respect to a series of what I will call mediations in which the originally formulated *Problematik* and the originally articulated stances are subjected of qualifications or determinations which each view demands of the other. However, I do not pretend to aim for a synthesis of the views for I will conclude that Marxism succeeds where phenomenology fails, at the most crucial point of difference.

So much for the schematic program of the paper; now for the substantive focus. The issues which I take to be central are almost too bald to be stated in less than a vague and general way. They are, simply, the question of how consciousness is related to reality. And where the schematic answer is that this relation is achieved by *praxis*, or by *action*, how one is to characterize this praxis or action. My conclusion will be that the phenomenologists fail to give an adequate answer to the latter question because they fail to realize either consciousness or praxis in its historical character, and thereby fail in their attempts to give consciousness a social or nonsubjective character.

1. The Genesis of Marxism and of Phenomenology

By *genesis* I do not mean the historical generation of phenomenology or Marxism in its concrete details, either as a history of ideas or in terms of the socio-historical matrix of the two philosophies. Though this is the concrete account of the origins of these two movements, I intend something more modest: an abstraction from this historical genesis in terms of a characterization of the typical *Problematik* or problem-setting in which each arose. In short, what problem or set of problems gives rise to phenomenology? What set to Marxism?

Again, abstractly, we may say that

phenomenology's problem is the reappropriation of the object. In response to the kind of objectivism which puts the objects of human knowledge or of human practice beyond the subject, phenomenology strives to effect a reconstitution of the subject-object relation as an *essential* relation—but essential from the side of the subject. The classical "object" is subjectivized in a recharacterization of "subjectivity" not as mere inwardness but as a structuring and creative activity which is to be studied not simply in its products—that is, not simply in its objectification or outward form—but, rather, from the side of the subject itself. Thus the "objects" are reconstrued in terms of what is to be found "in" consciousness, either from the point of view of its necessary conditions or its structures. Within the rationalist emphasis of phenomenology these are conceived as essences; within the existentialist strain as the concrete creations of human actions or projects. But in both they are modes of subjectivity in which the ego or the knowing-acting subject is the source and repository of these structures or conditions. The objectivity thus attained is a constructed or constituted objectivity, one with which the subject finds himself inextricably bound, from which he cannot absent himself without self-destruction, and, on another emphasis, one from which he cannot escape and in which he ultimately loses himself as a unique "I." The methodology of phenomenology therefore emphasizes the construction of the "world" or of a "life," namely, of the othersidedness of the ego as itself the inevitable concomitant of ego activity. In this, phenomenology turns out to be thoroughly Fichtean. The subject-object relation is a relation of and by a subject: "of" in the sense that the object is always "for-a-subject," and even its being "in-itself" is also, at the limit, an abstraction posited by a subject; and "by" in the sense that there are no passive subjects, that subjectivity is activity and the active positing of the other is the very being of subjectivity. In this way the "other" is always a clue to the character of the subject: the object can always be "read back," so to speak, as revealing the primordial or necessary conditions or structures of subjectivity itself. The relation with this "other"—whether it is realized as nothing else than the subject in its *own* otherness (and thereby the guarantee that all consciousness is ultimately self-consciousness) or whether it is realized as an intractable and totally alien "other" which stands beyond the subject as its delimitation, as what is ultimately "not-consciousness"—yet remains a relation with respect to a subject, or a relation in consciousness. It is easy to see where alternative influences can enter here: Hegelian, Kierkegaardian, Cartesian. But this is no more than a sketch and I will not pursue these alternatives.

By contrast, the genesis of Marxism lies in the critique of subjectivity not simply as a critique of the ego or of consciousness as the bearer of objectivity but as an argument against the theory of constitution or construction. The world, or a life, is not constituted by the activity of consciousness; rather, consciousness is constituted by a life or by the world. The ego is a product, not an agent; or in more cautious dialectical terms the ego is not an agent until it has been constituted. The world is not an achievement of the ego but, rather, the ego is an achievement of the world. In turn, the ego is then capable of reachieving this very world which generates it by way of reflection: it can then objectify what in the first place it has interiorized; it can project an image of the world from the fact that it is a subsumption or a product of this world. The world is therefore *not* an *other* for the ego or for consciousness, except on this reconstruction. The ontological stance is therefore totally different from that of phenomenology. The notion of "otherness" or "othersidedness" demands a subject for which the "other" *is* "other": the very logic of the concept "other" demands this. But this "otherness" is not constituted by the subject except as its own reconstruction of its own origin, as a subject. The world is therefore primordial, and primordial both to the ego and to its own reconstruction as an "other." The constituted world of the phenomenologist is therefore the image of the real world. But the phenomenologist takes this image for the reality of the world itself, and thereby makes a double error: he construes the ego as primordial, since the ego is primordial *for* the ego; and then he construes the world as the construction of the ego (albeit a necessary construction, involved in the very being of the ego itself).

In less metaphysical terms, the Marxist is a materialist in that he takes the world to exist independently of any relation to consciousness and therefore to exist primordially and prior to consciousness. He takes consciousness itself as a product of the activity of non-conscious and pre-conscious matter; and he takes the biologically live organism in its manifold of interactions with an environment, which includes other organisms both like it and unlike it, to be the context in which consciousness emerges. The specific context of biological life in which consciousness emerges is an interaction of organisms capable of reproducing their own existence and that of their species by the activity of production. Here animal drives for the satisfaction of life needs become something more than desires which are consummated without residue in sheer biological satisfaction. Instead, they give rise to means, to instruments, or tools. The drive therefore embodies itself in an activity which objectifies the need or, rather, which objectifies the *way* in which the need is met; namely, it objectifies the activity of satisfying a need in a teleological object or in the tool. This activity, then, is no longer mere animal activity but becomes production.

It is out of the activity of production that consciousness arises in the first place in the Marxist view. The activity of production, as a teleological activity embodied in a means of production and in the generation of relations of production which are involved in the utilization of such means, may be characterized as *praxis*, namely, as the distinctively human mode of self-reproduction. According to Marx, this involves two forms of organization, or rather a form of organization which has two aspects: that which has to do with the production of the means of existence and that which has to do with the reproduction of the species: production relations and family relations. It is out of this context that a necessarily social being is determined and a necessarily social instrumentality is developed: language, as an instrument of communication, and with it consciousness of a distinctively human sort, that is, thought. The separation of the ego, as a self-conscious agency or distinctive entity within this "ensemble of relations," is therefore a late achievement in this process, and not its origin. The ego is in effect constituted by this process of socialization and historicization of the animal. "History" becomes the self-conscious reconstruction of this genesis and of its sequence: but that there is a history before there is "history" is to say that there is a process of coming-to-be of the ego, before the ego can reflectively reconstruct this process.

In this theory of the genesis of the ego the ego's conscious activity becomes in turn an object of the ego. Since consciousness itself then serves as an embodiment or an objectification of praxis, it becomes the characteristic "tool" of conscious teleology, id est, an instrument of production and a necessary aspect of human labor. It becomes embedded, therefore, in the very structures which labor produces. And it is, moreover, capable of rediscovering itself there: it becomes, in effect, reflexive. It comes to know itself in its own objects insofar as consciousness, or the ego, is involved in the very character of production. The products of praxis are in this sense conscious products, but not, as such, mere products of consciousness or thought. Conscious praxis (all praxis is conscious) is the totality of human activity insofar as it is human—namely, insofar as it is not mere biological reflex, mere metabolism, or mere instinct—and therefore it is

"thought" or reflective consciousness only insofar as reflection is part of the process of human production itself. It is "theorized praxis," not in the sense that there is "dumb" or "blind" praxis, which then may be either "theoretical" or not, if by "theory" we mean the conscious teleology of human praxis.

Yet it becomes historically possible to separate the reflective consciousness from its role in praxis because the division of labor permits a concomitant division of the reflective component in the actual organization of production. The division of labor and class society, in the Marxist view, permits praxis to be fragmented: first, into its sheer mechanical component—its material component as the actual power to transform natural objects into objects for human use—and, second, into its rational or reflective component: the direction and employment of this power. The fullest articulation of this division comes about when the power to produce—labor power—becomes totally divorced from its teleology, namely, the production of use-values, and thereby becomes so-called alienated labor, whose teleological character is represented only in an abstracted form, namely, in the production of commodities or exchange values. According to a Marxist view, this division is the genesis of the abstraction of consciousness from living human praxis, and it is this abstraction which makes possible the reflection of consciousness upon itself as a praxis-free or purely theoretical activity of thought.[4] Yet even in this pure reflection of a divorced consciousness, praxis lives on as an abstraction, as a reflected-upon praxis, namely, as the "praxis" of thought itself, engaged in the "production" of its own "objects." It is the image of praxis which becomes the model for consciousness of itself: it "remembers itself," so to speak, in its origins, but only in this dim way. And so consciousness takes itself to be the agency, the source, the genesis of all activity. And it takes the objects of this activity to be its own so as to reveal consciousness to itself by means of its own objectifications. "praxis" becomes "theoretical praxis," the ghost of actual human praxis.

But Feuerbach had already unmasked this self-deception in *The Essence of Christianity* with respect to the image of man in religion and in theology, and Marx had followed Feuerbach's critique of the Holy Family with a critique of the earthly family. Feuerbach writes: "Ghosts are shadows of the past. They necessarily lead us back to the question: What was the ghost when it was still a creature of flesh and blood?"[5] The ghostly *Praxis* which appears to purely theoretical consciousness as its own (i.e., theoretical) activity is nothing but flesh-and-blood praxis of conscious production and reproduction of man divorced from its living reality and represented as merely conscious activity, that is, as the mere activity of consciousness itself.

Thus consciousness, which in its theological form takes itself to be the image of God's thought, transfers this godly creativity to itself as its own inner activity, indeed as its very nature. This is Descartes' first *cogito*. But it does so by the grace of God; it remembers its origin and appeals to it, not simply to preserve its own activity but rather to guarantee the objectivity of this activity as more than an idle dream or a thorough deception. This is Descartes' second *cogito*. Objectivity appears here in its masked form, not as the origin and object of praxis itself but as the abstract and metaphysical Being of God. For God is the origin of the activity, and thereby the guarantor of its objectivity. Thus far Feuerbach had gone in demythologizing the relation of the ego to its other, and Sartre follows him to this extent.

But even this account of the origin of the ego, remembering its birth abstractly and in this alienated form, is far from Marxism, though it has the features of a materialist genesis. What Marx adds is the historical dimension of this process in a reflection upon reflection which reveals its pre-reflective genesis. It is only in social practice that the ego becomes an ego, namely, becomes capable of the actual production of a world in its own image: not in reflection merely but in the world itself. As the *telos* of human action, the ego enters into real transformation and real reconstruction, into real subordination of the external world, or nature, to its needs. And thus the ego reconstructs this nature as an object according to its needs both in practice and in theory; its theory, the ego, becomes the reflex of its needs and, in turn, the determinant of its action. It is not simply determined but both determined and determining. Its freedom lies in its ability to meet needs by its teleological direction of action or by its intimate involvement with a socialized body, one which is already more than has made it and is the repository of skills, attitudes, social needs—in short, a human body. This ego is a historical body, one which acts in a concrete historical context and is an agent of this history, as well as a product of it. It is this dialectical two-sidedness of the humanized and socialized organism which sets the ego above nature: it transforms its past into conscious action toward a future.[6] But Marx goes further. Insofar as the ego is historical, it has no essence as such, apart from the history of its actions. And as such it is neither disembodied consciousness nor merely embodied consciousness; it is social and historical consciousness, and acts from social and historical needs which are concretely manifested in a society of a certain concrete type. Its theoretical awareness is therefore not of abstract and eternal essences but of its own historical character, which it expresses in its action. Such a consciousness or ego is therefore inevitably caught up in the web of its time and place, of its concrete situation. It transcends this parochialism only by means of historical action, id est, action which transforms this time and place into another, which changes the world. By contrast, the ego which is forever bound to its time and place and which either cannot engage in the transformation of its historical locale or (worse yet) attempts to preserve the present atemporally is bound to a theoretical consciousness which sees all praxis as its own, id est, as eternal and unchanging. It imposes this abstraction of history upon history, and becomes ahistorical. So, Marx argued, bourgeois economic theory took its present as an eternal present and read back its onesidedness or *stasis* into the very nature of things, into theories of nature and man as fixed essences in its own image.[7] Marx explains the social dynamic of this abstracted consciousness by a historical analysis, by showing the genesis of this mode of thought in the very situation of a historical period and in the praxis of a historical class.

In summary, then, Marxism takes the genesis of thought from beyond thought, and insofar as it does it is materialist. It takes the genesis of thought from beyond the thinker as an isolated individual and traces it to his social reality—the peculiar and distinctive construction of a world in which he finds his place. Insofar as Marxism does this, it is a historical materialism. It takes thought beyond thought in its history—in its relation to other thought, and as itself a process mediated by its history, by its material, by its objects, by what it derives from, by what it attains to, by what it interacts with. And insofar as Marxism does this it is dialectical.

In such a view, the phenomenologist is seen ultimately to derive thought from itself and all else from the activity of thought.[8] Phenomenology infects history with thought, infects the body with thought and the world with thought, and sees everything in an essential relation to consciousness, from which it cannot be rescued. In general, then, on this sharp antithesis Marxism is a materialist theory of consciousness; phenomenology is only the latest and perhaps the most subtle idealist theory of consciousness.

2. The First Mediation

Stated in its sharpest form, the antithesis appears as one between "objective" Marxism and "subjective" phenomenology. Marx himself paid homage to idealism when, in contrasting it with mechanistic materialism, he noted that idealism had developed the notion of self-activity, of agency, by contrast to the mechanistic conception of matter as dead, inert, mere extension. But the charge may be brought—indeed *has* been brought—against Marxism—if not against Marx, then against Engels; if not against Engels, then against Lenin; and if not against Lenin, then certainly against Stalin—that Marxism itself has fallen into the trap of "objectivism": that it has overlooked at best, and at worst deliberately destroyed, the subjective, active, agential, and therefore free nature of the human and has subjected it to a determinism borrowed from that very mechanistic physics which Marx himself held in disdain as undialectical. Marxism thereafter fails to deal with subjectivity except as a reflex, and therefore as a mere epiphenomenon, incapable of a truly dialectical interaction with its object. Thus subjectivity is not seen in its activity at all, except in an objectified form, as praxis, id est, as mere externality. Subjectivity is lost in the objectification of praxis. And whereas Marx *does* see labor, production, consumption, distribution, exchange, etc., as the activity of a "subject," this subject is an empty shell, an automaton. Though it may be an active subject, it is "active" in the sense that matter is active, or even self-active. The active subject has no subjectivity, no interiority. Its only "interiority" is a reflection of its external relations, and thus simply a displaced exteriority. So the constitutive activity of consciousness becomes, in the context of praxis, nothing but a mere reflection or epiphenomenon of praxis, and ultimately redundant as an agency in the world. And so Marx's claim to the efficacy and instrumentality of consciousness vanishes in this objectivism. It is all very well to say that when an idea grips the masses, it becomes a material force. But what is this "idea" but the ghost of an idea, an un-thing? Phenomenology, on the other hand, sees structures of the world, or life, or history in essential relation to an agential praxis—the praxis of consciousness itself—whereas Marx denigrates this human praxis, this self-conscious activity, as mere *work*, as mere externality.

To the extent that phenomenologists sometimes argue that Marx has this phenomenological sense of the ego, of the self-activity and interiority of consciousness, they attempt to save Marx from the Marxists: they counterpose a voluntaristic, existential, or Hegelian Marx to the crass "positivism" of Engels in the *Dialectics of Nature*, or of Lenin in *Materialism and Empirio-Criticism*. Here the early Lukács and the Karl Korsch of 1923 become relevant to the phenomenologist, as well as to revisionist or humanist Marxism.[9] For in this critical view the "active" or "subjective" side of Marxism, its "phenomenological" side, especially as it is found in the Feuerbachian and Hegelian Marx of the *Economic-Philosophic Manuscripts*, has not yet fallen into the patterns of scientism and determinism which empty man of his subjectivity and leave him merely a historical puppet, playing out a socially fated role.

3. The Second Mediation

The dialectical alternative to beginning from the "outside in," so to speak, is to move from the inside out. In eschewing the mere phenomenality of the self or its mere externality in the positivist tradition, phenomenology begins at the center, so to speak, with the activity of consciousness itself, or the ego, not merely "posited" but arrived at by stripping away all exteriority and all the standpoints which encumber the pure, presuppositionless activity of consciousness. Phenomenology thus begins with Descartes, with a series of "bracketings" which reduce or suspend the a priori presuppositions of one or another standpoint in order to get behind them to their constitutive genesis. In the *Krisis*, for example, Husserl subjects the mathematizing-Platonizing a priori of contemporary science to such a reduction in order to get to the life-world or world of "lived" existence, of which this scientific a priori is the idealization or reification.

Once we get to the life-world, another epoche, a suspension of its standpoint, perhaps gets us behind it to its presuppositions, as the philosopher proceeds to peel away the layers or accretions of construction to reach the primordial constitutive activity itself. But every concrete *Lebenswelt* has its standpoint, its empirical or lived praxis; and behind them all we seek what constitutes this praxis distinctively, until at the limit we have achieved the universal or transcendental *basis* of every possible reification and of every possible praxis; and here we find the transcendental, that is to say, the presuppositionless and inexpugnable subjectivity which is the primordial ground of every constitution.

"No object without a subject." Very well. But then *human* objectivity cannot be conceived except in its dependency on human subjectivity. What is part of the world for man is nevertheless what it is *for* man. And thus we have but two choices open to us: (1) that man, in his consciousness, is merely the reflex of the world, its mirror, or spectator, and subjectivity is passivity; or (2) that the subject is at the very least an activity of engagement which modifies or reconstructs the world, so that what is *given*, so to speak, is inextricable in its givenness from the relation to a subject. At the limit, we may conceive of this givenness as ultimately brutish, impenetrable, totally opaque to the subject. But then the subject is once again faced with passivity in the face of the given, or realizes its negativity, its "nothingness," in the face of this brute existence. What it "does," so to speak, is its own affair. And so, at worst, the subject is condemned to a meaningless play *within* subjectivity, forever alienated from being-as-such. Or the subject may take this being-as-such as ultimately meaningless and create itself, in spite of this, as a self-contained activity. The subject therefore makes its own life out of itself, out of its subjectivity, its willfulness, its activity as the *only* meaning-giving activity, against a background as black as the night of matter in Leibniz' *Monadology*. The "other," as

givenness, is totally other and hence beyond redemption. In effect, we arrive at
the Hegelian move of the *Logic:* that
being-as-such is nothing, is sheer negativity or abstract negativity—in effect,
non-existence.[10] Existence, by contrast,
is action. On the other hand, once objectivity is removed from mere brute givenness, once the activity of the subject is
seen as construction or constitution of its
own object, then the *nothing* is really nothing: it can be dispensed with, forgotten,
ignored. The world is then not merely
engaged by a subject but is constituted by
it. Or more precisely, the world becomes
a constitution of *subjects* which recognize each other, at least as "other" and
yet not intractable. A socialized
phenomenology, therefore, reintroduces
otherness in an optimistic mood as the
subject's otherness, not as isolated individual but as species-being or social—
therefore as a *thou*. With this move,
whether as *Lebenswelt* or as thou,
phenomenology finally reaches the point
at which Hegel and Feuerbach arrived
more than a century earlier. Sheer subjectivity, in its singularity, its aloneness,
ends in pessimism, despair, or in the ultimate self-reliance of the leap of faith.
Credo quia absurdum. Socialized subjectivity finds its faith in the otherness
of subjectivity, in a subjectivity suddenly rediscovered (after Kant, no less!)
as intersubjectivity. It is no surprise,
therefore, that Husserl's construction
of a social or even historical *noema* is
surprisingly like Russell's construction of
physics from sense data, as the "noema"
of a space of perspectives. Gurwitsch
writes: "Because of the intentionality of
consciousness, we are in direct contact
with the world." But which world? The
world which is essentially connected with
the intentionality itself, of course, since
the world comes into being out of this
intentionality itself. But then we are at a
dire point: the payment we have had to
make for rescuing the activity of the subject from either mere passivity or reflection, or from sheer inwardness and irrele-
vance to the world, is in effect to ransom
the world and objectivity to the sheer

constitutive activity of a subject, singular, social, or transcendental. It doesn't
much matter which, therefore, for the
schema is the same.

But in its method phenomenology is
intended to get behind this very presupposition itself, or at least to tell us where
to stop because we can go no further. It
has therefore transformed its very
methodology into an ontology: the ontology of the theoretical philosopher or the
Cartesian ego as the be-all and end-all
of—of what? Of itself? For only God
stands beyond it, and with the help of God
the ego has surrendered, once and for all,
its claim to centrality, to ultimacy, to
primordiality. The ontology of this
stance—if you like, the ontology of this
theoretical praxis—is the ontology of
pure theorizing or reflection: the dehis-
toricized and indeed dehumanized standpoint of speculation—timeless, static,
and ultimately divorced from the very
empirical praxis which it seeks to understand. For all its projecting, and acting,
and constituting, it becomes a disembodied activity, and its conception of
praxis is therefore a conception of a disembodied praxis. It is, in effect, a reification of theoretical praxis, but of a theory
divorced from real praxis, from which
theory takes its genesis in the first place
and to which it returns by transcending
itself as theory, or by negating its mere
theoreticity.

4. The Third Mediation

The first mediation took Marxism in its
objectivist form and, from a reconstruction of the criticism of this "positivist"
Marxism, argued that it lost the essential
character of subjectivity and that it transformed subjectivity into a mere shell, or
reflex of unconscious, or inert matter.
Therefore such a Marxism violated the
very dialectical character of subject and
object which ostensibly lies at the sources
of Marxism itself. The second mediation
took phenomenology in its subjective
form and argued to the ultimate en-
closedness of this subjectivity as a failure
to cope with the very problem of the rela-

tion of consciousness to its object, which is the origin of its *Problematik*. The third mediation is therefore obvious. It lies with an activist Marxism, that is, a Marxism in which the activity of the subject is fully realized, but not as an abstract and theorized praxis of consciousness. It seems to me that Marx offers this possibility in terms much less uncertain than one would presume from all the difficult discussions which have been generated by this question. The question is, simply, How does one get beyond the fatal egocentrism or idealism of phenomenology and yet preserve the content of real, and not merely reflected, interiority and agency? The question, rephrased, is how to put this interiority itself in touch with its own genesis, with its own transformation, and, thereby, how to avoid taking it as the ultimate and last refuge of ignorance? But this takes a metacritical, metaphilosophical move—"meta" not in the sense of yet "higher" levels of reflection but in the sense of that which dissolves the fated circularity of self-consciousness. This is to take the standpoint not of so-called "theoretical praxis"—a phrase Marx used in his dissertation to characterize philosophy[11]—but of a *theorized* praxis. It is, in essence, a very simple move; but the philosopher cannot make it. *Qua* philosopher, his praxis is *ultimately* theoretical, and no more. It cannot be more, is the philosopher is to remain a philosopher. Marx argues that the actual praxis of philosophy is the negation of philosophy: its dialectical negation, its transcendence, in political-social-human praxis; in the engagement not of theory, not of "criticism" in the theoretical sense, but of actual, practical criticism. In short, Marx's dissolution of the problem and his metacritical stance is so obvious, so absurdly plain, that only a philosopher could fail to grasp it. There is no solution for philosophy within philosophy. The attempt to get "beneath" the empirical praxis by epoche after epoche, the attempt to spin the world out of consciousness, or even to reconstruct it *in* consciousness, is doomed to failure. But here we have a paradox of a sort: the very critique of philosophy which argues for its transformation into a theorized praxis is still philosophy. But it is philosophy disabused—"disillusioned," as Marx liked to say, no longer caught in its own self-mystification. It is philosophy applied to the critique of what exists—and inevitably, therefore, a negation of its purely theoretical stance. There is no way beyond this, once Marx has done the metacritique of philosophy as *ideology*, namely, as the theorization of actual praxis, tied inevitably to its time, its place, its historical and social genesis *as* philosophy. It transcends itself only insofar as it is able to transcend its own condition, its own genesis, its own basis in a historical praxis, its own *class*-orientation, therefore. But it can do this only if it transforms its reality—not by reconstituting its world in thought but by reconstituting its world in reality by practical intervention, by the test of its validity, or of its truth. Philosophy does not measure itself against a given reality but against the very attempt to transform this given reality into something else.

The passivity and ahistoricity of phenomenology, despite its accent on the activity of the subject and on constitution, are in effect functions of its divorce from historical praxis. The divorce is not total, for historical praxis serves as a "world" for phenomenology, but a world reconstituted *in* thought, rather than constituted *by* thought as it claims. The constitution of a world, it is true, is the work of an active subject. But the subject is not a philosopher. He is a man. Moreover, his being is as a social being, as a historical being: his constituting activity is itself constituted by his history, which he transcends as he *makes* it. It is not received wisdom, and cannot be uncovered by reflection; it is achieved wisdom and therefore can only be won by practice in the world.

This presupposes a realism concerning the objectivity of existence, which is not derived from immediacy, from the *cogito*, but is rather the very condition for the structuring of a social and human consciousness. Man creates himself, certainly, but by his biological-historical activity and agency in which consciousness has both its genesis, and in turn, its agency.

NOTES

1. G. W. F. Hegel, *The Phenomenology of Mind*, tr. J. B. Baillie (London: George Allen & Unwin, 1910). Baillie is the obvious work, but there is much more in Hegel, especially in the earlier works, for example, *Jenensen Schriften*. Ludwig Feuerbach's *The Essence of Christianity*, tr. Marian Evans [George Eliot] (London, 1881) is the most directly phenomenological work, but see also the newly translated *Critique of Hegelian Idealism* in *The Fiery Brook, Selected Writings of Ludwig Feuerbach*, tr. with introduction by Zawar Haufi (Garden City, N.Y.: Anchor Books, 1972), and his *Gedanken über Tod und Unsterblichkeit, Sämmtliche Werke*, vol. 1, reprinted from the Bolin and Jodl edition of 1903-11 (Stuttgard-Bad Canstatt: Frommann Verlag, Günther Holzboog, 1960).

2. Among these works available in English are Georg Lukács, *History and Class Consciousness: Studies in Marxist Dialectics*, tr. Rodney Livingstone (London: Merlin Press, 1968; Cambridge, Mass.: MIT Press, 1973); Gajo Petrović, *Marx in the Mid-Twentieth Century* (Garden City, N.Y.: Anchor, 1967); Svetozar Stojanović, *Between Ideals and Reality: A Critique of Socialism and Its Future*, tr. G. Sher (New York: Oxford University Press, 1973); Adam Schaff, *Marxism and the Human Individual* (New York: McGraw-Hill, 1970). The Frankfurt school has its contemporary expressions in such works as Jürgen Habermas, *Knowledge and Human Interests*, tr. Jeremy J. Shapiro (Boston: Beacon Press, 1971); Alfred Schmidt, *The Concept of Nature in Marx*, tr. B. Fowkes (London: New Left Books, 1971); and in the various works of Horkheimer, Adorno, and Marcuse. Enzo Paci, *The Function of the Sciences and the Meanings of Man*, tr. P. Piccone and J. Hansen (Evanston: Northwestern University Press, 1972), represents recent "phenomenological Marxism" of the Italian variety.

3. Jean-Paul Sartre, *Critique De la Raison Dialectique* précédé de *Questions de Méthodes* (Paris: Gallimard, 1960), is the crucial work; the section, *Search for a Method*, is translated into English (tr. Hazel Barnes [New York: Knopf, 1963·). See also Maurice Merleau-Ponty, *Adventures of the Dialectic*, tr. Joseph Bien (Evanston: Northwestern University Press, 1973), and *Humanism and Terror*, tr. John O'Neill (Boston: Beacon Press, 1969).

4. This is not to say that reflective consciousness—i.e. theory—arises only with commodity production. Yet the requirement for theory, as Aristotle knew in the *Metaphysics*, is a degree of detachment from workaday praxis even when that theory is a theory of this praxis itself—as it is, for

example, when a priestly class is supported by a social surplus in order to intervene *theoretically* on behalf of this praxis. What is at issue here, however, is a theory of consciousness itself, taken as an abstracted object of reflection and divorced from its roots or applications in conscious praxis. Here, I think, the model of the alienated or detached commodity provides for the historical materialist the genesis of the (fetishistic) conception of consciousness itself as a detached and abstracted object of reflection, just as it is the development of a leisure class, not engaged in production, that provides the social concomitant of this abstraction. See my brief discussion of this point in *Conceptual Foundations of Scientific Thought* (New York: Macmillan, 1968). The psychological dialectic of this abstraction and reification of consciousness is most fully analyzed as a feature of religious and philosophical consciousness by Ludwig Feuerbach in (e.g.) *The Essence of Christianity* and *Principles of the Philosophy of the Future* (tr. Manfred Vogel [Bobbs-Merrill, 1966]), but there it is not given in any social or historical genesis.

5. Ludwig Feuerbach, *Das Wesen des Christentums*, vol. 1, ed. Werner Schuffenhauer (Berlin: Akademie-Verlag, 1956), p. 6. This, the critical edition, includes all the variants in the three editions. The quotation is from the foreword to the first edition (1841).

6. For a discussion of this see my "Telos and Technique: Models as Modes of Action," in Stanford Anderson (ed.), *Planning for Diversity and Choice* (Cambridge, Mass.: MIT Press, 1968), pp. 259-74.

7. See, for example, Karl Marx, *Contribution to the Critique of Political Economy*, ed. Maurice Dobb (New York: International Pubs. Co., 1971).

8. The change is most clearly relevant to transcendental phenomenology. Whether Merleau-Ponty escapes it remains, for me, an open question.

9. Georg Lukács, *History and Class Consciousness*; Karl Korsch, *Marxism and Philosophy*, tr. F. Holliday (London: New Left Books, 1970).

10. *The Logic of Hegel*, tr. W. Wallace (London: Oxford University Press, 1873), p. 161. Aron Gurwitsch, "Husserl in Perspective," in E. N. Lee and M. Mandelbaum (ed.), *Phenomenology and Existentialism* (Baltimore: The Johns Hopkins Press, 1967), p. 52.

11. "Notes to the Doctoral Dissertation (1839-41)" in *The Writings of the Young Marx on Philosophy and Society*, ed. and tr. by Lloyd D. Easton and Kurt H. Guddat (Garden City, N.Y.: Doubleday, 1967). p. 61.

Review of Dr. E. Husserl's
Philosophy of Arithmetic

GOTTLOB FREGE

The author decides in the Introduction that for the time being he will consider (only) cardinal numbers (cardinalia), and thereupon launches into a discussion of multiplicity, plurality, totality, aggregate, collection, set. He uses these words as if they were essentially synonymous; the concept of a cardinal number[1] is supposed to be different from this. However, the logical relationship between multiplicity and number (p. 9) remains somewhat obscure. If one were to go by the words "The concept of number includes the same concrete phenomena as the concept of multiplicity, albeit only by way of the extensions of the concepts of its species, the numbers two, three, four, etc.," one might infer that they had the same extension. On the other hand, multiplicity is supposed to be more indeterminate and more general than number. The matter would probably be clearer if a sharper distinction were drawn between falling under a concept and subordination. Now the first thing he attempts to do is to give an analysis of the concept of multiplicity. Determinate numbers, as well as the generic concept of number which presupposes them, are then supposed to emerge from it by means of de-

terminations. Thus we are first led down from the general to the particular, and then up again.

Totalities are wholes whose parts are collectively connected. We must be conscious of these parts as noticed in and by themselves. The collective connection consists neither in the contents' being simultaneously in the awareness, nor in their arising in the awareness one after another. Not even space, as all-inclusive form, is the ground of the unification. The connection consists (p. 43) in the unifying act itself. "But neither is it the case that over and above the act there exists a relational content which is distinct from it and is its creative result." Collective connection is a relation *sui generis*. Following J. St. Mill, the author then explains what is to be understood by "relation": namely that state of consciousness or that phenomenon (these expressions are supposed to coincide in the extension of their reference) in which the related contents—the bases of the relation—are contained (p. 70). He then distinguishes between primary and mental relations. Here only the latter concern us more closely. "If a unitary mental act is directed towards several contents, then with respect to it the contents are connected or related to one another. If we perform such an act, it would of course be futile for us to look for a relation or connection in the presentational content which it contains (unless over and above

Reprinted with permission of the publisher from *Mind*, 81(July 1972): 321-37; first published in *Zeitschrift für Philosophie und Philosophische Kritik*, 103 (1894): 313-32. Translated by E. W. Kluge.

this, there is also a primary relation). The contents here are united only by the act, and consequently this unification can be noticed only by a special reflection on it" (p. 73). The difference-relation, whereby two contents are related to one another by means of an evident negative judgment, is also of this kind (p. 74). Sameness, on the other hand, is (p. 77) a primary relation. (According to this, complete coincidence, too, would be a primary relation, while its negation—difference itself—would be a mental one. I here miss a statement of the difference between the difference-relation and collective connection, where in the opinion of the author the latter, too, is a mental relation because perceptually no unification is noticeable in its presentational content.) When one is speaking of "unrelated" contents, the contents are merely thought "together", i.e. as a totality. "But by no means are they really unconnected, unrelated. On the contrary, they are connected by the mental act holding them together. It is only in the content of the latter that all noticeable unification is lacking" (p. 78). The conjunction 'and' fixes in a wholly appropriate manner the circumstance that given contents are connected in a collective manner (p. 81). "A presentation...falls under the concept of multiplicity insofar as it connects in a collective manner any contents which are noticed in and by themselves" (p. 82). (It appears that what is understood by "presentation" is an act.) "Multiplicity in general...is no more than something and something and something, etc.; or any one thing and any one thing and any one thing, etc.; or more briefly, one and one and one, etc." (p. 85). When we remove the indeterminateness which lies in the "etc.," we arrive at the numbers one and one; one, one and one; one, one, one and one; and so on. We can also arrive at these concepts directly, beginning with any concrete multiplicity whatever; for each one of them falls under one of these concepts, and under a determinate one at that (p. 87). To this end, we abstract from the particular constitution of the individual contents collected together in the

multiplicity, retaining each one only insofar as it is a something or a one; and thus, with respect to the collective connection of the latter, we obtain the general form of multiplicity appropriate to the multiplicity under consideration, i.e. the appropriate number (p. 88). Along with this number-abstraction goes a complete removal of restrictions placed on the content (p. 100). We cannot explain the general concept of number otherwise than by pointing to the similarity which all number-concepts have to one another (p. 88).

Having thus given a brief presentation of the basic thoughts of the first part, I now want to give a general characterization of this mode of consideration. We here have an attempt to provide a naive conception of number with a scientific justification. I call any opinion naive if according to it a number-statement is not an assertion about a concept or the extension of a concept; for upon the slightest reflection about number, one is led with a certain necessity to such conceptions. Now strictly speaking, an opinion is naive only as long as the difficulties facing it are unknown—which does not quite apply in the case of our author. The most naive opinion is that according to which a number is something like a heap, a swarm in which the things are contained lock, stock and barrel. Next comes the conception of a number as a property of a heap, aggregate, or whatever else one might call it. Thereby one feels the need for cleansing the objects of their particularities. The present attempt belongs to those which undertake this cleansing in the psychological wash-tub. This offers the advantage that in it, things acquire a most peculiar suppleness, no longer have as hard a spatial impact on each other and lose many bothersome particularities and differences. The mixture of psychology and logic that is now so popular provides good suds for this purpose. First of all, everything becomes presentation. The references of words are presentations. In the case of the word "number," for example, the aim is to exhibit the appropriate presentation and to describe its genesis and composition. Objects are presentations. Thus J. St. Mill, with the approval of the author, lets objects (whether physical or mental) enter into a state of consciousness and become constituents of this state (p. 70). But might not the moon, for example, be somewhat hard to digest for a state of consciousness? Since everything is now presentation, we can easily change the objects by now paying attention, now not. The latter is especially effective. We pay less attention to a property and it disappears. By thus letting one characteristic after another disappear, we obtain concepts that are increasingly more abstract. Therefore concepts, too, are presentations; only, they are less complete than objects; they still have those properties of objects which we have not abstracted. Inattention is an exceedingly effective logical power; whence, presumably, the absentmindedness of scholars. For example, let us suppose that in front of us there are sitting side by side a black and a white cat. We disregard their color: they become colorless but are still sitting side by side. We disregard their posture: they are no longer sitting, without, however, having assumed a different posture; but each one is still at its place. We disregard their location: they are without location, but still remain quite distinct. Thus from each one we have perhaps derived a general concept of a cat. Continued application of this process turns each object into a less and less substantial wraith. From each object we finally derive something which is completely without restrictions on its content; but the something derived from the one object nevertheless does differ from that derived from the other object, although it is not easy to say how. But wait! This last transition to a something does seem to be more difficult after all; at least the author talks (p. 86) about reflection on the mental act of presentation. But be that as it may, the result, at any rate, is the one just indicated. While in my opinion the bringing of an object under a concept is merely the recognition of a relation which previously already obtained, in the present case objects are essentially changed

by this process, so that objects brought under the same concept become similar to one another. Perhaps the matter is to be understood thus, that for every object there arises a new presentation in which all determinations which do not occur in the concept are lacking. Hereby the difference between presentation and concept, between presenting and thinking, is blurred. Everything is shunted off into the subjective. But it is precisely because the boundary between the subjective and the objective is blurred, that conversely the subjective also acquires the appearance of the objective. For example, one talks of this or that presentation as if, separated from the presentor, it would let itself be observed in public. And yet, no-one has someone else's presentation but only his own, and no-one knows how far his presentation—e.g. that of red—agrees with that of someone else; for the peculiarity of the presentation which I associate with the word "red," I cannot state (so as to be able to compare it). One would have to have the presentations of the one as well as that of the other combined in one and the same consciousness; and one would have to be sure that they had not changed in the transfer. With thoughts, it is quite different: one and the same thought can be grasped by many people. The components of a thought, and even more so the things themselves, must be distinguished from the presentations which in the soul accompany the grasping of a thought and which someone has about these things. In combining under the word "presentation" both what is subjective and what is objective, one blurs the boundary between the two in such a way that now a presentation in the proper sense of the word is treated like something objective, and now something objective is treated like a presentation. Thus in the case of our author, totality (set, multiplicity) appears now as a presentation (pp. 15, 17, 24, 82), now as something objective (pp. 10, 11, 235). But isn't it really a very harmless pleasantry to call, for example, the moon a presentation? It is—as long as one does not imagine that one can change it as one likes, or produce it by psychological means. But this is all too easily the result.

Given the psychologico-logical mode of thought just characterized, it is easy to understand how the author judges about definitions. An example from elementary geometry may illustrate this. There, one usually gives this definition: "A right angle is an angle which is equal to its adjacent angle." The author would probably say to this, "The presentation of right-angledness is a simple one; hence it is a completely misguided undertaking to want to give a definition of it. In our presentation of right-angledness, there is nothing of the relation to another adjacent angle. True enough; the concepts 'right angle' and 'angle which is equal to its adjacent angle' have the same extension; but it is not true that they have the same content. Instead of the content, it is the extension of the concept that has been defined. If the definition were correct, then every assertion of right-angledness, instead of applying to the concretely present pair of lines as such, would always apply only to its relation to another pair of lines. All I can admit is (p. 114) that in this equality with the adjacent angle we have a necessary and sufficient condition for right-angledness." The author judges in a similar way about the definition of equinumerosity by means of the concept of a univocal one-one correlation. "The simplest criterion for sameness of number is just that *the same* number results when counting the sets to be compared" (p. 115). Of course! The simplest way of testing whether or not something is a right angle is to use a protractor. The author forgets that this counting itself rests on a univocal one-one correlation, namely that between the numerals 1 to n and the objects of the set. Each of the two sets is to be counted. In this way, the situation is made more difficult than when we consider a relation which correlates the objects of the two sets with one another without numerals as intermediaries.

If words and combinations of words refer to presentations, then for any two of these only two cases are possible: either they designate the same presentation, or they designate different ones. In the first case, equating them by means of a definition is useless, "an obvious circle"; in the other, it is false. These are also the objections one of which the author raises regularly. Neither can a definition dissect the sense, for the dissected sense simply is not the original one. In the case of the word to be explained, either I already think clearly everything which I think in the case of the definiens—in which case we have the "obvious circle"—or the definiens has a more completely articulated sense—in which case I do not think the same thing in its case as I do in the case of the one to be explained: the definition is false. One would think that the definition would be unobjectionable at least in the case where the word to be explained does not yet have a sense, or where it is expressly asked that the sense be considered non-existent, so that the word acquires a sense only through this definition. But even in the latter case (p. 107), the author confutes the definition by reminding us of the distinctness of the presentations. Accordingly, in order to avoid all objections, one would probably have to create a new root-word and form a word out of it. A split here manifests itself between psychological logicians and mathematicians. The former are concerned with the sense of the words and with the presentations, which they do not distinguish from the sense; the latter, however, are concerned with the matter itself, with the reference of the words.[2] The reproach that it is not the concept but its extension which is being defined, really applies to all the definitions of mathematics. So far as the mathematician is concerned, the definition of a conic section as the line of intersection of a plane with a cone is no more and no less correct than that as a plane whose equation is given in Cartesian coordinates of the second degree. Which of these two—or even of other—definitions is selected depends entirely on the pragmatics of the situation, although these expressions neither have the same sense nor evoke the same presentations. By this I do not mean that a concept and the extension of a concept are one and the same; rather, coincidence of extension is a necessary and sufficient condition for the fact that between the concepts there obtains that relation which corresponds to that of sameness in the case of objects.[3] I here note that when I use the word "same" without further addition, I am using it in the sense of "not different," "coinciding," "identical." Psychological logicians lack all understanding of sameness, just as they lack all understanding of definitions. This relation cannot help but remain completely puzzling to them; for if words always designated presentations, one could never say "A is the same as B." For to be able to do that, one would already have to distinguish A from B, and then these would simply be different presentations. All the same, I do agree with the author in this, that Leibniz' explanation "Eadem sunt quorum unum potest substitui alteri salva veritate" does not deserve to be called a definition, although I hold this for different reasons. Since every definition is an equation, one cannot define equality itself. One could call Leibniz' explanation a principle which expresses the nature of the sameness-relation; and as such it is of fundamental importance. I am unable to acquire a taste for the author's explanation that (p. 108) "We simply say of any contents whatever that they are the same as one another, if there obtains sameness in the ...characteristics which at that moment constitute the center of interest."

Let us now go into details! According to the author, a number-statement refers to the totality (the set, multiplicity) of objects counted (p. 185). Such a totality finds its wholly appropriate expression in the conjunction "and." Accordingly, one should expect that all number-statements have the form "A and B and C and ...Q is n," or at least that they could be brought into such a form. But what is it that we get exactly to know through the proposition "Berlin and Dresden and Munich are three" or—and this is supposed to be the same thing—through "Berlin and Dresden and Munich are something and some-thing and something"? Who would want to go to the trouble of asking, merely to receive such an answer? It is not even supposed to be said by this that Berlin is distinct from Dresden, the latter from Munich, and Munich from Berlin. In fact, in the second form at least there is contained neither the difference of Berlin from Dresden nor even their sameness. Surely it is peculiar that this form of number-predication almost never occurs in every-day life and that when it does occur, it is not intended as a statement of number. I find that there are really only two cases in which it is used: in the first case, together with the number-word "two", to express difference—"Rapeseed and rape are two (different things)"—in the other, together with the number-word "one" to express sameness—"I and the Father are one"—. This last example is particularly disastrous, for according to the author it should read, "are something and some-thing" or "are two". In reality we do not ask "How many are Caesar and Pompei and London and Edinburgh?" or "How many are Great Britain and Ireland?" although I am curious as to what the author would answer to this. Instead, one asks, for example, "How many moons does Mars have?" or "What is the number of moons of Mars?" And from the answer "The number of moons of Mars is two" one gets to know something which is worth asking about. Thus we see that in the question as well as in the answer, there occurs a concept-word or a compound designation of a concept, rather than the "and" demanded by the author. How does the latter extricate himself from this difficulty? He says that the number belongs to the extension of the concept, i.e. to the totality. "It is only indirectly that one can perhaps say that the concept has the property that the number...belongs to its extension" (p. 189). Herewith everything I maintain has really been admitted: In a number-statement, something is predicated of a concept. I am not going to argue over whether the assertion applies directly to a concept and indirectly to its extension, or indirectly to the concept and directly to its extension; for given the one, the other also obtains. This much is certain, that neither the extension of a concept nor a totality are designated directly, but only a concept. Now if the author used the phrase "extension of a concept" in the same sense as I, then our opinions about the sense of a statement of number would scarely differ. This, of course, is not the case; for the extension of a concept is not a totality in the author's sense. A concept under which there falls only one object has just as determinate an extension as a concept under which there falls no object or a concept under which there fall infinitely many objects—where according to Mr. Husserl, there is no totality in any of these cases. The sense of the words "extension of the concept moon of Mars" is other than the sense of the words "Deimos and Phobos"; and if the proposition "The number of Deimos and Phobos is two" contains a thought at all, at any rate it contains one which differs from that of the proposition "The number of moons of Mars is two". Now, since one never uses a proposition of the latter form to make a statement of number, the author has missed the sense of such a statement.

Let us now consider the ostensible genesis of a totality somewhat more closely (pp. 77 ff.). I must confess that I have been unsuccessful in my attempt to form a totality in accordance with the instructions of the author. In the case of collective connections, the contents are merely supposed to be thought or presented together, without any relation or connection whatever being presented between them (p. 79). I am unable to do this. I cannot simultaneously represent to myself redness, the Moon and Napoleon, without presenting these to myself as connected; e.g. the redness of a burning village against which stands out the figure of Napoleon, illuminated by the Moon on the right. Whatever is simultaneously present to me, I present to myself as a whole; and I cannot disregard the connection without losing the whole. I suspect that in my soul there just isn't anything which the author calls "totality", "set",

"multiplicity"; no presentation of parts whose union is not presented with them, although it does exist. Therefore it is not at all astonishing that Mr. Husserl himself later (p. 242) says of a set that it contains a configurative moment which characterizes it as a whole, as an organization. He talks of series (p. 235), swarms, chains, heaps as of peculiar kinds of sets. And no union is supposed to be noticeable in the presentation of a swarm? Or is this union present over and above the collective connection? In which case it would be irrelevant so far as the totality is concerned, and the "configurative moment" could not serve to distinguish kinds of sets. How does the author come to hold his opinion? Probably because he is looking for certain presentations as the references of words and word-complexes. Thus there ought to correspond a presentational whole even to the word-complex "redness and the Moon and Napoleon"; and since the mere "and" allegedly does not express a presentable relation or union at all, neither ought one to be presented. Add to this the following. If the union of the parts were also presented, almost all of our presentations would be totalities; e.g., that of a house as well as that of a swarm or heap. And hereby, surely, one notices only too easily that a number as a property of a house or of the presentation of a house would be absurd.

The author himself finds a difficulty in the abstraction which yields the general concept of totality (p. 84). "One must abstract completely...from the particularities of the individual contents collected together, at the same time, however, retaining their connection. This seems to involve a difficulty, if not a psychological impossibility. If we take this abstraction seriously, then of course the collective connection, rather than remaining behind as a conceptual extract, also disappears along with the particular contents. The solution lies at hand. To abstract from something merely means: not paying any particular attention to it."

The core of this exposition clearly lies in the word "particular." Inattention is a very strong lye which must not be applied in too concentrated a form, so as not to dissolve everything; but neither ought it to be used in too diluted a form, so that it may produce a sufficient change. Everything, then, depends on the proper degree of dilution, which is difficult to hit. I, at least, did not succeed in doing so.

Since in the end, the author himself really does admit that I am right after all—that in a number-statement there is contained an assertion about a concept—I need not consider his counterarguments in more detail. I only want to remark that he evidently has not grasped my distinction between a characteristic and a property. Given his logico-psychological mode of understanding, this is of course not surprising. Thus he comes to foist on me the opinion that what is at issue in the case of number-statements is a determination, the definition of a concept (p. 185). Nothing was farther from my mind.

Three reefs spell danger for naive, and particularly for psychological, views of the nature of numbers. The first lies in the question, how the sameness of the units is to be reconciled with their distinguishability. The second consists in the numbers zero and one; and the third, in the large numbers. Let us ask how the author seeks to circumnavigate these reefs! In the case of the first, he adduces (p. 156) my words, "If we want to let a number arise by collecting different objects, then we obtain a heap in which the objects are contained with just those properties in which they differ; and this is not the number. On the other hand, if we want to form a number by collecting what is the same, the latter will always coalesce into one and we shall never arrive at a multiplicity." It is clear that I have used the word "same" in the sense of "not different." Therefore the author's charge that I confuse sameness with identity does not apply. Mr. Husserl tries to blunt this antithesis by means of his hazy sameness: "In a certain respect, sameness does obtain; in another, difference. . . . A difficulty, or better, an impossibility would obtain only if the expression 'collection of what is the same' (which is intended to describe the genesis of a number) demanded absolute sameness, as Frege mistakenly assumes" (pp. 164, 165). Well, if the sameness is not absolute, then the objects will differ in one or the other of the properties with which they enter into combination. Now with this, compare the following: "The sameness of the units, as it results from our psychological theory, is obviously an absolute one. Indeed, already the mere thought of an approximation is absurd, for what is at stake is the sameness of the contents insofar as they are contents" (p. 168). According to the author, a number consists of units (p. 149). He here understands by "unit" a "member of a concrete multiplicity insofar as number-abstraction is applied to the latter" or "a counted object as such." If we consider all of this together, we shall be hard pressed to get clear about the author's opinion. In the beginning, the objects are evidently distinct; then, by means of abstraction, they become absolutely the same with respect to one another, but for all that, this absolute sameness is supposed to obtain only insofar as they are contents. I should think that this sameness is very far indeed removed from being absolute. But be that as it may, the number consists of these units which are absolutely the same; and now there enters that impossibility which the author himself emphasizes. After all, one must assume that this abstraction, this bringing under the concept of something, effects a change; that the objects which are thought through the medium of this concept—these very units which are absolutely the same—are distinct from the original objects, for otherwise they would resemble one another no more than they did at the beginning and this abstraction would be useless. We must assume that it is only through being brought under the concept of a something that these units which are absolutely the same arise, whether they appear through a metamorphosis out of distinct objects or whether they appear in addition to these as new entities. Therefore one would think that in addition to the remaining objects there are also units, sets of units over the above sts of apples. This, however, the author most emphatically denies (p. 139). Number-abstraction simply has the wonderful and very fruitful property of making things absolutely the same as one another without altering them. Something like this is possible only in the psychological wash-tub. If the author really has avoided this first reef, then surely he has done so more by way of magic than by way of science.

Further, Mr. Husserl adduces (p. 156) my words "If we designate each of the objects to be counted by 1, this is a mistake because what differs receives the same sign. If we supply the 1 with differentiating strokes, it becomes useless for arithmetic." To this he makes the following comment (p. 165), "However, we commit this mistake with each application of a general name. When we call Tom, Dick, etc., each a human being, this is the same case as that of the 'faulty notation' in virtue of which when counting, we write 1 for each object to be counted." If we did designate Tom by "human being" and Dick likewise, we should indeed be committing that mistake. Fortunately, we do not do that. When we call Tom a human being, we are thereby saying that Tom falls under the concept human being; but we neither write nor say "human being" instead of "Tom." What would correspond to the proposition "Tom is a human being" would be "Tom is a 1." If we call A, B in the sense of assigning the proper name B to A, then of course everywhere we say "A" we can say "B"; but then we may not give this very name "B" to still another object. This unfortunate expression, "common name," is undoubtedly the cause of this confusion. This so-called common name—better called concept-word—has nothing directly to do with objects but refers to a concept. And perhaps objects do fall under this concept, although it may also be empty without the concept-word referring any less because of this. I have already explained this sufficiently in sec. 47 of my *Foundations of Arithmetic*. Surely it is obvious that anyone using the proposition "All human beings are mortal" does not want to say anything about a certain chief Akpanya, of whom he has perhaps never even heard.

According to the author, $5 + 5 = 10$ means the same thing as "a set (any one, whatever it may be) falling under the concept five, and any other (why other?) set falling under the same concept yield, when combined, a set falling under the concept 10" (p. 202). To illustrate this to ourselves, we are to consider for example the fingers of the right hand as the first set, and a fountain-pen and the fingers of the right hand excluding the thumb as the other. It is possible that the author has here had Mr. Biermann as a teacher?[4]

We now proceed to the second reef, which consists in the numbers zero and one. The first way out is easily found. One says, "They aren't numbers at all." But now there arises the question "What, then, are they?" The author says, negative answers to the question "How many?" (p. 144) Answers like "Never" to the question "When?" "Not-many or 'no multiplicity' is not a particularization of manyness." Perhaps someone might even hit upon the idea that two is not yet a multiplicity but merely twoness (duality as opposed to multiplicity); that none, one and two, therefore, are the three negative answers to the question "How many?" In corroboration of this he would perhaps adduce the fact that two is the only even prime number. It is really asking a lot to want us to consider "one" a negative answer to the question "How many moons does the Earth have?" In the case of zero, the matter has more appearance of being correct. Exactly how are the answers "Never," "Nowhere," "Nothing" to the questions "When?" "Where?" "What?" to be understood? Obviously not as proper answers, but rather as refusals to answer, couched in the form of an answer. One says "I cannot give you a time, a place or an object of the kind wanted because there is none." According to this, an analogous reply to the question "How many?" would be "I cannot tell you such a number because there isn't one." Given my conception of the sense of a number-statement, this is what I should reply for example to the question "How many are Great Britain and Ireland?" I cannot regard either the answer "One" or the answer "Zero" as answers to the question "How many?" as synonymous with "There is no such number." How is it that there are here two negative replies? If to the question "Who was Romulus' predecessor on the throne of Rome?" one answers "No one," then one herewith denies that someone preceded Romulus. Therefore the negation belongs to the predicate, and its fusion with the grammatical subject—whence arises the appearance that "No one" designates a human being just as much as does "Romulus"—is logically incorrect. As is well known, the possibility of certain sophisms rests on this. One would think that such dangers also threaten with zero and one; but these are used just as are all other numbers, without special precautionary measures. Whence this difference? "Zero" is just as little a negative answer to the question "What is the number of Romulus' predecessors on the throne of Rome?" as "Two" would be. One does not thereby deny that there is such a number; rather, one names it. The author says, "To every unit there applies the number one" (p. 170) (presumably as a negative property!) and calls zero and one concepts (p. 145). Given this, one assumes that unit and one are concepts having the same extension. Or is it not the case that every one is a unit? Wherein do the thoughts of the two propositions "Tom is one" and "Tom is a unit" differ? To which one, then, does the number zero apply? Unnoticed and in concert with the author, we have again said "The number one!" There are here still many other puzzles left unresolved by the author, and I cannot admit that he has successfully avoided this reef.

We come to the third reef: the large numbers. If numbers are presentations, then the limited nature of our powers of presentation must also carry along with it a limitation of the domain of numbers.

Thus the author states, "It is only under extremely favorable circumstances that we can still have a real presentation of a concrete multiplicity of about a dozen elements" (p. 214). Now, at this point he introduces figurative or symbolic presentations as means of giving information, and the whole second part deals with these. Nevertheless, the author is forced to admit that "Naturally, not even now, when dealing with pure signs, are we completely unbounded; but we no longer feel these bounds" (p. 274). The finitude of the domain of numbers is thereby admitted. If numbers are presentations which I or someone else must form, then there cannot be infinitely many numbers; and no symbolism can remove this limitation. According to the author (p. 215), a symbolic presentation is a presentation by means of signs which uniquely characterize what is to be presented. "For example, we have a real presentation of the external appearance of a house when we are actually looking at it; we have a symbolic presentation when someone is giving us the indirect characteristic: the corner house on such-and-such sides of such-and-such streets." This refers to the case where something objective is present of which I am to make a presentation to myself; and for that very reason, this explanation does not fit our case at all well. To be sure, one cannot help but assume that according to the author, numbers are presentations: results of mental processes or activities (pp. 24, 46). But where is what is objective: that of which a number is a presentation? What is it that here corresponds to the house in the example above? And yet it is precisely this object that is the connecting link between a real and a symbolic presentation; it is this that justifies our saying that the symbolic presentation appertains to the real one, and it is this that is uniquely characterized by the signs when we have a symbolic presentation. The confusion of the subjective with the objective, the fact that no clear distinction is ever made between expressions like "Moon" and "presentation of the Moon," all this diffuses such an impenetrable fog that the attempt to achieve clarity becomes hopeless. I can only say that I have acquired the following impression of the author's opinion: If I want to have a symbolic presentation where I do not have a real one, I *idealize* (p. 251) my powers of presentation; i.e., I imagine or present to myself that I have a presentation which in fact I neither have nor can have; and what I thus imagine would be my symbolic presentation. So, for example, I can form a symbolic presentation by means of the sign "15," by presenting to myself that I am presenting to myself a set consisting of the elements of a set to which the number 10 belongs and the elements of a set to which the number 5 belongs, and then apply to this the procedure which according to the author produces the appropriate number. The presentations of the signs are incorporated into the symbolic presentations. "Here the sensible signs are not mere companions of the concepts, in the manner of linguistic signs. They participate in our symbolic constructions in a much more prominent manner—so much so, that they finally predominate over almost everything else" (p. 273, similarly p. 264). Herewith the author approaches very closely the opinions of Helmholtz and Kronecker. If this were correct, the numbers would change whenever we change the signs. We should have completely different numbers from the ancient Greeks and Romans. But would these symbolic presentations also have the properties which the real ones are supposed to have? Just as little, I think, as my presentation of a green meadow is green. Now, the author does of course note (p. 217) that a real presentation and a symbolic one belonging to it stand in a relation of logical equivalence. "Two concepts are logically equivalent if every object of the one is also an object of the other, and *vice versa*." He explains that it is on the basis of this that symbolic presentations can "go proxy for" the corresponding real ones. Here the confusion of presentation and concept interferes with our understanding. If we confine ourselves to the example of the corner-house, we may

presume that the "equivalence" is here supposed to consist in the fact that my real presentation and the symbolic one are referred to the same object (that very corner-house). Now, when can the latter "go proxy for" the former? Presumably, when I am talking about the corner-house itself, not about my presentation. In reading this book, I have been able to see how very difficult it is for the sun of truth to penetrate the fog which arises out of the confusion of psychology and logic. Happily, we here see the beginnings of such a penetration. It becomes overwhelmingly evident that our presentations matter very little here, but that instead it is the very thing of which we seek to make presentations to ourselves that is the subject of our concern, and that our assertions are about it. And expressions to this effect occur several times in the second part; which is the more remarkable, the less it really agrees with the author's whole mode of thought. We read (p. 214, bottom), "Even if we have not *really* given the concepts, at least we have given them in a *symbolic* way." Here, concepts appear as something objective, and the difference between real and symbolic concepts refers only to the way in which they are given. There is talk of *species* of the concept of number which are not accessible to us in any real sense (p. 265), and of *real* numbers, of numbers in themselves which are inaccessible to us in general (p. 295). We read (p. 254) about symbolic formations of numbers which belong to one and the same real number. Given the opinion of the author, one should expect "non-existent" instead of "real"; for if a number were a real presentation, in this case there would not be one. What are these "numbers in themselves" (p. 294), these "real numbers", if not objective numbers which are independent of our thinking; which exist even when they are not accessible to us (p. 296)? The author says (p. 295), "Any number whatever can be uniquely characterized...by means of diverse relations to other numbers, and each such characteristic provides a new symbolic presentation of this very number." Here the objective number "in itself" clearly plays the role of the corner-house in our example of the latter. It is not my presentation that is the number; rather, I form one or several presentations of one and the same number, or at least I try to do so. A pity that the author does not try to keep the expressions "A" and "presentation of A" clearly distinct. But if my presentation of a number is not that number itself, then the ground is herewith cut out from under the psychological mode of consideration insofar as the latter's aim is to investigate the nature of numbers. If I want to investigate a presentation, I have to keep it as unchanged as possible—which of course is difficult to do. On the other hand, if I want to investigate something objective, my presentations will have to conform as much as possible to the matter at hand, to the results of this investigation; in general, then, they have to change. It makes a tremendous difference to the mode of investigation whether the number-presentation is itself the object of the investigation, or whether it is merely a presentation of the real object. The author's procedure fits only the first case, whereas the last passages adduced above can only be interpreted as in-

stances of the second. If a geographer were to read a work on oceanography in which the origin of the seas were explained psychologically, he would undoubtedly receive the impression that the very point at issue had been missed in a very peculiar way. I have the same impression of the present work. To be sure, the sea is something real and a number is not; but this does not prevent it from being something objective; and that is the important thing.

In reading this work, I was able to gauge the devastation caused by the influx of psychology into logic; and I have here made it my task to present this damage in a clear light. The mistakes which I thought it my duty to show reflect less upon the author than they are the result of a widespread philosophical disease. My own, radically different position makes it difficult for me to do justice to his achievements, which I presume to lie in the area of psychology; and I should like to direct the attention of psychologists especially to Chapter XI, where the possibility of momentary conceptions of sets is discussed. But I consider myself insufficiently qualified to pass judgment in that area.

NOTES

1. Henceforth I shall take 'cardinal' to be understood [Trans.]

2. On this point, please compare my essay "On Sense and Reference" in *Zeitschrift für Philosophie und Philosophische Kritik*.

3. For strictly speaking, the relation does not

obtain in the case of concepts. Compare my essay "On Concept and Object" in *Vierteljahrsschrift für wiss. Philosophie* [16 (1892), pp. 192-205; Trans.].

4. Otto Biermann, Professor of Mathematics at the Deut. Techn. Hochsch. in Brünn; student of Weierstrass. [Trans.]

Phenomenology and Linguistic Analysis

ERNST TUGENDHAT

Ever since it was noticed in the Common Market countries that linguistic analysis is not reducible to logical positivism, parallels between analytic philosophy on the one hand and phenomenology and hermeneutics on the other have been noted. The title of this article could lead one to surmise that here, too, a comparative study is to be expected. But this is not my intention. The similarities between philosophical positions may fascinate future historians of philosophy. Contemporaries who philosophize within phenomenology, linguistic analysis, and hermeneutics have to draw out the latent contradictions. Philosophical positions differ from works of art in that, since the former make truth claims, they cannot coexist; rather, they must either exclude or complement one another. To the extent that this is brought to a decision in contemporary philosophical positions, presumably a new kind of philosophical position will take shape which we do not yet know anything about.

The confrontation between phenomenology and linguistic analysis which I intend to carry through is a comparatively simple undertaking. Settling accounts between linguistic analysis and hermeneutics would be more difficult, as well as more important. Linguistic analysis agrees more or less with phenomenology in regard to subject matter; they differ in their methods. Thus what is to be expected here is that the two positions do not complement but rather exclude one another, so that only one will survive the confrontation.

Hermeneutics is more comprehensive in subject matter than linguistic analysis and phenomenology. In its method, however, hermeneutics is closer to linguistic analysis, despite its origins in phenomenology. Linguistic analysis can be regarded as a reduced hermeneutics, as a first-floor hermeneutics. What linguistic analysis still lacks is a historical dimension and a comprehensive concept of understanding. Hermeneutics, in turn, lives dangerously in the upper story without especially troubling itself about the supportive capacity and the renovation of the floor below, which it has taken over from phenomenology or from an older tradition. The hermeneutical critique, and Heidegger's above all, of metaphysics in general and therefore of phenomenology too, bears only on their limitations; the inherited ground floor is protected like a monument and then either built upon or dug out underneath by the representatives of hermeneutics. Linguistic analysis has never pressed so far. Yet it does not want just to tear the building down, as positivism did. Rather, linguistic analysis believes it has new

This article appeared originally as "Phänomenologie und Sprachanalyse" in R. Bübner et al., eds., *Hermeneutik und Dialektik: Hans-Georg Gadamer zum 70. Geburtstag*, vol. 2 (Tubingen: J.C.B. Mohr, 1970), pp. 3-23. Translated by permission of the publisher and author. Translated by P. McCormick and F. Elliston. © 1976 McCormick and Elliston.

means and methods for a reconstruction that would be better able to bear the load.

What can be recognized hereby is what the confrontation between hermeneutics and linguistic analysis could accomplish for both sides, once it is adequately carried through. But it has also become clear that settling accounts between linguistic analysis and phenomenology at the same time prepares the other, more important confrontation precisely to the extent that hermeneutics is still based on phenomenology.

Of course, the confrontation between linguistic analysis and phenomenology can only be begun here. I limit myself to Husserl, and furthermore to his starting point.

For phenomenology as well as for linguistic analysis, both our understanding of the *meaning* (sense) of linguistic expressions and our reference (*Meinen*) to *objects* belong at the center of philosophical consideration; but with opposing priorities. For Husserl, the intentional "act" which "refers to" (*meint*) an object is the primary unit of consciousness. The intentional act and the correlative object make up, to use Heidegger's expression, the basic relationship of human "awareness" (*Erschlossenheit*). On the other hand, for linguistic analysis the primary unit of awareness is understanding the meaning of a sentence. While Husserl attempted to build the understanding of meanings—somehow—into the intentional relation to objects, linguistic analysis conceived the reference to objects as a *factor* in understanding the meanings of sentences. Here, then, we have a clear confrontation, as in a *chassé croisé*, which bears on the starting point of both positions.

I will not pursue this discussion from the standpoint of an uninvolved spectator but rather as a criticism of Husserl by the linguistic analyst. I let the critic open the attack on the terrain which is more favorable for him, that of meanings. If he succeeds in beating his adversary here, then in a second round he should try to attack him on his *adversary's* ground by trying to prove that starting with acts not only founders on meanings but even fails to provide an adequate understanding of our reference to objects.

I

1. In *Logical Investigations* (*LU* [German]; *LI* [English]), a work dedicated to basic questions in logic, the clarification of the meaning of a linguistic expression had to rank first. Therefore Husserl undertakes this clarification in the First Investigation, which bears the heading "Expression and Meaning." After distinguishing linguistic expressions from natural signs (*Anzeichen*) in the introductory sections, Husserl begins, in section 9, to introduce the concepts which are essential to him for the clarification of meaning. When a linguistic sign (*Zeichen*) is not only a perceptible "physical phenomenon" but a sign, and a sign of a special sort, this is owing to the fact that it is "apprehended" by someone as having a meaning, or, as Husserl also puts it, a meaning is "conferred" on the expression.

Scarely anyone would impugn this first step. But now the question immediately arises: What kind of activity or manner of behavior apprehends an expression as meaningful? When we know which meaning an expression has or in which sense someone intends an expression, we are accustomed to say that we understand the expression or that we understand its meaning, its sense. It would therefore have been natural to say that what confers meaning on the expression is an understanding. Not much ground would have been thereby won; but the direction would have been indicated as to how one must pose the question, namely: What is it to understand an expression?

But from the beginning Husserl sets out in another direction. What confers a meaning on an expression he calls an "act," the "meaning-conferring act" (*bedeutungsverleihenden Akt*). In the Fifth Investigation Husserl deals thematically with what an "act" is. Here the fundamental treatment of consciousness, on which the previous investigations and especially the first one are already based, is brought in. But now this fundamental treatment is no longer oriented toward linguistic expressions and their meanings. An introspective intuitive analysis, which is independent of language, arrives at the result that the basic phenomenon of consciousness is intentionality, the "referring directedness" (*meinendes Gerichtetsein*) to an object. 'Act' is introduced as a *terminus technicus* for "intentional experience."

From the side of linguistic analysis, a critical attack could start here. Such an introspective, intuitive analysis could be rejected. And what Husserl took as indubitable could be doubted—that there are such things as acts which we find and can "intuit" (*anschauen*) in ourselves. However, criticism of this global sort leads easily to a mutual lack of understanding and is unproductive. The criticism intended here can be counted as successful only when it can be assumed that the phenomenologist himself will recognize it as valid. On the present level of consideration, then, we can simply exercise *epoché* vis-à-vis Husserl's specifically "phenomenological," immanent-intuitive method. We merely hold to the peculiarity in the composition of *LU* which has been pointed out: since meanings are the theme of the entire work, the First Investigation immediately begins with the clarification of meaning; but this clarification is supported by concepts which stem from a fundamental treatment of consciousness which is carried through independently of the question of the meanings of linguistic expressions. No objection can be deduced from this, although difficulties can indeed be expected.

The first difficulty is easily overcome by Husserl. Since meaning-conferring consciousness is interpreted as an act, it would have been easy to construe meanings themselves as objects. But Husserl was sufficiently protected against this mistake through his study of Bolzano and Frege. In section 12 he declares: "Every expression...not only has its meaning; but it is also related to some kind of ob-

jects. . . . However the object never coincides with the meaning." And in section 13 he adds: "So that it also can be correctly said that the expression signifies (names) the object *by means of* its meaning."

Although Husserl does not make the mistake of conceiving the meaning as an object, nevertheless the expression is always supposed to refer to an object "by means of" its meaning. Obviously this conception is adequate for names, by which Husserl understands, in general, expressions which "could fulfill the simple subject function in a statement" (*LU*, 2: 1, 463; *LI*, 2: 625). For it is the function of such expressions to signify an object by naming. But since, quite generally, "meaning-conferring" consciousness is an act for Husserl, he is compelled by his point of departure to extend to all expressions this special characteristic of names which seems to distinguish them from other linguistic expressions. "Every expression...is also related to some object or other." This, then, is the specific conception which follows for Husserl's theory of meaning from starting with intentionality, and which plainly cannot be avoided in this approach: nominal expressions become the model for all expressions. Again, for the time being we can talk only of a difficulty, and whether the problems which follow from this difficulty are insurmountable remains to be seen.

2. Independently of this difficulty, the question arises about the ontological status of even nominal meanings. With intentionality as his point of departure, what possibilities remain for Husserl to understand anything which is not an object? The difficulty this question posed for Husserl is attested by the fact that it is one of the few points where the conception found in *LU* is replaced by another in *Ideas*.

When nominal expressions denoting the same object have different meanings, they appear to be distinguished by "their different way of referring to the object" (*LU*, 2: 1, 49; *LI*, 1: 289). Nevertheless, the meaning must be one and the same, as opposed to the plurality of the possible acts which belong to it. "The meaning hence is related to the actual acts of meaning" as their "species," just as "redness *in specie* is related to the strips of paper lying here which all 'have' this same redness" (*LU*, 2: 1, 100; *LI*, 1: 330). Within the only schema available, that of act and object, the meaning appears at first on the subjective side, although it is distinguished from it by the fact that it appears as a species of the act. This conception is surely untenable: a nominal meaning and the essence of the act that belongs to it indeed go together, but they are certainly not identical.

Thus it is understandable that Husserl repudiated this treatment in *Ideas* (sec. 94). But he now thinks that the mistake lies only in the fact that in *LU* he did not carry his point of departure with intentionality far enough. To every differentiation on the side of the act ("noesis") there corresponds, he now claims, a correlative differentiation on the side of the object as one of its "ways of being given." The object, together with its ways of being given, is now characterized as "noema." The "sense" is the noematic "object in its mode" (*Gegenstand im Wie*) of givenness (sec. 131).[1]

This conception appears to be quite appealing, at least in the case of nominal expressions. The fact that we can refer to an object in a definite way, for example, to the planet Venus as the evening star, is obviously connected with the fact that the object can be given to us in a definite way that is distinct from other ways in which the same object can be given to us (e.g., as the morning star). Whether this suffices to say that the meaning of the expression 'evening star' *is* the way in which the object is given appears doubtful. In particular, it seems that what is being surrendered in this "noematic" conception is the specific aspect of generality which we connect with the meaning of an expression and which was taken account of in the noetic conception. If the meaning of a nominal expression were understood, as it is likely to be from the point of view of linguistic analysis, as the rule for the use of the expression for the identification of the object referred to, then it could be said that both the possibility of noematic talk of a way of givenness determined through this identification rule and also the possibility of noetic talk of a corresponding reference are grounded in meaning, understood in this way. Yet the peculiar generality of a rule which is neither attained by "eidetic abstraction" nor understandable in terms of objects lies outside phenomenology's field of vision.

Thus it is very questionable whether, as is customary in phenomenological literature, Husserl's subsequent introduction of the "noema" should be valued as a step forward. It appears, rather, as a last attempt to construe what is not an object as quasi-objective and thereby to make oneself immune to everything which does not fit into the intentional subject-object schema. Like the talk of "objectivities" in *LU*, which are nevertheless not supposed to be "objects in the pregnant sense," the term 'noema' is an expression of embarrassment.

Yet the noematic interpretation of the meaning of *nominal* expressions may at least be taken as an understandable conception. But for the meanings of all *non-naming* expressions, this conception seems to become untenable. For when an expression does not signify an object, there is no object for which the meaning could be understood as its mode of givenness. With this, the present line of criticism merges into the one I postponed a little while ago and which concerns the pressure issuing from the phenomenological point of departure to assimilate all other meanings to nominal ones.

3. To what extent can such an assimilation be carried through? Let us first consider whole declarative sentences without paying attention to their various structures. Husserl explains in the First Investigation (*LU*, 2: 1, 48; *LI*, 1: 288) that there are two possibilities for understanding something as the object of a de-

clarative sentence. According to the first conception, the object of a sentence is that to which the subject of the sentence refers. According to the second, what can be understood as the object of the sentence is "the state of affairs" for which the statement as a whole is supposed to "stand." This second possibility was, of course, especially attractive to Husserl since it alone allows one to speak of an object that corresponds to the meaning of the whole sentence. According to the first conception, the object of a sentence is solely the object of the subject of the sentence, and no object would correspond to the meaning of the sentence as a whole.

Which conception is correct? Or are both possible? Here a distinction must be considered which Husserl introduces at the end of the First Investigation (sec. 34) and develops at more length in chapter 4 of the Fifth Investigation. "If we perform the act and live in it, as it were, we naturally refer to its object and not to its meaning" (*LU*, 2: 1, 103; *LI*, 1: 332). But we *can* always refer to the meaning "in a reflective act of thinking," and in that case we convert the meaning into an object. Thus if the meaning is simply understood, it is not an object but it can be transformed into one. The linguistic expression with which we then signify the meaning is not the original expression but a name. The objectification is expressed linguistically in a nominalization (5: sec. 35 f.; 6: sec. 39).

Thus we can nominalize a predicate like "is green" and speak of "the greenness." In a similar way, we can nominalize a sentence and then speak about the meaning of what was previously said. That the meaning is now an object is shown by the fact that the new expression is a possible sentence-subject of which, in turn, we can predicate something. For example, "The knife is blunt," "(This state of affairs) that the knife is blunt is irritating." The same objectification is, of course, also given when we simply say "He said something" or when we ask "What did he say?"

If these distinctions, which are Husserl's own but which are similarly found in Frege and in analytical philosophy,[2] are applied to the two possibilities Husserl mentioned for what can be conceived as the object of a statement, we arrive at the following. Both conceptions are correct, for both fulfill the criterion, also recognized by Husserl, that an expression stands for an object when it can function as the subject of true predications (*Ideas*, sec. 3; *LU*, 2: 1, 125; *LI*, 1: 352). But, as has now become clear, they meet this criterion in significantly different ways. If the sentence is spoken in unreflected discourse, only the first conception is possible. The second conception, according to which the object is a state of affairs, corresponds to the objectification of the meaning that is always possible, although (as Husserl explicitly says) it is derivative. It seems to be only a matter of nuance, but this nuance is decisive. If the object is constituted only in the subsequent objectification of meaning, then it is impossible to understand the meaning not yet objectified as something "by means of" which we refer to that object.[3]

Husserl never decided unambiguously between one or the other conception of what is to be regarded as the object of a declarative sentence. And now it is clear why it was impossible for him to do so. His semantic insight spoke unequivocally for the first view (object of the statement's subject); his starting point spoke just as unequivocally for the second view (state of affairs). The presupposition that "meaning conferring" consciousness is an act had to lead to the *hysteron-proteron* of projecting the object which results only from the subsequent objectification of meaning onto the original meaning-conferring consciousness.

One last doubt about the correctness of this criticism should now be taken into consideration. In the First Investigation Husserl gives, with the help of an example, a stricter elucidation of what is meant by the object of a statement in the sense of the state of affairs (*LU*, 2: 1, 48; *LI*, 1: 288). The two sentences, "a is larger than b" and "b is smaller than a," do not have the same meaning but "they express the same state of affairs." Is this not a very enlightening distinction, completely analogous to the one that holds for names which do not have the same meaning but signify the same object? Why, then, should we not say that by means of different meanings both sentences signify the same object, even though this object is presented *as* object only in a subsequent reflection?

However, the putative analogy is only apparent. The two sentences are connected by a narrower criterion than that which connects two names which signify the same object. The criterion by which it is decided whether two sentences express "the same state of affairs," in the sense Husserl intends here, is plainly the fact that they are analytically equivalent, and therefore their truth conditions are the same. The analogous relationship for nominal expressions is given when these denote not only the same object but when they denote it by means of the same conditions of identification. This criterion is satisfied, for example, by the two names 'John F. Kennedy's youngest brother' and 'the youngest son of John F. Kennedy's parents.' But obviously we can denote the same object just as well by other nominal expressions which are not connected analytically with these expressions (e.g., 'the senator who had an accident at Chappaquiddick'). An analogous equivalence relation is found in statements where they not only have the same truth conditions but the same truth value. But then one would have to say that all true statements denote one and the same object, and also all false ones. As is well known, Frege took this path, which, however, leads away from our normal understanding of 'object' and which, for Husserl's purposes, was not questioned.

Of course I do not want to contest the fact that it makes good sense to fix the meaning of the somewhat indefinite term 'state of affairs' in such a way that statements which have the same truth conditions express the same "state of affairs."[4] But the statement stands to the state of affairs, so defined as what is "said" by it, in an analogous relation—

not as the name stands to its object but, rather, as the name stands to "what is said"—if this too is so understood that what is said by several names is the same if, and only if, they express the same conditions of identification. Like what is said by a name, what is said by a statement is constituted only in the subsequent objectification already described.

4. The proof, until now pursued *in abstracto*, that Husserl's attempt to understand declarative sentences on the model of nominal expressions fails, may appear a bit academic. Granted that a weakness in Husserl's theory of meaning is visible here, and granted also that this weakness is a consequence of his point of departure, what are the consequences of such logical subtleties? These consequences become apparent when we consider the inner structure of statements. It can then also become clear that a completely new possibility for understanding is offered by linguistic analysis.

In chapter 6 of the Sixth Investigation Husserl developed the concepts which became fundamental for his view of the structure of statements. Starting with intentionality led him to understand the logical structure of a statement as a synthesis between objects, a synthesis in which an objectivity of a higher order is constituted. (In this context Husserl no longer speaks of the meaning of statements at all but only of "objectivities," which nevertheless become "objects in the pregnant sense" only through the modification of nominalization.) The synthesis is accomplished by an act, and by this act the synthetic objectivity is constituted. This act is "founded" on acts which represent the several elements of the synthesis. Husserl characterizes such a founded synthetic act as a "categorial act."

4.1 To what extent does Husserl clarify the structure of statements with these concepts? Let us consider the simplest form, predicative sentences. The narrow reciprocal connection which Husserl emphasizes between objects and expressions which can function as sentence subjects would have had to exclude speaking of predicates in such a way that they stand for objects. Husserl must have sensed this, for he avoids the question as best he can. On the other hand, his starting point left him no other possibility. And, in particular, the doctrine of categorial acts now rests on this presupposition. The categorial act synthesizes the objects of the acts on which it is founded. Were the categorial act founded in *one* act only, in the one which corresponds to the subject of the sentence, one could not speak of a synthesis. And when a second act is to be assumed on the side of the predicate, this means that the predicate also stands for an object.

But we do not depend here on speculation. In section 48 of the *Sixth Logical Investigation* Husserl carried through an analysis of predicative statements in which these statements are assimilated to statements in which something is said to contain something else as a part. The schema is "A is (has) a," with the form "a is in A" as converse (*LU*, 2: 2, 153; *LI*, 1: 793). In the case of the predicative sentences Husserl does not speak of parts simply but of "dependent moments." The Third Investigation, "On the Doctrine of Wholes and Parts," confirms this assimilation. The predicates stand for "dependent parts" of an object (sec. 2). Such an assimilation of course presupposes that the predicate ("a") is understood in its nominalized form. And so here too the subsequent transformation is projected back onto the original understanding.

Granted that one can say (and why should one not?) that the greenness is "in" (or "at" or "on") the meadow and, conversely, that the meadow has the greenness "in" or "at" it. One *can* say this *because* and *if* one can say that the meadow is green. And we do not verify this predicative sentence conversely by establishing that an object of a higher order (for this is what the greenness is) has some kind of a relation to the meadow. Furthermore, it is of course clear that the transformation of the predicative sentences into sentences about the relation of part and whole or other kinds of relational sentences leads to an infinite regress. "a is in A" is in its turn a predicative sentence, with a one-place or a two-place predicate, depending on how it is structured, but in any case a predicative sentence.[5] The form of the predicative sentence cannot be circumvented, Therefore, understanding a predicative sentence cannot consist in synthesizing two objects.

Husserl's theory of meaning has, then, foundered on the predicative sentence in a way which is manifestly irreparable within his system. Whoever considers the fundamental metaphysical significance which has belonged to the predicative judgment throughout the history of philosophy can no longer dispose of this result as a logical subtlety. Every philosophical starting point has its limits. But a starting point which does not allow understanding a predicative sentence must be abandoned.

How else can a predicative sentence be understood? We must proceed from the fact that such a sentence (in the simplest case of a one-place predication) has only *one* object, that of the subject of the sentence. As has been shown, it cannot be said that the person who utters the sentence with understanding connects this object with another object. Nor does he connect this object with something which is not an object. For as soon as we say that an object is connected with *something,* an object is already implied in the "something." Hence it is the traditional conception of a synthesis which is simply unusable for the elucidation of the predicative sentence.

Consequently, we have to seek the alternative solution at a more fundamental level. And we can do this by asking: When the person who utters the sentence with understanding does not *connect* the object for which the subject of the sentence stands with something, what does he do with it? The most natural answer seems to be: He characterizes it in a certain way, and he does this by classifying and distinguishing it by means of the predicate. The function of the predicate, then, does not consist in being the expression of an intentional act and in "representing" something. It consists simply in characterizing something in the sense just explained.

One might reply: If an object is characterized by means of a predicate, must not something be represented which the predicate stands for? But instead of postulating what must be the case on the basis of an allegedly self-evident presupposition, we should pay attention to what is the case and use this to question that presupposition. When we say with understanding "The meadow is green," we can connect a definite color intuition in perception or imagination with the predicate "is green." The predicate, however, is general. If it must stand for something and if this something must be capable of being represented, it cannot be a matter of sensory intuition. We would have to represent something which corresponds to the entire scope of the predicate. The nonsensible representation that is needed on this account is what Plato and Aristotle named *noein*. And in his theory of "eidetic abstraction" Husserl has tried to give a foundation to the existence of an "intuition of essences" in an analysis which he takes to be a phenomenological description but which, perhaps, is only a remarkable reconstruction of something which does not exist.

At any rate, I am unable to find any such representation within me. Moreover, it is doubtful whether the idea of a nonsensible seeing, conceived by analogy with our sensible seeing, is not just a round square. But, above all, we do not need such a representation to understand the understanding of predicates. We explain to someone the meaning of a predicate (and thereby reconstrue our own understanding) not by pointing to a general essence but by applying the predicate to different objects, whereby we explain the extent of its classificatory function, and by refusing its application to other objects, whereby we explain the extent of its discriminatory function.[6] Understanding the meaning of the predicate does not consist in seeing something but in mastering the rule which determines the application of the predicate. The generality of the predicate is a rule-generality, not a "general object."

To be sure, the meaning of a predicate, for instance "is green," can be explained to someone in the way just described only if he fulfills certain psychological (and physiological) conditions. To someone who is completely color blind, the meaning of this predicate cannot be explained. But whether these psychological conditions are fulfilled or not cannot be established by an inner seeing but only by whether one is able to learn the rule, just as with every other ability or talent.

The theory of predication which I have adumbrated is linguistic in the pregnant sense: it not only analyses language but leads to the result that the use of linguistic signs, instead of being merely a means of expression of something else, proves to be the element of understanding. The rule-guided use of signs takes over, at least in the case of predicates, the place which intentionality occupied for Husserl. In the case of predicates and predicative sentences, acts have proved to be ineffective—not just because they cannot be established in the inner forum (this assurance would be as unconvincing as its opposite) but because those who think they can establish such acts fail to clarify our understanding of predicates precisely because of this assumption.

4.2 What of the higher forms of statements? In section 51 of the Sixth Investigation Husserl deals with 'and' and also mentions, incidentally, 'or'. In the case of 'and', Husserl speaks of "the conjunctive connection of names or statements." Here too Husserl's primary orientation toward names is operative; that every conjunction of names is an implicit conjunction of sentences is overlooked. Since they are also expressions for "objectivities," the sentences are assimilated to the names, and conjunction is primarily explicitated in terms of names. Conjugating, too, is understood as a founded categorial act. It is an act in which we *"refer to the connection (Zusammen) of the objects A and B."*

This talk of a *Zusammen* is, of course, so vague that it must be characterized as useless. It is wholly unclear how Husserl could distinguish the "connection" referred to in a "conjugating act" from other logical and even intuitive modes of "connection." And again it is clear that this defect is not accidental but would inhere in every attempt to look for the meaning of 'and' and 'or' in some kind of synthetic representation. Inevitably, one would always be reaching back for intuitive images. Thus it becomes clear once more that the concept of nonsensory representation is senseless.

From the point of view of linguistic analysis, the meaning of 'and' and 'or', just as the meaning of the predicates, is seen in the rules which tie the statements which contain these words to definite truth-conditions. These truth-conditions are those which in propositional logic are represented by the so-called truth tables. The meaning of 'and' is determined by the fact that a sentence ("p and q") is true if both sentences of which it is composed are true, and that it is false in all other cases. To be sure, in this form the explanation is circular, since the *definiendum* reappears in the *definiens* in the word 'both'. It is impossible to introduce the sense of the word 'and' by means of other words without circularity. Nevertheless, we are able to explain to someone who knows neither the word 'and' nor an equivalent expression (and in this way we can reconstruct our own understanding) by *exhibiting*—analogously to what happened in the case of predicates—under what conditions a sentence ("p and q") is true and under what conditions it is false.

Our partner C observes, for example, that A asserts "p and q" and that B denies it. It then appears that "p" (or "q") is false; and A withdraws his assertion. In another situation it appears that "p" is true and also that "q" is true;[7] B withdraws his denial. And so on. On the basis of such examples, C can extract the rule that determines the meaning of 'and'. What is presupposed, of course, is that C

simply has the ability to learn these rules—not to represent together the objectivities "p" and "q" stand for (it is anyway unclear what this should mean).

In similar fashion, the meaning of the quantifiers ("all," "each") is explained,[8] whereas the idea that we can "represent" a universality in a synthetic act is again certainly obscure and probably senseless.

5. The theory of categorial acts has hereby been shown to break down at every level. (For the acts of ideational abstraction, the proof has not been given but only indicated. For categorial acts in the narrower sense, however, the failure of the theory seems to me proved.) The theory was a brilliant attempt to understand the meaning of connected expressions with the help of a hopelessly inadequate starting point. The apparent plausibility of Husserl's analyses derives from the manifest superiority of his theory over other accounts within the same traditional approach that is based on the schema "representation and object."[9]

Perhaps the question will be raised whether the alternative account given by linguistic analysis, which has been adumbrated, does not in its turn founder on the fact that it cannot explain the derivative objectification which is expressed in nominalization. However, it can explain it much better than Husserl could. The object that is referred to by a nominalized expression is neither a "synthetic objectivity" nor, as I have assumed hitherto with Husserl, the meaning itself. Rather it is *what-is-said* by a possible speaker in accordance with a definite rule, whereby "what-is-said" is defined in such a way that all possible utterances which have the same truth-conditions stand for an identical what-is-said. Defined in this way, what-is-said is, as for Husserl, an "ideal" object which, however, is not built up from syntheses of objects but is the result of an abstraction based on linguistic utterances in accordance with their conditions of use.

One might finally want to know

whether, with the categorial acts, Husserl's categorial intuition should go overboard too. Here a distinction is in order. To the extent that an intuition is an act and to the extent that it is even understood on the model of vision as a mental seeing, it must of course go overboard. Nevertheless, with his distinction between intuitive and signitive acts Husserl has pointed to a fundamental distinction which is not tied to these concepts and remains tenable even in the transformed perspective of linguistic analysis. This distinction manifests itself in the connection we have seen to obtain between the meaning and the truth-conditions of an expression. For example, predicates can only be introduced by explaining their truth-conditions—that is, by showing how their application can be verified. And yet we understand them in exactly the same way outside the verification-situation, which is not the situation of their normal use.

The rule for the normal use of a predicate consists, then, in a peculiar reference to the rule of the use of the predicate within a verification-situation. This reference corresponds to the reference of Husserl's signitive intention to its intuitive fulfillment, except that the members of the reference relation are no longer understood as acts. An analogous distinction obtains, *mutatis mutandis,* for names, just as for the whole predicative statement and for the different types of complex statements. Here, then, an idea that has been worked out by Husserl—an idea which is not specifically phenomenological—can be taken into the theory of meaning of linguistic analysis.

Clarification of the distinction that has been indicated might prove to be the core of a satisfactory theory of meaning in linguistic analysis and thereby, at the same time, an important part of a linguistic clarification of "awareness" (*Erschlossenheit*) in general.

II.

It was to be expected that the confrontation between phenomenology and linguistic analysis in terms of meanings would turn out unfavorably for Husserl, because linguistic analysis has an advantage because of its starting point. The opposite result could be expected in that area where Husserl's thought has its starting point: the reference to objects.

This expectation, nevertheless, will be disappointed. Starting with the reference to objects prevents not only a satisfactory clarification of meanings but, also, a satisfactory clarification of the reference to objects. This apparently paradoxical claim proves meaningful as soon as we consider the possibility that every reference to objects belongs, according to its own sense, in the context of the understanding of meanings. Husserl's definition points in this direction: an "object" is a "subject of possible true predictions" (*Ideas,* sec. 3; cf. *LU,* 2: 1, 125; *LI,* 1: 352). Nevertheless, Husserl never drew the conclusion from this explanation that the primary unit of consciousness is the understanding of a sentence, and that the mere reference to or naming of an object must be understood as essentially in need of supplementation. Husserl was again precluded from drawing such a conclusion by his starting point, since he started from the conception of the reference to an object as the primary unit of consciousness. But how could Husserl arrive at this conception in the first place, if, on the other hand, he regarded an object as a "subject of possible true predications"?

The reason seems to be that Husserl had, from the beginning, connected this first explanation of what is to be understood by "object" to a second explanation, according to which an object is essentially the correlate of a representing act, of an intentional experience. Here we again touch on the double starting point of the *LU,* which is externally evident in the discrepancy between the First Investigation that is oriented to language and the Fifth Investigation that is introspectively oriented and yet is made the foundation of the First. The first explanation of what is to be regarded as object gives a linguistic criterion; the second, which is the decisive one for Husserl, gives a psychological criterion.

But this characterization of Husserl's second (really his first) explanation of "object" does not yet suffice, for it is doubtful that this concept of object is the result of an unbiased analysis of those modes of consciousness which Husserl calls "intentional experiences." It is not at all obvious that the examples of such "experiences," which Husserl mentions where he introduces the concept of intentionality in the Fifth Investigation (*LU*, 2: 1, 366; *LI*, 2: 554), must be interpreted in such a way that they always have "direction towards an object," unless this object is understood as the secondary objectification of what is said by a statement. This is surely the sense in which we must interpret the example of "the statement [in which] something is stated." The same holds analogously for believing, wishing, and so on. But there are more complicated cases.

"In desiring," another example goes, there is "something desired." Here the surface grammar seems to conceal the fact that every desire of an object is a desire *to do* something with the object (to possess it, to consume it, and so on).[10] And now this *sentence* can be nominalized, so that we can again say that "something" is desired; but what we now mean by "something" is no longer the object but "to possess this object."

Thus a great number of those modes of consciousness which Husserl calls intentional have the "direction toward an object" which he emphasized only because they can be expressed in sentences and because these can be nominalized. This does not hold for all examples. For instance, it does not hold for "naming" or "hating." It suffices, however, to make this psychological criterion (which of course is based in turn on linguistic usage) useless for a unified explanation of what is to be understood by "object."

In fact, Husserl does not seem to have developed what I have called his second explanation of "object" from a descriptive analysis of "intentional experiences." Rather it is derived from an older belief which, ever since Plato, has been irritating philosophical thinking: the belief that all these modes of consciousness

are to be conceived after the model of seeing. Just as seeing has a visual image "before" it, philosophers have thought of the "object" as an analogous correlate of intentional consciousness which is interpreted as "representation."

How much Husserl was guided by this model appears in his conviction that "intuition" and "object" are "correlative concepts which belong together" (*Ideas*, sec. 3). A real object is a possible object of sense intuition; an ideal object is a possible object of a categorial intuition (*LU*, 2: 2, 142 ff.; *LI*, 2: 784 ff.). Of the latter I will not speak further. (No one will doubt that a real object is essentially a possible object of sense intuition). —But Husserl goes much further. Since he counts (*Sixth Logical Investigation*, sec. 42) everything which belongs to logical form as part of the domain of categorial acts, he must hold that a real object is constituted for us exclusively in sense intuition (sec. 47). This fits the model according to which an object is thought of on the analogy of a visual image. But it directly contradicts the conception that an object is essentially denoted by a subject-expression. For a subject-expression has a definite logico-linguistic form—namely, that form which allows the subject-expression to appear in a sentence in certain places and not in others. If an object is essentially the "subject of possible true predications," this form cannot be dispensable for the constitution of the object as object. On the contrary, it would have to be shown how the object, understood in this way, is constituted for us by the interdependence of language and perception—a task which has been successfully undertaken in recent linguistic analysis.[11]

Husserl gives two explanations of what is to be understood as an "object": (1) a subject of true predications and (2) the representatum of a representation. In the last analysis, then, these explanations cannot be coherently combined.[12] More precisely, the second explanation, which stems from an erroneous analogy, must be said to be an empty concept which is just as fictitious as the concept of "representation," which belongs with it. And whether a fictitious concept is compatible with another concept cannot be decided. But it is precisely this second explanation which became decisive for Husserl's starting point. While the first explanation calls unambiguously for a primacy of the sentence and, with it, of meaning against the object, the second makes the object appear as something independent, requiring no completion—just as little as an image does.[13]

We are therefore forced to conclude that Husserl failed in the clarification of meanings not simply because he started from the consciousness of objects; rather, he started from an isolated consciousness of objects because his enterprise was based on an untenable concept of "object."

Besides that first explanation of "object" as the subject of true predications, there are additional indications in Husserl that he felt the primacy of sentences over names. The most important is his penetrating analysis of "thetic qualities" (*Fifth Logical Investigation*, sec. 20; *Ideas*, sec. 103ff.). For Husserl, consciousness is so essentially positional—in any of the modalities, and be it that of "bracketing neutralization"—that for him there are no acts without thetic qualities. But surely it must be doubted that thetic qualities characterize our reference to objects. Rather, they appear to stand for the different attitudes, expressed in the utterance of a sentence, toward a state of affairs. The customary English term is therefore 'propositional attitude.' Had Husserl in his analysis of "intentional experiences" *set out* from the thetic qualities, the "intentional experiences" would have appeared as so many modes of the affirmation of sentences. But since the primary unit of consciousness was an

established fact for Husserl, he transferred the thetic qualities to the acts.

I cannot claim that the primacy of sentences over names has been demonstrated here. Nonetheless, this primacy seems to have become rather plausible. Whoever admits it has abandoned Husserl's starting point. The question, What then remains of phenomenology in Husserl's sense? can be left open.

If the understanding of sentences is demonstrated to be primary in comparison with the reference to objects, the further question arises: where is this understanding to be situated? That a sentence is the primary unit of meaning seems to be based on the fact that it is the smallest unit for intersubjective communication. (A name can be understood, but nothing can be communicated by just a name.) This fact seems to indicate that while the conception of the subject-object schema was based on the individual subject, from the outset the understanding of sentences belongs to intersubjective communication. In this case, while intersubjectivity is primary in this light, the "subject" is secondary. This, of course, must not simply be asserted but must be demonstrated in detail.

In any case, it ought to have become clear that linguistic analysis has not simply abandoned the tradition of transcendental philosophy but that it stands, at least latently, in opposition to it on a comparably fundamental level. The subject as starting point, just as orientation to the object, is contested by making the intersubjective communication in language the new universal system of reference. Formulated so generally, this is the same as the hermeneutic program, but in linguistic analysis it is carried through in a more elementary fashion.

NOTES

1. In *Ideas*, as in *LU*, Husserl speaks of the *sense* (*Sinn*) of acts as opposed to the *meaning* of expressions. The problem of meaning becomes less important in *Ideas* because Husserl thinks "the level of the expression [is] not productive" (sec. 124). Nonetheless, this level has the noteworthy

"distinction" of "mirroring as it were every other intentionality in form and content" (ibid.). We shall not discuss in the abstract whether this conception is correct. What matters is that in the fundamental treatment of theoretical consciousness in *Ideas* Husserl continued, *de facto* to use the basic concepts—concepts like "sense" and "thetic quality"—which he had developed in *LU* in relation to meanings (although even there they were developed partly in an analysis of acts in apparent independence of language). Therefore the concepts which are connected with the title "Meaning" have remained central in Husserl, in contrast to this title itself. And that they cannot be so easily separated from the use of linguistic expressions as Husserl thought will be shown below in a discussion of Husserl's analyses.

2. We will see (further on) that what is objectified in nominalization is not really the meaning but "what is said" (in a particular sense). In the case of statements, what is said is that of which we say it is true or false. But we cannot say of the meaning of the statement that it is true or false. To be sure, we can *also* objectify the meaning; however, this is not expressed linguistically in the nominalization of what is said but in the expression "the meaning of 'A'."

3. The situation can most easily be clarified by comparison with the ordinary nominal expressions. Even in a nominal expression, the meaning (or "what is said" by the expression) can be objectified. Thus we can, for example, transform the expression 'the Chancellor' into 'to be the Chancellor', and this nominalized expression can function as a sentence-subject. In nominal expressions we can therefore speak of two objects: (1) the object which is referred to by the expression in its ordinary usage (in our example 'the Chancellor') and (2) the objectified meaning. When Husserl speaks of the object of a nominal expression, he always—rightly—thinks of (1). But in the case of a predicate, for example "is green," (1) is lacking completely and only (2) is possible. And in an entire declarative sentence, (1) indeed is given, but only when the sentence is predicative, and even then the object is merely the object of the subject of the statement. In nominal expressions the reason why one can see so clearly that the object, in the sense of the objectified meaning, cannot be conceived of as the object of the meaning, and therefore not as an object the original expression stands for, is that in such cases both are actually given. Since, quite rightly, Husserl never said—in the case of names—that their object is their objectified meaning, it would follow that he must say other expressions do not stand for objects at all.

4. Cf. G. Patzig, "Satz und Tatsache," *Argumentationen: Festschrift für J. König* (1966).

5. Husserl tried to pass over this by taking the relational moment of relational sentences into the execution of the synthetic act, which led to an inextricable confusion of relations with aspects of logical form (cf. *LU*, 2: 2, 155 ff.; *LI*, 2: 795ff.).

6. Cf. P. Lorenzen at the beginning of most of his writings.

7. 'And also' is used here just as 'or' was used a moment ago in the description of the illustration. In the illustration itself, these words are not used.

8. Cf. Lorenzen, *Metamathematik*, sec. 2.

9. I hardly need to say that I now regard as a failure the attempt made in my book *Der Wahrheitsbegriff bei Husserl und Heidegger* (Berlin, 1967 [sec. 6-7]) to understand and to save the theory of categorial intuition.

10. Cf. A. Kenny, *Action, Emotion and Will* (London, 1963), chap. 9.

11. Cf. esp. P. F. Strawson, *Individuals* (London, 1959).

12. The lack of clarity and the ambiguity in the expression 'object' has had an irritating effect throughout German philosophy. Besides the two concepts I have discussed, a third concept plays a less important role in Husserl but, on the other hand, was decisive for Kant: *gegenständlich*, in the sense of "objectively." It is not an accident that this concept can be more easily expressed by an adverb than by a noun, for in reality it stands for a modal-like determination of a *statement* ("It not only appears to be the case that...but it is objectively so"). Even in Kant, however, this concept was combined with the other two (in his case without great damage) because of the lack of familiarity with sentences (cf., e.g., *Critique of Pure Reason*, A104).

The same ambiguity is also operative in the talk of an "objectification" (*Vergegenständlichung*). Heidegger's thesis about the objectification of being in modern philosophy is based primarily on the third concept of "object." Hence his "de-objectification" may lead to a conception (particularly in talk of "beings") which in turn is guilty of objectification in the sense of the first definition of "object."

13. It can be seen here that the alternative to a linguistic approach is not—as is customarily thought—some kind of a realistic approach but an approach which derives its orientation from metaphors taken from sense perception and especially from visual perception. The analytic approach is no less realistic; it is only less inward oriented, and necessarily so, because the inwardness of the "representation" is quasi-sensual and therefore loses touch with what has to be clarified, the linguistic structure of awareness.

The Phenomenological Reduction as Epoche and Explication

GUIDO KÜNG

A clear understanding of the notion of phenomenological reduction is crucial for any evaluation of the claims of Husserlian phenomenology. The phenomenological reduction is said to be the distinctive step (or steps) one has to take if one is to enter the realm of phenomenology proper. Husserl labored all his life to find the best way which would lead the non-phenomenologist into the new land he thought he had discovered. Commentators have classified the ways discussed by Husserl under at least three main headings:[1] the Cartesian way, the way through psychology, and the way through ontology. In each of these ways one is urged to perform a phenomenological reduction. But since the ways are different, the phenomenological reduction also varies somewhat for each approach. Husserl and his interpreters tried hard to clarify these subtle distinctions, but up to now their ways of speaking have proved to be rather opaque, especially to philosophers accustomed to the standards of clarity of analytic philosophy.

I will therefore try to sned some light on the different notions of phenomenological reduction by relating them to familiar notions of contemporary semantics, such as the distinction between sense and referent and the notion of explication. It will be seen, however, that in each case an analogical transposition from ordinary semantics to what I propose to call metaphysical semantics is involved. The propriety of this analogical transposition is in my estimation the crux in deciding the meaningfulness of Husserlian transcendental phenomenology.

The line of exposition will follow what I take to be some of the main turning points in the historical development of Husserl's thought.[2] But we are far from able to give a full developmental account of Husserlian philosophy. Further study of the texts still needs to be done and—especially—a precise record of the many important shifts in Husserl's philosophical terminology is still to be compiled.

1. Descriptive Psychology Based on Inner Perception

Brentano, Husserl's philosophical master, had taken up afresh the Lockean program of a careful reflective description of the immanently given of consciousness. The reflective grasp of the immanently given he called "inner perception" (*innere Wahrnehmung*), and, like Locke's "reflection," this inner perception was said to intuitively grasp the really occurring mental acts of different kinds: acts of simple presentation, of judgment, and of love and hate. Prominent among the objects of inner percep-

Reprinted with permission of the publisher and author from *The Monist*, vol. 59, no. 1(Jan. 1975): 61-80.

tion were the acts of external perception (*äussere Wahrnehmung*), such as perceiving a tree, hearing a noise, etc.

But the status of the objects of external perception proved at once to be problematic. For instance, was the green tree which we perceive in our garden to be counted among the objects of descriptive psychology? Brentano still adhered to the representationalist view which stressed the distinction between the green tree which we see and the invisible, colorless tree out there which is postulated by phsysics. He tried to describe the existence of the green tree as "in-existence" in the mind, but he soon had to admit that he could make no clear sense of this peculiar mental "in-existence." Husserl, on the other hand, started out as a scientific realist. He stressed that the green tree we perceive is identical with the tree investigated by physics, and he therefore claimed explicitly that the objects of external perception were *not* to be counted among the objects of descriptive psychology (or phenomenology, as he began to call it).[3]

A second major difficulty which concerned Husserl was the one raised by Natorp and Frege, namely their accusation of psychologism. It led Husserl to supplement Brentano's descriptive psychology with an explicit doctrine of abstraction involving the admission of an intuition of universal kinds ("*Species*") in order to account for the necessary character of for example, logical and ethical truths. Thus at the time of the *Logical Investigations* (first edition) the Husserlian descriptive psychology or phenomenology was based both on the inner perception of real mental particulars and on the intuitive grasp of ideal universals.

2. Phenomenology Presupposing a Universal Epoche

From 1904 to 1906 Husserl was led to reconsider, for various concurring reasons, his stand on the exclusion of the objects of external perception from the domain of phenomenology.

2.1. In actual practice the mental acts could not be phenomenologically described without also describing their objects. Natorp, whose writings the early Husserl had been studying very closely, had even held that (for instance) to describe the hearing of a tone was the *same* as to describe this tone.[4]

2.2. Husserl's attempts at giving the descriptive-psychological foundations of set theory and arithmetics had already in fact, included descriptions of intentional objects, namely of sets and numbers, and Husserl had thus been led to describe in detail the correlation between certain hierarchies of mental acts on the one hand and their objects of lower and higher categorial order on the other hand.

2.3. Husserl had already enlarged the domain of descriptive psychology by admitting not only real mental particulars but also ideal universals.[5]

2.4. The Munich group (students of Theodor Lipps, such as Alexander Pfänder and Johannes Daubert, who had greeted Husserl's *Logical Investigations* with enthusiasm) held that the new philosophy should not be limited to the description of the essences of mental particulars but should be concerned with the description of all essences whatsoever, including those of physical particulars. Meinong (another disciple of Brentano and founder of an influential group in Graz) also was proposing an all-comprehensive "theory of objects" (*Gegenstandstheorie*).

2.5. Furthermore, another most important consideration may have prompted Husserl to reevaluate his position on the status of the objects of *external* perception, namely the discovery that the status of the objects of *inner* perception was equally problematic. In 1894[6] Husserl had found that he could explain an intuitive grasp of a nonimmanent real particular in terms of an analogy with the interpretation of a symbol or picture. He found, for instance, that as we can "see" a mountain which is *not* present by interpreting the paint marks on a canvas which *are* present, so—in external perception—we are perceiving a tree which is *not* immanent in consciousness by interpreting the sensations (*Empfindungen*) which *are* immanent. It would seem therefore that Husserl assumed at that time that any intuitive grasp of a real particular was either an inner perception of what is immanently present or else a case where something immanently present serves as a basis for an interpretation. To his astonishment, Husserl discovered after 1905, in his analyses of inner time consciousness, that remembering could *not* be understood as an act of interpretation; that, for instance, remembering a past sound sensation could not be described as an interpretation of a presently immanent sound sensation but had to be described as a "direct" intuitive intending of a real particular which no longer existed.[7] This exploded the myth of the unproblematic nature of inner perception, because any perception whatsoever necessarily involves some retention of the immediate past. In other words, a restriction of the domain of descriptive psychology or phenomenology to actually immanent real particulars proved to be absolutely impossible since such a restriction would veto not only the use of external perception but that of inner perception as well!

The only way out of all these difficulties was to officially admit all intentional objects, namely, the intentional correlates of all mental acts, into the domain of phenomenology. But at the same time the proper nature of phenomenology had to be safeguarded, and a way had to be found to prevent its getting mixed up with physics and metaphysics.

Looking for a solution, Husserl could go back in history to Descartes, for whom the *cogito* had included not only the act of *cogitare* and the *ego* but also the idea or the *cogitatum qua cogitatum*. Actually, Husserl even went back to Descartes's philosophical ancestors, namely, the Skeptics. He read at this time two books which had just been published: Raoul Richter's *Der Skeptizismus in der Philosophie* (vol. 1 in Leipzig in 1904) and Albert Gödeckemeyer's ("Privatdozent in Göttingen") *Geschichte des griechis-* *chen Skiptizismus* (1905), and it seems that it was especially from the latter that he picked up the technical term *epoche* and incorporated it as a key term in his phenomenology.[8]

The skeptical term 'epoche' conveyed exactly (and more accurately than the Cartesian term 'doubt' what could guarantee that the phenomenological description of a physical object would not be confused with the kind of account that is given by physics: in a phenomenological description of the appearance of an external object one has to abstain from making any claims concerning the actual reality of this object; namely, all questions concerning actual reality have to be bracketed, set aside, left unanswered. For instance, I might accurately describe a present experience as one of seeing a round tower out there. If, later on, it should turn out that the tower in question was actually square, or that in actual reality there was no tower out there at all (that I had been having a haullucination), my previous description would still remain a true phenomenological description. All I would have to do would be to make sure that in my previous description I had been careful not to claim that there *actually* was a tower out there which *actually* was round.

Descartes and the Skeptics, as well as Husserl, found it both possible and philosophically necessary to give to this epoche an absolutely universal scope. They found it meaningful to guard the truthfulness of their descriptions of consciousness against not only the ordinary possibility that *some* external perceptions might turn out to be illusions or hallucinations but even against the metaphysical possibility that *all* external perceptions might be illusionary. Husserl explicitly envisioned the possibility that the belief in the actual existence of the material world might collapse entirely.[9]

In the winter semester 1906/7 Husserl for the first time described the phenomenological method as involving not merely the use of reflection and of intuition of universals but also as requiring the initial performance of a phenomenological reduction, namely, the adoption of a universal epoche.[10]

Actually the scope of the epoche is somewhat different, according to whether one follows the Cartesian way or the way through psychology. Following the Cartesian way, which might be called the way through epistemology, one approaches transcendental consciousness by first bracketing everything that can be doubted, namely, all transcendent referents, other minds included. By following the way through psychology, on the other hand, one starts out bracketing everything that does not belong in descriptive psychology, namely, all the physical referents, but not the other minds.

3. The Epoche and the Semantics of Sense and Referent

The epoche introduces a certain distinction between the external object as intentional object, namely, as appearance, and the external object as actual reality. But Husserl's predecessors had been unable to provide a satisfactory clarification of this distinction. The two models that were used to explain the relationship between actual reality and appearance were (a) the relationship between cause and effect and (b) the relationship between a pictured or signified thing and what is picturing or signifying the thing. But both the causal theory of the noumenon causing the phenomenon and the representationalist theory according to which the appearance is said to be a picture or a sign of absolute reality are unsatisfactory and have run into strong criticism, especially in contemporary philosophy. Actually Husserl is one of the fathers of this contemporary criticism, and it was for this very reason that he had from the start refused to distinguish *two* objects of external perception: a directly perceived immanent one and an inferred transcendent one.

The only appropriate model for the distinction between appearance and actual reality is—as far as I can tell—the semantical relationship between sense and refer-

ent. Since it is well known that the contemporary analysis of this semantical distinction has its origin in Frege, it is interesting to note that at this very point in his development Husserl took a renewed interest in Frege's views on sense.[11] In the summer semester of 1908 Husserl lectured on the theory of meaning (*Bedeutungslehre*)[12] and on this occasion was led to abandon his earlier view according to which meanings were a special sort of universal kinds (*species*). Instead he was led to admit that meanings, which he now called *ontic* meanings, were something *sui generis*, being neither real particulars nor universal kinds. Actually Husserl's views about meaning were now very similar to Frege's. But Husserl also took the further step of interpreting the troublesome notion of intentional object in terms of his newly found notion of ontic meaning or sense.[13]

But, unfortunately, while Husserl took a strong interest in the Fregean notion of sense, his phenomenological inclination prevented him from truly appreciating the importance of the notion of referent. Thus while discussing the Fregean examples, "the victor of Jena" and the "vanquished of Waterloo,"[14] Husserl did not introduce the actually existing Napoleon as the identical *referent* of the two expressions; instead he pointed out that the speaker *intends to refer* to the same *X*. That is; instead of introducing the Fregean notion of referent Husserl elaborated the phenomenological notion of the-identical-*X*-meant, namely, the notion of noematic pole. This noematic pole exists even in the cases where there is no referent, and thus, clearly, it still belongs on the level of the Fregean sense.

Thus while Husserl saw that the intentional object could be understood in terms of the notion of sense, it seems that he never fully realized that the notion of sense is necessarily connected with the notion of referent, and that if the intentional object is understood in terms of the notion of sense, then the *epoche* has to be defined as the provisional bracketing of all factual questions regarding the *referent*.

Probably it was just because of his adoption of the epoche that Husserl never discussed the notion of referent. But this was a mistake; Husserl should have realized that the *epoche* required only that all *factual questions regarding the actual existence* of the referent of external perception had to be bracketed, but that it did not rule out an investigation of the *notion* of referent. Another reason why Husserl did not elaborate the notion of referent may have been his above-mentioned early rejection of representationalism and the Kantian notion of the thing-in-itself. He should have realized, however, that a rejection of the notion of a thing-in-itself, "hidden behind" the phenomena, does not ipso facto entail the rejection of the notion of a referent, since the reference is *not* said to be "hidden behind" the sense but is described as being revealed through the sense.[15]

4. The Ordinary Notion of Referent and the Metaphysical Notion of Referent

One has to admit, however, that what is in question here is not the ordinary notion of referent but a metaphysical notion of referent. The basic referents in ordinary semantics constitute what is called the universe of discourse. But while Bertrand Russell had tried to identify the universe of discourse of his system with absolute metaphysical reality, this is no longer true of contemporary logicians. They hold, rather, that one and the same reality can be described in terms of different universes of discourse. This shows that the universe of discourse of a contemporary constructional system has to be under-

stood as being already a conceptualization of reality. Therefore the ordinary referents which compose a universe of discourse are, metaphysically speaking, already appearances and not metaphysical reality as it is in itself.[16]

The theory of sense and referent, as it is worked out in contemporary possible-world semantics, allows for singling out the actual world within the set of all possible worlds. But these possible worlds are not what may be called different possible conceptualizations; they are merely all the possible factual variations within the framework of a single conceptualization. These possibilities can cover the above-mentioned possibilities of *ordinary illusion and hallucination*, since they allow, for instance, for a distinction between these three kinds of possible worlds: (a) worlds where the above-mentioned tower is square, (b) worlds where the above-mentioned tower is round, (c) worlds where the above-mentioned tower does not exist at all. But ordinary possible-world semantics does not deal with the question of *metaphysical illusion*, namely with the possibility that an entire world picture, an entire conceptual scheme (an entire ontology), may be mistaken. (Notice that the possibility that *several different* conceptual schemes may be equally correct is left open. The notion of a metaphysical illusion merely presupposes the falsity of the claim that *all* conceptual schemes are equally correct.)

As a matter of fact, the metaphysical notion of referent involves a problematic transposition of the ordinary relationship between sense and referent to the metaphysical level:[17]

Ordinary Semantics		*Metaphysical Semantics*
Mental acts	...	Mental acts
Ordinary sense (incl. appearance in the ordinary sense) = ordinary noema:	...	Metaphysical sense (incl. appearance in the metaphysical sense) = metaphysical noema:
Ordinary ontic meanings	...	Ordinary ontic meanings
Ordinary noematic poles	...	Ordinary noematic poles
Ordinary referents	...	Poles of the metaphysical noema
		Metaphysical referent

What from the ordinary point of view is called a referent is, metaphysically speaking, still a kind of noematic pole. A metaphysical illusion, if there is such a thing, would be analogous to an ordinary illusion: just as in the case of an ordinary illusion there is an ordinary noematic pole but no ordinary referent which has the intended properties, in the case of a metaphysical illusion there would be the poles of the metaphysical noema (namely the referents in the ordinary sense) but there would be no counterpart with the intended determinations in actual metaphysical reality. Similar to the way in which the argument from ordinary illusion warrants the distinction between the ordinary sense and the ordinary referent; an argument from metaphysical illusion would justify a distinction between a metaphysical sense and a metaphysical referent.

Of course the correspondence between metaphysical semantics and ordinary semantics could never be a sameness relation, but can only be an analogy. The metaphysical notion of truth; for instance, must be quite different from the concept of truth in ordinary semantics. This is evident from the fact that any articulation is by definition a form of conceptualization (of sense), and therefore the metaphysical counterpart of the articulated plurality of the ordinary referents cannot be said to be an *articulated* plurality; the metaphysical analogue of the articulated plurality of the ordinary referents must rather be some sort of *preconceptual determinateness* of the metaphysical referent.[18] (Notice that I prefer to use the notion of metaphysical referent in the singular.)

5. Phenomenological Analysis as Analysis of Sense

With the admission of the intentional-object-as-such (the noema) into the domain of phenomenology, phenomenology became both noetic *and noematic* phenomenology. Noematic phenomenology even takes precedence over noetic phenomenology: the analysis of the noema requires only a reflection on the sense of what is before us,[19] whereas the

analysis of the noesis presupposes that consciousness has the ability of what might be described as "turning all the way back upon itself." Thus it is not astonishing to find Husserl now state that noematic phenomenology comes first and has to serve as a "guiding thread" for the more difficult analysis of the noesis.[20]

But noematic phenomenology is concerned with the analysis of intentional-objects-as-such, namely, with the analysis of sense. Therefore phenomenology as such is now primarily analysis of sense. This means that it is now much more closely related to analytic philosophy, whose chief method is the analysis of the meaning of linguistic expressions.[21]

Actually the results mentioned above (in sec. 2.5), according to which even the objects of so-called inner perception involve a process of constitution, suggest that not only noematic phenomenology, but noetic phenomenology as well, is concerned with the analysis of certain intentional-objects-as-such, and is thus nothing but analysis of sense.

One is tempted to say that all phenomenology is somehow noematic phenomenology, that noetic phenomenology is merely the special case where the noema involved is the noema of inner perception. But Husserl did not use this way of speaking, and it would really be misleading to adopt it. For, clearly, the sense in which noetic phenomenology could be described as an analysis of the noema of inner perception is *not* the same as the sense in which noematic phenomenology can be described as a description of noemata, for example, of the noema of external perception; it is, rather, the sense in which noematic phenomenology could be described as including a description of *the noema of the noema* of external perception.[22] Furthermore, to regard noetic phenomenology as a form of noematic phenomenology would mean to apply the epoche not only with respect to the external objects but also with respect to consciousness itself. But Husserl only advocated a demundanization of our notion of consciousness, and he did not mean to exclude factual statements concerning the demundanized transcendental stream of consciousness which is immediately present to the phenomenologist.[23] (Of course factual statements are excluded from the *eidetic* part of phenomenology, but that is another matter.) If one would argue that the epoche had to be applied with respect to the noetic acts simply because our reflective knowledge of these acts is likewise always mediated by a noema, a similar argument could be made which would require an epoche also with respect to all the noemata themselves; thus nothing would remain outside the scope of the epoche, which would be absurd.

However, the claim that phenomenology as such is nothing but analysis of sense is nevertheless true, because all phenomenology can indeed be characterized as being concerned with the analysis of the *constitution* of sense, namely, with the correlation between noesis and noema.

6. Phenomenological Analysis as a Form of Explication

One form of meaning analysis, described by analytic philosophers and practiced both by them and scientists in general, is what is called *explication*, namely, the move from expressions of ordinary language to explicitly defined expressions of a technical language, id est, to expressions of a language with an explicit system of exact definitions.[24] It is illuminating, I think, to view the step from ordinary descriptions to the descriptions of transcendental phenomenology as such a step of explication, that is, as a step of translation from ordinary ways of speaking into the highly technical language of transcendental phenomenology. For instance, instead of saying "I am seeing a green tree" a transcendental phenomenologist might report "My intentional acts of visual perception are directed toward a constituted perceptual noema Green Tree."

This characterization of phenomenological analysis as a kind of explication is in agreement with Husserl's emphatic claim that phenomenology is a strict science. But the most interesting feature of this way of specifying what phenomenology is doing is that no mention of performing an epoche has to be made. From this point of view, transcendental phenomenology is concerned not with setting certain kinds of non-phenomenological knowledge aside but with translating *all* our knowledge claims into a most accurate scientific language.

This corresponds exactly to what we find Husserl saying when he stressed the distinctive advantage of the way into phenomenology through ontology.[25] As a matter of fact, Husserl had become increasingly dissatisfied with the Cartesian way (and also with the way through psychology). The main reason for his dissatisfaction had been precisely the fact that the epoche involved seemed to obscure the really universal scope of phenomenological analysis. Husserl discovered, on the other hand, that if one followed the way through ontology, nothing had to be bracketed or excluded from phenomenology. If one follows the way through ontology (which might also be called the Kantian way), one is led into transcendental phenomenology by the aim of explaining the categories and necessary truths of our conceptual schemes. According to Husserl, this aim can be achieved by making explicit the constituting activity that is involved in building up our knowledge. From this point of view, phenomenology leaves nothing out; rather, it broadens (adds a new dimension to) our knowledge. From the point of view of this third way, the transcendental phenomenological reduction, id est, the step which brings us into transcendental phenomenology, is not an act of epoche. Rather, it is an act of conversion, of changing from the natural view of the world (which according to Husserl can easily degenerate into a mistaken naturalistic view) to the more perfect and more comprehensive transcendental view of the world.

Of course it remains true that physics is not phenomenology, and thus it still makes sense to recommend an epoche, an explicit bracketing of the results of physics, but only as far as this can be a *safeguard* that prevents a naturalistic confusion between phenomenology (i.e., conceptual analysis) and a scientific investigation of mundane matters of fact. The epoche is no longer the first step in the phenomenological method; it is now merely a useful accessory device to preserve methodological purity (to prevent a *"metabasis,"* i.e., to prevent slipping into the category mistakes of naturalism).

7. Logical Explication and Phenomenological Explication

However, just as we have seen that the phenomenological epoche is not an ordinary epoche bracketing factual questions concerning an ordinary referent, but a more problematic metaphysical epoche bracketing factual questions concerning the metaphysical referent, we find that transcendental phenomenology is not concerned with an explication of the kind we are familiar with from science or from the constructional systems of the logicians, but with a more problematic kind of explication.

In an ordinary explication the meaning of the explicata is said to be more explicit because each term has been assigned its exact place in an explicitly stated system of definitions. But transcendental phenomenology has as yet no explicitly stated system of definitions; such a logical systematization of it is still a totally unrealized desideratum. But one might say that in phenomenological "explication" the meaning of the "explicata" is more explicit in another sense, namely in the sense that each intentional object, each ontic meaning, is assigned its exact place in the accurately described "system" of transcendental constitution.

Carnap once attempted to do logical explication and this kind of phenomenological "explication" simultaneously, when in his book *The Logical Structure of the World* (1928) he tried to sketch an all-comprehensive constructional system of definitions. He wanted to give, by the same stroke, an account of a possible route of transcendental constitution.[26] But it seems in principle impossible that the train of definitions of some constructional system could be an adequate representation of the progression of transcendental constitution. The point is that while transcendental constitution is said to start from the *unarticulated* stream of experience, every constructional system must start from an already articulated universe of discourse. Carnap's *Aufbau*, for instance, has a universe of discourse of so-called elementary experiences (i.e., momentary cross sections of the stream of experience).[27]

I do not want to claim that the study of constructional definitions is of no help toward an understanding of the processes of constitution. Quite the contrary. It would seem that constructional methods—like definition by abstraction based on an equivalence relation—*are* methods operative in constitution, namely at higher levels of constitution. And the processes at the lower, prepredicative levels of constitution seem to have some as yet not exactly specified analogy to the processes occurring at the higher levels.

8. Phenomenology and Cartesian Epistemology

Husserl had become increasingly dissatisfied with the Cartesian way into phenomenology. Does this mean that he came to reject Cartesian epistemology as misguided or even outright nonsensical? Some interpreters of Husserl seem to argue this, but it remains a fact that Husserl did not categorically dismiss the Cartesian way.[28] It seems, therefore, that his criticism of the Cartesian way was not that it was wrong but merely that in actual practice it is not very effective in achieving what it is designed to achieve (namely to introduce the uninitiated to phenomenology), since it can give the wrong impression that the scope of phenomenology is very limited.

The point which has to be stressed, I think, is that phenomenology as such is not the same as epistemology.[29] Epistemology is the discipline which seeks to *assess the value* of our knowledge claims, while phenomenology is primarily a *descriptive*, not an evaluative, discipline. The relation of transcendental phenomenology (which describes transcendental consciousness and its activities of constitution) to epistemology is similar to the relation of ordinary psychology to an ordinary assessment of the reliability of our mental capacities. One can therefore argue that the Cartesian way is unsatisfactory as an introduction to phenomenology precisely because it prematurely burdens the beginner with difficult epistemological distinctions (such as the distinction between appearance and reality) and limits him unnecessarily (i.e., for purely epistemological reasons) to a solipsistic starting point. The limitation to a solipsistic starting point is unnecessary for phenomenology, but it is essential for an epistemology in the spirit of Descartes—and as far as I know Husserl never doubted that for epistemology the Cartesian approach is the only appropriate one.

One can, however, raise the further question, whether in light of certain results of his phenomenological investigations Husserl *should* have rejected the Cartesian approach to epistemology, though as a matter of fact he never rejected it. This question is very difficult; it is none other than the question whether the contemporary objections against the so-called myth of the given have succeeded in demolishing beyond repair the Cartesian program for epistemology— whether they render the Cartesian program irrevocably obsolete. I do not pretend to be able to give a decisive answer to this difficult question, but I believe that more attention to the semantical distinction between sense and referent can contribute toward a much needed clarification of the issue.

The phenomenological results which I have in mind and which concur with analogous findings in contemporary analytic philosophy are the ones mentioned above (in sec. 2.5), according to which not only in *external* perception but also in so-called *inner* perception we are faced with an already constituted noematic object. Does this not show that the myth of the given—namely, the notion of an unmediated, "naked," immanent given which could serve as the apodictically given starting point of all knowledge—is untenable?

To clarify the issue I would like to draw attention to the following four points.

8.1. Sense can still be made of the claim that inner perception, in contrast to external perception, refers to a *directly present* object.

The fact that inner perception also involves an already constituted intentional object does not entail that the referent of inner perception is not directly present. If the intentional object in question is understood to be a noematic object which belongs on the level of sense, and if one understands that the referent is not hidden behind the sense as one *thing* may be hidden behind another *thing*, it is still possible to make sense of the claim that inner perception is "perceiving" a "directly present" referent. On the other hand, external perception is "less direct," not in the sense that its referent would be "invisible" but simply in the sense that its referent is separated from the perceiver by a spatial distance.

Of course, in light of the analyses of inner time consciousness the situation turns out to be more complex than it was thought to be at first. If inner perception is reflection involving memory, then "directly present" cannot mean "really immanent now" but must mean either "immanently remembered" or "immanently present in the specious present," where the specious present includes an immediate past which is still intuitively "present" (i.e., retained by so-called "horizontal retentions"), but is not really (*reell*) present, since strictly speaking it is already past.

8.2. The claim that the intentional object of external perception is constituted on the basis of immanent sensations is still meaningful.

Since in perception we do not have the kind of freedom with respect to the object which we have in imagination, therefore a special limiting factor must be present in perception. In the case of inner perception this limiting factor can be identified with the directly present immanent referent. But in external perception, too, there must be a limiting factor which is *immanent*, because an external object which is transcendent can only be known by a human knower if it causes an effect in the knower. Husserl calls the immanent limiting factor of external perception "sensations" (*Empfindungen*).

8.3. The claim that we are not only able to reflect on the sense (the noematic objects) of our acts but that we are furthermore capable of reflecting on the noetic acts and sensations themselves (that we can have an inner perception of our acts and sensations) is not *prima facie* meaningless.

8.4. One may furthermore claim that we have a *non*reflective consciousness of our acts and sensations.

Especially if it is assumed that the knower is essentially consciousness, namely, that the knower must be conscious in one sense or another of everything which is immanent, then nonreflective consciousness of acts and sensations must precede any reflective consciousness (i.e., any inner perception) of them. And it would seem that we can find such a nonreflective awareness in our actual experience. Roman Ingarden, for example, has described it as a conscious "living-through" (*Durchleben*), and J.-P. Sartre too has given an account of unreflected consciousness (*la conscience irréfléchie*).[30] Husserl's descriptions of the sensations (*Empfindungen*) as experiences (*Erlebnisse*) which are a kind of nonintentional feelings (*nichtintentionale Gefühle*) also belong in this context.[31] Such a nonreflective living-through, however, though it is a form of consciousness, is *unlike* a perception, precisely because it involves no duality of perceiving act and perceived object. Such a pure "living present" includes no objectification, namely, no articulation, and therefore it is not knowledge in the proper sense of the word.

However, even to concede these four claims is not sufficient to remove the doubts concerning the Cartesian program for epistemology. Does the fact that the ultimate "given," namely the living present, is either merely lived through and thus not known in the proper sense of the word, or else is known, but only in reflection, when it is no longer really present, not cause the Cartesian program to collapse? For in neither of the two alternatives is the "given" given in the form of absolutely certain knowledge, and therefore there is no absolutely certain knowledge to start from.

This is, in my opinion, the heart of the question.

On the one hand, the Cartesian program does not seem to be totally misguided, because even if there is no absolutely certain knowledge there is nevertheless a genuine sense in which knowledge of what is immanent *does* have an epistemological priority, namely, is *in a certain respect* more certain than knowledge of what is transcendent. Knowledge of what is transcendent does in fact genetically presuppose (is in fact built on) an awareness of what is immanent, namely, is in fact based on a prereflectively lived-through living present of the really real stream of consciousness. On the other hand, however, it is also true that in another respect knowledge of what is transcendent is more certain than knowledge of what is immanent, since living-through is not knowing, and reflective inner perception—even if there is such a thing—is less reliable because it requires us to take an attitude which is much less natural for us than the attitude of external perception. Furthermore, intersubjective discussions about the public referents of external perception are much easier than a comparing of notes which describe the private referents of inner perception.

I am therefore inclined to think that a modified form of the Cartesian program has to be worked out, where the simplistic notion of the *absolute* certainty of inner experience is abandoned but where the epistemological importance of inner experience, with its specific and irreplaceable kind of certainty, is nevertheless recognized. It may therefore still be correct to require that the process of epistemological justification start from the solipsistic starting point of the living present of consciousness. But then the specific weakness of inner experience must also be taken into account; namely, one must check the account based on inner experience and see that it harmonizes with the convictions based on external perception. That is to say, one must strengthen the epistemological justification by making appropriate use of the specific kinds of certainty which are available in each type of experience.

NOTES

1. Cf. I. Kern, *Husserl und Kant*, *Phaenomenologica*, vol. 16 (The Hague: Nijhoff, 1964); R. O. Elveton, ed., "Introduction," in *The Phenomenology of Husserl: Selected Critical Readings* (Chicago: Quadrangle Books, 1970).

2. Cf. my paper "Husserl on Pictures and Intentional Objects," *Review of Metaphysics*, 26 (1973): 670-80.

3. E. Husserl, *Logische Untersuchungen* (1st ed.; Halle, 1901), 2: 11-12, 17, 387.

4. Cf. Kern, *Husserl und Kant*, pp. 356f.

5. Cf. E. Husserl, *Die Idee der Phänomenologie*, *Husserliana*, 2 (2nd ed.; The Hague: Nijhoff, 1958), p. 50.

6. E. Husserl, "Psychologische Studien zur elementaren Logik," *Philosophische Monatshefte* (Berlin), 30 (1894): 159-91, and Husserl's unpublished review of K. Twardowski's *Zur Lehre vom Inhalt und Gegenstand der Vorstellungen* (Vienna, 1894).

7. E. Husserl, *Zur Phänomenologie des inneren Zeitbewusstseins* (1893-1917), *Husserliana*, 10 (The Hague: Nijhoff, 1966), pp. 31f. and 269f. ("Zur Auflösung des Schemas Auffassungsinhalt-Auffassung").

8. I owe this information to Professor Spiegelberg. Cf. also H. Spiegelberg, *The Phenomenological Movement* (2nd ed.; The Hague: Nijhoff, 1965), p. 134; and P. J. Bossert, "The Origins and Early Development of Edmund Husserl's Method of Phenomenological Reduction," Ph.D. diss., Washington University, St. Louis (1973), pp. 98f., 128.

9. E. Husserl, *Ideas* (New York: Collier Books, 1962), sec. 49. Cf. also idem, *The Crisis of European Sciences and Transcendental Phenomenology* (Evanston: Northwestern University Press, 1970), sec. 40: "The difficulties surrounding the genuine sense of performing the total *epoche*. The temptation to misconstrue it as a withholding of all individual validities, carried out step by step."

10. Cf. the unpublished lecture notes "Einführung in die Logik und Erkenntniskritik," esp. MS F I 10 fol. 59b, for what is probably the first occurrence of *epoche* (see Bossert, op. cit, p. 128, who relies on E. Marbach), and MS F I 10 fol. 76a for the first discussion of the phenomenological reduction (see U. Claesges, "Einleitung," in E. Husserl, *Ding und Raum. Vorlesungen 1907*, *Husserliana*, 16 [The Hague: Nijhoff, 1973], pp. xiv-xv).

Excerpts from these lecture notes are published in E. Marbach, "Ichlose Phänomenologie bei Husserl," *Tijdschrift voor Filosofie*, 35 (1973): 518-559, and in E. Marbach, *Das Problem des Ich in der Phänomenologie Husserls*, *Phaenomenologica*, vol. 59 (The Hague: Nijhoff, 1974). On the origin of the reduction see also K. Schuhmann, *Die Dialekitk der Phänomenologie*, *Phaenomenologica*, vols. 56 and 57 (The Hague: Nijhoff, 1973).

11. In the winter of 1906/7 Husserl had his second exchange of letters with Frege, in which Frege insisted that logic deals with objective propositions (*Gedanken*). The letters are dated Oct. 30/Nov. 1, 1906, Frege to Husserl; Nov. 16, 1906, Husserl to Frege (this letter is lost); Dec. 9, 1906, Frege to Husserl. The first exchange of letters had taken place in 1891, after the publication of Husserl's *Philosophie der Arithmetik*.

12. MS F I 5.

13. Cf. D. Føllesdal, "Husserl's Notion of Noema," *Journal of Philosophy*, 66 (1969): 680-87.

14. MS F I 5 fol. 29b *f*.

15. Admittedly there is also the phenomenon of the "opacity" of the sense; cf. Quine's notion of "referential opacity" in *Word and Object* (Cambridge: M.I.T. Press, 1960), sec. 30. But to grant this opacity is not the same as to accept the Kantian notion of an unknowable thing-in-itself.

16. Cf. my paper "The World as Noema and as Referent," *Journal of the British Society for Phenomenology*, 3 (1972): 15-26.

17. Cf. the chart in my paper (op. cit., p. 16). There I had introduced for the first time the distinction between ordinary referents and metaphysical referents (referents *L* and referents *P*). But the specific problem of the analogy between ordinary semantics and metaphysical semantics had not been brought out, as is shown by the fact that in that chart, instead of the metaphysical referent being moved down to a fourth level, the ordinary referents are moved up one level. My distinction between ordinary noema and metaphysical noema has some similarity with Eugen Fink's distinction between the psychological and the transcendental noema; but Fink rejects the analogy between ordinary semantics and metaphysical semantics and claims explicitly that "the transcendental noema cannot refer to a being beyond"; that is, he does not accept the notion of a metaphysical referent. Cf. E. Fink,

"Die phänomenologische Philosophie Edmund Husserls in der gegenwärtigen Kritik," *Kantstudien*, 38 (1933): 319-83, esp. 364-65; English tr. in Elveton, ed., *The Phenomenology of Husserl*, pp. 73-147, esp. 123-25.

18. Cf. R. Ingarden, *The Literary Work of Art* (Evanston: Northwestern University Press, 1973), p. 159, wherein the author speaks of "the structure of the concreteness."

19. Husserl once called the reflection on the sense *"Be-sinnung,"* taking advantage of the etymology of this German word for contemplation. Cf. MS B III 12 IX fol. 178b from Oct. 22, 1908.

20. Compare this with Sellars' "Jonesean myth," according to which internal mental episodes are described in terms taken from our talk about external speech. W. Sellars, *Science, Perception and Reality* (London: Routledge, 1963), pp. 186ff.

21. Paul Ricoeur—in the paper "Phénomenologie du vouloir et approche par le langage ordinaire," read at the International Congress "Die Münchener Phänomenologie" in Munich (Apr. 13-18, 1971)—has also defended the claim that with the notion of the noema Husserl had reached the level of meaning, of what can be said, which is the starting point of analytic philosophy.

22. Husserl accepted, like Frege, that there are infinite hierarchies of sense: sense had in referring to this sense, sense had in referring to the sense had in referring to this sense, etc. Cf. the MSS F I 5 fol. 34b (1908), B III 12 fol. 118-21 (1917/18), B III 12 fol. 106b (1927), and E. Husserl, *Formale und transzendentale Logik* (Halle: M. Niemeyer, 1929), sec. 49.

23. Cf. E. Marbach, "Ichlose Phänomenologie bei Husserl," *Tijdschrift voor Filosofie*, 35 (1973): 546, wherein the author insists that the starting point of pure phenomenology is "transzendental-solipsistisch."

24. Cf. R. Carnap, *Logical Foundations of Probability* (Chicago: University of Chicago Press, 1950 [1st ed.], 1962 [2d ed.]), chap. 1. It is possible that Carnap took the words 'explication' and 'explicatum' from Husserl: cf. Husserl, *Formale und transzendentale Logik* (Halle: M. Niemeyer, 1929), pp. 50-51, and see also the entry "Explication" by Dorion Cairns in D. D. Runes, *Dictionary of Philosophy* (New York: Philosophical Library, 1942). But Carnap mentions also Kant and C. H. Langford; Kant speaks of the explication of concepts in the *Critique of Pure Reason* B 755-B 760. In the *Cartesian Meditations* ([3rd impr.; The Hague: Nijhoff, 1969]; German original: *Husserliana*, 1 [2d ed.; The Hague: Nijhoff, 1963] Husserl mentions *two* kinds of explication: (1) "Genuine phenomenological explication of one's own 'ego cogito' as 'transcendental idealism'" (title of sec. 41, p. 83; German text, p. 116: *"Die phänomenologische Selbstauslegung des 'ego cogito' als 'transzendentaler Idealismus'"*); (2) "Ontological explication" (in the title of sec. 59, p. 136; German text, p. 163: *"ontologische Explikation"*) which is characterized as "discovery of the apriori belonging to this world's universality" (p. 137, German text: *"die Herausstellung des zur Universalität < der realen Welt, d.h. der allgemeinen*

faktischen Struktur der gegebenen objektiven Welt, > gehörigen Apriori") and of which Husserl affirms that it is "not philosophical in the final sense" (*nicht im Endsinn philosophisch*) (ibid.). Thus Husserl distinguishes here precisely between transcendental phenomenological analysis understood as explication (*Auslegung*) on the one hand, and ontological analysis in the usual sense, also understood as explication (*Explikation, Herausstellung*), on the other hand.

25. Cf. Kern, *Husserl und Kant*, pp. 202f., 219f., 233 f.

26. R. Carnap, *Der logische Aufbau der Welt* (2d ed.; Hamburg: F. Meiner, 1961); English tr. in University of California Press (Berkeley) ed. (1967). Note that Carnap's word for "constructional system" was the German word *Konstitutionssystem*, and cf. also the references to Husserl and to other nonpositivistic philosophers.

27. Cf. to this N. Goodman, The *Structure of Appearance* (2d ed.; Indianapolis: Bobbs-Merrill, 1966), p. 155: "Carnap seems to hold that experience is originally given in a single stream and that lesser elements are known only through subsequent analysis. Others might argue that experience is no more given in one big lump than it is given in very minute particles, and that the single stream is as much the product of an artificial synthesis as the minimal particles are the products of an analysis. To me the debate seems a futile one, for I do not know how one would go about determining what are the originally given lumps." In my opinion it is important to realize that the noetic stream of experience *in itself* is not an ordinary referent but a metaphysical referent. As such it is neither articulated as one thing nor articulated as many things. This, of course, does not mean that it is chaotic; it must rather be said to have a "preconceptual determinateness" (cf. sec. 4 above).

28. Cf. Kern, *Husserl und Kant*, p. 209.

29. Concerning the proper place of epistemology, see R. Ingarden, *Über die Stellung der Erkenntnistheorie im System der Philosophie* (Halle: Karras, Kröber & Nietschmann, 1925). Cf. my paper "Zum Lebenswerk von Roman Ingarden: Ontologie, Erkenntnistheorie und Metaphysik" in H. Kuhn, E. Avé-Lallemant, and R. Gladiator, eds., *Die Münchener Phänomenologie, Vorträge des Internationalen Kongresses in München 13.-18. April 1971, Phaenomenologica* (The Hague: Nijhoff, [in print·).

30. R. Ingarden, "Ueber die Gefahr einer Petitio Principii in der Erkenntnistheorie," *Jahrbuch für Philosophie und phänomenologische Forschung*, 4 (1921): 545-68; J.-P. Sartre, "La transcendance de l'ego," *Recherches Philosophiques*, 6 (1936): 85-123. Cf. also Sellars' agreement with Chisholm concerning "the privileged access each of us has to his own thoughts." See "The Chisholm-Sellars Correspondence on Intentionality," reprinted in A. Marras, ed., *Intentionality, Mind and Language* (Urbana: University of Illinois Press, 1972), pp. 197-248, esp. 217.

31. Cf. E. Husserl, *Logical Investigations* (New York: Humanities Press, 1970), 2:572.

Phenomenology and Metaphilosophy

PETER MC CORMICK

Concluding his much remarked essay "Metaphilosophical Difficulties of Linguistic Philosophy," Richard Rorty sets out six different possibilities for the future of philosophy.[1] Each position is associated with one of the following: Husserl, Heidegger, Waismann, Wittgenstein, Austin, and Strawson. Besides the intrinsic attraction of such a general view in the hands of a meticulous philosopher like Rorty, what insists on immediate attention is just how these positions are to be differentiated. We discover that, before they are distinguished individually, the six positions can initially be grouped into three groups: (1) Husserl, (2) Heidegger, and (3) Waismann, Wittgenstein, Austin, and Strawson. And there are three groups, rather than two, or four, or whatever number, because these positions are finally to be distinguished in terms of only two programmatic issues. Thus (3) accepts both issues, (2) rejects both, and (1) accepts the first while rejecting the second.

What are these handy issues? The first I will call, somewhat artificially, the methodological issue and the second the criteriological issue. Rorty formulates the first, methodological nominalism, as "the view that all the questions which philosophers have asked about concepts, subsistent universals, or 'natures' which (a) cannot be answered by empirical inquiry concerning the behaviour or properties of particulars subsumed under such concepts, universals, or natures, and which (b) can be answered in *some* way,

can be answered by our asking questions about the use of linguistic expressions, and in no other way."[2] And the second issue, the criteriological one, can be described as the view that "clear-cut criteria of agreement about the truth of philosophical theses" must be demanded.[3] Consequently, positions (3) to (6) agree on both the methodological and the criteriological issues, whereas Heidegger rejects both issues while Husserl rejects the first and agrees with the second.

In this paper I wish to investigate some of the illustration and nuance which this summary suggestion requires, and if possible to reinterpret the second issue. I shall restrict myself here, however, to a discussion of Husserl and Heidegger only, leaving Rorty's third group for another occasion. It will prove useful to begin with some terminological clarifications about the words in my title, specifically the operative uses these words will have in the paper. Then I will consider an instance of both the characteristic kind of claim Heidegger is wont to make and the questions this kind of claim can easily be taken to generate. A similar illustration of a characteristic kind of claim that Husserl makes will occupy us at shorter length in section 3. With examples before us, we may then return to our starting point to reconsider the criteriological issue in more detail. I will suggest that this issue be construed more generally as a metaphilosophical one.

The broader concerns of this paper can

be put as a question: Can a particular phenomenological claim about perceptual objects, or about mental objects, or whatever, be criticized from a non-phenomenological viewpoint? It depends. If the claim is inside a set of paradigmatic assumptions about such things as the role of argument in philosophy, the nature of logic, concepts, and adequate evidence, then yes; if not, then no. What is central here is not whether a particular phenomenological claim is propounded inside a set of methodological assumptions. Rather, the corrigibility of the claim is a function of particular metaphilosophical views. Metaphilosophy, not methodology, determines the answer to the question.

1. Terms

I begin by clarifying the sense of both metaphilosophy and phenomenology that will be operative in this paper.

In the first place, we need some words about "metaphilosophy." The term 'metaphilosophy' is not synonymous with 'metatheory' in the sense in which the philosophy of science, or the philosophy of history, or the philosophy of law is a metatheory of science, or history, or law. Thinking about a metaphilosophical issue is not the same thing as thinking about some area of discourse or inquiry, but critically thinking within a particular area in a particular way.[4] Thus, as Lazerowitz first used the term in 1940, 'metaphilosophy' refers unambiguously, as he puts it, "to a special kind of investigation which Wittgenstein has described as one of the 'heirs' of philosophy."[5] The broad sense of the term today, Lazerowitz says, comes to construing 'metaphilosophy' as "the investigation of the nature of philosophy, with the central aim of arriving at a satisfactory explanation of the absence of uncontested philosophical claims and arguments."[6]

Now this account of metaphilosophy can quickly provoke objections, for many philosophers would want to maintain that investigating such general questions as "the nature of philosophy" seems pointless outside the context of quite particular, detailed work on quite specific philosophical problems. They might concede that determining just what is or is not to count as a philosophical problem is a question not without interest. But they would go on to insist that such a question most often comes into clearer focus when it is postponed at the outset of some particular inquiry. The point they would make, then, is not so much that metaphilosophy is too general to be philosophically rewarding. Rather, the point is that whatever interesting metaphilosophical issues there may be are interesting to the degree that they arise from the careful expression of philosophical particulars and then are reinserted into that context. In a word, metaphilosophy is not a separate specialization inside the domain of philosophy in the way that philosophy of history or epistemology are; rather, metaphilosophical issues are issues that can arise inside any philosophical specialization.

This qualification, which many would like to put on Lazerowitz's view of metaphilosophy, comes out fairly clearly in a characterization Husserl gave of his work in his foreword to the second edition of *Logical Investigations* in 1913. "For if these Investigations are to prove helpful to those interested in phenomenology," he writes, "this will be because they do not offer us a mere programme (certainly not one of the high-flying sort which so encumber philosophy), but that they are attempts at genuinely executed fundamental work in the immediately envisaged and seized things themselves. Even where they proceed critically, they do not lose themselves in discussions of standpoint, but rather leave the last word to the things themselves, and to one's work upon such things."[7]

We need not quarrel immediately, then, with talk of metaphilosophy if we take such qualifications into account. Where the quarrel might come, however, is in dealing with the second part of Lazerowitz's description, for it may not seem that once a philosophical claim is adequately justified with arguments we need do anything more than get on with looking at still further claims. But before we go on with that job, interesting issues may be involved in the reasons for concluding that the first claim is now viewed as uncontested. In other words, the paradigms for philosophical success may sometimes require examination, even in those cases where the paradigms seemed to have served us well by justifying our satisfaction with the way a particular claim has held up under scrutiny. Things are murky here. We shall need to come back to the matter later, when several examples will be at our disposal. In the meantime we may say that 'metaphilosophy,' as I shall be using the term, refers mainly to examining how criteria for the successful resolution of philosophical problems are to be appraised.

Now we need to specify just how the term 'phenomenology' will be used.

The usual problems with defining phenomenology are familiar to historians who wrestle with characterizing any large and loosely articulated group. We do not need to rehearse the various philosophical and nonphilosophical uses of the word 'phenomenology' before Husserl because this has already been done more than once. It will prove useful, however, to recall the strategy Spiegelberg has adapted to differentiate various senses of the word.[8]

Between 1913 and 1930, as is well known, Husserl and associates such as Geiger, Pfänder, Reinach, Scheler, Heidegger, and Becker edited the *Jahrbuch für Philosophie und Phänomenologische Forschung*. The *Jahrbuch* contained a statement of principle which Spiegelberg thinks was drafted by Husserl himself.[9] Several sentences in that statement deserve citing anew: "What unites [the editors] is the common conviction that it is only by a return to the primary sources of direct intuition and to insights into essential structures derived from them that we shall be able to put to use the great tra-

ditions of philosophy with their concepts and problems; and thus shall we be in a position to clarify such concepts intuitively, to restate the problems on an intuitive basis, and thus, eventually, to solve them, at least in principle."[10]

On the basis of this programmatic statement, Spiegelberg distinguishes four senses of phenomenology: the widest, the broad, the strict, and the strictest. The first includes those who accept the program without identifying themselves with the movement. The second or broad sense includes those who both accept the program and identify themselves with the movement. The third includes those in the broad sense plus those who would add a further feature to the program, namely, the study of the ways in which objects appear. And, finally, the fourth adds to the third sense still another feature, namely, the use of the phenomenological reduction to study the way the appearances of objects constitute themselves.

Now this description is not without difficulties. We are quite hesitant about saying that we understand the four features referred to here: direct intuition, essences, modes of appearance, reduction and constitution. These features mix traditional concepts which, however fruitful, are notoriously ambiguous (intuition and essences) with technical concepts that are operative in phenomenology alone (modes and reduction and constitution). It is of course precisely the ambiguity of the first set of concepts which allows different philosophers to commit themselves to a common program, while the tentative character of the second set allows them to call into question at least some of the conclusions their colleagues might wish to force on them.

For our purposes here, however, we do not need to sort through the various conceptual puzzles this program can easily seem to suggest. We need simply to specify the relevant sense of 'phenomenology' for what is to follow. Accordingly, we may say that 'phenomenology', as I shall be using the term, refers mainly to phenomenology in the third and strict sense—the view, that is, which embraces

(a) direct intuition, (b) essential features, and (c) modes of the appearance of objects. This view will include both Husserl and Heidegger, who are our immediate concern.

With these terminological questions clarified at least in a provisional way, I turn to a closer look at a characteristic Heideggerean claim. My concern will be to see in detail to what degree we can say that Heidegger rejects both methodological nominalism and the need for consensus about criteria for resolving philosophical problems.

2. Heidegger on Language

The last chapter of Heidegger's book *On the Way to Language* represents his most sustained meditation on language.[11] Before that meditation is focused on what I take to be the central claim in Heidegger's theory of language, a summary of that meditation in Heidegger's register should illustrate just what kinds of problems appraising Heidegger's central claim involves.

In this chapter, "The Way to Language" (hereafter "WL"), 'language' refers to speaking. Speaking, Heidegger maintains, is, above all, a texture of relationships, a self-recoiling matrix, a circle which moves in a definite direction. To the extent that we actively engage ourselves in this texture, which already necessarily implicates our speaking, the character and range of this self-recoiling and circular movement of speaking can be experienced from speaking itself.

The essence of language is the mode in which speaking exists. In its totality, the linguistic essence is what Heidegger calls "utterance" [*Sage*]. Utterance is saying when saying makes something manifest. Moreover, utterance is what lets us arrive at the essence of language precisely as language and not at anything other than language. Utterance is where speaking has its origin. Language, as it were, comes to pass in persons' speaking.

What comes to pass preeminently is what Heidegger calls the "event" [*Ereignis*]. The event is experienced in the man-

ifestation of utterance as what grants something. The event gathers the design of utterance and enfolds it in the articulativeness of a manifold manifestation. The essence of speaking as manifesting utterance reposes in the event. Hence the event is what determines the specificity of speaking; utterance is merely the manner in which the event speaks. But the unity of the linguistic essence, that is, utterance as the mode of the event, cannot be apprehended in propositions but only through a silence which is silent even about itself.

Finally, Heidegger holds that the classic theory of language develops into the theory of speaking as a relation between signifying and designating. From Aristotle through the Hellenistic time into the Stoic ascendancy, the signification of what manifests itself is transformed into its designation. But all signification finally stems from a manifestation. And it is this manifestation of utterance in the speaking of language which is both the essence of speaking as such and the coming to pass of that event in which the event reposes.

Now even when we reinsert these abbreviated remarks into their context an almost unending series of problems remains. For the moment I want to call attention to two kinds of difficulty only.

The first is terminological. When understanding first breaks down, one might suspect that Heidegger is using his terms in an unusual but nevertheless restricted way. But an attempt to use Heidegger's glosses of his own terms does not yield much clarity.[12] Rather, implicit definition simply compounds the initial difficulty. For where at first the sense of several items is confusing, implicit definition yields only additional items which are also confusing. What I want to indicate, then, by referring to the vagueness of some of Heidegger's terms in "WL" is not the fact that he uses words in unusual senses but that he does not enable us to determine just how these unusual senses are to be taken. This is one kind of difficulty.

There is another. Even when the reader

of "WL" decides that it is not unreason-able for a thinker to leave the unusual sense of words undetermined, he discovers that Heidegger justifies his claims in "WL" unsatisfactorily. Despite a reflective style which prefers the juxtaposition of various insights to their formal articulation, we can notice that Heidegger in some sense does argue various claims. The difficulty, then, is not the lack of argument. What is distracting is that some of these arguments would seem to involve both logical and factual error: conclusions do not always necessarily follow from premises, and premises are sometimes demonstrably false. More fundamentally, the problem is one of evidence since, even were Heidegger to present valid arguments consisting of true premises, the evidence for these premises would remain just as indispensable as before the revisions were undertaken. And what is problematic about this evidence is precisely its availability to other thinkers than Heidegger. What I want to indicate, then, by referring to the unsatisfactoriness of many of Heidegger's arguments in "WL" is not the fact that these arguments are inconclusive and invalid but that the evidence for some of their premises does not appear to be as manifest as Heidegger would have us believe. This is another kind of difficulty.

This twofold difficulty in reading "WL" is, of course, a difficulty for a certain kind of reader only. Were someone to decide that inconsistency, *petitio principii*, and non-sequiturs were not, at least in appraising Heideggerean claims, critical matters, then presumably he might proceed to make a more or less happy synthesis for himself of the numerous philosophically interesting remarks Heidegger makes. This, in fact, is what many have done. But someone else might want to suggest that until we ask just why our twofold difficulty with Heidegger's doctrine is not a critical matter, we beg the question whether there are any philosophically interesting remarks in that doctrine at all. For it is arguable that what makes a remark interesting precisely as philosophical is its availability to

more than one thinker. Whatever might be available to no other thinker than oneself, he might continue, surely can be nothing more than incommunicable. And the incommunicable is of philosophical interest to the degree that the reasons for its being incommunicable can themselves be communicated. Yet what makes these reasons communicable is our capacity to understand how the cardinal terms are limited and what is to count for or against the arguments these terms are used to formulate. Unless we can make it clear just why difficulties with Heidegger's terms and arguments are not critical matters, the question whether Heidegger's claims about speaking, nonobjectifying or otherwise, are of philosophical interest remains an open one.

The point of these general remarks can be seen in detail if we look at what I will take for now as a characteristic statement of Heidegger's central claim about speaking.

In order to reflect on the linguistic essence (*Sprachwesen*), to utter after (*nachsagen*) the linguistic essence what is its own, a transformation (*Wandel*) of language is required, a transformation which we can neither force nor discover. The creation of newly formed words and phrases does not yield the transformation. It touches on our relationship to language. This relationship is determined in accordance with the *Geschick* [with what comes to pass of being in each historical age], and in accordance with whether and how we are held in this relationship by the linguistic essence as the primitive tidings (*Ur-Kunde*) of the appropriating event (*Ereignis*). For the event—eventualizing, enduring, and retaining—is the relationship of all relationships. Therefore our uttering as an answering remains always in the mode of a relationship of relations. The coming into relation (*Ver-hältnis*) is thought here always in terms of the appropriating event and is no longer represented in the form of a mere relation (*Beziehung*). Our relationship (*Verhältnis*) to language is determined in terms of the manner according to which we belong in the appropriating event as the needed ones (*Gebrauchten*).[13]

The kinds of difficulty I have been trying to describe are evident in the first sentence of this text. It is clear that

Heidegger is using the term '*Sprachwesen*' in an unusual sense because his appositional remark, "to utter after the linguistic essence what is its own," however unusual in itself, suggests that the linguistic essence speaks. And yet, although we are not accustomed to refer to the essence of language as something that speaks, and despite a number of apparently related contexts in *On the Way to Language* where the same term occurs, Heidegger in fact nowhere indicates clearly how this unfamiliar sense of essence is to be taken. It is clear, however, that Heidegger is making a claim in this sentence when he writes that "a transformation of language is required." And yet when Heidegger's entire essay is scrutinized, when *On the Way* as a whole is studied thoroughly— even when the central problems of Heidegger's entire work are inventoried—nowhere is a satisfactory argument for this claim to be found.

Nevertheless, from what Heidegger tells us about this change we might presumably construct some kind of argument why such a transformation is needed. In this case we might argue something like this:

1. Man's relationship to language (speaking) is determined by man's relation to the manifestation of being.
2. But the manifestation of being changes from one age to another.
3. Man's relation to language (speaking) must also change from one age to another.

Now however many premises we may want to add to such a construction, the main point that needs making is that every formulation of such an argument remains at least one remove from Heidegger's text because Heidegger presents no argument of his own. A second point is that even a quite simple interpretation, such as the one above, can avoid neither terminological nor logical difficulties. A final point is that even when an argument for Heidegger's claim is extrapolated, and even could terminological

difficulties be circumvented, such extrapolation remains inconclusive. This inconclusiveness is the case not because of formal difficulties but because the evidence for the truth of Heidegger's premises seems generally unavailable.

To summarize what we have seen in Heidegger's case, we can say (1) Heidegger rejects methodological nominalism and (2) he rejects the criteriological issue. As to the first point, we need to note that Heidegger's question about language is a question about essence and hence a question which must come within the purview of the methodological nominalist. However, Heidegger's question is not an empirical one, to be turned over to the sciences. Nor is it a question about the ways we use words to talk about language. As to the second point, Heidegger rejects the criteriological issue in the sense that he does not demand clear-cut criteria for the resolution or even reformulation of philosophical problems. Nor, of course, does Heidegger demand any procedures for revealing decisions about the nature of such criteria nor for resolving disputes about such matters.

We need now to look at Husserl in the same light in which we have just considered Heidegger. Just as with Heidegger, so now with Husserl: I want to select a representative moment in Husserl's philosophy for closer inspection in light of our interest to illustrate and later to redefine the contrast between phenomenology and analytic philosophy.

3. Husserl on Psychologism

In May of 1900, just several weeks before Husserl published the first volume of *Logical Investigations*, he delivered a lecture at the University of Halle titled "On the Psychological Grounding of Logic." The topic of course was central to the whole series of concerns which had preoccupied him since Frege's review in 1893 of the first volume of *Philosophy of Arithmetic* (1891).[14] Moreover, the topic was to continue to preoccupy him through the successive editions of *Logical Investigations* into his mature work,

Formal and Transcendental Logic
(1927), and even to the time of his death,
as is evidenced by his posthumous *Experience and Judgement* (1939). What
makes this paper from 1900 of particular
interest for our purposes, however, is the
cogent and succinct summary of its contents, which was discovered and published in 1959.[15] Since the materials are
both centrally important to an abiding
theme in Husserl's work and are only just
now available in English, I don't hesitate
to cite them at length.[16] Here is a characteristic passage:

The following thesis characterizes
psychologism: the theoretical foundations of
logic lie in psychology. For it is unquestionable, so the argument goes, that the rules of
knowledge, as a psychological function, are to
be grounded only through the psychology of
knowledge..... If we concede the unquestionableness not of this argument but of the
proposition that a technique of knowing must
be dependent on a psychology of knowledge,
this in no way proves that all the theoretical
foundations of logic, above all the essential
ones, lie in psychology. The possibility remains open that perhaps yet another discipline
contributes to the grounding of logic, indeed in
a far more significant way insofar as out of it
springs the logical norms taken in a strict
sense, whose a priori character, moreover,
appears incompatible with origin from an empirical discipline. And here would be the place
for the historically controversial 'formal' and
'pure' logic which Kant and Herbart must
have had in mind when they straightway denied the dependence of logic on every other
discipline.[17]

Now this passage has a large context
which, as in the case of Heidegger, would
require careful examination if we were to
get to the bottom of the claims Husserl is
making here. Moreover, this passage is
not a series of isolated remarks which find
no echo in other parts of Husserl's philosophy as a whole. These other places
where Husserl discusses his views on
psychologism would also demand
analysis were we to situate the present
text in an entirely satisfactory way.[18]

Regardless of these more thorough attempts to understand the position Husserl is expressing here, at least several
points are in evidence. To begin with, we
should notice that Husserl is concerned
with a series of questions about the nature
of logic and the essence of logical laws.
The intitial point, then, is that here too the
methodological nominalist would be expected to want his say, just as in the case
of Heidegger's reflecting on the essence
of language. The second point that requires notice is the fact that this passage,
unlike the Heideggerean one, seems to
assume at least some clear-cut criteria for
solving philosophical problems like those
of logical psychologism. These criteria
are certainly not explicit in this text; but
the fact is that Husserl repeatedly formulates his view in terms of a particular argument whose validity or invalidity is
clearly open for inspection. So just as the
methodological issue is raised in this text,
we can also say the criteriological issue is
also in evidence here. We need, however,
to spell these points out.

On the question of methodological
nominalism, it is important to notice that
Husserl does not necessarily exclude any
scientific treatment of the nature of logical laws. What is at issue for Husserl,
rather, is whether any empirical treatment of these laws can be adequate. In
other words, Husserl wants to assume the
propriety of a distinction between empirical sciences and a priori sciences. The
former are to be excluded from consideration because of the a priori character of
logical laws. Only an a priori science,
therefore, will be adequate for dealing
with the nature of a priori laws. Whether
there is such a discipline as an a priori
science, or whether the concept itself of
an a priori science makes sense are questions he holds open here and considers in
detail only later, particularly in the early
chapter of the Prolegomena to his *Logical
Investigations*. The only point we need to
make here then is that Husserl does not
hand over questions about the nature of
logical laws to the empirical sciences because such sciences cannot address
themselves to the a priori character of
these laws. Nor does Husserl claim that
such questions are to be handled by concerning ourselves with the way we talk

about such laws. Rather, Husserl will later, in the *Logical Investigations* and elsewhere, insist on the effectiveness of an intentional analysis of the nature of logical laws. And he will couple this analysis to the idea of an a priori science which he will later come to call phenomenology. His position seems clear enough in this text, for the implications plainly suggest that neither the uses of language nor the procedures of the empirical sciences can successfully deal with questions about natures and essences. Husserl shares this view with Heidegger.

The second issue, the criteriological one, also requires more discussion. In contrast with Heidegger, Husserl in this passage shows his characteristic attentiveness to both terms and arguments. Thus he is careful to offer not so much a definition of psychologism as a brief and clear description of the psychologistic view. Moreover, where Husserl thinks it necessary to introduce unfamiliar terms, as when he refers to a "formal" or a "pure" logic, he calls attention to the fact that the terms are unusual by typographic means and then suggests historical parallels (Kant and Herbart) for the way in which he wishes to employ these unfamiliar terms. (In other passages the terms are in fact defined.) So when I say that Husserl is careful about his terms I mean that he both describes the meaning of the central terms in his arguments and qualifies the meaning of any unfamiliar terms he wishes to introduce into his argument.

This characteristic carefulness about terms suggests not so much that Husserl demands clear-cut criteria for the solution of philosophical problems, but that he makes it possible for other philosophers to follow his arguments with an eye toward their appraisal.

Also in contrast with Heidegger's characteristic practice is Husserl's attentiveness to argument. Again, what needs underlining is not that Husserl argues and Heidegger does not. This charge is usually false, and even when it is true the point is frequently irrelevant in light of the different purposes each author has.

Rather, the contrast to be drawn is between the way Husserl sets his argument up as opposed to Heidegger's way. In Heidegger's case, whether the conclusion follows from the premises is usually almost impossible to tell because the evidence for the truth of the premises seems accessible to no one but Heidegger himself. In Husserl's case, although the later practice of the reduction and imaginative variations will put an almost unbearable weight on too undifferentiated a concept of intuition, at least in his early work (particularly on psychologism) we are able to disagree with Husserl. We are able to ask, for example, whether Husserl is correct when he claims that "the essential foundations of logic lie in psychology" does not follow from "a technique of knowing must be dependent on a psychology of knowing." When I say, then, that Husserl is characteristically attentive to argument I mean that he orders his views in such a way that we are able to get on with the job of appraising the truth or falsity of these views. This characteristic carefulness about argument again suggests that Husserl makes it possible for philosophers to disagree with his views on other than simply intuitive grounds.

4. Phenomenology and Linguistic Analysis

Suppose, reconsidering the two issues under consideration here, we try to generalize the specific features we have turned up in examining a characteristic kind of statement from both Husserl and Heidegger. We recall that these features, nominalism and demand for criteria, can make difficulties for a certain kind of reader. What kind of reader? Call him, to continue Austin's interesting provocation, a "linguistic phenomenologist." And imagine him ideally after a sketch Rorty has given of the analytic philosopher.[19]

Our linguistic phenomenologist contends that "philosophical problems are problems which may be solved (or dissolved) either by reforming language, or by understanding more about the language we presently use."[20] This initial characterization suggests several starting points for discussion since Heidegger has proposed, if not a reform of language, at least a transformation of our relationship to the essence of language. Husserl, moreover, is continually preoccupied, particularly in his early work, with reformulating our traditional understanding of what logic is by examining the alternative ways of formulating logical laws.

Our linguistic phenomenologist might go on to add that, in his view, philosophy is characterized by a task, a demand, and a method. All three imply, though in differing degree, an understanding of philosophy as a particular kind of argumentative discipline whose past is confused and whose future is uncertain. If the principal task of such philosophy is solving philosophical problems, then such a task demands clear-cut criteria when attempts at solution are argued. How criteria which are themselves capable of rational agreement can be found is, someone might think, what distinguishes the views of our linguistic phenomenologist from those of his colleagues. The latter maintain that constructing ideal languages is the best procedure for solving philosophical problems, while the former hold that such problems are best solved by understanding the correct uses of ordinary language. What makes these different views collegial is methodological nominalism. And the point of methodological nominalism is that the accuracy and adequacy of our language cannot be checked satisfactorily since there are no "independent criteria for knowing what the phenomena are like, independent of our knowledge of how words are used."[21]

Now some of the views our linguistic phenomenologist holds are by no means without premises that both Husserl and Heidegger would want to question. The notions, for example, that philosophy is concerned with solving philosophical problems, that either ideal languages or ordinary language hold the key to philosophical success, and that independent criteria are not available are not as evident to Husserl and Heidegger as they seem to be to some linguistic phenomenological. However, there are, perhaps surprisingly, several apparent similarities. Husserl and Heidegger seem explicitly to reject an ideal language program when they insist on the need for a radical attempt to think through the foundations for the traditional understanding of logic. But this is not to say that they accept an ordinary language program, since the language Heidegger is concerned with is ordinary in a minimal sense indeed and the language Husserl is attentive to so often requires supplementing. Nevertheless, Heidegger seems to be proposing that ordinary language be used in some new sense, even if this sense is not best described as an ideal language. And Husserl too is careful to restrict his penchant for neologism as far as he can. Finally, although both Husserl and Heidegger reject methodological nominalism, they ask some of the questions that methodological nominalism is concerned with. For example, they are characteristically concerned with questions about essences and natures. Moreover, in Heidegger's case, though not in Husserl's, the point of methodological nominalism, the unavailability of nonlinguistic criteria, seems curiously similar to his understanding of what he calls, after Schleiermacher and Dilthey, the hermeneutic circle, the necessarily circular character of comprehensive understanding. Accordingly, Heidegger recognizes that an attempt to transform the relationship between the thinking of being and the essence of language is itself necessarily linguistic.

We need, then, to be more careful about discriminating phenomenological views from analytic ones in terms of the nominalism issue and the criteria issue. For we see that although generally useful in particular cases, such as Husserl's treatment of psychologism or Heidegger's treatment of the essence of language, some similarities can be more important than the differences. Further reflection shows, however, another way of distinguishing—I think more helpfully—between analytic philosophy and Husserl on the one hand and Heidegger on the

other. My suggestion, then, is that we set
aside the nominalism issue and try to re-
fine the issue about criteria.

5. A Metaphilosophical Difference

In the final chapter of his *Formal and
Transcendental Logic* Husserl raises a
series of questions about the relations between logic and the world. Since the passage is useful for grasping Husserl's mature views on the tortured problems of
changing paradigms for our understanding of logic, I cite the passage at some
length.

Objective (*objective*) logic, logic in the state of
natural positivity, is the first logic for us, but
not the final logic. Not only does the ultimate
logic reduce all the principles of objective
logic, as theory, to their original and
legitimate—thus transcendental-phenomenological—sense, and confer the dignity of
genuine science upon them: By the very fact
of doing so or beginning to strive, level by
level, toward that goal, it necessarily becomes
amplified. A formal ontology of any possible
world, as a world constituted in transcendental subjectivity, is a non self-sufficient
part of another 'formal ontology,' which relates to everything that exists in any sense: to
what exists as transcendental subjectivity and
to everything that becomes constituted in
transcendental subjectivity. But how the latter science can be developed, how the most
universal idea of a formal logic, as formal ontology and formal apophantics, can be satisfied within the absolute realm; how a logic
satisfying that idea becomes constituted
within the absolute and ultimate all-embracing science, within transcendental phenomenology, as a stratum necessarily belonging to it; what being-sense and what rank
on that basis the logic that grew up naturally
can claim as formal ontology; and what presuppositions of method restrict the legitimate
application of that logic—these are very profound philosophical questions.[22]

In this passage Husserl is concerned
with formulating a series of questions,
particularly about the nature of logic and
ontology, that will guide his concluding
formulation in *Formal and Transcendental Logic* of a theory of transcendental evidence. This is bold, and
cannot concern us here. But even outside

the context of Husserl's program we are
nonetheless struck by the unusual range
in his use of the word 'logic'. Consider
some of the expressions Husserl uses
here: 'objective logic', 'logic in the state
of natural positivity', 'the first logic,' 'not
the final logic,' 'the most universal ideal
of a formal logic,' and so on. The range of
these uses of one word, 'logic,' can
perhaps be seen more clearly if we formulate several sentences on the basis of this
passage. Here are three:

1. The ultimate logic reduces the principles of objective logic to their original and legitimate sense.
2. The most universal idea of a formal
   logic is the idea of a formal ontology
   and formal apophantics.
3. Objective logic, logic in the state of
   natural positivity, is not the final
   logic.

Now suppose someone calls attention
to this passage, or to one like it, and suppose that, after reflection, he concludes
that Husserl is recommending a particular construal of the word 'logic' as the
"ultimate" sense of that word. In short,
our reader believes that Husserl is making a particular claim, a claim which the
reader then sets out to appraise.

"Sets out to appraise this claim"
comes to something like this: he tries to
determine, minimally, whether an argument is being urged. That is, he asks
whether Husserl is holding that if certain
propositions are true, then at least one
other proposition is true on that account.
And he asks further whether Husserl is
holding that the first propositions are indeed true. Both features, we might imagine, are present; so he satisfies himself
that Husserl is arguing. He proceeds to
inquire whether the terms in this argument are sufficiently clear, that is,
whether the terms are not vague, where
'vagueness' refers to his inability to determine the extension of the relevant
terms. He investigates the kinds of sentences that make up the argument, settling, if possible, whether these sentences
are empirical or necessary ones. He sets

aside considerations of factual error to pursue logical concerns only. He inquires whether the argument is deductive or inductive, perhaps by determining whether the conclusion is claimed to follow necessarily from the premises or is propounded as an empirical conjecture only. He considers whether the argument is self-contained or in need of amplification, that is, whether all the argument's premises can be stated completely so that the truth or falsity of other sentences need not be considered to determine whether the conclusion logically follows. And he examines the validity of the argument, perhaps by investigating whether there is inconsistency (Are all the premises capable of being true?), *petitio principii* (Are the premises such that Husserl and his reader, independently of knowing whether their implied conclusion is true, can know the premises to be true?), or whether the argument's validity is vitiated by a variety of non-sequitur (Does the conclusion logically follow from these premises?). In short, Husserl's claim about logic is logically appraised.

I presume that even if we wish to qualify the understanding of its overly familiar details, we could agree on the reasonableness of this procedure.

Suppose now that someone else cites Heidegger on logic, asserts that a claim is being made, sets out to appraise this claim, and pursues roughly the same course followed with Husserl. Again I presume that we could also agree on the reasonableness of this procedure.

We could agree. But should we?

Consider several claims Heidegger makes about logic in *What Is Called Thinking?*[23]

4. Logic confuses us into believing that we already know what thinking is.[24]
5. Logic gives us instruction on what to understand by 'thinking'. But how does logic get to decide what is to be understood by 'thinking'?[25]
6. Logic must be transformed into "the question of the essential nature

of language—a question that is something else again than philosophy of language."[26]

What are we to make of such claims? Presumably, as philosophers; we are not necessarily to determine their historical accuracy, nor to examine first off their moral relevance, nor to pursue a dozen other kinds of consideration in their regard. We are, I take it, to appraise these claims.

Can we be more explicit? Yes. 'Appraise' here refers to nothing more (nor less) controversial than the way Strawson uses this term at the beginning of his book on logical theory.[27] That is, the term refers to the kind of criticism that does not deal with whether and how propositions square with facts but with whether and how they square with one another. Here, then, 'appraising' used in the narrow sense of 'logical appraisal' and in a context where the concepts of consistency, validity, soundness, equivalence, implication, entailment, inference, proof, and so on are most often operative. We may say, summarily, that 'appraisal' has to do preeminently with arguments.

I have asked the question What are we to make of such claims? And the reason why I've asked a question instead of getting on with the job is that I am not clear whether appraising these claims comes to the same thing as appraising the Husserlian claims. That this is the case does not follow from the fact that both sets of claims are about logic rather than about, say, the mind-body problem, nor does it follow from the fact that both sets of claims are odd claims about logic. These are similarities. However, there is more than one difference between these sets of claims. And the crucial one, I think, involves seeing that we do not know how to get on with appraising Heidegger's claims, whereas we do with Husserl's.

This is not to say that appraising Husserl's claims is easy; it is not. But once we recognize the familiar although complicated context of these claims in the development of the philosophy of logic in the late nineteenth century, against the backdrop of both Kant and Mill, we can at least get under way. Moreover, should we lose the path we need only turn to Husserl's masterful analyses in the *Logical Investigations* and in *Formal and Transcendental Logic* for some unmistakable indications of just what direction to take. In short, Husserl himself has shown us how to appraise claims like (1) to (3), whereas repeated study of Heidegger's texts yields no procedures for appraising claims like (4) to (6). Thus the philosophical point here is that Heideggerean claims—like (4) to (6)—seem to imply specifically different kinds of methodological difficulties in their appraisal than Wittgensteinian claims such as (1) to (3).

We have before us two kinds of claims: claims we know how to appraise without begging the question and claims we do not know how to appraise without begging the question. Now the difference between these two kinds of claims can be usefully termed a metaphilosophical difference.

If we adopt our earlier understanding of metaphilosophy, the metaphilosophical difference is no longer a difference in interpreting the appropriateness of appraising unlike sets of claims but a twofold difference about (a) the nature of philosophy and (b) the noncontroversial status of appraisal inside Husserlian phenomenology versus the unclear status of appraisal inside Heideggerean phenomenology. But the first point is too broad and the second point requires elaboration.

Recall three distinctions between metaphilosophical skepticism, metaphilosophical realism, and metaphilosophical pragmatism.[28]

Metaphilosophical skepticism is the view (A) that "in philosophical controversy, the terms used to state criteria for the resolution of arguments mean different things to different philosophers; thus each side can take the rules of the game of controversy in a sense which will guarantee its own success."[29] According to (A), a metaphilosophical difference amounts to construing the nature of philosophy as a game of controversy whose number, applicability, and relevance of rules are interpreted differently. But it is highly probably that neither Husserl's views of philosophy nor Heidegger's can be read in this light, since whether philosophy is in any sense a game is precisely what is in question when questions are raised either about the traditional understanding of logic (Husserl) or the appropriateness of appraisal (Heidegger).

Metaphilosophical realism is the view (B) that "philosophical arguments are, in fact, won and lost, for some philosophical positions prove weaker than others."[30] This view insists on the difference between philosophers who attend to coherence only and those who attend also to adequacy, that is, to something external to their systems. According to (B), a metaphilosophical difference amounts to different ways of taking the "something external" (say X) that limits retorting by redefinition. If we take X as "common sense," the metaphilosophical difference might well come to what convincing reasons there are for differing on how "common sense" is to be construed. But this difference, while indeed a philosophical difference, is not sufficiently general to qualify as a proper use of the term 'metaphilosophical'. If we take X as the history of philosophy, the metaphilosophical difference might well come to what convincing reasons there are for holding that a specific claim about the appropriateness of appraisal must at least make sense most of the things great philosophers have said about philosophical appraisal. But this difference is also insufficiently general. If, finally, we take X as the indefinite end of philosophical inquiry in the future, the metaphilosophical difference might well come to just what the substantive considerations are for differing on whether philosophical appraisal should be undertaken at all. This difference, clearly, is closer to the general question we have raised about whether some philosophical problems, such as how to interpret 'appraising', allow neither criteria nor anything like criteria for their solution.

Metaphilosophical pragmatism is the view (C) that since making communication possible is more important than truth or even agreement, philosophy comes to "formulating rules in terms of which to judge changes of rules."[31] According to (C), a metaphilosophical difference comes to agreeing that substantive considerations are available for construing philosophical truth as satisfaction of needs, but differing on whether criteria for rule changes are to be formulated on the basis of observation of actual patterns in rule changes or on the basis of proposing possible patterns for such changes on other than observational grounds. But the agreement in (C) depends on a view of truth which is arguably inconsistent with both Husserlian and Heideggerean claims about logic.

In short, the metaphilosophical difference between such claims refers to how the appropriateness of what we ordinarily understand by appraisal is to be judged. In the case of Husserlian claims, the term 'appraisal' is already inside a traditional and highly articulated interpretation of the indispensable role of argument in philosophy; in the case of Heideggerean claims, both the nature and the propriety of argument itself are what is in question.

6. Three Issues

That there can be differences at such a level and that there is some utility in calling such differences metaphilosophical is, I hope, reasonably plain. However, the interest in such differences remains to be spelled out.

My suggestion here must be brief. There are, I think, at least three substantive philosophical issues which understanding metaphilosophical differences in the way I have detailed suggests: a criteriological, a linguistic, and a historical issue.

The first issue, the criteriological one, may be put as a general question: Are other than strictly argumentative procedures available for appraising claims about the appropriateness of appraisal? When the question is put this way, I

think the answer must be no. One reason for such an answer is the intimate tie between how we use the terms 'argument' and 'appraisal'. In our universe of discourse an argument is an appraisal and, in the sense I stipulated earlier, an appraisal must involve argument. It does not help to point out that there are many different kinds of both argument and appraisal, precisely because we have limited these terms to quite specifically interrelated kinds. Were we to construe 'appraisal' more broadly than 'argument', or vice versa, perhaps a "no" answer would not be required.

However, a simpler move than this may be available if we simply reformulate the question in some such terms as the following: Are there any unambiguous procedures involving non-question-begging criteria for reaching agreement about what is to count as logical appraisal? Although this formulation drops the term 'argument', there may, on examination, turn out to be similar problems with the term 'criteria'.[32] However, such difficulties are not immediately evident. As it stands, this question is, I think, reasonably straightforward even if not transparent. The first issue then becomes just what an answer to such a question would look like.

The second issue, the linguistic one, may also be put as a general question, this time in the Heideggerean register: Does the very kind of thing a metaphilosophical difference seems to be require a transformation in the metaphilosopher's relation to his own language?

When put this way, the question does not allow an answer until we can be somewhat clearer about just what the terms 'transformation' and 'language' stand for. These terms, of course, can be taken variously. However, if we construe them along the lines the later Heidegger suggested, I think at least one issue the question purports to raise comes clear. We might take 'language' as the particular relationship between literal and figurative elements of discourse which a philosopher uses in trying to determine *whether* a specific formulation of a philosophical problem involves a metaphilosophical difference. And we might take 'transformation' as the shift from one particular relationship between literal and figurative elements of discourse to another in the attempt to *think through the consequences* of a metaphysical difference for the philosophical problem in question. On this interpretation I think the question can be answered with a tentative yes. The second issue then becomes whether the apparent reasons for such an answer do not raise questions of a different order about the intelligibility of what such an interpretation presupposes.[33]

The third issue, the historical one, we may put as follows: Are there kinds of metaphilosophical disagreements which cannot be resolved because of the preeminence of a particular paradigm of intelligibility, rationality, and argument in a particular historical epoch? Again, when the question is put this way, the answer I come up with is a tentative yes. The answer is yes because I think that metaphilosophical disagreements about the satisfactoriness or utility of alternative construals of, say, 'logical appraisal' necessarily involve different paradigms of, if not always intelligibility, at least argument and rationality. Given such an exaggerated importance of the various paradigms in these kinds of disputes, resolving the disputes would seem to entail revision of the paradigms. But where argument cannot be found even on the nature, kinds, and elements of one paradigm, such attempts at revision which seem to be called for only en-

counter the same problem of metaphilosophical disagreement at another point.

And the answer is tentative because at this level of reflection I think that, despite the reflex, it is virtually impossible to introduce the overworked distinction between philosophical disagreements which are in fact resolvable and which are resolvable only in principle. So even if there are disagreements about problems like freedom and determinism which seem at the moment to be unresolvable, we cannot on that basis alone and in this area claim for such problems "in-principle resolvability." For that would be to assume, minimally, that our criteria for judging successful resolution of such disagreements do not change. And it is precisely this assumption which our historical emphasis wants to disallow.

So much for three questions about metaphilosophical differences.

In the *Euthyphro* (7B-D) Socrates at one point distinguishes two kinds of disagreements: those which can be resolved and those which cannot. The latter not only set philosophers at odds with one another, they divide the gods. My suggestion is that what gives such disagreements their power to estrange even the gods is their necessity. The point, then, would be that metaphilosophical differences seem to be necessarily unresolvable. This means that Husserl's disputes about methodological nominalism are resolvable in principle whereas Heidegger's disputes both about nominalism and criteria are not.

NOTES

1. *The Linguistic Turn: Recent Essays in Philosophical Method* (Chicago, 1967), pp. 32-33.
2. Ibid., p. 24.
3. Ibid., p. 33.
4. See J. Moline, "On Philosophical Neutrality," *Metaphilosophy*, 1 (1970): 20.
5. M. Lazerowitz, "A Note on 'Metaphilosophy,' " *Metaphilosophy*, 1 (1970): 91.
6. Loc. cit.
7. *Logical Investigations*, tr. J. Findlay (New York, 1970), p. 45.

8. Herbert Spiegelberg, *The Phenomenological Movement: A Historical Introduction* (The Hague, 1965), pp. 1-23.
9. Ibid., p. 5, n. 1.
10. Cited in Spiegelberg, op. cit., p. 5.
11. *Unterwegs zur Sprache* (Pfullingen: Neske, 1959). Translations are my own.
12. See my paper "Heidegger's Meditation on the Word," *Philosophical Studies*, 18 (1969): 76-99.
13. *Unterwegs*, p. 267. An idea of the kinds of terminological problems one faces can be gotten

merely from inspecting the three different terms used here for 'relation' and 'relationship': *Verhältnis, Beziehung, Ver-hältnis*. A better idea can be had simply by trying to translate almost any central philosophical claim Heidegger makes from 1927 on.

14. G. Frege, "Review of Dr. E. Husserl's *Philosophy of Arithmetics*," tr. E. W. Kluge, *Mind*, 70 (1972): 321-37.

15. "Über Psychologische Begründung der Logik," *Zeitschrift für Phil. Forchung*, 13 (1959): 346-48.

16. Translated by T. J. Sheehan in *Husserl: Shorter Works*, ed. P. McCormick and F. Elliston (Notre Dame: University of Notre Dame Press, forthcoming).

17. Ibid., pp. 346-47.

18. On the issue of logical psychologism, see Dallas Willard, "The Paradox of Logical Psychologism: Husserl's Way Out," *American Philosophical Quarterly*, 9 (1972): 94-100.

19. Rorty, *The Linguistic Turn*, passim.

20. Ibid., p. 3.

21. Ibid., p. 31.

22. *Formal and Transcendental Logic*, tr. D. Cairns (The Hague: Nijhoff, 1969), p. 271 (italics omitted).

23. *What Is Called Thinking?* trans. F. D. Wieck and J. G. Gray (New York: Harper & Row, 1968).

24. Ibid., p. 45.

25. Ibid., pp. 153-54.

26. Ibid., p. 154.

27. Strawson, *An Introduction to Logical Theory* (London: Methuen, 1952), pp. 1-2.

28. R. Rorty, "Recent Metaphilosophy," *Review of Metaphysics*, 15 (1961): 299-318.

29. Ibid., p. 299.

30. Loc. cit.

31. Rorty, p. 301.

32. See J. F. M. Hunter's comments in his "Critical Notice of P. M. S. Hacker *Insight and Illusion*," *Canadian Journal of Philosophy*, 4 (1974): 201-11.

33. For a more detailed account of similar issues, see my paper "On Saying and Showing in Heidegger and Wittgenstein," *Journal of the British Society for Phenomenology*, 3 (1972): 27-35, and my book, *Heidegger: An Argumentative Reading* (Ottawa: University of Ottawa Press, 1976).

Further References

Idealism and Existentialism

Adorno, Theodore W. "Husserl and the Problem of Idealism." *Journal of Philosophy*, 37 (1940), 5-18.

Boehm, Rudolf. "Husserl et l'idéalisme classique." *Revue Philosophique de Louvain*, 57 (1959), 351-96.

Bosanquet, B. "Review of *'Ideen I.'* " *Mind*, 23 (1914), 587-97.

De Boer, Theodorus. "The Meaning of Husserl's Idealism in the Light of His Development." *Analecta Husserliana*, 2 (1972), 322-32.

Earle, W. "Phenomenology and Existentialism." *Journal of Philosophy*, 57 (1960), 75-84.

Edie, James M. "Transcendental Phenomenology and Existentialism." *Philosophy and Phenomenological Research*, 25 (1964-65), 52-63.

Gibson, W. R. Boyce. "The Problem of Real and Ideal in the Phenomenology of Husserl." *Mind*, 34 (1925), 311-27.

Gurwitsch, A. "A Non-Egological Conception of Consciousness." *Philosophy and Phenomenological Research*, 1 (1940-41), 325-38.

Hook, Sidney. "Husserl's Phenomenological Idealism." *Journal of Philosophy*, 27 (1930), 365-80.

Ingarden, R. *On the Motives Which Led Husserl to Transcendental Idealism*, tr. A. Hannibalsson. The Hague: Nijhoff, 1975.

Kockelmans, J. J. "World-Constitution: Reflections on Husserl's Transcendental Idealism." *Analecta Husserliana*, 1 (1971), 1-10.

Natanson, Maurice. "Phenomenology and Existentialism." *The Modern Schoolman*, 39 (1959-60), 1-10.

Scanlon, J. D. "Consciousness, the Structure and the Ego: *pro* Husserl *contra* Sartre." *Philosophical Forum*, 2 (1971), 332-54.

Spiegelberg, Herbert. "Husserl's Phenomenology and Existentialism." *Journal of Philosophy*, 57 (1960), 62-74.

Tymieniecka, Anna Teresa (ed.). "The Later Husserl and the Idea of Phenomenology: Idealism-Realism, Historicity and Nature," *Analecta Husserliana*, 2 (1972).

Husserl and Kant

Berger, Gaston. *The 'Cogito' in Husserl's Philosophy*, tr. K. McLaughlin. Evanston: Northwestern University Press, 1972.

De Oliveira, Manfredo Araugo. *Subjektivität und Vermittlung. Studien z. Entwicklung d. transzendentalen Denkens bei I. Kant, E. Husserl u. H. Wagner*. Munich: Fink, 1973.

Hartmann, Klaus. "Husserl und Kant." *Kanstudien*, 3 (1967), 370-75.

Ingarden, Roman. "A Priori Knowledge in Kant vs. A Priori Knowledge in Husserl." *Dialectics and Humanism*, 1 (1973), 5-18.

Kaufmann, F. "Cassirer, Neo-Kantianism, and Phenomenology" in *The Philosophy of Ernst Cassirer*, ed. Paul Schilpp. New York: Tudor, 1949, pp. 801-54.

Kern, Iso. *Husserl und Kant*. The Hague: Nijhoff, 1964.

Klein, Ted. "Husserl's Kantian Meditation." *The Southwestern Journal of Philosophy*, 5 (1974), 69-82.

Marbach, Eduard. *Das Problem des Ich in der Phänomenologie Husserls*. The Hague: Nijhoff, 1974.

Ricoeur, Paul. "Kant and Husserl." *Philosophy Today*, 10 (1966), 145-68.

Seebohm, T. *Die Bedingungen der Möglichkeit der Transzendental-Philosophie E. Husserls transzendental-phanomenologischer Ansatz, dargestellt im Anschluss an seine Kant-Kritik*. Bonn: H. Bouvier, 1962.

Husserl and Marxism

Desanti, Jean T. *Phénoménologie et praxis*. Paris: Editions Sociales, 1963.

Filipovic, Vladimir. "Die Sendung der Philosophie in unserer Zeit nach Marx und Husserl." *Praxis*, 3 (1967), 346-51.

Mays, Wolfe. "Phenomenology and Marxism" in *Phenomenology and Philosophical Understanding*, ed. Edo Pivcevic. New York: Cambridge University Press, 1975, pp. 231-50.

Nemith, Thomas. "Husserl and Soviet Marxism." *Studies in Soviet Thought*, 15 (1975), 183-96.

Pazanin, Ante. *Wissenschaft und Geschichte in der Phänomenologie Edmund Husserls*. The Hague: Nijhoff, 1972.

Piccone, P. "Phenomenological Marxism." *Telos*, no. 9 (1971), 3-31.

Schmueli, Efraim. "Can Phenomenology Accommodate Marxism?" *Telos* (1973), 169-80.

Tran-Duc-Thao. *Phénoménologie et matérialisme dialectique*. Paris: Editions Minh-Tan, 1951.

Vajda, Mihaly. "Marxism, Existentialism, Phenomenology: A Dialogue." *Telos*, no. 6 (1971), 3-29.

Husserl and Frege

Føllesdal, Dagfinn. *Husserl und Frege*. Oslo: Aschehoug, 1958.

McCarthy, T. A. "Logic, Mathematics and Ontology in Husserl." *The Journal of the British Society for Phenomenology*, 3 (1972), 158-64.

Mohanty, J. N. "The Frege-Husserl Correspondence." *The Southwestern Journal of Philosophy*, v. 5, no. 3 (Nov. 1974), 83-96.

———. "Husserl and Frege: A New Look at their Relationship." *Research in Phenomenology*, 4 (1974), 51-62.

Mortan, G. "Einige Bemerkungen zur Überwindung des Psychologismus durch G. Frege und E. Husserl" in *Atti XII Congr. intern. Filos*. Florence: Sansoni, 1961, 327-34.

Natorp, Paul. "Zur Frage der logischen Methode mit Beziehung auf Edmund Husserls Prolegomena zur reinen Logik." *Kantstudien*, 6 (1901), 270-83.

Pietersma, Henry. "Husserl and Frege." *Archiv für Geschichte der Philosophie*, 49 (1967), 298-323.

Pivcevic, Edo. "Husserl versus Frege." *Mind*, 76 (1967), 155-65.

Solomon, Robert C. "Sense and Essence: Frege and Husserl." *International Philosophical Quarterly*, 10 (1970), 379-401.

Husserl and Language

Bar-Hillel, Yehoshua. "Husserl's Conception of a Purely Logical Grammar." *Philosophy and Phenomenological Research*, 17 (1956-57), 362-69.

Derrida, J. *Speech and Phenomena*, tr. D. B. Allison. Evanston: Northwestern University Press, 1973.

Edie, James M. "Husserl's Conception of 'The Grammatical' and Contemporary Linguistics" in *Life-World and Consciousness: Essays for Aron Gurwitsch*, ed. Lester E. Embree. Evanston: Northwestern University Press, 1972, pp. 233-61.

Gutting, Gary. "Husserl and Logical Empiricism." *Metaphilosophy*, 2 (1971), 197-226.

Holenstein, Elmar. "Jacobson and Husserl." *The Human Context*, 7 (1975), 61-83.

Hulsmann, Heinz. *Zur Theorie der Sprache bei Edmund Husserl*. Munich: Pustet, 1964.

Küng, G. "The World as Noema and as Referent." *Journal of British Society for Phenomenology*, 3 (1972), 15-26.

Merleau-Ponty, M. "On the Phenomenology of Language" in *Signs*, tr. Richard C. McCleary. Evanston: Northwestern University Press, 1964, pp. 84-97.

Orth, Von Ernst Wolfgang. "Philosophy of Language as Phenomenology of Language and Logic" in *Phenomenology and the Social Sciences*, ed. Maurice Natanson. Evanston: Northwestern University Press, 1973, pp. 323-60.

Parret, Herman. "Husserl and Neo-Humboltians on Language." *International Philosophical Quarterly*, 12 (1972), 43-68.

Roche, Maurice. *Phenomenology, Language and the Social Sciences*. London: Routledge & Kegan Paul, 1973.

Verhaar, John W. W. "Phenomenology and Present-Day Linguistics" in *Phenomenology and the Social Sciences*, ed. Maurice Natanson. Evanston: Northwestern University Press, 1973, pp. 361-460.

Welton, D. "Intentionality and Language in Husserl's Phenomenology." *Review of Metaphysics*, 27 (1973), 260-98.

Husserl and Linguistic Analysis

Ayer, Alfred Jules. "Phenomenology and Linguistic Analysis." *Aristotelian Society Supp.*, 32 (1959), 111-24.

Gutting, Gary. "Husserl and Logical Empiricism." *Metaphilosophy* , 2 (1971), 197-226.

Ihde, Don. "Some Parallels between Analysis and Phenomenology." *Philosophy and Phenomenological Research*, 27 (1966-67), 577-86.

Meyn, Henning L. "Nonempirical Investigations in Husserl and Ordinary Language Philosophy." *Southwestern Journal of Philosophy*, 5 (1974), 245-59.

Ricoeur, Paul. "Husserl and Wittgenstein on Language" in *Phenomenology and Existentialism*, ed. Lee and Mandelbaum. Baltimore: Johns Hopkins Press, 1967, pp. 207-18.

Schmitt, Richard. "Phenomenology and Analysis." *Philosophy and Phenomenological Research*, 23 (1962-63), 101-10.

Taylor, C. "Phenomenology and Linguistic Analysis." *The Aristotelian Society*, 33 (1959), 93-110.

Tillman, F. "Transcendental Phenomenology and Analytic Philosophy." *International Philosophical Quarterly*, 7 (1967), 31-40.

Turnbull, R. "Linguistic Analysis, Phenomenology, and the Problems of Philosophy." *Monist*, 49 (1965), 44-69.

Van Peursen, Cornelis A. *Phenomenology and Analytic Philosophy*. Pittsburgh: Duquesnes University Press, 1972.

Wheatley, John. "Phenomenology: English and Continental" in *Existential Philosophy*, ed. D. Carr and E. S. Casey. The Hague: Nijhoff, 1973, pp. 230-42.

Husserl and Heidegger

Del-Negro, Walter. "Von Brentano über Husserl zu Heidegger." *Zeitschrift für philosophische Forschung*, 7 (1953), 571-85.

De Waelhens, Alphonse. *Phénoménologie et vérité*. Paris: Presses universitaires de France, 1953.

Gibson, W. R. Boyce. "From Husserl to Heidegger." *The Journal of the British Society for Phenomenology*, 2 (1971), 58-62.

Kersten, Frederick. "Heidegger and Transcendental Phenomenology." *The Southern Journal of Philosophy*, 11, no. 3 (1973), 202-15.

Kisiel, Theodore. "On the Dimension of a Phenomenology of Science in Husserl and the Young Dr. Heidegger." *The Journal of the British Society for Phenomenology*, 4 (1973), 217-34.

Kraft, Julius. *Von Husserl zu Heidegger*, Frankfurt: Verlag Öffentliches Leben, 1957.

Muth, Franz. Edmund Husserl und Martin Heidegger in ihrer Phänomenologie und Weltanschauung. (Diss., Munich) Temeswar: Schwabische Verlags-Aktiengesellschaft, 1931.

Picard, Yvonne. "Le Temps chez Husserl et chez Heidegger." *Deucalion*, 1 (1946), 93-124.

Schacht, Richard L. "Husserlian and Heideggerian Phenomenologies." *Philosophical Studies*, 23 (1972), 293-314.

Seeburger, Francis F. "Heidegger and the Phenomenological Reduction. "*Philosophy and Phenomenological Research*, 36 (1975-76), 212-21.

Smith, F. J. "Being and Subjectivity: Heidegger and Husserl" in *Phenomenology in Perspective*, ed. F. J. Smith. The Hague: Nijhoff, 1970, pp. 122-56.

Theunissen, Michael. "Intentionaler Gegenstand und ontologische Differenz. Ansätze zur Fragestellung Heideggers in der Phänomenologie Husserls." *Philosophisches Jahrbuch*, 70 (1963), 344-62.

Trépanier, E. "Phénoménologie et ontologie: Husserl et Heidegger." *Laval théologique et philosophique*, 28 (1972), 249-65.

Tugendhat, Ernst. *Über den Wahrheitsbegriff bei Husserl und Heidegger*. Berlin: De Gruyter, 1967.

Contributors

WALTER BIEMEL, Professor of Philosophy at the University of Aachen, has edited several volumes of the *Husserliana,* and is now general editor of Heidegger's works. He has published numerous articles and books including *Le Concept du monde chez Heidegger, Kants Begründung der Asthetik,* and *Analyzen zur Kunst der Gegenwart.*

JOHN B. BROUGH teaches philosophy at Georgetown University and has written several papers on Husserl's theories of time.

DAVID CARR taught philosophy at Yale University. He translated Husserl's *Crisis* and has recently published *Phenomenology and the Problem of History.*

EDWARD S. CASEY teaches philosophy at Yale University. In addition to articles on phenomenology and aesthetics, he is the author of *Imagining: A Phenomenological Study* (forthcoming).

FREDERICK A. ELLISTON has taught at Trinity College and York University and now teaches at Union College in Schenectady. He is coeditor of *Philosophy and Sex* and of *Husserl: Shorter Works* (forthcoming).

GOTTLOB FREGE, the founder of modern mathematical logic, influenced Husserl and profoundly affected the work of many philosophers, notably Russell and Wittgenstein.

ISO KERN teaches philosophy at the University of Heidelberg. He is the editor of the recent volumes by Husserl on intersubjectivity and the author of *Husserl und Kant* as well as *Idee und Methode der Philosophie.*

JOSEPH J. KOCKELMANS teaches philosophy at Pennsylvania State University. He is the editor of several anthologies and the author of many articles and books on phenomenology, including *Edmund Husserl's Phenomenological Psychology* and *Martin Heidegger: A First Introduction to His Philosophy.*

GUIDO KÜNG is Professor of Philosophy at the University of Fribourg in Switzerland. In addition to his work in logic and the foundations of mathematics he is the author of *Ontology and the Logistic Analysis of Language.*

LUDWIG LANDGREBE is Professor of Philosophy at the University of Cologne and Director of the Husserl Archives there. A student of Husserl and editor of his works, he has published many books and articles including *Der Weg der Phänomenologie, European Philosophy Today*, and *Phänomenologie und Geschichte*.

PETER MCCORMICK has taught at the University of Notre Dame and Denison University and now teaches at the University of Ottawa. In addition to articles on phenomenology he is the author of *Heidegger and the Language of the World* and the co-editor of *Husserl: Shorter Works* (forthcoming).

GARY B. MADISON teaches philosophy at McMaster University in Ontario. He has published articles on phenomenology, science and values, as well as *La phénoménologie de Merleau-Ponty*.

JITENDRANATH N. MOHANTY teaches philosophy at the New School for Social Research in New York. In addition to numerous articles he has published three books: *Edmund Husserl's Theory of Meaning, The Concept of Intentionality*, and *Phenomenology and Ontology*.

FREDERICK A. OLAFSON is chairman of the Philosophy Department at the University of California at San Diego. In addition to his work in phenomenology and social philosophy he is the author of *Principles and Persons*.

JEAN PATOČKA was Emeritus Professor at Charles University in Prague. He was a former student of Husserl and the author of many works on phenomenology, including *The Natural World as Phenomenological Problem* and *Introduction to Husserl's Phenomenology*.

HENRY PIETERSMA teaches philososohy at Victoria College at the University of Toronto. The author of articles on epistemology, he is presently writing a book on Husserl's views about truth.

ROBERT C. SOLOMON teaches philosophy at the University of Texas at Austin. In addition to his work in the philosophy of mind and phenomenology he is the author of *From Rationalism to Existentialism* and the editor of several collections.

ERNST TUGENDHAT was Professor of Philosophy at the University of Heidelberg and is now at the Max Planck Institute in Munich. He is the author of a work on Aristotle, *TI KATA TINOS*, and *Der Wahrheitsbegriff bei Husserl and Heidegger*.

H.L. VAN BREDA founded the Husserl Archives at Louvain and organized several international conferences on phenomenology. The editor and author of numerous papers on Husserl's works, he died in 1974.

CORNELIUS A. VAN PEURSEN is Professor of Philosophy at the University of Leiden and the author of articles and books on Leibniz, analytic philosophy, and phenomenology, including *Phenomenology and Reality* and *Phenomenology and Analytical Philosophy*.

Marx W. Wartofsky teaches philosophy at Boston University. He is the author of many works in the philosophy of science and is co-editor of the *Boston Studies in the Philosophy of Science*.

Donn Welton teaches philosophy at the State University of New York at Stony Brook and has published several articles on Husserl's theories of perception.

Dallas Willard teaches philosophy at the University of Southern California. In addition to articles on epistemology and logic he has translated several of Husserl's shorter works.

Index

absolute science, 248
  as key concept of phenomenology, 251-252
abstraction, 339
  concept of totality, 319
  and interpretation of scientific thought, 205-206
  and nature of numbers, 320-324
  and number-statements, 318-319
  and positive science, 146
  science and the life-world, 206
  and subject-object presentation, 315-318
acts
  difference between *Sinn* or noema and *Bedeutung,* 31-32
  as noema, 163
  as objective intentional experience, 162-163
  signitive and intuitive, 31-32, 334
Adorno, T., criticism of *eidos*, 150-152
anthropology, and horizon, 199-201
antiphilosophy, 262-264
appearance, 64
  concept of, 59
  objective sense, 59-60
  perception, 60
apperception (*also called* appresentation), 65-66, 221-222
  analogical appresentation, 222-223, 225-226
  synthetic unity, 274-275
  transcendental, 275
apperceptive transfer, 228-229
apprehension, 12
  constitution of "now perception" and primary memory, 86
  proto-apprehension, 61
  and time-consciousness, 6-7
Aristotle, 59, 119, 124, 129, 193, 207
  theoria, 102

Barbara syllogism, 2, 11
Bolanzo, B., 14
Brentano, F., 338-339
  and doctrine of intentionality, 161-162, 170
Camus, Albert, 256, 261
Cartesian Meditations, 5, 51, 104, 260, 277-279, 281
categorial act, 333-334
  and synthetic act, 330-331
Cogito (*also* cogitatum, cogitationes), 127-128, 273, 340
  as act of ego, 271-272
  parallelism with intentional act, 165
  and transcendental ego, 279-281
consciousness
  absolute consciousness, 94-95 98-99, 128-129
  absolute consciousness and apprehension schema, 88-89
  and combining of noema and *Sinn,* 177
  and concept of transcendental, 294-295
  and cultural world, 211
  and ego, 272-273
  and intentionality, 290
  and Marxian phenomenology, 306-307
  meaning-conferring act, 327
  modes of inner consciousness, 93-95
  and past, present, and future modes of perception, 84-86
  and predication, 334
  as a problem for philosophers, 297-298
  and theses of entities, 295
  and time-consciousness, 91-93
  time-consciousness and schema content of apprehension, 88-89
  as total of intentional experience and *Evidenz,* 49-50
  and two dimensions of immanence, 89-91

constitution, as part of explication and transcendental phenomenology, 344-345

Crisis, 129-130, 135, 142, 203-204, 210-211, 270, 280
and transcendental reduction, 281-282

Dasein, 241, 283, 300-302
Descartes, R., 43, 71, 77
as model of Husserl's reduction, 251
and notion of "epoche," 340-341
and phenomenological psychology, 298

ego (*also Erlebnisse*), 62
comments on Natorp's conception of pure ego, 271-272
development of concept of transcendental ego, 278-281
in four stages, 239-240
and genesis of Marxism, 305-308
and genetic phenomenology, 103-104
as pure presence, 258-259
real and pure ego compared, 273
reinterpretation of Kantian ego, 277
eidetic insight, 76
eidetic intuition and principle of variation, 153
eidetic necessity, 157-158
eidetic reduction, 292
eidetic variation, 19-20, 154-155
eidos, 78
and apprehension of the universal, 155
contrast between Husserlian and Aristotelian *eidos,* 154
and *de facto* ego, 279
doctrine of eidos, 150-153
and factual reality, 153-154
as primary substance, 157
Eley, L., criticism of Husserlian *eidos,* 154, 156-157
empathy
as characteristic of analogical apresentation, 223-224
and principle of verification, 225
epistemology, 4
contrast with transcendental phenomenology, 345-348
epistemic evaluation and perception, 4-5
epistemic situations in phenomenology, 39-43
and evaluation of external world, 46-47
and *Evidenz* (evident), 41, 50-51

epoche, 138
Cartesian development, 340-341
contrast with phenomenological epoche, 218
importance of, 245
new epoche and use of linguistics, 226-227
and referent, 341-342
thematic epoche, 217
the transcendental epoche, 296
Erlebnis (*also* lived experience), 216
lived experience and phenomenology, 291-293
essence
doctrine of, 47
epistemic features, 5
and positive science, 47-48
existentialism
and end of idealism, 260
and lived experience, 255-257
views of Heidegger and Husserl compared, 247-249
experience
and existentialism, 255-256
and intentionality, 335
explanandum, 216-217
explication, 245
as meaning analysis, 344-345

Feuerbach, L., 308
Føllesdal, Dagfin, interpretation of noema, 168, 173, 175-177
Formal and Transcendental Logic, 5, 61
and the question of logic and the world, 359-360
Frege, G., criticism of Husserl, 242-244
Galileo
mathematization of nature, 204, 206
and pure geometry, 204-206
geometry, Husserl's commentary on pure geometry, 204-206
Greek ideal, Greek rationalist tradition, 238

Heidegger, M., 240-241
compared views on tradition with Merleau-Ponty and Sartre, 261-262
contrast with Husserlian concepts, 259-260
and *Dasein,* 241, 283, 300-302
difference between Husserl and Heidegger's concept of